LOUIS

2nd edition
Richard Bizier

ULYSSES
TRAVEL PUBLICATIONS
Travel better... enjoy more

Series Director: Claude Morneau; *Project Supervisor:* Pascale Couture; *Editor:* Claude Morneau.

Research and Composition *Author:* Richard Bizier; *Louisiana Correspondant:* Charles Larroque; *Research Coordinator:* Roch Nadeau; *Research:* Paquerette Villeneuve, Gilles de Lalonde, Paul Haince, Roch Nadeau, Marie Rodrigue, Marie Tousignant.

Production *Design:* Patrick Farei (Atoll Direction); *Proofreading:* Jennifer McMorran, Sarah Kresh; *Translation:* Tracy Kendrick, Danielle Gauthier, Emmy Pahmer, Sarah Kresh; *Cartography:* André Duchesne, Patrick Thivierge (Assistant); *Layout:* Tara Salman; *Graphics:* Steve Rioux.

Illustrations *Cover Photo:* Rivera Collection Superstock; *Interior Photos:* Roch Nadeau, Steve Comeaux; *Chapter Headings:* Jennifer McMorran; *Drawings:* Lorette Pierson.

Special Thanks to Beverly Gianna and Christine DeCuir (New Orleans Metropolitan Convention and Visitor Bureau), Gérald Breaux (Lafayette Convention and Visitors Commission), Paquerette Villeneuve (main researcher), Charles Larroque (Louisiana correspondant), Jolème Adam, Pearl Arceneaux, Audrey and Maxie Broussard, JoAnne Clevenger, Robert Daffort, Joanne Kirkpatrick, Dany Madani, Jami Mitchell, Frank S. Rochefort, Marie Rodrigue, John Tessier, Elsie Begnaud-Trahan and Harry Trahan.

Thanks to SODEC and to the Department of Canadian Heritage for their financial support.

Distributors

AUSTRALIA:
Little Hills Press
11/37-43 Alexander St.
Crows Nest NSW 2065
☎ (612) 437-6995
Fax: (612) 438-5762

BELGIUM AND LUXEMBOURG:
Vander
Vrijwilligerlaan 321
B-1150 Brussel
☎ (02) 762 98 04
Fax: (02) 762 06 62

CANADA:
Ulysses Books & Maps
4176 Saint-Denis
Montréal, Québec
H2W 2M5
☎ (514) 843-9882, ext.2232
or 1-800-748-9171
Fax: 514-843-9448
www.ulysse.ca

GERMANY AND AUSTRIA:
Brettschneider
Fernreisebedarf
Feldfirchner Strasse 2
D-85551 Heimstetten
München
☎ 89-99 02 03 30
Fax: 89-99 02 03 31

GREAT BRITAIN AND IRELAND:
World Leisure Marketing
9 Downing Road
West Meadows, Derby
UK DE21 6HA
☎ 1 332 34 33 32
Fax: 1 332 34 04 64

ITALY:
Centro Cartografico del Riccio
Via di Soffiano 164/A
50143 Firenze
☎ (055) 71 33 33
Fax: (055) 71 63 50

NETHERLANDS:
Nilsson & Lamm
Pampuslaan 212-214
1380 AD Weesp (NL)
☎ 0294-465044
Fax: 0294-415054

SCANDINAVIA:
Scanvik
Esplanaden 8B
1263 Copenhagen K
DK
☎ (45) 33.12.77.66
Fax: (45) 33.91.28.82

SPAIN:
Altaïr
Balmes 69
E-08007 Barcelona
☎ 454 29 66
Fax: 451 25 59

SWITZERLAND:
OLF
P.O. Box 1061
CH-1701 Fribourg
☎ (026) 467.51.11
Fax: (026) 467.54.66

U.S.A.:
The Globe Pequot Press
6 Business Park Road
P.O. Box 833
Old Saybrook, CT 06475
☎ 1-800-243-0495
Fax: 1-800-820-2329

Other countries, contact Ulysses Books & Maps (Montréal), Fax: (514) 843-9448

"The bayous of Louisiana, in their peacefulness and beauty,
and in their mysterious tranquility, immediately gave me
the impression of having gone back to the beginning of time,
of having returned to the origins of the world."

Gilles Carle
Film-maker, *Le Diable d'Amerique*

TABLE OF CONTENTS

PORTRAIT OF LOUISIANA 13
    Geography 13
    History 16
    Politics 24
    Economy 24
    Population 24
    French in louisiana 25
    Culture 26
    Louisiana cuisine 30

PRACTICAL INFORMATION 37
    Entrance Formalities 37
    Customs 37
    Embassies and Consulates . . 38
    Tourist Information 39
    Finding Your Way Around . . 39
    Telecommunications 42
    Insurance 43
    Health 44
    Disabled Travellers 45
    Climate 46
    Money and Banks 47
    Accommodations 48
    Shopping 49
    Bars and Nightclubs 50
    Time Difference 50
    Public Holidays 50
    Drugs 50
    Electricity 50
    Emigrating to the
        United States 50
    Festivals 50
    Weights and Measures 51

GREATER NEW ORLEANS 53
    Finding Your Way Around . . 56
    Practical Information 63
    Exploring 68
    Outdoors 105
    Accommodations 107
    Restaurants 122
    Entertainment 139
    Shopping 149

THE PLANTATIONS
AND BATON ROUGE 155
    Finding Your Way Around . . 155
    Practical Information 160
    Exploring 161
    Parks 177
    Accommodations 177
    Restaurants 181
    Entertainment 186
    Shopping 188

BAYOU LAFOURCHE AND
TERREBONNE 191
    Finding Your Way Around . . 191
    Practical Information 194
    Exploring 195
    Parks 201
    Accommodations 201
    Restaurants 204
    Entertainment 206
    Shopping 209

ACADIANA: LAFAYETTE 211
    Finding Your Way Around . . 212
    Practical Information 214
    Exploring 218
    Parks 221
    Outdoor Activities 222
    Accommodations 223
    Restaurants 226
    Entertainment 231
    Shopping 234

BAYOU TECHE 237
    Finding Your Way Around . . 238
    Practical Information 241
    Exploring 242
    Parks 253
    Accommodations 254
    Restaurants 258
    Entertainment 263
    Shopping 266

ACADIANA:
NORTH OF LAFAYETTE 269
    Finding Your Way Around . . 269
    Practical Information 272
    Exploring 274
    Parks 285
    Accommodations 287
    Restaurants 290
    Entertainment 292
    Shopping 297

WESTERN ACADIANA 301
    Finding Your Way Around . . 301
    Practical Information 304
    Exploring 306
    Parks 315
    Accommodations 318
    Restaurants 323
    Entertainment 328
    Shopping 333

CROSSROADS 337
    Finding Your Way Around . . 337
    Practical Information 342
    Exploring 343
    Parks 353
    Accommodations 355
    Restaurants 360
    Entertainment 362
    Shopping 363

NORTHERN LOUISIANA 367
    Finding Your Way Around . . 367
    Practical Information 372
    Exploring 373
    Parks 385
    Accommodations 388
    Restaurants 393
    Entertainment 398
    Shopping 400

INDEX 402

Help make Ulysses Travel Guides even better!

The information contained in this guide was correct at press time. However, mistakes can slip in, omissions are always possible, places can disappear, etc. The authors and publisher hereby disclaim any liability for loss or damage resulting from omissions or errors.

We value your comments, corrections and suggestions, as they allow us to keep each guide up to date. The best contributions will be rewarded with a free book from Ulysses Travel Publications. All you have to do is write us at the following address and indicate which title you would be interested in receiving (see the list at the end of guide).

Ulysses Travel Publications
4176 Rue Saint-Denis
Montréal, Québec
Canada H2W 2M5
www.ulysse.ca
E-mail: guiduly@ulysse.ca

Canadian Cataloguing in Publication Data
Bizier, Richard

      Louisiana   (Ulysses travel guides)
      Translation of Louisiane.
      Includes index.
      ISBN 2-89464-161-3
1. Louisiana - Guidebooks. II. Title   III. Series.
F367.3B5913 1998 917.6304'63 C97-941475-X
ISBN 2-89464-161-3

TABLE OF SYMBOLS

🏝	Our favourites
☎	Telephone number
⇄	Fax number
≡	Air conditioning
⊗	Ceiling fan
≈	Pool
ℜ	Restaurant
⊛	Whirlpool
ℝ	Refrigerator
ℂ	Kitchenette
△	Sauna
#	Screen
☺	Exercise room
tv	Colour television
pb	Private bathroom
sb	Shared bathroom
ps	Private shower
hw	Hot water
½b	half-board (lodging + 2 meals)
bkfst	Breakfast

ATTRACTION CLASSIFICATION

★	Interesting
★★	Worth a visit
★★★	Not to be missed

HOTEL CLASSIFICATION

Unless otherwise indicated, the prices in the guide are for one room, double occupancy, in the high season.

RESTAURANT CLASSIFICATION

$	$10 US or less
$$	$10 US to $20 US
$$$	$20 US to $30 US
$$$$	$30 US or more

The prices in the guide are for a meal for one person, excluding taxes, drinks and tip.

All prices in dollars in this guide are in American dollars.

LIST OF MAPS

Alexandria   p 344
Baton Rouge   p 165
Bayou Lafourche and Terrebonne   p 193
Bayou Teche   p 239
Crossroads   p 339
Lafayette   p 219
Louisiana   p 10
Louisiana's Northern Parishes   p 11
Louisiana's Southern Parishes   p 12
Mid-City   p 86
Monroe   p 383
New France Prior to the Treaty of Paris of 1736   p 18
New Orleans   p 55
   Central Business District and the Warehouse District   p 84
      Restaurants and Hotels   p 116
   French Quarter (Vieux Carré)   p 69
      Restaurants and Hotels   p 108
   Garden District   p 88
   Greater New Orleans   p 97
   Uptown   p 94
North of Lafayette   p 271
Northern Louisiana   p 369
Plantation Country and Baton Rouge   p 157
Shreveport-Bossier City   p 374
Western Acadiana   p 303
Where is Louisiana   p 9

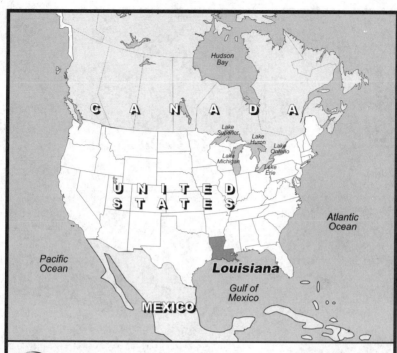

Hudson
Bay

C A N A D A

Lake Superior
Lake Huron
Lake Ontario
Lake Michigan
Lake Erie

U N I T E D
S T A T E S

Atlantic
Ocean

Pacific
Ocean

Louisiana

Gulf of
Mexico

MEXICO

***Where is
Louisiana?***

Louisiana

Capital: Baton Rouge
Population: 4,220,000 inhab.
Currency: American dollar
Area: 125,674 km²

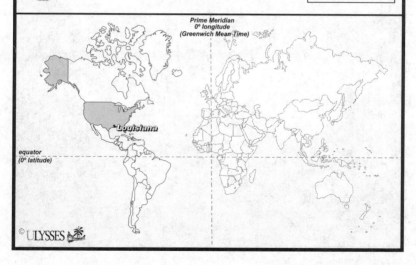

Prime Meridian
0° longitude
(Greenwich Mean Time)

Louisiana

equator
(0° latitude)

© ULYSSES

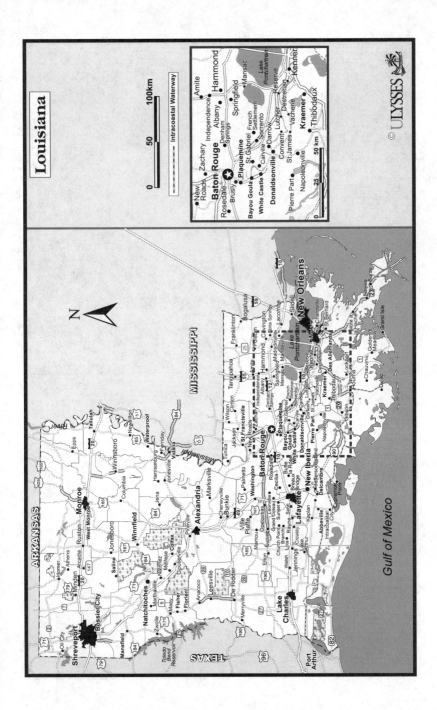

Louisiana

© ULYSSES

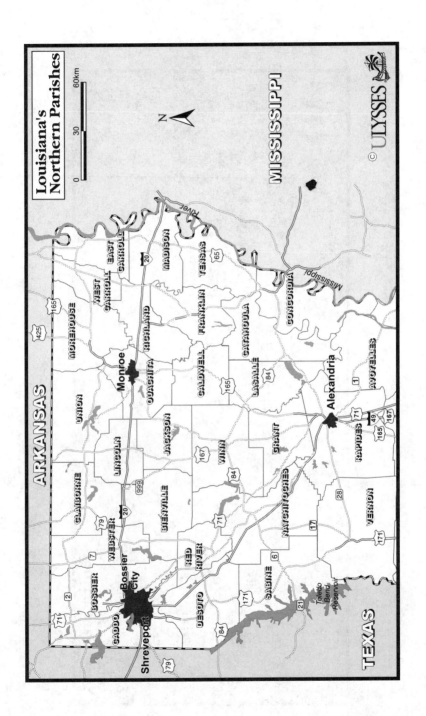

Louisiana's Northern Parishes

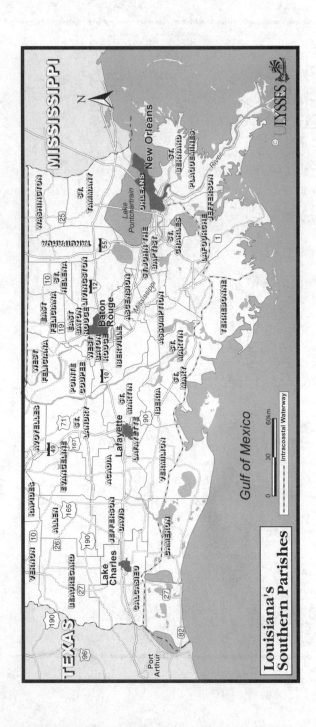

Louisiana's
Southern Parishes

PORTRAIT

Louisiana's colourful history recalls its many diverse inhabitants. The French who founded it in the 17th century, and then the Creoles, Africans, Spanish, Acadians and Americans, who settled over the next centuries, all contributed to its brilliance.

Compared to the territory it encompassed during the era of New France, contemporary Louisiana might seem minuscule. But this young southern state did not shrink away – crossing its length and width, a traveller quickly realizes that present-day Louisiana is large enough to lose oneself in, in beauty and in pleasure. To truly discover Louisiana, you really must delve into it, from Mississippi in the east to Texas in the west, and from the Gulf of Mexico in the south all the way to its northern border with Arkansas. An itinerary for this trip cannot be planned: Louisiana is a new

adventure every day, on the wharf of a little fishing port or in a café, in an anonymous crossroads town or on the square of a large city. Louisiana's southern climate contributes to its residents expansive character. Louisianians love tourists, and not mainly for commercial reasons. Do not hesitate to start conversations... you will be rewarded with famous southern hospitality and new friends.

GEOGRAPHY

The surface area of the state of Louisiana is 112,836 square kilometres. When it was a French colony, Louisiana (Haute-Louisiane and Basse-Louisiane) was an immense territory of 2,100,000 square kilometres, four times the actual area of France. French Louisiana then stretched from the Great Lakes to the Gulf of Mexico, hundreds of kilometres on either side of the Mississippi. Today this bygone colony is divided into 13 American states.

Louisiana is situated in the southern United States, wedged between Mississippi in the east, Arkansas in the north, the Gulf of Mexico in the south and Texas in the west. Louisiana, with its fertile river plains, receives abundant rains and enjoys a subtropical climate. The river bed of the Mississippi is bordered by dikes that protect neighbouring land from flooding. In addition to the Mississippi and the Gulf, Louisiana possesses many rivers, lakes, lagoons and bayous (of aboriginal origin, "bayou" means "slow-moving water"). These last are particular to Louisiana, and must not be confused with swamps. The Red River feeds the great lakes Pontchartrain, Maurepas, Borgne, Sabine and Calcasieu.

Louisiana's eastern border runs along the meandering Mississippi. From there, the southern state extends westward across vast plains interrupted only by stretches of water. An occasional rise in elevation indicates a subterranean salt deposit. You have to go to the north of the state, to the region of Shreveport-Bossier City, to discover even a timid hill of a maximum altitude of 70 metres, while in New Orleans the highest point is only five metres above sea level.

Geology

The land in southern Louisiana, is like a huge, floating blanket, and erecting buildings here requires true feats of engineering. Almost nowhere in the southernmost part of the state do the houses have basements; instead, they are set on concrete blocks, logs or other supports. The big buildings in New Orleans sit on foundations that plunge deep into the earth to the solid rock below the marshy terrain.

The highway linking New Orleans to Lafayette remains a masterpiece of ingenuity. Set on concrete piles, it runs over the series of swampy areas and bayous that stretch from New Orleans to Baton Rouge and from Maringouin to Lafayette. It spans a tiny portion of the enormous Atchafalaya basin, the largest stretch of swampland in America. Before the highway was built, travellers had to make a detour of several dozen kilometres to get to the districts of Breaux Bridge and Lafayette.

Numerous bayous wind their way through the countryside, cities and towns of Louisiana. There is water, water everywhere in this state, so don't be surprised when you see cemeteries with above-ground tombs in swampy areas. Eternal rest, fine, but not in the drink, thank you!

Flora

The subtropical climate of Louisiana, its multiple waterways and its persistent humidity are favourable to exuberant vegetation. Many indigenous plants inhabit the state's lagoons, forests and in marshes. In addition to these native species, transplants of various origins were imported for farming (practical and nutritious species) and for the pleasure of horticulture. Added to the local species of southern pine, pecan, walnut, oak and bald cypress, on which Spanish moss grows like garland, were fruit trees perfectly acclimatized to this humid climate.

During spring and summer, which stretches at least six months, swamps and ponds are bedecked with a multitude of aquatic plants. No one can resist the beauty of marvellous bouquets of water hyacinths, lotuses and water lilies forming multicoloured clusters of flowers – except for pleasure boaters who rip up these "awful" plants because they consider them a nuisance!

Magnolia Blossom

Louisiana counts an incredible number of public gardens. These are especially interesting for visitors who want to expand their knowledge of horticulture and be initiated to the basics of subtropical botany. Camellias, magnolias, azaleas, begonias, fuchsias and a multitude of other flowering plants abound in these magnificently maintained gardens.

Louisiana is like an immense garden throughout the year. Its subtropical climate promotes multiple flowering periods per cycle and per species. Whatever the season there is always a plant or a shrub in bloom somewhere.

In December and January, magnolias and camellias are in full bloom. Branches of azaleas and rhododendrons collapse under breathtaking bunches of flowers. Pansies border alleys. The Louisiana countryside is a profusion of evergreens. The apotheosis occurs in April, when the bayous are clothed in cloaks of flowering water plants.

Fauna

This land of water, earth and forests shelters exceptionally abundant fauna. Black bears, porcupines, squirrels, deer, hares, grey and red foxes, coypus, raccoons, wild pigs, armadillos, cougars, alligators, bobcats, American opossums, and many more species are omnipresent. Some forest insects, such as wood ticks, can carry disease, while on the ground and in swampy areas there are many venomous snakes; avoid walking too close to roadside ditches (for more information and advice see p 44).

A multitude of birds, including quail, doves and wild turkeys, resides permanently in Louisiana. To these are added geese, duck and other migrating birds from Central and South America and from northern regions. Snowy egrets, a species on the verge of extinction, are protected in an ornithological reserve on Avery Island.

Waterways, lagoons, bayous, ponds and swamps are as teeming with fish as is the Gulf of Mexico, where quantities of fish, shrimp, crabs, oysters, turtles and other marine species are caught. Crayfish and catfish are two of Louisiana's trademarks, and these are eaten throughout the state along with shrimp, soft-shell crabs and oysters.

In homage to its flora and fauna, Louisiana includes among its emblems the pelican, the magnolia and the bald cypress.

Brown Pelican

HISTORY

Pre-Columbian America was already inhabited by many peoples spread to the four corners of the continent before this immense territory was "discovered" and politically created by Europeans. These peoples included numerous autonomous communities, each with a distinct identity and rich culture. In present-day Louisiana once lived three large Native American groups: the Tunicas, the Caddos and the Muskogees. Experts assert that the ancestors of the native peoples of the Americas took advantage of the lowering of sea level – the long Pleistocene Age (which began about

1.75 million years ago and ended 10,000 years ago) created a ford between Asia and America – to cross Bering Strait and spread out across the vast American continent. These same experts surmise that the migrations of these Asiatic peoples took place about 25,000 years ago.

The first Europeans to explore the coasts of this part of the Gulf of Mexico were the Spaniards Alonzo de Pineda (1519) and Panfilo de Narváez (1528), although they did not dare adventure into the mysterious swamps inland. If we had to name the first European "tourist" the title would incontestably fall on Cabeza de Vaca, who, even if unwillingly, was the first to travel across this territory. De Vaca was part of an expedition launched by de Narváez, who was looking for gold in the area that is now Pensacola, a port town in Florida near the Alabama border. Many members of de Narváez's party were killed by natives. The treasurer de Vaca and two of his companions were captured on their small boat, which they had just boarded in an attempt to get closer to shore. After successfully escaping, Cabeza de Vaca travelled about 3,200 kilometres, across the territory that would two centuries later become Louisiana, to the Pacific Ocean. It was not until many years later that he met compatriots who brought him to Mexico and then home to Spain, where tales of his odyssey made him a celebrity. In the meantime, passing himself off as a "healer-sorcerer" he mastered the languages of the aboriginal peoples with whom he stayed during his long crossing.

The mouth of the Mississippi was not discovered until 1541. In April of that year Hernando de Soto, who had previously accompanied Francisco Pizarro in Peru, explored the area with his party.

The French

The St. Lawrence River and its many tributaries were important arteries of communication well before the arrival of Europeans. In 1534, 1535 and 1536, Jacques Cartier, the explorer from St. Malo, travelled up the St. Lawrence and realized the scale of importance the river held for the exploration of newly acquired French territories. From the moment of settlement in Acadia in 1604, and in Québec in 1608, and of the foundation of New France by Samuel de Champlain, traders, trappers, colonists, explorers and soldiers all used these same waterways. Navigating them, and penetrating further west inland each time, they discovered the Great Lakes and realized that they were a natural extension of the St. Lawrence. Following surveys of Lake Huron and Lake Erie, and then of Lake Michigan by Jean Nicollet in 1634, French explorers began to used this vast maritime network and it would play a predominant role in the history of New France and of Canada.

Nicollet, while desperately trying to reach China, opened the way to Louisiana... Louis Jolliet and Père Marquette discovered the Mississippi in 1673. In 1682, Cavelier de La Salle took possession of a territory that he named "La Louysiane" in honour of his king, Louis XIV. Colonization of Louisiana began tentatively in 1697, under the administration of Pierre Le Moyne d'Iberville, although its was his brother, Jean-Baptiste Le Moyne de Bienville, who definitively laid the foundations of the new colony. In its earliest period, Louisiana counted but a few hundred inhabitants.

Activity in this young French colony only really began after the foundation of New Orleans by de Bienville in 1718. Eight years later, in 1726, New Orleans had a population of almost 4,000, including colonists, slaves, soldiers and Native Americans, and began to have the appearance of a small maritime capital. New lands were cleared and planted with rice, tobacco, sugar cane, corn and cotton for export to Europe and to France's other American colonies.

The Creoles

The word "Creole", from the Spanish *criollo*, was originally intended to designate whites born in the colonies in the southern part of North America, as well as those living in the West Indies. As in the French West Indies, the sons and daughters of French planters born in New Orleans became genuine Creoles. One of the most famous Creoles was Empress Josephine, born Marie-Josèphe Tascher de La Pagerie in Trois-Ilets, Martinique. The term later came to refer to people of French or Spanish descent or (popularly) to someone of mixed French and Spanish and African descent.

In the course of its 38 years of Spanish rule (1762 to 1800), New Orleans never became hispanicized. During this period, Franco-Creole culture, education and traditions remained firmly intact throughout the city. The Spanish authorities left the cultural infrastructure in place and the soldiers, who had no choice but to marry

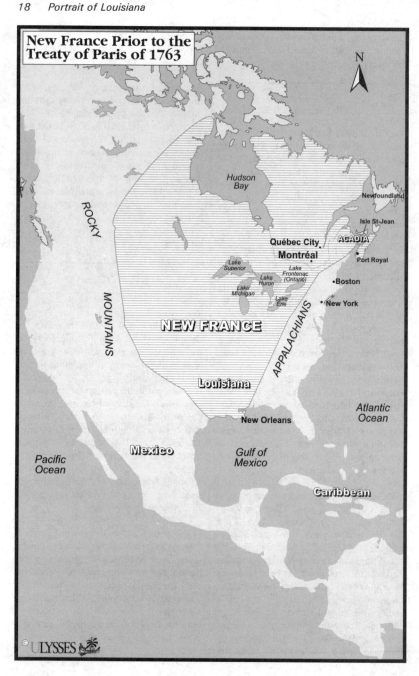

Creoles, were rapidly assimilated into the dominant French culture.

The Germans

The Germans recruited by the French settled in an area that had been farmed by natives (Taensas) and said to be a beautiful spot with fine land. The census of November 24, 1721 shows that the German families lived 12 leagues upriver from New Orleans, on the left, on an excellent stretch of land formerly occupied by *"Champs Sauvages"*, which were uncultivated lands that were nevertheless easy to clear. The man in charge of the German colonization, Karl Friedrich d'Arensbourg, founded the village of Des Allemands, on land granted to De Meuse. Other German villages were also established: Mariental, Augsburg and Hoffen. Under the French Regime, the majority of Germans were Catholic, but there were also a number of Calvinists, Lutherans and other Protestants. These settlers were recruited in Alsace and Lorraine, as well as in various parts of Germany, Switzerland and even Hungary. In 1734, referring to a Swiss regiment, Governor Bienville stated that it would be better to relocate them here than to send them back to France: "These Swiss are much more hard-working than the French. Furthermore, they'll have an easy time marrying into German families." This German-speaking population, soon joined by French-speaking colonists from France and parts of what would become known as Canada (present-day Québec, Acadia), ended up becoming bilingual and eventually assimilated into the Francophone majority. It wasn't difficult to integrate them, since their were no German-speaking priests or teachers, and most of them were illiterate; even their names were Frenchified. Interracial marriages took care of the rest. The Germans were industrious colonists and played an active role in Louisiana's economic development. Their main crops were rice, corn and indigo, and they also grew all sorts of market garden produce, which they sold at the French Market in New Orleans. The Germans were also involved in the sugar industry, used slaves to harvest cotton, and were major stockbreeders for their time.

The Spanish

The French occupation lasted 60 years. Under the terms of the Treaty of Fountainbleau (1762), France ceded Louisiana to Spain. However, the Louisianians were only informed of this two years later. The news was greeted with displeasure. On March 5, 1766, Antonio de Ulloa came to take possession of Louisiana in the name of the King of Spain. The new governor was so unpopular that he had to enlist the help of the last French governor, Charles-Phillipe Aubrey, to assert his authority. After being summoned to show his credentials to the Creole leaders and refusing to do so, Ulloa fled to Cuba. For 10 months, starting on October 27, 1768, Louisianians revolted against the Spanish, thus becoming the first colony in the New World to protest its subjugation. On August 18, 1769, however, Don Alejandro O'Reilly, accompanied by 2,056 soldiers, succeeded in imposing Spanish authority and established the Cabildo.

At that point, Spanish law replaced French law, and Spanish supplanted

Two Acadian Heroes

Joseph Broussard, known as Beausoleil, was one of the leaders of a movement that brought hundreds of Acadian detainees, prisoners from old Fort Beauséjour and from the camps in Halifax, by sea to the French Antilles and from there to the "Pays des Bayous" ("Bayou Land"). The boat that was used for these journeys was stolen from the English in a mutiny organized by Beausoleil during the Deportation.

In 1785, encouraged by the treaty signed the previous year between France and Spain (Louisiana had meantime fallen under the rule of the Spanish), Olivier Thériault left for Nantes to convince the Acadians who had settled there ten years earlier to join those in Louisiana. Thériault no doubt had a silver tongue, because he succeeded in bringing back 1,600 of the 2,000 "refugees". His project is the subject of a fresco by Robert Dafford, *L'Embarquement des Acadiens pour la Louisiane* ("The Departure of the Acadians for Louisiana"), which was completed at the same time as was the mural painting of the Acadian Monument. The two works were inaugurated simultaneously at twinned ceremonies – in Louisiana, for the fresco, and in Nantes, France, for the mural. The 20-metre mural has since been displayed outdoors, in Rue des Acadiens in the Ermitage neighbourhood of Nantes.

French as the official language. The Cabildo was made up of six *regidors* (councillors), an attorney general and a clerk. It was under the Spanish regime of O'Reilly, regarded as the father of Spanish Louisiana, that slavery was abolished.

The Acadians

In 1762 France ceded part of its Louisiana territory to Spain, in gratitude for the latter country's neutrality during the wars between France and England (the king of Spain, Charles III was the cousin of Louis XV). The next year, at the signing of the Treaty of Paris, it was England's turn to receive a piece of the Louisiana pie. By this time the population of Louisiana had risen to some 15,000 souls.

Driven from their northern home by the English, who appropriated their land and named the new territory Nova Scotia, Acadians deported in 1755 experienced many misadventures before some of them were finally able to settle in Louisiana. The hope of many Acadians was to reach still-French Louisiana, but English authorities had other ideas. Thus began the interminable saga of the Acadian people. Some were deported to France, others searched in vain for a peaceful haven in the English colonies from Massachusetts to South Carolina. Still others found their way to the French colonies in the Caribbean, and even to Guyana and South America. Neither the English nor the French knew how or where to relocate these people.

Spain finally ended the calvary of these martyred people, victims of the indifference and vicissitudes of history,

The *Code Noir*

In 1724, the French government instituted the *Code Noir*, which guaranteed certain rights to slaves and freed blacks. This code defined the responsibilities incumbent upon both slaves and masters, including, in the latter case, making sure that all slaves were baptized in the Catholic. Under its terms, slaves did not have to work on holidays or Sundays. The French *Code Noir* was decidedly more humane than those laws governing slavery in other Southern colonies (those under English and Spanish rule). This code remained in effect until the 1820s, after which the African-Americans were subject to the harsh laws prevalent in the Southern states.

in the 1870s. Back in France after spending many years in Louisiana, Peyroux de La Coudrenière became the spokesperson of the Acadians who, spread to the four corners of the earth, had as their greatest hope to be reunited with family members who had settled in the southern part of Louisiana, which had become Spanish territory. In Paris, de La Coudrenière met with the Spanish ambassador, to whom he submitted his proposal. The diplomat had a sympathetic ear, negotiations were initiated in the fall of 1783, and the plan became a reality. Charles III, the king of Spain, signed the agreement in 1784 and from May to October 1785 hundreds of Acadians boarded ships bound for New Orleans.

The Slaves

The European settlers forced the natives to do arduous work, one of several reasons why entire populations perished. The new arrivals brought many illnesses to the so-called New World that the immune systems of the indigenous peoples could not fight off. Exhausted, weakened and drained by the demands of the European conquerors, these communities were then abandoned to their sad fate.

Though huge numbers of natives died, the colonizers were more concerned about their shrunken work force than the death of these unfortunate and generally peaceable souls. The Europeans thus set their sights on Africa, and another kind of slavery emerged in the Americas.

Slave-trading was carried out in every European colony in the New World. The English, the Spanish, the French, the Dutch and the Portuguese purchased groups of Africans and installed them in slave quarters on their farmlands and plantations. According to a census taken in 1714, there were 111 whites, 134 natives and 10 blacks in Mobile (then part of French Louisiana) alone. And that was just the beginning...

The Americans

Well before France sold Louisiana to the United States in 1803, the Americans viewed the territory as the natural geographic continuation of their country. New Orleans lies at the mouth of the Mississippi, and this long river, which snakes its way from the north to the south, was rightly considered to be of strategic value. For reasons both military and economic, the young

The Civil War

In the fledgling American republic, each state enjoyed a certain degree of autonomy, and was thus responsible for decisions such as whether or not to abolish slavery within its borders. However, when a new state or territory joined the Union, Congress made such decisions for that region. The Northern states opposed slavery, which was not necessary for their economic growth and which they considered inhumane. However, in those states south of the Ohio, as well as those west of the Mississippi, where more and more cotton plantations were springing up, slavery provided landowners with an inexpensive workforce. Before long, a confrontation started brewing between the slave states of the South and the abolitionist states of the North.

The South first started protesting when Missouri was admitted to the Union as a slave state in 1821 following the Missouri Compromise, while efforts were being made to abolish the "peculiar institution" in states west of the Mississippi and in the North. In 1844, after several other states were admitted, the level of discontent reached its peak, and a secessionist movement that was prepared to break up the Union in order to maintain slavery took shape. In the 1860 elections, Republican candidate Abraham Lincoln, an avowed abolitionist, became President, thus excluding the pro-slavery democrats from power. Perceiving this election as provocation, the Southern states started seceding in 1861. They joined together as the Confederate States of America, naming Richmond, Virginia their capital city and declaring Jefferson Davis President. The Civil War lasted from the spring of 1861 to 1865.

The Southerners, who were better prepared, won many victories in the first two years of the war. They were outnumbered, however, by the Northerners, who occupied the entire territory west of the Mississippi; it was from there that the Union launched most of its attacks on the Confederates. Between Washington, the capital of the Union and Richmond, the capital of the Confederacy, the conflicts became bloodier and bloodier. The latter city was the scene of the decisive battle between the troops of Confederate General Robert E. Lee and those of Union General Ulysses Grant. The fighting lasted 10 days and resulted in Lee's surrender. This terrible war claimed 600,000 lives. Five days after it ended, on April 14, Abraham Lincoln, who had just begun his second term as President, was assassinated by an enraged Southerner, actor John Wilkes Booth. The outcome of the Civil War meant that the United States would remain intact. By 1863, in the middle of the war, the North had abolished slavery in all states where it was still legal, and in 1865, immediately after the war, slavery was officially banned in all parts of the United States.

Two of the eight Confederate generals, Braxton Bragg and Pierre Gustave Toutant Beauregard, were from Louisiana. It was under the command of the latter, a Creole, that the first shots of the Civil War were fired at Fort Sumter, in South Carolina, on April 12, 1861. Both had distinguished themselves during the Mexican War.

American republic coveted the region. As soon as the Louisiana Purchase had been concluded, the U.S. wasted no time encouraging a massive number of immigrants of Anglo-Saxon descent to settle in the region, first in the cities (New Orleans and Baton Rouge) and then gradually in the parishes along the Mississippi.

At the end of the first half of the 19th century, the "Anglos" continued moving into new regions—in St. Mary Parish, on the coast of the Gulf of Mexico and, in greater numbers, along the north part of the Atchafalaya River. "Sugar mania" prompted many other settlers to buy small farms from French farmers. The new arrivals replaced rustic buildings with immense agricultural facilities used for growing and processing sugar cane. The French farmers, for their part, moved to the prairies in the southwestern part of Louisiana. During the same period, many other immigrants arrived, though in fewer numbers than the Anglo-Saxons and Americans. Successive waves of German, Spanish, Irish, Italian and Slavic immigrants thus settled in American Louisiana.

In the years following the Civil War, there was a vast campaign to encourage new settlers to move to the prairies in the southwestern part of the state. Many German farmers from the American Midwest answered the call. These people were skilled at growing wheat and other grains; in Louisiana, they soon became expert rice-growers as well.

Another big wave of Anglo-Saxon immigration occured during the construction of the Southern Pacific railroad, in 1882. However, the preponderance of English-speakers became even more conspicuous after the discovery of oil in 1901, an upward trend that continued until after the Second World War.

Important Dates in the History of Louisiana

1763 The Treaty of Paris divides the enormous French territory of Louisiana. The eastern part joins the English colonies.

1801 Spain returns Louisiana to the French.

1803 November 30th, Napoleon Bonaparte, who has urgent need of funds for his military campaigns, sells Louisiana to the Americans for the sum of 80 million francs.

1804 March 26th, the American congress passes a law dividing Louisiana into Orleans territory, north of the 33rd parallel, and Louisiana territory, south of the 33rd parallel. This same year, Thomas Jefferson, president of the United States, names William Charles Cole Claiborne governor of the territory of Orleans, the first American to hold this post.

1810 Territorial disputes erupt between the Spanish and the Americans. Florida, still Spanish, reclaims the entire territory north of New Orleans and west to Baton Rouge. Governor Claiborne offers to leave the territory east of Pensacola to Florida, to cede the area of Mobile to Mississippi and to return the region of Baton Rouge to Louisiana.

1812 Louisiana joins the Union on April 8th, becoming the 18th state.

1814 The British occupy Louisiana.

1815 In New Orleans, buccaneer-patriot Jean Lafitte helps General Andrew Jackson push the English troops out of Louisiana.

1840 New Orleans becomes the fourth largest city in the United States and its port ranks second in importance.

1848 General Zachary Taylor, a Louisianian, is elected president of the United States.

1860 Abraham Lincoln is elected president of the United States.

1861 The State of Louisiana is created. Four days later, on the 23rd of January, the Baton Rouge Convention proclaims independence and the State of Louisiana becomes a republic.

1865 Louisiana is reintegrated into the United States.

1910 The first oil wells are drilled in Louisiana.

POLITICS

The state capital, Baton Rouge, is the seat of the state legislature, which consists of the Senate and the House of Representatives. The state is divided into districts made up of one or more parishes.

The judiciary includes the state Supreme Court, five courts of appeal and a number of district courts. It is interesting to note that Louisiana is the only American state to follow civil law, derived from the Napoleonic Code.

Each state has a governor and a lieutenant governor. In Louisiana, these offices are presently held by Mike

Foster and Kathleen Branco, respectively. The secretary of state and the attorney general are the two other most important figures in the state government.

In addition, each parish is governed by a board known as the Police Jury, whose members (the sheriff, coroner, clerk and assessor) are elected.

Finally, there are the state police, who monitor traffic on highways and major roads; the Sheriff's department, responsible for maintaining order and safety in the parishes, and the municipal or local police.

ECONOMY

Louisiana is a rich agricultural land. Corn, rice, wheat and other grain crops, soya, cotton, sugar cane, fruits and vegetables are all cultivated in abundance. The planting season begins in early January for tomatoes and extends through to October for cabbage; there are multiple harvests during the year. Oil, natural gas, petrochemicals, sulfur, salt, port industries, food processing, fishing and forestry also contribute a good deal to the state's economy. Close to 30% of the fish and seafood consumed in the United States is caught in Louisiana.

POPULATION

The population of Louisiana is approximately 4,400,000, largely concentrated in urban areas in 61 parishes. Not including residents of surrounding suburban sprawl (if the entire metropolitan area of New Orleans including Metairie is taken into account, the population of New Orleans rises to 1.2 million inhabitants), here are the population figures of Louisiana's five largest cities:

New Orleans:	487,000;
Baton Rouge:	230,500;
Shreveport-Bossier:	202,000;
Metairie:	149,500;
Lafayette:	109,000.

FRENCH IN LOUISIANA

Society and Culture

During a national census a few years ago, 898,716 residents of Louisiana identified themselves as being of French descent. This figure represents about 21% of the 4.4-million-strong population of the state. A little less than half of these are of Acadian ancestry, and one quarter of them still speak French in the home. Unfortunately, the survey did not take into account the thousands of Creoles and Native Americans who also speak French, so the exact number of Francophone Louisianians is difficult to establish.

Lafayette Parish is home to the largest number of Acadian descendants, followed by Calcasieu, Lafourche, Acadia and Vermilion Parishes.

At present, Louisiana is officially a bilingual state, and French is taught in all elementary schools. As is clear, even if the greatest proportion of Francophone Louisianians are of Acadian descent not all of them are. Other French-speaking people have heritages that are Native American,

French, African, Spanish, German, Metis and Irish.

After the Louisiana Purchase, New Orleans would not resist assimilation for long. Attempts by New Orleanians to maintain the French language in the courts and in the legislature lasted some time – resistance on the part of Creoles was particularly strong – but the English language imposed itself and gradually the use of French diminished. Nonetheless, throughout the rest of Louisiana, French remained the official language until the turn of the century and groups of all ethnic backgrounds were integrated into the French culture. It is not uncommon to find people of French ancestry with English names. What little French that is spoken in Louisiana now is very particular and not always understandable to Francophones from France, Québec or elsewhere.

French Toponyms

Throughout Louisiana, in the west and south of New Orleans and Lake Pontchartrain, the names of parishes, towns, villages and localities illustrate the amplitude of the influence of French on the culture of Louisiana.

Acadiana

In 1971 a group of representatives in the Louisiana legislature proposed to officially name the part of the state that is the centre of Francophone culture "Acadiana".

The Flag of Acadiana

Carencro native Judge Allen Maurice Babineaux was the originator of the idea to create a distinctive flag for Acadiana, an idea that came to fruition when it was officially adopted by the Louisiana legislature in 1974. In 1962, during a family trip to the Northern Acadia (in the Maritime provinces of Canada), he had noticed that the Acadian flag was flown throughout New Brunswick. This sight motivated him to promote the idea of a flag for the descendants of Acadians in Louisiana.

The flag was designed by Thomas J. Arceneaux and refers as much to the history as to the culture of Acadiana. Three lilies on a blue background symbolize France; a gold castle on a red background refers to Spain, which welcomed Acadians in Louisiana; a gold star on a white background (*Maris Stella*) represents Our Lady of the Assumption, the patron saint of the Acadians, and is also symbolic of Cajun participation in the War of American Independence.

Acadiana, where the highest concentration of people of Acadian descent lives, is in southeast and south-central Louisiana. It begins past Baton Rouge, the state capital. Its main city and symbolic capital is Lafayette (formerly called "Vermillon").

Joie de vivre (joy of living) is a characteristic of Cajun culture. Although the most important festival on the calendar is still Mardi Gras, in terms of cultural fairs, Cajuns have not given up their place. For five years now, during the month of April, the streets of downtown Lafayette have been enlivened by the clamour of the Festival International de la Francophonie, which brings together people from almost all French-speaking countries.

CULTURE

Writers and Louisiana

Louisiana has been the birthplace of several writers, attracted a number of others and inspired many. African-American writers from Solomon Northup, author of *Twelve Years a Slave*, published in 1853, to contemporary novelist Ernest Gaines, have never overlooked the humiliation inflicted upon their people. In another vein, a number of musicians have left behind memoires or told others their recollections for publication; these include Sidney Bechet, Jelly Roll Morton and Louis Armstrong, whose book *Growing up in New Orleans* was published in 1952.

At the age of 23 years, Frank Scott Fitzgerald (1896-1941) wrote his first novel, *This Side of Paradise*, in an apartment facing Lafayette Cemetery in

New Orleans. No commemorative plaque identifies the apartment. The poet Andrei Codrescu, in his introduction to the anthology *New Orleans Stories: Great Writers on the City* (1992), points out that if a plaque were hung at every place that an author had lived, the city would be covered in them. Of Romanian origin, Codrescu has made New Orleans his adoptive home... "The city might be small, but it is so lively that one doesn't even notice."

Truman Capote (1924-1984), a novelist with a fantastic imagination, was born in New Orleans and lived for some time in the Garden District, to which he returned in many of his works. One of these, the short story *Dazzle* is about the occult powers of a woman who dabbles in witchcraft to whom he confides his secret desire to "be a girl".

Anne Rice, a contemporary author whose works include novels and short stories (*The Feast of All saints* and *The Vampire LeStat*), lives in the "Crescent City" and probably best describes the everyday characters of New Orleans.

Tennessee Williams' *A Streetcar Named Desire*

The famous play by Tennessee Williams, *A Streetcar Named Desire*, for which he won the Pulitzer Prize in 1947, opens on the following setting, lovingly described by the author: "The exterior of a two-story corner building on a street in New Orleans which is named Elysian Fields and runs between the L&N tracks and the river. The section is poor but, unlike corresponding sections in other American cities, it has a raffish charm. The houses are mostly white frame, weathered grey, with rickety outside stairs and galleries and quaintly ornamented gables. This building contains two flats, upstairs and down. Faded white stairs ascend to the entrances of both.

"It is first dark of an evening early in May. The sky that shows around the dim white building is a peculiarly tender blue, almost a turquoise, which invests the scene with a kind of lyricism and gracefully attenuates the atmosphere of decay. You can almost feel the warm breath of the brown river beyond the river warehouses with their faint redolences of bananas and coffee. A corresponding air is evoked by the music of Negro entertainers at a barroom around the corner. In this part of New Orleans you are practically always just around the corner, or a few doors down the street, from a tinny piano being played with the infatuated fluency of brown fingers. This 'blue piano' expresses the spirit of the life which goes on here."

Longfellow's *Evangeline*

Born in 1807 in Portland, Maine, the poet Henry Wadsworth Longfellow wrote his first verses in 1841. In 1847, inspired by an Acadian legend, he wrote a long poem that is still on the curricula of American schools, *Evangeline*. Longfellow was well aware of the dramatic odyssey that was lived almost a century earlier by the Acadian people. Acadia was on the border of his native New England, and, in the years following the Great Deportation, many Acadians passed difficult years in this part of the American country, which was still under British control in the years following 1755. The writings of the era and the tales relating the exodus told in people's homes no doubt supplied Longfellow all the elements of his composition, which is at its core about the massive deportation of the Acadians. *Evangeline*, in fact, traces their long journey through the North American continent, their arrival in Louisiana and the long years that drifted by before the heroine, Evangeline, was reunited with her fiance, Gabriel, in St. Martinville, Louisiana.

Longfellow's poem is a heart-wrenching portrayal of lost dreams. The main character is Evangeline Bellefontaine, who lives in Grand-Pré and is engaged to Gabriel Lajeunesse. When the English arrive and load the Acadians onto boats, Evangeline and her beau are separated. Evangeline spends the rest of her life searching the colonies for her fiancé until, in her old age, she loses hope and joins the church. As a nun tending to the poor and the sick, she is finally reunited with her girlhood love. Gabriel is old and bedridden. He recognizes Evangeline and then dies. The lovers' last meeting is set in Louisiana, in a St. Martinville hospital, right near Bayou Teche.

For northern Acadians as much as for southern Cajuns, the legend rings true. To them, Longfellow's romantic characters are far from just fictional, and it is not even in doubt that these personages really existed under the names Emmeline Labiche and Louis Arsenaux.

Jazz and African-American

It all started in New Orleans. It was here that the traditional African musical styles took root and evolved into jazz, blues and gospel.

The oldest African-Americans still remembered the rhythms and instruments used in the ceremonies and rituals they took part in before being rounded up and sold into slavery in the white world. On Congo Square, where they were permitted to gather on Sundays, slaves would spend hours performing inspired dances to the sounds of big cylindrical drums, tom-toms carved out of tree trunks, square drums, castanets made out of bones, calabashes, triangles, as we are told by jazz historian Arnaud Bienville, whose name summons up the memory of the founder of New Orleans. Though never written down, the music they made was nonetheless coded; like all music it was based on a specific rhythmic structure, and only within that structure did imagination take over. This music would always retain these characteristics, which made it ideal for improvisation

Music, in general, played a big role in New Orleans, which had its own opera companies, symphony orchestras and even, toward the end of the 19th century, a Creole symphony orchestra made up entirely of black musicians; New Orleans was the birthplace of a phenomenon unknown elsewhere – that of the black Creole. Originally, the term "Creole" designated a white person born in the West Indian colonies. In French Louisiana, however, in spite of the *Code Noir* drawn up at Versailles in 1724, slave owners were not punished for their transgressions, and when they fathered mulatto children, they often had them baptized, assigned them less strenuous tasks and even freed them.

By around 1800, there were at least 2,000 of these freed black Creoles living in New Orleans, some of whom

Louis Armstrong

Montréal writer and art critic Paquerette Villeneuve had the opportunity to meet famous jazzman Louis Armstrong and converse with him when he was visiting Montréal. Here is what she has to say about him, and about jazz...

Louis Armstrong, born in New Orleans in 1900, would become internationally recognized as a symbol of the New Orleans style. In his autobiography, *Growing up in New Orleans*, he speaks of a wonderful childhood. They were poor with all of the consequences that entails, but there was music everywhere. Armstrong lived on Gravier Street, in the old neighbourhood of St. Mary, with his mother Mayann (short for Mary Ann), who did laundry for white people. He would leave the neighbourhood to sell coal.

Out of this mix of misery and music Armstrong created a remarkable synthesis. Composer Erik Satie was undoubtedly thinking of Armstrong when he said in the twenties that what he loved about jazz was that it brought you its sadness and it didn't give a damn!

All through his life, Louis Armstrong, "Pops" or "Satchmo" as his innumerable friends and acquaints called him, was welcomed everywhere with the same warmth he himself exuded.

were able to take advantage of the same musical instruction available to whites.

The music of this small population took its roots from the very heart of Africa and remained profoundly anchored in the hearts and memories of newly arrived Africans who became slaves in America, forced to toil in cotton fields under merciless masters. They were allowed to chant, since despite the harsh sun these rhythms seemed to encourage them in their work, and their songs would later open avenues to freedom for them. Like all great seaports, New Orleans had its share of pleasure parlours and eventually black music was introduced as one of their attractions.

In France the arrival of black musicians in the cabarets of Montmartre inspired the enthusiasm of greats like Claudel and Ravel. French author and diplomat Paul Claudel had given African music, which would one day offer America jazz, a definition that harmonized perfectly with its profound sensuality. "The lanterns are out, the shrill oboe is quiet, but to the quick beat of sticks, rich with the continuous rumbling of the drum, the procession continues its tumult and its dance. What is that beating? It bursts and falls, flees, returns, and at times it is a racket as though impatient hands were rattling the sword suspended between two worlds, and at other times it is solemn under spaced out beats, echoing the clash in full voice." As for the composer Maurice Ravel, it was the saxophone in particular that enchanted him, although he also wrote a sonata for piano and violin entitled *Blues*.

Cajun Traditions

Culturally there are many common points between Creoles (black or mixed) and Cajuns. Music, despite young roots, occupies an important place in the lives of Cajuns and Creoles. Some musicians claim the line of Luderin Darbonne, Harry Choates and Iry LeJeune – pioneers of traditional Cajun music – as their heritage; others' influences include Amédée Ardoin, Moïse Dugas, Adam Fontenot and Clifton Chénier.

Clifton Chénier did not invent "zarico" (the name comes from the French word *"haricot"*, which means "bean", specifically from an old expression that is used to describe tough times: *"les z'haricots sont pas salés"*, which translates literally as "the beans are not salted"). He did modernize and popularize this form of musical expression inspired by Cajun and Afro-Caribbean music, rock and roll, and rhythm and blues and he perfected washboard playing technique.

The influence of Chénier and his Red Hot Louisiana Band was significant for many. On St. Antoine Street in Lafayette Nathan Williams' Zydeco Cha Chas debuted at the El Sido Club, and the band remains one of the absolute best of the style. According to radio host John Broussard, the band's popularity is so great that during a trip to New York the press was unanimous in acclaiming its talent. To really swing and appreciate the Zydeco Cha Chas requires a trip to the El Sido (see the chapter "Acadiana: Lafayette", p 231).

On Saturdays in Eunice, from 9am to noon, there is a Cajun jam session in the shop of renowned accordion-maker and musician Marc Savoy. Musicians and singers, men and women, beginners and professionals from the four corners of Louisiana meet on these joyful Saturday mornings in Eunice. For three hours the instruments of twenty musicians, including piano, fiddle, guitar, bass, cello, and "ti-fer" blend in renditions of traditional songs.

LOUISIANA CUISINE

Nowhere else in the United States does the cuisine rival that of Louisiana. Creole, African-American and Cajun food is consumed like an open history book: jambalaya is derived from Spanish paella, shrimp, crab and okra gumbo are steeped in African flavours, the brown roux of Savoie is from the French repertoire, and crayfish étouffée is half-Creole, half-French. Some preparation and cooking methods are similar to those used since time immemorial by native Americans. This fusion has produced an original cuisine, some of the specialties of which – Tabasco sauce, pecan pie, Creole shrimp and oysters Rockefeller, to name a few – have become standards all over the world.

Gourmet Glossary

Andouille: Not comparable to the French *andouille*, which is prepared with pork chitterlings or tripe. The smoked, Louisianian *andouille* is made of pork meat and spices; it is used to spice up various dishes including the famous gumbo.

Beignet: Of French origin, this square-shaped doughnut is sprinkled with icing sugar and served hot and always with a *café au lait*.

Boudin: This is not a traditional *boudin* made with pig's blood, but rather is a sausage made of rice, onion, spices and herbs, among other ingredients.

Café au lait: Coffee with steamed milk, a favourite beverage of New Orleanians, which, like at the famous Café du Monde, is deliciously accompanied by beignets.

Calas: A fried pastry made of flour, rice and cinnamon, served with syrup at breakfast.

Court-bouillon: The Creole court-bouillon includes tomatoes, onion, garlic, pepper and hot peppers and is used to cook fish such as snapper, redfish, and red sea bream.

Creole: Probably of Spanish origin, this sauce has a base of tomatoes, garlic and sweet peppers. It is used in many culinary preparations including the famous Creole shrimp.

Papillote: A method called en papillote that consists of cooking – usually steaming – foods in parchment paper.

À l'étouffée: A method that consists of cooking foods in a sealed casserole dish.

Filé: Obtained by grinding sassafras leaves, this powder, similar to ground bay leaves, is used to season sauces and gumbos.

Gumbo: Traditional okra soup. To a spicy broth seasoned with a brown roux, are added *andouille*, crayfish, shrimp, oysters, crab and duck to taste. White rice is added to the soup bowl.

Gumbo z'herbes: Mustard greens and spinach are added to the usual okra gumbo.

Jambalaya: Similar to Spanish *paella*, it is composed of rice, sausage, seafood and tomatoes. The name jambalaya comes from the French *jambon*, which means ham, and the African *ya*, which means rice.

Maque-choux: A dish with a base of fresh corn and vegetables.

Mirliton: This vegetable from the squash family, called *chayotte* in Haiti and *christophine* in Guadeloupe and Martinique, is stuffed with ham or shrimp.

Muffaletta: An Italian sandwich-meal made of cold cuts, olives and cheese.

Pain perdu: As its French name suggests, this recipe uses slightly stale bread slices that are soaked in a mixture of milk, sugar and eggs and then browned on the stove (also known as French toast).

Po'boy: A contraction of "poor boy", this sandwich – or inexpensive meal – is made from a baguette of French bread stuffed with fried oysters, shrimp, soft-shell crab or crayfish and seasoned with hot pepper sauce.

Pralines: A favourite with New Orleanians, this candy is made of sugar, butter, cream and pecans.

Roux: Obtained by cooking flour in oil or butter, a roux heightens many Creole and Cajun dishes including the famous gumbo.

Sauce Piquante: A sauce made of a roux watered down with white wine to which are added tomatoes, hot peppers and a hint of vinegar.

Soft-Shell Crab: Every spring, blue crabs shed their shell. For a few weeks, before the crabs' new armour has hardened, fishermen gather them up off the coast. The crabs are then savoured by New Orleanians, who prepare them in all kinds of ways—in salads, in sauces, grilled, breaded and fried.

Tasso: Smoked pork, sliced into thin strips and dried, tasso is often an ingredient in gumbo and is used to season myriad dishes.

CAJUN MENU

Soup
Duck and Sausage Gumbo

Appetizer
Marinated Crab Salad

Main Course
Cajun Jambalaya
and
Corn Bread

Dessert
Pecan Pie
or
Dame Broussard's Cane Syrup Cake

THE RECIPES

DUCK AND SAUSAGE GUMBO
Serves 8
Preparation time: 20 minutes
Cooking time: about 2 hours, 15 minutes

This dish can be served as a soup or as a meal and is a favourite of Cajuns and Louisianians generally. The recipe can also be prepared with crab, shrimp, okra or chicken. The hardy soup is seasoned with ground sassafras ("poudre filé"), which tastes like and replaces bay leaves. To it is added a brown roux flavoured with grilled almonds; since the preparation of this last item is very time consuming it is replaced here by grilled flour. The cooked rice is added at the end.

375 g (3/4 lb) Toulouse or spicy Italian sausages cut into 1 cm (1/2") pieces
Corn oil, as needed
1 1-kg (2-lb) duck, cut into 8 pieces
Salt and freshly ground pepper, to taste
125 ml (1/2 cup) grilled flour
2 onions, finely chopped
4 small green onions, finely chopped
2 cloves of garlic, finely chopped
1 stick of celery, with top, finely diced
1 large green pepper, finely chopped or shredded
3 L (12 cups) of hot water
3 ml (1/2 tsp) Tabasco sauce
8 ml (1 1/2 tsps) Cayenne pepper (optional)
1 small bunch of parsley, finely chopped
5 ml (1 tsp) of sassafras (or ground bay leaf)
1 L (4 cups) cooked white rice

In a heavy-bottomed pot cook the sausages over a low flame, stirring them to extract the grease. Gradually increase the heat to brown them, turning them often. Once the sausages are well browned, drain them and put them aside.

Add oil to the sausage drippings until there is 125 ml (1/2 cup) of liquid in the pot. Remove the fat from the pieces of duck, dry them, salt, pepper, and lightly flour them; cook in the sausage drippings. Turn frequently until the pieces are golden brown. Drain and put aside.

Drain off some of the fat from the pot. Saute the onions, the green onions, the garlic and the celery. Stir often and cook for 5 minutes over a medium fire. Add the green pepper. Gradually add the water, stirring, and bring to a boil.

Mix some of the broth into the grilled flour; pour the mixture into the pot, whisking continuously. Add the sausages, the duck, the salt, the Tabasco sauce, and the cayenne pepper. When the soup reaches a boil again, lightly cover the pot and let it simmer on low heat for 2 hours.

Take the pot off the burner, skim the fat off the broth, and add the parsley and sassafras or ground bay leaf. Adjust the seasoning (gumbo is usually quite spicy). More Tabasco sauce and cayenne pepper can be added, or they can be omitted altogether, to taste. Serve the rice on the side, for people to add at will.

MARINATED CRAB SALAD
Serves 6
Preparation time: 5 minutes
Marinate overnight in the refrigerator

Cajuns are partial to seafood and fish, which can be found everywhere, even in little grocery stores. This refreshing crab salad is served as an appetizer or as a light meal.

90 ml (6 tbsps) cider vinegar
Salt and freshly ground pepper, to taste
125 ml (1/2 cup) corn oil
125 ml (1/2 cup) water
1 medium onion, minced
500 g (1 lb) crabmeat
Lettuce leaves
Assorted vegetables, for decoration

In a bowl, dissolve the salt in the vinegar, add the pepper, and gradually whisk in the oil. Add the water, onion and crabmeat. Marinate overnight in the refrigerator.

The next day, spread the lettuce leaves on a serving plate, place the crabmeat on them. Decorate with tomatoes, radishes, cucumbers or other vegetables as desired.

CAJUN JAMBALAYA
Serves 6
Preparation time: 15 minutes
Cooking time: 45 minutes

Jambalaya is another favourite in Louisiana. It consists of rice and, depending on one's inspiration, meat, smoked sausage, fish and seafood. The name is derived from the French *"jambon"*, meaning "ham", and the African *"ya"*, meaning "rice"; It is said that Acadians added *"à la"* creating the compound "jamb-à-la-ya".

125 g (1/4 lb) bacon, sliced and cut into 2.5-cm (1") pieces
1 medium onion, minced
2 green peppers, seeded and cut into 2.5-cm (1") slices
375 g (1 1/2 cups) uncooked rice
4 cloves of garlic, minced
625 ml (2 1/2 cups) tomatoes, peeled, seeded, and cut into big pieces
3 ml (1/2 tsp) Tabasco sauce (or to taste)
Pinch of thyme
Salt and freshly ground pepper, to taste
500 ml (2 cups) chicken stock
250 g (1/2 lb) cooked smoked ham, cut into 5 cm X 1 cm (2"X3/8") slices
500 g (1 lb) medium raw shrimp, shelled and de-veined
Fresh parsley, finely chopped, for decoration

Preheat the oven to 180° C (350° F). In a casserole dish, cook the bacon until it is brown but not crunchy; drain and put aside. Cook the onion in the bacon drippings over a low flame until clear. Add the green peppers; gently simmer. Stir in the rice; when it becomes milky and slightly opaque, add the garlic, the tomatoes, the Tabasco sauce, the bacon, the thyme, the salt and the pepper. Pour in the chicken broth and bring to a boil; add the ham. Cover and bake for 20 minutes or until the rice is tender.

Ten minutes before removing from the oven, add the shrimp. Serve in the casserole dish or on a hot platter. Sprinkle with parsley.

NOTE: If the rice seems to dry during the simmering stage, add some chicken stock.

CORN BREAD
Makes about 16 slices
Preparation time: 5 minutes
Cooking time: 20-25 minutes

At any good Louisiana supper, corn bread is a must. This recipe can be doubled (add 10 minutes cooking time) or tripled (add 15 minutes).

250 ml (1 cup) corn flour (or corn meal)
250 ml (1 cup) flour
3 ml (1/2 tsp) salt
Pinch of sugar
20 ml (4 tsps) dried yeast (baking powder)
250 ml (1 cup) 2% milk
1 egg, beaten
30 ml (2 tbsps) melted butter
Butter, to grease the pan

In a bowl, mix the corn meal, flour, salt, sugar and baking powder. Blend in the milk, the egg, and the melted butter. Mix well in a mixer or with a whisk, until smooth.

Preheat the oven to 220° C (425° F). Grease a 20-cm baking square (8"X8"). Pour the mixture into the pan and bake 20 to 25 minutes. Let cool before cutting.

PECAN PIE
Serves 6
Preparation time: 10 minutes
Cooking time: 40 minutes

This delight comes to us from the land of the pecan, the southern United States. It is said that this dessert is a variation of sugar pie, introduced to Louisiana in the 18th century by Acadian deportees. To the original sugar pie was added raw-cane-sugared pecans and corn syrup.

250 ml (1 cup) brown sugar
15 ml (1 tbsp) softened butter
30 ml (2 tbsps) flour
3 eggs
250 ml (1 cup) corn syrup
Pinch of salt

5 ml (1 tsp) vanilla or 15 ml (1 tbsp) rum
250 ml (1 cup) pecans
1 pie crust bottom

Preheat the oven to 180° C (350° F). Blend the brown sugar and the butter, and then add the flour. Add the eggs one at a time and the corn syrup; beat well, then add the salt, the vanilla or the rum, and the pecans.

Pour the mixture into the pie crust. Bake 40 minutes. Let cool. Serve with vanilla ice cream, if desired.

DAME BROUSSARD'S CANE-SYRUP CAKE
Serves 8
Preparation: 10 minutes
Cooking time: 45 minutes to one hour

Audrey Broussard confided in me her famous cane-syrup cake recipe during a family dinner in Lafayette, the capital of Acadiana.

250 ml (1 cup) cane sugar (if unavailable, white sugar)
250 ml (1 cup) cane syrup (if unavailable, molasses)
2 eggs
500 ml (2 cups) flour
5 ml (1 tsp) baking soda
125 ml (1/2 cup) corn oil
5 ml (1 tsp) vanilla
250 ml (1 cup) boiling water
125 ml (1/2 cup) pecans

Whisk together the sugar, syrup, eggs, flour, baking soda and oil. Mix the vanilla and the water, and stir into the first mixture, then add the pecans, blending it all well.

Preheat the oven to 180° C (350° F). Butter and flour a rectangular cake pan and pour in the batter. Bake 45 minutes to one hour, until a knife comes out of the cake clean.

PRACTICAL INFORMATION

I nformation in this section will help visitors from English-speaking countries better plan their trip to Louisiana.

ENTRANCE FORMALITIES

Travellers from Canada, the majority of western European countries, Australia and New Zealand do not need visas to enter the United States. A valid passport is sufficient for stays of up to three months. A return ticket and proof of sufficient funds to cover your stay may be required. For stays of more than three months, all travellers, except Canadians and citizens of the British Commonwealth, must obtain a visa ($120 US) from the American embassy in their country.

Caution: as medical expenses can be very high in the United States, travel health insurance is highly recommended. For more information, see the section entitled "Health" (p 44).

CUSTOMS

Foreigners may enter the United States with 200 cigarettes (or 100 cigars) and duty-free purchases not exceeding $400 US, including personal gifts and one litre of alcohol (you must be 21 years of age to drink alcohol). There is no limit on the amount of cash you are carrying, though you must fill out a special form if you are carrying the equivalent of more than $10,000 US. Prescription medication must be placed in containers clearly marked to that effect (you may have to present a prescription or a written statement from your doctor to customs officials). Meat and its by-products, all kinds of food, seeds, plants, fruits and narcotics can not be brought into the United States.

For more ample information, contact:

United States Customs Service: 1301 Constitution Avenue Northwest, Washington, DC 20229, ☎ (202) 566-8195.

EMBASSIES AND CONSULATES

United States Embassies and Consulates Abroad

Australia
United States Embassy: Moonah Place, Canberra, ACT 2600, ☎ 270-5000.

Belgium
United States Embassy: 27 Boulevard du Régent, B-100 Brussels, ☎ (2) 513-3830, ⬛ (2) 511-2725.

Canada
United States Embassy: 2 Wellington Street, Ottawa, Ontario, K1P 5T1, ☎ (613) 238-5335, ⬛ (613) 238-5720.

United States Consulate: Place Félix-Martin, 1155 Rue Saint-Alexandre, Montréal, Québec, H2Z 1Z2, ☎ (514) 398-9695, ⬛ (514) 398-9748.

United States Consulate: 360 University Avenue, Toronto, Ontario, M5G 1S4, ☎ (416) 595-1700, ⬛ (416) 595-0051.

United States Consulate: 1095 West Pender, Vancouver, British Columbia, V6E 2M6, ☎ (604) 685-4311.

Germany
United States Embassy: Deichmans Aue 29, 53170 Bonn, ☎ 228-3391.

Great Britain
United States Embassy: 24 Grosvenor Square, London W1A 1AE, ☎ (171) 499-9000.

Ireland
United States Embassy: 42 Elgin Road, Ballsbridge, Dublin 4, Ireland, ☎ 660-8922, 668-8085 or 668-8858.

Italy
United States Embassy: Via Veneto 121, 00187 Roma, ☎ (06) 46741, ⬛ (06) 46742217.

Netherlands
United States Embassy: Lange Voorhout 102, Den Haag, ☎ (70) 310-9209, ⬛ (70) 361-4688.

New Zealand
United States Embassy: 29 Fitzherbert Terrace, Thorndon, Wellington, ☎ 472-2068.

Spain
United States Embassy: C. Serrano 75, Madrid, 28006, ☎ (91) 577-4000, ⬛ (91) 587-2239.

Switzerland
United States Embassy: 95 Jubilaeumsstrasse, 3005 Berne, ☎ 31-43-70-11.

Foreign Consulates and Delegations in Louisiana

Belgium
There is no Belgian consulate in Louisiana; address inquiries to the consulate in Houston: 2929 Allen Parkway, Office 2222, Houston, Texas 77019, ☎ (713) 529-0775, ⬛ (713) 224-1120.

Canada

The Canadian consulate closest to Louisiana is located in Atlanta: 235 Peachtree Street, Northeast 100-Colony Square, Office 1700, Atlanta, Georgia, 30361-6205, ☎ (404) 255-8470, ≈ (404) 532-2050.

Great Britain

British consulate: 321 St. Charles Ave., 10th floor, New Orleans, LA 70130, ☎ (504) 586-8300.

Netherlands

Dutch consulate: 643 Magazine Street, New Orleans, LA 70130, ☎ (504) 596-2838, ≈ (504) 596-2800; mailing address: P.O. Box 60643, New Orleans, LA 70160-0643.

Spain

Spanish consulate: 2102 World Trade Center, 2 Canal Street, New Orleans, LA 70130, ☎ (504) 525-4951, ≈ (504) 525-4955.

Switzerland

Swiss consulate: 1620 Eighth Street, New Orleans, LA 70115, ☎ (504) 897-6510.

TOURIST INFORMATION

Louisiana Office of Tourism: 666 Foster North Street, P.O. Box 94291, Baton Rouge, LA 70804, ☎ 1-800-334-8626 (1-800-33-GUMBO).

CODOFIL – Council for the Development of French in Louisiana, 217 rue Principale, Lafayette, LA 70501, ☎ (318) 262-5810, ≈ (318) 262-5812.

FINDING YOUR WAY AROUND

By Car

The good condition of the roads and the low price of gasoline compared to gas prices in Europe and Canada make driving an ideal mode of independent transportation in Louisiana. Excellent maps are available in travel book stores, or, once arrived in Louisiana, at gas stations.

A few tips:

Driver's License: In general, European driver's licenses are valid, but it is preferable to obtain an international driver's license, which may be acquired by contacting the Royal Automobile Club of Belgium (R.A.C.B.).

Canadian driver's licenses are completely valid in the United States. Take note that many states are linked to Québec police forces by a computer network for the control of traffic infractions. A ticket remanded in the United States is automatically reported to a file in Québec.

Driving Code: Careful: traffic coming from the right does not have the right of way. Instead road signs at intersections indicate right of way. "Stop" signs are scrupulously respected. A "Stop" sign with a rectangle that reads, "4-way'" means that every one must stop at the intersection and no particular lane has the right of way. Stops must be made even when there is no apparent danger. When two cars arrive at a "Stop" sign at the same time, the right of way on

PRACTICAL INFORMATION

Table of Distances
By the Shortest Route

Example : The distance between New Orleans and Baton Rouge is 129 kilometres or 80 miles
1 mile = 1.6 kilometres
1 kilometre = 0.6 mile

© ULYSSES

					Alexandria	Alexandria
				Baton Rouge	180/112	Baton Rouge
			Lafayette	87/54	125/78	Lafayette
		Monroe	311/193	291/181	138/86	Monroe
	New Orleans	452/281	216/134	129/80	309/192	New Orleans
Shreveport	513/319	164/102	359/223	385/239	204/127	Shreveport

the right rule applies. In all other cases the car that arrived first has the right of way.

Traffic lights are most often on the far side of the intersection. Be careful to stop before the intersection or the crosswalk.

In Louisiana it is permitted to make a right turn on a red light when the lane is clear (you must stop first, however). Intersections where this is not permitted are marked with signs that reads, "No Turn on Red". When a (yellow) schoolbus stops with its flashing lights lit, it is obligatory to stop regardless of the direction you are travelling in. Failure to stop for a schoolbus is considered a serious offence.

The wearing of seat belts is obligatory.

Highways are free, except for most thruways. Interstate highways are designated by an "I" followed by a number.

The speed limit is 55 mph (88 kph) on most highways, and 65 mph (104 kph) on interstates.

The highway patrol is particularly zealous all over Louisiana. Be vigilant on the outskirts of towns and cities.

A triangular, yellow "Yield" sign means you must slow down and cede right of way to vehicles crossing your path.

A round, yellow sign with a black cross and the letter "R" on it indicates a level crossing.

Gas Stations: since the United States is an oil-producing country, gasoline is plainly cheaper than it is in Europe or Canada.

Car Rental

The agency **HATA** (☎ 1-800-356-8392) is a free hotel and car rental reservation service (see "Accommodation", p 48).

Car-rental agencies are located at the airport and at various places in the city. To rent a car, a tourist must have a valid driver's license and a major credit card. Rates start at $31 per pay and $150 per week for an economy-class car with unlimited mileage.

By Bus

Bus, along with automobile travel, is probably the best mode of transportation. Well organized and inexpensive, bus lines cover most of Louisiana.

For schedules and routes, contact the local Greyhound outlet (see below).

In Montréal the Voyageur Colonial company represents Greyhound (☎ 514-842-2281).

In Toronto information is available at the Go Transit Terminal (☎ 416-393-7911).

On most bus lines smoking is forbidden. In general children five years of age and younger travel for free. People aged 60 years and over are eligible for significant discounts. Animals are forbidden.

Greyhound Bus Lines: 1001 Loyola Avenue, New Orleans, ☎ (504) 525-6075 or 1-800-231-1222.

Hotard Coaches: 2838 Touro Street, New Orleans, ☎ (504) 944-0253.

Routes and Schedules

The Greyhound bus route begins in California, crosses Texas and Louisiana, where it links most major cties, then travels through Mississippi to wind up at the southern tip of Florida.

There are five departures daily from the cities listed below.

One-way fares:

Lafayette – New Orleans: $22
Baton Rouge – New Orleans: $13
Lafayette – Baton Rouge: $10
Lafayette – Lac-Charles: $14
Alexandrie – Lafayette: $27.50
Shreveport – Alexandrie: $23
Shreveport – Monroe: $18

By Train

In the United States, the train is not always the least expensive way to travel, and it is certainly not the fastest. (It takes about 30 hours to travel from New York to New Orleans.) It can be interesting for long distances, however, as it is very comfortable (try to get a seat in a panoramic car to take advantage of the scenery). For schedules and destinations contact AMTRAK, the present owner of the rail network in the United States (toll free in North America ☎ 1-800-972-7245).

AMTRAK train station: Union Passenger Terminal, 1001 Loyola Avenue, New Orleans, ☎ (504) 528-1610.

By Plane

Plane is certainly an expensive mode of transportation, but some airlines, especially regional ones, regularly offer special fares (low season, short stays). Be a smart shopper and compare prices. For precise details on variuos destinations, contact local tourist offices.

PRACTICAL INFORMATION

Moisant Airport/New Orleans International Airport *(900 Airline Hwy., exit 228 from the I-10, Kenner, ☎ 464-2650 or 464-3547)* is named for the famous New Orleans aviator and is the most important airport in Louisiana. It provides links with the major cities of North America, Central American and South America.

All essential services are found here: car rental, automatic teller machines, bars, restaurants, souvenir shops. There is also a New Orleans Tourist Office counter, a welcome centre for visitors and the Louisiana Tax Free Shopping counter, where out-of-state travellers can be reimbursed for sales tax paid during their stay.

Hospitality is a Louisiana tradition and is apparent from the moment of visitors' arrival.

Many flights of large airline companies arrive at New Orleans International Airport (Moisant).

Aeromexico: ☎ 524-1245 or 1-800-237-6639.
American Airlines:
☎ 1-800-433-7300.
Aviateca Airlines: ☎ 1-800-327-9832.
Continental Airlines: ☎ 581-2965 or 1-800-525-0280.
Delta Airlines: ☎ 529-2431 or 1-800-221-1212.
Lacsa the Airlines of Costa Rica: ☎ 468-3948 or 1-800-225-2272.
Northwest Airlines Inc.:
☎ 1-800-225-2525.
Southwest Airlines: ☎ 834-2337 or 1-800-531-5601.
Trans World Airlines:
☎ 1-800-221-2000.
United Airlines: ☎ 466-1889 or 1-800-241-6522.

USAir: ☎ 454-2668 or 1-800-428-4322.
ValuJet: ☎ 1-800-835-8538.

By Bicycle

In the realm of the automobile, it is preferable for cyclists to stick to secondary roads: the Louisiana countryside is full of lovely sights, and it is useless to try to bicycle on major highways.

Hitchhiking

At your own risk! It is inadvised to hitchhike in Louisiana; after too many bad experiences, motorists are very mistrustful of hitchhikers. People who use this form of transportation are identified as itinerants. On the other hand, hitchhikers never know what sort of person is picking them up. In brief, hitchhiking is risky.

TELECOMMUNICATIONS

The **area code** for New Orleans and environs, Baton Rouge, plantation country, Lafourche Bayou and Houmas is **504**. In the rest of the state – Acadiana, Caffefour and northern Louisiana – the area code is **318**. When calling from within the calling area you need not dial the area code. Numbers beginning with 1-800 and 1-888 are toll free from within the United States and, unless otherwise stated, Canada.

To reach an operator, dial 0. If you use the operator to make a local call, and you do not have a telephone card, it will cost $0.80.

A local call costs $0.25 from a public phone; keep change handy, although you can also use calling cards and credit cards.

For long-distance calls within North America, dial 1 + the area code + the local number.

For long-distance calls outside of North America, dial 011 + the country code + the area code + the local number.

Country Codes

Australia	61
Belgium	32
Germany	49
Great Britain	44
Holland	31
Italy	39
New Zealand	64
Spain	34
Switzerland	41

It is generally less expensive to use your own telephone company's direct service access number.

Canada Direct: 1-800-555-1111
AT&T Canada: 1-800-957-9000

British Telecom Direct Access Numbers:
From a SPRINT phone:
1-800-825-4904
From an MCI phone: 1-800-854-4826
From an AT&T phone:
1-800-445-5688

INSURANCE

Cancellation Insurance

Your travel agent will usually offer you cancellation insurance when you buy your airline ticket or vacation package. This insurance allows you to be reimbursed for the ticket or package deal if your trip must be cancelled due to serious illness or death. Healthy people are unlikely to need this protection, which is therefore only of relative use.

Theft Insurance

Most residential insurance policies protect some of your goods from theft, even if the theft occurs in a foreign country. To make a claim, you must fill out a police report. It may not be necessary to take out further insurance, depending on the amount covered by your current home policy. As policies vary considerably, you are advised to check with your insurance company. European visitors should take out baggage insurance.

Life Insurance

Several airline companies offer a life insurance plan included in the price of the airplane ticket. However, many travellers already have this type of insurance and do not require additional coverage.

PRACTICAL
INFORMATION

Health Insurance

This is the most useful kind of insurance for travellers, and should be purchased before your departure. Your insurance plan should be as complete as possible because health care costs add up quickly. When buying insurance, make sure it covers all types of medical costs, such as hospitalization, nursing services and doctor's fees. Make sure your limit is high enough, as these expenses can be costly. A repatriation clause is also vital in case the required care is not available on site. Furthermore, since you may have to pay immediately, check your policy to see what provisions it includes for in such a situation. To avoid any problems during your vacation, always keep proof of your insurance policy on your person.

HEALTH

General Information

Vaccinations are not necessary for people coming from Europe or Canada. On the other hand, it is strongly suggested, particularly for medium or long-term stays, that visitors take out health and accident insurance. There are different types, so it is best to shop around. Bring along all medication, especially prescription medicine. Unless otherwise stated, the water is potable throughout Louisiana.

Be careful of the sun. Even when you do not feel it you are susceptible to sunburn. Louisiana is at the same latitude as Cairo: sunscreen is a must!

Snake and Insect Bites

The subtropical climate and the abundance of expanses of water and forest make Louisiana a preferred habitat of snakes, insects and mosquitoes.

The venimous water moccasin is quite common in marshy areas such as bayous, cypress groves, paddy fields and ditches. Like most reptiles, and wildlife generally, snakes fear humans. So as not to disturb snakes, one must walk carefully in areas such as those mentioned above. Walkers should wear good rubber boots when adventuring in the habitat of the famous water moccasin.

Mosquitoes, an insect well-known to Canadian readers, are abundant in summer. Wherever there is water you will find these annoying blood-sucking insects. A simple insecticide is the best antidote to this unpleasantness.

When walking through woods, you must be on guard for ticks. Not only does this tiny insect bite, it also transmits disease. In case of tick bite, it is recommended to slip a few specimens into a hermetic container and take them immediately to the nearest pharmacy or clinic to be analysed. Wood ticks stick to the skin and must be cautiously removed with tweezers.

Do not get too close to alligators (or "cocodries", as they are called in the Cajun language), as, despite their sleepy appearance, they are always on the look-out. If you are chased by an alligator, try not to run in a straight line, but rather zigzag; alligators charge straight at their prey and it is difficult for them to change directions.

In the city as well as in the countryside, there are red ant piles. Avoid them, since red ants can cause a skin irritation similar to a burn, hence their name, "fire ants".

A brochure on the particularities of Louisianian flora and fauna is available from the Acadiana Park Nature Station *(☎ 318-261-8448).*

In case of emergency, including snake bites and poisoning, see the telephone numbers below.

Emergencies

In case of emergency, dial 911, or 0 to obtain the operator's assistance.

In case of poisoning, throughout the state: ☎ 1-800-256-9822; in the area of Monroe: ☎ (318) 325-6454; in the area of Lac-Charles: ☎ (318) 478-6800.

In case of medical emergency in the Lafayette region, call Ask-a-Nurse: ☎ (318) 231-2900.

There is also an automated telephone information service in Lafayette that provides instructions regarding what to do in a variety of situations: ☎ (318) 262-5854. Once you have dialled this number you will be prompted to dial the number that corresponds to your situation; for example, for animal bites dial 1080, for ant bites dial 3063.

Important telephone numbers may be found in the yellow pages of the telephone books of Lafayette and of the other towns in Louisiana.

Safety

Unfortunately, American cities are not always the safest, this does not mean, however, that you should spend your trip barricaded in your hotel room.

Upon arriving, simply inquire about which neighbourhoods are to be avoided, no matter what the time of day. By taking the necessary precautions, there is no reason to worry about your safety. If, however, you are unlucky remember to dial **911** for all emergencies.

DISABLED TRAVELLERS

The State of Louisiana has enacted legislation requiring the respect of the rights of disabled people.

There are parking zones reserved for disabled motorists with special parking permits. Those without these permits who park in these reserved zones are issued $50 tickets.

Accessibilty for people with limited mobility or in wheelchairs is a recognized requirement in all public spaces in Louisiana: hotels, motels, restaurants, museums, golf courses, parking lots, etc.

The following national American organization can also provide useful information for disabled travellers: **Society for the Advancement of Travel for the Handicapped** *(347 5th Avenue, Suite 610, New York, NY 10016, ☎ 212-447-7284).*

PRACTICAL INFORMATION

Services for Disabled People in Louisiana

Louisiana State Rehabilitation Services: ☎ 1-800-737-2875 *(24-hour service)*.

The following organizations are open every day from 8:30am to 5:30pm.

In New Orleans:
Resources for Independant Living: 1555 Poydras Street, New Orleans, ☎ 522-1955 *(Mon to Fri 8:30am to 5:30pm)*.

Advocacy Center for the Elderly and Disabled: 210 O'Keefe Avenue, Suite 700, New Orleans, LA 70112, ☎ 522-2337 or 1-800-960-7705.

In Lafayette:
Department of Disabilities: ☎ (318) 262-5610.

Southwest Louisiana Independent Living Center: ☎ (318) 269-0027.

Office for Persons with Disabilities: ☎ (318) 232-3463 or 261-5548.

Southwest Louisiana Education and Referral Center: 439 Heymann Blvd., Lafayette, LA 70505, ☎ (318) 232-3463 or 261-5548.

Affiliated Blind of Louisiana: 409 Sainte-Marie Blvd. West, Lafayette, LA 70506, ☎ (318) 234-6492.

Advocacy Center for the Elderly and Disabled: 515 College Road South, Suite 130, Lafayette LA 70503, ☎ (318) 237-7380.

CLIMATE

The climate encountered in Louisiana is essentially hot and humid during the summer, from the beginning of May to the end of September. It is ideal, if possible, to visit the region in the spring or fall, in order to avoid the torrid heat waves and high general humidity of summer and rather enjoy warm, sunny days and cool nights. Winters are mild. Whatever the time of year you should pack a good raincoat.

Most public places in Louisiana, including hotels and restaurants are air-conditioned, sometimes to excess. It is recommended to keep your shoulders covered so as not to get chilled.

Temperature

Average Maximum and Minimum Temperatures (°C/°F):

January:
    19 and 9 / 66.2 and 48.2
February:
    19 and 10 / 66.2 and 50
March:
    22 and 13 / 71.6 and 55.4
April:
    25 and 17 / 77 and 62.6
May:
    29 and 20 / 84.2 and 68
June:
    32 and 24 / 89.6 and 75.2
July:
    32 and 24 / 89.6 and 75.2
August:
    32 and 25 / 89.6 and 77
September:
    31 and 23 / 87.8 and 73.4
October:
    27 and 19 / 80.6 and 66.2

November:
   21 and 13 / 69.8 and 55.4
December:
   18 and 10 / 64.4 and 50

The best time to visit Louisiana is between October and May; June, July, August and September are very humid and sometimes uncomfortable.

MONEY AND BANKS

Money

The monetary unit is the dollar ($), which is divided into cents (¢). One dollar = 100 cents.

Bills come in one-, five-, 10-, 20-, 50- and 100-dollar denominations; and coins come in one- (penny), five- (nickel), 10- (dime) and 25-cent (quarter) pieces.

Dollar and fifty-cent coins exist, as does a two-dollar bill, but they are very rarely used. Virtually all purchases must be paid in American currency in the United States. Be sure to get your travellers' cheques in American dollars. You can also use any credit card affiliated with an American institution like Visa, MasterCard, American Express, Interbank, Barclay Bank, Diners' Club and Discovery. **Please note that all prices in this guide are in American dollars.**

Banks

Banks are open Monday to Friday from 9am to 3pm.

Banks can be found almost everywhere, and most offer the standard services to tourists. Most automatic teller machines (ATMs) accept foreign bank cards so that you can withdraw directly from your account (check before to make sure you have access) and avoid the potentially high charges of using a real teller. Most machines are open at all times. Cash advances on your credit card are another option, although interest charges accumulate quickly. Money orders are a final alternative for which no commission is charged. This option does, however, take more time. The easiest and safest way to carry your money, however, remains travellers' cheques.

Non-residents cannot open bank accounts. People who have acquired resident status, permanent or otherwise (immigrants, students), can open bank accounts and must present their passports and proof of their resident status.

Exchanging Money

Several banks readily exchange foreign currency, but almost all charge a **commission**. There are exchange offices, on the other hand, that do not charge commission, but their rates are sometimes less competitive. These offices often have longer opening hours. It is a good idea to **shop around**.

Credit Cards

Most credit cards are accepted at stores, restaurants and hotels. While the main advantage of credit cards is that they allow visitors to avoid

Exchange Rates

$1 CAN	= $0.70 US	$1 US =	$1.43 CAN
1 £	= $1.63 US	$1 US =	0.61 £
$1 Aust	= $0.65 US	$1 US =	$1.55 Aust
$1 NZ	= $0.57 US	$1 US =	$1.75 NZ
1 guilder	= $0.49 US	$1 US =	2.05 guilders
1 SF	= $0.68 US	$1 US =	1.48 SF
10 BF	= $0.27 US	$1 US =	38 BF
1 DM	= $0.55 US	$1 US =	1.82 DM
100 pesetas	= $0.65 US	$1 US =	154 pesetas
1000 lire	= $0.56 US	$1 US =	1791 lire

carrying large sums of money, using a credit card also makes leaving a deposit for car rental much easier and some cards, gold cards for example, automatically insure you when you rent a car. In addition, the exchange rate with a credit card is generally better, and at many banks and some exchange bureaux you can get cash advances with your credit cards. The most commonly accepted credit cards are Visa, MasterCard, and American Express. Visa International has a 24-hour telephone service in case of loss or theft of your credit card.

Visa International: ☎ 1-800-847-2911 or 1-800-336-8472.

American Express: ☎ 1-800-528-5200.

MasterCard: ☎ 1-800-826-2181.

 ACCOMMODATIONS

Types of Accommodation

Hotels: A few luxury establishments, large international chains such as Le Meridien, Holiday Inn, Crown Plaza, with restaurants for various budgets. Many downtown and along highways. International-style service.

Motels: Located on access roads. Separate room for two to four people, with television, private bath, and parking.

Bed and Breakfasts: Lodging in host's home, either in a detached building or in a charming plantatation house. Furnishings are often antique. Light breakfast, or American-style breakfast (eggs, bacon, sausages, etc.), is graciously served.

Cabins: These individual cottages with kitchenettes are still available, but harder and harder to find.

Campgrounds: They are numerous. Budget for $5 and less for state-run campgrounds and about $12 for private ones.

Youth Hostels: Members of the American Federation of Youth Hostels.

Reservations and Rental

The HATA agency, open every day from 8:30am to 10:30pm, makes hotel and motel reservations and can take care of car rental.

If you are interested in a particular area, HATA will suggest hotels and take care of the reservations.

HATA: ☎ 1-800-356-8392, toll free all over North America

 SHOPPING

Check with shopkeepers whether they are members of Louisiana Tax Free Shopping, a state-run program by which tourists can be reimbursed sales tax paid during their visit.

Louisiana is the only state with such a program. The simplest strategy is to pick up the directory of participating stores and establishments (there are over one thousand of them) at:

Louisiana Tax Free Shopping: 2 Canal Street, New Orleans, LA 70130, ☎ 568-5323.

At the time of purchase, you will be given a form to fill out which you hand in, with your receipts, before you leave Louisiana. Refunds of less than $500 are made immediately, in cash, at the Refund Center of New Orleans International Airport; amounts of more than $500 are paid by cheque and sent by mail to visitors' homes.

Business Hours

Post Offices: Monday to Friday, 8:30am to 4:30pm, and Saturday, 8:30am to noon.

Stores

Stores are generally open Monday through Saturday, from 9:30am to 5:30pm or 6pm. Supermarkets, on the other hand, are open later, and in some cases are open 24 hours a day, 7 days a week.

What to Buy

New Orleans offers many Mardi Gras souvenir shops, art galleries and antique stores.

You can buy practical Native American crafts, and in Acadiana you can visit artisans right in their studios.

Taxes

Unlike in Europe, prices are advertized not including sales tax. Keep this in mind when planning your budget, as in New Orleans added sales tax can be as much as 9% of the price of the item. See the explanation of Louisiana Tax Free Shopping, above.

Tipping

In general, tipping applies to all table service (no tipping in fast-food restaurants), as well as service in bars and nightclubs, and taxi service. The tip is usually about 15% of the bill

PRACTICAL INFORMATION

before tax, but varies, of course, depending on the quality of service. The tip is not included in the bill; you must calculate it yourself and leave it on the table for the waiter or waitress.

 BARS AND NIGHTCLUBS

Some establishments charge an entrance fee, especially when there is a band. Tipping is not obligatory, but it is appreciated; if you do decide to tip, 10% to 15% is the norm.

Note that the legal drinking age is 21.

TIME DIFFERENCE

Louisiana is in the Central Time Zone, six hours behind Greenwich Mean Time. Noon in New Orleans is 1pm in Montréal, 7pm in Paris, and 10am in Los Angeles.

PUBLIC HOLIDAYS

The following is a list of public holidays in the United States. Most stores, administrative offices and banks are closed on these days. **In addition to these holidays, Mardi Gras is a public holiday in Louisiana.**

New Year's Day (January 1)
Martin Luther King, Jr.'s Birthday (third Monday in January)
President's Day (third Monday in February)
St. Patrick's Day (March 17)
Patriots Day (April 19)
Memorial Day (last Monday in May)
Independence Day (July 4)
Labor Day (first Monday in September)

Columbus Day (second Monday in October)
Veterans' Day (November 11)
Thanksgiving (fourth Thursday in November)
Christmas (December 25)

DRUGS

The United States has a strict policy on drugs and they are forbidden (even "soft" drugs). Drug users and dealers caught with drugs in their possession risk severe consequences.

ELECTRICITY

Voltage is 110 volts throughout the United States, as in Canada. Electrical plugs are two-pinned and flat. Visitors from outside North America will need a transformer and a plug adapter. These are available here.

EMIGRATING TO THE UNITED STATES

Inform yourself at the immigration office of the United States embassy or consulate in your home country.

FESTIVALS

See the "Entertainment" section of the chapter on the region of interest.

WEIGHTS AND MEASURES

The United States use the imperial system:

Weights
1 pound (lb) = 454 grams (g)
1 kilogram (kg) = 2.2 pounds (lbs)

Linear Measure
1 inch = 2.54 centimetres (cm)
1 foot (ft) = 30 centimetres (cm)
1 mile = 1.6 kilometres (km)
1 kilometres (km) = 0.63 miles
1 metre (m) = 39.37 inches

Land Measure
1 acre = 0.4 hectare
1 hectare = 2.471 acres

Volume Measure
1 U.S. gallon (gal) = 3.79 litres
1 U.S. gallon (gal) = 0.83 imperial gallon

Temperature
To convert °F into °C: subtract 32, divide by 9, multiply by 5
To convert °C into °F: multiply by 9, divide by 5, add 32

PRACTICAL INFORMATION

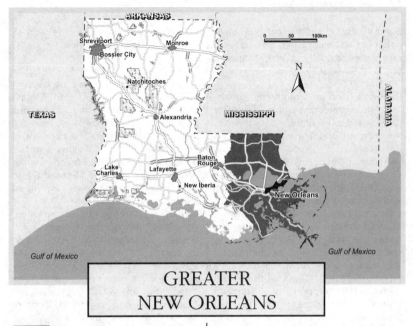

GREATER
NEW ORLEANS

he history of **New Orleans ★★★** is intertwined with that of New France. Jean-Baptiste Le Moyne de Bienville laid the city's foundations in 1718. Preceding him were Louis Joliet and Père Marquette in 1673, and Cavelier de La Salle in 1682. In 1697, under Pierre Le Moyne d'Iberville (Jean-Baptiste's brother), the colonization of Louisiana began. In 1762, France ceded Louisiana to Spain, to be returned it in 1800. November 30th, 1803, Napoleon sold the 2,600,000 square-kilometre territory of Louisiana to the United States for 80 million francs.

New Orleans was profoundly marked by the French presence; even during the Spanish occupation, French maintained precedence. Today French is hardly ever heard within its boundaries. If, on a stroll, one should by chance hear French spoken, it is only because

Louisianan Acadia is not far from the city.

Many are the Cajun musicians and singers who appear in the restaurant-cafés of this city which is the birthplace of so many performers. New Orleans, a meeting ground for widely divergent cultures over the last three centuries, was apt for the hatching of an original fusion. Here were born Louis Armstrong and Sidney Bechet. Also renowned for its restaurants, New Orleans boasts of being the culinary capital of the United States; its Creole cuisine is a fusion of Native American, French, African and Spanish.

New Orleans seems to rise up out of the twists and turns of the Mississippi. The river and the proximity of the Gulf of Mexico both favoured the city's development. Indeed, as soon as it was founded, New Orleans became an important economic pivot between

Europe and the fledgling European colonies in America. Today, its port ranks second in the United States in terms of tonnage handled.

Renowned for its gastronomy, music, festivals, architecture and history, New Orleans is like no other place on earth. All sorts of epithets can be used to describe it: magical, boisterous, debonair, flamboyant, even decadent. A 19th-century chronicler called it the most cosmopolitan of provincial cities and the most provincial of cosmopolitan cities. Ensconced on a curved stretch of land between the Mississippi and Lake Pontchartrain, it has a distinctive, almost insular location that has also earned it the nickname "Crescent City". Due to the city's complicated topography, standard points of reference are of little use here; fashionable Uptown is located to the west, commercial Downtown to the east. The city is bounded to the north and south by the shores of Lake Pontchartrain and the Mississippi, respectively.

New Orleans has succeeded in preserving its rich heritage. Its French Quarter, or Vieux Carré, is of impressive size and boasts a remarkable number of period houses. The architecture here reflects French and Creole, more than Spanish, influences. With its inner courts decked out with flowers, finely worked balconies, charming streets and public squares, New Orleans is truly enchanting. Around Jackson Square (the former Place d'Armes), dominated by the spires of St. Louis Cathedral, and throughout a maze of streets with names like Bienville, Toulouse, Bourbon, Dauphine, Conti, Ursulines, Levée, Dumaine, Chartres and

Esplanade, the historic area reveals all sorts of unexpected charms.

Feverish New Orleans is without a doubt one of the most captivating urban centres in the United States. Even those visiting the marvellous Mississippi city for the first time fall madly in love with it. The richness of its architecture, the fabulous diversity of its cultural heritage (French, Creole, African-American and Spanish), its unique gastronomy and its proud inhabitants... everything here is harmonious, delightful, sensuous. Americans adore New Orleans more than any other city. Each day, thousands of tourists flood into the Vieux-Carré or French Quarter. They come from all over the country—New York, Boston, Los Angeles and Chicago—by bus, chartered flight or car. Just as others make a pilgrimage to Mecca, Americans go to New Orleans to get back to their roots in a place that has been instrumental in shaping their culture. And no one from anywhere else in the world will ever feel completely lost in New Orleans, with its myriad cultures; everyone has roots here.

New Orleans, the city of music, thrilled to the sounds of jazz greats like Louis Armstrong and Sidney Bechet. In the New Orleans of Tennessee Williams, you'll catch yourself looking for *A Streetcar Named Desire*. New Orleans is a city even more beautiful than you'd think, a city that leaves no one indifferent.

North of New Orleans

Between 1840 and 1930 New Orleanians crossed Lake Pontchartrain to restore themselves in the little

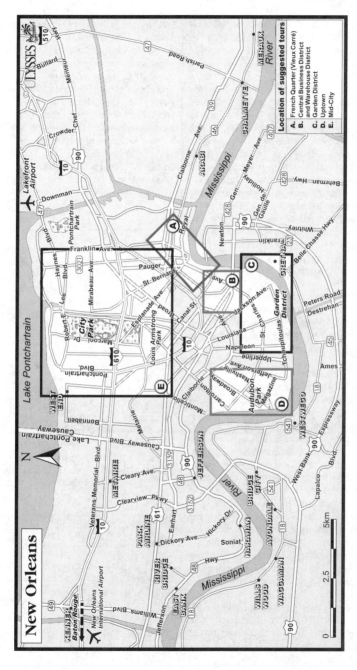

villages of St. Tammany Parish. The exceptionally high concentration of ozone in its pure springs turned the region into a favourite with those seeking escape from hectic city life or from areas in which yellow fever was endemic.

Today visitors take the Lake Pontchartrain Causeway, which, with its two spans of more than 42 kilometres, is the longest such construction in the world. Urban folk, happy for a change of rhythm, leave behind the feverish pace of the city for the scenic roads of the countryside and the welcoming bed and breakfasts that replace glass and steel hotels.

The population of St. Tammany is 145,000, spread through many small municipalities. Bedroom communities, high-tech centres and tiny rural agglomerations all possess an old-fashioned charm made up of history, old stone and peaceful nature.

West and north of New Orleans are the parishes of Livingston, St. Helena, Tangipahoa and Washington. A vast rural land the economy of which is anchored by forestry, agriculture and the dairy industry. Bogalusa was once the site of the largest sawmill in the world. After the Civil War, descendants of Italian immigrants began cultivating strawberries; Hammond, was the shipping centre for these crops. The State of Mississippi borders the northern and eastern parishes along the banks of the Pearl River. The Bogue Chitto Wildlife Reserve also hugs the shores of this river, which is perfect for canoeing and other water sports.

Following an uprising against the Spanish in 1810, (the Spanish then occupied this area of Louisiana, which at the time was part of the parishes of East and West Feliciana, and the parish of Baton Rouge), this territory gained independence and the fledgling State took the name Republic of West Florida. This sovereignty was short-lived – it lasted barely three months, from September 24 to December 7 – but long enough for Governor Williams C. C. Clairborne to bring the mini-republic under the banner of the United States. The region is still commonly known as the "Florida Parishes".

South of New Orleans

The territories of the parishes of St. Bernard, Plaquemines and Jefferson, stretching on either side of the Mississippi, are in large part constituted of huge stretches of swampland, lakes and bayous. For example, of the 967,000-hectare area that makes up the parish of St. Bernard, only 12,500 hectares are not swampy, making this region an excellent place for hunting and fishing. Plaquemines was created by alluvial deposits from the Mississippi. Its rich soil and its geographic location on the Gulf favour the cultivation of citrus fruits, and of the famous "Creole tomato", a particularly tasty and juicy variety that is harvested in May. This area is also rich in subterranean gas and oil deposits.

FINDING YOUR
WAY AROUND

The area code for New Orleans and surroundings is 504, although it is not necessary to dial this prefix when you are calling from within the area. Numbers beginning with 1-800 are toll free.

New Orleans is very easy to reach. **New Orleans International Airport (Moisant)**, 16 kilometres (10 miles) west of the city, serves all of the major international airlines, while private planes and charters pass through the airport in the east on Lake Pontchartrain (**Lakefront Airport**). Interstate 10 (I-10) and Highways LA 61 and LA 90 cross the city, which is also accessible by train and national coach lines. New Orleans is also a port of call for cruise ships that navigate the Gulf of Mexico and the Caribbean Sea.

New Orleans is situated about 145 kilometres or 90 miles from the Gulf of Mexico and stretches along the Mississippi. The city is built around the French Quarter. Down the river, or "downtown", are Faubourg Marigny and the suburbs of Arabi and Chalmette, site of the famous Battle of New Orleans. Algiers Point and Gretna compose a suburb facing the French Quarter on the west bank of the Mississippi. West of the French Quarter and up the river, or "uptown", is the Central Business District, which was once known as *Faubourg Sainte-Marie*. Further along are the Garden District and Tulane and Loyola Universities, Audubon Park and Zoo, and the residential neighbourhoods around Magazine Street and Carrollton Avenue (the area around Carrollton and St. Charles is called Riverbend). Next come the municipalities of Metairie and Kenner, in which is located New Orleans International Airport (Moisant). Between downtown and Lake Pontchartrain, the northern border of the city, are found the Faubourg Tremé and Mid-City, mainly African-American neighbourhoods.

From the I-10 the city can be reached via Exits 234A (Claiborne), 234B (Poydras) or 234C (Superdome), 235A (Vieux Carré-French Quarter and Orleans Avenue), 235B (Canal Street) and 236A (Esplanade Avenue).

Airports

Moisant Airport/New Orleans International Airport *(900 Airline Hwy., Exit 228 from the I-10, Kenner,* ☎ *464-2650 or 464-3547)*. See p 42.

Lakefront Airport *(Exit 241 from the I-10,* ☎ *242-4110)* receives charter and private flights.

Taxi fares are set by the city at $21 for a trip from the airport to most downtown locations for two people; for three or more passengers budget for about $8 per person.

Louisiana Transit provides public bus service linking the airport and downtown every half hour for $1.50 (the trip is about 45 min). The bus stop is on the upper-level ramp. For the return trip to the airport, a stop is located at the corner of Elk Place and Tulane Avenue, facing the public library. The last bus leaves at 6:20pm. Information: ☎ 737-9611.

The **New Orleans Tour Airport Shuttle** takes passengers downtown from Moisant Airport in less than 45 minutes *($10;* ☎ *522-3500 or 1-800-543-6332)*.

By Train

For schedules and destinations contact **AMTRAK**, the present owner of the rail network in the United States *(toll free*

in North America ☎ *1-800-972-7245).*
See p 41.

AMTRAK train station: Union Passenger Terminal, 1001 Loyola Avenue, New Orleans, ☎ 528-1610.

By Bus

For information on routes and schedules contact the offices of the following companies (see also p 41).

Greyhound Bus Lines: 1001 Loyola Avenue, New Orleans, ☎ 525-6075 or 1-800-231-2222.

Hotard Coaches: 2838 Touro Street, New Orleans, ☎ 944-0253.

By Taxi

Taxi metres are regulated and the fare demanded for a trip is not negotiable. The regular fare is $2.10 plus $0.20 for every 1/5 mile or 40 seconds, plus $0.75 for every additional passenger. There is a small surcharge for luggage. Disputes can be addressed to the New Orleans taxi drivers' association.

United Cabs Inc.: 1630 Euterpe Street, New Orleans, ☎ 522-9771 or 1-800-323-3303.

Checker Yellow Cabs: ☎ 943-2411.

Liberty Bell Cabs: ☎ 822-5974.

By Public Transportation

New Orleans offers many types of public transit. Each requires exact change. The **Regional Transit Authority**

- **RTA** *(*☎ *248-3900)* offers a **Visitour Pass**, available in most hotels, for $4 per day or $8 for three days of unlimited bus and streetcar travel.

Regional Transit Authority (RTA): 6700 Plaza Drive, ☎ 248-3900 or 569-2700.

The **Riverfront Streetcar** ★ *($1.50 one way; Mon to Fri 6am to midnight, Sat and Sun 8am to midnight)* runs along the river for easy access to river-front activities. Inaugurated in 1926, this nine-station circuit is the oldest in the city. Antique cars in rich gold and red colours, familiarly known as "the ladies in red", permit about 5,500 passengers per day to enjoy the cultural and commercial attractions of the river front. Here is a list of the stops:

1st stop: Esplanade Avenue
2nd stop: French Market (at the Halle des Légumes - Vegetable Market)
3rd stop: French Market (at Decatur Street)
4th stop: Jackson Square, St. Louis Cathedral and the Cabildo
5th stop: Woldenberg Riverfront Park and Aquarium of the Americas
6th stop: Aquarium of the Americas, Canal Street Wharf and Ferry
7th stop: the *Creole Queen* paddle-wheel boat and the Poydras Street entrance to Riverwalk
8th stop: Julia Street entrance to Riverwalk and the New Orleans Convention Center
9th stop: historic Warehouse District

St. Charles Streetcar ★★ *($1; 24-hour service)* follows St. Charles Avenue from Canal Street past Loyola University (run by Jesuits), Tulane University (home of the oldest business faculty in the United States), the Garden District and Audubon Park to Carrollton Avenue.

Public Buses serve the entire city *($1, $0.10 extra for transfers)* and take exact change or passes.

The **Central Business District Easy Rider** *($0.30; Mon to Sat 6:30am to 6pm)* stops along Poydras and Canal Streets, as well as at the Convention Center.

By Ferry

Three ferries shuttle between the shores of the Mississippi. The Canal Street Ferry is free for foot passengers and one dollar for cars. It docks at Canal Street, near the French Quarter and takes passengers to Algiers Point. A second ferry, on Jackson Avenue, south of the Garden District, serves Gretna. The third ferry leaves from Chalmette.

By Car

Car Rental

The agency **HATA** (☎ 1-800-356-8392) is a free hotel and car rental reservation service (see "Accommodation", p 49).

Car-rental agencies are located at the airport and at various places in the city. To rent a car, you must have a valid driver's license and a major credit card. Rates start at about $30 per day and $150 per week for an economy-class car with unlimited mileage.

Alamo Rent A Car: 225 E Airline Highway, New Orleans, ☎ 469-0532 or 1-800-327-9633.

Avis Rent A Car: 2024 Canal Street, New Orleans, ☎ 523-4317 or 1-800-331-1212.

Budget Rent A Car: 1317 Canal Street, New Orleans, ☎ 467-2277 or 1-800-527-0700.

Dollar Rent A Car: 1910 Airlines Highway, Kenner, ☎ 467-2285 or 1-800-800-4000.

Hertz Rent A Car: 901 Convention Center Boulevard, Office 101, New Orleans, ☎ 568-1645 or 1-800-654-3131.

National Car Rental: 1020 Airline Highway, Kenner, ☎ 466-4335 or 1-800-227-7368.

Value Rent A Car: 1701 Airline Highway, Kenner, ☎ 469-2688.

Car Service and Assistance

American Automobile Association (AAA): 3445 North Causeway Boulevard, Metairie, New Orleans, ☎ 838-7500 or 1-800-222-4357.

CBD Chevron Services: 447 Rampart North, New Orleans, ☎ 568-1177.

Mardi Gras Truck Stop: 2401 Elysian Fields, New Orleans, ☎ 945-1000.

Parking

For any questions concerning parking downtown: ☎ 826-1854 or 826-1900.

In New Orleans, particularly in the French Quarter and the Central Business District, parking places are rare and precious. Restrictions are

GREATER NEW ORLEANS

many, and some of the signs are easier to understand than others. If you have the misfortune of having your car towed, something authorities are quick to do, here is the address of the municipal pound:

Claiborne Auto Pound, 400 North Clairborne Avenue, New Orleans, ☎ 565-7450 or 826-1900.

Parking Lots

Dixie Parking Service, Inc.: ☎ 523-4521.

Downtown Parking Service: ☎ 529-5708.

By Bicycle

The streets of New Orleans are particularly busy, so bicycling is much more pleasant in Audubon Park, City Park, and along the shores of Lake Pontchartrain. **Crescent City Cyclists** (☎ 276-2601) provides information on cycling activities.

Bicycle Rental

Some rental centres organize excursions in parks or in the Garden District, outings to the bayous or to plantations in the environs of New Orleans. Rental rates vary, but budget for between $3.50 and $5 per hour, or between $12.50 and $15 per day.

French Quarter Bicycles: 522 Dumaine Street, French Quarter, New Orleans, ☎ 529-3136.

Joe's Bike Shop: 2501 Tulane Street, New Orleans, ☎ 821-2350.

Michael's: 618 Frenchmen Street, Faubourg Marigny, New Orleans, ☎ 945-9505.

Olympic Bike Rentals & Tours: 1618 Prytania Street, New Orleans, ☎ 523-1314 *(every day 8am to 7pm)*.

Services for Disabled People in Louisiana

Gray Lines *(☎ 587-0861)* offers tours of New Orleans with adapted transportation.

Olympic Bike Rental and Tours *(☎ 523-1314)*, as well as specializing in bicycle rental, rents wheelchairs. Free delivery.

Around New Orleans

Metairie and Kenner

These two cities between the Missippi and Lake Pontchartrain constitute the western suburbs of New Orleans and are easily accessible via Interstate 10 (I-10). New Orleans International Airport is in Kenner.

Slidell

Slidell is the first town east of New Orleans, at the intersection of the I-10, I-12 and I-59 highways. From New Orleans, travel 50 kilometres on Interstate 10 (I-10) to the Slidell exit. US 11 crosses the town.

Lacombe

This town is on the north side of Lake Pontchartrain, halfway between Slidell

(16 km east) and Mandeville (15 km west). It can be reached by US 190 or by I-12, Lacombe exit.

Mandeville

From New Orleans, take I-10 west to exit 228 and cross the Lake Pontchartrain Causeway *($1 per car)*; Mandeville is right at the end of the bridge, 56 kilometres from New Orleans.

Madisonville

Madisonville is 16 kilometres from Mandeville via Highway US 190, and then LA 22 from Chinchuba. Madisonville can also be reached directly from the north end of the Lake Pontchartrain Causeway.

Covington

From New Orleans take the Lake Pontchartrain Causeway and continue on Highway US 190 for 13 kilometres. Covington is a total of 65 kilometres north of New Orleans and seven kilometres north of I-12. The sweetness of the air here is a product of the large pine forests surrounding the town and, in these polluted times, has made Covington very popular.

Abita Springs

Leaving Covington on the east side of town take LA 36 East five kilometres to Abita Springs; from Mandeville, take LA 59 North. From New Orleans, after getting off the Causeway continue on US 190 and then take I-12 eastward to the exit for Abita Springs and Highway LA 59 North.

Bogalusa

This forest town is in the northeast part of the state, 113 kilometres from New Orleans, in Washington Parish, at the Mississippi border. There are two routes by which to reach it: from Covington, take LA 21 North 48 kilometres to Bogalusa; from New Orleans, take I-10 East and, once past Slidell, take I-59 North five kilometres to the intersection with LA 41 (at the Pearl River exit), which you take 40 kilometres to LA 21 North: Bogalusa is 21 kilometres away.

Folsom

This little town is in the heart of the rural region north of Covington. From Covington, take State Highway LA 25 North 16 kilometres.

Franklinton

Franklinton is 24 kilometres north of Folsom on LA 25.

Robert

Robert is 25 kilometres west of Covington on US 190. Alternately, take exit 47 from I-12.

Hammond

Hammond is a crossroads town 80 kilometres from New Orleans: Interstates 12 and 55 and Highways US 190 and US 51 all intersect here.

GREATER
NEW ORLEANS

Southeastern Louisiana University is based in Hammond. From New Orleans, take I-10 west to I-55, which you then take 48 kilometres to Hammond. Highway US 190 goes to the downtown area.

Albany

From Hammond, take US 190 West or I-12 West for 16 kilometres.

Ponchatoula

The abundant Spanish moss on the trees in this area is the basis for Ponchatoula's name, which, in the language of the Choctaw means "hanging moss". From Hammond, US 51 South leads to LA 22 East which you take two kilometres to Ponchatoula.

Springfield

Springfield is 11 kilometers from Ponchatula on LA 22 West, or 11 kilometres from Albany on LA 43 South.

Independence, Amite, Tangipahoa and Kentwood

From Hammond follow US 51 North to Independence (20 km), Amite (31 km), Tangipahoa (50 km) and Kentwood (56 km). These towns are also accessible via I-55 which runs parallel to US 51.

Loranger

From Independence take LA 40 eastward 13 kilometres to Loranger.

Chipola

Chipola is 29 km west of Kentwood via LA 38.

Chalmette, Violet, Pointe a la Hache and Bohemia: the East Bank of the Mississippi

From New Orleans, take Rampart St. (in the French Quarter), which turns into St. Claude Avenue, and then into LA 46, before reaching Chalmette 11 kilometres southeast of the city. There is ferry service between Chalmette and Gretna.

There are many villages along the river, among them Violet and Poydras, and, continuing along LA 39, Pointe a la Hache and Bohemia, 85 kilometres from New Orleans.

Port Sulphur, Buras, and Venice: the West Bank of the Mississippi

From New Orleans, cross the Mississippi on the Greater New Orleans Bridge (US 90) and continue on the West Bank Expressway to the Lafayette exit, from which you take the Belle Chasse Highway. From Belle Chasse, LA 23 runs alongside the Mississippi for over 100 kilometres to its estuary at Venice, passing through Port Sulphur and Buras. A ferry at Belle Chasse and another at Pointe a la Hache West link the two banks of the river.

Crown Point, Jean Lafitte, and Lafitte

From New Orleans, take the West Bank Expressway to the Barataria exit, and then take Barataria Boulevard 27 kilometres to Crown Point.

Continuing on LA 45 you will reach the villages of Jean Lafitte and Lafitte.

Barataria

From Jean Lafitte, cross the bridge over Bayou des Rigolettes and take LA 301 two kilometres north.

PRACTICAL INFORMATION

The area code for Greater New Orleans is 504. You do not need to dial it for local calls. All telephone numbers beginning with 1-800 and 1-888 are toll-free when dialed from within the United States and in some cases from within North America.

Tourist Information

New Orleans Metropolitan Convention and Visitors Bureau, Inc.: 11520 Sugar Bowl Drive, New Orleans, LA 70112, ☎ (504)-566-5031 or (504) 566-5011, www.nawlins.com.

New Orleans Tourist Information: ☎ 1-800-NEW-ORLEANS or ☎ 1-800-639-6753 *(24-hour service)*.

Welcome Center: 529 Saint Anne Street, New Orleans, LA 70112, ☎ (504) 568-5661 or (504) 566-5031. *(Mar to Nov 10am to 6pm, Dec to Feb 9am to 5pm)*

Airport Hospitality Center: New Orleans International Airport, Baggage Claim area *(every day 10 am to 10pm)*.

Metairie

AAA Tourist Center: 3445 Causeway Blvd. North, ☎ 838-7500 *(Tue, Thu and Fri 8:30am to 5:15pm, Mon and Wed 8:30 to 7pm)*

Emergency Assistance: ☎ 1-800-453-7198 in North America.

African-American Tourism Organizations

Greater New Orleans Black Tourism Network, Inc. *(Louisiana Superdome, 1520 Sugar Bowl Drive, New Orleans, LA 70112,* ☎ *504-523-5652 or 1-800-725-5652, www.gnobtn.com)*. There is good reason for New Orleans to be identified with African-American culture and with jazz. With a black population that is 60% of the total population, New Orleans is the largest city of colour in the United States, a fact that is reflected at the administrative level. For 15 years, New Orleans has had black mayors, a mark of societal progress on the background of the cruel diaspora experienced by Africans brought to America.

The Greater New Orleans Black Tourism Network offers tours that emphasize the influence of African-American culture on the city. Famous the world over as the cradle of Jazz, New Orleans owes this distinction to a rather unique phenomenon that occurred in a wasteland northeast of the city known as the "plaines du Congo" that served as a fairground and a Native-American ball field during the week. On Sunday, the Lord's day, blacks were permitted to meet there, to dance and to play the African instruments that lived in their memories: tomtoms, calabash, triangles and the bamboo drum called "bamboula", in a dance phenomenon that was destined to progressively to lead to jazz. Jazz, the music of poor exiles as able to express explosive joy as melancholic languor, would leave profound marks not only on the places where we rejoice, but also on those where we commune with ourselves. Among the celebrated names of black music in New Orleans, are Louis Armstrong, the big band singer and trumpet-player, and the uncontested queen of gospel, Mahalia Jackson. Laughter and prayer, these two poles of the spectrum of human activity, show a strong African influence, one of the rich sources of the cultural originality of Americans.

Mythic Congo Square, now Louis Armstrong Park, is still a site of musical exchange and improvisation. The most important event in this sphere is still the New Orleans Jazz and Heritage Festival in April, a climactic point in the city's tourism calendar. For those that miss it, the many Social Aid & Pleasure Clubs organize annual fall parades with bands of all sorts and musicians of all ages.

The contribution of African-Americans is equally strong during Mardi Gras. This festival period that begins on Epiphany (January 6) and reaches its apogy in the days preceding Lent attracts visitors from the world over. The arrival of the Krewe of the Zulu King is among the festival's most important moments. It begins at dawn with the arrival of the "king", by barge on the Mississippi, and runs until dusk (St. Charles Ave. and Canal St.). There is also the parade of torch carriers and then the second line made up of all those who follow the procession, including musicians who go all out trying to attract more atention than the

"official" paraders. The French Quarter, conceived by Pierre Le Blond de La Tour and built in 1718 by Adrien de Pauger, is the popular setting of good times with these thousands of celebrants, dancing to the rhythm of the festival that brings back so much French, African, native, Cajun and North American history.

Roots of New Orleans *(reservations: ☎ 504-596-6889 or 504-523-7818)*, a name reminiscent of Alex Haley's *Roots*, offers a half-day "discovery" tour that includes a Creole lunch *(departure at 9am: adults $25, children $19, meal included; departure at 1:30pm: adults $19, children $15)*.

Global Resources, Inc. *(P.O. Box 50601, New Orleans, LA 70150; contact John Hankins, ☎ 504-861-0170)* specializes in cultural tourism.

Conventions and Events

Expo Emphasis! *(4429 Bienville Ave., 70119, ☎ 504-488-5825, ⊷ 504-488-5830)* specializes in the organization of conventions and expositions in New Orleans. Contact Bobby Bergeron directly; he organizes every aspect of the preparation and success of the event, from the stay to the layout of the hall, transportation, meals, even guided tours of the city.

Emergencies

Police, Fire and Ambulance Emergency Number: ☎ 911

Eighth District Police Station: 24 hours a day; 334 Royal Street, French Quarter, ☎ 822-2222.

Safety Tips

Some sections of New Orleans are best avoided at night, and little recommended during the day for people who are alone. These include the northern part of the French Quarter and the streets around St. Louis Cemetery No. 1 and No. 2, as well as any poorly lit street in the French Quarter. The same thing goes for the area north of St. Charles Avenue between the West Bank Expressway and Audubon Park, but especially between Jackson and Louisiana Avenues, and for the area south of Magazine Street.

It is also recommended to keep your car doors locked while driving in the city, to leave nothing of value in your car and to be careful at stoplights.

In May 1997 two people who were attending a convention were visiting a very busy section of the French Quarter by car when they were shot at. Only one of the victims survived this villainous and gratuitous attack, which is just one example among so many instances of crime in the city.

Fire Department: ☎ 581-3473

New Orleans Dental Association: ☎ 834-6449

Travellers' Aid Society: ☎ 525-8726

Hospitals

There are three hospitals located close to the French Quarter and downtown:

Touro Infirmary: 1401, Foucher Street, New Orleans, ☎ 897-7011 *(open 24 hours a day, emergency entrance on Delachaise Street, at the corner of Prytania Street)*. The centre is located near St. Charles Avenue. Credit cards are accepted.

Medical Center of Louisiana: 1532 Tulane Avenue, New Orleans, ☎ 568-2311.

Tulane University Medical Center: 1415 Tulane Avenue, New Orleans, ☎ 588-5268.

Pharmacies

Walgreen pharmacies *(open 24 hours a day)* sell, among other things, a product called "XS", which is particularly useful as a cure for that carnival hangover. There are Walgreen stores all over the city; here are a few addresses:

134 Royal Street.

4001 General De Gaulle Avenue, ☎ 368-8171.

1429 St. Charles Avenue, ☎ 561-8458.

3057 Gentilly Boulevard, ☎ 282-2621.

3311 Canal Street, ☎ 822-8073 or 822-8070.

9999 Lake Forest, ☎ 242-0981.

GREATER NEW ORLEANS

Banks

First National Bank of Commerce: 210 Baronne Street, ☎ 561-1371 or 1-800-462-9511.

Hibernia National Bank: 313 Carondelet Street, ☎ 586-5552.

Shearson Lehman Brothers: 909 Poydras Street, Suite 1600, ☎ 585-3902.

Whitney National Bank: 228 St. Charles Avenue and 430 Chartres Street, ☎ 586-7272.

American Express Co.: 158 Baronne Street, ☎ 586-8201.

Automatic Teller Machines

First National Bank of Commerce (FNBC): 240 Royale Street and 801 Chartres Street.

Hibernia National Bank: 701 Poydras Street.

Whitney National Bank: 228 St. Charles Avenue.

Exchanging Money

Several banks readily exchange foreign currency, but almost all charge a **commission**. There are exchange offices, on the other hand, that do not charge commission, but their rates are sometimes less competitive. These offices often have longer opening hours. It is a good idea to **shop around**.

At the airport: **Whitney National Bank** *(Mon to Thu 8:30am to 3pm, Fri 8:30 to 5:30pm)* and **Mutual of Omaha** *(every day 6am to 7pm)* are on the upper level of the main terminal.

Downtown: **Continental Currency Exchange Inc.** *(Mon to Sat 10am to 9pm, Sun 11am to 5pm)* is in Riverwalk Market; **Thomas Cook Currency Services** *(111 St. Charles Ave.,* ☎ *524-0700)* is one block from the French Quarter.

Post Office

Main Post Office: 701 Loyola, ☎ 589-1111 or 589-1112.

Climate

New Orleans enjoys a subtropical climate. Between December and February average maximum and minimum temperatures are about 19° C and 10° C (66.2° F and 50° F); from March to May they are about 25° C and 17° C (77° F and 62.6° F); from June to September they are about 32° C and 24° C (89.6° F and 75.2° F); from October to November they are about 16° C and 24° C (59° F and 75.2° F).

Child Care

In addition to child-care services, these agencies offer tourist activities and entertainment options specially designed for children:

Accent Arrangements: ☎ 524-1222.

Dependable Kid Care: ☎ 486-4001.

The **New Orleans Metropolitan Convention and Visitors Bureau, Inc.** (see p 63) *(☎ 566-5031 ou 566-5011)* sells a five-dollar booklet of suggestions for activities and sights that are of interest to children.

Radio Stations

WWOZ - 90.7 FM
1201 St. Philip Street, ☎ 568-1239.
Traditional jazz and rhythm and blues.

KMEZ (Big Easy 102.9 FM)
1450 Poydras Street, Suite 440,
☎ 593-6376.
Soul music and classics from the sixties and seventies.

WWNO - 89.9 FM
University of New Orleans, ☎ 280-7000 or 286-7000.
Classical and jazz.

Around New Orleans

Jefferson Parish Tourism: 1221 Elmwood Harahan Park Blvd., Metairie, ☎ 736-6417 or 736-6400. *(Mon to Fri 8:30am to 4:30pm)*

Kenner Convention & Visitors Bureau: 2100 3rd Street, Suite 10, Kenner, LA 70062, ☎ 464-9494 or 1-800-231-5282 from the United States.

Kenner Office of Tourism: 2100 3rd Street, Suite 11, Kenner, LA 70062, ☎ 468-7228 or 1-800-473-6789 from the United States.

North of New Orleans

St. Tammany Parish Tourist & Convention Commission: 600 Highway US 190 North, Suite 15, Covington, LA 70433, ☎ 892-0520 or 1-800-634-9443 *(every day 8:30am to 4:30pm)*. This office can provide tourist information on the towns of Madisonville, Mandeville and Slidell, as well as on Covington, the county seat of St. Tammany Parish.

Bogalusa Chamber of Commerce: 608 Willis Avenue, Bogalusa, LA 70427, ☎ 735-5731.

Tangipahoa Parish Tourist Commisssion: 42271 Morrison Blvd. South, Hammond, LA 70403, ☎ 542-7520 or 1-800-542-7520 from the United States *(Mon to Fri 9am to 5pm, Sat and Sun 10am to 4pm)*. The parish of Tangipahoa includes the municipalities of Amite, Hammond, Independence, Kentwood, Loranger, Ponchatoula, Robert and Tangipahoa.

Amite Chamber of Commerce: 100 West Oak Street, Amite, ☎ 748-5537 *(Mon to Fri 9am to 5pm, on weekend address inquiries to the police station across the street)*.

South of New Orleans

Jefferson Parish Tourist Information Center: at the corner of Loyola and I-10 in Kenner, ☎ 468-8227 *(every day 8am to 5:30pm)*. Jefferson Parish includes the towns of Metairie, Kenner and Westwego, and the villages of Crown Point, Barataria and Lafitte.

Plaquemines Parish Office of Tourism: P.O. Box 829, Port Sulphur, LA 70083, ☎ 564-2761 or 564-2925. Plaquemines

GREATER
NEW ORLEANS

Parish runs along the Mississippi from Belle Chasse to the mouth of the river.

Plaquemines Parish Economic Development: 104 New Orleans Street, Belle Chasse, LA 70037, ☎ 394-0018.

St. Bernard Parish Tourist Commission: 8201 W. Judge Perez Drive, Chalmette, LA 70043, ☎ 278-4242 *(Mon to Fri 9am to 4:30pm)*.

 EXPLORING

The French Quarter (Vieux Carré) ★★★

The French Quarter (Vieux-Carré Français) boasts an impressively rich architectural heritage. From its elaborate balconies and blooming courtyards, the quarter displays its charms, at once French, Spanish and Creole; one cannot help but compare this cultural mosaic to that of the French- and Spanish-speaking Caribbean islands. In Jackson Square (the old Place d'Armes), the spires of elegant St. Louis Cathedral dominate the landscape. From the square to the middle of the park, painters at their easels confer a certain *je ne sais quoi* to the area, with its evocative street names like Decatur, Conti, Dauphine, Bienville, Bourbon, Ursulines, Chartres, Toulouse, Dumaine, etc. Situated on the banks of the Mississippi River, the **French Quarter** combines past and present in a peaceful, verdant setting. In its midst is **Jackson Square**, a former military parade site, in front of **St. Louis Cathedral** with its tall steeples and white façade, which now watch an endless procession of musicians, artists and horse-drawn-carriage drivers stream by. The **equestrian statue of**

Andrew Jackson, the general who saved New Orleans from British invaders during the War of 1812, also stands before the Cathedral. To the right and left (respectively) of the Cathedral, visitors can admire the **Presbytère** and the **Cabildo**, an old guardroom that later became the seat of the Spanish Colonial government, and the site of the signing of the Louisiana Purchase in 1803. These two buildings are now part of the Louisiana State Museum, as are the **Lower Pontalba Building** and the **Upper Pontalba Building**, red brick structures, adorned with quintessential cast-iron balustrades, that were the first apartment buildings built in the United States.

This very particular type of nineteenth-century architecture is characteristic of New Orleans. The buildings' façades are decorated with delicate balustrades, veritable cast-iron embroideries in which complex designs harmoniously intermingle. This fashion was initiated by the Spanish after the fire that ravaged the city in 1788.

On that score, the famous and imposing **Labranche Building** (Édifice La Branche) *(700 Royal Street)* should not be overlooked. Also worth seeing are **Lafitte's Blacksmith Shop** (La Forge Lafitte) *(941 Bourbon St.)*, a typical example of the brick-and-post cottage, and the Greek Revival **Beauregard-Keyes House** *(1113 Chartres St.)*, two examples of typical eighteenth-century Louisiana architecture and masonry.

Another interesting building in the French Quarter is the **Hermann-Grima House** *(320 St. Louis St.)*. Built in the Georgian style in 1831, which was then much in fashion along the

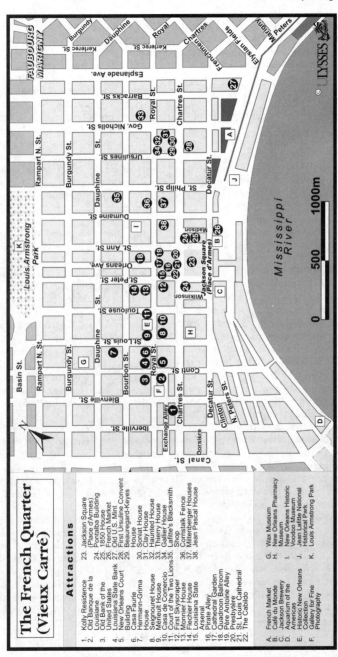

The French Quarter (Vieux Carré)

Attractions

1. Kolly Residence
2. Old Banque de la Louisiane
3. Old Bank of the United States
4. Louisiana State Bank
5. New Orleans Court Building
6. Casa Faurie
7. Hermann-Grima House
8. Soniat House
9. Clay House
10. Haunted House
11. Seignouret House
12. Mérieult House
13. Casa de Comercio
14. Court of the Two Lions
15. Louisiana State Arsenal
16. Pirate Alley
17. Cathedral Garden
18. Quadroon Ballroom
19. Père Antoine Alley
20. Presbytère
21. St. Louis Cathedral
22. The Cabildo
23. Jackson Square (Place d'Armes)
24. Pontalba Building
25. 1850 House
26. French Market
27. Old U.S. Mint
28. First Ursuline Convent
29. Beauregard-Keyes House
30. Clay House
31. Thierry House
32. Haunted House
33. Gallier House
34. Lafitte's Blacksmith Shop
35. Cornstalk Fence
36. Miltenberger Houses
37. Jean Pascal House
38.

A. French Market
B. Café du Monde
C. Jackson Brewery
D. Aquarium of the Americas
E. Historic New Orleans Collection
F. Gallery for Fine Photography
G. Wax Museum
H. New Orleans Pharmacy Museum
I. New Orleans Historic Voodoo Museum
J. Jean Lafitte National Historical Park
K. Louis Armstrong Park

Louisiana coastline, it opens its doors to visitors for whom demonstrations of Creole cooking are held from October to May. Reservations are required.

The French Market
(Le Marché Français)

The French Market has always been known as such, even though it was first a Native American trading post. Under the Spanish regime, in 1791, it was transformed into an indoor market. German/Creole market gardeners – Germans who came during the French regime – were the first to supply the public market with food; they were later followed by Italians. As early as 1831, a train skirting the Elysian Fields (Champs Élysées) from the French Market (Marché Français) ran all the way to Lake Pontchartrain. Thanks to President Roosevelt, the old French Market was restored in 1936. With its Old Butcher's Market (Halle des Boucheries), built in 1813, its Vegetable Market (Halle des Légumes) in 1822, its Red House (Maison Rouge), encompassing the original bazaar, and its new Kitchen Market (Halle des Cuisines), the French Market makes up a fascinating whole. The French Market also houses the Flea Market, where local hand-crafted wares can be purchased. Cafés set themselves up here in 1860. The Café du Monde is its oldest tenant. Delicious beignets and its popular *café au lait*, a robust chicory-flavoured coffee, can be savoured here. The French Market extends over several blocks between Decatur Street and North Peters Street.

The **French Market** ★★★ (Le Marché Français) spreads over five blocks of houses along Decatur Street and North Peters Street; here, visitors will find secondhand shops, restaurants and, a most remarkable place, a two-hundred year old market that displays fresh meats, incredibly aromatic spices as well as fresh fruits and vegetables 24 hours a day. Visitors will also find the venerable **Café du Monde** here, a place where you can treat yourself to a full-flavoured coffee and a beignet (French sugar doughnut) any time of day or night.

Right nearby stands the **Jackson Brewery** *(620 Decatur St.)*, commonly known as **Jax.** This old factory converted into a picturesque shopping arcade has about one hundred shops and boutiques under its roof.

The **Aquarium of the Americas** ★★★ *(adults $9.75, seniors $7.50, children 2-12 years of age $5; every day 9:30am to 5pm; Canal St., ☎ 861-2537)*. Over 100,000 species of birds, fish and reptiles, in their natural habitats, can be admired here.

This beautiful, resolutely modern facility is very popular and is close to Woldenberg Riverfront Park and its promenade, which follows along the banks of the Mississippi River. Here, visitors mingle with families and hundreds of school children from neighbouring states arriving by school bus. The place is certainly worth a visit, but be forewarned, the cost of parking in the adjacent lot proves to be almost as high as the price of admission itself! It is therefore preferable to use the tram skirting the river (the Riverfront Streetcar), which can be taken from the French Market.

Typical house in the French Quarter

From its very entrance (upon passing through the turnstile), the Aquarium of the Americas offers explorers the planet's wondrous submarine worlds. On the ground floor, visitors first pass beneath a huge vaulted aquarium in which the moray eel, the skate, the boxfish and the shark swim about above visitors' heads and on either side of the glass arch. The visit continues through different ocean ecosystems and climatic microcosms, set up in order to accommodate species from the "coralline" waters of the Caribbean and the Pacific, as well as those from the polar oceans of the Arctic and the Antarctic.

Upstairs, two parrots greet visitors in the Amazon River Basin exhibit, a re-creation of the moist, humid environment of this South American region. The sturgeon catfish, the arapaima, the *pacu*, the boxfish, the carnivorous piranha in their own special tank (their scales are a veritable mosaic of gold and silver nuggets) and finally the black-and-white-spotted leopard ray are all to be found here. Farther along, visitors encounter Arctic and Antarctic species such as affable, child-pleasing penguins with their little tufts of yellow hair. Other areas reproduce the sea bed of the Gulf of Mexico. In one tank, between the pillars of a replica of an oil rig, metal rods are completely encrusted with coral. The astonishing saw shark and the giant sea turtle swim in its waters. In other aquariums, blue jellyfish, unquestionably the most magnificent of their kind, flutter their colourful umbrellas, while other tanks re-create the murky ocean depths, enabling visitors to better observe certain species of phosphorescent fish.

The Aquarium of the Americas shelters many other residents such as spiders, snakes (terrestrial and aquatic), tortoises and turtles, as well as a rare white alligator. Under a guard's vigilant eye, young and old alike can gently pet a harmless baby shark raised in an aquarium built especially for this purpose!

The **Historic New Orleans Collection** ★★ *($2; Tue to Sat 10am to 4:45pm; 533 Royal St., ☎ 523-4662)*. Historic site, museum and research centre on the history of the state and the city itself. Guided tours of the gallery and the residence.

The **Gallery for Fine Photography** ★★ *(free admission; Mon to Sat 10am to 6pm, Sun 11am to 6pm; 322 Royal St., ☎ 568-1313)* displays a very beautiful collection of photographs from the late 1800s to the present. Works by Lartigue and by Henri Cartier-Bresson as well as those by jazz portraitist Herman Leonard and photos of Mardi Gras can all be viewed here, among others. Practically every theme is tackled and a new exhibit is presented every month.

The **Louisiana State Museum** ★★★ *(for each museum: adults $4, seniors and students $3, free for children under 12; for the museum complex: $10 and $7.50; Tue to Sun 10am to 5pm; 701 Chartres St., ☎ 568-6968)*. This museum occupies a certain number of historic buildings in the French Quarter. The **Old United States Mint** *(400 Esplanade Ave.)* is dedicated to jazz and Mardi Gras; the **Presbytère** *(701 Chartres St.)* presents exhibitions pertaining to the history of Louisiana;

the **1850 House** (Maison 1850) *(523 St. Ann St.)* specializes in the period preceding and following the American Civil War. (See also "Walking Tour of the French Quarter", p 74)

The **Musée Conti Wax Museum** ★ *(adults $5.75, seniors and students $5.25, children $3.50; every day 10am to 5pm; 917 Conti St., ☎ 525-2605 or, from the US, 1-800-233-5405)*. Heroes, villains and celebrities such as the humanist and writer Mark Twain and the naturalist painter John James Audubon are in effigy here, not to mention great mock-ups of historic events: Napoleon signing the Louisiana Purchase, Lafayette visiting the city in 1825 and the Battle of New Orleans, to name but a few.

The **New Orleans Pharmacy Museum** ★★ *(adults $2, seniors and students $1, free for children under 12; Tue to Sun 10am to 5pm; 514 Chartres St., ☎ 524-9077)*. Founded in 1950, this museum is a replica of the first chemist shop built here in 1823. The dispensary and carved rosewood counters are filled with retorts and huge blown-glass jars whose contents sometimes prove disturbing: virtually unidentifiable multicoloured fluids, grigris and roots of all kinds.

The **New Orleans Historic Voodoo Museum** ★★ *(adults $5, seniors and students $4, guided French Quarter tour $18, guided cemetery tour $10; every day 10am till dusk; 724 Dumaine St., ☎ 523-7685)*. In this unique museum, all the secrets of this mysterious religious practice, which originated in Africa, are disclosed. Here, visitors will see the most mysterious of objects, age-old evidence of good and evil spells...

Current names	Original French names
Exchange Passage	place des Échanges
Esplanade Avenue	avenue de l'Esplanade
Elysian Fields	avenue des Champs-Élysées
St. Louis Cemetery No. 1	cimetière Saint-Louis no. 1
Central Business District	Faubourg Sainte-Marie or Ville Gravier
Pirate Alley	passage des Pirates
Père Antoine Alley	passage du Père Antoine
Jackson Square	Place d'Armes
Bourbon Street	rue de Bourbon
Love Street	rue d'Amour
Burgundy Street	rue de Bourgogne
Chartres Street	rue de Chartres
Iberville Street	rue de la Douane
Governor Nicholls Street	rue de l'Hôpital
Decatur Street	rue de la Levée
Piety Street	rue de la Piété
Victory Street	rue de la Victoire
Good Children Street	rue des Bons-Enfants
Greatmen Street	rue des Grands-Hommes
Felicity Street	rue Félicité
Barracks Street	rue du Quartier
Rampart Street	rue du Rempart
Royal Street	rue Royale
St. Andrew Street	rue Saint-André
St. Philip Street	rue Saint-Phillipe
St. Peter Street	rue Saint-Pierre
St. Ann Street	rue Sainte-Anne
St. Mary Street	rue Saint-Marie
French Quarter	Vieux-Carré Français

GREATER NEW ORLEANS

The **Jean Lafitte National Historical Park and Preserve - French Quarter Folklore Center** ★★★ (Le Parc national et réserve historique Jean-Lafitte - Centre de folklore du Quartier Français) *(every day 8am to 5pm; 916 North Peters St.,* ☎ *589-2636)*. Exhibitions and shows are presented here as are demonstrations of all kinds. This is also the point of departure for guided tours of the French Quarter – the oldest district in New Orleans, classified as a National Historical Landmark – and of the Mississippi Delta region.

Louis Armstrong Park ★★★ *(north of the French Quarter, between St. Peter and St. Philip Streets)*, dedicated to this great jazz musician and inaugurated by his widow in 1980, lies on the former Congo Square. The **Municipal Auditorium** and the **New Orleans Theater for the Performing Arts** are also here.

**Historic Street Names
in the French Quarter**

Just as the French Quarter's precious architectural heritage is scrupulously preserved by the State, as are its other neighbourhoods and districts, so are street names maintained with equal resolve by the city of New Orleans. On each of the street signs, the original French name appears above the more recent appellation. Some streets and squares have commemorative name plates bearing Spanish appellations; these names, such as Calle Real for Royal Street and Plaza de Armas for Place d'Armes (now Jackson Square), were added during the Spanish occupation of Louisiana. The list in the box below offers examples of historical and modern appellations of a few streets, squares, places and districts.

**Walking Tour of
the French Quarter ★★★**

Visiting the French Quarter or Vieux Carré on foot is much more enjoyable than doing so by car. By strolling along its main boulevards, through its streets and alleys, visitors will discover the charms of New Orleans' historic district, also known as "The Crescent City" on account of its location around a bend in the Mississippi. Put aside at least three hours for this stroll, or more if you wish to take your time and window shop, or have something to eat or drink in one of the many cafés in the area. The numbers will enable you to locate places worth visiting on the French Quarter map.

The Kolly Townhouse - The First Ursulines Convent - Charity Hospital (1) *(301 Chartres St., at Bienville)*. Jean-Daniel Kolly, the Elector of Bavaria's financial adviser and one of the investors in the *Compagnie des Indes Occidentales*, had this *hôtel particulier* built in 1718, soon after the founding of New Orleans. Kolly resided here for about ten years. It was then home to the Ursulines, until 1749 when they took possession of their new convent on Chartres Street. The building's final occupant was the Charity Hospital, New Orleans' first hospital.

Go back up Bienville Street to Royal Street; take a right and stop at no. 334.

The **Banque de la Louisiane (2)** *(334 Royal St.)*. This magnificent building was built in 1826, in what was then the financial district, to house the Banque de la Louisiane. It has since been used as the seat of the government of the State of Louisiana, by the American Legion and, more recently, as the French Quarter police station.

Cross Royal Street to no. 343.

The **Old Bank of the United States (3)** *(343 Royal St.)*. It is in this edifice, built in 1800, that the first Bank of the United States opened. The building is adorned with magnificent windows and lacy wrought-iron balconies, attesting to the talent of artisans in that era.

Continue along Royal Street to Conti Street.

The **Louisiana State Bank (4)** *(403 Royal St.)*. The bank's monogram, LSB, is still visible in the balconies' wrought ironwork. The building was erected in 1821 according to the plans of the Frenchman Benjamin Larobe, one of the architects of Washington's Capitol.

Cross Royal Street to no. 400.

The **New Orleans Court Building (5)** *(400 Royal St.)*. This white-marble edifice dates from the beginning of the century. It once housed the State Supreme Court and is now occupied in part by the Wildlife Museum as well as by the U.S.'s fifth judicial district court of appeal. The building was entirely renovated in 1997.

Cross Royal Street again to no. 417.

Casa Faurie also know as **Morphy House (6)** *(417 Royal St.)*. This *hôtel particulier* was erected in 1801 for the maternal grandfather of the Impressionist painter Edgar Degas. Purchased four years later by the Banque de la Louisiana, it was resold in 1819 to David Gordon, who was to make it the centre of New Orleans high-society. General Andrew Jackson was the guest of honour at lavish parties thrown here during his second passage through the city, in 1828. By 1841, Gordon was ruined and the building, sold at auction, was to become the property of Judge Alonzo Morphy. Today, it houses the famous restaurant Brennan's (see "Restaurants", p 127).

Turn left on St.Louis Street and head to no. 820.

The **Hermann-Grima House ★ (7)** *(adults $5, seniors and students $4, 8-18 years of age $3, free for children under 8; Mon to Sat 10am to 4pm; 820 St. Louis St.)*. The house was built in 1831 by architect William Brand for the wealthy merchant Samuel Hermann; it is a rare example of American architecture in the French Quarter. Thirteen years later, it fell into the hands of the lawyer and notary Felix Grima, who added the outbuildings. The house and stunning horse stables are well preserved. Another original detail is its Creole-style open kitchen. Today, cooking classes and Creole culinary demonstrations are held here on Thursdays, from October to May. The building now billets a women's religious association.

Go back to Royal Street and turn left.

The **Seignouret House** (Maison Seignouret) **(8)** *(520 Royal St.)*. It was François Seignouret, a wealthy wine merchant originating from Bordeaux, who had this splendid residence built in 1816. A skilled cabinet maker, Seignouret also built a few pieces of furniture on which he discreetly added an S, his last initial. One such example can be discerned in the frieze of the wrought-iron balcony upstairs. A radio and television station now occupies the space.

Cross the street.

The **Merieult House** (Maison Mérieult) **(9)** *($2; Mon to Fri 9am to 5pm; 533 Royal St.)*. Here stands the oldest house on Royal Street, built in 1792 for the merchant Jean-François Mérieult. The Merieult House was one of the few to survive the fire that ravaged the city two years after its construction.

Apparently, during a stay in Europe, Jean-François Mérieult's bride, Catherine McNamara, received an offer for a large sum of money from Napoleon in exchange for her beautiful, naturally red hair. The Emperor wished to offer it as a gift to the Turkish Sultan, whose beloved wanted desperately to be admired as a redhead. But the lovely Catherine did not let herself be swayed, and returned to Louisiana with a full head of hair.

In the rear courtyard of the Merieult House is another beautiful building, the **Williams Residence**, built in 1888.

The Merieult House, now the property of the Kemper and Leila Williams Foundation, contains a magnificent collection of prints, old maps and other documents relating to the history of New Orleans.

Cross Royal Street once again.

Casa de Comercio (10) *(536 Royal St.).* This building, built soon after the December 1794 fire, which destroyed the city's core, is a significant example of Spanish architecture in New Orleans.

Head to the intersection of Toulouse Street.

The Court of Two Lions (11) *(537 Royal St. and 710 Toulouse St.).* The building derives its name from the two stone lions supporting the high portal from which Toulouse Street can be seen.

Continue along Royal Street.

The **First Skyscraper** (Le Monnier House, La Maison Le Monnier) ★ **(12)** *(640 Royal St.).* The first house built in 1811 by Dr. Le Monnier had three floors, making it more or less "Louisiana's first skyscraper". The doctor's consulting room, on the top floor, is considered one of New Orleans' architectural gems.

Turn left on St. Peter Street.

Le Monnier House (13) *(714 St. Peter St.).* Constructed in 1829 for Dr. Yves Le Monnier, it was then purchased in 1860 by Antoine Alciatore, who converted it into a boarding house. Gastronome and *cordon bleu* chef, Alciatore offered such an exquisite *table d'hôte* that New Orleans' upper crust flocked to his place in droves, so much so he decided to open a restaurant. Success was immediate and Antoine's quickly achieved international renown.

Antoine's is still in existence, only a stone's throw from here, and Antoine Alciatore's descendants now run it (see "Restaurants", p 127).

Continue on to 718 St. Peter Street.

The **Flechier House** (Maison de Flechier, Garnier House) ★ **(14)** *(718 St. Peter St.).* This house was built soon after the 1794 fire, for the planter Étienne-Marie de Flechier. A bar now occupies the premises. French and Spanish interior courtyards abound in the French Quarter; the one in the Flechier House is truly magnificent and well worth a visit.

Head back toward and cross Royal Street.

The **Louisiana State Arsenal** ★★ **(15)** *(adults $4, seniors and students $3, free for children under 12; Tue to Sun 9am to 5pm; 615 St. Peter St.).* This structure was the prison (*calabozo*) at the time of the Spanish occupation. In the early 1800s, the State of Louisiana set it up as an arsenal and military academy, attended by the sons of the best Creole and American families. The building, which has aged fairly well, now houses the Louisiana State Museum (see p 72).

Take a few steps back up to Royal Street and turn right on Cabildo Alley, which leads to Pirate Alley.

Pirate Alley (16) was originally called Ruelle d'Orléans, Sud. It is here that General Jackson supposedly arranged to meet the buccaneer brothers Pierre and Jean Lafitte to discuss the city's plan of defence against British troops. The present alley dates from 1831. The great novelist William Faulkner lived there as a youth.

Head toward Royal Street and stop at Orleans Street.

The **Cathedral Garden (17)** *(at Royal St. and Orleans St.)* lies behind a wrought-iron gate. Inside visitors will see the monument erected in honour of the sailors who died after volunteering to fight a yellow-fever epidemic.

Head for no. 717 on Orleans Street.

The **Quadroon Ballroom** (Salle de Bal D'Orléans) **(18)** *(717 Orleans St.).* A small village founded in 1718 under the French regime, New Orleans has since become one of the U.S.'s principal cities. The opening of the Théâtre Français in 1817 marked an important date in its history. Its director, Davis, intended to add a lavish opera house, a restaurant and a casino, which could compete with the best European establishments. However, the Civil War, which ruined the New Orleanian aristocracy, put an end to these lavish designs. In 1881, the nuns of the Holy Family Order made this their mother house and opened a school here as well. And in 1964, another sign of the times, the "ballroom", as it has always been called, was sold to a hotel complex. Despite the transformations it has sustained, the historic ballroom still stands, though it is now shorn of its original decor.

Return to Royal Street, turn left; at the edge of Cathedral Garden is Père Antoine Alley.

Père Antoine Alley (19) *(between the Cathedral and the Presbytère).* This alley was laid out in 1831. No one here ever refers to it as Orleans Alley (its official name), but rather, as Père Antoine Alley: in memory of the beloved Spanish monk. The same holds true for the Cathedral Garden, better known to its users as "Père Antoine's garden".

Continue on to Chartres Street and Jackson Square. When facing the Cathedral, the Presbytère (the grey building) is on the right.

The **Presbytère** ★★ **(20)** *(adults $4, seniors and students $3, free for children under 12; Tue to Sun 9am to 5pm).* The Spanish Capuchins' monastery erected on this site did not escape the fire that ravaged the city in 1788. In 1791, Don Andrès Almonester y Roxas had El Casa Curial ("the Presbytère") built on its foundations, as a residence for the priests of the neighbouring St. Louis Cathedral. Construction work was not finished until 1810, seven years after the colony became American.

Despite its name, "the Presbytère" has never been used as such, and when local authorities acquired it in 1853, it was to house the courthouse. It is now part of the Louisiana State Museum complex (see p 72). Though the Presbytère's artisans were mainly Spanish and American, a French influence clearly predominates.

GREATER NEW ORLEANS

St. Louis Cathedral ★ (21), the oldest cathedral in the United States, was built between 1849 and 1851, according to plans by J.N.B. de Pouilly; Pope Paul VI granted it the status of minor basilica in 1964, and Pope John Paul II celebrated mass there during his visit to the United States in 1987. The St. Louis Cathedral is the third church to be erected on this site. The first was swept away by a hurricane in 1722, and the second was destroyed by fire.

To the left is the Cabildo.

The **Cabildo** (Spanish Governing Council) **★★ (22)** *(adults $4, seniors and students $3, free for children under 12; Tue to Sun 9am to 5pm)*. Under the Spanish regime, the Cabildo's buildings served as the home of the Spanish colonial government, until they were destroyed by the fire that ravaged the city in 1788. Don Andrès Almonester y Roxas had them rebuilt before the end of the century, and a magnificent, quintessentially Spanish wrought-iron balustrade, created by Marcelino Hernández, still graces the historic Cabildo.

This building has seen many governments file through its doors. The French, who had preceded the Spanish, returned; the United States government gave it up to the Confederates for a time, before also returning. The deed by which France sold Louisiana to the United States of America (the Louisiana Purchase) was signed here, in the Sala Capitular. The "Iberville Stone", symbolizing the colony in 1699, as well as a death mask of the Emperor Napoleon can also be admired here.

The park and the square are known as Jackson Square.

Jackson Square (Place d'Armes) **★★(23)**. It was called "Place d'Armes" under the French; it was "Plaza de Armas" to the Spanish and, toward the middle of the nineteenth century, it was officially transformed, with the usual attendant ceremonies, into **Jackson Square**. The equestrian statue of General Jackson, which has dominated the square since 1856, was the work of sculptor Clark Mills. It commemorates Jackson's victory over the British during the famous Battle of New Orleans in 1815, which took place in Chalmette, about 10 kilometres from here.

From here, you can see the two imposing buildings on either side of Jackson Square.

The **Pontalba Buildings ★ (24)** *(bordering Jackson Square on each side)*. The wealthy merchant Don Andrés Almonester y Roxas was one of the most important figures of the time when Louisiana was a Spanish colony. In 1849, his daughter, the baroness Micaela Almonester de Pontalba, had the edifice built. With its ground floor giving out on Jackson Square (then known as Place d'Armes), it was designed to house luxury boutiques with the aim of attracting the local wealthy clientele. Forsaking their old-fashioned stalls in the French Quarter, shopkeepers responded to the proposition with enthusiasm, and visitors from all across Louisiana and even from other states soon flocked there.

You'll spot the 1850 House, on St. Ann Street, in the centre of the Pontalba Buildings.

The **1850 House ★ (25)** *(adults $4, seniors and students $3, free for* *children under 12; Tue to Sun 10am to 5pm; 525 St. Ann St.).* The central part of one of the Pontalba Buildings has been entirely restored on its three floors. Its refined decor and period furniture allow visitors to get a fair idea of how the New Orleanian upper crust lived in the mid-18th century.

Upon exiting the 1850 House, turn left on St. Ann Street. At Decatur Street, head straight to the narrow building adjoining the French Market.

The **French Market** (Le Marché Français) ★★★ **(26)**, see p 70.

Continue your stroll to Esplanade Avenue and stop at no. 400.

The **Old United States Mint** ★★ **(27)** (Le Vieil Hôtel de la Monnaie des États-Unis) *(adults $4, seniors and students $3, free for children under 12; Tue to Sun 9am to 5pm; in the 400 block of Esplanade Ave.).* Fuerte San Carlos stood here in the 18th century. In 1839, the U.S. government had the US Mint built. The building is now part of the Louisiana State Museum complex. The great moments of jazz and Mardi Gras are illustrated in a permanent exhibition (see p 72).

Head back via Decatur Street and turn right at Ursulines Street. Chartres Street is one block away.

The **Old Ursuline Convent** (L'Ancien Couvent des Ursulines) ★★ **(28)** (see also no. (1), 301 Chartres St., p 74) *(adults $4; seniors and students $2; free for children under 8; Tue to Fri guided tours at 10am, 11am, 1pm, 2pm and 3pm, Sat and Sun at 11:15am, 1pm and 2pm; 1114 Chartres St.).* This is one of the oldest buildings in the Mississippi Valley. The

Ursulines, who arrived in New Orleans in 1727, had it built in 1749. The convent became the city's first Catholic school, the first orphanage and the first institution to welcome Native Americans and African-Americans. The Ursulines occupied the building until 1827. The Louisiana State Legislature succeeded them from 1831 to 1834, and in 1846, the convent was re-attached to St. Mary's Italian church.

Cross the street.

The **Beauregard-Keyes House** (Maison Le Carpentier - Maison Beauregard) ★★ **(29)** *(adults $4, seniors and students $3, children under 12 $1.50; Mon to Sat 10am to 5pm; 1113 Chartres St., ☎ 523-6722).* After having purchased the land from the Ursulines, Joseph Le Carpentier built this house in 1827 for his daughter and her husband, the notary Alonzo Morphy.

General of the Confederate Army, Pierre-Gustave Toutant Beauregard, affectionately nicknamed "the great Creole" as much for his military prowess as for his capricious disposition, spent the rough winter of 1866 that followed the South's defeat and the end of the Civil War in a small room in this house. The novelist Frances Parkinson-Keyes, author of several works inspired by life in Louisiana and the tribulations experienced in this very place by the celebrated General, lived here in the late 1800s.

Continue along Chartres Street.

Soniat House (Maison Soniat du Fossat) ★ **(30)** *(1133 Chartres St.).* This *hôtel particulier* was erected in 1829 for the Louisiana planter Joseph

The Statuary of New Orleans

Like all great cities in the world, New Orleans has wished to pay homage to its heroes and heroines by erecting monuments in their honour.

The one raised in memory of **Jean-Baptiste Le Moyne, Sieur de Bienville**, stands in the heart of the French Quarter, in the little triangular park bordered by North Peters, Conti and Decatur Streets. The memorial recalls the fact that the man who founded New Orleans in 1718 was "Born in Montréal (Québec) on February 23rd, 1680 - Died in Paris (France) on March 7th, 1767".

The equestrian statue of democrat **Andrew Jackson**, hero of the Battle of New Orleans in Chalmette and president of the United States of America from 1829 to 1837, stands in Jackson Square. The monument is adjacent to a group of sculptures representing the four seasons, a somewhat unexpected subject matter in a city that knows but one: perpetual summer. Near Lafayette Square are the statues of **Benjamin Franklin** and the former head of Congress **Henry Clay**. Another statue, depicting **Molly Marine**, cast in concrete in 1943 (the only material that could be spared in this time of war) and now covered in bronze, stands on the corner of Canal Street and Elk Place. This monument is an homage to the female pioneers of the American Army. At City Park's entrance, visitors can see the equestrian statue of **General Pierre-Gustave Toutant Beauregard**. Lee Circle *(1000 St. Charles Ave.)* is dominated by a high column surmounted by the bronze statue of the "unfortunate" Confederate leader **General Robert E. Lee**. This monument, weighing some three tons, is the work of sculptor Alexander Doyle.

The sizeable African-American population forms the majority in New Orleans and has not forgotten the righteous fight lead by the Reverend Martin Luther King Jr. for the civil rights and integration of blacks. A monument to **Martin Luther King Jr.** therefore graces the intersection of the main thoroughfare bearing his name and Claiborne Avenue. It was also an absolute must to honour the man who proved to be one of the most prestigious ambassadors of New Orleans and the true originator of classic jazz, **Louis "Satchmo" Armstrong**. This luminary, for his part, has his statue in the park bearing his name (formerly Congo Square), which is situated on Rampart Street, between St. Ann and St. Peter Streets.

In New Orleans, as in all other cities of multiple origins, monuments and public squares also testify to ties woven throughout history. Near the International Trade Mart, for instance, is the gilded bronze statue of **Joan of Arc**, given by the French government. Other tokens of international friendships include the statue of **Sir Winston Churchill**, set up in British Place and, on the central median of Basin Street, those of Latin American heros **Simón Bolívar** (donation from Venezuela), **Benito Juárez** (donation from Mexico) and **General Francisco Morazón** (donation from Honduras).

Soniat du Fossat, a full-fledged member of the New Orleanian aristocracy. Around 1860, a face-lift to the building had the original wrought-iron gates replaced by the wonderful filigree work seen today. The Soniat House now houses a charming little hotel of the same name (see "Accommodations", p 110).

Head toward Governor Nicholls Street and, from there, turn left.

The **Clay House** (31) *(618-620 Governor Nicholls St.)*. John Clay had this residence built in 1828 to house his family. John was the brother of Henry Clay, the fierce supporter of American protectionism who presided over Congress from 1810 to 1820. The building at the end of the garden was added in 1871 and served as a school as of 1890.

Head to the corner of Governor Nicholls and Royal Streets, where you will find a "haunted" house promising customary chills and thrills for fans of this genre.

The **La Laurie House**, also known as **"The Haunted House"** (32) *(1140 Royal St.)*. Edmond du Fossat innocently had this house built in 1830, then sold it to Barthélemy de Macarty (also called Maccarty or McCarty on old documents), who bequeathed it to his daughter Delphine. After marrying de La Laurie, Delphine threw very popular parties here and all of New Orleans praised her as an excellent hostess. But, in 1833, one of the servants brought a complaint against her mistress, claiming she had been severely lashed. That a slave's complaint was heeded is extraordinary in itself, and Delphine was, at the very least, fined. Had the magistrates

suspected something? The following year, a fire broke out on the premises. All the neighbours rushed over to help the inhabitants of the house. They yelled, they hammered at doors and windows, but to no avail. Could the La Lauries have already succumbed? Or were they simply away? This was not the time to speculate, however, and the rescuers broke down the double-locked door. A ghastly scene met their eyes. In the smoke-filled room, seven miserable servants were found chained and horribly mutilated.

In the next day's paper, Madame La Laurie was openly suspected of having set fire to the house herself. A roaring mob gathered around the house of the torturer couple, determined to hang them high and raze this accursed place to the ground. At that very moment, a carriage carrying the La Lauries suddenly appeared from the courtyard. They fled the city to avoid public condemnation and were never seen again.

It is said that Delphine La Laurie died in Europe a few years later, and that her body was brought back to New Orleans to be buried here in secret.

Though the house was later entirely renovated, it is still said to be haunted. To this day, more than one New Orleanian affirms having heard the moaning and yelling of the torture victims along with the clanging of chains and the snapping of whips. Better to abstain from prowling about this house at the stroke of midnight, or at any time of night for that matter!

Fellow visitor... Take a deep breath, be careful crossing Royal Street and return to Governor Nicholls Street.

GREATER NEW ORLEANS

Gallier Hall

Thierry House (Maison Thierry) **(33)** *(721 Governor Nicholls St.)*. This house dates from 1814 and once belonged to Jean-Baptiste Thierry, the editor of the newspaper the *Courrier de la Louisiane*. Greek Revival in style, it is the first and one of the most interesting constructions of this style in Louisiana.

Return to Royal Street.

Gallier House ★★ (34) *(adults $5, seniors and students $4, children $3; Mon to Sat 10am to 4pm; 1132 Royal St., ☎ 523-6722)*. The son of a highly renowned architect who, moreover, left behind interesting memoirs, James Gallier Jr. was also to mark New Orleanian architecture during the whole period preceding the Civil War. We are indebted to this father and son for several buildings, including St. Patrick's Cathedral *(724 Camp St.)*, Gallier Hall *(545 St. Charles Ave.)*, the Pontalba Buildings and the St. Charles Hotel. The house has been restored, decorated and furnished in the style of the 1860s. Its balconies are made of wrought iron with a pattern of lovely roses.

Take Ursulines Street and turn left on Bourbon Street to the intersection of St. Philip Street.

Lafitte's Blacksmith Shop (35) *(941 Bourbon St.)*. The first notarized deed relating to this house dates back to 1772. The Lafitte brothers had opened this shop as a cover for their much more profitable activities as privateers in the neighbouring waters of the Gulf of Mexico, or more precisely, in swampy Barataria Bay. They attempted to redeem themselves by participating in the famous Battle of New Orleans, doing so with a courage that actually was to their credit.

Continue along Royal Street.

The **Cornstalk Fence ★ (36)** *(915 Royal St.)* stands before the hotel of the same name. The first house built on this site dates at least as far back as 1731, for it appears on a city map drawn up by Gonochon that year. It was replaced by a residence to be occupied from 1816 to 1826 by François Xavier Martin, first Chief Justice of the State Supreme Court. This magistrate was to be the author of the very first history book on Louisiana. The group of Victorian buildings seen today were built in 1850. The wrought-iron portal at the entrance gate, with motifs of cornstalks and ears of corn entangled with morning glories, is magnificent.

The **Miltenberger Houses (900-906-910 Royal Street) (37)**. The three houses built in 1838 for Mrs. Miltenberger were meant for her three sons. In 1910, it was her great-granddaughter Alice Heine who occupied them all. This interesting heiress first wed the Duke of Richelieu, before becoming a princess, through her second marriage to Prince Louis of Monaco.

Take Dumaine Street and head to no. 632.

Madame John's Legacy - Jean Pascal House (38) *(632 Dumaine St.)* Is a lovely raised house, with a recessed balcony. The first construction dates back to 1726. After the great fire on Good Friday of 1788, which razed almost the whole of New Orleans to the ground, Madame John entrusted the rebuilding to Robert Jones, a renowned artisan. The Spanish officer Manuel de Lanzos was its first tenant. This house (much like the Old Ursuline Convent) is rightly considered one of the most beautiful examples of Creole architecture in the entire Mississippi Valley; this style, developed in the French West Indies, was to influence many Louisiana architects. The building is now the property of the State of Louisiana, which had it transformed into a museum. Unfortunately, access to the museum is strictly reserved for student groups and community groups. These privileged few can admire a magnificent collection of period furniture (see "The Louisiana State Museum", p 72).

Here ends our stroll through the French Quarter (Vieux Carré), but by all means continue exploring the streets and alleyways on your own...

Central Business District and Warehouse District ★

West of the French Quarter is the Central Business District, a downtown area that is often associated with Canal Street. Just south of the Central Business District, the Warehouse District, whose industrial buildings were until recently in disuse, has become home to artists and galleries.

The **Contemporary Arts Center ★★ (1)** *(adults $5; Mon to Sat 10am to 5pm, Sun 11am to 5pm; 900 Camp St., ☎ 523-1216).* The Center exhibits contemporary art in all its forms: alternative theatre, music, visual arts, and more.

The **Virlane Foundation Collection ★★ (2)** *(free admission; 1055 St. Charles Ave., at Lee Circle).* This private organization has made it its objective to spur public interest in the

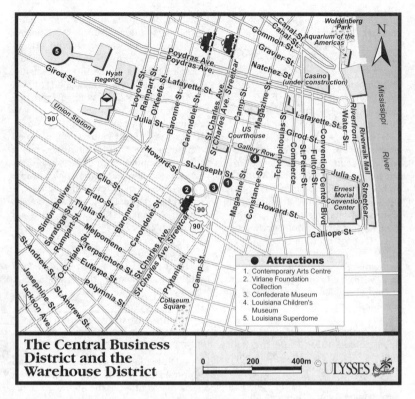

The Central Business District and the Warehouse District

Attractions

1. Contemporary Arts Centre
2. Virlane Foundation Collection
3. Confederate Museum
4. Louisiana Children's Museum
5. Louisiana Superdome

0   200   400m © ULYSSES

arts and, more particularly, in contemporary sculpture. The collection consists of works from universally known artists from all over the world; these works are exhibited in the square around the K&B Building and in the building itself. Explanatory booklets and detailed maps are distributed free of charge. In addition to a sculpture by British artist Henry Moore *(Reclining Mother and Child)*, visitors can take pleasure in observing the movement of the helicoidal piece *Flight* by American Lin Emery (to whom is credited a similar work in front of the New Orleans Museum of Art), *The Virlane Tower* by Kenneth Snelson, a structure whose metal bars are supported and joined together by a steel cable that seems to defy gravity, or again, *Bus Stop Lady*, a life-size woman waiting for the bus, whom we cannot help but greet. In short, over 70 creations can be viewed here.

The **Confederate Museum** ★★★ **(3)** *(adults $4, children under 12 $2; Mon to Sat 10am to 4pm; 929 Camp St., ☎ 523-4522)*. Built in 1891, this is the oldest museum in Louisiana. Thousands of priceless mementos can be seen here: weapons, uniforms, flags dating back to the Civil War and even the personal effects of Northern heroes.

Louisiana Children's Museum ★★ (4) *($5; Tue to Sat 9:30am to 5pm, Sun noon to 5pm; 420 Julia St., ☎ 523-1357).* Educational museum for children. Good news, the museum features hands-on, participatory exhibits!

Louisiana Superdome ★★ (5) *($6; seniors $5, 5-10-year-olds $4; guided tours 10am, noon, 2pm and 4pm; Sugar Bowl Drive, 1500 Poydras St., ☎ 587-3808 or 587-3810).* Built in 1975, it can accommodate up to 80,000 people; it is the largest building of its kind in the world. This is where big sports events, mega-concerts and more take place.

The **Canal Street Ferry ★★★** *(free for pedestrians, cars $1; 6am to midnight, departures every 30 min).* Operated by the Louisiana department of transport, the ferry takes pedestrians and drivers to Algiers Point on the west bank of the Mississippi. This service has been offered without interruption since 1827.

Algiers Point ★★★. In 1719, Bienville, the founder of New Orleans, was assigned this region, which is adjacent to the Vieux Carré on the other side of the Mississippi. Algiers Point was originally a landing site for slaves arriving from Africa. A suburb was built here between 1840 and 1900, and due to its particular character, in 1978 it was classified an American historical heritage site. Additional tourist information is available on site. A walking tour of the area is particularly interesting.

Mid-City ★★★

North of the French Quarter and the Central Business District is the Mid-City area, stretching, from east to west, between City Park and Metairie Cemetery, which leads to the suburb of the same name.

The **Sun Oak ★ (1)** *($5; by appointment; 2020 Burgundy St., ☎ 945-0322)* in the historic Faubourg Marigny. Creole cottage with neoclassical ornamentation. Beautiful collection of French, Creole and Cajun furniture. Decorative arts. Large park; accommodations.

Esplanade Avenue - Bayou St. John - Lakefront ★★★. If the Garden District of St. Charles Avenue is the architectural expression of New Orleanians of American origin, the district that stretches from the French Quarter to the Bayou St. John is in large part made up of the magnificent residences of old French families. At 2306 Esplanade Avenue, you'll see what was, for a brief period during the winter of 1872, the residence of Impressionist painter Edgar Degas, who had come to visit his financier brothers in New Orleans.

New Orleans Museum of Art ★★★ (2) *(adults $6, seniors $5, 3-17-year-olds $3; Tue to Sun 10am to 5pm; 1 Lelong Drive, City Park, ☎ 488-2631).* The New Orleans Museum of Art (NOMA) owes its existence to a generous patron. Son of a rich family of planters from Jamaica, Isaac Delgado, born in 1837, left his native island at the age of 14 years. He came to join his uncle Samuel in New Orleans, who was making a fortune in the sugar industry. Having become rich in his turn, Isaac

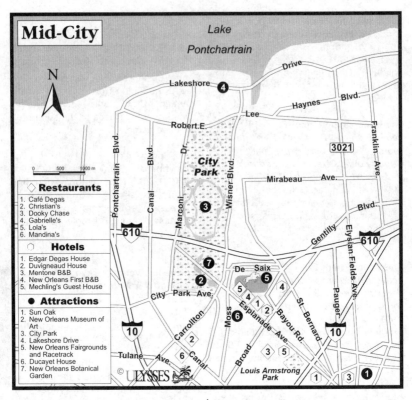

Mid-City

Lake Pontchartrain

N

Drive

Lakeshore ❹

Haynes Blvd.

Lee

Robert.E.

Franklin Ave.

Pontchartrain Blvd.

Canal Blvd.

Marconi Dr.

City Park

Wisner Blvd.

3021

Mirabeau Ave.

0   500   1000 m

◇ **Restaurants**
1. Café Degas
2. Christian's
3. Dooky Chase
4. Gabrielle's
5. Lola's
6. Mandina's

∩ **Hotels**
1. Edgar Degas House
2. Duvigneaud House
3. Mentone B&B
4. New Orleans First B&B
5. Mechling's Guest House

● **Attractions**
1. Sun Oak
2. New Orleans Museum of Art
3. City Park
4. Lakeshore Drive
5. New Orleans Fairgrounds and Racetrack
6. Ducayet House
7. New Orleans Botanical Garden

Blvd.

Gentilly

Elysian Fields Ave.

610

610

❸

❼

De Saix

❺

❷

5 4

5 4

2 1

6 ❻

City Park Ave.

Carrollton

Moss

Esplanade Ave.

Bayou Rd.

St. Bernard

Pauger

10

10

2

Tulane Ave.

6 Canal

Broad

3 5

© ULYSSES

Louis Armstrong Park

1 3 ❶

Delgado showed great generosity toward his adopted city. At the beginning of the century, he made large donations to charitable organizations, and in 1905, remitted $180,000 to the Charity Hospital. A true art lover, Delgado handed over a sum of $150,000 in 1910 so that a fine arts museum worthy of the city he was so fond of could be built in City Park.

The imposing building, whose lobby is flooded with daylight, is the work of Samuel A. Marx. This architect has lent this structure, whose architrave is supported by four huge columns, a Greek style adapted to the subtropical clime. As for the collection, it is distributed according to theme throughout the many rooms on both levels. The museum boasts an abundance of treasures from all eras and all continents, including a rich collection of Renaissance art, obtained in October 1952 thanks to a donation from the Samuel H. Kress Foundation.

Among the pieces museum visitors can enjoy are magnificent pre-Columbian sculptures; a rich collection of glass and earthenware; European, American and Chinese pottery; remarkable 17th-century paintings from the famous Cuzco Peruvian school; several works from the great Flemish, Dutch, Italian and French masters as well as those of contemporary American painters; works painted by Edgar Degas during his stay in New Orleans with his maternal uncle Michel Musson; bronzes from this same artist as well as Rodin; 18th- and 19th-century furniture; and more. The museum also boasts the Courtyard Café and Museum Shop. An amusing aside: the museum uses *Van Go* vans to transport its works.

City Park ★★★ (3). This 750-hectare park stretches from Esplanade Avenue, north of the French Quarter, right up to Lake Pontchartrain. This land was once part of the Louis Allard plantation. It is a choice spot for all outdoor sports. Eight-hundred-year-old oak trees surround lagoons where visitors can abandon themselves to the pleasures of fishing. Other activities here include horseback riding and golf.

Lakeshore Drive ★★ (4) skirts New Orleans' sizeable lake: Lake Pontchartrain, which is 60 kilometres long and 40 kilometres wide. The **Lake Pontchartrain Causeway ★** spans this large body of water.

The **New Orleans Fairgrounds and Racetrack (5)** *(admission fee; Wed to Sun from Nov to Apr; 1751 Gentilly Blvd.,* ☎ *944-5515)* has been open since 1872, which makes it one of the oldest in the U.S. Its entrance, the work of architect James Gallier, was built in 1859 for an agricultural fair. It is here that the Louisiana Derby takes place. Bets are placed on thoroughbred horses racing at this track and others; all of these races are simultaneously broadcast. No children under 6 years of age allowed.

Longue Vue House and Gardens ★★ *(adults $7, seniors $6, students and children $3; Mon to Sat 10am to 4pm,*

last guided tour 3:45pm; Sun 1pm to 4:15pm, last guided tour 4:15pm; 7 Bamboo Road, ☎ *488-5488 or 486-7015)*. Built in 1942 by the wealthy New Orleanian Edgar Stern, this Greek Revival estate has a Spanish patio surrounded by English gardens, thus showing the historical course of the city in its own way. It contains a beautiful collection of French and English 18th- and 19th-century furniture.

Ducayet House (Maison Ducayet) **★★** *(adults $3, seniors $2, under 12 yrs $1; Wed to Sun 10am to 3pm; 1440 Moss Street,* ☎ *482-0312)*, a plantation house in the Caribbean colonial style, was constructed around 1800 by the aristocratic Ducayet family. The property was later acquired by the second mayor of New Orleans, James Pitot.

The **New Orleans Botanical Garden ★★** *(adults $3, 5-12 yrs $1, guided tour by reservation;* ☎ *483-9386)* is adorned with statues and fountains reminiscent of the Art Deco era. Next to the oaks and magnolia trees, the park is home to splendid azalea and camellia gardens as well as a pond of water-lilies.

The Garden District ★★★

Following the sale of Louisiana in 1803, many of the city's inhabitants did not appreciate the massive influx of "Americans". Those who lived in the French Quarter (Vieux Carré) jealously guarded the exclusivity of their neighbourhood – these same Creoles had however lived with the Spanish – even enlarging their territory toward Faubourg Marigny. So the Americans settled in Faubourg Sainte-Marie, now the Central Business District. The

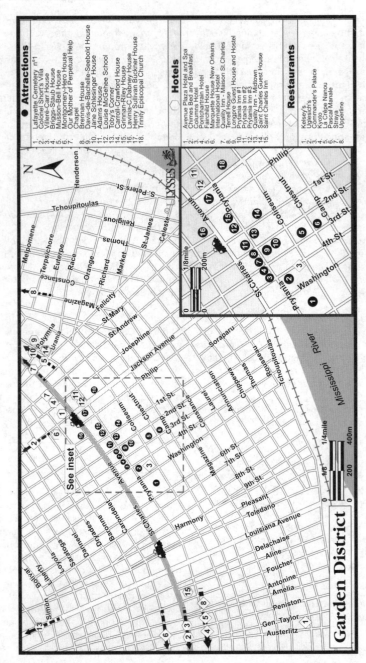

● Attractions

1. Lafayette Cemetery n°1
2. Colonel Short's Villa
3. Villeré-Carr House
4. Briggs-Staub House
5. Musson-Bell House
6. Mrs. Mother's Hero House
7. Our Mother of Perpetual Help Chapel
8. Brennan House
9. Davis-de-Bachelle-Seebold House
10. Jane Schlesinger House
11. Adams House
12. Lucinda McGehee School
13. Toby's Corner
14. Carroll-Crawford House
15. Grinnan-Riley House
16. Lavinia-C Dabney House
17. Henry Sullivan Buckner House
18. Trinity Episcopal Church

◇ Hotels

1. Avenue Plaza Hotel and Spa
2. Chimes Bed and Breakfast
3. Columns Hotel
4. Pontchartrain Hotel
5. Fairchild House
6. Marquette House New Orleans
7. Quality Inn - Maison St-Charles
8. International Hostel
9. Terrell House
10. Longpre Guest House and Hostel
11. Prytania Inn #1
12. Prytania Inn #2
13. Prytania Inn #3
14. Quality Inn Midtown
15. St-Charles Guest House
Saint Charles Inn

◇ Restaurants

1. Kelsey's
2. Uglesich's
3. Commander's Palace
4. Kyoto
5. La Crèpe Nanou
6. Pascal Manale
7. Straya
8. Upperline

Garden District

newcomers prospered in the business district and then developed the residential areas of Uptown and the Garden District. These rich merchants had their opulent houses built, not at the edge of the street like those in the French Quarter, but further back, allowing for magnificent gardens at the front as well as at the back of their houses.

Definitely one of the best ways to see the Lower Garden District, the Garden District and Uptown is from the St. Charles Streetcar from Canal Street *(at Carondelet)*. For the modest price of one dollar, the route and the reduced speed allow you to discover this wonderful part of the city in less than two hours. For a more in-depth visit, we suggest walking. The streetcar has existed since 1835 (run by electricity since 1893) and has contributed greatly to the rapid development of this area of the city, particularly to the expansion of St. Charles Avenue.

Lafayette Cemetery No. 1 ★★ **(1)** *(1400 Washington Ave.)* has been in existence since 1833 and was then the property of the City of Lafayette before it's annexation to New Orleans. Because the interment of "Americans" in the cemeteries near the French Quarter was less desirable, many people of German (not the descendants of colonists who came to settle in Louisiana in the eighteenth century but, rather, immigrants who came to New Orleans much later) and Irish origin were buried here. In 1852, yellow fever was raging and over 2,000 victims were then interred in this single cemetery. Most of the tombs are fairly modest monuments. In 1970, the City of New Orleans undertook to restore some tombs and, with the aim of making the place more attractive, had

a lovely row of magnolias planted along a path at the cemetery's entrance.

From the cemetery's exit, on Washington Avenue, head for Prytania Street, then to Fourth Street. Turn right...

Colonel Short's Villa (2) *(1448 Fourth St.)* was built in 1859. Four years later, at the height of the Civil War, the house was seized by Federals while its rebel owner was away. The structure is graced with lacy wrought-iron balconies and a railing whose distinctive motifs are reminiscent of cornstalks. It is said that the colonel's wife so greatly missed Kentucky that her husband procured this gate for her, evoking the corn fields from her distant land. This lovely portal, forged by the Wood and Perot Foundry in Philadelphia, brings the one at the 915 Royal Street house, in the French Quarter, to mind.

Return to Prytania Street and cross the street.

The **Villeré-Carr House (3)** *(2621 Prytania St.)* was built around 1870 in typical Greek Revival style for one of the members of the prominent New Orleanian Villeré family. Its porch and angular windows harmoniously blend with this lovely architectural whole, particularly sought-after at the time.

Continue your stroll along Prytania Street.

The **Briggs-Staub House (4)** *(2605 Prytania St.)* is one of the rare Gothic constructions in the city. It was erected in 1849, and its architecture shows the European influences of the time.

Take Third Street and head to no. 1331.

Edgar Degas in New Orleans

In 1872, Edgar Degas came to New Orleans, whence his mother, née Musson, originated and where his brothers, Achille and René, had established themselves as cotton merchants.

The place enchanted him. *"Nothing pleases me more than the black women of all shades, holding little white babies that are oh so white in their arms, in white houses with fluted wooden columns and in orange-tree gardens and the ladies in muslin in front of their little houses and the steamboats with two smokestacks, as high as the twin chimneys of factories, and the fruit merchants with full and overflowing shops, and the contrast between the bustling and so affluent offices and the huge brute strength of the black population, ... etc. And the lovely pure blooded ladies and the lovely quadroons and the black women who are so well built!"*, he wrote to a Parisian friend.

His letters are generally written on paper with the *de Gas Brothers* letterhead, his brothers having kept the original name to make a good impression in the elegant circles in which they moved. The painter, for his part, renounced it. *"Those among the nobility are not in the habit of working. Since I wish to work, I will therefore retain a common name"*, he explained.

His correspondence aptly reflects high society in New Orleans, which was rather shaken up after the Civil War. In a letter to his friend Rouart dated December 5th, he deplores the absence of the traditional opera season in speaking of his blind cousin, Estelle, who had married his brother René and who was pregnant. *"Poor Estella who is a musician was counting on it. We would have rented her a ground-floor box where she would never have missed a performance until the time she was to give birth."* He goes on to emphasize how, *"In its place, we have a comedy, drama, vaudeville troupe, where there are many fairly talented performers from Montmartre"*.

Degas was to take several family "scenes" from his stay home with him. These scenes inspired major paintings such as *Portrait dans un Bureau (Portrait in an Office)*, more commonly known as *Le Bureau de Coton à La Nouvelle-Orléans (The Cotton Office in New Orleans)*, his first work to make it into a French museum, the one in Pau, to which it still belongs. In this painting, we see the brothers loafing, René nonchalantly reading the paper as his associate Achille leans against a wall staring off into space, while the merchants bustle about. The two brothers ultimately went bankrupt and it was, ironically, Edgar the successful artist who assumed their debts in order to save the honour of their family name.

The **Musson-Bell House (5)** *(1331 Third St.)*, erected in 1850, was commissioned by the wealthy cotton merchant Michel Musson, the celebrated painter Edgar Degas' uncle. The house is magnificently girdled by elaborate wrought-iron balconies. This place was witness to a particularly tragic conjugal story. In 1872, Edgar and his brother René arrived from France to visit their maternal family. René fell madly in love with his cousin Estelle, who sadly had been blind since the age of 12. Because they were first cousins, René and Estelle obtained a papal dispensation to live out their happiness without religious constraint. Four children were born of their union. Every afternoon, a friend of Estelle's came by to read to her and took advantage of her visits to court René. Succumbing to her charms, René abandoned Estelle and his children. Beside himself with rage, Estelle's father disowned his son-in-law and adopted his grandchildren, giving them the name of Musson, and crossed the Degas name from his family for good. Estelle's name and likeness were, however, immortalized in a painting by Edgar entitled *Le Portrait d'Estelle (Estelle's Portrait)*, which can still be admired in the New Orleans Museum of Art (see p 85).

Continue to no. 1213.

The **Montgomery-Hero House (6)** *(1213 Third St.)*. This splendid residence was built around 1868, perhaps even before the Civil War, by Archibald Montgomery. From the time of Montgomery's death in 1885 until 1977, the house belonged to the Hero family. Its green shutters as well as the fine white columns rising from the front and side porches distinguish this lovely

home, restored in all the elegance of its era by the Reynoirs, its last proprietors.

Retrace your steps back to Prytania Street and head to the Chapel.

Our Mother of Perpetual Help Chapel (7) *(2521 Prytania St.)*, first built as a private residence in 1856, was then converted into a chapel to cater to the needs of the Redemptorist priests.

Continue along Prytania Street.

The **Brennan House (8)** *(2507 Prytania St.)*, with its stunning Corinthian columns, dates from 1852. The wealthy owners of the time turned to a Viennese artist to decorate the magnificent ballroom, their pride and joy, in gold leaf.

Go back across Prytania Street.

The **Davis-De Bachelle Seebold House - Women's Guild of the New Orleans Opera Association (9)** *(2504 Prytania St.)* was first home to Edward Davis, who had commissioned its construction in 1858. Dr. Hermann de Bachelle Seebold and his wife, music lovers and patrons of the arts, acquired it in 1944. Upon Mrs. Seebold's demise, the opera association inherited this residence flanked by an octagonal turret, one of the few to be opened to the public (reservations are required). Every piece of furniture dates from the time of the original owners.

Continue along Prytania Street. Turn right at Second Street.

Part of the **Jane Schlesinger House (10)** *(1427 Second St.)* was once attached to the residence of a large plantation. The annex was moved and joined to the building under construction in the 1850s. Four-metre-high French doors giving directly onto the balcony and almost reaching the ceiling are one of its distinctive features.

Retrace your steps to Prytania Street and turn right.

The **Adams House (11)** *(2423 Prytania St.).* Having acquired a piece of land on François de Livaudais' plantation in 1860, the merchant John I. Adams had this residence built there, and lived in it as of 1896. The two (front and side) porches are lined with a series of white colonnades.

Cross Prytania Street once again.

The **Louise McGehee School (12)** *(2343 Prytania St.),* also known as Bradish-Johnson House, is the work of architect James Freret. It displays lines highly influenced by the French *École des Beaux-arts*, where the master studied from 1860 to 1862. Freret built this residence in 1872 for the wealthy sugar-cane planter Bradish Johnson. In 1929, it was converted into a private school for girls.

Across the street is **Toby's Corner (13)** *(2340 Prytania St.),* also called the Toby-Westfeldt House. It is said to be one of the oldest residences in the Garden District. Its style is inspired by Creole cottages in the Caribbean. During its construction in 1838, its owner, an affluent businessman originally from Philadelphia, took great care to have his house raised in order to protect it from floods, which are all too common in New Orleans.

Head toward First Street and turn right.

The **Carroll-Crawford House (14)** *(1315 First St.),* erected in 1869 in the Italianate style by its first owner Samuel Jamison, later housed Joseph Carroll, a cotton magnate who came from his native Virginia to acquire more wealth in New Orleans. Magnificent balconies and a wrought-iron railing adorn this beautiful pastel residence.

Return to Prytania Street.

The **Grinnan-Riley House (15)** *(2221 Prytania St.).* It is to architect Henry Howard, who designed a great number of buildings in New Orleans, that the Englishman Robert A. Grinnan entrusted the construction plans of his *hôtel particulier*. Also of interest is that the coat of arms on the front door is similar to that at the Nottoway plantation (situated in White Castle), also designed by Howard.

Go back up First Street to St. Charles Avenue.

The **Lavinia C. Dabney House (16)** *(2265 St. Charles Ave.),* erected in 1856-57, is the work of the architectural firm Gallier, Turpin & Associates. As of 1893, the Dabrey residence was inhabited by Jonas O. Rosenthal's family, who occupied it until 1952. That same year, it became the see of the Episcopal Church until 1972.

Continue your stroll along St. Charles Avenue until you reach Jackson Avenue.

The **Henry Sullivan Buckner House (17)** *(1410 Jackson Ave.)* was built in 1856 by the famous architect Lewis E. Reynolds. With its grandiose balconies graced with colonnades girdled by elaborate ironwork, it is one of the most majestic residences in the Garden District. Soulé College, a private school, occupied this beautiful property until 1983.

Trinity Episcopal Church (18) *(1329 Jackson Ave.)*. Construction work on this imposing church in the Gothic style, commissioned to architect George Purves, began in 1852. In 1873, major alterations were made to the church's actual façade, steeple and portal, the joint work of architect Charles L. Hilger and the building contractor Middlemiss.

Uptown ★★★

The **Milton H. Latter Memorial Library (1)** *(Mon to Sat 10am to 5pm, Sun 12:30pm to 4:30pm; 5120 St. Charles Ave., ☎ 596-2625)*. Built in 1907, it was first the residence of the silent-film actress Marguerite Clark. The Latter family then bought the house and donated it to the city in 1948, in memory of their son who died in World War II. The library is open to the public and is worth a visit.

Head to the intersection of St. Charles Avenue and Walnut Street.

Tulane University - Gibson Hall (2) *(6823 St. Charles Ave.)* was erected in 1893-94. The plans were drawn up by architects Harrod and Andry, and came in first in a contest held throughout the State of Louisiana. The winners were also awarded the task of creating the other campus pavilions, namely Tillton Hall *(left of Gibson Hall)*, built in 1901, and Dinwiddie Hall *(right of Gibson Hall)* in 1936. The University was founded in 1834 and was then called the Medical College of Louisiana before becoming the University of Louisiana. In 1884, it

was renamed once again, this time after Paul Tulane, one of its principal benefactors. That same year, the State of Louisiana chose not to maintain the university as a public institution, and Tulane University thus became private.

The **Amistad Research Center (3)** *(Mon to Sat 8:30am to 5pm; Tillton Hall, Tulane University, ☎ 865-5535)* is a large archive on the history of ethnic minorities in the U.S., dealing with, among other things, race relations and the civil rights movement.

The **Middle American Research Institute & Art Gallery ★★ (4)** *(free admission; Mon to Fri 8:30am to 4:30pm; Tulane University, 6823 St. Charles Ave., ☎ 865-5110)* has been around since 1924 and presents an exhibition on the pre-Columbian and Hispano-American eras. An interesting collection of Mayan and Guatemalan art is featured here, and visitors are free to consult the books and documents in the impressive library dedicated to Central America.

Continue along St. Charles Avenue.

With the exception of its Law Faculty, located on St. Charles Avenue at Broadway Street, the **Loyola University campus (5)** *(6363 St. Charles)* borders Tulane University's and stretches out thus to Calhoun Street. In the middle of the campus stands the imposing Gothic-style Holy Name of Jesus Church. Since its foundation by the Jesuits in 1911, the University has distinguished itself with its law and communications programs. The latter faculty is housed in the Louis J. Roussel pavilion.

Cross St. Charles Avenue toward Audubon Park.

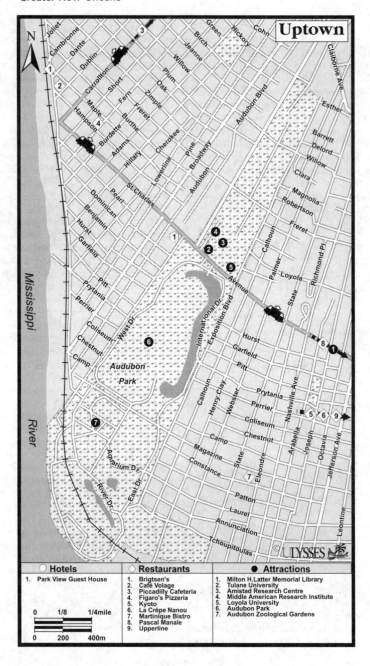

Uptown

Mississippi River

Audubon Park

○ **Hotels**	◇ **Restaurants**	● **Attractions**
1. Park View Guest House	1. Brigtsen's	1. Milton H.Latter Memorial Library
	2. Café Volage	2. Tulane University
	3. Piccadilly Cafeteria	3. Amistad Research Centre
	4. Figaro's Pizzeria	4. Middle American Research Institute
	5. Kyoto	5. Loyola University
	6. La Crêpe Nanou	6. Audubon Park
	7. Martinique Bistro	7. Audubon Zoological Gardens
	8. Pascal Manale	
	9. Upperline	

0   1/8   1/4mile

0   200   400m

© ULYSSES

Audubon Park ★★★ (6) is across the street from both Tulane and Loyola Universities. It stretches from St. Charles Street to the Mississippi's north shore, encompassing the zoological gardens of the same name, which are bordered by Walnut and Calhoun Streets.

This land once belonged to Jean-Baptiste Le Moyne Sieur de Bienville, before becoming the property of the planter Étienne de Boré, the first mayor of New Orleans and the man who discovered how to granulate sugar in industrial quantities, changing the Louisiana industry forever. The city acquired the land in 1871. In 1884-85, plans to organize the World's Industrial and Cotton Centennial Exhibition got underway. This was to highlight the hundred-year anniversary of this industry. The megalomaniac pretensions of this event's organizers seemed to know no bounds and they had, most notably, the largest building in the world built for the occasion, a building whose exhibition hall had a surface area of 14 hectares. The ridiculous amounts of money disbursed made the event a financial disaster. Nothing remains of these buildings today. A few years later, Frederick Law Olmsted (the creator of Central Park in New York City and Mont-Royal Park in Montréal) was entrusted with the task of planning this magnificent park. Its name commemorates the famous John James Audubon, artist and ornithologist, and his contribution to New Orleans.

Audubon Park is one of the largest urban parks in the United States, not to mention one of the most famous. The park is dotted with lagoons and fountains, and several of its oaks date back from the time of the de Boré plantation. Besides the visit to the Audubon Zoological Gardens (see below), many outdoor activities can be practised here: golf, tennis, cycling, running, walking and horseback riding. One of the running tracks has signs at every fifteenth post or so, indicating the warm-up exercises to do during this activity. The park also offers picnic areas, a swimming pool, children's playgrounds, and more.

Visitors can reach the Audubon Zoological Gardens by walking across Audubon Park and following the golf course on the right, when facing the park on St. Charles Avenue. Count on a 45-minute to one-hour walk. Using the shuttle service that runs from St. Charles Avenue to the Zoological Gardens is another option.

The **Audubon Zoological Gardens ★★★ (7)** was once considered one of the vilest of its kind in the U.S. The deplorable conditions in which its inmates lived aroused outraged protests from animal lovers. Fortunately, this situation has since radically changed, and the zoological gardens now enjoys an excellent reputation. The zoo pays special attention to natural habitats, thereby encouraging reproduction. Over 1,800 different species can be observed here, including white alligators in an exhibit named the "Louisiana Swamp". Other areas reproduce the environment of a Cajun bayou with its flora and fauna. In this exhibit, visitors learn, among other things, how the famous Spanish moss is gathered and used as stuffing for furniture; the zoo also boasts a mock-up of a fishing camp, equipped with shrimping nets and crayfish traps, as well as a dredger used to collect oysters from the Gulf of Mexico. Farther along, for those who are so

GREATER NEW ORLEANS

John James Audubon (1785-1851)

Celebrated naturalist and artist John James Audubon has been honoured time and again in the place names of Louisiana. Born Jean-Jacques in 1785 in Santo Domingo, now Haiti and the Dominican Republic, he is of French origin. After studying in France, Audubon made his first trip to the United States in 1805. The following year, he returned and became a naturalized American by marrying Lucy Bakewell whom he had met in Pennsylvania during his first trip. Audubon settled in Louisiana in 1821, first in New Orleans, then in St. Francisville, at the Oakley plantation, where he worked for four months as a tutor to the three sisters of Mrs. Percy, a naval officer's widow. Here, John James Audubon did 82 of the 435 watercolours of his famous "The Birds of America" series. The remainder of the drawings were done while travelling through a vast territory stretching from Florida (he bought a house for himself in Key West and resided there as of 1832) all the way to Québec. He produced a great number of drawings, sketches and paintings all through his life. His most famous work, *The Birds of America*, in four volumes and containing 435 plates, is most certainly the most expensive collection in the world since it was auctioned in London for several million pounds in 1984.

inclined, is the wonderful world of reptiles. The largest snake species in the world, from the giant cobra, which can reach up to six metres in length, to the green anaconda, sometimes measuring up to 12 metres, wow 'em at the Reptile Encounter. A brand new exhibition entitled *Butterflies in Flight* presents a video on the metamorphosis and the migrations of butterflies. Visitors then enter a hothouse (or aviary) in which thousands of exotic butterflies flutter freely. In proximity of the hothouse, under the shade of centuries-old trees, the statue of John James Audubon watches over his friends from the animal kingdom and their visitors.

The **Lower Garden District** starts at Lee Circle. At the centre of the circle is a monument in honour of General Robert E. Lee, head of the Confederate armies during the American Civil War. On the left is the **Zion Lutheran Church** *(1924 St. Charles Ave.)*, built out of wood in 1871. On the right, the K&B Plaza houses the Virlane Foundation Collection (see p 83).

Sacred Heart Academy *(4521 St. Charles Ave.)* is a private school, created in 1899 for young girls. The wings of the huge building are connected by wide covered walkways surrounding a flowering garden. Above the entrance gate, in wrought iron, is the French inscription "Sacré-Coeur".

Around New Orleans

Metairie

Lafreniere Park *(free admission, every day 6am to sundown; 3000 Downs Blvd., Metairie, ☎ 838-4389)*. This 62-hectare park is equally suited to both nature lovers and athletes. Botanists will love the landscaped gardens and the rich local flora. Fans of outdoor activities can rent boats, bikes

Jackson Square (Place d'Armes) and St. Louis Cathedral, from North Peters Street
in New Orleans - Roch Nadeau.

Ornate wrought-iron balconies in the French Quarter - R.N.

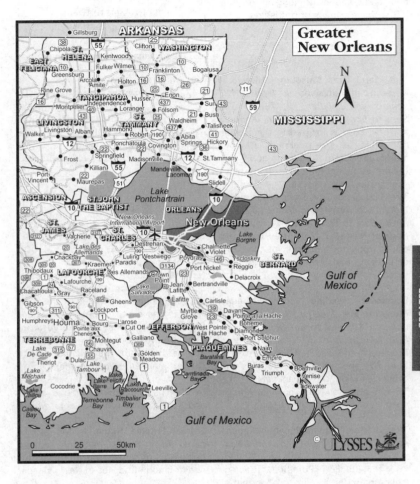

and pedal-boats, go jogging on the paths, have picnics or go fishing.

Kenner

The **Mardi Gras Museum - Historical Museum of Louisiana** ★ *(adults $3, seniors and children $2; Tue to Sat 9am to 5pm; 1922 Third St., Kenner, ☎ 468-7258)* is located in the former home of ex-sheriff Frank Clancy. Memorabilia from the "green gold" era, the era of bounty hunters, is on display.

The **Louisiana Toy Train Museum** ★ *(adults $3, seniors and children $2; Tue to Sat 9am to 5pm; 519 Williams Blvd., Kenner, ☎ 468-7223)*. They have toy trains from the beginning of the 19th century, hands-on exhibitions and videos.

Louisiana Wildlife and Fisheries Museum ★★ *(adults $3, seniors and children $2; Tue to Sat 9am to 5pm, Sun 1pm to 5pm; 303 Williams Blvd., Kenner, ☎ 468-7232)*. This is a reserve with 700 species of birds, reptiles and other indigenous animals; the 56,775-litre aquarium houses various species of fish from the region.

The **Jefferson Downs Racetrack** *(opens at 6:30pm, Apr to mid-Nov; 1300 Sunset Blvd., Kenner, ☎ 466-8521)*. Pure-bred racing. Children under 12 are not permitted and 12- to 17-year-olds must be accompanied by an adult. The old train tracks alongside the Hippodrome were converted into a trail bordered by parkland.

Visits to Agricultural and Industrial Facilities

The Louisiana Seafood Exchange *(by appointment, Mon to Sat 7am to 3pm; 428 Jefferson Highway, Kenner, ☎ 834-9393)*. Wholesaler of a wide variety of fresh seafood. New Orleans-style restaurant, with po'boys, hot meals, boiled or poached seafood (take out).

Slidell

Slidell is the most populous town in St. Tammany Parish with 25,000 inhabitants, most of whom work in New Orleans. Near the Mississippi border, from which it is separated by a 28,000-hectare swamp fed by the Pearl River in the east, it abuts the **Bogue-Chitto National Wildlife Reserve** ★★. The city was founded in about 1880 and is home to the **Stennis Space Center**, a NASA computing centre.

In Slidell's Old Town, antique shops and art galleries rub shoulders with a little museum and a former prison. **Salmen-Fritchie House** is the former home of a Swiss immigrant whose brickyard provided the material for construction of houses in New Orleans.

Lacombe

This town, situated between Mandeville and Slidell, was founded in 1700 by Choctaw Indians who chose this site for its rich vegetation. The region's microclimate is caused by high levels of atmospheric ozone.

At the **Bayou Lacombe Museum** *($2; every day 9am to 5pm)*, housed in the oldest schoolhouse in the parish, tools, furniture and everyday objects of the Choctaw Indians are exhibited.

Mandeville

This little agglomeration of 7,000 residents, founded in 1840 by Bernard Marigny de Mandeville, is today a simple bedroom community at the north end of the Lake Ponchartrain Causeway. The lakeshore has been landscaped with playing fields and pedestrian paths.

Just southeast of Mandeville is **Fontainebleau State Park ★**, which occupies 1,080 hectares of lakefront land. The ruins of an old sugar mill can be visited here.

Madisonville

Madisonville is the oldest locality on the shores of the Tchefuncte River, dating from 1811, and was once a centre of maritime activity. Today it is a choice holiday spot with a population of under one thousand residents.

The **Madisonville Museum ★** *(free; Sat and Sun noon to 2pm; 201 Cedar Street, ☎ 845-2100)* is located in the old courthouse and exhibits documents related to life in western St. Tammany Parish.

At the mouth of the Tchefuncte River is an old lighthouse that has been converted into the **Otis House Museum** *(free; every day 9am to 5pm)* by the St. Tammany Historical Society.

Covington

This town of 8,000 residents, founded in 1813, is the county seat of the parish and is very popular with artists and writers.

Hundreds of antique everyday objects are exhibited in an old general store (1876) which now houses the hardware store and museum, **H. J. Smith's Son Museum ★** *(free; Mon, Tue, Thu and Fri 8:30am to 5pm, Wed 8:30am to noon, Sat 8:30am to 1pm; 308 Columbia St. North, ☎ 892-0460)*. Objects for sale include oxen yokes, cast-iron cookware, oak chairs and kerosene lamps.

Christ Church, erected in 1846, is a small chapel built entirely of wood. The interior includes an upper gallery that once was reserved for slaves.

St. Joseph Abbey ★★ *(every day 8am to 11am and 1:30pm to 5pm; St. Benedict, Old River Road, north of Covington, ☎ 892-1800)* is a centenarian Benedictine monastery, seminary and retreat. The church was built in 1931 and its interior walls are covered with murals by Dom Gregory de Wit, a Dutch monk and artist. Also on the site is a Creole villa, dating from 1840, which was the house of the first owners who sold the property to the monks of the Order of St. Benedict. Church services include Gregorian chant.

Abita Springs

During times of epidemic, New Orleanians retreated to Abita Springs. On the shore of the Abita River is a building that dates from 1888. The

River Boat Tours

There are many guided river tours of the Mississippi and of the bayous around New Orleans.

The first paddleboats appeared in 1812 and made New Orleans the first stopover in the transportation of cotton. Later, they would serve as a mode of transportation of goods (furniture, French wine, books) and of famous passengers: artists, opera singers and actors.

From February to December, the **Delta Queen** ★★★ (☎ 586-0631 *or toll free in North America 1-800-543-1949)*, the **Mississippi Queen** ★★★ and the **American Queen** ★★★ offer cruises of three to 11 days between New Orleans and Saint Paul, Minnesota, including plantation visits and stops in Natchez and Viksburg, Mississippi.

The **Natchez** ★★ *(during the day, adults $14.75, children 6-12 years old $7.25; evenings, adults $18.75, children 6-12 years old $10.75, 3 and under free; 11:30am, 2:30pm and 7pm, departure from the Jax Brewery wharf,* ☎ *586-8777 or toll free in North America 1-800-233-2628)* makes two-hour cruises every day that include Creole buffets and jazz concerts *(adults $38.75, 6-12-year-olds $19.25).*

The **Creole Queen** ★★ *(adults $14-$18, children $7-$10 depending on the time; 10:30am, 2pm and 7pm;* ☎ *524-0814 or toll free in North America 1-800-445-4109)* offers daily, guided tours leaving from the Canal Street Wharf to the historic site of the Battle of New Orleans in Chalmette. A Creole buffet is served and there is also a two-hour cruise with a jazz concert *(adults $39, children $18).*

The **Cajun Queen** ★★ *(adults $12, 2-12-year-olds $6; 10:30am and 2pm;* ☎ *524-0814 or toll free in North America 1-800-445-4109)*, a replica of a 19th-century paddle-wheel boat, leaves the wharf at the Aquarium of the Americas, on Poydras Street, for a one-and-a-half-hour cruise that brings passengers to the French Quarter, the Chalmette Battlefield (site of the Battle of New Orleans), plantations and bayous.

The **Cotton Blossom** ★★ *(adults $14.50, children $7.25; every day 11am to 4pm; departure from Jackson Brewery, 1300 World Trade Center,* ☎ *586-8777 or toll free in North America 1-800-233-2628)* offers cruises on the Mississippi, the Intercoastal Waterway, and the Barataria-Lafitte bayou. Creole meals are available for a supplemental charge.

The **John James Audubon** ★★ *(10am, noon, 2pm and 4pm; departure from the wharf at the Aquarium of the Americas,* ☎ *586-8777)* has eight departures daily to Audubon Zoo *(return trip including zoo admission: adults $16.50, children $8.25; aquarium visit additional $1; return trip adults $10.50, children $5.75; one way $8.50 and $4.50).* The evening cruise includes a visit to the Aquarium and a deluxe dinner *(adults $45.50, children $25; without meal adults $39.50, children $22; departures from the wharf at the Aquarium at 8pm and 10pm).*

The **Crown Point Swamp Tour ★★** includes transportation from your hotel to the wharf, located about 20 minutes from downtown New Orleans. The hour-and-a-half cruise meanders bayous, the natural habitat of alligators, owls and racoons *($20, $35 with hotel pick-up; departures 10am and 2pm, ☎ 592-0560)*.

R.V. River Charters offers barge cruises for tourists who want to use their recreational vehicles for stopovers *(10-12 days; $2,775 to $3,650 for two people; ☎ toll free in North America 1-800-256-6100)*. This formula is becoming increasingly popular. People board in their RV's and nonchalantly meander the great Mississippi River and its many bayous. The cruise crosses the Atchafalaya basin and Cajun Country, stopping at the most interesting points to take stock of local culture: dance, music, cooking and other tourist attractions.

GREATER NEW ORLEANS

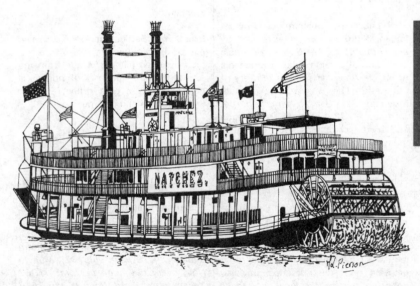

Paddlewheeler

Abita Brewery brews its beer with the area's famous springwater.

Bogalusa

Located in one of the "toes" of foot-shaped Louisiana, Washington Parish is mainly an agricultural region and one of its principal industries is the production of paper. Bogalusa, which is a Native American word that means "black stream", owes its existence to the forestry industry. Some sights of interest include the **Town Hall** *(202 Arkansas Ave.)*, **Mayor Sullivan's Home** *(223 South Border Dr.)*, and the **old train station**.

The **Louisiana Museum of Ancient Indian Culture** ★★ *(weekends, by appointment; ☎ 732-4008)* possesses a collection of objects linked to the lives of Native Americans in the territory of Louisiana. The **Bogue Lusa Pioneer Museum** *(Sat 10am to 4pm, Sun 1pm to 4pm; ☎ 732-4238)* exhibits antique and historical objects. Both of these museums are in Cassidy Park.

Folsom

Folsom is a rural region north of Covington known mainly for the raising of exotic livestock: llamas, austriches, emus and Arabian horses. The dairy industry, pecan plantations, mushroom growing and tree nurseries are also important parts of the local economy.

The **Global Wildlife Center** ★ *(free admission; guided tour: adults $8.95, seniors $7.95, 2-11-yr-olds $6.95; every day 9am to dusk; on LA 40, 15 km east of Folsom; or, take exit 47 from I-12, then take LA 442 north for 17 km and turn right onto LA 40,*

continue 1.6 km; ☎ 624-9453) Over 600 animals, some of them endangered species, roam free in this 360-hectare reserve. Explore it carefully. Accommodation and horseback riding can be arranged.

Zemurray Gardens ★★ *($3, seniors and children $2; Mar and Apr, every day 10am to 6pm; on LA 40, 15 km east of Folsom, ☎ 878-2284)* offers an initiation to indigenous plants, giant bamboos, azaleas and camelias in a 30-hectare park amid great pines and Greek statues. There are also an eight-hectare lake and hiking trails here.

Franklinton

Mile Branch Settlement ★★ *(admission fee; by appointment; ☎ 839-6485)* is a reconstructed pioneer village from the turn of the 19th century with houses, a general store, a post office, a sugar mill, a church and a forge.

Hammond

Hammond, with its population of 18,000, is the largest town in the area. Southeastern Louisiana University is based here and every year it hosts **Fanfare**, a cultural fair.

Kliebert's Turtle & Alligator Farm *(adults $4, 3-12-yr-olds $2; Mar to Nov, every day noon to 7pm; 41067 Yellow Water Road West, ☎ 345-3617 or 1-800-854-9164, ≈ 542-9888)* is home to about 5,000 alligators and 15,000 turtles and offers tastings of sausages and of alligator steak with hot sauce.

Albany

Albany *(on US 190)* is home to the oldest Hungarian community in the United States. The **Hungarian Harvest Festival** is held here the last week of October and features exhibitions dedicated to Hungarian cultural heritage, traditional crafts and cooking.

Springfield

The **Courthouse** *(near LA 22)* was originally built in 1832 as a colonial home and was later used as the courthouse of Livingston Parish.

The **Old Louisiana Turnpike** ★★ *(LA 43, heading north toward Greensburg)* is one of the most scenic routes in the area. It connects Springfield and Greesburg via Albany and Montpelier.

Independence

The area of Independence was colonized by Italians who practiced large-scale strawberry cultivation. The historic neighbourhood of the town has preserved a lovely group of turn-of-the-century homes and shops. There is an **Italian Museum** *(by appointment; ☎ 878-4664)* in a 19th-century church, and the **Italian Festival** *(last weekend in April)* highlights exhibitions, music, dance, and cuisine.

Amite

Amite is the county seat of Tangipahoa Parish ("ear of corn" in Choctaw). The countryside here is a little bit hilly, in contrast to regions to the south. Pine forest are cut through with cattle pastures and dairy farms. Strawberry fields and peach orchards also figure prominently in the area.

Blythewood Plantation ★★ *($4; by appointment; 300 Elm St., ☎ 345-6419 or 748-8183)* is a three-story colonial house built in 1885 with a widow's walk, columned verandas, and antique furniture.

Tangipahoa

Camp Moore State Commemorative Area ★ *(adults $2, 6-14-yr-olds $1, under 6 free; US 51, ☎ 229-2438)* was the site of a Confederate camp during the Civil War. The encampment was established north of New Orleans, in a region that was plainly healthier than the mosquito-infested swamps south of the city.

Manchac ★★

Between the Mississippi River and Lake Pontchartrain, west of New Orleans, cross the Bonnet Carre Spillway. Going north on I-55 you will come to a strand of land between Lake Pontchartrain and Lake Maurepas on which sits the fishing village of Manchac.

Just north of Manchac, **Joyce Wildlife Refuge** offers an interesting boardwalk promenade of many dozen metres through a bayou. This environment is perfect for the development of aquatic plants and shelters more than 100 bird species; mammals such as opossum, muskrat and otter; and reptiles such as alligators, 15 species of snake, and turtles. An information pamphlet is available at the **Tangipahoa Parish Tourist Commission** *(2612 Morrison Blvd. South, Hammond, ☎ 542-7520)*.

GREATER NEW ORLEANS

St. Bernard Parish

The Spanish presence, which had a strong influence in this region, endowed the area with a rich architectural heritage. Chalmette, site of the Battle of New Orleans, is home to a national historic park. Also an excellent area for hunting and fishing, St. Bernard Parish is full of inviting little fishing villages from which it is possible to plan deep-sea fishing excursions.

Chalmette

Jean Lafitte National Historical Park and Preserve, Chalmette Unit *(free; every day 8:30am to 5pm; 8606 St. Bernard Hwy. West,* ☎ *589-4430)* is the site of the famous Battle of New Orleans, the last major confrontation in the War of 1812 against the English. There is a historical interpretive centre here with audiovisual documentation, and you can tour the battlefield, with its reconstructed redoubts, and the national cemetery.

Chalmette is also home to **Beauregard House** (1833), a building evocative of a bygone way of life on the shores of the Mississippi.

St. Bernard

Jean Lafitte National Historical Park and Preserve, Isleños Unit ★★ *(free; every day 8:30am to 5pm; 1357 Bayou Rd.,* ☎ *682-0862)*. In 1777, the Spanish permitted Isleños (as were called the inhabitants of the Canary Islands) to emigrate to Louisiana. This centre presents exhibitions on their way of life and their contribution to the develpment of the region.

Plaquemines Parish

The peninsula at the mouth of the Mississippi juts out into the Gulf of Mexico. Visitors enjoy roaming roads along the river, lounging on the docks of marinas, and crossing the mighty Mississippi on one of the ferries that link its two banks. These scenic roads run through citrus orchards and are dotted with fruit stands where you can stop to stock up on provisions of sweet produce. Hunting and fishing are also popular in this area; Empire and Venice are departure points for deep-sea fising expeditions.

Southeast of Buras and Triumph on a point that juts into a bend of the Mississippi, is **Fort Jackson** (1832). The annual **Plaquemines Festival**, **Orange Festival**, and **Independence Day** *(4th of July)* celebrations are held in the fort's enclosure.

West Pointe a la Hache

Identified on maps as Judge Perez Lake, **Lake Hermitage** ★★ is 40 kilometres from New Orleans, on a little gravel road between Myrtle Grove and West Pointe a la Hache. This road crosses a landscape of bayous and little fishing villages – a very lovely route.

Empire

Passionate fishers come in great numbers to Empire, the "Plaquemines Capital of Seafood", during the **Empire - South Pass Tarpon Rodeo** *(inscription fee; third weekend in Aug)* to try to capture the trophy awarded to the best fisher of this combative opponent.

Buras

Citrus fruit orchards line the high ground on the banks of the Mississippi along LA 23.

Restored **Historical Fort Jackson ★★** *(free; Mon to Fri 10am to 4pm, Sat and Sun 11am to 5pm; LA 23, about 7 km south of Buras, ☎ 657-7083)* was built between 1822 and 1832 to protect New Orlreans and the Lower Mississippi.

Next to Fort Jackson is a **monument to Robert Cavelier, Sieur de La Salle**, a French Canadian explorer born in Montréal who discovered this area in 1682 and named it *Louisiane*.

OUTDOORS

Cycling

Since New Orleans' streets are very busy, it's particularly pleasant to cycle in Audubon Park, City Park and along Lake Pontchartrain. Information on cycling activities is available through **Crescent City Cyclists** *(☎ 276-2601)*.

Canoeing

At **City Park** *($5 per hour; ☎ 483-9371)*, you can rent a canoe and explore lagoons and subtropical wildlife.

Fishing

You can go fishing for perch or catfish in the waters of **City Park** *(adults $2,*

under 16 $1; ☎ 483-9371). A permit is required and can be purchased on site.

For information on New Orleans fishing permits (including Lake Pontchartrain), contact the **Wildlife and Fisheries Department** *(1600 Canal Street, ☎ 568-5636)*.

Swimming

Since the Gulf of Mexico is about 100 kilometres from New Orleans it's not exactly a seaside resort. Also, the thin layer of earth covering the southern Louisiana region doesn't allow for the construction of swimming pools. However, certain hotels have pools: small ones if built in the hotel's courtyard and bigger ones in some of the larger hotels where they are located on the upper floors, if not the top floor or roof itself. To cool off on those scorching hot or extraordinarily humid days, or for swimmers who want to stay in shape, it's better to choose a hotel with a pool because public pools in New Orleans are practically nonexistent.

You will have to go outside New Orleans to find a public swimming pool. The **Bayou Segnette State Park** swimming pool *(adults $8, under 12 yrs $4; 7777 West Bank Expressway, Westwego, ☎ 736-7140)* attracts big crowds. There are picnic tables and a playground.

St. Bernard State Park *($2; Highway Saint Bernard, LA 39 South, Poydras, ☎ 682-2101)* is over 180 hectares in size and offers, as well as a swimming pool, picnic tables, walking trails and campgrounds.

Walking

Most public parks in New Orleans have walking trails. Walking is by far the best way to see the city and the surrounding area. The **French Quarter**, the **Garden District** and **Algiers Point** are great places to walk while discovering this historic city's many points of interest. Don't forget to take a supply of water or some other refreshment.

One hour from New Orleans, **Jean Lafitte Park** *(☎ 689-2002 or 589-2330)* has a large number of trails. Some of the paths go through swamps and archaeological sites.

 Tennis

Tennis lovers will find courts at **Audubon Park** *(6400 to 6900 St. Charles Avenue)* and at **City Park**.

 Golf

The following golf courses are open to the public:

Audubon Park: 473 Walnut Street, New Orleans, ☎ 865-8260 *($10; 18 holes)*.

Brechtel: 3700 Berhman Place, Westbank, ☎ 362-4761 *($8; public 18-hole course)*.

City Park: 1040 Filmore Street, New Orleans, ☎ 483-9396 *($15; four 18-hole courses, driving range)*.

Excursions

The **Air Reldan** ★★ company *(starting at $25 per person; 8227 Lloyd Steaman Drive, suite 120, ☎ 241-9400)* offers flights over New Orleans during the day or night. Since there are no beaches in Louisiana, the company offers charter flights to the sunny beaches of nearby Florida.

Air Tours on the Bayou ★★ *(every day; 1 Coquille Drive, Belle Chasse, south of New Orleans, ☎ 394-5633)* flies over the city and surrounding swamps. The plane lands in the middle of the swamps or on bayous.

A number of small and large businesses offer trips on the bayous where you can admire the alligator kingdom and cypress trees. The only problem is figuring out which one to choose. Contact **Captain Terry's Swamp Tour** *(☎ 471-4933)* or **Lil Cajun Swamp Tours** *(adults $16, seniors $14, children $12, with transportation to hotel $15 and $30; departures 10am, noon, 2pm; Highway 301, Crown Point, ☎ 689-3213 or 1-800-725-3213)*, with Cyrus Blanchare, known as "Cyrus the Cajun", captain of the *Moonlight Lady*, a boat that can carry 60 passengers. Tours visit the swamps of Jean Lafitte National Park and last two to four hours.

Fun-Day Bayou Tours ★★ *(adults $18, under 12 yrs $12, with transportation to hotel $38 and $18, meal included; leaves the dock at 9:30am and 1:30pm except Sun morning; ☎ 471-4900)*, offers a guided tour of the Segnette Bayou and the swamps located half an hour away from New Orleans. A traditional meal of rice and beans with sausages is offered on Miss Mary's islet. You are also urged to visit her garden.

Private excursions and photo-safaris (camera included) are available through **Captain Nick's Wildlife Safaris** ★★ *(☎ 361-3004 or 1-800-375-3474)*. Their boats are small, holding from one to four passengers. They will pick you up at your hotel.

 ACCOMMODATIONS

Whether you are looking for a simple *pied-à-terre* or something more luxurious, New Orleans offers a wide choice of hotels, motels and bed and breakfasts to suit all budgets.

Whether you just want to rent a small room or would prefer to stay in a historic manor, **Bed and Breakfast Inc.** *(1021 Moss Rd., New Orleans, LA 70152-2267,* ☎ *488-4640 or 1-800-749-4640 from the U.S.,* ⌨ *827-5391)* can provide all of the necessary information and make reservations.

New Orleans Bed & Breakfast and Accommodations *(P.O. Box 8163, New Orleans,* ☎ *838-0071)* reserves rooms, apartments, furnished flats and houses.

You can get information on all the different hotels in the Southern Comfort chain in the New Orleans metropolitan area and make reservations through the **Southern Comfort** reservation service *(P.O. Box 13294, New Orleans,* ☎ *861-0082 for information or 1-800-749-1928 for reservations)*.

Most of the major hotel chains are represented in New Orleans, especially in the Central Business District. They obviously do not have the character and ambience that a smaller hotel has, but they offer good quality, service and comfort.

The French Quarter and Faubourg Marigny

St. Peter Guest House *($50-$180 bkfst incl.;* ≡, *pb, tv; 1005 St. Peter St., 70116,* ☎ *524-9232 or 1-800-535-7815 in North America,* ⌨ *943-6536 or 523-5198)*. The wrought-iron balconies of this beautiful 19th century building overlook the French Quarter. There are 17 rooms and 11 suites with period decor.

The **Nine-O-Five Royal Hotel** *($65 and up;* ≡, *pb, K; 905 Royal St., 70116,* ☎ *523-0219)*, constructed in 1890, is one of the oldest small hotels in the French Quarter. Its European character, courtyard and balconies looking over Royal Street make it very charming. Credit cards are not accepted.

The **New Orleans Guest House** *($79-$99 bkfst incl.; pb; 1118 Ursulines St., 70116,* ☎ *566-1177)* is a Creole cottage dating from 1848 with a pleasant courtyard in which breakfast is served. The owners are very friendly. There is private parking.

Rue Royal Inn *($75-$145;* ≡, *pb, K, ℝ; 1006 Royal St., 70116,* ☎ *524-3900 or 1-800-776-3901 in North America,* ⌨ *558-0566)* is a beautiful Creole house from the 1830s. It offers luxurious suites with balconies and rooms that open onto a courtyard.

The **French Quarter Suites** *($79-$119 bkfst incl.;* ≡, *pb, tv,* ≈; *1119 Rampart North St., 70116,* ☎ *524-7725 or 1-800-457-2253 from the U.S.,*

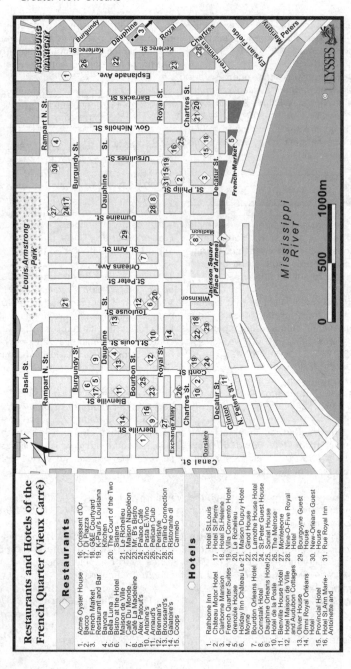

Restaurants and Hotels of the French Quarter (Vieux Carré)

◇ Restaurants

1. Acme Oyster House
2. Bacco
3. French Market Restaurant and Bar
4. Bayona
5. Bella Luna
6. Bistro at the Hotel Maison de Ville
7. Café Du Monde
8. Café La Madeleine
9. Alex Patout's
10. Antoine's
11. Arnaud's
12. Brennan's
13. Broussard's
14. Galatoire's
15. Coops
16. Croissant d'Or
17. Di Piazza
18. G&E Courtyard
19. K-Paul's Louisiana Kitchen
20. The Court of the Two Sisters
21. Le Richelieu
22. Maison Napoléon
23. Mr. B's Bistro
24. Palace Café
25. Pasta E Vino
26. Pelican Club
27. Peristyle
28. Praline Connection
29. Ristorante di Carmelo

◉ Hotels

1. Rathbone Inn
2. Château Motor Hotel
3. Clairborne Mansion
4. French Quarter Suites
5. Grenoble House
6. Holiday Inn Château Le Moyne
7. Bourdon Orleans Hotel
8. Cornstalk Hotel
9. Dauphine Orleans Hotel
10. Hotel de la Poste
11. Bienville House Hotel
12. Hotel Maison de Ville and Audubon Cottages
13. Olivier House
14. Omni Royal Orleans Hotel
15. Provincial Hotel
16. Hotel St.Ann Marie-Antoinette and
17. Hotel St.Louis
18. Hotel St Pierre
19. Hotel St.Helene
20. Villa Convento Hotel
21. Le Richelieu
22. Maison Dupuy Hotel
23. Girod House
24. Lamothe House Hotel
25. St.Peter Guest House
26. Soniat House
27. The Melrose
28. Inn-O-Five Royal Hotel
29. Bourgoyne Guest House
30. New-Orleans Guest House
31. Rue Royal Inn

Our Favourites

For warm atmosphere:
>Le Meridien (p 117) and Le Richelieu (p 110).

For New Orleans architecture:
>Hotel Maison de Ville and Audubon Cottages (p 112), Soniat House (p 110), and the Rue Royal Inn (p 107).

For attractive decor:
>Chimes B&B (p 114), Grenoble House (p 111), the Dauphine Orleans Hotel (p 111), Hotel Maison de Ville and Audubon Cottages (p 112) and Soniat House (p 110).

For pleasant courtyards:
>Chimes B&B (p 114), Hotel de la Poste (p 112), Maison Dupuy (p 113), and Soniat House (p 110).

For sophisticated character:
>Claiborne Mansion (p 111), the Bourbon Orleans Hotel (p 113), the Omni Royal Orleans Hotel (p 112), the Pontchartrain Hotel (p 115), Le Meridien (p 117), The Melrose (p 113), and the Monteleone (p 112).

For a warm welcome:
>The Avenue Plaza Hotel and Spa (p 115), Chimes B&B (p 114), Villa Convento Hotel (p 110), Le Meridien (p 117), Le Richelieu (p 110), New Orleans Guest House (p 107).

For period antiques:
>Claiborne Mansion (p 111), Grenoble House (p 111), Cornstalk Hotel (p 110), Girod House (p 111), Duvigneaud House (p 115), and Soniat House (p 110).

For affordable prices:
>Comfort Inn/Downtown Superdome (p 116), French Quarter Suites (p 107), the Nine-O-Five Royal Hotel (p 107), New Orleans Guest House (p 107), and Prytania Inn I, II and III (p 113).

For the most attractive lobby:
>The Hyatt Regency Hotel (p 117).

For romantic atmosphere:
>The Melrose (p 113).

For terraces and balconies:
>Hotel de la Poste (p 112), the Omni Royal Orleans Hotel (p 112), Girod House (p 111), Soniat House (p 110), Rue Royal Inn (p 107).

For views of the city and the Mississippi:
>The Westin Canal Place Hotel (p 118).

GREATER NEW ORLEANS

↵ *522-9716)*, located close to the French Quarter, offers rooms that are modest but comfortable.

The picturesque **Château Motor Hotel** *($79-$129 bkfst incl.; ≡, pb, tv, ≈, ℜ; 1001 Chartres St., 70116, ☎ 524-9636, ↵ 525-2989)* is located in the heart of the historic French Quarter. Free parking.

Villa Convento Hotel *($89-$155 bkfst incl.; ≡, pb, tv; 616 Ursulines St., 70116, ☎ 522-1793, ↵ 524-1902)* is a lovely Creole house built in 1848. This family guest house offers very proficient European-style service.

The **Rathbone Inn** *($90-$145 bkfst incl.; ≡, pb, K, tv; 1227 Esplanade Ave., 70116, ☎ 947-2101 or 1-800-947-2101 in North America, ↵ 947-7454)* is an elegant manor that was constructed in 1850. Well situated in the attractive and historic Faubourg Marigny, the Rathbone has eight cozy rooms and two magnificent suites. Private parking.

Lamothe House Hotel *($90-$195 bkfst incl.; pb, K; 621 Esplanade Ave., 70116-2018, ☎ 947-1161 or 1-800-367-5858 in North America, ↵ 943-6536)*, a hotel tucked away in a grove of oak trees, is well situated one block from the French Quarter. Its 11 rooms and 9 suites are furnished in old-fashioned style. Every aspect of the place evokes the charm of the Victorian era – it's pleasant, but a bit stiff.

🏨 **Le Richelieu** *($95-$150; ≡, ⊗, pb, tv, ℝ, ≈, ℜ; 1234 Chartres St., 70116, ☎ 529-2492 or 1-800-535-9653 in North America, ↵ 524-8179)* is a highly recommended, wonderful establishment that has earned a four-diamond rating from the AAA auto club. Le Richelieu is

located near the Ursuline Convent, the French Market, Faubourg Marigny and elegant Esplanade Avenue. Romantic charm, exceptional service and relatively reasonable prices for the French Quarter merit this hotel particular acclaim. The hotel bar, which also serves as dining room, opens onto a beautiful, flowered courtyard and a pool. At night this marvellous spot is a favourite meeting place in the French Quarter. Everyone on the staff is exceptionally kind. Room service is available on request and there is free parking.

The **Hotel St. Pierre** *($109-$129 bkfst incl.; ≡, pb, ≈; 911 Burgundy St., 70116, ☎ 524-4401 or 1-800-225-4040 in North America, ↵ 524-6800)* includes two 18th-century Creole cottages in a peaceful, shady courtyard. Free parking.

The **Cornstalk Hotel** *($115-$155 bkfst incl.; ≡, pb; 915 Royal St., 70116, ☎ 523-1515, ↵ 522-5558)* is located in the heart of the French Quarter. This elegant little hotel, declared a historic landmark, offers 14 rooms furnished with antiques, stained-glass windows, fireplaces and canopy beds. Set back a bit from the road, behind a pleasant garden, the hotel is easily recognized by its wrought-iron fence with corn motifs.

🏨 **Soniat House** *($120 and up bkfst incl.; pb, ≡, tv; 1133 Chartres St., 70116, ☎ 522-0570 or 1-800-544-8808 in North America, ↵ 522-7208)* is quiet, luxurious and enthusiastically recommended. The historic character of the Soniat du Fossat House, which was built in 1829 for plantation owner and New Orleans aristocrat Joseph Soniat du Fossat, has been maintained in this unique hotel.

Rooms and suites are furnished with antiques from France, Great Britain and Louisiana. Breakfast is served in the charming, rustic courtyard. From the beautiful wrought-iron balcony that overlooks Chartres Street there is a view of the Old Ursuline Convent, a masterpiece of New Orleans' architectural heritage (see p 79). Across the street is another historic house, which originally belonged to Joseph Soniat du Fossat's son and which has also been converted into a hotel by the owners of this establishment. This second house also has a magnificent, abundantly flowered courtyard with a lovely fountain.

Olivier House *($125 and up; ≡, pb, tv, ≈, K; 828 Toulouse St., 70112-3422, ☎ 525-8456, ⇥ 529-2006)* is an attractive building that dates from 1836 and is listed in the National Register of Historic Places. It offers large rooms with high ceilings and antique furniture. The hotel opens onto a lush yard.

The **Holiday Inn Château Le Moyne** *($139 and up; ≡, pb, tv, ≈, ℜ; 301 Dauphine St., 70112, ☎ 581-1303 or 1-800-465-4329 in North America, ⇥ 523-5709)*, located close to the French Quarter, offers, apart from its rooms, some lovely suites in Creole cottages. The rooms are all tastefully decorated; some have brick walls, canopy beds and fireplaces, and they all feature ceiling-height windows adorned with floral-patterned drapes.

Hotel Saint-Louis *($139 and up; ≡, pb, ⊛, ℜ; 730 Bienville St., 70130, ☎ 581-7300 or 1-800-535-9111 in North America, ⇥ 524-8925)*. Everything here is reminiscent of the New Orleans of bygone days: the Louis XVI decor of the restaurant, the fountains, the subtropical flora, etc.

🏨 **Grenoble House** *($145-$195; ≡, pb, tv, ≈, K; 329 Dauphine St., 70112, ☎ 522-1331, ⇥ 524-4968)* is a delightful little 17-suite hotel with enchanting decor. The suites are distributed among the three original sections of the estate: the masters' residence, the servants' wing and rooms, and the slave quarters. All of the suites have sofa-beds as well as beds. The kitchenettes are equipped with modern facilities (conventional or microwave oven, stove, refrigerator and dishwasher). Children under the age of 12 are not admitted.

🏨 **Girod House** *($145-$225 bkfst incl.; ≡, pb, K; 835 Esplanade Ave., 70116, ☎ 522-5214 or 1-800-650-3323 in North America, ⇥ 522-7288)* is a well-preserved Creole residence that is pleasantly decorated with antiques. This distinctive little hotel offers five rooms and six suites. Every suite includes a bedroom, a living room, a kitchenette and a bathroom. The two largest suites have balconies that overlook either elegant Esplanade Avenue or the rustic courtyard. Rooms and suites combine Creole comfort and luxurious 19th-century furnishings.

🏨 **Claiborne Mansion** *($150-$250; ≡, pb, tv, ≈; 2111 Dauphine St., 70116, ☎ 949-7327 or 1-800-449-7327 in North America, ⇥ 949-0388)*, a small hotel located across from Washington Square in Faubourg Marigny, has nine spacious, inviting rooms in a sober yet tasteful decor of neutral tones. Some rooms are furnished with canopy beds.

🏨 **Dauphine Orleans Hotel** *($150 and up; ≡, pb, tv, ≈; 415 Dauphine St.,*

GREATER
NEW ORLEANS

70112, ☎ *586-1800 or 1-800-521-7111 in North America, ⇌ 586-1409).* Upon arrival, guests are greeted with a complimentary refreshment. Tea is served every afternoon. The hotel has 109 rooms. The "Dauphine" part of the hotel, dating from the beginning of the 19th century, houses 14 magnificent rooms with original exposed ceiling beams and brick walls. The other rooms, with their pale-coloured walls, beige carpeting and flowered bedspreads also have a lot of character. Rooms are equipped with a number of small appliances such as irons and hair dryers.

The adorable **Hotel de la Poste** *($150 and up; ≡, pb, tv, ≈, ℜ; 316 Chartres St., 70130,* ☎ *581-1200 or 1-800-448-4927 in North America, ⇌ 523-2910)* has about one hundred rooms, each with a balcony overlooking the courtyard or the street. The decor of the rooms is simple but cozy, with dark-wood furniture. The Hotel de la Poste boasts an excellent restaurant, Bacco, renowned for its fine Italian cuisine with strong Creole accents (see p 125).

At the **Monteleone** *($150 and up; ≡, pb, tv, ≈, ℜ; 214 Royal St., 70140,* ☎ *523-3341 or 1-800-535-9595 in North America, ⇌ 528-1019)*, you will discover the advantages that a high-calibre hotel has to offer. The spacious rooms were renovated in 1996. Light-coloured walls provide a contrast to the finely crafted dark-wood furniture. Some rooms have canopy beds.

The **Omni Royal Orleans Hotel** *($169 and up; ≡, pb, tv, ≈, ℜ; 621 St. Louis St., 70140,* ☎ *529-5333 or 1-800-843-6664 in North America, ⇌ 529-7089)*. During major events such as Mardi Gras, certain rooms of this hotel offer no respite since it is located in the heart of the action in the French Quarter. The rooms are decorated with wallpaper in a light, striped design with a flowered band, and some of them have canopy beds. There is a pool on a roof-top terrace, from which there is a striking view of the French Quarter.

The **Bienville House Hotel** *($175 and up; ≡, pb, tv, ≈, ☉, ℜ; 320 Decatur St., 70130,* ☎ *529-2345 or 1-800-535-7836 in North America, ⇌ 525-6079)* is a charming little establishment, and a few of its rooms have balconies. Recently, the building and its 83 rooms were completely renovated. Bedspreads with subtle prints and curtains with flower designs in pink tones complement dark, finely crafted wood furniture. Across from the Aquarium of the Americas and Riverfront, close to Bourbon Street and Jackson Square, the hotel benefits from one of the best locations in the French Quarter. Free parking.

Hotel Maison de Ville and Audubon Cottages *($180 and up, bkfst incl.; ≡, K, pb, ℜ, 727 Toulouse St., 70130,* ☎ *561-5858 or 1-800-634-1600 in North America, ⇌ 528-9939)*. Located in the heart of the French Quarter, this establishment, of refined architectural beauty, is comprised of 16 rooms and 7 cottages. Originally, John James Audubon and his family lived in the house. He created some of his most beautiful sketches, drawings and paintings here. The principal residence and the outbuildings have all been carefully restored. The varied decor of the rooms – some rustic, some luxurious – reflects different periods in the history of the South. Children under the age of 12 are not admitted. Free parking.

The **Bourbon Orleans Hotel** *($185-$250; ≡, pb, tv, ≈, ℜ; 717 Orleans Ave., 70116, ☎ 523-2222 or 1-800-521-5338 from the U.S., ⌖ 525-8166)* is a luxurious hotel in the tradition of 19th-century Europe, with Queen-Anne period antiques and marble bathrooms. Bedspreads and curtains are made of sumptuous floral-patterned fabrics that are set off nicely by bright carpeting.

The **Maison Dupuy Hotel** *($185 and up; ≡, pb, tv, ≈, ℜ; 1001 Toulouse St., 70112, ☎ 586-8000 or 1-800-535-9177 in North America, ⌖ 566-7450)* has 198 rooms and suites, arranged in seven 19th-century cottages which have retained their old-fashioned character despite recent renovations. The spacious rooms have European-style decor. The floral-patterned bedspreads and curtains complement the light-coloured walls. Many rooms have French windows that open onto the pool in the magnificent courtyard. The garden is full of wonderful banana, orange and grapefruit trees. Sunday brunches at the hotel restaurant, Le Bon Créole, are accompanied by jazz.

🐌 The **Melrose** *($250 and up; ≡, pb, tv, ≈; 937 Esplanade Ave., 70116, ☎ 944-2255, ⌖ 945-1794)*. The splendid rooms of this elegant historic house are luxuriously decorated. Wealthy romantics can stay in the "Donecio Suite" for the modest price of $425! The hotel provides transportation to and from the airport.

Uptown and the Garden District

Longpre Guest House and Hostel *($12 in the dormitory, $35 for a room; sb, K;*

1726 Prytania St., 70130, ☎ 581-4540) is located between the French Quarter and the Garden District and is close to the St. Charles streetcar. The hundred-year-old house is a bit run down and now houses a youth hostel. This is no-frills accommodation: either a bed in a dormitory or a small private room.

Marquette House New Orleans International Hostel *(2253 Carondelet St., 70130, ☎ 523-3014)*, a member of the American Youth Hostel Association, has 160 beds, most of them in dormitories *($14-$17; sb)*, and a few in private rooms *($28-$31; ≡, pb)*. There are also two-bedroom suites with living rooms and kitchenettes *($40-$70; ≡, pb, K)*.

Prytania Inn I *($40 and up; pb, 1415 Prytania St., 70130, ☎ 586-0853)*. Although the decor is somewhat stark, this modest little hotel offers comfortable clean rooms. Under the same administration, **Prytania II** *(2141 Prytania St.)* and **Prytania III** *(2127 Prytania St.)* offer slightly more expensive accommodation.

The **Saint Charles Guest House** *(single $45-65, double $65-$85, continental bkfst incl.; ≡, pb or sb, ≈; 1748 Prytania St., 70130, ☎ 523-6556)* is small, simple hotel near the Lower Garden District and the streetcar. The house is somewhat old-fashioned and offers no luxuries. Clients tend to be fairly young, sometimes bohemian, low-budget travellers – this is one of the cheapest places to stay in New Orleans. There are 26 rooms overlooking a pretty, sunny courtyard and a pool.

Saint Charles Inn *($50-$90 bkfst incl.; pb; 3636 St. Charles Ave., 70115,*

☎ *899-8888, 1-800-489-9908 in North America,* ≈ *899-8892).* Although the entrance to this hotel is squeezed between a restaurant and a café, you will find the recently renovated rooms inside very inviting.

The **Quality Inn - Maison Saint-Charles** *($65 and up;* ≡, *pb,* ≈; *1319 St. Charles Ave., 70130,* ☎ *522-0187 or 1-800-831-1783 from the U.S.,* ≈ *525-2218)* is comprised of six historic buildings around a charming courtyard. The modest rooms are impeccable despite the industrial-quality carpeting and nondescript furniture. A good place to stay if you are on a fixed budget.

Fairchild House *($75-$100 bkfst incl.; pb, tv; 1518 Prytania St., 70130,* ☎ *524-0154 or 1-800-256-2043 from the U.S.,* ≈ *568-0063)* is a magnificent neoclassical residence built in about 1841 and it is close to the Garden District. It has only 14 Victorian-style rooms. The decor is warm and inviting, and guests are welcome to enjoy the charming courtyard. Private parking.

Quality Inn - Midtown *($75 and up;* ≡, *pb, tv,* ≈, ℜ; *3900 Tulane Ave., 70119,* ☎ *486-5541 or 1-800-228-5151 in North America,* ≈ *488-7440).* The rooms are comfortable and the prices are among the most affordable. Clients can take advantage of free shuttle service to various points in the French Quarter. Free parking.

The **Columns Hotel** *($75-$175 and up, bkfst incl.; pb or sb,* ≡; *3811 St. Charles Ave., 70115-4638,* ☎ *899-9308 or 1-800-445-9308 in North America,* ≈ *899-8170)* is listed in the National Register of Historic Places. The very same grand staircase that

leads to the rooms can be seen in the film *Pretty Baby*. Although the furnishings are somewhat sparse, the rooms shine like a new penny! Nineteen rooms are available, nine of which have private bathrooms. Every Thursday night, the hotel bar hosts a jazz-rock band. On Sundays there is a brunch with mellow jazz.

The **Park View Guest House** *($90-$120 and up;* ≡, *pb, tv,* ℜ; *7004 St. Charles Ave., 70118,* ☎ *861-7564,* ≈ *861-1225),* located on the edge of Audubon Park, was constructed for visitors to the World's Industrial and Cotton Centennial Exhibition in 1884. The rooms on the St. Charles Avenue side of this charming Victorian house have period furniture. The other rooms have less character but offer a magnificent view of the park. All 23 rooms are clean and comfortable. Breakfast is served in the dining room, which offers a splendid view of the park.

Chimes Bed & Breakfast *($90-$125 bkfst incl.;* ≡, *pb; 1146 Constantinople St.,* ☎ *899-2621 or 1-800-749-4640 from the U.S.)* are attractive suites, with private bathrooms, that can house up to six people. Smoking is permitted outside only. Charles, the Lebanese owner, also works as the head waiter at Arnaud's, in the French Quarter (see p 127). He is very friendly and loves to chat. A charming place to stay, the Chimes is highly recommended by the authors of this guide and easily accessible via the St. Charles streetcar, which can also take you to the heart of the French Quarter in a matter of minutes.

Terrell House *($100-$125 bkfst incl.;* ≡, *pb, tv; 1441 Magazine St., 70130,* ☎ *524-9859),* erected in 1858, has been converted into a nine-room guest house. The house maintains its old-fashioned character and its furnishings appear to be authentic. It is located in the residential Lower-Garden District, also the site of many galleries and antique shops. Two dogs keep watch over a lush English garden. Your hosts will make restaurant and guided-tour reservations for you upon request.

🏨 **Avenue Plaza Hotel and Spa** *($125 and up; ≡, pb, tv, ≈, ℜ; 2111 St. Charles Ave., 70130, ☎ 566-1212 or 1-800-535-9575 in North America, ⌨ 525-6899)*. The hotel's spacious and inviting rooms have recently been renovated. Some of them are decorated with attractive Art Deco furniture.

🏨 The **Pontchartrain Hotel** *($150 and up; ≡, pb, tv, ℜ; 2031 St. Charles Ave., 70140, ☎ 524-0581 or 1-800-777-6193 in North America, ⌨ 529-1165)*, a luxurious European-style hotel, is located in the heart of the Garden District. As well as offering standard rooms, there are a few romantic suites. Prince Aly Khan and Rita Hayworth stayed in one of this illustrious hotel's suites during their honeymoon in New Orleans.

Mid-City

🏨 The **Degas House** *($100-$200 bkfst incl.; pb; 2306 Esplanade Ave., ☎ 821-5009)*, built in 1854, exhibits Italian-inspired style. The painter Edgar Degas stayed here in 1873, while visiting his mother's family. It was during his time in New Orleans that Degas painted *Le Portrait d'Estelle* (owned by the New Orleans Museum of Art, see p 85) as well as *Le Bureau de coton de La Nouvelle-Orléans*. The house has been renovated in keeping with its original character. Rooms on the second floor are spacious and furnished with antiques; one has a large private balcony. Although the rooms on the third floor have a bit of an attic feel, they have the advantage of being less expensive.

The **New Orleans First B & B** *($100-$125 bkfst incl.; pb; 3660 Gentilly Boulevard, ☎ 947-3401)* is a splendid Art-Deco-style house flanked by magnificent oaks. The three rooms are rented to non-smokers only.

Mechling's Guest House *($125 and up, bkfst incl.; ≡, pb, 2023 Esplanade Ave., 70116, ☎ 943-4131 or 1-800-725-4131 from the U.S.)*, a Victorian-style historic manor from the 1860s, is close to the French Quarter.

Duvigneaud House *($135 bkfst incl.; pb, tv, K; 2857½ Grand Route St. John, close to St. John Bayou, 70116, ☎ 821-5009, ⌨ 948-3313)* is a plantation residence built in 1834 that has been completely restored. The spacious, homey, four-person suites have high ceilings and wood floors. Rooms are furnished with antiques and guests have access to a pretty courtyard. Almost all services and facilities for an extended stay are available (laundry, housekeeping, grocery store a few blocks away). The house is located near Esplanade Avenue and City Park. Free parking.

Central Business District

The **YMCA International Hotel** *($50 and less; ≡, tv, pb, ℜ, ☺, ≈; 920 St. Charles Ave., 70130, ☎ and ⌨ 568-9622)* is a favourite among budget travellers, fans

GREATER NEW ORLEANS

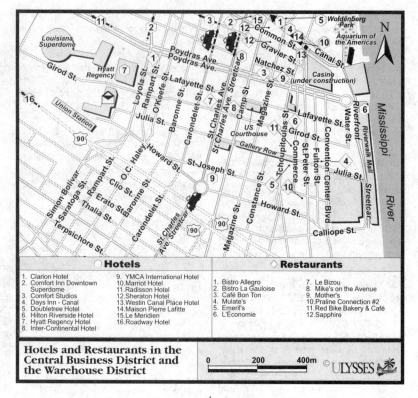

○ Hotels

1. Clarion Hotel
2. Comfort Inn Downtown Superdome
3. Comfort Studios
4. Days Inn - Canal
5. Doubletree Hotel
6. Hilton Riverside Hotel
7. Hyatt Regency Hotel
8. Inter-Continental Hotel
9. YMCA International Hotel
10. Marriot Hotel
11. Radisson Hotel
12. Sheraton Hotel
13. Westin Canal Place Hotel
14. Maison Pierre Lafitte
15. Le Meridien
16. Roadway Hotel

◇ Restaurants

1. Bistro Allegro
2. Bistro La Gauloise
3. Café Bon Ton
4. Mulate's
5. Emeril's
6. L'Economie
7. Le Bizou
8. Mike's on the Avenue
9. Mother's
10. Praline Connection #2
11. Red Bike Bakery & Café
12. Sapphire

**Hotels and Restaurants in the
Central Business District and
the Warehouse District**

0   200   400m   © ULYSSES

of Jack London and Jack Kerouac, and the young at heart in general.

Comfort Studios *($55-$105; pb, ≈, tv, ≈, ⊛, ℝ, 346 Baronne St., 70112-1627, ☎ 524-1140 or 1-800-228-5150 in North America, ⇆ 523-4444)*, located four blocks from the French Quarter, is ideal for people looking for comfortable rooms at reasonable prices. Free parking.

The **Comfort Inn Downtown Superdome** *($65-$90; ≈, pb, tv, ℝ, ℜ; 1315 Gravier St., 70112-2003, ☎ 586-0100 or 1-800-535-9141 in North America, ⇆ 588-9230 or 527-5263)* benefits from an ideal location, mid-way

between the Superdome and the French Quarter. Rooms are simple and inviting, all equipped with contemporary furnishings. Every room has useful small appliances such as irons, hair dryers and microwave ovens.

The **Clarion Hotel** *($89-$109; ≈, pb, tv, ≈, ⊙, ℜ; 1500 Canal St., 70112, ☎ 522-4500 or 1-800-824-3359 from the U.S., ⇆ 525-2644)*, a highly rated hotel located close to the Superdome, offers free shuttle service to the French Quarter. Rooms are tastefully decorated, mostly in pastel tones and have attractive, finely crafted dark-wood furniture. The hotel offers families a list of reliable people who provide child-care services.

The **Days Inn - Canal** *($95-$135; ≡, pb, tv, ≈, ℜ; 1630 Canal St., 70112, ☎ 586-0110 or 1-800-232-3297 in North America, ≈ 581-2253)* is only a few minutes away from the French Market, close to the I-10 (exit 235B). This 211-room, eight-floor hotel has classic decor. Each standard room is furnished with either one king-size bed or two large beds. All the rooms are comfortable, adorned with wall-to-wall carpeting, and equipped with a chest of drawers and small appliances (hair dryers, coffee machines, voice message service). Free parking.

The **Doubletree Hotel** *($129 and up; ≡, pb, tv, ≈, ℜ; 300 Canal St., ☎ 581-1300 or 1-800-222-8733 in North America, ≈ 522-4100)*, less expensive than other hotels in the same category, has the advantage of being situated just a few minutes from the French Quarter. The lobby of this 363-room hotel is unassuming, but the rooms are cozy. Their pale wood furniture is well matched with the pastel-coloured curtains and bedspreads.

🛏 **Le Meridien** *($185 and up; ≡, pb, tv, ≈, ℝ, ☉, ℜ; 614 Canal St., ☎ 525-6500 or 1-800-543-4300 in North America, ≈ 586-1543)*. This luxurious, up-market hotel has 494 spacious, elegant, comfortable rooms. A work table completes the furnishings that are composed, most notably, of an easy chair and a sofa whose colours harmonize with the drapes and the bedspread. Modern luxury is combined with all the traditional charm of the South. The rooms on the upper floors of this 30-floor building offer a superb view of the city. Staff members see to every detail of guests' needs, right down to the complimentary toiletries in the washrooms. An outdoor pool and an exercise room are on the eighth floor. The hotel has a bistro, **La Gauloise** (see p 129), and numerous conference rooms with all necessary services for business people. Jazz performances are presented every evening and during the hotel's famous Sunday brunches.

The **Hilton Riverside Hotel** *($185 and up; ≡, pb, tv, ≈, ℝ, ☉, ℜ; 2 Poydras St., ☎ 561-0500 or 1-800-445-8667 in North America, ≈ 568-1721)* is definitely one of the biggest hotels in the city with more than 1,500 rooms. Furnishings are contemporary, and the decor in the standard rooms is comfortable, if not especially creative. The "concierge rooms", designed for business people, are equipped with fax machines. Suites are also available, some with pool tables and private terraces. Other services and facilities include bars, tennis courts, a health club and two pools.

Hyatt Regency Hotel *($185 and up; ≡, pb, tv, ≈, ℝ, ☉, ℜ; 500 Poydras St., ☎ 561-1234 or 1-800-233-1234 in North America, ≈ 587-4141)*. The lobby and lounge areas are spacious and bright, creating a luxurious and comfortable environment. Rooms are large and tastefully decorated. Some rooms are specially designed for women and, apparently out of chivalry, are located near the elevators. Other amenities include bars, a health club and a beauty salon.

Hotel Inter-Continental *($185 and up; ≡, pb, tv, ≈, ℝ, ☉, ℜ; 444 St. Charles Ave., ☎ 525-5566 or 1-800-332-4246 from the U.S., ≈ 585-4387)*. A few blocks from the French Quarter, the comfort and elegance found here are the reasons for this international chain's distinguished reputation. Approximately 450 vast rooms with simple, inviting decor are available. Some of the rooms are designed for people with physical disabilities. Everyone on the hotel's staff shows great concern for the well-being of guests. Other services and facilities offered are bars, a health club and a beauty salon.

The **Marriott** *($185 and up;* ≡*, pb, tv,* ≈*,* ℝ*,* ◎*,* ℜ*; 555 Canal St.,* ☎ *581-1000 or 1-800-228-9290 in North America,* ↩ *523-6755)*, a modern hotel with 1,300 rooms and 54 suites, is located a few steps away from the French Quarter. The Marriott often hosts important conferences. The rooms are comfortable and very well equipped. Those on the upper floors have a spectacular view of the city, the French Quarter and the Mississippi. The staff is very courteous.

The **Radisson Hotel** *($185 and up;* ≡*, pb, tv,* ≈*,* ℝ*,* ◎*,* ℜ*; 1500 Canal St.,* ☎ *522-4500 or 1-800-333-3333 in North America)*, part of another large hotel chain, is listed in the National Register of Historic Places. The warmth and ambience of the South are present in every one of the 759 spacious, elegantly decorated rooms. The dark tones of the wood furniture blend well with attractive floral fabrics. The Radisson offers a number of luxurious suites, as well as rooms for people with physical disabilities. Staff members speak many languages. Reception and service are among the most courteous. The hotel offers guests free shuttle service to the French Quarter.

The **Sheraton Hotel** *($185 and up;* ≡*, pb, tv,* ≈*,* ℝ*,* ◎*,* ℜ*; 500 Canal St.,* ☎ *525-2500 or 1-800-325-3535 in North America,* ↩ *592-5615)* is another hotel in demand for mega-conferences. The enormous lobby was designed to accommodate the comings and goings of thousands of people. The 1,100 comfortable rooms are functionally furnished. Staff members make every effort to pay particular attention to each visitor.

🦐 The **Westin Canal Place Hotel** *($185 and up;* ≡*, pb, tv,* ≈*,* ℝ*,* ◎*,* ℜ*; 100 Iberville St.,* ☎ *566-7006 or 1-800-228-3000 in North America,* ↩ *553-5133)*. This hotel's expansive rooms are attractively decorated in pastel colours; each has a marble fireplace and a large marble bathroom. From the outdoor pool, on the 30th floor, there is a fantastic panoramic view of the city. The restaurant Le Jardin offers room service 24 hours a day and weekly Sunday jazz brunches. Among the other facilities offered are a fully equipped exercise room and two bars.

Around New Orleans

Close to Downtown

Quite close to downtown, the **Mardi Gras Campground** *($15-$25;* ≈*; 6050 Chef Menteur Hwy., exit 240B from the I-10,* ☎ *243-0085)* is a AAA-rated campground with 200 tent sites. There are also a guaranteed security service, showers, laundry facilities and public transportation to downtown.

Jude Travel Park *($19 and up;* ≈*,* ⊛*; 7400 Chef Menteur, exit 240B from the I-10,* ☎ *241-0632 or 1-800-523-2196 in North America,* ↩ *245-8070)*. This "Good Sam" campground has 43 shady sites for recreational vehicles, showers, washrooms, and laundry facilities. It is located close to bus routes and there is a car-rental agency on site, a shuttle to the French Quarter and a security service.

The **Parc d'Orléans Travel Park 1** *($50 and less; ≈; 7676 Chef Menteur Hwy., 70126, exit 240B from the I-10, ☎ 241-3167 or 1-800-535-2598 from the U.S.)* is a 74-site campground with showers, washrooms and laundry facilities. Transportation to the French Quarter and guided tours are offered.

The **Parc d'Orléans Travel Park 2** *($50 and less; ≈; 10910 Chef Menteur Hwy., exit 240B from the I-10, ☎ 242-6176 or 1-800-535-2598 from the U.S.)*, open all year, has 125 sites, showers, washrooms and laundry facilities. Shuttle service to the French Quarter and guided tours are also available.

Metairie

KOA New Orleans West *($21 for tents, $27 for recreational vehicles; ≈; 11129 Jefferson Hwy.: from the I-10, take exit 223A-Williams, travel south on Williams to Jefferson Hwy. and take it east, ☎ 467-1792)*, located on the Mississippi riverbank, is open all year. There are 96 sites, showers, washrooms, laundry facilities, a playground and a grocery store. Many of the sites are paved, shaded from the sun and bordered by grass.

Kenner

The **Seven Oaks Plantation** *($85-$95 bkfst incl.; pb; 2600 Gaylynn Dr.,* ☎ *888-8649)* is 20 minutes from the French Quarter. A Caribbean Creole plantation house built on the ruins of the Seven Oaks Plantation, it offers two rooms furnished with antiques and a very attractive living room with a fireplace and many Audubon paintings. A tour of the plantation is included in the rate and credit cards are accepted.

Slidell

KOA New Orleans East *($21; ≈; exit 263 from I-10, 7 km west of the intersection of hwys. I-10, I-12 and I-59, ☎ 643-3850)* is open-year round and offers 142 sites, showers, washrooms, laundry facilites, a playground, and a grocery store. Cottages are also available. Tours of New Orleans leave from the campground.

Salmen-Fritchie House *($75-$95, bkfst incl.; 127 Cleveland Ave., ☎ 643-1405)* is a restored 1895 manor house with five rooms furnished with antiques. It is surrounded by two hectares of giant trees: oaks, pecans, and magnolias.

Mandeville

Fontainebleau State Park *($12-$15; P.O. Box 152, Mandeville LA 70448, ☎ 624-4443)*, on Lake Pontchartrain, has 130 well-maintained sites, picnic areas, a playground, walking trails, and a sailboat launch.

Madisonville

Fairview-Riverside State Park *($12-$15; P.O. Box 856, Madisonville, ☎ 845-3318)*, on the picturesque

Tchefuncte River, has 82 landscaped campsites, picnic areas, playgrounds and washrooms. There are also more rustic campsites.

River Run *($55-$65 bkfst incl.; sb; 703 Main St.,* ☎ *845-4222)* is a welcoming establishment right on the Tchefuncte River, with three rooms and a common bathroom. Canoes and bicycles may be rented to explore the surrounding area.

Covington

Bell Plantation Guest House *($40-$50 bkfst incl.; pb; 204 24th Ave. West,* ☎ *893-7693)* is near the centre of town. This beautiful Victorian house has high ceilings and two elegantly decorated rooms.

Riverside Hills Farm Bed & Breakfast *($80 bkfst incl.; sb; 96 Gardenia Ave., Covington LA 70433,* ☎ *892-1794)* is a charming guardhouse (1903) on a beautiful five-hectare property with a pond. This peaceful spot offers guests three rooms, accommodating up to six people *($15 per additional person)* and a living room.

Folsom

Tchefuncte Campground *(Route 40, 8 km west of Folsom, near the Global Wildlife Center,* ☎ *796-3654)* has ten sites for recreational vehicles *($15)*; 100 tent sites with water and electricity *($13)*; and summary sites in an oak grove by the river *($11)*. There is a grocery store, fishing and a swimiming pool. This is a very beautiful spot for camping, with the clear water of the Tchefuncte River perfect for a refreshing swim. Native American powwows are held here.

Robert

Yogi Bear's Jellystone Park *($12-$15; exit 47 from I-12, 5 km north on LA 445,* ☎ *542-1507)* is open year-round. There are 302 sites and all of the amenities: electricity, showers, washrooms, laundry, playground, swimming pool, grocery store, fishing, boat rental, walking trails, and rollerblading paths.

Hammond

KOA New Orleans/Hammond *($21; ≈; exit 28 from I-55 South, 2855 Club De Luxe Rd.,* ☎ *542-8094)* offers 59 completely maintained campsites with showers, washrooms and a laundry. There is also a playground and a grocery store where you can rent a boat for fishing or exploring.

The **Pink Panther RV Park** *($21; ≈; exit 35 North from I-12, 5.5 km west of Hammond,* ☎ *1-800-735-3460)* is open year-round. Its 54 sites are specially laid out for recreational vehicles with showers, washrooms and a laundry. There is a playground adjoining the pool and there are also hiking trails. There is fishing boat and pedalboat rental. Guided tours of the area are offered.

Amite

Sweethall *($40-$50 bkfst incl.; pb; 313 Hickory St.,* ☎ *748-8612)* is a Cajun guesthouse, built in the 1940s, with an original guest room.

Elliot House *($50-$80 bkfst incl.; pb; 545 Duncan Ave. North,* ☎ *748-8553)* is a turn-of-the-century house with three-metre-high ceilings and a columned gallery. It sits on a two-hectare wooded lot in an older residential neighbourhood. The house has preserved most of its original furniture. There is a guest room with a private washroom and a two-room suite with a shared washroom. Credit cards are accepted.

The **Greenlawn** *($50-$85 bkfst incl.; pb; 200 Chestnut St. East, ☎ 748-8946 or 748-9062)* is a registered landmark building from the late 19th century. Its unique architecture includes superimposed verandas. The guesthouse counts three suites. Credit cards are accepted.

Blythewood Plantation *($70-$100 bkfst incl.; pb or sb, ctv; 300 Elm St., 345-6419 or 748-8183)* is also a registered landmark. It is a centenarian building with five guest rooms, two of them with private washrooms. Beautiful Victorian furniture decorates the house, which also has a confernece room. Dinner is prepared by reservation and credit cards are accepted.

There are other bed & breakfasts in the Amite region. For more information, or to make reservations, contact the **Amite Bed & Breakfast Association**, by mail, care of the Amite Chamber of Commerce, P.O. Box 383, Amite, LA 70422, or by telephone, Caroll Glasgow, ☎ 748-5537.

Kentwood

The **Great Discovery Campground** *($15-$20; ≈; exit 61 from I-55, another 4 km on LA 38, ☎ 229-7194)* is open year-round and has 48 sites equipped with electricity, toilets and showers. There is a playground, a swimming pool, picnic areas, and trails. The grocery store also rents out fishing equipment. It is

possible to go horseback riding in the area.

Westwego

On the west bank of the Mississippi, **Bayou Segnette State Park** *($15 and up; 7777 West Bank Expressway, ☎ 736-7140)* offers 100 campsites *($12)* and 20 cottages *($65; max. 6 people)*. There is also a huge wave pool, a playground, picnic areas and a boat launch. Barataria Bay is accessible via Bayou Segnette. Visa and MasterCard are accepted.

Delacroix

Delacroix Island *($45 per person bkfst incl.; pb; P.O. Box 133, Delacroix Island, LA 70085; ☎ 684-3866)* is at the End of the World Marina on Delacroix Island, 24 kilometres south of New Orleans. Accommodation consists of a one-room house on stilts, surrounded by Spanish-moss-covered trees. There is excellent fishing on Bayou Terre aux Boeufs. In addition to breakfast, sandwiches for fishing trips and supper are included in the rate.

Venice

The **Venice Marina** *($12-$15; on LA 23, ☎ 534-9357)* is a fully equipped marina with easy access to the river. There are eight campsites, five of which are fully serviced and three of which are equipped with water and electicity only. Fuel and ice are available, as are fishing guides and boats. For fising information call the 24-hour telephone service, ☎ 534-7701.

RESTAURANTS

Restaurants abound both in and around the French Quarter, serving Creole, French, African-American (soul food) or Cajun cuisines. New Orleans is a city to indulge (oneself) in where gourmets are sure to make all sorts of delectable discoveries. Unless otherwise indicated, all major credit cards are accepted in the following establishments.

The French Quarter and Faubourg Marigny

For the locations of these establishments, see map on p 108.

The world-famous **Café du Monde** *($; 24 hours a day; 800 Decatur St., French Market, ☎ 581-2914)*, located right in front of the French Market, near the riverfront promenade, has been around since 1860. Its chicory-flavoured *café au lait* (coffee with steamed milk) is served with tasty beignets. It is relatively inexpensive; you can eat here for as little as $5 at noon or in the evening. Good value for your money.

A small, rather plain restaurant, **Coops** *($; 1109 Decatur St., French Quarter, ☎ 525-9053)* serves good gumbo and delicious po'boys.

The **Croissant d'Or** pastry shop *($; every day 7am to 5pm; 615-617 Ursulines, French Quarter, ☎ 524-4663)* offers a lunch special that might include delicious green-pea soup with a ham and cheese sandwich, served with salad. It is best to avoid the microwave-oven-heated sandwiches. The coffee is mediocre, but the croissants and brioches

prepared by Maurice Delechelle are exceptional for New Orleans. Classic French pastries are also available here. The lovely interior courtyard with its fountain is the ideal place to eat when the temperature allows, but should be avoided on very humid days. Good value.

Acme Oyster House *($-$$; lunch $5 to $10/person; 724 Iberville St., French Quarter, ☎ 522-5973)*. Generations of New Orleanians have passed through this restaurant over the years. The establishment specializes in fresh fish and seafood; it is particularly renowned for oysters, shrimp and catfish. Accepted credit cards: Visa, American Express.

Café de la Madeleine *($-$$; every day, morning to night; 547 St. Ann St., French Quarter, ☎ 568-9950)* is close to what used to be Place d'Armes but is now Jackson Square. Both its ambiance and breakfast are French. This bistro and café, which is also a bakery, boasts wonderful bread, baked right on the premises, in a wood-burning oven. Expect to pay about $5 for breakfast.

Napoleon House *($-$$; Mon to Thu 11am to midnight, Fri and Sat 11am to 2am, Sun 11am to 7pm; 500 Chartres St., French Quarter, ☎ 524-9752)*. It is said that this residence, dating from 1791, had been reserved for the Emperor Napoleon, should he come to seek refuge in Louisiana. Having a cocktail in the charming back courtyard is a must. With classical music playing in the background, patrons can enjoy good sandwiches; a small, inexpensive menu *($5)* is also offered.

The café of the **Le Richelieu** hotel *($-$$; every day 7am to 9pm;*

Our Favourites

For their trendy side:
Emeril's (p 130), Palace Café (p 125), Peristyle (p 127), Mike's on the Avenue (p 130), and Straya (p 131).

For their warm ambiance:
Bacco (p 125), Bayona (p 124), Café Degas (p 133), Économie (p 129), Martinique Bistro (p 132), and Upperline (p 133).

For its balcony:
K-Paul's (p 126).

For their lovely interior courtyards:
Bayona (p 124), Bistro at the Hotel Maison De Ville (p 126), Café Volage (p 131), Broussard's (p 126), Brennan's (p 127), G & E Courtyard (p 126).

For their inviting decor:
Upperline (p 133) and Sapphire (p 130).

For their preppy side:
Brennan's (p 127), Antoine's (p 127), Commander's Palace (p 133), Galatoire's (p 126).

For their dinner concerts:
Bistro La Gauloise - Le Meridien (jazz) (p 129), Mulate's (Cajun music) (p 129) and Praline Connection #2 (gospel) (p 128).

For their romantic ambiance:
Bayona (p 124), Bella Luna (p 124), Arnaud's (p 127), Bistro de Ville (p 135) and Upperline (p 133).

For the best French cuisine:
Bistro de Ville (p 135).

For their service:
Christian's (p 134), Emeril's (p 130), G & E Courtyard (p 126), K-Paul's (p 126), Praline Connection (p 124) and Upperline (p 133).

For their healthy menu:
Bella Luna (p 124), Croissant d'Or (p 122), Kim Son (p 138), Mr. B's Bistro (p 124) and Mike's on the Avenue (p 130).

For its view of the Mississippi:
Bella Luna (p 124).

For their quintessential New Orleans surroundings:
Acme Oyster House (p 122), Café du Monde (p 122), Coops (p 122), Galatoire's (p 126), Mother's (p 128), Napoleon House (p 122) and Uglesich's (p 130).

For their breakfasts:
Le Richelieu (p 122) and Mother's (p 128).

GREATER NEW ORLEANS

*1234 Chartres St., French Quarter,
☎ 529-2492)* serves good breakfasts,
even at night. The mood on the terrace,
which faces a lovely interior courtyard
and its pool, is pleasant and fancy-free.
The bar crowd consists of local
regulars. Sandwiches and steaks are
featured on the menu. Everyone here is
very friendly, from the big boss Frank
S. Rochefort to the manager Joanne
Kirkpatrick, the barman Armand and
the waiter Michael (an ace at
breakfast), as well as Lester, the waiter
who takes over in the evening.

Praline Connection *($$; Sun to Thu
11am to 10:30pm, Fri and Sat 4pm to
midnight; 542 Frenchmen St. at
Chartres St., in the Faubourg Marigny,
☎ 943-3934)* features Creole specialties
and family fare typical of Southern
Louisiana. The Creole and African-
American (soul food) cuisines are
excellent, the ambiance is relaxed and
the bill is never high. Featured dishes
include gumbo, Creole-style stuffed
crab, stuffed peppers, crayfish étoufée,
grilled chicken, jambalaya, rice with
lima beans, bread pudding with praline
sauce and sweet-potato pie. The
restaurant also has a sweetshop where
clients can purchase cookies and the
most famous pecan pralines in all of
Louisiana (an old recipe whose origins
date back to the French Colonial era).

A very talented chef presides at
Bayona *($$-$$$; Mon to Fri 11:30am
to 1:30pm, Mon to Sat 6pm to
10:30pm; reservations required;
430 Dauphine St., French Quarter,
☎ 525-4455)*. Susan Spicer prepares
exquisite meat and fish dishes, inspired
by early fruits and vegetables, which
prove to be both successful and
flavourful. Patrons have the choice of
eating in the charming dining room or
the magnificently flowering interior

courtyard, all the while being lulled by
the gentle murmur of the fountain. On
the fixed-price dinner menu: rabbit
aiguillette in a pecan crust with a
mustard glaze; braised sea kale with
mustard; young rabbit and Portobello
mushroom cream soup; lemon sole with
spicy red beans and fresh coriander
pesto with avocado "salsa"; ginger-
rhubarb cake with custard, fresh
blackberries and crème fraîche.
Excellent California wines are offered
by the glass. Good value.

Bella Luna *($$-$$$; every day 6pm
to 10:30pm, until 9:30pm on Sun;
reservations recommended; 914 North
Peters St., French Quarter,
☎ 529-1583)* is located behind the
French Market. This fashionable
restaurant, with lovely table settings
and a well-trained staff, offers an
unobstructed view of the Mississippi.
Chef Horst Pleifer's cuisine reveals
Creole and European flavours. Savoured
dishes included shrimp soup garnished
with carrots julienne, mussels, roasted
garlic, fresh basil and dill; fresh peach,
strawberry and blackberry sorbet;
redfish in a cashew crust with *beurre
blanc* and blood orange; Tahitian vanilla
crème brulée with a banana biscuit and
chocolate ice cream. Good value.

Mr. B's Bistro *($$-$$$; every day,
lunch and dinner; 11:30am to 3pm and
5:30pm to 10:30pm, brunch on Sun
10:30am to 3pm; 201 Royal St.,
French Quarter, ☎ 523-2078)*. With its
marble tables scattered throughout a
large dining room and lunchtime
clientele of bureaucrats and business
people, this establishment is warmly
reminiscent of a Parisian bistro. Waiters
don the customary service uniform:
black vest, white shirt, bow tie and
long white apron. The concoctions of

Michelle McRaney, the talented chef whose menu changes with the season, are flavourful and aromatic and inspired by New Orleans' Creole and French culinary heritages. Savoured dishes included cream of crayfish and cauliflower soup; "jambalaya pasta" with fettucini and spinach, fresh tomatoes, Gulf shrimp, chitterlings (smoked sausage), duck, beef and chicken; bread pudding with whiskey sauce. The restaurant offers a few good Louisiana wines. Service is prompt and amiable. Live jazz is featured during brunch on Sundays.

Bacco *($$-$$$$; breakfast $5-$10, lunch $10-$15, dinner $15-$20; Mon to Sat 7am to 10am, 11:30am to 3pm and 5:30pm to 10:30pm, brunch on Sun 10:30am to 3pm; reservations recommended; 310 Chartres St., French Quarter, ☎ 522-CIAO or 522-2426)* is located right next to the Post Office. Gothic arches, Venetian chandeliers and Baroque-style murals are part of the eccentric and extravagant decor. The place is pleasant nonetheless; service is courteous and attentive toward a relaxed clientele of all ages. Here, Italian-inspired Creole cuisine is prepared, or is that Creole-inspired Italian cuisine? No matter what the definition, the presentation of the dishes is exquisite and you are sure to be pleased with the food. A few of their specialties include oyster and eggplant ravioli; crawfish pizza; pasta with wild mushrooms and herbs; "jambalaya" risotto; barbecued duck or lamb. The restaurant also offers valet parking. Languages spoken: Italian, Spanish and English. Good value.

The **Pelican Club** *($$-$$$$; every day from 5:30pm on; 312 Exchange Alley, ☎ 523-1504)* offers a fixed-price menu at $19.50 (a 17% tip is added for groups of eight or more) between 5:30pm and 6pm. The large bar and its round tables make it reminiscent of a private club in the Edwardian era. The menu features little crawfish and shrimp cakes; escargots and crawfish *à la duxelle* of mushrooms, with a tequila, garlic and butter sauce; smoked and roasted duck supreme with mushroom ravioli; fillet of fish in a pecan and coconut crust; vanilla and brandy *crème brulée*; orange and sour cream cheesecake.

Alex Patout's *($$$; every night 5:30pm to 10pm; 221 Royal St., French Quarter, ☎ 525-7788)* serves cuisine typical of Southern Louisiana, prepared with local ingredients. The menu features Louisiana-style won tons; shrimp in a remoulade sauce; seafood and smoked tasso (dried-meat) pasta; Cajun-style roast duck étoufée; suckling pig; sautéed crawfish; bread pudding and brownies. The soberly decorated 125-seat dining room is most welcoming. One unfortunate drawback is that groups making their way to the other dining rooms (which are spread out over three levels) have to pass behind your table. Service, however, is very amiable. Reservations are recommended. Parking is available. Good value.

Unless you want to wait in line, it's best to make reservations at the **Palace Café** *($$$; Mon to Sat 11:30am to 2:30pm, every day 5:30pm to 10pm; brunch on Sun 10:30am to 2:30pm; 605 Canal St., French Quarter, ☎ 523-1661)*. The service and decor are reminiscent of great Parisian cafés, and the cuisine is both Creole and French. On the menu: shrimp and pasta Provençale; shrimp barbecued in Abita beer (a good local beer); Maine lobster

GREATER NEW ORLEANS

or grilled fish; bread pudding with white chocolate.

Galatoire's *($$$-$$$$; Tue to Sat 11:30am to 9pm; Sun noon to 9pm; 209 Bourbon St., ☎ 525-2021).* The *ne plus ultra* of New Orleans cuisine, this restaurant is prized for its lunchtime fare. The establishment does not take reservations – first come, first served! To avoid the queue, show up after 1pm. Men are required to wear a tie at dinner.

G & E Courtyard *($$$-$$$$; Fri to Sun 11am to 2:30pm, Tue to Thu and Sun 6pm to 10pm, until 11pm Fri and Sat; 1113 Decatur St., French Quarter, ☎ 528-9376)* serves Italian food that is good though inconsistent from lunch to dinner; dishes here are invariably seasoned with vinegar – sometimes a bit too much. In any case, this does not seem to deter clients. Indeed, its interior courtyard is very popular, though only the lucky ones manage to snare a table there. Nevertheless, the air conditioned interior is charming and its two carriage gateways open out on the street, allowing patrons to observe the constant stream of motley tourists walking past. Lovely fresh artichokes are charmingly arranged on a shelf, but these merely serve as decoration and are nowhere to be found on the menu. The dishes are artfully presented and beautifully cooked. The menu features such dishes as Caesar salad with fried oysters; shrimp tempura with deep-fried straw potatoes; roasted pullet with rosemary; lamb sausages with tomato and basil pasta.

K-Paul's Louisiana Kitchen *($$$-$$$$; Mon to Fri 11:30am to 2:30pm and 5:30pm to 10pm, closed Sat and Sun; 416 Chartres St., French Quarter, ☎ 524-7394, reservations* 596-2530).This establishment owes its good reputation to the famous Cajun chef Paul Prudhomme. The restaurant is on two levels: the upstairs and balcony are for those with reservations; the ground floor looks more like a bistro. The kitchen is open and a double of Paul, only thinner but still well-padded, presides there. The menu is peppered with Cajun and Creole classics as well as original dishes, composed of early produce and fresh products from the market. Among dishes not to be missed are the traditional chicken and sausage gumbo, the famous blackened fish (the celebrated chef Prudhomme's creation) and the gorgeous sweet potato and pecan pie with Chantilly cream, laced with cognac and Grand Marnier.

The **Bistro at the Hotel Maison de Ville** *($$$$; Mon to Sat 11:30am to 2:30pm, Sun to Thu 6pm to 10pm, Fri and Sat 11am to 11pm; reservations required; Hotel Maison de Ville, 727 Toulouse St., French Quarter, ☎ 528-9206),* recreates a Parisian bistro atmosphere (very popular in New Orleans) and can accommodate 40 people in its dining room and 20 more on its pleasant flowered courtyard. Excellent wine list and tastings by the glass.

Broussard's *($$$$; every night 5:30pm to 10pm, brunch and jazz on Sun 10:30am to 2pm; 819 Conti St., French Quarter, ☎ 581-3866)* is a must with its very European cachet and lovely flowering courtyard set with tables. New owners have taken over. Among the treats are crab and shrimp cheesecake; Napoleon sea perch and Broussard veal. Reservations are required. Diners can be served in English, French, Spanish, German or Italian.

Antoine's *($$$$; approx. $50; Mon to Sat 11:30am to 2pm and 5:30pm to 9:30pm, closed Sun and public holidays; 713 St. Louis St., French Quarter, ☎ 581-4422)*. This restaurant, well-known on both national and international levels, has been around since 1840. Since Antoine Alciatore of Marseilles first opened it, the establishment has been run by five generations of his descendants. The famous Rockefeller oysters were first created in this very restaurant. The establishment has several reception rooms, and some can accommodate up to 700 people. The rather rustic decor features countless photographs of celebrities who have set foot here. The menu is made up of French and Creole classics (the menu is in French) and its dishes are well-prepared and particularly delicious. Service is very professional. The staff speaks French, Spanish and English.

Arnaud's *($$$$; approx. $50, not including wine, service and taxes; reservations recommended; parking at 912 Iberville St.; lunch Mon to Fri 11:30am to 2:30pm, dinner Sun to Thu 6pm to 10pm, Fri and Sat 6pm to 10:30pm, brunch on Sun 10am to 2:30pm, closed for lunch Sat; 813 Bienville St., French Quarter, ☎ 523-5433)* was founded by Arnaud Cazenave in 1918 and now belongs to the Casbarians. The Cazenaves enjoyed celebrating Mardi Gras, and from 1937 to 1968, Irma Cazenave never missed the festivities; she made her own dazzling costumes as well as those of her husband. She was queen of the Carnival on several occasions. Upstairs, a museum exhibits Dame Cazenave's fabulous collection. The Gulf of Mexico is teeming with fish, crustaceans and seafood and these fresh products are prepared in a variety of ways: Arnaud

shrimp, potted turtle, oysters Suzette, Bourgeois crawfish mousse, seafood court-bouillon, shrimp and eggplant casserole, *pompano* in a crust, alligator with hot sauce, Provençale frog's legs. Meat dishes include quail in red wine sauce, Rochambeau braised chicken, rack of lamb diablo, Caën-style tripe, and more. Cheeses, salads, classic desserts and Arnaud's *café brûlot* round off this dazzling menu. Service is impeccable.

Brennan's *($$$$; approx. $40, including wine, service and taxes; reservations required; every day brunch 8am to 2:30pm, Tue to Fri lunch 11:30am to 2:30pm and dinner 6pm to 10pm; 417 Royal St., French Quarter, ☎ 525-9711)* is renowned for its breakfasts and brunches. All the same, it is hardly a gourmet's paradise; their eggs Benedict are smothered by a mass of béchamel sauce, and their other preparations are as heavy as they are uninspired. It is very expensive and quite disappointing. The dining rooms do, however, give out on a magnificent and serene subtropical garden, with a fountain, banana trees, flowers and plants, that is best enjoyed with good friends. This place is a must when visiting New Orleans. Among the overpriced items offered for breakfast, brunch or dinner: oyster soup, Creole-style onion soup, eggs *sardou*, eggs *hussarde*, Rockefeller oysters, Chantecler fillet steak, grill-smoked red mullet, Cajun pepper chicken, Gulf shrimp chitterlings, chef Roussel's sautéed veal, lemon tartlets and bananas Foster.

The talented chef Anne Kearny officiates at **Peristyle** *($$$$; lunch Fri 11:30am to 2pm, dinner Tue to Thu 6pm to 10pm, until 11pm Fri and Sat; 1041 Dumaine St, French Quarter,*

☎ *593-9535)*. Her French-inspired cuisine has retained a distinctive New Orleans flavour, as demonstrated by the earthiness of the cream of mushroom soup, well-seasoned with pepper and chillies. The crab and horseradish salad is served on a bed of roasted beets with marinated red onions. The grilled puppy drum fillet, a Gulf of Mexico fish, is well-prepared and served on a bed of sticky rice with tomatoes and spinach, enhanced by a spoonful of pesto; a shrimp and saffron sauce surrounds this delightfully prepared dish. Among the fabulous desserts is the lemon pudding, spread over sponge cake and garnished with crystallized lemon rinds and blackcurrant jam. Good French and American wines. Service is rather aloof, however. An affluent and stylish clientele of all ages frequents this dining room, which makes itself out to be a bistro despite the austerity of the place; many come out of curiosity and some are confined to small spaces here and there.

Central Business District and Warehouse District

The following establishments are located on the map on p 116.

Red Bike Bakery & Café *($; Mon to Fri 11am to 3pm, Tue to Thu 6pm to 9:30pm, until 11pm Fri and Sat; 746 Tchoupitoulas St.,* ☎ *529-2553)* serves home-made bread as well as turkey or sausage gumbo soups, sandwiches and a few cooked meals such as fettucini with mushrooms, sesame chicken, and more.

Café Bon Ton *($-$$; 11am to 2pm and 5pm to 9:30pm; 401 Magazine St., at Natchez,* ☎ *524-3386)*. Since 1953, the Pierces have been preparing dishes here derived from family recipes: "Bon Ton" red snapper, crawfish étouffée, shrimp and oysters in every shape and form as well as wonderful bread pudding.

Mother's restaurant *($-$$; Mon to Sat 5am to 10pm, Sun 7am to 10pm; 401 Poydras St.,* ☎ *523-9656)* is close to Riverwalk. Traditional New Orleans cuisine is prepared here. Mother's is the best restaurant in the world for smoked ham. The establishment offers a wide choice of po'boys, with ham, of course, but also with roast beef, crawfish, oysters or chicken. The standard American breakfast is served at all times. Cafeteria-style setting.

Bolstered by the success of their enterprise in the Faubourg Marigny, Curtis Moore and Cecil Kaigler, have opened **Praline Connection #2** *($-$$; every day 11am to 10pm; 901 and 907 South Peters St., between St. Joseph and North Diamond,* ☎ *523-3973)* in a huge space, in a soulless neighbourhood where renovation efforts are being carried out. In addition to the restaurant, a stage is set up for jazz, R&B and gospel groups (see "Entertainment", p 143). The trademark black and white room is surrounded by a backdrop of façades of Creole houses. The food is the same as on Frenchmen Street, but not as tasty, that is heavy and mostly deep-fried family fare. On the menu: head cheese, battered with deep-fried soft-shell crab; peppers stuffed with sausage and shrimp; meat loaf; barbecued pork chops (huge and overcooked on this occasion) with hot sauce; fried chicken in brown sauce. Everything is well-seasoned with chillies. The restaurant also serves deep-fried alligator... The bread pudding with praline sauce is not to be missed.

Bizou *($-$$$; lunch and dinner, except Mon; 701 St. Charles Ave., ☎ 524-4114)* was opened by Daniel Bonnot, former chef-owner of the Chez Daniel restaurant, now the Bistro de Ville, in Metairie. In this bistro, the cooks transform the classics in their own way, but not always with success. The vichyssoise was nothing more than a purée of cream and green onions, the spring roll (sushi) was bland and the garnishes usually found in Niçoise salad were conspicuously missing. For lunch, it is perhaps best to have one of their delicious sandwiches, as the regulars do. On the afternoon of our visit, the waiter was neither eager nor friendly.

The decor at **Bistro Allegro** *($$; every day 11:30am to 2:30pm; 1100 Poydras St., room 101, ☎ 582-2350)* is Art Deco. As it is right downtown, business people crowd in at lunch time. Here, Creole cooking is influenced by Italian cuisine and the fusion of the two, it is said, is utterly harmonious. Free parking. The staff speaks French, Spanish, Italian and English.

Mulate's *($$; every day 11am to 11pm, Mon to Fri lunch Cajun buffet; 201 Julia St., ☎ 522-1492)* is situated in the Warehouse District, across from the convention centre. This restaurant is very popular with tourists. Unfortunately, the cuisine is not what it used to be, but the music is authentic and the performers are genuine Cajun musicians and singers from Lafayette, Abbéville, St. Martinville, Eunice or New Iberia. The ambiance is terrific. Reservations are recommended.

Bistro La Gauloise *($$-$$$; breakfast $5-$15, lunch $10-$20 and dinner $15-$30; every day 6:30am to 10pm; Le Meridien, 614 Canal St., ☎ 527-6712)*, the famous bistro in the Meridien hotel, faces bustling Canal Street, across from the French Quarter. The ambiance is warm and relaxed. À la carte dishes, a daily menu and a buffet are offered, providing something for everyone. On the menu: crawfish gumbo; shrimp Provençale; "vetiver" lamb (in a cabbage leaf); seafood pennine with olive oil and basil; grilled veal chop seasoned with tarragon, served with spinach gnocchi; bread pudding; Creole-style cheesecake. The place is renowned for its Sunday brunch, livened by a jazz band *(10:30am to 2:30pm, valet parking at 609 Common Street)*.

Those who do not know their way around the neighbourhood may have trouble locating the entrance to the **Économie** restaurant *($$-$$$; Tue to Fri 11:30am to 2pm and 5pm to 10pm, until 11pm Fri and Sat; 325 Girod St., at Commerce St., ☎ 524-7405)*. The restaurant is set in buildings that once flourished as warehouses and factories. Despite the neighbourhood's monotony, the inside reveals an amazing ambiance and Mexican colours adorn the walls on which lovely paintings by contemporary artists hang; in short, it is attractive, vital and fresh. The chef-proprietor Keith Mallini – whose father and mother are Italian and Japanese, respectively – demonstrates perfect skill in the kitchen. What a treat to find a genuine and delicious vegetable soup, a Caesar salad made with spinach and enhanced with a perfect dressing. The menu offers several choices: salmon, crawfish, chicken, guinea fowl and pork. They also serve an excellent New York strip steak, nice and rare if you so desire, with a true cream, pepper and cognac sauce; this tasty cut of meat comes with fried scalloped potatoes and sautéed snowpeas. The *crème brulée* and the gargantuan chocolate truffle cake with custard are equally divine. All this and more can be enjoyed at marble-topped tables. Good value.

Sapphire *($$-$$$$; lunch $7-$12, dinner $14-$30; 228 Camp St., ☎ 571-7500).* Good things are being said about this newcomer; though it has yet to prove itself. Poached oysters in hollandaise sauce, Peking duck and rack of lamb are a few selections from its menu. The restaurant was designed by Mario Villa, a New Orleans artist.

Mike's on the Avenue *($$$$, lunch $$-$$$; Mon to Fri 11:30am to 2pm, every day 6pm to 10pm; 628 St. Charles Ave., Lafayette Hotel, ☎ 523-1709)* is run by the very esteemed and very popular chef Mike Fennelly along with Vicky Bayley. The dining room is decorated with watercolour paintings by the chef himself, who also holds a degree in architecture. The restaurant is on the hotel's ground floor and its dining room opens out on Lafayette Square and Gallier Hall. The clientele mainly consists of business people. The food here is a blend of Californian, Mexican, Japanese and Louisianian cuisines. This fusion is rather successful, as demonstrated by the delicious rice rectangles (sushi) stacked like sandwiches with nori seaweed, blackened tuna, a remoulade of crawfish and smoked salmon; the grilled tomato tortilla soup appears as a delectable creamed, peppered and spiced purée with a faintly smoky flavour; strips of trout tempura are served with pecan rice and a purée of green onions that is somewhat bland but impressively presented; for dessert, there is the traditional New Orleans bread pudding served in a pie crust, covered in raisins and chocolate sauce (a real treat!) and *crème brulée* made

with real cream. The bread is home-made. It is less expensive at lunch. Apparently, Mike Fennelly is about to open a restaurant in California: let us just hope this won't affect the St. Charles Avenue establishment.

Emeril's *($$$-$$$$; lunch $10-$15, dinner $15-$20; Mon to Fri 11:30am to 2pm, Mon to Sat 6pm to 10pm; reservations required; 800 Tchoupitoulas St., ☎ 528-9393).* Housed in an old warehouse, the restaurant is currently enjoying great popularity and people come here from all across the United States. Groups of stylish patrons gather around large tables; jeans, casual jackets and other unconventional attire are prohibited. Creole and American *nouvelle cuisine* are featured here. Service is warm and friendly and most of the waiters are Latino. Real gourmets, however, will find the flashy cuisine disappointing. The staff speaks Spanish, French, German and English.

Uptown

Piccadilly Cafeteria *($-$$; every day 11am to 8:30pm; 3800 South Carrollton Ave., ☎ 482-0776).* There are several Piccadillys in Louisiana. Many daily specials are offered here, with something for everyone. No credit cards accepted.

Uglesich's *($-$$; Mon to Fri 9:30am to 4pm; 1238 Barron St., ☎ 523-8571).* Small places that are little known to tourists – their neighbourhoods being somewhat disreputable – often have pleasant surprises in store for visitors. Large onion and potato sacks are piled up between the tables in this café, with its concrete floors and look of an old neighbourhood grocer's shop. For lunch, patrons come and eat shrimp or oyster po'boys at the counter. A mixed clientele of business people, blue-collar workers and students crowd the dining room to savour gumbo enhanced by brown roux, spicy crawfish bisque, fresh oysters in their half shells from the Gulf of Mexico or a soft-shell crab sandwich. Between orders, the amiable Karin peels and cuts up the potatoes, the major ingredient of some of the best fries in town. No credit cards accepted. Good value.

After having travelled around the world, Felix Gallerani finally settled in New Orleans. For the last few years, the affable host has been the heart and soul of **Café Volage** *($-$$$; Sun brunch $12.95; every day 11am to 3pm and 4pm to 10pm; 720 Dublin St., Riverbend district, one street west of Carrollton, ☎ 861-4227)*. He has built a lovely terrace behind the little "shotgun" house, classified as a historic monument. The place, however, is a bit run down and could certainly use a thorough cleaning. A small menu offers Italian, French and Creole specialties. Among these are onion or gumbo soup; seafood fettucini in wine and cream sauce; veal scallopini Marsala; steak and fries (the fries are home-made); chocolate mousse or *crème brulée*. The host, holding court at a table like a prince upon his throne, welcomes patrons with a huge Havana cigar in the corner of his mouth!

Pizzas, pasta, and a terrace beneath the trees, that is what you'll find at **Figaro's Pizzeria** *($$; Mon and Tue 11:30am to 10:30pm, until 11:30pm Fri and Sat, noon to 10pm Sun; 7900 Maple St., two streets north of* St. Charles Ave., just after Audubon Park, ☎ 866-0100). The restaurant makes Neapolitan-style pizza with garlic butter and Mozzarella cheese, and a choice of toppings such as shrimp, smoked salmon, spinach, feta cheese, etc. Standard American pizza garnished with tomato sauce, pepperoni, green peppers, onions and mushrooms is also served as are a few pasta dishes. For dessert: New York cheesecake, fudge pie, brownies and peanut-butter pie.

Eating at **Straya** *($$; Sun to Thu 11am to midnight, until 2am Fri and Sat; 2001 St. Charles Ave., ☎ 593-9955; 4517 Veterans Boulevard, Metairie, ☎ 887-8873)* is somewhat like dining in a discotheque. Star-studded black tables and gaudily-coloured couches are dispersed throughout a vast space, dotted with Hollywood-esque gilded banana trees. In this galactic universe, the star theme dominates all accessories. The current trend for fusion cuisine is apparent here, with a selection of Creole, Eurasian, Cajun and Californian cuisines to which are added Italian and Japanese touches. Servings are huge. A few specialties include nori seaweed California rolls; sushi made of rice, crab and avocado with horseradish and ginger; crispy pizza topped with cheese; fillet of trout in an almond crust; barbecued shrimp fettucine; roasted chicken; tiramisu crepe; bread pudding laced with white chocolate and apple pizza with Amaretto cream. Patrons are warmly greeted and service is as sparkling as the decor. Good Californian wines served by the glass.

At the very popular bistro-creperie **La Crepe Nanou** *($$-$$$; every day 6pm to 10pm, until 11pm Fri and Sat; 1410 Robert St., between Magazine and St. Charles, ☎ 899-2670)*, the menu is in French (it features the classic *escargots de Bourgogne*). Specialties include whole grilled fish; *moules marinière* (mussels cooked in white wine); onion soup; Greek chicken and rice soup; leg of lamb and veal scallopini. There are also crepes, of course: with crab and spinach; ratatouille; cheese and onion; crawfish; beef bourguignon and about fifteen different dessert crepes.

Kelsey's *($$-$$$; Tue to Fri 11:30am to 2pm, Fri and Sat 5:30pm to 10pm; 3923 Magazine St., ☎ 897-6722)* with its warm French-café ambiance is set in a very quaint neighbourhood full of charming boutiques. Randy Barlow's fusion cuisine draws its inspiration as much from Cajun and Creole schools as it does from other cuisines world-wide. Perusing his menu is tantamount to a culinary tour of the world, as the following savoured dishes attest to: cream of artichoke hearts and mushroom soup; chicken and chitterlings gumbo; tomatoes and *provolone* cheese on a bed of lettuce and red onions, with a mustard vinaigrette; oyster, Brie and herb tartlet; crawfish fritters with honey and Meaux mustard sauce; stuffed breast of smoked duck; soft-shell crab stuffed with seafood and green mayonnaise; chocolate nut cake and lemon pie.

Kyoto *($$-$$$; lunch Mon to Fri 11:30am to 2:30pm, Sat noon to 3:30pm, dinner Mon to Thu 5pm to 10pm, until 10:30pm Fri and Sat; 4920 Prytania St., ☎ 891-3644)* is currently the most popular sushi place in town; what matters here is the freshness of the ingredients. Besides the rolls, there are shrimp tempura; *miso*, noodle, shrimp and vegetable soups; as well as chicken or beef teriyaki and sashimi.

The affable Hubert Sandot of the **Martinique Bistro** *($$-$$$; fixed-price menu $23.50; every day 5:30pm to 9:30pm; 5908 Magazine St., ☎ 891-8495)* is quite loquacious, and a real charmer who enjoys chatting with the customers. He prepares a few classic French dishes and improvises with a range of Italian, Caribbean or Indian dishes, depending on deliveries. The menu features such items as leek and carrot soup; eggplant with goat cheese; endives with nuts, apples and blue cheese; steamed mussels cooked in white wine and herbs; sautéed shrimp with dried mangoes and curry as well as Provençale braised leg of lamb. This warm and friendly little restaurant remains a place worth visiting in New Orleans. Good value.

One of New Orleanians' great favourites remains **Brigtsen's** *($$$$; Tue to Sat 5:30pm to 10pm; 723 Dante St., at Leake Ave., Riverbend District, ☎ 861-7610)*, comfortably nestled in a lovely cottage in the residential district of Riverbend. Its chef, Frank Brigtsen, prepares innovative food inspired by Cajun and Creole cooking that is the delight of gourmets; it is best to make reservations. The menu features tomato, crouton and blue cheese salad with avocado vinaigrette; rabbit and sausage gumbo; "Bienville" oyster gratin; zucchini flowers stuffed with ricotta, crawfish and mushrooms, flavoured with basil oil; grilled fish, crispy crab with Parmesan and lemon purée; blackened tuna with smoked corn sauce; sautéed veal and crawfish with mushrooms, topped with Parmesan sauce; bread and banana pudding with rum sauce; pecan pie with caramel sauce; champagne zabaglione with fruit and a hint of crème fraîche.

At the **Upperline** restaurant *($$$-$$$$; Wed to Sun 5:30pm to 9:30pm, brunch on Sun 11:30am to 2pm from $13.50 to $22.50; 1413 Upperline St., near Magazine St., ☎ 891-9822)*, JoAnn Clevenger, the owner, is only too happy to take the time to chat with customers; she likes to share and it is with this enthusiastic spirit of generosity that diners are invited to her table. The place is positively dazzling and adorned with paintings by Martin LaBorde (see p 150). The beautiful bouquets on each of the tables come from the small flower garden surrounding the house. Chef Richard Benz's cuisine is particularly flavourful; there are two gumbos: seafood and okra gumbo or the more intense duck and chitterlings gumbo, enhanced by a spicy roux. The restaurant's fine hors d'oeuvres include fried green tomatoes with shrimp remoulade and fried veal sweetbreads on crisp corn polenta, served on a bed of mushrooms with *demi-glace* sauce. Main courses include grilled Gulf fish with warm Niçoise salad, tapenade and basil lemon-butter; braised lamb in wine, with saffron risotto and *gremolata*; port and garlic crispy duck. A couple of tasty desserts: *tarte Tatin* with apple sorbet and chocolate truffle cake.

Commander's Palace *($$$$; $40-$50; Tue to Fri 11:30am to 2pm, Sat 11am to 2pm, Sun 10am to 2pm, every night 6pm to 10pm; 1403 Washington Ave., ☎ 899-8221)*, situated in the historic Garden District, enjoys an excellent reputation with New Orleanians. Without being jingoistic, some even classify it as the best restaurant in the country – and they truly believe it. The establishment offers classic Creole cuisine, and its chef occasionally tries his hand at unexpected concoctions. The restaurant's Victorian style is very appealing. The dining rooms can accommodate up to 100 guests; other lovely little private rooms are ideal for smaller, more intimate gatherings.

Mid-City

Café Degas *($-$$; lunch and dinner $5-$10; every day 10:30am to 2:30pm and 5:30pm to 10:30pm, brunch Sat and Sun; 3127 Esplanade Ave., ☎ 945-5635)*. This friendly little place, on elegant Esplanade Avenue, bears the name of the celebrated French painter, engraver and sculptor Edgar Degas, whose brothers, who still signed their name de Gas, endeavoured to make their fortune here. This restaurant's honest prices make it ideal for those on limited budgets. Specialties include shrimp and couscous salad with mustard vinaigrette; smoked trout with garlic mayonnaise; veal sweetbreads *à la grenobloise*; a variety of omelettes; rack of lamb; sirloin steak with shallots; key-lime pie and chocolate and peanut butter pie. Good value.

Some restaurants don't look like much and **Lola's** *($-$$; every day 6pm to 10pm; 3312 Esplanade Ave., facing Gabrielle's, ☎ 488-6946)* certainly falls into this category. Though it's run down and its few rows of tables lack decor, it does offer a wide range of specialties such as garlic soup; grilled squid; beef, vegetarian or Valencia-style paella; grilled tuna; spinach linguine; *caldereta* (lamb stew with tomatoes, wine and peppers) and caramel cream with nougat icing.

Gabrielle's *($$-$$$; fixed-price lunch menu $16.95; Fri 11:30am to 2pm, Tue to Sat 5:30pm to 10pm; 3201 Esplanade Ave., ☎ 948-6233)* stands apart from other establishments and, with its modern cuisine, attracts numerous devoted patrons. Taking magnificent Esplanade Avenue to get there is a truly enchanting experience. The menu features fillet of rabbit wrapped in prosciutto, in a mustard sweet and sour sauce; crawfish *enchilada* with cheese; blackened ribeye steak with crispy bacon and *shitake* étouffée with grilled red pepper and horseradish sauce; grilled red snapper with roasted garlic and crab meunière; pork chop with a Root beer, pear and caramelized onions glaze; upside down apple pudding with vanilla sauce; and home-made ice cream.

Christian's *($$-$$$$; Tue to Fri 11:30am to 2pm, Tue to Sat 5:30pm to 10pm; reservations recommended; 3835 Iberville St., ☎ 482-4924)*. Christian Ansel and Henry Bergeron could not have found a more noble location than the old Lutheran church, built in 1914, in which to relocate their restaurant, previously in Metairie. The welcoming building retains its stained-glass windows as well as the original woodwork, and offers delicious Creole and French cuisine. Savoured dishes included "Roland" oysters with garlic and mushrooms; okra gumbo; onion soup with Parmesan and croutons; swordfish with artichokes and mushrooms sautéed in black butter; angel hair pasta with shrimp, crawfish and artichoke hearts, in a tomato-flavoured cream and butter sauce; as well as chocolate profiteroles. Service is very warm and attentive. Take care, the man at the table next to you could be the owner's son, listening in on your comments! Good value.

Around New Orleans

Metairie

Coffee Rani *($; every day 11am to 8pm; 2324 Veterans Memorial Hwy., between Bonnabel and Causeway Blvds., ☎ 833-6343)* offers light, healthy meals, consisting of salads and of a variety of original, hearty sandwiches.

The Lebanese restaurant **Byblos** *($$; Mon to Sat 5:30pm to 9:30pm; 1501 Metairie Rd., ☎ 834-9773)* offers authentic dishes, such as traditional chick-pea puree (*hommos*), eggplant puree (*baba ghanouj*), stuffed grape leaves, brochettes (*kebab*) served with rice, and, for dessert, delicious *Mihallabiïa* (Lebanese blancmange).

Buster's New Orleans Kitchen *($$; lunch, Mon to Fri 11am to 2:30pm; dinner, Mon to Thu 5pm to 9pm, Fri and Sat 5pm to 10pm; 3044 Ridgelake Drive, ☎ 836-2881)* has a traditional atmosphere created by original woodwork and photographs hung on the walls. Creole and Cajun cuisines are prepared.

Sid-Mar's Restaurant *($$; Tue to Sun 11am to 10:30pm; 1824 Orpheum St., ☎ 831-9541)* is set in a fishing village just minutes from the big city. It has a screened-in porch that faces Lake Pontchartrain. Regional cuisine and seafood, either boiled or prepared in a court-bouillon, are served.

Straya *($$; Sun to Thu 11am to midnight, until 2am Fri and Sat; 2001 St. Charles Ave., ☎ 593-9955; 4517 Veterans Boulevard, Metairie, ☎ 887-8873)*. See p 131.

🦐 **Bistro de Ville** *($$-$$$; Tue to Sat 5pm to 9pm, French guitar player Fri and Sat; 2037 Metairie Rd, Exit 229-Bonnabel off Highway 1-10 heading south, ☎ 837-6900)* is a small restaurant that seats 70 and looks like a Parisian bistro. This used to be the restaurant Chez Daniel. The new owner is Daniel's former sous-chef and she offers Creole cuisine imbued with French and Mediterranean flavours. One dining room wall depicts a country dinner scene inspired by French impressionists. The restaurant is situated in Metairie, 15 minutes from downtown New Orleans.

Charley G's Seafood Grill *($$$; Sun to Fri 11:30am to 2:30pm and 5pm to 9:30pm, Sat 5pm to 10pm; Heritage Plaza, 111 Veterans Memorial Hwy., ☎ 837-6408)* is on the ground floor of an office building. The contemporary, multi-level decor lends it a comfortable, inviting atmosphere. New Orleans classics, such as duck gumbo, crabcakes and grilled fish, becoming more and more difficult to find in Louisiana, fill the menu. The Sunday jazz brunches here are renowned.

Ruth's Chris Steak House *($$$$; every day 11:30am to 10pm; 3633 Veterans Memorial Hwy., at the corner of Causeway Blvd., ☎ 888-3600)* is a New Orleans institution. Gigantic portions of meat are charcoal grilled and covered in seasoned butter or Bordelaise sauce. These are accompanied by French fries, or potatoes au gratin, and salad.

Kenner

Andy Messina's *($$; Mon to Sat 11am to midnight, Sun noon to 10pm; 2717 Williams Blvd., ☎ 469-7374)* has been serving Creole, Cajun and Italian cuisine

seafood dishes, at affordable prices, for three generations of Messinas now.

Southshore Seafood Restaurant *($$; Mon to Thu 11am to 2pm and 5pm to 10pm, Fri and Sat 11am to 10pm; 2000 West Esplanade Ave., ☎ 467-2735)*, on the south shore of Lake Pontchartrain, is famous for the freshness of the seafood it serves grilled and boiled.

Slidell

Honey Island Restaurant *($-$$; every day 5am to 10pm; 55154 Route US 90, ☎ 649-4807)* serves Cajun specialties for breakfast, lunch and diner. It is also possible to go on a swamp tour from the restaurant; tours leave at 9am, 11:30am and 2pm.

The **Piccadilly Cafeteria** *($-$$; every day 11am to 8:30pm; 104 Route US 190 West, ☎ 646-0566)* is part of a chain of establishments that propose a multitude of regional dishes. Credit cards are not accepted.

The **Boiling Point** *($$; Mon, Tue and Thu to Sat 11am to 10pm, Sun 11am to 9pm; 2998 Pontchartrain Drive, ☎ 641-5551)* is a neighbourhood restaurant that serves boiled and fried seafood and po-boys.

Vera's Restaurant *($$; Wed, Thu, and Sun 11am to 9pm, Fri and Sat 11am to 10pm; 337 Lake View Drive, ☎ 643-9291)* is one of the oldest seafood restaurants in Slidell with a splendid view of Lake Pontchartrain.

GREATER NEW ORLEANS

Lacombe

Sal & Judy's *($$-$$$; Tue to Sun 11:30am to 9:30pm; route US 190, ☎ 882-9443)* offers generous portions of seafood prepared Italian style. This restaurant is very popular, so it is best to make reservations.

La Provence *($$$$; Tue to Sun 5pm to 9pm; 25020 Route US 190, ☎ 626-7662)* is renowned as one of the best French restaurants in the region. It is much frequented by New Orleanians who make the hour-or-so-long trip for the divine lamb.

Mandeville

Coffee Rani *($; every day 8am to 6pm; 3510 Route US 190, at the intersection of LA 22, ☎ 674-0560)* offers light healthy meals, consisting of salads and of a variety of original, hearty sandwiches.

Roy's Diner *($; Mon to Fri 6am to 3pm, Sat and every 2nd Sun of the month 7am to noon; 23245 Kilgore St., ☎ 892-2667)* offers home cooking including a traditional Louisiana family breakfast.

Figaro's Pizzeria *($$; Mon and Tue 11:30am ot 10:30pm, until 11:30pm Fri and Sat, Sun noon to 10pm; 2820 Causeway Blvd., at the intersection of Route US 190, ☎ 624-8500)*. See p 131.

On the shore of Lake Pontchartrain, **Bechac's** *($$-$$$; Mon to Sat 11:30am to 3pm and 5pm to 9:30pm except Tue, Sun noon to 8pm; 2025 Lakeshore Dr., ☎ 626-8500)* proposes New Orleans Creole dishes in a turn-of-the-century house with period decor. The balcony overlooking the lake is the perfect spot for Sunday brunch.

Benedict's Restaurant *($$-$$$; Tue to Fri 11:30am to 2:30pm and 4:30pm to 9:30pm, Sat 4:30 pm to 9:30pm, Sun buffet 11:30am to 3:30pm; 1144 Lovers Lane, ☎ 624-5070)* is a beautiful plantation house that offers traditional Creole cuisine as well as seafood and steak.

Camelia Beach House Restaurant *($$-$$$; 2025 Lakeshore Dr., ☎ 626-8500)* is in a Caribbean-style two-story cottage (1834). Steak, seafood, lamb, partridge and pasta are prepared. The balcony overlooks Lake Pontchartrain.

Trey Yuen *($$-$$$; every day 5pm to 10pm; 600 North Causeway Blvd., ☎ 626-4476)* is an innovative Chinese restaurant that has become quite popular. The vegetable, seafood and meat dishes are very refined. As well, the restaurant is located right by the causeway to New Orleans.

Madisonville

Friends on the Tchefucte *($; 213 Madison St. North, ☎ 845-5301)* is a reasonably priced establishment that serves copious portions of grilled fish, crab with almonds, and, wonder of wonders, a cake made with five kinds of chocolate called Death by Chocolate!

Friends on the Tchefucte *($$; Tue to Thu and Sun 11am to 9pm, Fri and Sat until 10pm; 407 St. Tammany St., ☎ 845-7303)*, Madisonville's second restaurant with this name, is admirably situated on the Tchefuncte River and can be reached by boat or by road.

Boiled seafood in season, steak and daily specials are savoured indoors or on the dock.

Morton's Seafood *($$; Mon to Fri 11am to 9pm, Sat and Sun 11am to 10pm; 702 Water St., ☎ 845-4970)* has a view of the river and serves fried and boiled seafood as well as fresh oysters on the half shell.

Covington

Coffee Rani *($; every day 8am to 5:30pm; in the Kumquat Library, 226 Lee Lane, ☎ 893-6158)* is perfect for a meal on the go: soups, sandwiches, salads, seafood dishes, pasta and French pastries. This friendly café exhibits the work of local artists.

Courthouse Café *($; Mon to Fri 6am to 3:30 pm, Sat 7am to noon; 323 New Hampshire St. North, ☎ 893-4041)* is located, as its name indicates, near the courthouse. It is not unusual to see judges, lawyers and local notables here. The ambiance is relaxed and the kitchen prepares good breakfasts as well as daily specials, po-boys, and hamburgers.

Tyler Downtown Drugs Soda Fountain & Café Cabaret *($; Mon to Fri 8:30am to 6:30pm, Sat 9am to 5pm; 322 Florida St. North, ☎ 892-7220)* is an old-fashioned drugstore counter where patrons quench their thirsts with milkshakes.

Schwing's Seafood Gallery *($-$$; Mon to Thu 11am to 9pm, Fri and Sat to 11pm; 1204 21st St. West, ☎ 892-3287)* is a neighbourhood restaurant that serves steak, seafood, barbecued pork ribs and a great variety of po-boys.

Licata's Restaurant and Seafood Market *($$; Tue to Fri 11am to 10pm, Sat and Sun 11am to 11pm; 1102 Route US 190 North, ☎ 893-1252)* serves boiled and fried seafood and Italian dishes in a family atmosphere. The gumbo and the crawfish *étouffée* have made this spot famous. Adjoining the restaurant is a seafood market.

Gauthier's Market Café *($$$; Tue to Fri 11:30am to 2pm, Tue to Thu 5pm to 9pm, Fri and Sat to 10pm, Sun brunch 10:30am to 2pm; The Market, 500 Theard St. North, ☎ 867-9911)* is worth a side trip from New Orleans, but seating is limited and it is not unusual to have to wait for a table. The cuisine is *"nouveau"* New Orleanian, strongly influenced by French and Italian currents. There is a Sunday jazz brunch.

Bush

Grey Barn Antiques & Tea Room *($-$$; Wed to Sat 11am to 3pm, Sun 11:30am to 3pm; 81590 Route LA 21, 21 km from Bogalusa, ☎ 886-3271)* sells and displays antiques and serves traditional fare, sandwiches and desserts.

Hammond

Coffee Rani *($; every day 8am to 6pm; 112 Thomas St. West, ☎ 345-1203)* offers light healthy meals, consisting of salads and of a variety of original, hearty sandwiches.

The **Morrison Cafeteria** *($-$$; Mon to Sat 11am to 8pm, Sun 11am to 6:30pm; 2000 Railroad Ave. Southwest, ☎ 542-0588)* has a variety

GREATER
NEW ORLEANS

of daily specials. Credit cards are not accepted.

The **Iron Skillet** *($-$$; 24 hours a day; 2100 Railroad Ave. Southwest, ☎ 345-6741)* is the intersection of highways I-12 and US 51. It has a rustic decor, an all-you-can-eat buffet, and it serves breakfast, sandwiches, Louisiana barbecue, steak and daily specials.

Trey Yuen *($$-$$$; every day 5pm to 10pm; 2100 Morrison Blvd. North, ☎ 345-6789)* is an innovative Chinese restaurant that has become quite popular for its vegetable and seafood dishes.

Pontchatoula

Paul's Old Town Café *($; every day 4am to 4pm; 100 Pine St. East, ☎ 386-9581)* serves country-style breakfasts and lunches and accepts credit cards.

Manchac

Middendorf's *($$; Mon to Sat 10:30am to 9:30pm, Sun 10:30am to 9pm; exit 15 from I-55 North, ☎ 386-6666)*, on Lake Maurepas, has been run by the same owners for 55 years. The eternal specialties are as well loved today as ever: fried fillet of catfish, fried soft-shell crab, and boiled or court-bouillon crab.

Amite

Cabby's Restaurant-Tavern *($-$$; Mon to Sat 11am to 10pm, Sun 11am to 2pm; 225 Central Ave. Northwest,* ☎ 748-9731)* has a country decor and a patio on which diners savour steaks, seafood and sandwiches. From Sunday to Friday there is a buffet.

Gretna

Gretna is less than a half hour from downtown New Orleans. Visitors can get there by taking the Greater New Orleans Bridge, which links the two cities. **Kim Son** *($-$$; Mon to Sat 11am to 3pm and 5pm to 10pm; 349 Whitney Ave., first exit off West Bank Expressway after the bridge, keeping to the right, second light on the left, behind the Oakwood Shopping Center, ☎ 366-2489)*, a delicious Vietnamese and Chinese restaurant, is worth the trip. For those who love this type of cuisine, this is unquestionably one of the best Asian restaurants in or around New Orleans. Savoury spring rolls, complemented with coriander when there is no fresh mint, are prepared here. The seafood soup as well as the vegetable and soya soup are tasty, the chicken strips sautéed with citronella and broccoli are delectable, and the Singapore noodles are judiciously seasoned with curry. The staff here speaks Vietnamese, Chinese and English. Good value.

Cannon's Restaurant *($$; Mon to Thu 11am to 10pm, Fri and Sat 11am to 11pm, Sun noon to 9pm; 19717 West Bank Expressway, Oakwood Shopping Center, ☎ 364-1047)* is the site of the invention of Cajun popcorn salad. Also on the menu are steaks, seafood, hamburgers, chicken dishes, pasta and various salads.

La Pointe Restaurant *($$$; Mon to Thu 11:30am to 2:30pm and 5pm to 10pm, Fri and Sat 11:30am to 2:30pm and*

5pm to 11pm, Sun brunch 10am to 3pm, supper 4:30pm to 10pm; *2 Bermuda Wharf St.,* ☎ *362-2981)* serves regional American cuisine: seafood, chicken, pasta. Reservations are recommended.

Westwego

Tchoupitoulas Plantation Restaurant *($$-$$$; breakfast Mon to Fri 11:30am to 3pm, supper Thu to Sat 5:50pm to 9pm, Sun 11:30am to 5pm; 6535 River Road, Waggaman,* ☎ *436-1277)* is established in a plantation house that dates back to 1812 and serves Creole cuisine: veal, duck, crab, shrimp and steak.

Chalmette

The **Piccadilly Cafeteria** *($-$$; every day 11am to 8:30pm, closed Christmas; 3200 Paris Rd.,* ☎ *271-6860)* in Chalmette, like all of the establishments of this chain, offers an excellent selection of local dishes and a great variety of salads. Credit cards are not accepted.

If those hunger pangs hit while in Chalmette, the friendly and inexpensive **Rocky and Carlo's** cafeteria *($-$$; open late every day; St. Bernard Highway West,* ☎ *279-8323)* is sure to satisfy your appetite. The restaurant features family fare, with a menu consisting of macaroni and cheese, hamburger steak with onion sauce, and white beans and pork. The place is hardly luxurious, but very popular at lunch time. No credit cards accepted.

Crown Point

The **Restaurant Des Familles** *($$; Tue to Sun 11:30am to 9pm; at the intersection of LA 45 and LA 3134,* ☎ *689-7834)* is near Jean Lafitte National Historic Park and enjoys a breathtaking view of the bayou. Cajun cuisine is served in abundant portions for reasonable prices.

  ENTERTAINMENT

Just before the first world war, jazz was born in New Orleans, and whether it's blues, ragtime, old Creole songs or haunting spirituals, it always gets your blood flowing. Fans should hit **Bourbon Street**, in the **French Quarter**: a long-established spot for all-night revelry to explosive and nostalgic music.

Bars and Nightclubs

The French Quarter and Faubourg Marigny

The **Café Brazil** *(2100 Chartres St., Faubourg Marigny,* ☎ *947-9386)* is considered one of the best places in the city for dancing to reggae and Afro-Caribbean music. Julia Roberts has been spotted there.

At the Royal Sonesta Hotel's **Can Can Café** *(300 Bourbon St., French Quarter,* ☎*553-2372)*, the Silver Leaf Jazz Band plays traditional Dixieland from Thursday to Sunday.

The **Café Istanbul** nightclub *(cover charge; 534 Frenchmen St., Faubourg Marigny,* ☎ *944-4180)* is open every night, with dancing on Fridays and Saturdays. As well as English, they

The Captain's Tour

In the social atmosphere of New Orleans' cafés it's easy to meet interesting characters. This is how, one night at the Hotel Richelieu's bar in the French Quarter, we were approached by Captain Roger C. Johnson, who, having learned that we were from Québec (he has a pied-à-terre in the port of Québec City), invited us for a tour of his favourite spots. The Captain, who has been frequenting the French Quarter for 30 years, knows a lot of out-of-the-way spots that the average tourist might not otherwise find. Here's the route he suggests, preferably not all at once.

In the bars...

We start with **The Blacksmith Shop** *(914 Bourbon St., French Quarter,* ☎ *523-0066)*, practically the oldest bar in the United States and the only one to escape the numerous fires that have ravaged the city. Regular customers; sometimes a pianist in the evening.

At **Molly's on the Market** *(1107 Decatur St., French Quarter)*, beside Coops, you will be greeted by Jim Monaghan. Thursday is media night. From 10pm to midnight, newspaper and television people get together with a guest bartender each time. This guest could be the city mayor, the state governor, a member of Congress or someone else making headlines at the time.

The Captain likes the **Chart Room** *(at the corner of Chartres St. and Bienville, French Quarter)* for its fine cocktails at reasonable prices.

For a little "buffet" break, he recommends **Lord V.J.'s Bar** *(at the corner of Bienville and Decatur, French Quarter)*. On Monday nights, the regulars indulge in delicious corn bread and red beans.

Johnny Whites *(733 St. Peter St., French Quarter)* and **Johnny Whites Sports Bar** *(at the corner of Toulouse St. and Bourbon St., French Quarter)* are both open all the time. They have a regular clientele; at the Sports Bar, you can see rebroadcasts of big sporting events.

At **Bar 711** *(711 Bourbon St., French Quarter)*, the late-night bartender "Freak", has great sideburns and a sense of humour, and knows about everything that goes on in the city.

Maison Napoléon *(500 Chartres St. at St. Louis, French Quarter,* ☎ *524-9752)*. "One of the best bars in the world." Good background music, good food, good service. No jukebox. The house was built to welcome Napoleon who died before being able to visit. Say "hello" to the manager, Ray Fox (an aspiring writer), on behalf of the Captain.

At **Giovanni's - The Sequel** *(625 St. Phillip St., French Quarter)*, you can expect the unexpected. Here, say "hello" to Johnny (Giovanni) on the Captain's behalf. On Wednesdays and Sundays, between 9pm and 3am, you can replenish your proteins during an evening of liberal liquor consumption with a juicy steak.

The **Richelieu** bar, at Arnaud's restaurant *(813 Bienville St., French Quarter)*, is a favourite for a quiet afternoon drink.

speak Italian and Turkish here. Parking is available after 8pm. The only Turkish restaurant in Louisiana is on the main floor. They are open for lunch and dinner and offer traditional Turkish hors-d'oeuvres, lamb, grilled chicken and salads. There is live music at lunch.

At **Checkpoint Charlie** *(501 Esplanade Ave., Faubourg marigny, ☎ 947-0979)*, you can munch on a Charlie Burger while listening to live music.

The **Club Second Line** *(216 Bourbon St., French Quarter, ☎ 523-2020)*, open every night, is one of the rare spots in New Orleans where they present Dixieland as well as contemporary jazz.

The **Famour's Door** *(339 Esplanade Ave., Faubourg Marigny, ☎ 522-7626)*, in existence since 1934, is one of the oldest bars on Esplanade Avenue. There is jazz in the afternoon and evening, and dancing to jazz and blues.

The **Hard Rock Café** *(418 Peters St. North, French Quarter, ☎ 529-5617)*. All the big cities of the world have Hard Rock Cafés. In New Orleans, Fats Domino's piano hangs over the guitar-shaped bar and you can even see Elton John's shoes.

The **Hotel Fairmount** *(123 Baronne St., French Quarter, ☎ 529-7111)* has three different bars, each with its own music: The **Fairmount Court**, The **Sazerac Bar** which is a bit more stylish, and **Bailey's** for the end of the evening.

The **House of Blues** *(225 Decatur St., French Quarter, ☎ 529-2624)* is the latest trend for its music as much as its food. Different artists perform each week.

Howlin' Wolf *(828 South Peters St., French Quarter, ☎ 523-2551)*. This bar was converted from an old cotton-seed warehouse. They offer shows by contemporary rock bands.

Jimmy Buffet's in the **Margaritaville Café at Story Ville** *(1104 Decatur St., French Quarter, ☎ 592-2560)* features different solo artists or groups each week. They also serve some traditional dishes.

Maxwell's Toulouse Cabaret *(615 Toulouse St., French Quarter, ☎ 523-4207)* is renowned for the quality of its artists. You will find the New Orleans style at its best here. Harry Connick, the father of the famous singer of the same name, takes time off from his job as New Orleans' district attorney to sing here two nights a week.

The **Palm Court Jazz Café** *(1204 Decatur St., French Quarter)* presents high-calibre jazz seven nights a week. Danny Barker, considered one of the best banjo players in the world, plays here regularly. You can also listen to their exceptional collection of rare and out-of-print records. Prices for both the drinks and their local cuisine are among the most reasonable.

Preservation Hall *(726 St. Peter St., French Quarter)* remains the definitive choice for traditional jazz. A different group plays here every night, bringing together grand masters for unforgettable jam sessions. There's neither food nor drinks, only jazz.

Rhythms *(227 Bourbon St., French Quarter, ☎ 523-3800)* offers intoxicating blues in an old courtyard

GREATER NEW ORLEANS

enhanced with a babbling fountain and beautiful wrought-iron balconies.

The **Snug Harbor** *(626 Frenchmen St., Faubourg Marigny,* ☎ *949-0696)* presents two shows a night, at 9pm and 11pm, of contemporary jazz and rhythm and blues.

Uptown

Carrollton Station *(8140 Willow St.,* ☎ *865-9190)* is a small quiet bar that nonetheless attracts talented singers and musicians.

Jimmy's Music Club *(8200 Willow St.,* ☎ *866-9549)* presents all different styles of music indiscriminately (rock, reggae, rap, etc.).

The **Maple Leaf Bar** *(8316 Oak St., past South Carrollton St.,* ☎ *866-5323)* is open seven days a week. Their program includes blues on Wednesdays, Cajun music on Thursdays and poetry readings on Sunday afternoons.

At **Michaul's Live Cajun Music Restaurant** *(701 Magazine St.,* ☎ *529-3121)* you can take free Cajun dancing lessons, and then move up to the huge dance floor.

Muddy Water's *(8301 Oak St., past South Carrollton St.,* ☎ *866-7174)* welcomes young aspiring musicians as well as larger bands on tour. Relaxed atmosphere and original decor.

Tipitina's *(501 Napoleon Ave.,* ☎ *895-8477)*, which witnessed the growth of the Neville Brothers and Professor Longhair, has shows every night. You will find the best local and regional rock bands, New Orleans funk, gospel, zydeco, rhythm and blues, jazz, Cajun and reggae music.

The **Victoria Lounge** in the Columns Hotel *(3811 St. Charles Ave.,* ☎ *899-9308)* offers a plush setting that accommodates professionals of all ages.

The Warehouse District

Mulate's *(201 Julia St., by South Peters St.,* ☎ *522-1492)*. At this establishment, which also doubles as a Cajun restaurant (see p 129), all kinds of Louisiana Cajun singers and groups perform every night.

On the third floor of the **Hilton** *(2 Poydras St., close to the French Quarter,* ☎ *523-4374)* you'll find famous jazz-man **Pete Fountain's** nightclub.

At the **Jazz Meridien** *(Hotel Meridien, 614 Canal St.,* ☎ *525-6500)*, a jazz pianist performs during the week and a Dixieland band on weekends.

Favourites of the Gay Community

In New Orleans, most of the establishments visited by members of the gay community are located in the French Quarter and are easy to spot. The most popular small café, the **Bourbon Pub** *(801 Bourbon St., French Quarter,* ☎ *529-2107)*, is open 24 hours a day.

Café Lafitte in Exile *(901 Bourbon St., French Quarter,* ☎ *522-8397)*, one of the oldest and most popular meeting places, is open all the time. A disc jockey plays the music.

Charlene's *(940 Elysian Field, Faubourg Marigny,* ☎ *945-9328)*, although outside the French Quarter, offers an atmosphere that is worth going out of your way for. Friendly advice: take a cab!

The **Golden Lantern** *(1239 Royale St., French Quarter,* ☎ *523-6200)* is an old corner pub.

The **Good Friends Bar** *(740 Dauphine St., French Quarter,* ☎ *566-7191)* has all the charm of the French Quarter and offers a quiet ambience, perfect for conversation.

Rawhide *(740 Burgundy St., French Quarter,* ☎ *525-8106)* plays the best music in town and squeezes in a crowd with a fondness for dressing in leather.

Other Styles...

Karaoke fans can get themselves recorded on video performing their favourite songs at both the **Cat's Meow** *(701 Bourbon St., French Quarter,* ☎ *523-1157)* and at **White Horse Bar & Grill** *(526 St. Louis St., French Quarter,* ☎ *566-1507)*.

The **Mid-City Lanes Rock'n'Bowl** *(4133 South Carrollton St.,* ☎ *482-3133)*, where you can dance to a live band or sample steamed shrimp or crawfish between games, has been a local attraction since it opened in 1941.

Cultural Activities and Festivals

Gospel

For the best gospel in town, go to the **St. Stephen Baptist Church** during Sunday services *(Sun 8am and noon; 7pm on the 2nd, 4th and 5th Sundays of the month; 2308 South Liberty St., in the Mid-City area, seven streets north of St. Charles St., access from Philip St.,* ☎ *822-6800)*. Their singing is sometimes broadcast on local radio stations *(Mon-Fri 9:15am on WYLD 940 AM and 10:45am on KKNO 1750 AM)*. The church has a devout following among local blacks.

The **Praline Connection #2 Gospel and Blues Hall** restaurant *($19.95; Sun 11am and 2pm; 901-907 South Peters St., Warehouse District,* ☎ *523-3973)* offers gospel performances during their Sunday brunches.

Films

There are a number of movie theatres in New Orleans. Among them are the theatres of **Canal Place** *(333 Canal St.,* ☎ *581-5400)*, located close to the French Quarter. The **Prytania** *(5339 Prytania St.,* ☎ *895-4513)* presents mostly repertory films. There is an **IMAX** theatre *(*☎ *581-4629)* a few steps away from the Aquarium of the Americas. Finally, **Movie Pitchers** *(3941 Bienville Ave.,* ☎ *488-8881)* shows mostly foreign films.

Dance and Opera

The **New Orleans Ballet Association** *(*☎ *522-0996)* is the only professional

GREATER NEW ORLEANS

dance ensemble in New Orleans. They perform at the Theater of the Performing Arts. At the same theatre, the **New Orleans Opera Association** *(☎ 529-2278)* presents operas.

Theatre

The **Saenger Performing Arts Centre** *(143 North Rampart St., French Quarter, ☎ 524-2490)*, a superb renovated theatre, puts on Broadway shows.

The **Petit Théâtre du Vieux-Carré Français** *(616 St. Peter St., French Quarter, ☎ 522-2081)* is the oldest surviving theatre troupe in the United States. Every year in March, the famous Tennessee Williams Festival takes place here.

The **Marigny Theatre** *(616 Frenchmen St., Faubourg Marigny, near Chartres St., ☎ 944-2653)* has a reputation for choosing the most avant-garde plays.

The **Contemporary Arts Center** *(900 Camp St., near Julia St., ☎ 523-1216)* presents experimental theatre.

The **Southern Repertory Theater** *(Canal Place, 333 Canal St., 3rd floor, ☎ 861-8163)* offers regional works as well as classics.

Casinos

Although casinos were legalized in 1993, their presence continues to be controversial among residents. There are currently four casinos that are open 24 hours a day, seven days a week in the New Orleans metropolitan area; most have been set up on boats. Theoretically they must leave the dock for gambling to be permitted, though in practice things don't always work that way!

For fans of games of chance, the **Flamingo Casino New Orleans** boat *($5 entrance fee; cruises 11:45am to 1:15pm, 2:45pm to 4:15pm, 5:45pm to 7:15pm; Poydras St. Pier, adjacent to the New Orleans Hilton Riverside and to the Riverwalk Market, ☎ 587-7777)* offers 1000 square metres of floor space on its four decks and is able to accommodate up to 2,400 passengers. There are more than 100 slot machines, video lottery terminals, blackjack tables, roulette wheels, etc.. They also offer a restaurant, jazz and a free shuttle to downtown hotels. There is free parking with validation from the ticket office at the Hilton, the World Trade Center or at Riverwalk.

On Lake Pontchartrain, close to Lakefront airport, **Bally's Casino Lakeshore Resort** *(1 Stars and Stripes Boulevard, South Shore Harbor, ☎ 248-3200)* also has a large selection of slot machines and gaming tables for dice games, mini-baccarat, roulette, blackjack, etc..

Located in Kenner, on Lake Pontchartrain, the **Treasure Chest** *(5050 Williams Boulevard, ☎ 443-8171)* is a replica of a nineteenth-century paddleboat. They recently invested five million dollars to renovate the interior.

On the right bank of the Mississippi, anchored at the Harvey Canal Pier, the **Boomtown Belle Casino** *(4132 Peters Route, Harvey, ☎ 366-7711)*, a 75-metre, three-deck ship, has 850 video lottery terminals, 50 gaming tables, as well as a dance floor, a bar and a café.

Mardi Gras in New Orleans ★★★

Mardi Gras became part of Louisiana history as of March 3rd, 1699. In that year, the French explorer Pierre Le Moyne, Sieur d'Iberville, named an area near the future New Orleans "Bayou Mardi-Gras". As of 1740, under the French regime, masquerade balls took place in New Orleans, then were banned by the Spanish governors. Prohibition continued with the Americans as of 1803. Nevertheless, the Creole population ignored this ban and revived the tradition of the masquerade ball in 1823.

Four years later, the first Mardi Gras parade made its way through the streets and the tradition has repeated itself every year since. One of the most spectacular and surprising elements of the parade is the "Indian Mardi Gras". Blacks strut about in clans with hand-made, glittering feathered and beaded costumes. Next come the Tchopitoulas, the Pocahontas and other colourfully-clad traditional native characters, and of course there are the popular zulus.

There are also a few rules to follow during the Mardi Gras parade: use plastic glasses only, no glass or metal allowed; no streamers to be thrown from balconies; don't park your car along the parade route, in fact parking regulations change during the parade so to avoid a $100 ticket or, worse, getting your car impounded *(400 Claiborne Ave., ☎ 826-1900)*, double-check that you are legally parked; wear comfortable clothes and shoes; and don't carry your valuables with you. Finally portable toilets can be found throughout town.

Mardi Gras is the festive period preceding the fast or Lent. It falls 46 days before Easter.

In Louisiana, parish rulings declare the season officially open 12 days before Mardi Gras itself. There are about 70 parades in the four parishes - Orleans, Jefferson, St. Bernard and St. Tammany - during this period.

Since 1872, the colours of Mardi Gras are purple which represents justice, gold symbolizing power and green for faith.

Every year, each krewe chooses a different theme for their floats and masks. "Krewe" comes from the word "crew", probably "hispanicized". They are non-profit organizations, often associated with charity groups whose main goal is to contribute to the preparation and financing of floats before presenting them at Mardi Gras. The originator of this venerable tradition, the krewe of Comus was born in 1857. In honour of this, the krewe of Comus concludes the Mardi Gras procession.

Krewes parade with a captain at the head, on horseback or in a convertible. The captain is followed by officers, then the king and queen, accompanied sometimes by a few dukes and always by young girls, and behind them, the float with costumed krewe members on it. All this is followed by bands, dance troupes, clowns and public entertainers, etc.. In all, there are over 3000 participants.

Kings and queens get chosen in a different manner from one krewe to another. For some it's done by a draw, but regardless of the method, most require a monarch. The King of Carnival is chosen by a committee from the School of Design, the parade's sponsor.

Arrive early because space is limited and good spots are precious, and be careful when the doubloons and necklaces start getting thrown from the floats, because there's a lot of jostling to catch them. Also think about stocking up on sandwiches and water because it's as hard to break through the crowd as it is to find a free table at a restaurant. St. Charles Avenue, between Napoleon Avenue and Lee Circle gets transformed into a huge picnic area for the whole family. The crowd is more restless toward Canal Street and in the French Quarter.

New Orleanians prefer attending the Metairie Mardi Gras, whose parades rival those of their own city.

Lundi Gras, a recent addition, takes place the day before at Spanish Plaza, adjacent to Riverwalk *(Poydras St.)*. This is where, at around 5pm, Rex, the King of Mardi Gras, arrives. The program for this first evening includes a masquerade ball, fireworks and a concert.

Mardi Gras is always more fun in disguise. There is even a competition reserved for visitors for the best costume. To participate, contact Mardi Gras **Maskathon** *(☎ 527-0123)*. There is a good selection of masks at the French Market.

On the day of Mardi Gras, watch for bands going by, they call them marching clubs. The traditional Jefferson City Buzzards and Pete Fountain's Half-Fast Walking Club are the most famous. The parade starts at 8:30am with the arrival of the Zulus and then at 10am, the most

spectacular event of the day occurs, the arrival of Rex, the King of Carnival, followed by 200 thematic floats.

During Mardi Gras, the public transportation service, the **RTA** *(☎ 560-2700)*, offers day-passes *($3)*.

The costume competition near the bar Rawhide, at Burgundy and St. Ann, is one of Mardi Gras' most popular shows. It starts at noon. Two pieces of advice: come early and leave the kids at home!

Calendar of Events

January

Sugar Bowl Football Classic *(Jan 1; Superdome, 1500 Sugar Bowl Drive, LA 70112, ☎ 525-8573)*. The Sugar Bowl is the final match between the two best American college football teams. In celebration of it there is a colourful parade in the city's streets.

Beginning of the Mardi Gras season *(starting Jan 6)*.

Black Arts and Martin Luther King Jr. Festival *(mid-Jan; Tulane University, office of multicultural affairs, ☎ 596-2697)*. Peace Week.

February

Festival of the Zulu Family *(day before Mardi Gras 10am to 5pm; Woldenberg Park, ☎ 822-1559)*. More Mardi Gras festivities.

Lundi Gras (Fat Monday) on Spanish Plaza *(Riverwalk, ☎ 522-1555)* celebrates the eve of Mardi Gras with fireworks and a masquerade ball (a mask is required).

Mardi Gras *(☎ 566-5068 or 525-6427)*. Festivities and parades throughout the city streets and the French Quarter.

March

St. Patrick's Day Parade *(mid-Mar; French Quarter, ☎ 525-5169)*. As in a lot of major American cities, this Irish holiday is celebrated in fine splendour in the French Quarter.

St. Patrick's Day Parade in the Irish Channel area *(mid-Mar; ☎ 565-7080)*. Another neighbourhood, another Irish gathering, another party!

Black Heritage Festival *(mid-Mar; Audubon Zoo, ☎ 861-2537)*. For two days, this event highlights the cultural, musical, artistic and gastronomical contributions of the black community.

St. Joseph Day Festivities *(mid-Mar; St. Joseph Tabernacle, Piazza d'Italia, at Poydras and Tchoupitoulas, ☎ 891-1904)*. This day celebrating the patron saint of workers is also celebrated in grand style.

The **Crescent City Classic** *(3rd weekend in March; ☎ 861-8686)* is a 10 kilometre foot race starting at Jackson Square and finishing at Audubon Park.

The **Tennessee Williams Literary Festival** *(last weekend in March; Conference Services of New Orleans University, ☎ 286-6680 or 581-1144)* focuses on the works of the famous writer, born Thomas Lanier, author of, among others, *A Streetcar Named Desire* and *Suddenly Last Summer*. For three days there are various theatre productions, poetry recitals and other cultural activities taking place in the city that the writer loved so much and where he wrote his early plays including *The Glass Menagerie*.

The **Earth Festival** *(last weekend in March, 9:30am to 6pm; Audubon Zoo, ☎ 861-2537)*. Even spring's reawakening is a reason to celebrate in New Orleans!

April

At the **French Quarter Festival** *(☎ 522-5730)*, there are a dozen or so bands on as many stages. Refreshments, fireworks, etc..

Spring Festival *(☎ 581-1367)*. For five days the public is invited to visit historic sites and houses, plantations, etc.. The festival opens with a parade of horse-drawn carriages.

The **Jazz and Heritage Festival** *(last weekend in April; New Orleans Hippodrome Fairgrounds, ☎ 522-4786)* is one of the most popular celebrations in the world. For ten days, more than 4,000 artists, musicians, chefs and artisans share their talent with more than 250,000 visitors.

Uptown Free Street Festival *(1st weekend in April; New Orleans Jazz and Heritage Foundation, ☎ 522-4786)*. There is a lot of frenzied crowd participation at this huge celebration devoted to music.

May

Greek Festival *(last weekend in May; Greek Cultural Centre, 1200 Robert E. Lee Boulevard, ☎ 282-0259)*. This event presents folk dancing, music and art exhibitions.

GREATER NEW ORLEANS

June

Reggae Riddums Festival *(2nd weekend in June; City Park, ☎ 367-1313)*. This festival brings together reggae and calypso performers from around the world.

Carnival Latino *(last weekend in June; and Mississippi River Front and Canal, ☎ 522-9927)*. Throughout the four days of this festival you can hear bands from Latin America, Spain and Portugal.

Great French Quarter Tomato Festival *(1st weekend in June; French Market, ☎ 522-2621)*. A number of popular events are presented with the tomato as central theme; June is tomato season here.

Zydeco Bay-Ou *(3rd weekend in June; Crown Point, ☎ 689-2663)*. A number of shows are presented with zydeco singers and musicians.

July

Independence Day *(Riverfront, ☎ 528-9994)*. The fourth of July is celebrated with various activities and performances that always attract a diverse and joyous crowd.

Wine and Food Experience *(end of July; Ernest N. Morial Convention Center, 900 Convention Boulevard, ☎ 529-9463)*. Wine-tastings and a variety of foods are offered in the French Quarter. Approximately 40 restaurants participate in this event.

August

International Festival of African Heritage *(end of Aug and beginning of Sep; ☎ 949-5600 or 949-5610)*. Festivities are devoted to African-American art of all forms and disciplines.

October

Swamp Festival *(Audubon Zoo and Wodenberg Park, ☎ 861-2537)*. For two weekends, the zoo offers free admission. You can also enjoy some Cajun food and examine distinctive swamp wildlife.

Festival of Film and Video *($3-$6; 365 Canal St., ☎ 523-3818)*. For one week, various film and video productions from all over the world are shown. The festival takes place at the Canal Place theatres.

Festa D'Italia *(☎ 891-1904)*. Celebrating, it's something that Italians do so well!

Gumbo Festival *(beginning of Oct; Bridge City, Westwego, ☎ 436-4712)*. There's gumbo, music and... more gumbo!

Gay Pride Weekend *(Oct 11 and 12; ☎ 1-800-345-1187)*. A very lively weekend for the gay community. A parade, dancing and shows are held at Washington Square.

Hallowe'en *(Oct 31; ☎ 566-5055)*. Throughout the city costume parties are organized but the most popular is the one in the French Quarter. There is also a parade.

Boo at the Zoo *($10; Oct 29 to 31; Audubon Zoo, 6500 Magazine St., ☎ 871-2537)*. Special Hallowe'en activities are organized at the Zoo. Profits go to the city's children's hospital.

Octoberfest *(all month)*. Approximately 20 establishments in the city serve beer and German food. You can also polka at the Deutches Haus *(☎ 522-8014)*.

November

Luling Suckling Pig Festival *(1st weekend in Nov; on the west bank of the river, route US90, Luling)*. This festival celebrates the suckling pig. The highlight is of course tasting it either roasted or prepared in a variety of other ways.

Celebration in the Oaks *(evenings, end of Nov to beginning of Jan; City Park)*. The park's trees are decorated with hundreds of thousands of lights. This brilliant spectacle is accompanied by music.

December

Creole Christmas *(☎ 522-5730)*. The public is invited to take part in carolling at Jackson Square, candlelight walks, bonfires and Christmas celebrations.

New Year's Eve at Jackson Square *(Jackson Square, ☎ 566-5046)*. New Orleanians and visitors get together to say goodbye to the year and ring in a new one.

Orange Festival and Parish Persimmon Fair *(1st weekend in Dec; Port Sulphur, ☎ 656-7752)* proposes food, music, a catfish-cooking contest, a duck-calling competition and a *fais do-do*, a traditional Cajun dance.

 SHOPPING

More than one thousand New Orleans businesses participate in the state's sales-tax-reimbursement program. Simply present your passport and airplane ticket at the time of purchase to receive the tax-refund voucher that is filled out and submitted to **Louisiana Tax Free Shopping (LTFS)** at the New Orleans International Airport (Moisant). Amounts of less than $500 are reimbursed in cash; larger amounts are paid by cheque sent to the visitor by mail.

Neighbourhoods

Each New Orleans neighbourhood has its own specialty. The French Quarter, essentially a tourist area, brings together many different businesses from the most elegant gallery to the simplest souvenir stand. Uptown, a residential district, is known for the row of antique shops on Magazine Street; there are also a number of restaurants, food markets and a few cafés here. In the Riverbend neighbourhood, around Carrollton Street and St. Charles Avenue, there are a few good restaurants, jazz clubs and clothing stores.

Shopping Centres

A main point of interest for window-shoppers is **Canal Place Fashion Mall**, with more than 60 stores and cafés. Of course **Jax**, or **Jackson Brewery**, is also a choice spot for shoppers.

The recently opened **New Orleans Centre**, near the Superdome and the Hyatt Hotel, offers three floors of elegant boutiques under a glass dome.

On the site of the 1984 Universal Exposition along the Mississippi, **Riverwalk** is a market of 140 stores,

GREATER NEW ORLEANS

boutiques and restaurants that allows you to do your shopping while enjoying a unique view of the river.

Galleries and Antique Shops

Royal Street is the address of about 40 of the over 60 boutiques and galleries in the French Quarter that specialize in antiques of all kinds. Paintings, jewellery, furniture, glass, porcelain, bronze, etc., whether for decoration or collection, authentic or reproduction, there is something for all tastes if not for all budgets. There's no point in naming them all: the best thing to do is stroll along and enjoy the ambience.

Like Royal Street, **Julia Street**, in the Warehouse District, is renowned for its many galleries. They are located near the Contemporary Arts Center.

A Gallery for Fine Photography *(322 Royal St., ☎ 568-1313)* sells posters by American and international photographers.

The **French Antique Shop** *(225 Royal St., ☎ 524-9861)* specializes in pieces from the 18th and 19th centuries: light fixtures, marble, porcelain, bronze.

At **Dixon & Dixon** *(237 Royal St., ☎ 524-0282 or 1-800-848-5148)* you can find exceptional collections of paintings, Oriental rugs, European and Oriental porcelain and antique jewellery.

Endangered Species *(619 Royal St., ☎ 568-9855)* sells sculpted ivory figures, ritual objects, icons and masks.

The **Morton M. Goldberg Auction Galleries** *(547 Baron St., ☎ 882-7422)*, one of the most important auction houses in North America, offers imported furniture, paintings and various other objects. They regularly hold estate auctions.

La Belle Gallery *(309 Chartres St., ☎ 529-3080)* houses one of the most important collections of African-American art in the United States.

Martin LaBorde Gallery *(631 Royal St., ☎ 587-7111)* exhibits paintings by the artist. His richly coloured works display a Mexican influence, for example, in those that represent a figure floating freely through the air. Some of LaBorde's paintings can be seen at the cozy **Upperline** restaurant (see p 133).

The portrait artist **Johnny Donnels** *(634 St. Peter St., ☎ 525-8550)* presents work from throughout his career, spanning over fifty years, as well as an attractive collection of photographs of New Orleans.

Macon Riddle *(☎ 899-3027)*, an expert consultant, conducts visits to antique shops and galleries on Royal and Magazine Streets.

Magazine Street is a paradise for antique enthusiasts. Stretching over almost 10 kilometres, boutiques, arcades and galleries offer ceramics, pewter pieces, glassware, and other old objects.

Bookstores

Book Star *(414 North Peters St., French Quarter, ☎ 523-6411)* has a wide selection of books including a complete section on the history, culture and food of Louisiana and New Orleans.

The ideal place to hunt down a book of recipes from rural Louisiana and New Orleans is **Aunt Sally's Praline Shop** *(810 Decatur St., French Quarter,* ☎ *524-3373 or 524-5107).*

At the **Arcadian Books & Art Prints - Librairie d'Arcadie** *(714 Orleans St., French Quarter,* ☎ *523-4138)* the pleasant and erudite owner Russel Desmond, a history and literature enthusiast, proposes the best authors "for the study of French and Francophone Louisiana": Barry Ancelet *(Contes Bilingues 'cadiens et créole)*, Jeanne Castille *(Moi, Jeanne Castille de la Louisiane)*, Maurice Denuzière *(Je te nomme Louisiane)*, and the Reverend Mother Saint Augustin de Tranchepain *(Relation du voyage des premières Ursulines à La Nouvelle-Orléans et leur établissement en cette ville* - published in 1859*).*

Louisiana Cookbooks

Local cuisine in Louisiana is an important preoccupation and you will probably want to take home a few books dedicated to Cajun, Creole, southern or African-American cooking. Here is a list of some of the most popular books in New Orleans.

Creole Gumbo and All That Jazz: New Orleans cuisine.

River Road Recipes I: Two million copies sold since 1959.

La Bonne Cuisine: Creole cuisine of New Orleans.

The Little New Orleans Cookbook: New Orleans' cuisine.

La Bouche Créole I: Authentic Creole recipes.

Commander's Palace Cookbook: Recipes from the gastronomic mecca of New Orleans.

Recipes & Reminiscences of New Orleans I: Written by the Ursuline nuns of New Orleans.

The Best of New Orleans: A marvellous little book, fully illustrated with beautiful colour photos, bringing together the best Creole and Cajun recipes from New Orleans and Louisiana, including a few from Paul Prudhomme and from prominent restaurants such as Antoine's.

Music

Tower Records - Video *(every day 9am to midnight; Jackson Brewery, 408-410 North Peters St., at Decatur,* ☎ *529-4411).* Excellent selection of local music.

Record Ron's *(every day 11am to 7pm; 239 Chartres St.,* ☎ *522-2239; 1129 Decatur St.,* ☎ *524-9444).* One of the largest selections of vinyl: pop, R & B, jazz, soul, Dixieland, rock, blues, gospel, Cajun, etc.. Credit cards accepted.

Rock & Roll Records *(10am to 10pm; 1214 Decatur St.,* ☎ *561-5683).* Records (33, 45 and 78 rpm), cassettes, compact discs and videos.

Louisiana Music Factory *(every day 10am to 7pm; 225 North Peters St., French Quarter,* ☎ *523-1094).* Regional music, books, photos, videos and posters.

Food, Coffee and Wine

At **Aunt Sally's Praline Shop** *(810 Decatur St., French Quarter)*, you can buy cookbooks, jars of pepper sauce, other pickles and preserves, and typical local foods. Just look for the glassed-in counter facing the street where staff prepare mountains of sugary pralines.

You'll find good coffee just about everywhere in New Orleans; **Community** coffee is roasted according to tradition.

At **Croissant d'Or** *(7am to 5pm; 615-617 Ursulines St., French Quarter, ☎ 534-4663)*, Maurice Delechelle, a French-pastry chef, prepares delicious (and huge) butter croissants, chocolate croissants, Danish pastries and other treats. The café also serves quiche and a small menu of daily lunch specials (soup, sandwich and salad). The building has a lovely courtyard, but it can be very hot on humid days. Thankfully, the café has air conditioning.

The **Vietnamese Farmer's Market** *(Sat mornings; 13344 Chef Menteur Hwy, Route US 90, at the east exit of the city, ☎ 254-9646)* is the most interesting vegetable market in New Orleans. You have to get there early.

You can't visit New Orleans without stopping in at the historic **French Market** *(Decatur St., French Quarter)*. In addition to local produce there is produce from other states: Texas oranges, Georgia peaches and California grapes, to name a few. Garlic braids and small jars of pepper sauce are popular items.

It's not easy to find good cheese in New Orleans. **Martin Wine Cellar** *(3827 Baron St., two streets north of St. Charles Ave., Uptown, ☎ 899-7411)* imports Stilton, goat cheese, Brie and Parmesan. They also have one of the largest selections of wine in New Orleans and a sandwich counter.

The **Praline Connection** restaurant *(542 Frenchmen St., Faubourg Marigny)* has a gift shop where they sell products from New Orleans including traditional, chocolate and coconut pralines.

Progress Grocery *(912 Decatur St., French Quarter, ☎ 525-6627)*, best known for its muffalettas (sandwiches of Italian meats, cheeses and olive salad), also carries some groceries, cigarettes, magazines and newspapers.

At the **Saint Roch Seafood Market** *(2381 St. Claude Ave., east of the French Quarter at St. Roch St., ☎ 943-5778 or 943-6666)*, you can get locally caught fish and seafood including soft crab (in season), shrimp, crawfish, oysters, etc..

Vieux Carré Wine and Spirits *(422 Chartres St., French Quarter, ☎ 568-9463)* is run by an Italian who started out in the catering business in New Orleans. It stocks a wide variety of good wines from many different countries and a large selection of beers.

Photography

Photography stores throughout the city offer developing, a number of them in the area of Canal Street near Decatur, Chartes and Royal and on the other side of Canal. Professionals will find a good selection of film at the **Liberty**

Camera Center *(337 Carondelet St., one street north of St. Charles, between Gravier and Union, ☎ 523-6252).*

Mardi Gras

You can relive the atmosphere of Mardi Gras throughout the year by visiting the **Louisiana State Museum** (see p 72) *(751 Chartres St., ☎ 568-6972 or 568-6978),* with its permanent collection of costumes, old floats, documents and accessories (invitation cards, decorations) dating back to the last century.

You can get a closer look at and a better feel for costumes, masks and other finery at the following specialty shops.

The **Accent Annex** *(1120 Jeff Davis Parkway South, ☎ 821-8999 or 838-8818)* wholesales all kinds of decorations and objects.

Barth Brothers *(4346 Poche Court West, ☎ 254-1794)* is a business that has made Mardi Gras celebration an art in itself. They specialize in the design and construction of elaborate floats. Their work is exhibited at the Museum of American History in Washington.

Blaine Kern's Mardi Gras World *(233 Newton St., Algiers Point, ☎ 361-7821)* makes floats and sells all the requisite Mardi Gras accessories.

Jefferson Variety Store *(239 Iris Ave., Metairie, ☎ 834-5222).* Costumes and doubloons, which are tokens used in Mardi Gras festivities.

Costume Headquarters *(3635 Banks St., ☎ 488-9523 or 488-6959).* All sorts of costumes, wigs and masks for rent.

Garage Antiques and Clothing *(1234 Decatur St., French Quarter, ☎ 522-6639)* specializes in selling Mardi Gras accessories; you'll find a wonderful selection of old costumes and masks. The owner, Marcus Fraser, is up on all the latest trends.

Neighborhood Art Gallery *(2131 Soniat St., ask for Sandra Berry, ☎ 891-5537).* This African-American artists' co-op exhibits members' work.

Bergen Galleries *(Sun to Thu 9am to 9pm, Fri and Sat 9am to 10pm; 730 Royal St., ☎ 523-7882 or 1-800-621-6179).* The largest selection of Mardi Gras posters, new and old. They can be shipped anywhere in the world.

Little Shop of Fantasies *(523 Dumaine St., French Quarter, ☎ 529-4243)* has one of the most dazzling selections of Mardi Gras masks.

French Market Flea Market *(every day; at the corner of St. Peter and Decatur, ☎ 522-2621).* At this 200-year-old market you will find a bit of everything, including Mardi Gras masks.

Rumors *(513 and 319 Royal St., French Quarter, ☎ 525-0292 or 523-0011)* is a favourite spot for buying Mardi Gras masks. There's a large selection of earrings, from the most classic to the most eccentric.

GREATER NEW ORLEANS

Florist

The staff at **Scheinuk The Florist** *(2600 St. Charles Ave., at Washington Ave., ☎ 895-3944 or 1-800-535-2020)* takes care of customers without delay. An attractive selection of cut flowers and tastefully arranged bouquets are offered at reasonable prices.

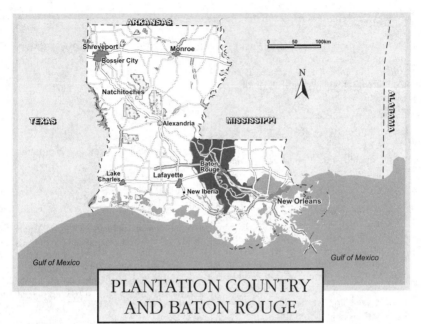

PLANTATION COUNTRY
AND BATON ROUGE

The land along the serpentine Mississippi River was a veritable El Dorado for cotton and sugar cane farming. Thanks to an endlessly renewable work force, planters were like kings here, ensconced in sumptuous houses surrounded by vast stretches of farmland - a situation they enjoyed right up until the Civil War. Few plantations remain in operation, and the old houses, now listed as historic landmarks, have been turned into museums and hotels.

Almost all the big plantations are located on the banks of the Mississippi, between Natchitoches and Pointe a la Hache, west of New Orleans. These majestic estates can not only be admired from the outside; many are open to the public, and some even offer accommodations.

The economic development of Baton Rouge, the capital of Louisiana, was largely determined by its location on the banks of the Mississippi. Numerous industrial plants (carbon-black operations and petrochemical refineries) set up shop here in order to take advantage of the Mississippi waterway and the city's extensive port installations, which make Baton Rouge the fourth largest port in the United States.

 ## FINDING YOUR WAY AROUND

The East Bank of the Mississippi

The set of directions below will take you from the New Orleans riverfront to St. Francisville.

Take the I-10 West out of New Orleans. Just past Kenner, get on the I-310, then exit at St. Rose. From there, take LA 48 to Destrehan, Good

Hope and then Norco. From Norco, LA 44 will take you through LaPlace, Reserve, Garyville, Lutcher, Remy, Convent, Romeville, Central, Union and Burnside.

River Road

The single name "River Road" refers to the various highways that run along either side of the Mississippi. These are studded with magnificent plantations, which were built here so that their owners could take the greatest possible advantage of the river, a waterway of central importance during the steamboat era. Unfortunately, the levees constructed to protect the area from the Mississippi's floodwaters make it hard to see across the river. A large number of petrochemical plants are also clustered between New Orleans and Baton Rouge.

Next, get on LA 75, which runs through Darrow, Geismar, Carville and St. Gabriel. Follow LA 30 to Baton Rouge, then US 61 to St. Francisville.

Destrehan

After taking the I-10 West out of New Orleans, pick up the I-310 just past Kenner. After 11 kilometres, take the Destrehan exit and get on LA 48/River Road.

LaPlace

Forty-eight kilometres from New Orleans, the I-10 intersects with US 51 South, the continuation of the I-55, which leads to the centre of LaPlace, a town of 24,000 people. Exit 206 (LA 3188) of the I-10 also leads to downtown.

Reserve

From LaPlace, take LA 44 along the river to Reserve, located five kilometres away.

Lutcher

From Reserve, take LA 44/River Road for 16 kilometres. A quicker route is to take US 61; 12 kilometres after LaPlace, pick up LA 641 and continue to Gramercy, then take LA 44 for a few kilometres. From the I-10, take Exit 194.

Convent

From Lutcher, take LA 44/River Road for 32 kilometres. Convent is the parish seat of St. James Parish.

Burnside

Burnside is located 27 kilometres from Convent on LA 44/River Road. It is also possible to reach Burnside without following the river: take Exit 182/Donaldsonville off the I-10, then follow LA 22 for five kilometres.

Darrow - Carville - St. Gabriel

From Burnside, take LA 75; Barrow is located eight kilometres away, Carville 28 kilometres and St. Gabriel 36 kilometres. From St. Gabriel, take LA 30 Baton Rouge (23 km).

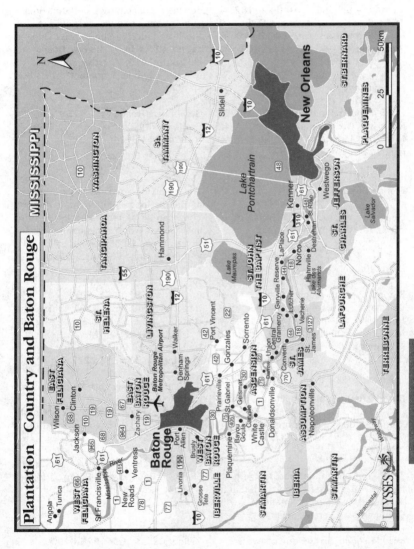

Plantation Country and Baton Rouge

Sorrento - Gonzales - Prairieville

Get off River Road to reach Sorrento, located after the I-10 (Exit 182 or 187/US 61), then take US 61 11 kilometres to Gonzales and 10 more to Prairieville.

Port Vincent

Upon leaving Prairieville, take US 61 North for two kilometres, then LA 42 for 16 kilometres. Port Vincent is located in Livingston Parish.

French Settlement

Head out of Port Vincent and take LA 16 South for eight kilometres.

Baton Rouge

Baton Rouge, the capital of the State of Louisiana, is located 125 kilometres from New Orleans and 85 kilometres from Lafayette by the I-10, and 150 kilometres from Slidell by the I-12.

Airport

Baton Rouge Metropolitan Airport: 9430 Jackie Cochrine Avenue, Terminal Building, Baton Rouge, LA 70807, ☎ (504) 355-0333 or 357-4165

The Baton Rouge Metropolitan Airport, located 18 kilometres north of Baton Rouge, is served by American Eagle, Continental Express, Delta Airlines, Northwest Airlink and USAir. There is a shuttle service to the downtown area.

Buses

The **Greyhound/Trailways** bus company provides service between Baton Rouge and the major towns in Louisiana. A trip from Baton Rouge to New Orleans costs $13; from Baton Rouge to Lafayette, $10. For the departure or arrival schedule, contact the bus station:

Greyhound/Trailways: 1253 Florida Boulevard, Baton Rouge, ☎ (504) 383-3124

Car Rentals

The following agencies have a branch at Baton Rouge Metropolitan Airport. They can all be reached toll-free from anywhere in North America, except for Hertz, whose 1-800 number only works within the United States.

Avis: ☎ 1-800-331-1212
Budget: ☎ 1-800-527-0700
Hertz: ☎ 1-800-654-3131 within the United States only, Canada ☎ 1-800-263-0600
National: ☎ 1-800-227-7368
Thrifty: ☎ 1-800-367-2277

Other agencies have offices downtown:

Enterprise Rent-A-Car: 8121 Florida Boulevard, Baton Rouge, ☎ (504) 929-7560

University Ford Rent-A-Car: 7787 Florida Boulevard, Baton Rouge, ☎ (504) 925-1309

Taxis

Yellow Cab: ☎ (504) 926-6400

Public Transportation

Capital Transportation City Bus: 2222 Florida Boulevard, Baton Rouge, LA 70802, ☎ (504) 336-0821

Denham Springs - Walker

These two towns are located east of Baton Rouge. Denham Springs is 25 kilometres from the capital by the I-10, Walker 34. The distances are about the same on the I-12.

Zachary

Zachary is 24 kilometres from Baton Rouge by LA 19 North.

St. Francisville

St. Francisville is 48 kilometres from Baton Rouge by US 61 North.

Tunica - Angola

From St. Francisville, drive five kilometres on US 61 North, then pick up LA 66 (30 kilometres to Tunica, 32 kilometres to Angola).

Jackson

From St. Francisville, head east on LA 10 for 18 kilometres.

Wilson

From Jackson, continue on LA 10 East for three kilometres, then take LA 68 East for 13 kilometres. To reach Wilson from Zachary, take LA 19 for 32 kilometres.

Clinton

From Jackson, drive 20 kilometres on LA 10 East.

The West Bank of the Mississippi

From Westwego, across the river from New Orleans, LA 18/River Road follows the Mississippi for over 100 kilometres, as far as Donaldson, passing through Luling, Hahnville, Edgard and Vacherie along the way. In Donaldson, take LA 1 and continue to White Castle, Plaquemine, Port Allen (50 km) and New Roads (110 km).

Hahnville

From Destrehan, take the I-310 bridge over the river and head west on LA 18/River Road for five kilometres to Hahnville, the parish seat of St. Charles Parish.

Vacherie

From Hahnville, continue on LA 18/River Road for 40 kilometres. From New Orleans, take the I-10 for 65 kilometres to Exit 194. A bridge spans the river at Lutcher; on the other side, you'll be five kilometres east of Vacherie.

St. James

From Vacherie, take LA 18/River Road 13 kilometres to St. James.

THE PLANTATIONS AND BATON ROUGE

Donaldsonville

From St. James, continue on LA 18/River Road for 18 kilometres, then take US 70 for 10 kilometres to Donaldsonville. To reach Donaldsonville faster, take the I-10, then pick up US 70, 72 kilometres from New Orleans, and continue for 24 kilometres.

White Castle

Take LA 1 North out of Donaldsonville and continue for 18 kilometres.

Bayou Goula

From White Castle, take LA 1 for six kilometres, then LA 405 for three more.

Plaquemine

Plaquemine is 20 kilometres from White Castle by LA 1. At Plaquemine, you can catch a ferry across the river; it will drop you off near LA 75/River Road, between St. Gabriel and Baton Rouge.

Brusly - Port Allen

By continuing on LA 1 from Plaquemine, you'll reach Brusly after 13 kilometres and Port Allen after 20. Port Allen lies across the river from Baton Rouge and is the parish seat of West Baton Rouge Parish.

Grosse Tete - Rosedale

Grosse Tete is 24 kilometres from Port Allen by the I-10 West. It is possible to reach Grosse Tete from Plaquemine by taking LA 77 North.

Rosedale - Livonia

From Grosse Tete, take LA 77 North three kilometres to Rosedale and 19 more to Livonia. Livonia is located on US 190, which runs through Port Allen and Baton Rouge (40 km).

New Roads

Head northward out of Port Allen on LA 1 and continue for 56 kilometres. There is a ferry service from New Roads to St. Francisville.

Ventress

From New Roads, head east on LA 415 for three kilometres, then turn right on LA 413, which leads to Ventress (1 km).

PRACTICAL INFORMATION

The area code is 504.

Emergencies

For the police, the fire department or ambulance service, dial 911.

Hospital

Baton Rouge General Medical Center: 3600 Florida Boulevard, Baton Rouge, LA 70806, ☎ 387-7000

Young musicians in the French Quarter - R.N.

Laura Plantation in Vacherie - R.N.

Louisiana, the kingdom of hot sauce - R.N.

Tourist Information

Louisiana Office of Tourism: 900 Riverside Drive, Baton Rouge; Mailing address: P.O. Box 94291, Baton Rouge, LA 70804, ☎ 342-8119 or 1-800-33-GUMBO within North America *(Mon to Fri 8am to 4:30pm)*

State Capitol Tourist Information Center: In the New State Capitol, State Capitol Drive, Baton Rouge, ☎ 342-8147 *(every day 8am to 4:30pm)*

Baton Rouge Convention and Visitors Bureau: 275 South River Road (in the New State Capitol), Baton Rouge, ☎ 383-1825 or 1-800-527-6843 within the U.S. *(every day 8am to 5pm)*

St. James Historical Society Culture & Heritage Center Museum: 1988 LA 44, Lutcher; Mailing address: P.O. Box 426, Gramercy, LA 70052, ☎ 869-9752

Ascension Parish Tourist Center: 6474 Highway 22, Sorrento, LA 70778, ☎ 675-8687

Iberville Chamber of Commerce, Iberville Parish Tourist Office: 57730 Main Street, Plaquemine; Mailing address: P.O. Box 248, Plaquemine, LA 70765-0248, ☎ 687-7158, 687-3560 or 1-800-233-3560 within the U.S.

West Baton Rouge Tourist Commission: 2855 I-10 (Frontage Road), Port Allen, LA 70767, ☎ 344-2920 or 1-800-654-9701 within North America *(every day 9am to 5pm)*

West Feliciana Parish Tourist Commission: Mailing address: P.O. Box 1548, St. Francisville, LA 70775, ☎ 635-6330

East Feliciana Parish Tourist Commission, Feliciana Chamber of Commerce: Mailing address: P.O. Box 667, Jackson, LA 70748, ☎ 634-7155

Pointe Coupee Chamber of Commerce and Office of Tourism: LA 1, 10 kilometres south of New Roads, ☎ 638-3500 or 638-9858 *(Tue to Fri 10am to 3pm, Sat 10am to 4pm, Sun noon to 4pm)*

 EXPLORING

The East Bank of the Mississippi

Destrehan - Reserve

This part of Louisiana, one of the first to be settled, is the jumping-off point for our tour of the plantations. The first stop on the itinerary is Destrehan Plantation, which is the oldest estate on the tour and hosts an annual festival. Later comes the San Francisco Plantation House, which has an impressive wrap-around balcony on the roof, lending the place an extravagant air.

Toward the bedroom community of LaPlace, visitors will find the Bonnet-Carré Canal, which links the Mississippi to Lake Ponchartrain and was built in order to control the flow of the river.

Destrehan Plantation ★★ *(adults $5, seniors and students $3, ages 6-12 $2; guided tours every day 9:30am to 4pm, except on holidays; P.O. Box 5, 13034 River Road, Destrehan, LA 70047, ☎ 764-9315 or 524-5522)* is located just 16 kilometres from New Orleans International Airport (Moisant), on LA 48/River Road, between St. Rose and

San Francisco Plantation House

Destrehan. The house, built in 1787 in the French colonial style and given a Greek Revival remodeling around 1830, is listed as the oldest plantation home in the lower Mississippi Valley. It is flanked by stately live oaks and decorated with lovely antiques.

Ormond Plantation ★ *(adults $5, seniors $4, children $2.50; every day 10am to 4pm; 13786 River Road, Destrehan, ☎ 764-8544)* boasts a magnificent house built around 1790. With its cob walls, it is typical of plantation homes built during the French era and has antique furnishings. Collections of dolls, canes and guns are displayed here as well.

St. Charles Borromeo Catholic Church *(River Road)* has jealously preserved its 18th-century cemetery.

The galleried, Creole-style **San Francisco Plantation House ★★** *(adults $6.50, ages 12-17 $3.75, ages 6-11 $2.50; guided tours every day 10am to 4pm, except on holidays; LA 44, Reserve, LA 70084, ☎ 535-2341)*, built in 1856, is listed on the National Register of Historic Places. Considered an architectural masterpiece, it is truly impressive, with its numerous volutes, wrought-iron railings and monumental roof supported by fluted columns. Its 22 rooms contain lovely 18th-century furniture.

Lutcher - Grand Point - Convent

The **St. James Historical Society Culture & Heritage Center Museum ★★** *(free admission; 1988 LA 44, Lutcher, ☎ 869-9752)* is a former pharmacy that has been converted into a museum about St. James Parish. The local tourist information center is also located here.

The **Manresa House of Retreats** *(LA 44/River Road, Convent)* was built in 1931 in the same Gothic Revival style as Jefferson College. A Catholic retreat, it is run by the Jesuits. Outside retreat periods, the grounds are open to the public.

St. Michael's Catholic Church ★★ *(Convent)* houses a replica of the grotto in Lourdes made of bagasse, a material derived from sugar cane. The hand-carved altar is from the 1867 World's Fair, held in Paris.

Tours of Agricultural and Industrial Facilities

The **Perique tobacco farm** *(free admission; by appointment; 39412 Hwy. 642 West, Grand-Point, ☎ 869-3098)*, in St. James Parish, is the only place where the famous Perique tobacco is grown. An Acadian deportee, Pierre Chenet, known as "Perique", was the first to cultivate and market this fragrant tobacco, which his descendants are still growing today, two centuries later. The farm is open year-round, but June and July are the busiest months and therefore the most interesting for anyone wishing to learn more about this tobacco, a favourite among connoisseurs.

The **Judge Poche Plantation House** *(admission fee; by appointment; Convent, ☎ 562-3537)*, built in 1870, is an example of the Victorian style.

Burnside - Darrow

Tezcuco Plantation ★★ *(adults $5, seniors and ages 13-17 $3.50, children* $2.50; guided tour, every day 9:30am to 4:30pm; B&B and restaurant: every day 9am to 5pm; both closed on Thanksgiving, Christmas and New Year's Day; 3138 LA 44/River Road, 9 km south of Burnside, ☎ 562-3929)* is a Greek Revival house dating from 1855 and decorated with friezes and elaborate wrought-iron balconies. It has a circular drive lined with century-old oaks and magnolias. Tezcuco was one of the last plantations to be built before the Civil War and is listed in the National Register of Historic Places.

The **River Road African-American Museum & Gallery** *(Wed to Sun 1pm to 5pm; on the grounds of Tezcuco Plantation, Burnside; ask for Kathe or Darryl Hambrick, ☎ 644-7955)* deals with the history of slavery on plantations, as well as the daily lives of the descendants of slaves over the years.

Houmas House Plantation and Gardens *(adults $6.50, ages 12-17 $4.50, children $3.25; catering service; guided tours; group discounts; Feb to Oct 10am to 5pm, Nov to Jan 10am to 4pm, closed Thanksgiving, Christmas and New Year's Day; 40136 LA 942, Darrow, LA 70725, ☎ 437-7841 or 522-2262)* is a Greek Revival mansion which was built in 1840 and restored in 1940. It is known for its magnificent spiral staircase and its antique furniture, made by Louisiana craftsmen. The house, surrounded by luxuriant gardens, is listed on the National Register of Historic Places.

Carville

The **Gillis W. Long Hansen's Disease Center** ★★ *(LA 75, 5445, Point Clair Rd., ☎ 642-4740 or 1-800-642-2477* *within the U.S.)*, the only hospital in North America to specialize in the treatment of leprosy, is located here. It is possible to tour this hundred-year-old facility *(☎ 642-7771)* and the administrative offices at **Indian Camp**, an old plantation house.

St. Gabriel

St. Gabriel Church ★★ *(LA 75, ☎ 642-8441)* is the oldest Catholic church in Louisiana. It was built in 1770 by Acadians who settled here after the Deportation, and its bell is said to have been a gift from the Queen of Spain.

Sorrento - Gonzales

In the early 18th century, many colonists from France, Germany and Spain settled on the banks of the Mississippi. In 1760, they were joined by deported Acadians. Toward the end of the century, the colonists migrated inland to the banks of a small bayou called New River. Tee Joe Gonzales established the first post office there in 1887. Farms and cotton plantations gradually developed in the area. Today, Gonzales, the most multi-ethnic of Louisiana's small towns, lies at the heart of plantation country and is thus an excellent base for touring this region steeped in history.

The Village 'Cadien *(free admission; Sun to Thu 6am to 9pm; Fri and Sat 6am to midnight; 6490 LA 22, Sorrento, ☎ 675-8068)* is a collection of Cajun-style cypress buildings near River Road. Contemporary art gallery, antiques and restaurant. Swamp tours upon request.

The **Tee Joe Gonzales Museum** ★★ *(Wed to Fri 1pm to 5pm; 728 N. Ascension St., Gonzales)*, set up inside an old train station, highlights the heritage of Ascension Parish.

The **Gonzales Tourist Information Center** has its offices in the museum *(664-6000)* and organizes tours of five plantations every April.

French Settlement

French Settlement was named after the French immigrants who settled here in the early 20th century. The **Creole House Museum** ★★ *(3rd Sun of each month, by appointment; LA 16, behind the town hall, ☎ 698-6114)* is devoted to these pioneers (genealogical documents, antique furniture, photographs and assorted objects).

Baton Rouge ★

Baton Rouge is the capital of the State of Louisiana. The Amerindians who first lived here called it Istrouma, meaning "red-painted stick". According to legend, the city owes its present name to explorers Pierre Le Moyne, Sieur d'Iberville, and his brother Jean-Baptiste Le Moyne, Sieur de Bienville, who, during an expedition on the Mississippi in 1699, supposedly saw a post stained with animal blood. This *bâton rouge* ("red stick" in French) marked the boundary between the territory of the Goulas and that of the Houmas, a fact that the explorers supposedly recorded on their map.

The city founded on this site in 1719 was originally called Dironbourg. The English renamed it New Richmond after the Treaty of Paris in 1763. It wasn't

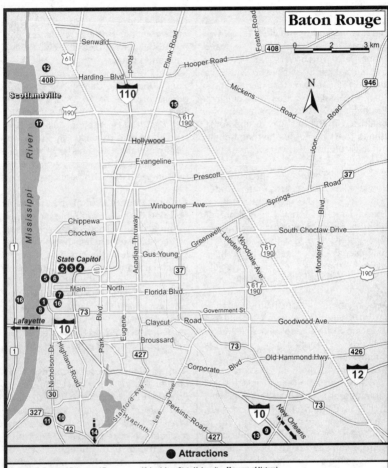

Baton Rouge

Senwald

61

408

Harding Blvd

110

Scotlandville

190

17

Mississippi River

15

61 190

Hollywood

Evangeline

Prescott

Winbourne Ave.

Chippewa

Choctwa

Acadian Thruway

Gus Young

State Capitol

2 3 4

5 6

7

1 16

16

8

Lafayette

10

73

Park Blvd

Eugene

Main North

Florida Blvd.

Government St.

Claycut Road

Broussard

427

Nicholson Dr.

Highland Road

30

327

11 10

42

14

Stafford Ave.

Hyacinth

Lee Drive

Perkins Road

Corporate Blvd.

73

13 9

10

New Orleans

427

Hooper Road

Mickens Road

408

Road

Foster Road

Plank Road

946

N

0   1   2   3 km

61 190

Springs

Road 37

Greenwell

Lobdell

Wooddale Ave.

South Choctaw Drive

Monterey

61 190

37

190

Goodwood Ave.

Old Hammond Hwy.

426

12

73

● **Attractions**

1. Spanish Town and Beauregard Town
2. State Capitol - Visitor's Center - Fort San Carlos
3. Governor's Mansion
4. Old Arsenal Museum
5. LASC Riverside Museum
6. Louisiana Arts and Science Center - Old Governor's Mansion
7. Louisiana's Old State Capitol
8. Destroyer USS Kidd
9. Louisiana State Archives
10. Louisiana State University - Museum of Natural Sciences - Geoscience Complex - Louisiana State University Stadium and Union Gallery
11. Magnolia Mound
12. Southern University
13. Rural Life Museum
14. Hilltop Arboretum and Louisiana State University
15. Laurens H. Cohn Memorial Arboretum
16. St.James Episcopal Church
17. Samuel Clemens Steamboat

© ULYSSES

THE PLANTATIONS AND BATON ROUGE

until 1817, nearly a century after it was founded, that it became Baton Rouge again.

The **historic part of the city (1)** has two sections: **Spanish Town** ★ and **Beauregard Town** ★. The first was created by the Spanish who withdrew to Baton Rouge, which remained under Spanish jurisdiction after the Louisiana Purchase in 1803. Spanish Town is small, but it still has lots of character, thanks to its numerous historic houses and its little cobblestone streets.

Beauregard Town was named after pioneer Elias Beauregard, who founded it in 1806. In the late 19th century, turrets and wooden "gingerbread" decorations were added to the houses in the area. The law firms and small businesses now located here have revived the air of respectability originally sought by Beauregard.

Most of the important historic sites in Baton Rouge are clustered around the **Louisiana State Capitol** ★★★ **(2)**. This building, completed in 1932, is impossible to miss; at 34 stories, it is the tallest capitol in the country. Ironically, the man responsible for this ambitious project, Huey P. Long, was later assassinated on the ground floor. Guided tours *(free admission; Mon to Sun 8am to 4:30pm)* are available. Visitors can see the chambers and the place where Senator Long was assassinated, as well as taking in a **panoramic view of Baton Rouge** ★★ from the observation platform on the 27th floor *(Mon to Sat 10am to 4pm, Sun 1pm to 4pm)*. At the souvenir shop, Bernice Economou will be glad to tell you about Senator Long's funeral, which she attended, and other events in Louisiana's history, both past and present.

The **Governor's Mansion (3)** *(free admission; by appointment; Mon to Fri 9am to 11pm and 2pm to 4pm; 1001 Capitol Access Rd., ☎ 342-5855)* is the state governor's official residence. Built in 1963, it resembles a Greek Revival plantation house.

The **Visitors' Center** ★★ *(free admission; Tue to Sat 10am to 4pm, Sun 1pm to 4pm; N. Riverside Dr., ☎ 342-1866)*, located in building C of the **Pentagon Barracks**, next to the Capitol, traces the history of these Greek Revival buildings, which were built in the early 19th century.

Also on the grounds of the Capitol is **Fort San Carlos** ★, with its star-shaped foundations. This Spanish fort protected the parishes north of New Orleans under the Spanish regime, which lasted from 1779 to 1810 here.

The **Old Arsenal Museum** ★ **(4)** *(free admission; Mon to Sat 10am to 4pm, Sun 1pm to 4pm; in the Capitol gardens, ☎ 342-0401)* used to be the fort's powder magazine.

At the **LASC Riverside Museum** ★★ **(5)** *(adults $1.50, children $0.75; Tue to Fri 10am to 3pm, Sat 10am to 4pm, Sun 1pm to 4pm; Front St. and North Blvd., ☎ 344-5272)*, a replica of the train station once located on the **site of the Battle of Baton Rouge** houses an interesting collection of Egyptian sarcophagi.

The **Old Governor's Mansion** ★★ **(6)** *(adults $1.50, students $0.75, seniors and children free; Sat 10am to 4pm, Sun 1pm to 4pm; 502 North Blvd., ☎ 344-5272)* was built by former Governor Huey P. Long. Antique furniture and exhibitions.

Go ahead and use the streetcar to tour the downtown area; it's free. Make sure not to miss Louisiana's **Old State Capitol** ★★★ **(7)**, a Gothic Revival castle topped with a dome of muticoloured glass, which Mark Twain dubbed the "horror on the Mississippi". Today, the Old Capitol houses the **Louisiana Center for Political and Government History** *($5; Mon to Sat 10am to 4pm; Sun noon to 4pm; ☎ 342-0500)*.

At the foot of Government Street, visitors can tour the **U.S.S. Kidd** ★★ **(8)**, a World War II destroyer *(adults $5, children $3.50; every day 9am to 5pm; 305 S. River Rd., ☎ 342-1942)*. The dock is built so that almost the entire structure of the 112-metre-long vessel is visible when the water is low.

The **Louisiana State Archives** ★★ **(9)** *(free admission; Mon to Fri 8am to 4:30pm; Sat 9am to 5pm; Sun 1pm to 5pm; 3851 Essen Lane, ☎ 922-1206)* will interest archivists, librarians and history buffs alike, since it contains scores of historical documents dating back to the 17th century.

Louisiana State University (10) is located two kilometres southwest of the capital, between Highland Road and Nicholson Drive. There are several museums and a 3,500-seat stadium on the campus.

Memorial Tower, erected in 1923 in memory of Louisianians who died in World War I, houses the **LSU Museum of Art** ★ *(free admission; Mon to Fri 9am to 4pm, Sat 10am to noon and 1pm to 4pm, Sun 1pm to 4pm; ☎ 388-4003)*. Here, visitors can admire an impressive collection of engravings from the 17th century to the first half

of the 19th. The museum also has a collection of antique silver and Newcomb pottery, among other things.

Right nearby, in **Foster Hall**, the **Museum of Natural Science** ★ *(free admission; Mon to Fri 8am to 4pm, Sat 9:30am to 1pm; 119 Foster Hall, ☎ 388-2855)* displays dioramas of Louisiana wildlife, as well as specimens of reptiles and other animals. The **Museum of Geoscience** ★ *(adults $3.50, seniors $2.50, children $1.50; 144 Howe-Russell Geoscience Complex, ☎ 388-1934 or 388-6884)* in the **Geology Building**, exhibits minerals, fossils and archeological pieces, as well as objects used by natives in their daily life.

Also noteworthy on campus are a majestic alley of oak trees planted in memory of students who died in World War II and two burial mounds believed to date back to 3,800 B.C.

Northwest of the campus, visitors can tour **Magnolia Mound** ★★ **(11)** *(adults $3.50, seniors $2.50, students $1.50, children $0.75; Tue to Sat 10am to 4pm, Sun 1pm to 4pm, 2161 Nicholson Dr., ☎ 343-4955)*, one of the oldest plantations in the state (1791). The magnificent French-Creole house, surrounded by oaks and magnolias, looks out over the river. Its interior boasts magnificent woodwork and lovely period furniture. Open-hearth cooking presentations *(Oct to May, Tue and Thu)*.

The **LSU Stadium** *(tours permitted; inquire at the souvenir shop, ☎ 388-3202)* bears the mysterious nickname "Death Valley". Residents of Baton Rouge are big football fans, and their team, the Tigers, was one of the best in the country for many years.

When the 68,000-seat stadium is full of fans cheering like crazy every time their team makes a good move, you can't hear yourself think. Hence its original nickname, "Deaf Valley", which students quickly transformed into "Death Valley".

In the LSU Union, right by the stadium, the **Union Gallery** presents art and craft exhibitions. Mike, the Tigers' mascot, lives in a cage near one of the neighbouring buildings. The Tigers took their name from a batallion of Louisiana Zouaves who became famous for their courage and fighting spirit.

Southern University (12) *(free admission; by appointment, Jun and Jul Mon to Fri 8am to 5pm; ☎ 771-2430)*, founded in 1880, is the biggest African-American university in the United States. It has a museum of fine arts, a jazz institute and a library that hosts exhibitions on African-American cultural heritage.

The **Rural Life Museum ★★ (13)** *(adults $3, children $2; Mon to Fri 8:30am to 4pm; 6200 Burden Lane, ☎ 765-2437)* is a reconstructed village complete with a police station, a school, a blacksmith's shop, a gristmill and a smokehouse. The infirmary and slaves' cabins add a grim note to the atmosphere. The property, which covers 180 hectares, is also home to a center for agricultural research.

The five-acre **LSU Hilltop Arboretum (14)** *(free admission; every day from dawn to dusk; 11855 Highland Rd., ☎ 767-6916)* is home to a variety of rare trees and plants native to this region, many of which are labelled to satisfy visitors' curiosity. Contributions welcomed (when you leave).

The **Laurens H. Cohn Memorial Arboretum ★★ (15)** *(free admission; every day 8am to 5pm; 12056 Foster Rd., ☎ 775-1006)* covers six and a half hectares and boasts a large collection of indigenous flora, which grows outdoors, as well as a greenhouse containing orchids and tropical plants.

The Gothic Revival **St. James Episcopal Church (16)** *(Mon to Fri 8:30am to 3:30pm; 208 N. 4th St., ☎ 387-5141)* was completed in 1853.

Visitors can enjoy an hour-long cruise in the Baton Rouge harbour aboard the ***Samuel Clemens* (17)** *(at the Florida Blvd. docks, adults $6, children under 12 $4; every day Apr to Aug 10am, noon and 2pm; Sep, Dec and Mar Tue to Sun; closed Jan and Feb; ☎ 381-9606)*, a steamboat bearing Mark Twain's real name. "Catfish" cruises are also available *(adults $13, children $8; Tue, Thu and Sat evenings)*.

Norfolk Tours *(424 Lovers Lane, ☎ 383-2215 or 1-800-626-6957 within the U.S.)* offers guided tours of the state capital *($15 per person; every day 10am to noon)*, plantation tours *($25 per person)* of Nottoway *(Mon and Thu)*, Rosedown and St. Francisville *(Wed and Fri)*. Swamp boat tours *($25 per person, 2pm to 6pm)* are also available. You can be picked up at your hotel. Reservations recommended.

Tiger Taxi and Tours *(☎ 921-9199 or 635-4641)*. Tours of the city, the plantations and the swamps.

Denham Springs

This former spa town is the headquarters of the **National Association of Louisiana Catahoula**

Dogs. The Catahoula dog, a breed identified specifically with Louisiana, is a mix between a breed of fighting dog introduced by explorer Hernando de Soto and an indigenous breed. Museum; dog show on the last Sunday of March.

Zachary

The **McHugh House Museum** *(free admission, contributions welcomed; Mon to Fri 10am to 1pm and by appointment; 4524 Virginia St., ☎ 654-1912)*, a venerable Victorian located 16 kilometres from Baton Rouge, contains documents on life in Zachary during the first half of the 20th century.

US 61, north of Baton Rouge, will take you to the **Port Hudson State Commemorative Area** *($2, seniors and children under 12 free; every day 9am to 5pm except New Year's Day, Thanksgiving and Christmas; 756 W. Port Hudson Rd., about 12 km west of Zachary, ☎ 654-3775)*, the site of one of the most terrible sieges of the Civil War. The battlefield is now a park. On a 10-kilometre historical trail, visitors will find fortifications, an interpretive centre an observation tower and three picnic areas. Guided tours and re-enactments of Civil War battles *(3rd week of March)*.

Numerous victims of the Civil War lie buried in the **Port Hudson National Cemetery** *(LA 3133, west of US 61)*.

St. Francisville ★★★

It is worth taking a tour of historic St. Francisville. The loop formed by Royal and Ferdinand Streets is lined with no fewer than 140 houses of historical interest. Many private homes are open to the public during the Audubon Pilgrimage in mid-March *(☎ 635-6300)*.

The **West Feliciana Historical Society Museum ★★** *(free admission; 364 Ferdinand St., ☎ 635-6330)* is the best place to start off a tour of St. Francisville. Tourist information, ticket office for Audubon Pilgrimage.

The Gothic-style **Grace Episcopal Church ★★** *(Ferdinand St.)* was built in 1858 in order to replace a wooden church erected 30 years earlier. It is noteworthy for its stained-glass windows, its impressive chandelier and its organ, which was installed in 1860 and is one of the oldest still in use.

Our Lady of Mount Carmel Church ★ was built in 1871 according to a design by the great Confederate military commander Pierre Gustave Toutant Beauregard.

Propinquity ★ *($4; by appointment; 523 Royal St., ☎ 635-6540)* is an elegant and exquisitely furnished, restored antebellum house (1809). Accommodations available.

The antebellum **Barrow House ★** *(524 Royal St., ☎ 635-4791)* has been converted into a B&B.

The **Methodist church ★** was built in 1899 to replace an earlier building damaged in a flood.

The St. Francisville Area

Oakley Plantation House - Audubon State Commemorative Area ★★ *(grounds: admission fee, seniors admitted free; every day Oct to Apr*

THE PLANTATIONS AND BATON ROUGE

9am to 5pm, Apr to Oct 9am to 7pm for the grounds, 9am to 5pm for the house; P.O. Box 546, St. Francisville, LA 70775; 11788 LA 965 E., 5 km from US 61 and 4 km south of St. Francisville, ☎ 635-3739). The Creole house, decorated with period furnishings, stands in the centre of a 50-hectare estate. The site commemorates the life of painter and ornithologist John James Audubon. Upon arriving in Louisiana in 1821, the famous naturalist painter, a native of the island of Santo Domingo (Haiti), lived here and tutored the younger sisters of Mrs. Percy, the widow of a navy officer. Here, he drew 82 of the 435 plates for his famous *Birds of America*.

Rosedown Plantation and Gardens ★★ *($9 house and gardens, $5 gardens only; Mar to Oct 9am to 5pm, Nov to Feb 10am to 4pm; mailing address: P.O. Box 1816, St. Francisville, LA 70775; 12501 LA 10/Great River Rd., at US 61, ☎ 635-3332).* A lovely Greek Revival house (1835) surrounded by 12 hectares of gardens and paths inspired by those of Versailles.

The Myrtles ★★ *(adult $6, children $4; every day 9am to 5pm; P.O. Box 7747, US 61, St. Francisville, LA 70775, ☎ 635-6277)* takes its name from the luxuriant, fragrant vegetation that surrounds it. Myrtle, a shrub native to Mediterranean regions, seems to have found its ideal climate here. The house is known for its balconies, adorned with lacy ironwork, and for the decorative plasterwork in its rooms. The Myrtles is reputed to be one of the most haunted houses in the country. Restaurant, B&B.

Butler Greenwood ★ *($5, children free; Mon to Sat 9am to 5pm, Sun 1pm to 5pm; 8345 US 61, just north of St. Francisville, ☎ 635-6312),* which dates from 1790 and has been owned by the same family ever since, is still a working plantation. Original Victorian parlor; extensive grounds and gardens. B&B.

The **Afton Villa Gardens ★** *($4; Mar to Jun; every day 9am to 4:30pm; Oct to Nov, Tue to Sun; 9247 US 61, 6 km north of St. Francisville, ☎ 635-6773 or 861-7365)* lie on either side of the longest live-oak avenue in Louisiana. Thousands of tulips and daffodils bloom here in the spring.

At **Catalpa Plantation ★** *($5, ages 6-12 $2.50; every day 10am to noon and 2pm to 4pm; closed Dec and Jan; 9508 US 61, 8 km north of St. Francisville, ☎ 635-3372),* a magnificent live-oak avenue leads to a Victorian cottage filled with antiques and family souvenirs. Guided tours led by a member of the fifth generation.

The Cottage *($5; US 61, 8 km north of St. Francisville, ☎ 635-3674),* one of the region's best-preserved plantation houses, still has its original furnishings. Built in 1795, it has numerous outbuildings. B&B.

Greenwood Plantation ★★ *($5 house and grounds, $1.50 grounds only; every day Mar to Oct 9am to 5pm, Nov to Feb 10am to 4pm; 6838 Highland Rd., 5 km from LA 66 and 13 km from US 61, towards Angola, ☎ 655-4475 or 1-800-259-4475 within the U.S.)* is a magnificent house that has been used as a setting for many television productions and films. The original house, built in 1830, survived the atrocities of the Civil War, but was ravaged by fire in 1960; only its 28 Doric columns were left standing.

Richard Barnes, the present owner, began to restore the house according to the original plans in 1968. The project was completed in 1984 and *National Geographic* has since called the house the finest example of Greek Revival architecture in southern Louisiana. While you're there, make sure to taste Mr. Barnes's flavourful coffee. A 40-kilometre bike ride of the plantation *($20 bkfst incl.; mid-May)* is possible. All necessary equipment may be rented at the house (tandems, hybrid bicycles, etc.).

Highland Plantation House ★ *($4; by appointment; Highland Rd., off LA 66, north of St. Francisville, ☎ 635-3001)*, the ancestral home of the Barrow family, is distinguished by its Italianate architecture.

The **Locust Grove State Commemorative Area ★** *(free admission; every day 9am to 5pm; north of St. Francisville, off US 61, ☎ 635-3739)* is a cemetery containing the graves of General Ripley and Sarah Knox Taylor, the wife of Confederate President Jefferson Davis.

The **Feliciana Bike Touring Agency** offers bicycle tours of the region *($21 per person; mid-Apr; 11734 St. Ferdinand St., St. Francisville, ☎ 635-0083)*. The "Cemeteries and Haunted Houses" tour includes stops at the Locust Grove cemetery, The Myrtles and Grace Episcopal Church. Total distance covered: 29 kilometres.

The **Catalpa, Oakley and Cottage Bicycle Tour** *($26 bkfst incl.)* offers a chance to visit three antebellum houses. Total distance covered: 37 kilometres.

Tunica - Angola

A few kilometres north of St. Francisville, on LA 66, the scenic route known as the **Tunicas Trail** comes to a dead-end at Angola, the state penitentiary, located on the former site of the Angola Plantation. The **Angola Rodeo** *(admission fee; Sunday afternoons in Oct)* is "the wildest cowboy show in the South".

The **Angola Crafts Fair** *(free admission; late Apr to early May; on the rodeo grounds, ☎ 655-4411)* is held in the prison, which is open to the public during this period *(adults $1, children $0.50)*. You can even do the jailhouse rock, since inmate bands provide music for the event.

Just before Angola, you'll find a small community of Tunica Indians, who live on the site where their nation's treasures were discovered. At Marksville, in Avoyelles Parish, visitors can admire objects found at a burial ground on the east bank of the Mississippi.

Jackson - Wilson - Clinton

In the early 19th century, West Feliciana Parish was part of the breakaway Republic of West Florida. It was recovered by the United States in 1810.

The parish seat of East Feliciana since 1824, **Clinton** was one of the first places in the region where cotton, introduced by English-speaking farmers from the south, was cultivated. Architecture buffs can admire the **Court House**, a Greek Revival building with an octagonal dome, built in 1840. It is also possible to visit the **Marston House** *(by*

THE PLANTATIONS AND BATON ROUGE

appointment; admission fee;
☎ 683-5594), **St. Andrews Episcopal Church** and the Gothic Revival **Woodside Cottage**, as well as the Greek Revival **Woodside House** *(Woodville Rd.)*. The Confederate cemetery is also worth a stop.

The Greek Revival **Milbank Historic House ★** *(adults $4, children and seniors $3.50; every day 10am to 4pm; mailing address: P.O. Box 1000, 102 Bank St., Jackson, LA 70748;* ☎ *634-5901)*, located in the heart of old Jackson, has a fine collection of antique furniture.

The **Republic of West Florida Museum ★★** *($2; Tue to Sun 9am to 5pm; Old Hickory Village, E. College St., Jackson,* ☎ *634-7155)* presents exhibitions on wildlife and local history: an original cotton gin, a sugarcane press, old farm implements and Native American objects.

Glencoe Plantation ★ *(13 km west of Clinton, P.O. Box 178, Wilson, LA 70789,* ☎ *629-5387)* is an imposing Victorian originally built in 1870, then reconstructed in 1898 after being destroyed by fire. With its multicoloured stained-glass windows, diagonal wood panelling in its dining room and imposing porches, it is truly a must-see.

Oakland Plantation ★ *(adults $5, seniors $4.50; open to groups by appointment, LA 963 between the 68 and the 19, near Wilson,* ☎ *692-5960)* features a lovely two-story brick house dating from 1827. Its woodwork and dining room are particularly noteworthy.

The West Bank of the Mississippi

Hahnville

Hahnville was founded by German-speaking settlers from Alsace-Lorraine. The parish in which it is located, St. Charles, used to be called **Côte-des-Allemands** (Lake des Allemands, Bayou des Allemands and the town of Des Allemands can still be found here), *Allemand* being the French word for German. Michael Hahn was the Federal governor of Louisiana during the Civil War; the Confederates had their own governor.

The **Keller Home Place Plantation House** *(by appointment, 9am to 5pm; LA 18,* ☎ *783-2123)* was built around 1790. With its big wrap-around porch, it resembles the French colonial architecture of the West Indies.

Vacherie - St. James

The town of St. James was originally the seat of the parish of the same name. In 1869, however, it lost its title to Convent, which is located on the banks of the river, near the Sacred Heart Convent.

Laura Plantation ★★★ *(adults $7, children and teenagers $4; group discounts; every day 9am to 5pm; closed Thanksgiving, Christmas and New Year's Day; 2247 LA 18, on River Road, Vacherie, LA 70090,* ☎ *265-7690)*, the "Belle Créole" of the Mississippi, has unfortunately been unoccupied since 1984; faithful to tradition, its successive occupants made French the language spoken at the plantation until their departure in 1984. Its acquisition by a group of history enthusiasts including the architect and historian Norman Marmillion, himself a descendant of a rich aristocratic Louisiana family, ensured the preservation of this beautiful heritage site, built in 1805, which would have otherwise deteriorated with time and inevitable acts of vandalism.

After being partially restored, the plantation house was opened to the public in 1994. Though other buildings are still being fixed up, this is definitely the most inviting of all the plantations. Lesser known than some other "star" plantations, it is nonetheless more interesting, thanks to its authentic Creole character (how many other plantation houses are painted in such bright colours?) and its history, the details of which are supported by extensive research. The fascinating anecdotes told by the guides during the tours were taken from old documents (5,000 pages' worth!) consulted at the National Archives of Paris and from *Memories of Laura*. These memoires, written by Laura Locoul and spanning nearly two centuries, relate the daily lives of two-centuries' of plantation residents. The document was found in St. Louis, Missouri in 1993. There has been no attempt to disguise the fact that slaves were used on the plantation, and the site of the former slave cabins is moving testimony to the hardships that African-Americans had to endure.

Upon request, Laura Plantation also offers five thematic tours of the estate: Creole architecture, the feminine presence and matriarchy on the plantation, Creole slaves: folklore and craft traditions, the daily lives of children on a Creole plantation and French wine tastings at Laura Locoul's.

Oak Alley Plantation ★★★ *(guided tours; adults $6.50, students $3.50, children $2; Mar to Oct 9am to 5:50pm, Nov to Feb 9am to 5pm, closed Thanksgiving, Christmas and New Year's Day; restaurant and cabins for overnight stays; 3645 LA 18, Vacherie, LA 70090, ☎ 265-2152 or 1-800-442-5539 within the U.S.)* is a Greek Revival mansion, built on River Road in 1837-1839. It is world-famous for its alley lined with live oaks, which were already a century old when the house was built, and its 28 Doric columns, each over two metres around. One of the most impressive attractions on the tour.

St. James Catholic Church and Cemetery ★★. The church dates from the 19th century. It was on the site of its cemetery, one of the oldest in Louisiana, that the first Acadians settled in this region after being deported from their native land in 1755.

Donaldsonville ★★★

Founded in 1750 on the banks of Bayou Lafourche, Donaldsonville is the oldest town in Louisiana after Natchitoches and New Orleans. A large number of Acadians came to this area in 1758, and the Francophone presence is still very evident here.

Over 600 of the houses, shops and other buildings in the historic district were built between 1865 and 1933 *(tourist information: Donaldsonville Chamber of Commerce, ☎ 473-4814)*.

The **Ascension Catholic Church** *(716 Mississippi St.)* was built in 1772, during the reign of Spanish monarch

THE PLANTATIONS AND BATON ROUGE

Charles III. It has the oldest religious archives in Louisiana.

St. Peter's Methodist Church *(at the corner of Houmas and Claiborne)* has been the spiritual centre of Donaldsonville's black community since it was built in 1871. In sugar-cane country like this, there is always a large African-American population made up of descendants of slaves brought here to work on the plantations.

The **Parish Prison** *(at the corner of Chetimatches and Nicholls)* no longer serves the purpose for which it was built, but it did so for over a century.

B. Lemann & Brothers Inc. *(between Mississippi St and Railroad Ave.)*, built in 1836, is the oldest department store in Louisiana. Its wrought-iron balconies and its elaborate ornamentation give it a great deal of charm.

Part of the **Evan Hall Sugar Mill** *(LA 1 N.)* dates back to the era of Evan Hall Plantation.

White Castle - Bayou Goula - Plaquemine ★★★

This part of the tour covers the sugarcane country east of the Atchafalaya basin, home of several plantations, including Nottoway, whose palatial architecture earned it the nickname "White Castle". Iberville Parish, for its part, was named after the French explorer. It was one of the first places the deported Acadians settled.

Nottoway Plantation ★★ *(adults $8, children $3; museum: every day 9am to 5pm, restaurant: 11am to 3pm and 6pm to 9pm, closed Christmas; P.O. Box 160, LA 1, White Castle, LA*

70788, ☎ *545-2730 or 545-2409 or in Baton Rouge,* ☎ *346-8263)* dates back to 1859. The house, a mix of Greek Revival and Italianate styles, has 64 rooms, making it the largest in Louisiana. Its grounds cover 15 hectares. A 300-seat restaurant can be found on the premises, and rooms are available for rent.

The **Madonna Chapel**, on the road to Plaquemine, is said to be the smallest church in the world *(LA 405, Bayou Goula)*. Formal Mass on August 15, Assumption Day (the Acadian national holiday).

Tally-Ho, also on LA 405, is the reconstructed caretaker's house of the plantation of the same name, which burned down.

At the **Plaquemine Locks** ★ *(free admission; Mon to Fri 8am to 4pm; Plaquemine,* ☎ *687-0641)*, visitors will find an interpretive centre focussing on the history of the river as a navigable waterway. Picnic area and observation tower.

The **Plaquemine Town Hall** ★ *(at the corner of Main and Church)* is a Greek Revival building dating from 1849.

There are several plantation houses in the Plaquemine area: the Greek Revival **St. Louis Plantation** *(admission fee; May 1 to Nov 15, 9am to 5pm except Sun)*, on River Road; the **Variety Plantation Cottage** *(by appointment,* ☎ *659-2510)*, on Bayou Road; **Live Oaks Plantation** and its slave church, at Grosse Tete; and the two restored houses of **Old Turnerville** *($5; groups of 10 or more; 23230 Nadler St., Plaquemine,* ☎ *687-5337)* on LA 1.

Brusly

The small community of Brusly is located between Port Allen and Plaquemine, on the west bank of the Mississippi. Here, visitors can admire a 350-year-old live oak listed in the register of the Louisiana Live Oak Society. Also noteworthy are the **Lockman, Antonio and Cazenave houses**, all built in the previous century. The **St. John the Baptist Church cemetery**, which dates from the mid-19th century, is also worth a visit.

Cinclare Plantation, right near Brusly *(LA 1)*, is home to one of the oldest sugar mills in southern Louisiana.

Port Allen

Port Allen, across the river from the state capital, is the parish seat of West Baton Rouge Parish. Baton Rouge's extensive port facilities, which make the city the fourth largest port in the country, are located here *(☎ 387-4207)*.

West Baton Rouge Museum ★★ *(free admission; Tue to Sat 10am to 4:30pm; Sun 2pm to 5pm; 845 N. Jefferson Ave., ☎ 336-2422)*. The Aillet House, a French Creole cottage from the 1830's, slave quarters and a sugar mill have been transformed into a museum about daily life during the plantation era.

Allendale Plantation *(US 190 W.)* was built in 1852 by Henry Watkins Allen, a former state governor.

Poplar Grove Plantation *(admission fee; guided tours by appointment for groups of 20 or more; 3142 N. River Rd., ☎ 899-8087)* was built specially for the

Banker's Pavilion at the 1884 World's Industrial and Cotton Exposition. At Christmas time, the old slave cabins and the mill are lit up, and the plantation is open to the public.

The **Port Allen Locks** *(every day 9am to 4pm)* connect the Mississippi to the Intracoastal Waterway.

Rosedale

Rosedale, which lies between Grosse Tete and Maringouin, is also located in Iberville Parish. Its roads run alongside the bayous and through a rural landscape. The famous I-10, built on piles, starts here. This masterpiece of engineering, which runs over the Atchafalaya basin for over 30 kilometres, stops at Henderson, just before the Cajun capital, Lafayette.

Live Oaks Plantation ★ *($5, by appointment; Mar to Jun every day 9am to 4:30pm, Oct to Nov Tue to Sun; LA 77, ☎ 648-2346)* boasts a lovely house surrounded by live oaks, azaleas and camellias, and looking out onto a picturesque bayou. An unusual tomb and a slave chapel can also be found on the property. Listed in the National Register.

New Roads

New Roads, with its 5,000 inhabitants, is the parish seat of Pointe Coupee Parish. This peaceful region, where time seems to have stopped in the 19th century, has a tranquil atmosphere and a number of resorts. Vacationers are particularly fond of False River, whose calm waters are perfect for water sports. C-shaped False River was created in the 18th century, when the

THE PLANTATIONS AND BATON ROUGE

Mississippi changed course significantly. It is flanked on both sides by fertile land, which led to the development of magnificent estates like Parlange Plantation, erected in 1750. The region abounds in agricultural riches: corn, sugar cane, soy beans, market garden produce, pecans, cotton, livestock, etc.

The little town of New Roads is quite charming. Strolling down the narrow streets of its historic neighbourhood, visitors will be pleased to discover a large number of splendid houses with tree-lined drives.

On the way there, stop by the pretty **Pointe Coupée Parish Museum**, on LA 1.

St. Mary's Catholic Church ★ *(free admission; 348 W. Main St., ☎ 638-9665)* is a historic building dating from 1823. The nearby cemetery *(New Roads St.)* was laid out in 1865.

At the **Pointe Coupée Antique Show & Sale** *($4 per person; late Apr; Scott Civic Center, ☎ 638-9858)*, which lasts three days, visitors can browse among paintings, jewellery, porcelain, crystal, lace, silver, and rustic and Victorian furniture. Cooking and recipe-trading are also part of the event.

It is possible to tour the **H.C. Bergeron Pecan Shelling Plant** *(free admission; Nov to Apr, Mon to Fri 8am to 3pm, LA 1, ☎ 638-9626 or 638-7667)*. Products available for sale on the premises.

East and South of New Roads

Wickliffe Plantation ★ *($5; by appointment; LA 415, 5 km east of New Roads, ☎ 638-9504)* features a Creole house built in 1820 for a sugar-cane planter. The plantation now specializes in pecans.

LeBeau House ★ *($5 per person; open to groups by appointment; LA 414, Jarreau, near the south end of False River, ☎ 627-5466)* is a lovely Creole cottage (1840) furnished with graceful antiques. Its magnificent grounds are graced with century-old oaks.

Bonnie Glen ★★ *(adults $5, children $2; by appointment; LA 1, on False River, a few kilometres east of New Roads, ☎ 638-9004)*, a plantation house, was built between 1825 and 1834 and has remained in the same family ever since. Cob walls, large porches on the façade and facing the yard. Barn and cabin dating from the 18th century.

The **Villa de Mon Cœur** ★ *($5; Tue to Sat 10am to 4pm; 7739 False River Dr., Oscar, LA 1, 13 km south of New Roads, ☎ 638-9892)* is a traditional two-story house with lovely gardens. It is possible to have tea here as well *(afternoon tea: $10; Fri and Sat noon to 4pm)*.

Parlange Plantation ★★ *(adults $5, children $2.50; every day 9am to 5pm by appointment; LA 1, near LA 78, ☎ 638-8410)* is one of the most gorgeous residences in the False River area. A colonial house made of brick and cypress, it was built in 1750 by ancestors of the present owners.

The **Pointe Coupée Parish Museum and Tourist Center** ★★ *(free admission; contributions welcomed; Mon to Fri 9am to 3pm, Sat 10am to 3pm; LA 1, 10 km south of New Roads, ☎ 638-9858)* is typical of Louisiana architecture of the 18th and 19th centuries. The museum focusses on the cultural and historical links between Québec, the rest of Canada, and France.

The **Chérie districts** ★ *(3645 Gladiola St., #6, 16 km south of New Roads, Baton Rouge, LA 70808; speak to Ruth Laney, ☎ 344-8803).* It was here that African-American novelist Ernest J. Gaines, author of *The Autobiography of Miss Jane Pitman* and *Bloodline*, made into a film by Volker Schlondorff in 1983, was born. The Chérie districts remain a constant source of inspiration for the author. Today, there is hardly anything left but a small church, two slave cabins and a cemetery containing the graves of five generations of slaves who worked on River Lake Plantation.

North of New Roads

St. Stephen's Episcopal Church ★ *($2; by appointment; LA 418, near Innis, 31 km north of New Roads, ☎ 638-9858),* a brick building dating from 1848, is listed in the National Register. Visitors will find a tomb of the unknown Civil War soldier and a historic cemetery here.

St. Francis Chapel ★ *($1; by appointment; River Rd., between New Roads and Morganza, ☎ 638-8165)* is a Catholic oratory that was built in 1895 on the vestiges of an earlier church (1760). It was moved to its present site in 1930.

PARKS

The East Bank of the Mississippi

The **Baton Rouge Zoo** *(adults $2, ages 5-17 $1, under four free; every day except Christmas and New Year's Day, 10am to 5pm, 10am to 7pm during summer; I-110 then LA 67, ☎ 775-3877)* is home to nearly 1,000 species of birds and other animals from every continent. A small train and a tram carry visitors about.

At the **Blue Bayou Water Park** *(18142 Perkins Rd., Baton Rouge, Exit 66 off the 10, ☎ 753-3333),* visitors can go for a swim and enjoy a variety of other wet activities.

St. Francisville

The Bluffs on Thompson Creek *($40 on weekdays, $50 on weekends; every day until nightfall, closed Christmas; mailing adress: P.O. Box 1220, St. Francisville, LA 70775, LA 965, at Freeland Rd., east of St. Francisville, ☎634-3410).* Golf course designed by Arnold Palmer, tennis courts, croquet and accommodations. Credit Cards accepted.

ACCOMMODATIONS

The East Bank of the Mississippi

Burnside

Tezcuco Plantation *($60-$150 Creole bkfst incl.; ≡, pb; 3138 LA 44,*

Darrow, LA 70725, ☎ 562-3929) rents out 16 rooms in the big house, as well as a few cabins on the grounds. Wine, coffee or tea is served to guests upon their arrival.

Prairieville

The **Tree House in the Park** *($100 bkfst and dinner incl.; pb, ≈, ⊚; mailing address: 16520 Airline Hwy., Prairieville, LA 70769; ☎ 622-2850 or in Baton Rouge ☎ 335-8942)* is a Cajun cottage in the swamps with a big bedroom, a waterbed and a private whirlpool bath on the terrace. Guests can enjoy an outing on the Amite River in a two-person kayak. Boat landing and fishing pier.

Baton Rouge

Knight's R.V. Park *(US 190, 11 km east of Baton Rouge, ☎ 275-0679)*, open year-round, has 35 R.V. sites, showers, restrooms and laundry facilities.

Like all big cities, Baton Rouge has hotels, motels and bed and breakfasts in all different price ranges. Big chains like Holiday Inn *(☎ 1-800-HOLIDAY within North America)*, Hampton Inn *(☎ 1-800-HAMPTON within North America)*, Hilton *(☎ 1-800-HILTONS within North America)* and Wilson Inn *(☎ 1-800-WILSONS within North America)* have international reservation services and compete to offer guests all sorts of bonuses: complimentary breakfasts, no charge for teenagers, etc.

The **Plantation Inn** *($35-$70; ≡, ≈, ℜ, pb, ctv; 10330 Airline Hwy., Exit 2 off I-12, ☎ 293-4100)* is a 175-room hotel

located east of downtown Baton Rouge, near an expressway (US 61).

The **Belmont Hotel** *($40-$90; ≡, ≈, ℜ, pb, ctv; 7370 Airline Hwy., Exit 2 off I-12, ☎ 357-6812 or 1-800-272-8300 within the U.S.)* is located near the major roads leading to the airport.

The 120-room **Hampton Inn** *($45-$70; ≡, pb, ctv, ≈; 10045 Gwendale Dr., Baton Rouge; Exit 2 off I-12, ☎ 924-4433, ☎ 1-800-HAMPTON within the U.S.)* is located east of the city, at the intersection of Airline Highway and the I-12.

The 140-room **Hampton Inn** *($50-$70 bkfst incl.; ≡, pb, ctv, ≈; 4646 Constitution Ave., College Drive Exit off I-10, ☎ 926-9990 or 1-800-HAMPTON within the U.S.)* offers a standard level of comfort.

The **La Quinta Motor Inn** *($55-$70; ≡, pb, ctv, ≈; 2333 S. Acadian Thrwy., Exit 157B off I-10, ☎ 924-9600 or 1-800-531-5900 within North America)* is located near downtown Baton Rouge.

The **Howard Johnson Plaza Suite Hotel** *($60-$80; ≡, ≈, pb, tv; 2045 N. Third St., ☎ 344-6000 or 1-800-487-8157 within North America)* is located downtown, three blocks from the Capitol.

The **Holiday Inn South** *($60-$90; ≡, ≈, ℜ, ⊘, pb, ctv; 9940 Airline Hwy., ☎ 924-7021 or 1-800-HOLIDAY within North America)* has a big indoor garden, two restaurants, two bars and a recreation room.

The **Hilton Hotel** *($75-$97; ≡, ≈, ℜ, △, ⊘, pb, ctv; 5500 Hilton Ave., College Drive Exit off I-10, ☎ 924-5000 or*

1-800-621-5116 within North America) has 298 rooms and is located next to the downtown area.

Denham Springs

The **KOA - East Baton Rouge** *(≈; Exit 10 off I-12, LA 16 S. for 1 km, then west for 0.5 km, Denham Springs, ☎ 664-7281 or 1-800-292-8245 within the U.S.)*, open year-round, has 72 fully equipped R.V. sites and 102 other sites with electricity only. Showers, restrooms, laundry facilities, playground, grocery store, excursions.

St. Francisville

The **Green Acres Campground** *(LA 965 E., 5 km from US 61 S., ☎ 635-4903)* is fully equipped and well laid-out.

The **Ramada Inn - St. Francisville** *($55 to $80; ≡, ≈, ℛ, pb, ctv; at the junction of US 61 and LA 10, ☎ 635-3821 or 1-800-523-6118 within the U.S.)* has 101 rooms.

Those travellers wishing to spend the night in an opulent, historic house can refer to the following listings for East and West Feliciana Parishes:

The **Wolf-Schlesinger House - St. Francisville Inn** *($55-$65 bkfst incl.; pb, ≈, ℛ; mailing address: P.O. Box 1369, St. Francisville, LA 70775; 118 N. Commerce St., ☎ 635-6503 or 1-800-488-6502 within the U.S.)* is located next to the historic district. A nine-room Victorian house, it looks out onto a typical New Orleans-style courtyard.

The **Lake Rosemound Inn** *($60-$92 bkfst incl.; ℛ; 10473 Lindsay Lane, St.*

Francisville, LA 70775, 20 km north of St. Francisville, ☎ 635-3176) has four rooms with a view of the lake. No smoking.

The Garden Gate Manor *($65-$90 bkfst incl.; ≡, pb; 204 Poydras St., St. Francisville, LA 70760, ☎ 638-3890 or 1-800-487-3890)* is considered to be one of the 10 best period B&Bs between Houston, Texas and Mobile, Alabama. A Victorian house restored in 1912, it has seven large rooms and sumptuous bathtubs. Gardens, gastronomic breakfasts and afternoon tea.

The **Printer's Cottage** *($60-$75 bkfst incl.; ≡, pb; mailing address: P.O. Box 299, St. Francisville, LA 70775; 533 Royal St., ☎ 635-6376)*, located in the historic district, is a Creole cottage with two guestrooms.

There are two B&Bs behind **Butler Greenwood** *($75-$100 bkfst incl.; ≡, pb; 8345 US 61, St. Francisville, LA 70775; ☎ 635-6312 or 1-800-749-1928 within the U.S.)* plantation house. One was the original detached kitchen (1790) and the other, which has a view of the pond, was the cook's cottage (19th century). Credit cards accepted through the Reservation Service.

The Myrtles *($75-$130 bkfst incl.; ≡, pb; mailing address: P.O. Box 1100 LA 61, St. Francisville, LA 70775; ☎ 635-6277)* is a luxurious 12-room house. Candle-lit dinners upon reservation.

Green Springs Plantation *($80-$110 bkfst incl.; ≡, pb; 7463 Tunica Trace, St. Francisville, LA 70775, ☎ 635-4232 or 1-800-457-4978 within the U.S.)* is a recently built Feliciana-style cottage with three guestrooms and a magnificent view of the pastures. There is a native burial mound right near by. One of the breakfast specialties is spinach Madeline. No smoking.

🦀 **The Lodge at the Bluffs** *($85-$120 bkfst incl.; ≡, pb, ≈; mailing address: P.O. Box 1220, St. Francisville, LA 70775; LA 965 at Freeland Rd., 10 km east of St. Francisville, ☎ 634-3410 or (888) 634-3410 within the U.S.)* has 29 luxurious suites with 19th-century decor. Golf and tennis.

Hemingbough *($85-$105 bkfst incl.; ≈, pb; LA 965, 3 km south of St. Francisville; mailing address: P.O. Box 1640, St. Francisville, LA 70775; ☎ 635-6617)* is a peaceful country getaway whose 90 hectares of property include a 15-hectare lake. Eight rooms and two suites with period furnishings.

The Cottage *($90 bkfst incl.; ≈, pb, ≡, ℜ; mailing address: P.O. Box 1816, St. Francisville, LA 70775; LA 68, ☎ 635-3110)* is located on 160 hectares of land and is surrounded by century-old oaks. This magnificent house, erected in 1795, is listed in the National Register of Historic Places. A pool and a restaurant have been added.

Jackson

🦀 **Asphodel Plantation** *($55-$80 bkfst incl.; ≡, pb, ≈, ℜ; 4626 LA 68, Jackson, LA 70748, ☎ 654-6868)* is made up of several houses and other buildings, earning it the name "Asphodel Village". The rooms, decorated with period furnishings, are in the lovely Greek Revival plantation

house. Some of them include sitting rooms, and a few even have fireplaces. There are some more modest rooms on the second floor. One of the houses, the Levy House, contains a restaurant and a conference room.

The **Milbank Historic House** *($75 bkfst incl.; ≡, ℜ, pb, cb; 102 Bank St.; mailing address: P.O. Box 1000, Jackson, LA 70748; ☎ 634-5901)*, located in the heart of old Jackson, is a Greek Revival mansion (1825) decorated with quality antiques.

The West Bank of the Mississippi

Vacherie

Oak Alley Plantation *($85-$115 bkfst incl.; ≡, pb; 3645 LA 18/River Rd., Vacherie, LA 70090, ☎ 265-2151)* has six charming cabins set beneath the trees on its grounds. No smoking.

White Castle

The **White Castle Inn** *($55-$75 bkfst incl.; ≡, pb; 55035 Cambre St., White Castle, LA 70788, ☎ 545-9932 or 545-2271)* was erected in 1897 as a bank. It was converted into a house in 1945, then into a B&B in 1990.

🦀 **Nottoway Plantation** *($95-$250 bkfst incl.; ≡, pb; mailing addres: P.O. Box 160, White Castle, LA 70788; ☎ 545-2730 or 346-8263)* is the biggest plantation house in the South (64 rooms). There are 13 guestrooms altogether, some in the mansion and others in the restored caretaker's cottage.

Plaquemine

The **Bayou Bait Shop, R.V. Park/Cabins** *(LA 75, Bayou Sorrel, 21 km south of Plaquemine, ☎ 659-7060)*, open year-round, has 40 sites, 30 of which are equipped for R.V.s. Electricity, showers, restrooms, laundry facilities, grocery store, gas pump, fishing, landing stage. Ten air-conditioned cottages with bedclothes and dishes.

The **Old Turnerville B&B** *($60-$65 bkfst incl.; ≡, pb; 23230 Nadler St., Plaquemine, LA 70764, ☎ 687-5337)*, a cottage built over a century ago, is located in the beautiful village of Plaquemine. It has a big veranda with a swing and rocking chairs on it and rooms furnished in old-fashioned style. A tour of the lovely neighbouring houses is available.

Port Allen

The **Cajun Country Campground** *(4667 Rebelle Ln., 3 km from Exit 151 off I-10, 7 km west of Baton Rouge, ☎ 383-8554)*, open year-round, has 77 R.V. sites, showers, laundry facilities, a grocery store and a gas pump. Campers are offered a complementary Cajun supper on Saturday night. Fishing.

The **Newcourt Inn** *($35-$60; ≡, pb, ctv, ≈; LA 415 Exit 294 off I-10, ☎381-9134, ☎ 1-800-826-3375 within the U.S.)* is a decent 148-room hotel at the west edge of Port Allen.

A Cottage at Poplar Grove Plantation *($95-$125 bkfst incl.; pb, K; 3142 N. River Rd., Port Allen, LA 70767, 3 km north of Port Allen, ☎ 344-3913)* is, as indicated by its name, a restored Creole cottage (1840) on Poplar Grove Plantation. Located near the river, it offers a rural atmosphere and a view of the cane fields. It has one guestroom, a kitchenette, a sitting room and a porch with a swing, as well as an attic with a small tub. Tour of the house and continental breakfast included.

New Roads

The **Pointe Coupée Bed & Breakfast** *($60-$70 bkfst incl.; ≡, pb, 401 Richey St., New Roads, LA 70760, ☎ 634-6254 or 1-800-832-7412 within the U.S.)* has two restored houses: a Victorian dating from 1902 and a Creole cottage dating from 1835. Antique furniture. Suites with fireplace available. Six guestrooms. Wine upon arrival. No smoking.

 Mon Rêve Bed & Breakfast *($65 and up, bkfst incl.; ≡, pb; 9825 False River Rd./LA 1, New Roads, LA 70760, ☎ 638-7848 or 1-800-324-2738 within the U.S.)*. The present owner's great-grandmother loved this Creole house (1820) so much that she nicknamed it *"mon rêve"* (my dream). It has a lovely porch looking out onto False River and a small dock for guests.

The **River Blossom Inn** *($65-$85 bkfst incl.; ≡, pb; 300 North Carolina St., New Roads, LA 70760, ☎ 638-8650)* has four spacious guestrooms decorated with antiques. Southern-style breakfast. Tea or wine upon arrival. Smoking areas.

✕ RESTAURANTS

As many restaurants are closed on Thanksgiving, it should be noted that this holiday is always on the last Thursday of November in the United

States, not, as in Canada, on the second Monday of October.

The East Bank of the Mississippi

Burnside

The Cabin *($$; Mon to Wed 8am to 3pm, Thu 8am to 9pm, Fri and Sat 8am to 10pm, Sun 8am to 6pm; LA 44 at LA 22, ☎ 473-3007)* cooks up good Cajun cuisine and does a wonderful job with seafood from the Gulf of Mexico. Closed holidays.

French Settlement

The candle-lit dining room at the **Bordelon's Restaurant** *($$$; Wed to Thu 5pm to 9pm, Fri and Sat 5pm to 10pm, Sun noon to 9pm, closed Christmas and Easter; 14476 Oak St., ☎ 698-3804 or 695-6903)* offers a splendid view of the Amite River. Creole cuisine, steak and local seafood.

Baton Rouge

The **Coffee Call** - College Drive *($; Mon to Thu 6am to 2am, Fri and Sat around the clock, Sun 6am to 12:30am; closed Christmas; 3010 College Dr., ☎ 925-9493)* serves traditional café au lait with New Orleans-style beignets. Po-boys and excellent home-made soup at lunchtime. No credit cards.

The **Coffee Call** - Catfish Town *($; Mon to Fri 6am to 6pm, Sat and Sun 7am to 6pm; 110 St. James St., Catfish Town - shopping mall by the river, ☎ 383-3461)* serves café au lait with New Orleans-style beignets, as well as po-boys. Lunch buffet Monday through Friday. No credit cards.

Poor Boy Lloyds *($; Mon to Fri 6:30am to 4pm; 210 Florida Blvd., ☎ 387-2271)* is where civil servants who work downtown get together. Breakfast, table d'hôte, seafood and po-boys. The place is fairly busy at lunchtime, then quiets down after 1pm.

There are **Picadilly Cafeterias** *($-$$; every day 11am to 8:30pm, closed Christmas; six locations: 3332 S. Sherwood Blvd., Cortana Mall, Bon Marché Mall, Westmoreland Village and Delmont Village, ☎ 5474 Essen Ln., ☎ 293-9440)* in most towns in southern Louisiana; all offer a good choice of regional dishes. No credit cards.

Ellington's *($-$$; Howard Johnson Hotel, 2045 N. Third St. ☎ 344-6000)* serves up homestyle cooking and has live jazz on Saturday nights.

Carlino's Restaurant *($-$$; Mon to Fri 7:30am to 2pm; 392 Florida Blvd., ☎ 387-5148)*, located downtown, specializes in breakfast, but also has a table d'hôte and makes good po-boys, salads, sandwiches, muffulettas and hamburgers. Relaxed atmosphere.

The Louisiana House of Representatives Dining Hall *($-$$; Mon to Fri 7am to 2pm; Louisiana State Capitol, ☎ 342-0371)* is located in the basement of the Capitol. Standard offerings, cafeteria-style service. Soup and salad counter, daily menu, breakfast. Closed holidays.

Patrons of **Phil's Oyster Bar** *($-$$; Mon to Sat 10:30am to 9:30pm; 5162 Government St., ☎ 924-3045)* tuck into seafood, oysters on the half-shell and po-boys, as well as Italian and Louisiana cuisine.

Maggio's - College Drive *($-$$$; every day 11am to 11pm; 5294 College Dr., ☎ 926-1462)* is one of the best Italian restaurants in Baton Rouge hands down, and is equally renowned for its grill and super-fresh fish. Closed holidays.

The **Café Louisiane** *($$-$$$; every day 11am to 10pm; 2246 S. Acadian Thrwy., ☎ 343-2148)* serves up all the classics of Louisiana cuisine. The menu also includes a whole range of seafood dishes, po-boys, rib steaks, salads and desserts.

Juban's Restaurant *($$-$$$; lunch Mon to Fri 11:30am to 2pm, dinner Mon to Sat 5:30pm to 10pm, closed Christmas; 3739 Perkins Dr., ☎ 346-8422)* serves Louisiana cuisine. House specialties include "Hallelujah" crab and gumbo. New Orleans French Quarter ambiance.

Navia's New Orleans Seafood Restaurant *($$-$$$; Tue to Thu 11:30am to 9pm, Fri 11:30am to 2pm and 4pm to 6pm, Sat 4pm to 10:30pm; 145 Ben Hur Rd., ☎ 768-7444)*. After leaving New Orleans for a trip towards the Mississippi Valley, you'll find an excellent spot for gluttons and gourmets alike. Typical New Orleans ambiance. Everything here is reminiscent of the Crescent City: the apéritifs, the cuisine (the seafood is particularly good) and the music (Louis Armstrong, Louis Prima and Fats Domino are featured on the jukebox).

Ralph & Kakoo's Seafood Restaurants - Airline Highway *($$-$$$; Mon to Thu 11:30am to 2pm and 5pm to 10pm, Fri 11:30am to 2pm and 5pm to 10:30pm,* Sun 11:30am to 9pm; 7110 Airline Hwy., ☎ 356-2361) serve seafood from the Gulf of Mexico, prepared Cajun style. Closed holidays.

The **Chalet Brandt Restaurant** *($$-$$$; Mon to Fri 11:30am to 2pm, Mon to Sat 5pm to 10pm; 7655 Old Hammond Hwy., ☎ 927-6040)* is owned by Betsy and Erik Brandt. Erik, the son of a Swiss businessman, was trained at the American Culinary Institute in New York. The menu includes a few Swiss specialties and an excellent duck with Madeira and blueberries, which is highly recommended by the friendly maitre d', Bill.

Mamacita's Restaurant and Cantina *($$-$$$; 24 hours a day; 7524 Bluebonnet Rd., ☎ 769-3850)* specializes in fajitas grilled on prosopis wood, as well as shrimp and fish. Friendly Southern atmosphere.

Serop's Restaurant *($$-$$$; Mon to Fri 11am to 2pm and 5pm to 10pm, Sat 5pm to 10pm; 4065 Government St., ☎ 383-3658)* serves Lebanese cuisine. Closed holidays.

Carnivores take note: **Ruth's Chris Steak House** *($$$; Mon to Fri 11:30am to 11:30pm, Sat 4pm to midnight; 4836 Constitution St., ☎ 925-0163)* is the best place to go for red meat and grilled food. Good wine list.

The **Maison Lacour** *($$$-$$$$; Mon to Fri 11:30am to 2pm and 5:30pm to 11pm, Sat 5:30pm to 10pm; 11025 N. Harrell's Ferry Rd., ☎ 275-3755)* is a 1920s-style building with five 50-table dining rooms. It serves traditional French cuisine, as well as a few classic Louisiana dishes.

The atmosphere is elegant and refined and appropriate dress is required. It's expensive – one might even say very expensive – but seeing as they take credit cards...

🦅 The **Mansur's Restaurant** *($$$-$$$$; lunch Mon to Fri 11:30am to 2pm, dinner Mon to Sat 5:30pm to 10pm; 3044 College Dr., ☎ 923-3366)* serves Creole and French cuisine: veal, lamb, quail, steak, lobster and other seafood prepared New Orleans-style. Live piano music every night. Reservations recommended; elegant attire required. Fortunately, they take credit cards here!

Denham Springs

At **Crawford's Restaurant** *($$; Mon to Thu and Sat 10:30am to 9pm, Fri 10:30am to 10pm; 2313 S. Range St., ☎ 664-1412)*, the Crawford family offers catfish and seafood specialties, a table d'hôte, po-boys and excellent homemade desserts. Closed holidays.

St. Francisville

The **Bayou Sara Coffee & Tea Co.** *($; Tue to Sun 8:30am to 6:30pm; 215 Ferdinand St., ☎ 635-5446)* serves espresso, cappuccino, ice cream and desserts. Souvenirs and funny t-shirts. No credit cards.

🦅 At **Glory B's Diner** *($; Mon to Fri 10am to 7pm, Sat 10am to 4pm; 116 Ferdinand St., ☎ 635-4764)*, customers pick up their food at a counter, cafeteria-style. New Orleans-style po-boys, made with hot French bread. Fresh home-made desserts. Closed holidays.

D'Johns *($-$$; Sun to Thu 11am to 9pm, Fri and Sat 11am to 10pm; US 61, ☎ 635-6982)* has all the charm of a country inn. The walls are decorated with Audubon prints and works by local artists. House specialties: seafood, steak and grilled meat dishes.

🦅 The **Magnolia Café** *($$-$$; Mon to Sat 10am to 4pm; 121 E. Commerce St., ☎ 635-6528)* serves sandwiches, a soup of the day, salads, pizza and Mexican cuisine. Homemade pies baked fresh daily. Closed holidays.

Mattie's House *($$; every day 5:30am to 9pm; The Cottage, US 61, ☎ 635-3674)* cooks up shrimp and chicken dishes and homemade bread and desserts. Closed holidays.

The **Wolf-Schlesinger House - St. Francisville Inn** *($$-$$$; every day 7am to 9am, Tue to Sun 11am to 2pm, Wed to Sat 5pm to 9pm; 118 N. Commerce St., ☎ 635-6502 or 1-800-488-6502 within the U.S.)*, a Victorian dating from 1880, offers a breakfast buffet every morning. Other specialties are crepes, quiche, fried chicken and several Creole dishes, including gumbo and crawfish in season.

🦅 The **Clubhouse at the Bluffs** *($$$; Mon to Fri 7am to 9pm, Fri and Sat until 10pm, Sun until 8pm; closed Christmas, LA 965 E. at Freeland Rd., 10 km east of St. Francisville, ☎ 634-5088)* serves fine Louisiana and European cuisine. The dining room looks out onto a golf course designed by Arnold Palmer. Dinner served on the indoor patio or outside on the terrace. Accommodations available.

Jackson

🐚 **The Inn at Asphodel** *($$; every day 7:30am to 9am and 11:30am to 3pm, Wed to Sat 5:30pm to 7:30pm, Thu, Fri and Sat until 9pm; LA 68, ☎ 654-6868)* is an old house that belonged to a wealthy planter. Southern cuisine.

Jackson Bear Corner Restaurant *($$-$$$; dinner Wed to Sat 5:30pm to 9pm, Sun buffet 11am to 2pm; LA 10, ☎ 634-2844)*, set up inside a faithfully restored building dating from 1820, serves continental cuisine. Closed holidays.

The West Bank of the Mississippi

Vacherie

🐚 If you'd like to have a meal after visiting Laura Plantation or Oak Alley, make sure to stop at the friendly store run by the Breaux family, who fish on the area bayous and lakes. At the **B & C Seafood - Market of Cajun Delights** *(2155 LA 18/River Rd., Vacherie, LA 70090, ☎ 265-8356)*, customers choose their own fish or seafood at the counter. Their selection is then weighed and cooked up Cajun or Creole style. Possible dishes include alligator, frog's legs, clams, crab, etc. The store also sells scores of prepared products, such as Cajun boudin, smoked sausages, tasso, bread pudding, spices, wild blackberry jelly, pepper jelly, fig spread and vinaigrettes.

The **Oak Alley Plantation Restaurant** *($$; lunch every day 11am to 3pm; 3645 LA 18/River Rd., ☎ 265-2151)* is located on the grounds of the

plantation, in a pretty, relaxed setting. Traditional Southern cuisine.

Donaldsonville

At **Ruggiero's on the Avenue** *($$; Tue to Fri 11am to 9:15pm, Sat 5pm to 9:15pm; 206 Railroad Ave., ☎ 473-8476)*, the Ruggiero family serves up regional specialties: seafood, steaks, chicken, pasta and po-boys. Lunchtime table d'hôte. Closed holidays.

🐚 **Lafitte's Landing Restaurant** *($$$-$$$$; Sun 11am to 8pm, Mon 11am to 3pm, Wed to Sat 11am to 3pm and 6pm to 10pm, closed Christmas and New Year's Day; 10275 LA 70, access road at Sunshine Bridge, ☎ 473-1232)* is the domaine of Louisiana chef John Folse, who, like chef Paul Prudhomme, creates menus based on typical Louisiana ingredients. The building itself, a former Cajun plantation house (1797), is very interesting; according to local legend, pirate Jean Lafitte used to be a regular visitor here.

Brusly

Swab's Family Restaurant *($-$$; Mon to Thu 11am to 9pm, Fri and Sat 11am to 10pm; 4631 Raymond LaBauve Rd., ☎ 749-3423)* is renowned for its homestyle Cajun cuisine. It also serves seafood and steaks and has a buffet.

Port Allen

Ethel's Seafood Village *($$; Tue to Fri 11am to 9:30pm, Sat and Sun 3pm to 10pm; Exit 151 off I-10 E., 2901 Frontage Rd., ☎ 334-0968)* has a warm atmosphere. Steaks, seafood and assorted specialties. Closed holidays.

Livonia

Though **Joe's Dreyfus Store Restaurant** *($$-$$$; Tue to Sat 11am to 2pm and 5pm to 9pm, Sun 11am to 2pm; LA 78, between Livonia and New Roads, ☎ 637-2625)* is located in an out-of-the-way spot, Louisianians don't mind travelling over 50 kilometres to savour the chef's fabulous specialties. The building is a former general store constructed in the 1920s.

Ventress

Located on LA 413, near False River Island, **Dailey's Seafood - Bar & Grill** *($$; Mon to Fri 5pm to 10pm, Sat and Sun 11am to 2pm and 5pm to 11pm; 8204 Island Rd., ☎ 638-9222)* has a family atmosphere. The place claims to serve the best crawfish in Louisiana. The house specialty is seafood, boiled or fried. Oyster bar. No credit cards.

New Roads

Lyn-Z's Café *($-$$; lunch Mon to Fri 11am to 2pm, dinner Wed to Sat 5pm to 11pm, closed Easter, Thanksgiving and Christmas; 2371 Hospital Rd., ☎ 638-4580)* is very popular with local residents. On the menu: seafood and Cajun dishes. Lunch specials and weekend table d'hôte.

The **Coffee House Creole Cafe** *($$; Mon to Fri 11am to 2pm, Wed and Thu 5pm to 8pm, Fri 5pm to 10pm, Sat noon to 10pm; Sun noon to 3pm; 124 W.Main St., ☎ 638-7859)* is a former bank in the heart of the historic district.

Creole cuisine, meal and lodging packages (exchange with Pointe Coupee B&B possible). Shop on the premises: antiques, cookbooks devoted to Louisiana cuisine, and objets d'art.

Morel's Restaurant *($$; every day 10am to 10pm, closed Christmas and New Year's Day; 210 Morrison Pkwy., ☎ 638-4057)* is located in the heart of New Roads and offers a sweeping view of False River. Grilled and fried seafood; steaks, po-boys, table d'hôte and home-made soups.

 The Oxbow on False River *($$$; Tue to Fri 11am to 2pm and 5pm to 9pm, Sat 5pm to 9pm, Sun 11:30am to 8pm, closed New Year's Day, Thanksgiving and Christmas; LA 1, south of New Roads, ☎ 627-5285)*. After exploring this historic downtown district, "Les Quartiers Chérie", treat yourself to a stop at this elegant restaurant. Lovely view of False River. Fresh seafood, steaks and Louisiana cuisine.

ENTERTAINMENT

The East Bank of the Mississippi

Baton Rouge

Catfish Town. The warehouses at Baton Rouge's historic old port have been restored and now house attractive shops, restaurants and nightclubs. The process is still underway; two of the most recent additions are the **Music Hall - Club Louisiane**, where artists from Louisiana and elsewhere perform in a venue able to accommodate over 400 people *(nightly)* and the **Pilot House Restaurant & Brewery**, which has room for 200 in its restaurant and some 120 more in its brasserie (beers brewed on the premises according to traditional methods).

The *Belle of Baton Rouge* **riverboat casino** sets out from the Argosy pier for cruises on the Missisippi, just like back in the days when paddlewheelers used to travel back and forth between St. Louis and New Orleans. The *Belle of Baton Rouge* is a faithful reproduction of one of these famous boats. It is 9,000 square metres and has three decks, two smokestacks and an operational paddlewheel *(five three-hour cruises every day, starting at 9am; midnight cruises Thu to Sat)*.

Mulate's *($$; every day 11am to 10:30pm, closed Christmas; 8322 Bluebonnet Rd., 767-4794)*. Like the three other Mulate's, this one hosts live Cajun bands every night. Meal included in the cover charge.

On Stage - Nightclub and Cafe *(Quality Inn, 10920 Mead Rd., ☎ 293-9370)*. Live music every night.

Theatre buffs will be pleased by the variety of offerings at the **Centroplex Theater for the Performing Arts** *(220 St. Louis St., ☎ 389-4953)*. Other cultural activities take place at the **Louisiana State University Theatre** *(Raphael Semmes Rd., ☎ 388-5118)*.

Walker

The Old South Jamboree *(cover charge; US 190, 13 km east of Baton Rouge)* has live country music every other Saturday.

Calendar of Events

Festivals

In plantation country, as elsewhere in every parish in Louisiana, every week, month and season is an excuse for a festival. For more information on these countless events, contact the **Louisiana Asociation of Fairs & Festivals** *(601 Oak Ln., Thibodeaux, LA 70301, ☎ 1-800-940-1462 within the U.S.)* or the **Louisiana Office of Tourism** *(P.O. Box 94291, #5091, Baton Rouge, LA 70804-9291, ☎ 342-8119)*.

Some of the most interesting festivals are described below.

May

The Premier Symphony Summerfest ★★ *(adults $15, children $8; during summer, starting in May; Hemingbough, near US 61 in St. Francisville, ☎ 635-6617 or in Baton Rouge, ☎ 926-8181)*, a series of outdoor concerts featuring outstanding artists like Lou Rawls and Emmylou Harris, is held in a 96-hectare park that is perfect for family picnics. Reservations recommended.

June

On the last weekend of June, the town of Gonzales, the Jambalaya Capital of the World, welcomes over 100,000 visitors for its **Jambalaya Festival** ★★ *(Gonzales Civic Center, 219 S. Irma Blvd., Gonzales, ☎ 647-5779)*. This event abounds in music and activities of all different sorts. Its high point is a cooking contest, during which blue-ribbon chefs feverishly compete to become the "World Jambalaya Champion" (in case anyone's forgotten, jambalaya is *the* Louisiana dish).

August

The **Baton Rouge Blues Festival** ★★★ *(on the weekend before Labour Day)*. Baton Rouge prides itself on being a blues capital, and its festival, which attracts up to 100,000 people, is one of the biggest in the entire United States. The rhythms of jazz, traditional Cajun music and zydeco can also be heard during this gigantic event, which offers a chance to appreciate the talents of chefs as well as musicians.

October

The **International Acadian Festival** ★ *(3rd weekend of October; at the Plaquemine locks, ☎ 687-7319)* commemorates the arrival of the Acadians in this region through a variety of festivities (historical exhibitions, crafts, music, food, etc.).

 SHOPPING

The East Bank of the Mississippi

Landmark Antiques *(every day 10am to 6pm; Catfish Town, near the USS Kidd,*

☎383-4867) is a collection of over 70 antique shops, almost all of which take credit cards.

The Louisiana Art & Artists' Guild: The Guild Gallery *(free admission; Tue to Fri noon to 5pm and by appointment; ☎ 928-2960)*. This non-profit organization runs a gallery intended to acquaint the public with the work of local artists. The exhibitions change monthly. Closed holidays.

The **Neubig Art Gallery** *(free admission; Mon to Sat 9am to 4:30pm and by appointment; 16950 Strain Rd., Exit 7 off I-12, 1.6 km farther north on O'Neal Ln., ☎ 275-5126 or 1-800-446-4209 within the U.S.)* is a big studio-cum-gallery located in a park. It belongs to Louisiana artist Henry Neubig, who has developed a technique of using mud in his paintings. He offers demonstrations of this technique for groups of 10 to 50. Closed holidays.

The West Bank of the Mississippi

Grosse Tete

The **Midway Grocery** *(LA 77, Grosse Tete Exit off I-10 W., ☎ 648-2222)*, a former country grocery store, sells an array of quality Louisiana products: boudin, brown roux, head cheese, etc. It is located on a scenic highway leading to New Roads.

Jackson

Feliciana Cellars Winery and Vineyards
(Mon to Fri 10am to 5pm, Sat 9am to 5pm, Sun 1pm to 5pm; 1848 Charter St., LA 10, ☎ 634-7982 or 634-5771) sell eight different regionally produced wines, both red and white, varying in flavour from dry to sweet. Their names - Évangeline, La Salle, Audubon, Blanc du Bois - are evocative of Louisiana. A few beers are also brewed on the premises.

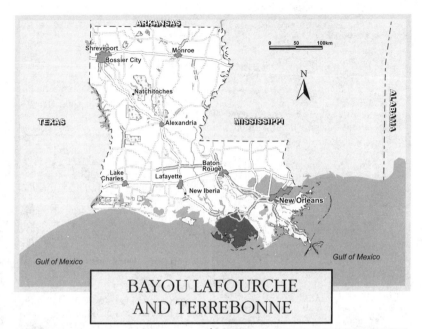

BAYOU LAFOURCHE AND TERREBONNE

Highway US 90 heads from New Orleans to Lafayette through Terrebonne, Lafourche and Assumption parishes – the bayou country of southernmost Louisiana. Houma is the county seat of Terrebonne, and Thibodaux, on Bayou Lafourche, is the county seat of Lafourche.

The source of Bayou Lafourche is the Mississippi River from which it flows into the Gulf of Mexico with Highway LA 1 running alongside its whole length. Plantations, sugar refineries, monumental churches and swamps line this 180-kilometre-long route, nicknamed "the longest road in the world", and the further south you go, the more Francophones you encounter.

 FINDING YOUR WAY AROUND

Houma

Houma is on Highway US 90 East, 175 kilometres east of Lafayette and 90 kilometres west of New Orleans.

By Bus

Only cities along US 90 have bus service; contact Greyhound/Trailways (☎ 873-8573) for information.

By Train

The region's train station is in Schriever, between Houma and Thibodaux. Contact Amtrak (☎ 1-800-872-7245) for information.

Service Stations

Jeffery's Truck and Auto Repair: 250 Robert Street, Houma, ☎ 851-6098 *(service 24 hours a day)*

Schexnayder's Shell Service Station: 1800 Grand-Caillou Road, Houma, ☎ 504-872-0390

Terrebonne Motors: 202 Saint Charles Street, Houma, ☎ 504-876-5100 *(minor repairs)*

In Lafourche Parish, especially on the LA 1 and in the town of Grand Isle, watch your speed because the police are keen on writing tickets.

Before crossing over to Grand Isle, which is very isolated, stock up on supplies at Cut Off, Galliano or Golden Meadow, where the selection and prices are better.

South of Houma

Chauvin - Cocodrie

From East Main Street in Houma, follow LA 24 six kilometres to the junction with LA 56, which will take you to Chauvin (26 km), and Cocodrie (50 km) on the Gulf of Mexico.

Pointe-aux-Chênes - Montegut - Isle de Jean-Charles

From Houma, take East Main Street/LA 24 to Bourg. Past Bourg continue on LA 55 to Pointe-aux-Chênes (16 km) and Montegut (3 km further). From Pointe-aux-Chênes, take LA 665 17 kilometres to reach Isle de Jean-Charles.

Dulac

Dulac is 32 kilometres south of Houma via LA 57. From Houma, Grand Caillou Road becomes the LA 57 which joins LA 56 further south, heading toward Cocodrie.

Northwest of Houma

Gibson - Morgan City

Gibson is 38 kilometres from Houma, along Highway US 90 West, and Morgan City is 22 kilometres further.

Morgan City - Pierre-Part - Paincourtville

From Morgan City, LA 70 runs alongside swamps for 30 kilometres before reaching the small fishing village of Pierre Part. Paincourtville and Bayou Lafourche are about 20 kilometres further on LA 70.

North of Bayou Lafourche

From Paincourtville to Thibodaux: Napoleonville - Supreme - Labadieville - Thibodaux

From Paincourtville, LA 1 goes down Bayou Lafourche on the west side (right bank), to Napoleonville (8 km), Supreme (20 km), Labadieville (23 km) and Thibodaux (37 km).

On the left bank, LA 308 runs along Bayou Lafourche passing Plattenville, Freetown and Thibodaux.

In this area, four bridges link the two sides of the bayou: at Paincourtville (LA 70), Supreme, Labadieville and Thibodaux.

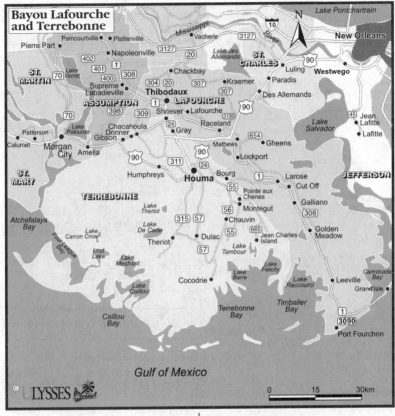

Bayou Lafourche and Terrebonne

Schriever - Thibodaux

From Houma, take West Park Avenue/LA 24 West 25 kilometres to Schriever and another five kilometres to Thibodaux.

Chackbay - Kraemer

From Thibodaux, take LA 20 East 11 kilometres to Chackbay. About six kilometres further, you will come to Highway LA 307, which you take 16 kilometres to Kraemer and which continues south to Raceland.

Des Allemands

From Houma, take US 90 East toward New Orleans for 38 kilometres.

South of Bayou Lafourche

From Thibodaux to Grand Isle: Raceland - Mathews - Larose - Cut Off - Galliano - Golden Meadow - Leeville - Grand Isle

From Thibodaux, staying on LA 1 along Bayou Lafourche, drive south toward the Gulf of Mexico. You will come across Raceland (24 km), Mathews (32 km), and the most picturesque part of the trip, Larose (55 km), Cut Off (60 km), Galliano (72 km), Golden Meadow (78 km), Leeville (95 km) and Grand Isle (125 km).

LA 308, on the left bank, goes to Lafourche (7km), Jay (Valentine) (50 km), Ludevine (55 km) and Golden Meadow.

You can cross over to the opposite shore by bridges at Thibodaux, Jay, Cut Off, Galliano and Golden Meadow.

Raceland

Raceland is 18 kilometres from Houma. Take US 90 West, and then LA 3199.

Gheens

Gheens is set back a bit from Bayou Lafourche on the east side. Take the bridge from US 90 to LA 308 and Clotilda. From Clotilda, follow LA 654 12 kilometres.

Port-Fourchon

Port-Fourchon is a small fishing village on the Gulf of Mexico. Twelve kilometres south of Leeville, take LA 3090 for five kilometres.

PRACTICAL INFORMATION

The area code is 504

Emergency

Police, fire, ambulance
☎ 911

Hospitals

Lady of the Sea General Hospital: 200 134th Place West, Cut Off, LA 70345, ☎ 632-6401

Terrebonne General Medical Center: 936 Main Street East, Houma, LA 70360, ☎ 873-4141

Tourist Information

Houma-Terrebonne tourism office: P.O. Box 2792, Houma, LA 70361, ☎ 868-2732 or 1-800-688-2732 from North America, houmatourism@cajunnet.com *(at St. Charles St. and the US 90).*

Lafourche Parish Tourism Office: P.O. Box 340, Raceland, LA 70394, ☎ 537-5800

Guided Tours

Charter Time, USA *(P.O. Box 2018, Galliano, LA 70354; ask to speak to Dennis Sandras, ☎ 798-7609 or 632-7184).* Ocean and fresh-water fishing; scuba diving for fishers or photographers; equipment rental; accommodation on the beach; tours in English, French, Spanish and German.

In the Houma-Terrebonne region, a number of outfitters offer fishing-boat rentals and guide services. A complete list of these is available from the **Houma-Terrebonne Tourist Information Office** *(St. Charles St., Houma,* ☎ *868-2732).*

The Marsh Cat Guide Service *(Grand Isle; contact Ms. Arlen Authement,* ☎ *787-2235)* offers hunting and fishing trips on a five-metre inflatable dinghy.

There are charter fishing excursions from **Marina Bon Voyage** *(2488 LA 1, Boudreaux Lane,* ☎ *787-3179).*

At **Griffin's Station & Marina** *(LA 1 South, Leeville,* ☎ *396-2415)* you will find fresh seafood, fishing equipment and guides.

Captain T-Man Cheramie *(P.O. Box 293, Cut Off, LA 70345,* ☎ *798-7166 or 632-5000).* There is a professional guide service here for both fresh- and salt-water fishing. You can also take boat trips.

Charlie Hardison and Son *(Route 1, P.O. Box 360, Golden Meadow, LA 70357,* ☎ *396-2442)* offers fishing trips on the Gulf of Mexico and on the bayous.

At **Bonne Chance - fishing** *(Captain Bobby Chouest,* ☎ *787-2602),* sea-trout and Louisiana-perch fishing enthusiasts can charter boats for up to four people. Night fishing trips also available.

★ EXPLORING

Houma ★★

Houma has two evocative epithets: **Venice of America** and **Swamp Capital**. It's an outstanding location for fresh- and salt-water fishing, and a favourite spot for hunters, with ducks and geese in abundance. The rich flora and fauna of the area can be discovered during an organized walk around the swamps. This region is also very fertile as attested to by its many sugar-cane plantations.

The **Historic District ★★** of Houma, dating back to 1840, is resplendant with beautiful Victorian and Art-Deco buildings of particular note are the **post office**, **St. Francis de Sales Cathedral**, the **Magnolia Cemetery** and **St. Matthew's Episcopal Church**. Literature and videos on attractions are available from the **Houma-Terrebonne Tourist Office** *(St. Charles St.,* ☎ *868-2732).*

The **Southdown Plantation House/Terrebonne Museum ★★** *(adults $4, students and seniors $2, children 12 and under $1; Tue to Sat 10am to 3pm; at the corner of St. Charles and Route 311,* ☎ *851-0154)* includes a magnificent 18th-century English manor, whose 20 rooms are open to the public, flanked by two turrets. The museum offers information on Cajun history, an interesting collection of birds and an exhibition of Mardi Gras accessories.

BAYOU LAFOURCHE AND TERREBONNE

Visits to Agricultural or Industrial Sites

Motivatit Seafood ★★ *(guided tours for groups only by reservation; $5 per person to visit one of the sites and $7.50 for both; Mon to Sat 7am to 5pm; at the corner of Palm and Gum Sts., Houma, ☎ 868-7191).* Visit the seafood and crustacean (oysters, crabs, crawfish) processing and packaging plants. The factory is located beside the shipyard.

The **Magnolia Plantation ★★** *(groups by appointment only; Schriever, 24 km north of Houma on Route 311, ☎ 446-1493)* has a neoclassical house shaded from the sun by immense magnolia trees. It was used as a hospital during the American Civil War.

The **Arboretum ★** next to **Le Jardin sur le Bayou** bed and breakfast (see "Accommodation", p 202) *(by appointment only; 256 Lower Country Dr., Bourg, ☎ 594-2722),* is a lovely garden on the bayou which can be visited by making arrangements with the owners.

Cajun Tours of Terrebonne *(709 May Avenue, Houma LA 70362, ☎ 872-6157).* Learn about Cajun cultural and architectural heritage through tours of the parish.

Guided Tours

The **Coup-Platte Hunting and Fishing Camp** *(212 Midland Dr., Houma, LA 70360; ask to speak to Terry Trosclair, ☎ 868-7940 or 868-7865 and dial 0611 after the message)* offers duck

hunting in season *(Nov to Jan; $150 per day)* as well as sea-trout fishing all year *($70 per day).*

If you want to visit the swamps, the Houma-Terrebonne region offers some of the most interesting choices:

The Adventures on a Bayou Circle ★, **ABC Driving Tour of Terrebonne Parish ★** *(contact the Houma-Terrebonne tourist information centre, St. Charles St., P.O. Box 2792, Houma, LA 70361, ☎ 868-2732, ☎ 1-800-688-2732 in North America).* There's a brochure here for motorists indicating important sites to visit: plantations, Native American cemeteries, a seafood processing and packaging plant, shrimp boats in action, a cypress grove, swamps, etc.

Hammond's Cajun Air Tours ★ *($30 per person; 1200 Dunn St., Houma, ☎ 872-1423)* offers flights over the coastal region and the swamps. Aboard the hydroplane you can see birds, alligators and free roaming deer; a bit further on are drilling platforms in the gulf, bays where pirates, including the famous Lafitte brothers, once sought refuge, shrimp boats at work and a fort dating from the Civil War. You can choose to land on an isolated lake, on the beach or even at the door of a bayou restaurant. The trip takes abut three hours.

Annie Miller's Swamp & Marsh Tours ★★★ *(adults $15, children $12; schedule depends on the season; departure from the Bayou Delight restaurant, US 90 West, ☎ 879-3934).* Annie Miller Tours are renowned: Mrs. Miller, an experienced guide who benefits from an excellent reputation, has the ability to "call" the alligators, which she attracts to the boats to the delight of her fellow passengers. She speaks both English and French. The trip lasts from two to two and a half hours.

A Cajun Man's Swamp Tour ★★★ *(adults $15, children $10; spring and summer; every day 8am to sundown; fall and winter; 10am to 2pm; Bayou Black Marina, US 90 West, 16km from Houma; contact "Black" or Sondra Guidry, ☎ 868-4625).* From this fifty-passenger boat, you can observe alligators in the water and eagles in the sky. Mr. Guidry, the guide, speaks French and English, and he also plays the accordian and sings Cajun songs. The trip lasts from 1.5 to 2.5 hours, depending on passengers wishes.

Atchafalaya Basin Backwater Adventure *($25 per person; every day 11am; 6302 N. Bayou Black Dr., outside Gibson, 36 km west of Houma, ☎ 575-2371)* offers a two-hour tour of the swamps around Gibson in the company of Jon Faslun, a guide who is as knowledgeable about the evolution of local wildlife as he is about the many medicinal plants that grow in the area.

Bayou Black Swamp Tours *(hydroplane tour $35 per person, boat tour $15; every day 5am to 2pm; ☎ 575-2315)* offers flights over the area in a hydroplane with a few stops on the swamps. The plane ride lasts one and a half hours, as does the boat tour, during which you can do a bit of fishing.

Cajun Tours of Terrebonne (Land and Swamp) *($10 and $20; every day; 709 May St.; speak to Mrs. Sandra Pellegrin, ☎ 872-6157).* Alligator-watching in a private swamp.

Munson's Cypress Bayou Swamp Tours *(adults $15, 5-17-yr-olds $10; every day 9am to 6pm; 4328 Grand-Caillou Rd.; 11 km south of Houma on LA 57, ☎ 851-3569)* offers boat tours of a private cypress grove. The trip takes two hours and allows you to discover and admire alligators ("cocodrils" or "cocodries"), coypu, racoons, birds and vegetation typical to the bayou.

South of Houma

Pointe-aux-Chenes - Dulac - Chauvin - Cocodrie

Visitors interested in the Acadian culture of Southeast Louisiana will want to meet two residents of **Pointe-aux-Chenes** ★★★ *(LA 55, 13 km southeast of Houma).* Ms. Laïse Ledet *(722 LA 665, Pointe-aux-Chenes, close to the church, ☎ 594-4385)* is the most precious source of information on the history of Terrebonne. You can easily call for an appointment with this woman in her seventies who loves to share her knowledge. She founded the first school for Houma Indian children. Until then, native children had the right to go to neither white nor black schools. Ms. Ledet's cousin, Dovie Naquin *(house indicated by sign beside the Wildlife & Fisheries office, ☎ 594-2690),* is Terrebonne's storyteller par excellence. He tells stories about "cocodril" hunting, in which he still participates at the age of 80. He also plays the accordian and the harmonica. Call in advance, and on your way out you can leave a contribution in the little saucer.

The **Houmas Indian Center** ★★★ *(LA 57, Dulac, by LA 55)* is a cooperative store that sells craftwork made by natives from **Isle Jean-Charles** *(take LA*

665 to the end along the Pointe-aux-Chenes bayou, ☎ *563-7483).*

The **Boudreaux Canal General Store** *(Mon to Fri 7:30am to 4pm, Sat 7:30am to noon; LA 56, Chauvin),* which was built around 1940, has attractive antiques as well as some native craft pieces.

Sportman's Paradise *(every day 5am to 9pm; 6830 LA 56, Chauvin,* ☎ *594-2414),* with eight boats, is the biggest fishing-trip outfitter in Louisiana. The company also operates a marina, a restaurant and a motel.

The **Louisiana Universities Marine Consortium** ★★ *(free admission; Mon to Fri 8am to 4:30pm; 8124 LA 56, Chauvin,* ☎ *851-2800)* is an aquatic museum presenting specimens from both fresh water, like the bayous, and the warm salt water of the Gulf of Mexico. From an observation post there's a panoramic view of the coast.

Northwest of Houma

Gibson

Wildlife Gardens ★★ *(adults $8, children $3.25; every day 10am, 1pm and 3:30pm; 5306 N. Bayou Black Dr., ask for Mrs. Betty Provost,* ☎ *575-3676).* This wildlife refuge, located in a natural swamp, offers guided walking tours. There are demonstrations of the making of duck-hunting decoys. Their trapping cabins and alligator farm are very interesting for visitors; accommodation, including breakfast is available. The tour takes about an hour and a half.

Pierre-Part ★★

If you go around Lake Palourde and Lake Verret on your way out of Bayou Teche country on your way to New Orleans, you will come across Bayou Lafourche country at Pierre Part (LA 70). Because of its isolation, in the middle of the swamps, this area has remained very Francophone and the Cajuns here live from fishing like their ancestors did. In 1882, a flood ravaged Pierre-Part, destroying the church. Only the statue of the Virgin Mary escaped; still today, the faithful address their prayers to her in hope of protecting themselves against inclement weather.

The language immersion program offered at the Pierre Part school has promoted a revival of French in Assumption Parish. Ms. Carole Aucoin, the previous director of the establishment, instituted this project, of which she is rightfully very proud, and is still actively involved.

Bayou Lafourche Area

When travelling down Bayou Lafourche, you will see beautiful antebellum Victorian and Queen-Anne houses. Sugar-cane cultivation and fishing in the Gulf of Mexico contribute in large part to the economy of this area of very hardworking people.

Visits to Agricultural or Industrial Sites

The **Indian Ridge shrimp processing company** ★★ *(May to Dec, by appointment;* ☎ *594-3361).* An interesting visit to learn more about the different techniques used in processing and packaging shrimp.

Napoleonville - Supreme

Built in 1846, the house at **Madewood Plantation** ★★★ *(adults $5, children $3; every day 10am to 4:45pm; 4250 LA 308, approximately 7 km from Napoleonville,* ☎ *1-800-375-7151 from the U.S.)* is considered one of the most beautiful examples of neoclassical architecture. A traditional family cemetery is on the grounds. Accommodation is offered in the nine bedrooms of the residence. Madewood is 26 kilometres from the Sunshine bridge, which crosses the Mississippi on LA 70 and links up with Interstate 10 (Baton-Rouge - New Orleans). The tour lasts 45 minutes.

Thibodaux ★★

Thibodaux, the county seat of Lafourche Parish, was founded in 1820. The historical tour of the city is a must.

Tour of the Thibodaux old city ★★. The old houses that line Canal Boulevard all have interesting verandas adorned with architectural ornamentation. You should also see: **St. Joseph's Cathedral** *(7th St.),* **St. John's Espiscopal Church** *(at Jackson and 7th Sts.),* **Lafourche Courthouse,**

Dansereau House and **St. Joseph's Catholic Cemetery.** For more information, contact the **Thibodaux Chamber of Commerce** *(1048 Canal Boulevard,* ☎ *446-1187).*

Laurel Valley Plantation Village ★★★ *(entrance fee; spring and summer; Tue to Fri 10am to 4pm, Sat and Sun noon to 4pm; fall and winter; 11am to 4pm; LA 308, 9.6 km/6 miles south of Thibodaux,* ☎ *446-7456)* is the site of one of the largest intact sugar-cane plantations; more than 70 slave cabins stand on its grounds. The plantation also houses the **Museum of Rural Life** and the **General Store**, which showcases and sells work by local artisans.

Wetlands Acadian Cultural Center - Jean Lafitte National Historical Park and Preserve ★★★ *(free admission; Mon 9am to 7pm, Tue to Thu 9am to 6pm, Fri to Sun 9am to 5pm; 314 Sainte Marie St. - along the Bayou Lafourche,* ☎ *448-1375).* The cultural centre, part of the national park, presents exhibitions on Acadian artisans from the coastal area: boat builders, fishers and farmers. There are demonstrations of boat-building, music, and craftwork, and a film illustrates the diversity of Acadian culture in Southeast Louisiana. The tour takes from one hour to an hour and a half. Monday-night Cajun-music jam sessions, from 5:30pm to 7pm, are very popular.

Kraemer ★

On LA 307, between US 90 and LA 20, is the small community of Kraemer, a departure point for interesting excursions.

Jean Lafitte - Pirate and Patriot

Jean Lafitte is one of those characters whose story has naturally ripened into legend. This firebrand of the seas was born in France in about 1780 and died around 1825, and was undoubtedly very busy in the years between. He arrived in the French Antilles at a very early age with his older brother Pierre and received letters of marque from the South American republic of Cartagena, permitting him to attack English and Spanish enemy ships to his own profit. At the beginning of the 1800s, he settled in New Orleans as a blacksmith, a good cover for his smuggling and slave-trading buinesses. In search of networks in which to sell his spoils, he soon discovered the advantages of Barataria Bay, whose swampy waters opening into the Gulf of Mexico made it impenetrable. It was here that he formed his band of *baratariens* (a French word of Spanish origin meaning "swindlers"), which the English sollicited to help invade New Orleans in 1814. (New Orleans had been American since the treaty with Napoleon of 1803.) More concerned with escaping legal recourse for his smuggling activities, he offered his services instead to General Jackson in exchange for a pardon that he earned easily with his passionate fighting at the head of his men. For this reason he is considered by many to be a hero of the young American republic.

Next Lafitte founded the town that would later become Galveston, Texas, before returning to piracy and finally disappearing, in about 1825. Jean Lafitte's name is still not listed in the *Petit Larousse* dictionnary, but it was immortalized by Hollywood. The 1937 film "Buccaneers", by the famous director Cecil B. de Mille, features Lafitte as the hero, and in 1958 Anthony Quinn made a new version of this film with Yul Brynner in the leading role.

Patriot or pirate, Jean Lafitte's presence is still strongly felt in Louisiana, where a national historic park and a number of streets and public places are named after him.

Torres Cajun Swamp Tours *($10; every day 9am to 5pm, by reservation; 101 Torres Rd.; LA 307, 30 km northeast of Thibodaux,* ☎ *633-7739)* are guided by a genuine alligator hunter. The trip takes about two hours.

Zam's Swamp Tours & Cajun Cookin' *($12.50 adults, $6 children; every day 10:30am and 3:30pm; 135 Bayou Rd.; exit LA 307 at the bridge 20 min from Thibodaux, take Bayou Rd.,* ☎ *633-7881)* offers boat trips in a natural swamp. You can visit the

museum, see live alligators, eat some Cajun food and, from the Tregle family, get a glimpse of French culture in Bayou Lafourche country. The guided tour takes about two and a half hours.

Des Allemands ★

This region between Bayou Lafourche and New Orleans is named the "Côte des Allemands" as a reminder of the Germans that moved here during the time of the French regime, near the middle of the 18th century. The area is famous for its catfish, and the **Louisiana Catfish Festival** (see p 207) is held here each year on the second weekend of June.

Lockport

Juliana's Cajun Cruises (☎ 532-6538) explore the swamp country and bayous.

Golden Meadow - Port-Fourchon - Grand Isle

Grand Isle, the only inhabited island in Louisiana, has beautiful sandy beaches; in the distance, in the Gulf of Mexico, you can see oil-drilling platforms. Places to swim are extremely rare in Louisiana, so beach fans ignore rigs that obscure the horizon. Campers appreciate the island's calm and amateur ornithologists enjoy the multitude of birds that seek refuge here.

In the heart of Golden Meadow, *Petit-Caporal* ★, built in 1854, is the oldest existing shrimp boat in Louisiana.

Port Fourchon is a fishing port on the Gulf of Mexico with calm beaches and superb sunsets.

Grande Terre Island *(east of Grand Isle)* is only accessible by boat and is best explored on foot: you can see old **Fort Livingston**, built just before the Civil War, and the **Lyle S. Saint-Amant marine laboratory**. There's also a **fish farm** open during the week.

 PARKS

Houma

Houma aquatic park *($8, after 5pm $5, every day 10am to 6pm; at the intersection of LA 311 and St. Charles St., north of Houma, ☎ 872-6143 or 872-6144)*. With its waterslides and pools, this park is the ideal place when it's hot! There is also minigolf.

Grand Isle

At **Grand Isle State Park** ★★ *(on Grand Isle, ☎ 787-2559)* you can get a lot of information on the history and geology of the island, go swimming and fishing, camp on the beach or have a picnic.

ACCOMMODATIONS

Houma

Since Louisiana is subject to long periods of heat and humidity, all residences, businesses and public buildings have air conditioning.

 The **Association 'Cadienne de Bed and Breadkfasts "Le Français à la Maison"** *($37 to $57 bkfst incl.; pb; 815 Funderburk Avenue, Houma, LA 70364; speak to the head of the association, Ms. Audrey Babineaux George, ☎ 879-3285, 868-9519 or 879-3033)*. This network is an association of Cajun bed and breakfasts that offer complete breakfasts and other meals upon request. Credit cards are not accepted.

🏚 **Houma Grand Manor** *($42, $47, $55 and $61 bkfst incl.; pb; 217 Lynwood Dr., Houma, LA 70360, right near the Houma-Terrebonne tourist office, ☎ 876-5493)* is a charming two-bedroom house. The generous hostess, Cecilia Rodriguez, offers copious breakfasts; lunch is available on request. Mrs. Rogriquez, a genuine Cajun, loves chatting with customers. There is laundry service. Smoking is allowed outside only!

🏚 **La Petite Maison de Bois** *($45 bkfst incl.; group rates; 4084 Southdown Mandalay, Route 90 west of Houma, ☎ 879-3815 or 876-1582)* is a pleasant Cajun house with a view of Bayou Black.

Le Jardin sur le Bayou *($80 bkfst incl.; pb; 256 Lower Country Dr., a few kilometres southeast of Houma, close to the LA 24, Bourg, LA 70343, ☎ 594-2722)*. Dave and Jo Ann Coignet's house is close to a bird sanctuary that is a registered state protected area; it's a wonderful spot for amateur and professional ornithologists. There is a marvellous garden on the Coignet property.

The **A-Bear Motel** *($21-$27; ≡, pb, tvc; 341 New Orleans Boulevard, ☎ 872-4528)* offers all the standard motel conveniences.

The **Economy Inn** *($23; ≡, pb, tvc, ℜ; 224 S. Hollywood Rd.., ☎ 851-6041)* is part of a hotel chain that offers all modern comforts at low prices.

The **Sugar Bowl Motel** *($26-$34; ≡, pb, tvc, ℜ; 625 E. Park Ave., ☎ 872-4521)* is another inexpensive establishment. Credit cards are accepted.

At **Bernard Whitney** *(2706 E. Main St., Houma, ☎ 873-7629)*, there are 18 fully equipped sites for recreational vehicles, a gas station and laundry facilities.

Thibodaux

Court-Capri *(6 km from Houma on US 90 East, turn left onto LA 316; drive for 6 km to 101 Court-Capri, ☎ 879-4288 or 1-800-428-8026 from the U.S.)* has 45 camp sites as well as washrooms, showers, a pool, laundry facilities, fishing, a dock and trails. Guided tours of the swamps, plantation visits, Mardi Gras, etc.. Open all year.

Bayou Neuf Camping *(open all year; LA 56, between Houma and Chauvin, ☎ 594-2628)*. As well as their four basic camping sites, they offer six-person chalets with water, electricity, washrooms and showers. Grocery store, dock, fishing, marina, swamp excursions.

Lovell House B & B *($60 bkfst incl.; 221 W. 7th St., Thibodaux, LA 70301, ☎ 446-2750)*. In the heart of Thibodaux, the inviting house of Charlene and Richard Elmore offers a prime example of Cajun hospitality. The Elmores are fluent in German and French as well as English.

Chauvin

The **Marina Coco** *($20 per night; LA 56, Cocodrie, 45 km south of Houma, ☎ 594-6626)* is owned by the same person as is the Motel Co-Co. There are 17 sites for recreational vehicles, water, electricity, a grocery store, a dock and fishing. Open year round.

The **Motel Co-Co** *($50 per person; $100 for four people, motel or shared appartment-condominium; flat rates available; ≡, pb, tvc, ℜ, 106 Pier 56, ☎ 594-6626 or 1-800-648-2626 from the U.S.)* is suitable for all budgets.

Gibson

Linda's Campground *(open all year; $10 tent, $12 RV; US 90, ☎ 575-3934)*. There are 17 camping sites here as well as sites outfitted for recreational vehicles. Amenities available include water, washrooms, and laundry services.

At **Wildlife Gardens** *($50 bkfst incl.; group rates; ≡, pb; 5306 N. Bayou Black Dr., 22.4 km/14 miles west of Houma, ☎ 575-3676)*, there are three fully equipped chalets on a natural swamp. The Cajun breakfasts at James and Betty Provost's house are huge and delicious. From the balcony of the house you can throw food to the alligators: they'll be grateful. Trails, small touring boats. Smoking outside only. Credit cards not accepted.

Napoleonville

Madewood Plantation - Bed & Breakfast *($85 bkfst incl.; ≡, pb, 4250 LA 308, ☎ 369-7151)*. The house has kept its original wood stairs and high ceilings. Candlelight dining.

Larose

At the **Gaudreaux Bed & Breakfast** *($85 bkfst incl., seasonal rates; pb, sb; 1313 11th St., ☎ 693-4316)* visitors stay in a fully equipped Cajun cottage. There's a lovely pond nearby.

Cut Off

The 11-hectare property of **À la Maison Hassell - Bed & Breakfast** *($85 bkfst incl.; group rates; pb, ®, K; 550 E. 74th St., Cut Off, LA 70345, ☎ 632-8088)* opens onto Bayou Lafourche. It is possible to rent a six-bedroom chalet with a complete kitchen. The breakfast is traditional American and thus generous. Smoking is allowed outside only. Credit cards are not accepted.

Galliano

The **Grand Isle State Park** *(park fee: $2 adults, $1 children; P.O. Box 741, Grand Isle, LA 70358, ☎ 787-2559)* is located right at the end of the island. There are approximately 100 camp sites on the beach *($10; no water or electricity hook-ups for RVs)* with washrooms and communal showers. Picnic sites, swimming, fishing on the sea or from the dock.

Cigar's Marina - Camping *(after the bridge, when arriving on the island, ☎ 787-3220)*, as well as the marina offers a grocery store and a restaurant.

At the **Cajun Inn Motel** *($25-$37; ≡, pb, tvc; LA 1 West, W. 217th St., ☎ 475-5677)*, they speak both English and French.

Grand Isle

At **Roussel's Beach Front Camp Ground**
*(P.O. Box 263, Grand Isle, LA 70358;
☎ 787-3393)*, the property of Edna and
Rodney Roussel, all services are offered
for recreational vehicles.

The **Cajun Holiday Motel** *(from $40; ≡,
pb, K, ≈; 2002 LA 1, ☎ 787-2002)*
offers 16 fully equipped cottages.

The **Offshore Motel** *(from $40; ≡, pb,
tvc, K; at the centre of Grand Isle,
☎ 787-3178)* is close to the Gulf of
Mexico.

Rates for **cotages on Grand Isle** are
between $55 and $130 per day,
depending on the size, whereas motel
rooms start at $40.

There are nine **Seabreeze Cottages** *($$;
pb, K; 3210 LA 1, ☎ 787-3180)*; each
has two bedrooms and a living room.
Rates vary according to the season.

 The **Bruce Apartments** *($-$$; daily,
weekly or monthly rental; pb; LA 1, on
the left after the post office,
☎ 787-3374 or 632-5133)* overlook the
beach. Services include laundry and a
seafood-preparation area is among the
facilities. Prices are very reasonable.

Bridge Side Cabins and Marina *($-$$;
pb; LA 1, at the Grand Isle bridge,
☎ 787-2418 or 787-2419)*. Here you
can rent fully equipped cottages. The
property can accommodate recreational
vehicles and there are two docks for
fishers.

Sun and Sand Cabins *($-$$; ≡, pb, tvc,
K; P.O. Box 1094, Grand Isle, LA
70358; 2 km past the Caminada*

bridge, ☎ 787-2456). Each of these
cabins has two bedrooms, a patio and
a living room. Each is also equipped
with an outdoor seafood-preparation
area and a picnic table. Bedding is
supplied but not towels.

✕ RESTAURANTS

Houma

At the **French Loaf** *($; 1508 W.
Park Ave., Houma, ☎ 851-6000)*, they
prepare excellent daily specials,
delicious grill dishes, and po-boy
sandwiches. Credit cards are not
accepted.

At **Dave's Cajun Cuisine** *($; Mon
10:30am to 2pm, Tue to Thu and Sat
and Sun 10:30am to 9pm, Fri 10:30am
to 10pm; 2433 W. Main St.,
☎ 868-3870)* you can sample a variety
of seafood including soft-shell crab,
gumbo and salads, all reasonably
priced.

Dula and Edwin's Cajun Restaurant *($;
Tue to Sun 10am to 10pm; 2426
Bayou Blue Dr., ☎ 876-0271)* serves
delicious potatoes stuffed with
seafood, crawfish *court-bouillon* and
crab, accompanied by live Cajun music
every Tuesday night.

The **Bayou Delight** *($-$$; Mon to Thu
and Sun 10am to 9pm, Fri and Sat
10am to 10pm; 4038 Bayou Black Dr.,
across from Annie Miller's dock,
☎ 876-4879)* is an inviting spot that
serves traditional Cajun cuisine,
incuding alligator with hot sauce,
gumbo, spicy crawfish *court-bouillon*
and steamed shrimp. There's a live
Cajun band every Friday and Saturday.

The **Highway 24 Seafood Restaurant** *($-$$; Mon to Thu 10:30am to 9pm; Fri and Sat 10:30am to 9:30pm; close to the airport, Bourg, ☎ 563-7483)* specializes in fried okra, crab *croquettes*, crawfish or shrimp either fried or prepared in a *court-bouillon*.

At **Eastway Seafood West** *($-$$; Sun to Thu 11am to 9pm, Fri and Sat 11am to 10pm; 1029 W. Tunnel Blvd., ☎ 876-2121)*, you feel like you're part of the family. They serve seafood and Cajun dishes: steamed shrimp or crawfish, gumbo, and alligator with spicy sauce.

At this **Picadilly Cafeteria** *($-$$; every day 11am to 10:30pm; 1704 Park Avenue, ☎ 879-4222)*, as at all Piccadilly Cafeterias, local cuisine is carefully prepared.

Chauvin

The **Bayou Breeze** *($; every day; 7am to 9pm; 5531 Hwy 56, ☎ 594-3388)*. Here you can sample seafood and family-style Cajun dishes.

La Trouvaille *($-$$; Oct to May, Wed to Sun, lunch; ☎ 594-9503 or 879-8005)*. The food is strictly home-made and the ambience is particularly warm and inviting. There is live music on the first Sunday of the month throughout the fall. The Dusenberry family, who own this establishment, are experts in traditional Cajun singing. Credit cards are not accepted.

Sportman's Paradise *($-$$; LA 56, on Bayou Petit-Caillou, ☎ 594-2414)* serves fresh seafood from the Gulf of Mexico in a hunting-lodge-style building. The restaurant is open for breakfast, lunch and supper, but hours vary depending on the season. Credit cards are not accepted.

Rouse Supermarket - Bakery *($; 2737 W. Main St., ☎ 868-5033)* is the only place in town to get a famous "porridge pie": a donut pastry with cream filling.

Dulac

The owner of **Annie's Restaurant** *($; every day, 8am to 10pm; 5550 Grand Caillou Rd., via LA 57)* serves seafood dishes and traditional Cajun meals. Credit cards are not accepted.

Cocodrie

Point Cocodrie Inn *($$; Sun to Thu 6am to 9pm, Fri and Sat 6am to 10pm; 8250 Hwy 56, ☎ 594-4568)*. The house specialties are seafood and fish and the menu includes daily specials of authentic Cajun dishes.

The **Marina Coco - Seafood** *($$-$$$; every day 6am to 9pm; ☎ 594-6626)* is located close to the port. The menu includes very fresh fish and seafood, grill dishes, shrimp cooked in wine, and oysters.

Labadieville

Nubby Duck's *($; every day; LA 1, ☎ 526-8869)* is a venerable old diner that offers Cajun cuisine and other Southern specialties: fried chicken, jambalaya, salads, grilled chicken and corn bread.

The **Bayou Dairy Bar** *($; LA 1)* serves hamburgers, shrimp gumbo, okra gumbo and refreshing ice-milk drinks.

Thibodaux

At **Politz** *($-$$; Tue to Fri 11am to 1:30pm, Sun 11am to 2pm, Tue to Sat 5pm to 9pm; 535 N. St. Marie St., ☎ 448-0944)*, the menu is limited to seafood, hamburgers and gumbo.

Chackbay

Boudreaux's *($; 507 Route 20, ☎ 633-2382)* puts the spotlight on Cajun cuisine and alligator specialties.

Kraemer

Edwina's *($; beside Zam's Swamp Tours, ☎ 633-5628)* specialties are alligator, seafood and turtle. Credit cards are not accepted.

Des Allemands

The atmosphere is relaxed at **Spahr's Seafood** *($$; Mon to Thu 9am to 9:30pm, Fri to Sun 9am to 10pm; 52 Route US 90 West, ☎ 758-1602)*. Nearby, there's a view of alligators, turtles and other swamp dwellers. Specialties include catfish Des Allemands, alligator with hot sauce, frog's legs, and gumbo.

Lockport

Blackie's Po-boy *($; LA 1, ☎ 532-5117)*. Blackie's shrimp and oyster po-boys are famous and attract quite a crowd at lunch-time. Credit cards are not accepted.

Golden Meadow

 Randolph Cheramie *($$; Wed to Sun 11am to 9pm; 806 S. Bayou Dr., ☎ 475-5272)*. This French-bistro-style restaurant offers seafood, steak and Southern Louisiana dishes.

Grand Isle

At **Cigar's Cajun Cuisine** *($; every day 10am to 11pm; past the Grand Isle Bridge, ☎ 787-2188)*, Bobby and Levita Cheramie prepare seafood and Cajun dishes. The marina next door is fully equipped to meet all fishing and camping needs.

Camardelle's Seafood restaurant *($; 5am to 8pm; LA 1, Cheniere, ☎ 787-3222)* is right by the Gulf. It serves crabmeat, steamed shrimp, crawfish tails, seafood *court-bouillons*, and soft-shell crab.

ENTERTAINMENT

Calendar of Events

February - March

Mardi Gras Parades

Houma *(Don Kinnard, P.O. Box 1995, Houma, LA 70361, ☎ 868-3806)*. The program varies from one year to the next but there's always a traditional parade.

Thibodaux *(Nathalie Dantin, P.O. Box 340, Raceland, LA 70394, ☎ 537-5800)*. Mardi Gras is the most anticpated event of the year. To make sure you don't miss any of the festivities, contact the organizer.

April

The **Blessing of the Shrimp Fleet** *(Mr. A. Dupré Jr., ☎ 446-FAIR, Dulac)*. Traditional procession of fishing boats in the harbour and annual blessing of the shrimp boats.

May

The **Fireman's Fair** *(Thibodaux)*, celebrated since 1857, has become a much-loved tradition over the years. The fair includes a parade, carousel rides, music, an auction and communal meals. It is held in the first week of May.

The **Louisiana Praline Festival** *(Houma)*. For the occassion, celebrants make the world's biggest praline. Music, crafts and food are also on the agenda. The first weekend in May.

June

The **Louisiana Catfish Festival of Des Allemands** *(Rev. Leszczynski, P.O. Drawer G, Des Allemands, LA 70003, ☎ 758-7542)*. Early June is catfish season: there's dancing, singing and eating... catfish!

The **Gheens Bon Mangé Festival** *(Mr. Lindel Toups, Raceland, LA 70394, ☎ 532-5889)*, during which there is so much to drink and eat, is irresistible.

The town puts on this huge annual festival during the first week of June.

July

Grand Isle International Tarpon Rodeo *(Mr. Nickie Candies, Grand Isle, ☎469-7700)*. Every year at the end of July, this gathering brings together over 3,000 tarpon fishing enthusiasts. To them nothing is more exciting than catching a "silver acrobat", as they call the tarpon. The rodeo attracts about 15,000 visitors to Grand Isle each year.

August

The **Blessing of the Fishing Boats** *(Golden Meadow)* is an old Acadian tradition kept in most of the small fishing ports on the Gulf of Mexico. It takes place during the first week in August every year.

During the **Cajun Heritage Festival** (Galliano), the third weekend in August, there are demonstrations by local artisans of craftwork including miniature-boat building and the making of duck-hunting decoys. Also on the agenda are competitions, music and cooking.

September

The **Houma Indian Pow Wow Festival of Houma** *(Janie Luster, 2247 Brady Dr., Theriot, LA 70397, ☎ 872-2917)*, the first week of the month, celebrates the cultural heritage of the Houmas with dance performances and traditional native songs.

The **Cajun Heritage Festival** *(James Lynch, Cut Off, ☎ 475-7491)* is held during the second week of September. It takes place in Cut Off and includes music, dancing and the chance to sample a multitude of regional dishes.

October

The **Raceland Sauce Piquante Festival** *(Larry Babin, 114 1st St., Raceland, LA 70394, ☎ 537-7638)* coincides with hot-pepper-harvest time at the beginning of October. And why not mark the occassion with a hot sauce festival? After all, the condiment is a permanent fixture on the table of any Louisianian!

Louisiana Gumbo Festival of Chackbay *(Johnny Louviere, Thibodaux, LA 70301, ☎ 633-7789)*. In the first week of October, the national dish of Cajuns and all Louisianians, has its own festival... and Cajuns certainly live it up!

The **Louisiana Oyster Festival of Cut Off** *(Otis Pitre, ☎ 632-3800)* takes place in the second week of October, right in season for famous Gulf of Mexico oysters. These delicious oysters are prepared in every possible way.

Raceland Fireman's Festival *(Richard Hackworth, 131 S. Service Rd., ☎ 537-3524)*. On the third weekend of October, there is a multitude of activities at this flamboyant firefighters' festival including a bazaar, games, and carousel rides.

The **Mathews Festival of Lafourche Living** *(☎ 537-5800)* is an hommage to traditional life in Bayou Lafourche country. Artists' exhibitions, parades of people in period costumes, demonstrations in cane-syrup production, regional food, bands, a butcher shop selling seasonal meats, and other activities take place at this colourful festival on the third weekend of October.

French Food Festival *(Henri Boulet, Larose Civic Center, 307 E. 5th St., Larose, ☎ 693-7355)*. During the last week of October there are cooking contests, culinary demonstrations and tastings galore.

November

At the **Raceland Cajun Heritage Festival** *(Hamilton Dantin, 115 Lowerline Rd., Raceland, LA 70394, ☎ 537-3236 or 537-5444)*, during the first week of November, there are performances by singers and musicians from Louisiana's Acadian community.

December

Not to be missed, **A Bayou Christmas** *(Galliano)* is a dazzling and colourful event: the procession of boats decked out in Christmas finery on Bayou Lafourche is magical. The second weekend of December.

Christmas at Laurel Plantation *(Laurel Valley Village LA 308, 9.6 km/6 miles south of Thibodaux; contact Ruby Landry, ☎ 447-2902)*. During the holidays the village is adorned with spectacular lighting and multicoloured decorations.

SHOPPING

Houma

La Trouvaille *(LA 56, south of Houma, near Chauvin, ☎ 594-9503)* promotes itself as *the* shop for local crafts.

Schriever

The **Bourgeois Supermarket** *(Mon to Fri 7am to 5:30pm, Sat 7am to 3pm; Route 20, ☎ 447-7128)* prepares, among other things, excellent smoked meats.

Thibodaux

The **Laurel Valley General Store** *(Tue to Sun 10am to 4pm; LA 308, ☎ 446-7456)* is an attractive old-fashioned general store where there's always a little something to buy.

Mathews - Cut Off - Golden Meadow

Adam's Fruit Market *(every day 6:30am to 6:30pm; 5013 LA 1, Mathews, ☎ 532-3265)* offers a whole range of local products, including cane syrup, honey, fishing accessories and souvenirs.

Glen Pitre's Côte-Blanche Productions *(at the edge of the Bayou Lafourche, Cut Off, across from W. 69th St., ☎ 1-800-634-4104 or 1-800-375-1400 from the U.S.).* Glen Pitre, a Cajun film-maker, owns this store which has the most complete selection of products from Louisiana. Côte-Blanche is mostly a catalogue shopping service (books, records, films, videos, souvenirs, cards, food, etc.).

Dufresne's Bakery *(every day 5am to 7pm; 1706 W. Main St., Golden Meadow, ☎ 798-7780)* has a large stock of fresh breads, cookies, delicious pecan pies and many other local delicacies.

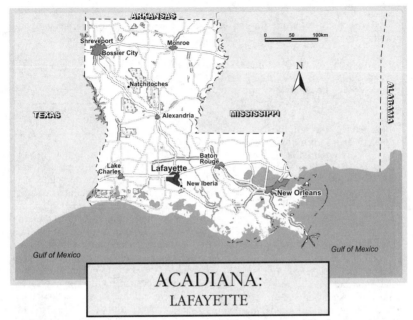

ACADIANA:
LAFAYETTE

Louisiana's Acadian Region, or "Acadiana", alone occupies 22 of the 61 administrative regions or "parishes" in Louisiana. Its somewhat-unofficial borders form a triangle whose base runs along 200 kilometres of the jagged coastline; the east side follows the Mississippi past New Orleans to peak at Avoyelles Parish, approximately 125 kilometres northwest of New Orleans; from there the west side cuts across to the Texas border.

As big as it is though, Acadiana does not include any of Louisiana's large cities. Lafayette, its capital, comes fourth in size after New Orleans, Baton Rouge and Shreveport-Bossier City. It is surrounded by hamlets, mostly transformed into bedroom communities, like Broussard, Carencro and Pont Breaux. Nonetheless, it is a very lively area, ideal for enjoying Cajun and Creole food and music. Southern

Louisiana's Cajun capital, Lafayette, has a metropolitan population of 150,000 and is the hub of the area. It lies between the Atchafalaya basin and the Cajun Prairie, on the edge of the Bayou Vermilion, named for its reddish-coloured waters. Its first inhabitants were the Acadians. Deported in 1755 from their land, which was later named New Brunswick, Prince Edward Island and Nova Scotia, they first established themselves on Bayou Teche. Following conflicts with the aristocratic Creole community, they moved west, to the site of the present city, where Bayou Tortue meets the Vermilion "River", called Bayou Vermilion in the North. In 1812, there was a disagreement between Jean Mouton, an Acadian, and John Reeves, an English speculator, who each wanted to establish the city on their territory. Mouton prevailed, providing the land on which the church and the courthouse would be erected.

In 1836, the city was granted its charter and was named Vermilionville.

In 1756 the river was opened to navigation. A century later, Vermilionville became an important location for both culture and trade.

Train service started in the city in 1880, three years before it arrived in San Francisco. It was in 1884 that Vermilionville took the name of the famous French hero of the War of Independence, the Marquis de La Fayette.

The discovery of oil in 1900 in Anse-la-Butte (Pont Breaux) attracted the large oil companies, who preferred it to distant Texas. In 1959, The Heymann Oil Center was home to no less than 250 businesses, and from 1960 to 1970 the population almost doubled, growing from 40,000 to 70,000 inhabitants. This increase, linked to the rise in the student population of the University of Southwest Louisiana, favoured the emergence of arts and culture.

In the 1980s, the drop in oil prices led to the city's economic collapse. In 1986 there were more bankruptcies than during the depression.

Over the last few years, Lafayette definitely appears to be experiencing a growth in economic activity. The unemployment rate is one of the lowest in the state and, in June of 1997, the financial magazine *Money* ranked the Lafayette region as the second best place to live in Louisiana after New Orleans.

Tourism makes a significant contribution to Lafayette's economy thanks to a growing interest in Cajun and Creole music and food.

FINDING YOUR WAY AROUND

Lafayette

Lafayette is a two-hour drive from New Orleans. It's easy to get to by bus, train or plane. To fully appreciate it's location in the geographic heart of Cajun country, it is best, of course, to travel by car. The first thing to do upon arriving is to arm yourself with a map of the city since the streets are an inextricably tangled web. As in New Orleans, they radiate out from the river and intersect at chaotic angles. Newer highways and their sideroads have been superimposed on the US 90 and the old Abbeville Route (LA 167).

The I-10 passes north of Lafayette, crossing the state from east to west. The 103B exit will take you to the Evangeline Thruway Southeast, which goes south passing by downtown Lafayette.

Approaching from the north, take the I-49 which turns into the Evangeline Thruway Southeast to Lafayette.

From the south, take the US 90 which turns into the Evangeline Thruway Northwest to Lafayette.

The main street, Jefferson, is east of the Evangeline Thruway.

Airport

Lafayette is served by the following airline companies: American Eagle

(☎ 1-800-433-7300), Atlantic Southeast Airline (Delta connection) (☎ 1-800-282-3424), Continental (☎ 1-800-523-0280), Northwest Airlink (☎ 1-800-225-2525) and USAir (☎ 1-800-428-4322). The airport is south of the city and can be reached by taking the US 90.

Lafayette Regional Airport
200 Terminal Drive
☎ (318) 266-4400

By Bus

Greyhound Bus Lines (*315 Lee Ave., Lafayette,* ☎ *318-235-1541*) provides service to cities along the main highways. The Lafayette - New Orleans trip costs $22; Lafayette - Baton Rouge, $10; Lafayette - Lake Charles, $14; and Lafayette - Alexandria, $27.50.

From Lafayette to New Orleans: Departures from the airport: 9am and 2pm; departures from the central station: 7am, 8:30am, 9:45am, 12:30pm and 1:30pm.

By Train

Amtrak: ☎ 1-800-872-7245 (from the U.S.)

From Lafayette to New Orleans: leaves at 3:33pm and arrives at 7:35pm (Sun, Tue, Thu).

From New Orleans to Lafayette: leaves at 1:20pm and arrives at 4:28pm (Mon, Wed, Fri).

IMPORTANT: Trains leave as soon as cars are unloaded and passengers have boarded.

The train to New Orleans continues on to Florida, first to Jacksonville then to Miami.

Car Rental

There are a number of agencies including:

Agency Rent-a-Car: 3909 West Congress Street, ☎ (318) 988-0186

Avis: 100 John Glenn Drive, Lafayette, ☎ (318) 234-6944

Budget: 1711 Jefferson Street, Lafayette, ☎ (318) 233-8888

Hertz: Regional Airport, Lafayette, ☎ (318) 233-7010

National Car Rental System: Regional Airport, Lafayette, ☎ (318) 234-3170

Airport Thrifty: 401 East Pinhook Road, Lafayette, ☎ (318) 237-1282 or (318) 989-9933

Acadiana Auto and Truck Rental: 2433 Cameron Street, Lafayette, ☎ (318) 237-6121

Rent a Wreck: 4480 Johnston Street, Lafayette, ☎ (318) 981-7433 or 1-800-554-7433 from the U.S.

Stan's Rent a Van: 2500 Footage Road Northeast, (along the Evangeline Thruway), Lafayette, ☎ (318) 237-5729

Enterprise Rent-a-Car: 135 James Comeaux Road, Lafayette, ☎ (318) 237-2864

Taxis

AAA Cab: ☎ (318) 264-9709
Acadian Cab: ☎ (318) 264-9709
Acadiana Yellow Cab:
☎ (318) 237-5701
Affordable Cabs of Acadiana:
☎ (318) 234-2111
City Cab Inc.: ☎ (318) 235-7515
City Dixie Cab: ☎ (318) 235-7517
Dixie Cab: ☎ (318) 237-3333

Public Transportation

City of Lafayette Transportation
☎ (318) 261-8570

Service Stations

D & S Automotive: 304 South St.
Antoine Street, Lafayette,
☎ 1-800-296-8028

Gauthier's R.V. Center Inc.: Highway
I-49, exit at Pont-des-Moutons Road,
Lafayette, ☎ (318) 235-8547 or
1-800-235-8547 *(parts and service for
recreational vehicles)*

A-1 Discount Towing: 407½ Pecan
Grove Road, Lafayette,
☎ (318) 232-2124 *(open 24 hours a
day; credit cards accepted)*

Ace Towing: ☎ (318) 896-6135 *(open
24 hours a day; credit cards accepted)*

Benoit Towing: 200 Pecan Grove Road,
Lafayette, ☎ (318) 235-0327

Grossie Car Repairs: 503 Mudd
Avenue, Lafayette, ☎ (318) 234-3761
(Mon to Fri 8am to 5pm)

Carencro

From Lafayette, take I-49 north for
eight kilometres or go north on
University Street.

Faul's Towing and U-Haul: 4129 St.
Joseph Street, Carencro,
☎(318) 873-3622 or 896-0041*(service
24 hours a day; used car rental)*

Broussard

From Lafayette, take the Evangeline
Thruway Southeast or US 90, for eight
kilometres. You can also get to
Broussard by Pinhook Road, or LA 182.

Milton

From Lafayette, take Johnston Street,
or LA 167, in the direction of Abbeville,
to Maurice. There, take LA 92 east for
five kilometres.

PRACTICAL
INFORMATION

The area code is 318

Tourist Information

**Lafayette Convention and Visitors
Commission:** 1400 Evangeline Thruway
Northwest, P.O. Box 52066, Lafayette,
LA 70505, ☎ 232-3808, 232-3737,
1-800-346-1958 from the U.S.,
1-800-543-5340 from North America,
⇰ 232-0161, *(every day 9am to 5pm)*
e-mail address: lcvc@aol.com, webiste:
www.lafayettetravel.com

Emergencies

Police, fire, ambulance
☎ 911

Police

Lafayette Parish Sheriff's Office:
☎ 232-9211

Ambulance

Acadian Ambulance Service,
Emergency: ☎ 911, ☎ 267-1111

Hospitals

Columbia Medical Center of Southwest Louisiana: 2810 Ambassador Caffery Parkway, Lafayette, ☎ 981-2949

Lafayette General Hospital: 1214 Coolidge Street, Lafayette, ☎ 289-7991, *(in the Oil Center Building)*

Our Lady of Lourdes Regional Medical Center: 611 St. Landry Street, Lafayette, ☎ 289-2000, *(between Johnston and Congress Streets)*

Charity Hospital, University Medical Center: 2390 West Congress Street, Lafayette, ☎ 318-261-6000

Women's & Children's Hospital: 4600 Ambassador Caffery Parkway, Lafayette, ☎ 981-9100, *(south of Kaliste Saloom Rd.)*

Banks

Bank 1 One: 200 West Congress Street, Lafayette, ☎ 236-7000, *(bank transactions and currency exchange)*

The First National Bank: 600 Jefferson Street, Lafayette, ☎ 265-3200

The Whitney National Bank: 911 Lee Avenue, Lafayette, ☎ 364-6000

Post Offices

Central: 1105 Moss Street, Lafayette, ☎ 269-4800

Downtown Branch: 101 Jefferson Street, ☎ 232-4910

Oil Center Branch: 1031 Coolidge Boulevard, Lafayette, ☎ 234-3822

Southside Branch: 3523 Ambassador Caffery Parkway, Lafayette, ☎ 988-3732

Broussard Post Office: 4200 Route US 90 East, Broussard, ☎ 837-6651

Carencro Post Office: 809 Bernard Street, Carencro, ☎ 896-6884

Associations

Association for Acadiana International Relations, *(Association des relations internationales d'Acadiana)*, Ms. Iva Clavelle, University of Southwest Louisiana (USL), P.O. Box 42849, Lafayette, LA 70504-2849, ☎ 233-4550

Créole Inc., (Creole cultural association), Mr. Melvin César, P.O. Box 2505, Lafayette, LA 70502, ☎ 232-9076 or 232-6216

The World Acadian Congress of Louisiana in 1999

In August of 1994, in New Brunswick, sometimes called Northern Acadia, the first World Acadian Congress was held. This was the largest international gathering of Acadian people since the *"Grand Dérangement"* (Great Upheaval) in 1755. The event drew more than 300,000 members of the Acadian diaspora to this Canadian maritime province, once a part of Acadia with its neighbouring provinces Nova Scotia and Prince Edward Island. Fortified by its great success, the second edition will take place in Louisiana in the summer of 1999.

From July 31 to August 15, 1999, French Louisiana's tricentennial and the thirtieth anniversary of the Council for the Development of French in Louisiana (CODOFIL), the World Acadian Congress will hold a number of events in all of Acadiana's 22 parishes: pairing up twin cities and villages with other Acadian and Francophone municipalities in North America and Europe, gatherings of Acadian and Cajun families from all over the world, festivals (film, theatre, music, food) and conferences. The closing ceremonies will end with a huge concert at the Lafayette Cajundome, on National (and international) Acadian Day, the 15th of August.

For information regarding congress activities, contact:
Mr. Brian Comeaux, World Acadian Congress of Louisiana in 1999, CMA-Louisiane, P.O. Box 3804, Lafayette, LA 70502-3804, ☎ 234-6166, ⇆ 233-9353

FrancoFête 1999

FrancoFête (Francophone Festival) 1999 was created by the Council for the Development of French in Louisiana (CODOFIL) and is sponsored by the Louisiana Tourism Office. Events in all regions start on January 1st 1999, bringing in this new year, French Louisiana's tricentennial, and end on the last day of the same year, that is, on December 31, 1999.

For any information regarding FrancoFête activities, or to participate in events, contact Mr. Curtis Joubert, at the **Louisiana Tourism Office** *(P.O. Box 94291, Baton Rouge, LA 70804-09291;* ☎ *504-342-6799 or 457-5864)*.

The Greenhouse Senior Center, Ms. Claire Hernandez, 110 Evangeline Thruway Northeast, Lafayette, LA 70501, ☎ 261-8456, *(recreation center for seniors)*

Newspapers

The **Lafayette Daily Advertiser** is the only daily newspaper in the Cajun capital. Their Friday edition has a list of the upcoming week's interesting events.

The **Times of Acadiana** (☎ 237-3560), a free weekly newspaper, has the most complete listings of cultural events. It is available at the tourist information center and in all public places (supermarkets, restaurants, etc.).

Soccer

The **Lafayette Swampcats** soccer team *(season from Jun to Aug; $5 to $25; Lafayette Cajundome,* ☎ 265-2100).

Locksmiths

Lafayette Locksmith Service: 411 Kaliste Saloom Road, Lafayette, ☎ 261-5464 or 1-800-737-7091 from the U.S.

Bonnet's Key & Lock: 410 West St. Mary Boulevard, Lafayette, ☎ 233-6644 *(open 24 hours a day)*

Hardware Stores

Guidry Hardware *(Mon to Fri 7am to 5pm, Sat 7am to 1pm; 1818 Jefferson St., Lafayette,* ☎ 234-5263). You'll find everything here, from nuts and bolts to crawfish-cooking equipment.

Guided Tours
"Francophone Louisiana"

Allons à Lafayette! ("Let's go to Lafayette!") *(127 Baudoin St., Lafayette, LA 70503;* ☎ 988-5003). Specializing in welcoming and providing accommodation to Francophone visitors, they offer guided tours of the Cajun capital in French, social events and traditional meals.

Acadiana To Go *(619 Woodvale Ave., Lafayette, LA 70503,* ☎ 981-3918) organizes guided excursions in French throughout Cajun country.

The **International - Tour of Louisiana** *(P.O. Box 52449, Lafayette, LA 70505-2449,* ☎ 233-3972, ⚬ 233-3952). Eight-, nine- or eleven-day tours with guides that speak the language of their clients. The tour takes you to a number of cities, museums, plantations and monuments, and there are also evenings at nightclubs, breakfast at a native reserve, a discovery cruise on the Atchafalaya, an evening of jazz aboard the *Natchez*, and more.

Public transit isn't very extensive in Louisiana (almost everyone drives a car), but there is a very valuable means of transportation for visitors without cars.

Yellow/Checker and Affordable Cabs *($9 to $100 per person depending on the route; 200 Johnston St., Lafayette,* ☎ 237-6196) offer tours of Lafayette and Cajun country in vans (7 passengers); they pick you up at your hotel. They offer the following routes: the **Acadian Village**, **Vermilionville**, the **Acadiana Shopping Centre**, **Henderson**, **Fred's Lounge** in Mamou, and the **Liberty Theatre** in Eunice. Call the owner, Allen Picard, for prices of the various itineraries they offer.

The **French Louisiana Bike Tours** *(604 East Pinhook Rd., Lafayette, LA 70501,* ☎ 232-5854 *or 1-800-458-4560 from the U.S.;* ⚬ 232-6688) offers interesting package tours of Cajun country which involve cycling between 48 and 90 kilometres a day. Groups of eight to fourteen

A Bird's Eye View of Louisiana ★★★

There is a company that offers a fascinating **flight over the coastal swamps and the Atchafalaya basin in an airplane.** Contact **Lafayette Aero Inc.** *($99 for 3 passengers, lasts 1 hour; 123 Grissom Dr., leaves from Lafayette Airport, ☎ 234-3100).* The Cessna 172 flies at a low altitude over the coastal swamps of Cypremort Point, heads east to Franklin and comes back toward Bayou Teche, continues to Henderson and the Atchafalaya basin. The pilot, Martin Angelle, flies low enough so that you can photograph, film or just admire the rich wildlife of this distinctive environment where, among others, wild turkeys and stags abound.

people ride through small country villages, swamp regions, prairies, etc. Excursions are well planned; there are stops at the best tourist spots in the area (inns, authentic cuisine, music, dance). They offer three tours: **The Tour of Cajun Country** *($750 for 5 days, breakfast and lunch included; Oct, Mar, Apr);* **The Cajun Music-Food Tour** *($595 for four days, breakfast, lunch and tickets for the Liberty Theatre included; Oct, Nov, Mar, Apr);* **Mardi Gras by Bike!** *($750 for four days, breakfast, lunch and some dinners included; Mardi Gras costume; Ticket to the Liberty Theatre, the Mardi Gras Ball and the Run-Up to Mardi Gras).* They also rent bikes: $89 for three days. Credit cards accepted for deposit only.

Cajun Country Tours *(Mon to Fri 9am to 5pm; 2020 Pinhook Rd., office 201, Lafayette,   ☎   235-8000   or ☎ 1-800-364-0924 from the U.S.).* Guided tours for groups or individuals.

Other Guided Tours

Jean Lafitte National Park *(every day 8am to 5pm)* also offers guided tours that last one hour: see below in "Exploring".

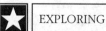

EXPLORING

Lafayette ★★

Louisiana's Acadian capital, universal crossroads of French-speaking communities, is also a university town with a lot of cultural activity. Lafayette, which was called Vermilionville from 1836 to 1880, jealously guards everything associated with its heritage. Acadian descendants, who make up the largest part of its population, are eager to help visitors discover all facets of their culture and all the wonderful places linked to their moving history.

Acadian Cultural Center at Jean Lafitte National Park ★ (1) *(Surrey St. close to the US 90 across from the airport, ☎ 232-0789).* With their exhibitions and excellent film about the Great Upheaval, a historical framework of the deportation of the Acadians by the English in 1755, the centre offers the most comprehensive information about Cajun history and culture. It is thus the best place to start when doing a tour of the city.

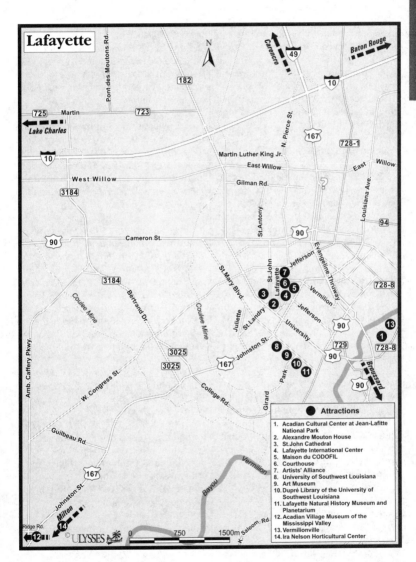

Lafayette

N

Attractions

1. Acadian Cultural Center at Jean-Lafitte National Park
2. Alexandre Mouton House
3. St.John Cathedral
4. Lafayette International Center
5. Maison du CODOFIL
6. Courthouse
7. Artists' Alliance
8. University of Southwest Louisiana
9. Art Museum
10. Dupré Library of the University of Southwest Louisiana
11. Lafayette Natural History Museum and Planetarium
12. Acadian Village Museum of the Mississippi Valley
13. Vermilionville
14. Ira Nelson Horticultural Center

© ULYSSES

0   750   1500m

Alexandre Mouton House ★ (2) *($3 adults, $2 seniors, $1 children; Tue to Sat 9am to 5pm, Sun 3pm to 5pm; 1122 Lafayette St., ☎ 234-2208)*. This residence, which formerly belonged to Alexandre Mouton, the first democratic governor of the state, was built in 1800 and is now listed in the National Register of Historic Places. There are objects relating to the American Civil War, as well as period furniture and Mardi Gras costumes.

St. John Cathedral ★ (3) *(every day 6am to 6pm; 914 St. John St., ☎ 232-1322)*. This building of gothic inspiration, dating from 1916 is the seat of the Diocese of Lafayette. There is an impressive 500-year-old oak next to it. You can also visit the cemetery, whose oldest tombstones are inscribed in French.

Lafayette International Center *(735 Jefferson St., Lafayette, ☎ 268-5474)*. A statue of General Alfred Mouton stands in front of the old city hall, now the site of the Lafayette's Office for the Promotion of Business and International Trade.

Maison du CODOFIL ★ (4) *(217 W. Main St., Lafayette, ☎ 262-5810)*. The Council for the Development of French in Louisiana was created in 1968 by James Domengeaux. This public agency works to promote French, especially in the area of youth education. It is located in Lafayette's attractive old city hall.

Lafayette Moments in Time ★ (5) *(free admission; Mon to Fri 8:30am to 4:30pm; Courthouse, 800 Buchanan St., Lafayette, ☎ 233-0150)*. This collection, started by Court Clerk O.C. Guillotte, includes over 8,000 photographs that illustrate life in the area during the last century. The collection is on the second floor of the Courthouse.

Artists' Alliance ★ *(Wed to Fri 11am to 5pm; 121 W. Vermilion St., Lafayette, ☎ 233-7518)*. Located in an old hardware store, this visual arts centre presents travelling exhibitions or works by local artists.

The **University of Southwest Louisiana (USL) ★ (7)** *(Mon to Fri 9am to 4pm, Sun 2pm to 5pm; 101 Girard Park Dr., Lafayette, ☎ 482-5326)* has exhibits of contemporary art, decorative arts and permanent collections in the Foundation building.

Dupré Library of the University of Southwest Louisiana ★ *(Mon to Thu 7:30am to 11pm, Fri 7:30am to 6pm, Sat 10am to 6pm, Sun 2pm to 11pm; at the corner of St. Marie Blvd. and Hebrard Blvd., Lafayette, ☎ 482-6039)*. In the entrance, press clippings and photographs provide a precious source of information on the oil industry, genealogy and culture of the area.

Museum of Natural History - Planetarium ★★ (8) *($2.50 adults, $1 5-17 years old; Mon, Wed, Thu 9am to 5pm, Tue 9am to 9pm, Sat and Sun 1pm to 5pm; 637 Girard Park Dr., Lafayette, ☎ 268-5544)*. The museum presents interesting exhibitions on the environment, interactive exhibits and a "discovery room". Various presentations at the Planetarium on Mondays and Tuesdays.

Acadian Village - Museum of the Mississippi Valley ★★ (9) *($5 adults, $4 seniors, $2.50 6-14 years old, every day 10am to 5pm; 200 Green Leaf Dr., when exiting off Ridge Rd. from Lafayette, ☎ 981-2364 or*

1-800-962-9133 from the U.S.) Authentic setting of a 19th-century Acadian community; almost all original structures.

Vermilionville★★ (10) *($8 adults, $6.50 seniors, $5 students; every day 10am to 5pm, closed Dec 25 and Jan 1; 1600 Surrey St., Lafayette, ☎ 233-4077 or 1-800-99-BAYOU from the U.S.).* Nine-hectare park between the Bayou Vermilion and the Lafayette Airport; Acadian village with a plantation, school, chapel, etc. Craft demonstrations, concerts, exhibitions, conferences and other Cajun and Creole cultural events. The centre also has a restaurant: **La Cuisine de Maman**, that offers meals for $7.

Azalea Trail ★ *(☎ 232-3737).* Guided tour through the streets of Lafayette to parks and other sites celebrated for their azaleas: in bloom from mid-March to Mid-April.

The Crepe Myrtle Trail ★ *(starts at the northern outskirts of Lafayette).* A trail approximately 40 kilometres long that runs along the Vermilion River. You can take this route which has shady areas with pastures and horse farms by either bike or car. Cyclists will appreciate the flat terrain, minimal traffic and clearly indicated signs.

Ira Nelson Horticultural Center *(free admission; Mon to Fri 7am to 4pm; 2206 Johnston St., Lafayette, ☎ 482-5339).* Numerous tropical and sub-tropical varieties of plants from Louisiana.

Broussard

Founded in 1884, Broussard takes its name from Valsin Broussard, a direct descendant of Alexandre Broussard de Beausoleil, one of the first Acadians to arrive in Louisiana in 1765. The old Côte Gelée has changed a lot since the time of horse-drawn carriages and plantations. Now it's just a Lafayette subdivision with a lot of oil-company offices. The *Beau Soleil Broussard, A Driving Tour* pamphlet suggests a pleasant tour of the city by car. By following the directions, you will discover the elegant architecture of the following houses: Melançon, Ducôté, Bernard, Valsin, Broussard, Yongue, Charles Billeaud *(W. Main St.)*; André Billeaud, Alphonse Comeaux, Paul Billeaud, Breaux and Pineau *(E. Main St.)*; A.A. Comeau *(E. Madison St.)*; Alesia, Martial Billeaud, Jr., Janin *(Morgan Ave.)*; Edmond Comeaux and Marguerite Roy Saint-Julien *(E. 2nd St.)*; as well as the Sainte-Cécile School, the Sacred Heart Church, the Ducrest Building, the Saint Julien Building and the Janin store.

Acadiana Zoo *($6 adults, $3 children; 9am to 5pm; 6 km south of Broussard, LA 182, ☎ 837-4325).* The zoo has created a natural habitat for wild animals.

 PARKS

Lafayette

The **Acadiana Park Nature Station ★★** *(Mon to Fri 9am to 5pm; Sat and Sun 11am to 3pm; E. Alexander St., ☎ 261-8348; to get there, from the Evangeline Thruway North, take Willow St. to Louisiana Ave., then turn left onto Louisiana until you reach Alexander St.; turn right, 800 m further: the park is on the left).* This nature station on the Vermilion River, allows you to get acquainted with the area's wildlife, vegetation, geography and history. Cajun naturalist Bill Fontenot is the best person to take you on a tour of the station; call in advance to reserve his services.

Girard Park *(St. Marie Blvd. and Park Girard Circle)*. This municipal park is endowed with beautiful oak trees, a peaceful pond, many picnic sites, outdoor barbecues and tennis courts. YMCA with a pool open during the summer. Girard Park is adjacent to the University of Southwest Louisiana campus. Acadian festivals take place here in September. The Natural History Museum and Planetarium are behind the park.

 # OUTDOOR ACTIVITIES

 ## Golf

The **Municipal Park Golf Course** *(1121 Mudd Ave., Lafayette, ☎ 268-5557)*. This 18-hole golf course is open to the public.

The **"Old Oaks of Lafayette"** Public Golf Course *(1600 Highway 89, Youngsville (Lafayette), ☎ 837-1159)*. An 18-hole course five minutes from downtown Lafayette. Open to the public.

The **Lafayette Golf Links** *(1040 E. Broussard Rd., Lafayette, ☎ 984-1556)*. Another 18-hole golf course close to Lafayette.

 ## Horseback Riding

In the Lafayette area, particularly in the black Creole community, there are a number of **trail riding** ★★★ associations. Fuelled by a fine diet of zydeco music, dancing and Creole food, you ride for three days, generally Friday to Sunday. Contact Don or Charles Cravins at the KFXZ radio station *(☎ 318-232-5363)* for information.

  ## Hunting and Fishing

Provost Adventures Outfitters *(P.O. Box 31892, LA 70593, ☎ 988-6531)* offer hunting and fishing trips. They specialize in hunting wild dove, duck, goose, turkey, alligator and deer. Vans available.

Hunting enthusiasts who are in Lafayette in September or October won't have to go far to hunt wild dove. Cajun Maxie Broussard *(☎ 232-9785)* guarantees an interesting hunting experience even if you don't come back with a satchel full of game. Maxie is a Cajun storyteller *par excellence*, and his hunting stories alone are worth it. It costs about $40 per day, including a "po-boy" sandwich at registration time, and refreshing drinks during the trip. Maxie Broussard's property (Palais des Vaches and Pacaniere) is located on Neuville Road, at the Verot School Road exit (at Youngsville, southeast of Lafayette).

ACCOMMODATIONS

Lafayette

Since Lafayette is the capital of Cajun country, staying with a Cajun family offering lodging and breakfast is particularly enjoyable for visitors. Most of these places also have special rates for week-long stays.

Note: Except where mentioned, credit cards are not accepted at tourist inns and bed and breakfasts. However, they are accepted at most hotels and motels. Due to Louisiana's subtropical climate during the long hot summer months, all establishments have air conditioning.

Park Acadiana Camping *($; 1201 E. Alexander St., Lafayette, ☎ 234-3838).* This is the most attractive camp site in Lafayette, right beside the Nature Station. The campground has about 69 sites. Fully equipped with electricity and all services.

Alleman Center *($; 303 New Hope Rd., Lafayette, ☎ 984-6110).* Right beside the enchanting Acadian Village, this campground has 80 sites with hook-ups. All services are available.

Smith's Lodge *($; LA 96, Broussard, 2 km from the LA 182, on the left toward St. Martinville, ☎ 837-6286)* is attractively located near a stream in an agricultural environment. It's a peaceful spot with many sites and all services.

Maxie's Mobile Valley Camping *($8 tent, $10.55 RV; US 90 South, Broussard, 6 km south of the airport,* ☎ *837-6200)* offers 70 sites with hook-ups and all services.

KOA Camping of Lafayette *($15.50 tent, $18.50-$22.50 RV, $27-$35 cabins; exit 97 from the I-10, Scott,* ☎ *235-2739).* This campground, recognized by KOA as one of the best in the United States, offers 175 campsites with hook-ups and services; mini-golf, fishing, row boat rental. Cassettes are available with information about Lafayette's history.

The **Lafayette Inn** *($18-$30; ≡, pb, tvc; 2615 Cameron St., Lafayette,* ☎ *235-9442)* is a small, simple, well-maintained motel that is close to downtown.

The **Acadian Motel** *($20-$28; ≡, pb, tvc; 120 N. University Ave., Lafayette,* ☎ *234-3268)* offers fine-quality accommodations and has the advantage of being close to downtown Lafayette.

The **Red Roof Inn** *($35-$50; ≡, pb, tvc; 1718 N. University Ave., Lafayette,* ☎ *233-3339 or 1-800-843-7663 from North America)* is located close to the I-10. This economical hotel offers 108 clean, comfortable rooms.

The **Days Inn** *($42-$47; ≡, pb, tvc, ≈, ℜ; 1620 N. University Ave., Lafayette,* ☎ *237-8880 or 1-800-325-2525 from North America),* which is close to the I-10, has 120 rooms and one fully equipped suite.

The **Lafayette Oil Center Travelodge** *($45-$48; ≡, pb, tvc, ≈, ℜ; 1101 W. Pinhook Rd., Lafayette,* ☎ *234-7402 or 1-800-255-3050 from North America)* is a 61-room hotel located south of the city. Airport shuttle and parking.

The **Acadian Bed and Breakfast** ($45-$85 bkfst incl.; pb, tvc; 127 Vincent Rd., Lafayette, ☎ 856-5260). Léa and Raymond LeJeune offer a complete breakfast and an evening meal with all the delights that Cajun cooking has to offer. For Cajun music fans, Lafayette's most popular dance hall, Randol's is conveniently located nearby.

The **Cypress Tree Inn** ($47-$49; ≡, pb, tvc, ≈, ℜ; 2501 SE Evangeline Thruway, Lafayette, ☎ 234-8521). The Evangeline Thruway is a major artery but this modern comfortable hotel, once belonging to the Ramada chain, is nevertheless well situated close to downtown and City Park. The rooms are comfortable and they have conference rooms. Free parking.

🦐 **Cajun Country Home B & B** ($55-$75 bkfst incl.; pb or sb; 1601 LaNeuville Rd., Youngsville (Lafayette), LA 70508; exit 100 from I-10 and follow Ambassador Caffery Pkwy for 14 km to Verot School Rd. or LA 339, turn right, continue for 1 km to LaNeuville Rd., turn left and drive for 1 km until you reach a sharp left turn; the house is straight ahead; ☎ 856-5271). This warm and inviting, pure Cajun-style house, comes highly recommended. Built in 1830, it is Maxie Broussard's ancestral farm. Now, Audrey and Maxie Broussard welcome visitors with great kindness. The beautiful 50-hectare farm is a dream come true if you want to enjoy the outdoors but still be close to the bustle of Lafayette city. On this pastoral site, where cows are set out to pasture just steps away from the house, a large vegetable garden, mulberry trees, beautiful oaks as well as imposing hickory trees adorn the property in majestic fashion. In May, the orchard provides juicy peaches, which Mrs. Broussard uses to make the succulent jam that is served at breakfast with delicious butter croissants from Poupart's, Lafayette's famous French bakery. Cajun and American breakfasts are also offered. It's wonderful to sit in the shade of the oak trees, on the small flowered terrace, and admire the peaceful scenery; this is also where smokers are to be found since smoking is not allowed in the house. Visitors can do their laundry for a few extra dollars, and use the outdoor barbecue on the terrace.

The **Quality Inn** ($59-$69; ≡, pb, tvc, ≈, ℝ; 1605 N. University Ave., Lafayette, ☎ 232-6131 or 1-800-752-2682 from North America) is located close to the I-10 and has 153 rooms. Conference rooms available. Airport shuttle.

🦐 The **Auberge Creole** ($60 bkfst incl.; pb or sb; 204 Madison St., Lafayette, LA 70501, ☎ 232-1248). In the Creole quarter, close to downtown Lafayette, Creole Ruby Henderson welcomes guests to her charming residence which has six large rooms. This establishment, every room of which is decorated with attractive period furniture, is highly recommended. Mrs. Henderson will teach you all the secrets of zydeco and gospel music, and how to make the best gumbo, a dish she prepares wonderfully. Although the inn is non-smoking, you can smoke outside. Parking available.

The **Holiday Inn Central Holidome** ($60-$70; ≡, pb, tvc, ≈, ℜ; 2032 NE Evangeline Thruway, Lafayette, ☎ 233-6815 or 1-800-942-4868 from North America), a 242-room hotel,

St. John Cathedral in Lafayette - R.N.

A zydeco band in downtown Lafayette - R.N.

offers a shuttle service to and from the airport.

🏠 **Rest House Bed & Breakfast** *($60-$85 bkfst incl.; pb or sb; 218 Vincent Rd., Lafayette, LA 70508, ☎ 856-6958).* On the property of this big city bungalow, also highly recommended, multicoloured myrtle bushes, magnificent oaks and great hickory trees abound. The owner, Mrs. Mildred Doucet, has three rooms available including one with a private entrance facing the garden. The amiable hostess, a highly skilled cook, loves to satisfy the choosy palates of her guests (with foods from her garden) with jalapeño pepper jelly, strawberry butter, fig cake with cane syrup, shortbread, quiche, spicy vinegar, etc.. Morning biscuits and French croissants are served nice and hot.

T'Frère's House Bed & Breadfast *($75-$90 bkfst incl.; pb, tvc, ℝ; 1905 Verot School Rd., Lafayette, ☎ 984-9347).* This lovely old Victorian-style house, built in 1890, is an oasis of tranquillity in an urban setting. They offer an airport shuttle upon request. Parking.

Alida's Bed & Breakfast *($75-$100 bkfst incl.; pb; 2631 SE Evangeline Thruway, 3 km south of the airport, Lafayette, ☎ 264-1191 or 1-800-922-5867 from the U.S.; internet address: http://cust.iamerica.net/alidas),* is a beautiful house, in Queen-Anne style, belonging to Doug and Tanya Greenwall. Laundry service is available.

🏠 **Au Bois des Chênes** *($75-$105 bkfst incl.; pb, K, tvc; 338 N. Sterling St., Lafayette, ☎ 233-7816)* is one of the 100 best bed & breakfasts in North America. It occupies the splendid old coach houses of the historical Charles Mouton plantation (1890). They speak English, French and Spanish. Airport shuttle service. Parking.

The **Best Western Hotel Acadiana** *($85; ≡, pb, tvc, ≈, ℝ; 1801 W. Pinhook Rd., Lafayette, ☎ 233-8120 or 1-800-874-4664 from the U.S.)* is a comfortable, 300-room hotel located close to the regional airport with a number of conference rooms for business people or professionals.

🏠 The **Sunny Meade Bed and Breakfast** *($85-$125 bkfst incl.; pb, ≈, ⬝; 230 Topeka Rd., Scott, LA 70583, ☎ 873-3100 or 1-800-833-9693 from the U.S.).* Listed as a historical monument, this cozy Victorian house, also highly recommended, is hidden away in the pastoral countryside of Scott, only a few kilometres away from Lafayette. It's an extremely calm and restful place. The Cajun hosts, Charles and Barbara Primeaux offer four big, inviting rooms, each with a private bathroom. Sunny Meade has a good reputation for its breakfasts and guests heartily partake of their corn bread, "couche-couche" (a cereal with milk), home-made jam and bread, French toast and biscuits. This place attracts many Francophones from all over the world, undoubtedly because the hosts speak French.

Jane Fleniken's Country French B & B *($90-$120 bkfst incl.; pb; 616 General Mouton St., Lafayette, LA 70501, ☎ 234-2866).* This elegant house, resembling an old French manor, is entirely furnished with beautiful antiques. They offer two rooms, both of which have their own private bathrooms.

Carencro

The **Bechet Homestay Bed & Breakfast** *($80 bkfst incl.; sb or pb; 313 N. Church St., Carencro, ☎ 896-3213)* has five rooms in a Victorian-style house and another room fixed up in an attractive separate cottage. Languages spoken: English, French, Spanish and Italian.

La Maison du Campagne *($95-$140 bkfst incl.; pb, ≈, 825 Kidder Rd., Carencro, north of Lafayette, ☎ 896-6529 or 1-800-895-0235 from North America)* is another beautiful Victorian house located in a pleasant country setting.

Broussard

The Maison d'André Billeaud House Bed & Breakfast *($85-$125, bkfst incl.; pb; 203 E. Main St., Broussard, LA 70518, ☎ 318-837-3455)* is a historical residence located 10 minutes from downtown Lafayette and five minutes from the regional airport. The host, Craig Kimball, also runs a catering service so you can be sure breakfasts are good.

La Grande Maison *($85-$195 bkfst incl.; pb; 302 E. Main St., Broussard, ☎ 837-4428 or 1-800-829-5633 from the U.S.)* is Victorian in character and houses seven rooms. Normand and Brenda Fakir run this attractive establishment.

Milton

Cajuns operate many bed & breakfasts, but they are often a bit outside of the city. Such is the case with the Bordeaux family's pleasant **"Country Cottage"** *($75 for 2 people; $100 for 4 people; ≈, pb, tvc, K; 311 Grand St./LA 92, Milton, ☎ 856-5762)*. The cottage has two bedrooms, a living room and a kitchenette with a microwave oven and a barbecuing area; washer and drier supplied. The Bordeaux's always greet you with a warm welcome.

 RESTAURANTS

As well as the Cajun food, which is first-rate here, you can't leave Lafayette without trying some authentic Creole cuisine. This chapter lists many "soul food" restaurants as well as a number of other types of restaurants.

Lafayette

The **Poupart's Bakery** *($; Tue to Sat 7am to 6:30pm, Sun 7am to 4pm; 1902 Pinhook Rd., close to Kaliste Saloom Rd., Lafayette, ☎ 232-7921)*. The Poupart's, of French origin, have been supplying people of the area with their "daily bread" and delicious pastries for a generation. Their exceptional butter croissants are served at the breakfast tables of many of Lafayette's family-run bed and breakfasts. They have seating so you can relax and enjoy one with a fine coffee.

Café Chez Laura *($; Mon to Fri 11am to 2pm; 918½ Voorhies St. behind the Langlinais grocery store, close to Congress St., Lafayette, ☎ 234-3915)*. This popular and inviting restaurant was opened by Creole Laura Broussard, who unfortunately died a few years ago. The café remains a family business with Dot and Harold Broussard presiding over the kitchen. Patrons storm the premises at lunch time. If you don't arrive early enough, that is before 11:30, there's a good chance that you'll have to get your lunch "to go". Very friendly atmosphere.

Café Dwyer *($; Mon to Fri 4am to 4pm, Sat 4am to 2pm; 323 Jefferson St., Lafayette,* ☎ *235-9364).* This cafeteria-style restaurant has been the most popular in Louisiana for close to 70 years. Business people, families, workers and Cajun artists all cross paths here; the singer Zachary Richard is known to eat here from time to time. The chef, who is also the son of the owner, greets customers as they enter. Delicious breakfasts, roasted meats, chicken stew and various sauces. Warm atmosphere and fast service.

Charlie's & Pearl's Penny Saver Seafood *($; Tue to Sat 9am to 6pm; 2022 Moss St., Lafayette,* ☎ *234-9973).* We highly recommend this establishment. This Cajun market has everything: a butcher shop/delicatessen, a fish store, a grocery store and a snack bar where 1,800 savory crab or crawfish fritters and 6,000 Cajun-style hot dogs, smothered in explosive meat and tomato sauce, are devoured every week. The counters are overflowing with hot sauce, Louisiana rice, fine coffee, cayenne pepper, cane syrup, Creole spices, kidney beans, black eyed peas, spicy sausages, gumbo filet, brown sauce, marinated Cajun-style quail eggs, white pudding, sweet potatoes, okra, swordfish, catfish, crawfish, tuna, prawns and crab. Their refrigerated fish and seafood counter is

full of delicacies from the Gulf of Mexico and Louisiana's lakes and rivers. At lunch, Pearl adds wonderful *court bouillon* fish dishes to the small daily menu. All in all, it's a must while in Lafayette!

The Country Cuisine *($; Tue to Sat 10am to 8pm, Sun 11am to 2pm; 709 N. University Ave., Lafayette,* ☎ *269-1653).* Arthur Williams prepares the best Creole boudin in Lafayette. In the morning, the smoke can be seen rising from their chimney from afar. Barbecues and pork rinds are other house specialties.

Earl's Supermarket and Deli *($; Mon to Fri 11am to 2pm; Sun 10:30 to 2pm; 510 Verot School Rd., Lafayette,* ☎ *237-5501).* Counter service. "Poboys", seafood lunches, roast chicken. Barbecues on Sundays.

Cedar's Grocery *($; Mon to Fri 9am to 6pm, Sat 9am to 4pm; 1115 Jefferson St., Lafayette,* ☎ *233-5460).* Lebanese and Mediterranean cuisine, counter service. Specialties: New Orleans *muffulettas*, *gyros*, spinach pies, *kibbes*.

Olde Tyme Grocery Store *($; 218 W. St. Mary Blvd., Lafayette,* ☎ *235-8165).* This little market has a snack bar, where the best oyster and shrimp "po-boys" in Lafayette are to be found. At lunch time, it's a favourite spot for workers and students; people also come with their families.

Judice Inn *($; 3134 Johnston St., Lafayette,* ☎ *984-5614).* Run by the Judice family since 1947, this establishment was a long-time neighbour of the drive-in. Great for connoisseurs of hamburgers, home-fries, chips and beer.

Léger's Meat Market *($; Mon to Fri 6am to 6pm; Sat 6am to 4pm; 1008 E. Simcoe St., Lafayette, ☎ 318-232-7630)*. The Léger family is proud of their boudin, which contains less fat due to a process they developed which involves wringing it out after it's made. Some restaurants in New Orleans list "Léger's boudin" on the menu.

At **Louvière's** *($; Mon to Fri 10am to 2pm; 1015 Lamar St., at Jefferson, Lafayette, ☎ 235-6258)* the menu changes every day. The main dishes are crawfish stew, prawns, *court bouillon*, pork and beef. The dining room alone is worth the trip for its collection of bayou alligator engravings.

Jack's Restaurant *($; Mon to Sat 11am to 3pm; 200 Madison St., Lafayette, ☎ 237-5273)*. With its five tables, this little hole-in-the-wall doesn't look like much but it is a very charming place. If you're on a small budget you'll love it: for only a few dollars, you can get good Creole dishes cooked by Patrick Jack's mother, Creole. Patrick, the owner, will tell you about the best places to go for local zydeco music. On the menu, depending on the day, you'll find gumbo, Creole stuffed chicken, meatballs, steamed crawfish, crawfish fettuccine, braised steak, etc. You can eat in or take out.

Lindon's *($; Mon to Thu 10am to 9pm, Fri and Sat 10am to 2:30am, Sun 6pm to 1am; 313 E. Simcoe St., Lafayette, ☎ 232-4526)*. The best deal in Lafayette for Creole food: in fact, all the dishes, barbecues, pork roast and other things, are offered at the same price: $4.30. Visiting night owls will enjoy spending the wee hours of the morning in the company of local night owls. Credit cards are not accepted.

Savoy's Famous Boudin *($; Mon to Fri 7am to 5:30pm; Sat 8:30am to 3pm; 2832 Verot School Rd., Lafayette, ☎ 984-0920)*. The Savoys make good boudin, pork rinds, smoked sausages, poultry, barbecues, *tasso* and *andouille* (in winter).

The **Chavis Barbecue Service** *($; every day 8am to 9pm; 407 Brooks St., Lafayette, ☎ 233-1318)*. This is John Chavis' place, undisputed master chef of the barbecue.

T-Coon's *($; Mon to Fri 11am to 2pm; 740 Jefferson St., Lafayette, ☎ 232-3803)*. The best Cajun food in downtown Lafayette: jambalaya, rabbit in hot sauce, fricassee, rice and kidney beans, shrimp "po-boys", salads, homemade bread.

Piccadilly Cafeterias *($-$$; every day 11am to 8:30pm; 100 Arnould Blvd, Lafayette, ☎ 984-7876; 838 Coolidge St., Lafayette, ☎ 232-4317)*. Cafeteria-style service. Carefully prepared regional dishes.

Creole Lunch House *($-$$; Mon to Sat 11am to 7:30pm, Sun 11am to 3pm; 713 12th St., Lafayette, ☎ 232-9929)*. Raymond and Merline Herbert from the Maison Creole serve their famous stuffed bread, corn bread and rice with sauce. Cafeteria service. Another location *(Northgate Mall, ☎ 318-232-8605)*.

The Hub City Diner *($-$$; Mon to Fri 7am to 10pm, Sat and Sun 8am to 10pm; 1412 S. College Rd., Lafayette, ☎ 235-5683)*. Named after Lafayette's pseudonym, this fifties-style diner (they even celebrate Elvis week!) serves fast food with a Cajun twist.

Lagneaux *($-$$; Mon to Thu 5pm to 10pm, Fri to Sun 5pm to 11pm, 445 Ridge Rd., 2km west of Ambassador Caffery Parkway, Lafayette, ☎ 984-1415)*. Lagneaux is on the road that leads to Acadian Village. All-you-can-eat seafood buffet. This restaurant is very popular among local Cajuns.

🦞 **Miss Helen's Cajun Seafood Restaurant** *($-$$; every day 11am to 10pm; 109 Benoit Patin Rd., Scott, ☎ 234-3536; 3151 Johnston St., Lafayette, ☎ 989-7001)*. This restaurant close to the KOA campgrounds serves authentic Cajun cuisine: catfish, crawfish étoufée, steamed shrimp, seafood gumbo, bread pudding, etc. Miss Helen, deservedly considered one of the grand dames of Acadian cuisine in Louisiana, is a first-rate chef of the same calibre as Enola Prudhomme, sister of the renowned chef Paul Prudhomme.

Pete's *($-$$; every day 11am to 2am; 3903 Johnston St. and 1311 Pinhook Rd., Lafayette, ☎ 981-4670 and 237-6415)*. It's young and it's a challenge: the hamburgers are huge.

Dean-o's Pizzeria *($-$$; Mon to Fri 11am to 11pm, Sat and Sun 11am to 1am; 305 Bertrand Dr., Lafayette, ☎ 233-5446)*. Unique family restaurant with a good variety of unusual pizzas (shrimp, crawfish, etc.).

Poppa T's *($-$$; Mon to Sat 8am to 6pm; Sun 8am to 1pm; 1508 N. Bertrand Dr., Lafayette, ☎ 235-9432)*. Fine local cuisine to take out (for a picnic in Girard Park). Specialties: boneless chicken, boudin, sausages, sausage bread.

Ruby's *($-$$; Mon to Fri breakfast 7am to 9:30am and lunch 10am to 2pm, Sun 10:30 to 2pm; 520 Kaliste Saloom Rd.; 1601 Eraste Landry Rd., Lafayette, ☎235-2046; Mon to Fri 10:30 to 2pm, 315 Louis XIV St., Lafayette, ☎ 989-0222)*. All the Ruby's restaurants offer Cajun and Creole family cuisine. On the menu: pork roast, crawfish étoufée, turkey wings, stewed rabbit.

The Golden China *($$; every day 11am to 2pm; Mon to Thu 5pm to 10pm; Fri and Sat 5pm to 11pm; 3822 W. Congress St., Lafayette, ☎ 981-3661)*. Chinese food with Cantonese, Sechuan and Cajun seasonings. Specialties: soft-shell crab in a creamy Chinese sauce, "volcano" shrimp, Hunan-style catfish, orange beef.

Prejean's *($$; Sun to Thu 11am to 10pm, Fri and Sat 11am to 11pm; 3480 US 167 North, just south of the Evangeline Downs racetrack, Lafayette, ☎ 896-3247)*. Cajun food: eggplant, catfish, alligator.

Poor Boy's Riverside Inn *($$; Mon to Thu 11am to 10pm; Fri 11am to 11pm; Sat 5pm to 11pm; 240 Tubing Rd., exit from Highway 90 East, 4 km from the airport, Lafayette, ☎ 837-4011)*. Authentic Cajun cuisine: oysters on the half-shell, crabmeat, crawfish, prawns, steaks.

Randol's *($$; Sun to Thu 5pm to 10pm, Fri and Sat 5:30pm to 10:30pm; 2320 Kaliste Saloom Rd., Lafayette, ☎ 981-7080)*. There was a time when you had to go to Mulate's in Breaux Bridge for good food and dancing. Now it's possible in downtown Lafayette at Randol's, a large, 500-seat restaurant. The decor is more modern but the music is just as great (especially the band Jambalaya); and the crowd is a winning combination of tourists and Cajuns.

Café Tee-George *($$-$$$; Mon to Fri 11am to 2pm and 5pm to 9pm, Sat 11am to 10pm; 6155 Johnston St., Lafayette, ☎ 993-1103).* This new Cajun restaurant, just south of the Acadiana Mall, has a rustic decor and an attractive collection of old commercial signs recalling old-time rural Louisiana. They serve traditional Cajun food and the best fish and seafood in the country. The owner is painter George Rodrigue, a well known personality in the Louisiana art world. The famous "blue dog" and the painting with people in front of majestic moss-covered oaks, are only a couple of his known works. There is a Cajun band on Friday and Saturday evenings (see "Entertainment", p 232).

Cajun Pier *($$-$$$; every day, 11am to 2pm and 5pm to 10pm; 1601 W. Pinhook Rd., ☎ 233-8640).* This restaurant offers a multitude of salad items and dressings at their salad counter, as well as Cajun food, seafood and grillades. The dining room has a large mural featuring the stars of Cajun politics such as a previous senator, Dudley LeBlanc and the ex-governor, Edwin Edward. They have happy hour specials *(5:30pm to 7pm)* and zydeco performances *(Fri and Sat from 9pm)*. The owner Ken Guilbeau is also a breeder of race horses.

Café Vermilionville *($$$; Mon to Fri 11am to 10pm, Sat 6pm to 10pm, jazz brunch on Sundays until 2pm; 1304 W. Pinhook Rd., Lafayette, ☎ 237-0100).* This charming restaurant, on the edge of Bayou Vermilion, is located in a historical house dating

from 1818; it was even occupied by the Northern forces during the American Civil War. The renowned chef, Michael Richards, an authentic Cajun, prepares savoury Cajun, Creole and French dishes with his personal touch. On the menu: swordfish, red snapper, red perch and a shrimp dish with Kahlua (coffee liqueur). This restaurant is known for the freshness of its food, the favourite sauces and wonderful country soups. The smoked turkey and the gumbo *andouille* are divine.

Charley G's Seafood Bar and Grill *($$$; Mon to Thu 11am to 2pm and 5:30 to 10pm, Fri until 11pm, Sat 5:30pm to 11pm, Sun 11am to 2pm; 3809 Ambassador Caffery Pkwy, Lafayette, ☎ 981-0108).* Specialties: Grilled seafood, turtle soup, crab and tuna fritters. Classic jazz and piano-bar on the weekends; brunch and jazz on Sundays. Reservations recommended.

I Monelli Italian Restaurant *($$$; Tue to Fri 11:30am to 2pm, Tue to Sat 5:30pm to 10pm; 4017 Johnston St., Lafayette, ☎ 989-9291).* Northern-Italian and continental cuisine. Specialties: artichoke crawfish, stuffed rainbow trout, ricotta and spinach tortellini.

Carencro

Enola Prudhomme's Cajun Café *($-$$; Tue to Sat 11am to 10pm, Sun until 2:30pm; 4676 NE Evangeline Thruway, Carencro, ☎ 896-7964).* Enola's inviting Cajun house is a traditional structure located right in the country, on a service road that runs alongside the Lafayette/Baton Rouge highway. Sister of famous New Orleans

Cajun chef Paul Prudhomme, Enola prepares wonderful eggplant stuffed with shrimp and crawfish accompanied by cheese sauce, cheese bread and sour cream dressing. And that's just one of the exquisite dishes on the menu. Enola has won many prizes for her roast pork stuck with garlic cloves and her oyster po-boy. Like her brother Paul, Enola, at times, acts as an ambassador of Cajun cuisine at foreign culinary events.

Paul's Pirogue *($$; Sun to Thu 5pm to 10pm, Fri and Sat 5pm to 11pm; 209 E. St. Peter St., across from the church, Carencro, ☎ 896-3788)*. This restaurant is known for its crawfish *court bouillon*. Reservations are recommended.

Broussard

Chez Norbert *($; Mon to Fri 10:30 to 2pm; 521 Ave. C, when exiting from the Evangeline Thruway, direction of St. Martinville, Broussard, ☎ 837-6704)*. The Norberts, John and his wife, serve different dishes every day: barbecues, jambalaya, chicken, crawfish pie, seafood on Fridays.

Chez Alcide *($-$$; lunch Mon to Fri 11am to 2pm, Thu to Sat 6pm to 10pm; 101 2nd St., Broussard, ☎ 839-0044)*. This beautiful Victorian house, which until recently was called "Le Bistro de Broussard", continues to offer fine regional cuisine at very reasonable prices. Specialties: daily gumbo, grill and catfish. Some sections are reserved for smokers. Reservations are recommended.

ENTERTAINMENT

Lafayette

Downtown Alive! Every Friday from April to June and from September to November, between 5:30pm and 8:30pm, students and office workers alike gather to dance outside on Jefferson and Vermilion Streets. The restaurants are open and you can drink beer on the street while listening to excellent zydeco, Cajun and rock bands.

Zydeco

Cajun Pier *(9pm; 1601 W. Pinhook Rd., ☎ 233-8640)*. A stage is set up near the bar and various zydeco bands perform, featuring Zydeco Joe, Jean-Pierre and the Zydeco Angels, etc. Every night from 5:30 to 7pm, a lot of people come here for happy hour. They also serve food (see "Restaurants", p 230).

Club El Sido *(1523 N. St. Antoine St., Lafayette, ☎ 235-0647)*. On Fridays, Saturdays and sometimes Sundays, Nathan Williams, the owner's brother, plays here with his Zydeco Cha Chas, one of the best zydeco bands in Lafayette, perhaps even Louisiana or the United States. Other highly-acclaimed bands are also on the bill. It all starts around 10pm.

Hamilton's *(1808 Verot School Rd., Lafayette, ☎ 984-5583)* is a dance hall that has been open since the 1920s. Mr. Hamilton has been the director for around thirty years. Creole bands.

Cajun

Back to Back *(Thu to Sat 9:30pm, Sun 3:30pm; 201 Pine St., Lafayette, ☎ 232-9500 or 232-0272).* On Sunday nights, this nightclub, located at the back of Northgate Mall, has Cajun and "swamp pop" bands to get the large crowd dancing. The cover charge varies depending on the band.

Café Tee-George *(Fri and Sat 8pm to 10pm; 6155 Johnston St., Lafayette, ☎ 993-1103)* presents the best Cajun musicians. You can get meals too (see "Restaurants", p 230).

Préjean *(every evening 7:30 to 9:30, Sat until 11pm; 3840 Route 167, north of Lafayette).* Seafood restaurant and dancing.

Randol's *(2320 Kaliste Saloom Rd., Lafayette, ☎ 981-7080).* Seafood restaurant: music, shows and dancing starting at 8pm every night. The most popular spot in Lafayette for Cajun dancing.

Vermilionville *(1600 Surrey St., Lafayette, ☎ 233-4077).* Jam sessions on Saturdays from 10:30am to 12:30am and Sundays at 2pm. Cajun bands. Cover charge varies depending on the band.

Country

The Yellow Rose *(Wed to Sat 10am to 2am; 6880 Johnston St., at the southwest end of Lafayette, ☎ 989-9702).* At this renowned venue, for a fraction of the price of a show at a concert hall, you can dance and listen to the country's best-known performers.

Mixed Clubs (Gay and Straight)

Metropolis Club *(every night; 425 Jefferson St., Lafayette, ☎ 233-6320).* This club which is right downtown has an extremely diverse clientele. Tourists, transvestites, professionals and workers all gather here to hear a good variety of music.

Other Events

Antler's *(5:30pm to 10pm; 555 Jefferson St., Lafayette, ☎ 234-8877).* There's *fais do-do* dancing in the street on Friday nights during the Downtown Alive! season. Wide variety of bands (blues, zydeco, Cajun, rock, etc.), drinks and food all available at this bar that has preserved its old-time charm.

Poet's Restaurant and Bar *(119 James Comeaux Rd., Pinhook Plaza, Lafayette, ☎ 235-2355).* This is the most popular bar for rock and progressive music. Happy hour is from 2pm to 7pm, Monday to Saturday. Bands on Mondays, Tuesdays and Thursdays. Good blues bands on Thursday nights.

Grant Street Dance Hall *(113 W. Grant St., Lafayette, ☎ 237-8513 or 237-2255).* Some of the greatest names in Louisiana's music scene such as Clifton Chenier, Dr. John, Zachary Richard, Beausoleil, etc. have played at this old warehouse. Grant Street Hall isn't open all the time, but when it is, the shows are always of excellent quality.

Carencro

Evangeline Downs *($1, $2, $2.50; Apr to Sep; Fri and Sat 7:15pm, Sun*

1:15pm and Mon 6:45pm; Highway I-49 North, exit 2, Carencro, ☎ *896-7223).* Purebred racing with purses of $40,000 to $125,000. Air conditioned, restaurant, video poker.

Calendar of Events

Lafayette, like Louisiana's Cajun country in general, is known for the number and diversity of its annual festivals. Nowhere else in Louisiana are there so many activities, cultural gatherings and joyous Cajun festivities where they "let the good times roll". Here are some of the major events. For more information on the festivals in this part of the state, contact the **Lafayette Convention and Visitors Commission** *(P.O. Box 52066, Lafayette, LA 70505;* ☎ *232-3808).*

December - January

Christmas at Acadian Village *(entrance fee; 200 Green Leaf Dr., at the exit from Ridge Rd. from Lafayette,* ☎ *981-2364, 232-3808 or 1-800-962-9133 from the U.S.).* Starts the last week in November and goes until Christmas. Not to be missed.

Vermilion Christmas Candles *(Lafayette).* Exhibitions and gatherings starting a bit before mid-November and continuing until Christmas.

Lafayette Annual Winter Exhibition. Third week in January. It's rodeo draws a large audience.

February - March

Louisiana Boudin Festival *(Arceneaux Park, Broussard).* Three weeks before Mardi Gras.

Mardi Gras in Acadiana

Lafayette's Mardi Gras celebration is the second largest after New Orleans'. As in New Orleans, local associations or "krewes" compete in outlandishness. The parades, which everyone can attend, go down Jefferson Street, from Surrey Street to Blackham Coliseum. The Bonaparte Krewe parades on the previous Saturday at 6pm. The day before Mardi Gras, the Queen's parade takes place at 6pm, and on the day of Mardi Gras, you can catch beaded necklaces and doubloons at the King's parade.

The Vermilionville Courir de Mardi Gras *(entrance fee;* ☎ *233-4077).* Food sampling, music, etc.. Two weeks before Mardi Gras.

The Blooming of the azaleas in Lafayette. Around the third week of March to mid-April.

April - May

The Louisiana Flower Festival. Second week of April.

The Festival International de la Louisiane *(P.O. Box 4008, Lafayette, LA 70502,* ☎ *232-8086).* This Francophone festival, the biggest in the United States, takes place in Lafayette's historic district. Food, music, films and works of art from all Francophone countries are honoured. There are more than 600 artists and craftspeople from Africa, the French

Antilles and Louisiana as well as Creole-speakers from Europe. The event takes place during the fourth week of April. Every year there is a different theme: "Revelations of the Diaspora" in 1995, "World Carnival" in 1996, "American Indians" in 1997, "Latin Roots" in 1998, "300 Years of French in Louisiana": in 1999, etc.

Zydeco Fantasy *($5 adults, $2 children; Blackham Coliseum, Johnston St., ☎ 234-9695).* Zydeco music by the best bands in Southern Louisiana. Last week of May.

August-September

The *Fête Nationale des Acadiens*. On August 15th, in Lafayette and all the parishes in Cajun country.

The Cajun Festival - Cajun French Music Association (CFMA) *($5; Blackham Coliseum, ☎ 896-8186).* The CFMA's mission is to promote Cajun music, language and culture, which is accomplished by means of eight regional groups covering the territory from New Orleans to Houston, Texas. During the festival, a prize called "The Cajun" is awarded to the best writer or performer of Cajun music for the year. The festival takes place on the third weekend of August. The Lafayette Chapter of the CFMA also holds a Mardi Gras Dance *(Harry's Club, Breaux Bridge, ☎ 231-6597),* on the Saturday before Mardi Gras, and an evening of dancing on the last Saturday of June.

Summerfest *(Carencro, ☎ 837-FEST).* On the trailer park and campgrounds: regional food, fairground, merry-go-round. The event is held between the first and the last weekend of August depending on the year.

Acadian Festivals, around mid-September, consisting of six events: The Acadiana commercial exhibition, Downtown Alive festivities, the Acadian music festival, the craft festival, the seniors festival and the Bayou food festival. Contact the Lafayette Convention and Visitors Commission *(☎ 232-3808)* for information.

October-November

The **Acadian Village Music Festival ★** *(☎ 232-3808).* Representatives from various cultural groups in Louisiana present everything that makes up Cajun culture: humour, music and food. Second weekend of October.

SHOPPING

Lafayette

Jefferson is the main shopping street in Lafayette. There are many small shops, restaurants and nightclubs.

Duty-Free Shopping

Louisiana is the only American state where visiting foreigners are exempt from paying taxes on their purchases. In metropolitan Lafayette, there are no less than 80 shops that participate in Louisiana Tax Free Shopping program (LTFS) (see "Practical Information", p 49) Call to obtain a list of these shops *(☎ 232-3737).*

Antiques

Old Fashion Things *(402 SW Evangeline Thruway, Lafayette,* ☎ *234-4800)*. This boutique specializes in heavy antique furniture.

Ruins & Relics *(900 Evangeline Dr., Lafayette,* ☎ *233-9163)* offers everything for collectors: furniture, glassware, etc.

Baked Goods

The **Poupart Bakery** *(1902 Pinhook Rd., close to Kaliste Saloom Rd., Lafayette,* ☎ *232-7921)*. The Pouparts prepare all sorts of delicious breads and pastries. They have an excellent reputation within Lafayette and throughout Cajun country. Bread, butter croissants and pastries are baked fresh daily. You can get them to go, or enjoy your delicacies on the spot with an espresso or *a café au lait*. Closed on Mondays.

Shops

The **Cajun Country Store** *(every day 10am to 6pm; 401 E. Cypress St., at Johnston, Lafayette,* ☎ *233-7977)*. A vast selection of recipe books, spices, condiments, craftwork, cassettes, t-shirts and souvenirs are sold at this LTFS-member store.

The **Horseman Store** *(on I-49, across from Evangeline Downs, Carencro,* ☎ *896-4848)*. This store has a complete selection of Western-style clothing: for the cowboy or cowgirl in us all!

Shopping Centres

The **Acadiana Mall** *(Mon to Sat 10am to 9pm, Sun 12:30pm to 6pm; 5725 Johnston St.,* ☎ *984-8240; from I-10, take the exit 100 to Ambassador Caffery)*. This mall has more than 100 shops and large stores like Sears, Maison Blanche, etc..

Acadiana Flags

Evangeline Specialities *(Mon to Fri 8am to 5pm; 210 E. 3rd St., Lafayette,* ☎ *232-3898)*. This stationery shop is one of the few places where you can get an official Acadiana flag.

Ice-Cream

Borden's Ice-Cream *(every day, 11am to 10pm, 1103 Jefferson St., Lafayette,* ☎ *235-9291)*. For many years, this ice-cream counter has made Lafayette's sub-tropical climate a bit more tolerable thanks to their large selection of refreshing treats: milk shakes, sundaes and ice-cream, etc.

Food Stores

Sid's One Stop *(803 Martin Luther King Jr. Dr., Lafayette,* ☎ *235-0647)*. In the heart of the lively black Creole area, Sid Williams' supermarket is full of irresistible pork and other Creole products. People will travel miles on their knees to come here to stock up on pork rinds and crunchy pork chips seasoned with vinegar and cayenne pepper, the best in all southern Louisiana; it's better to find out in advance which days these famous pork

---

A Gourmet Paradise

At **Charlie and Pearl's Penny Saver Seafood**, Charlie and Pearl Arcenaux's "grocery store/butcher shop/fish market/snack bar" *(2022 Moss St., Lafayette, ☎ 234-9973; also see "Restaurants", p 227)*, the shelves and counters abound with Cajun and Creole products: hot sauces, Louisiana rice, cane syrup, cayenne pepper, all sorts of spices, kidney beans, black-eyed peas, gumbo "filé", brown sauce, marinated Cajun-style quail eggs, white boudin, spicy sausages, sweet potatoes, okra, crab, tuna, swordfish, catfish, crawfish, shrimps, etc.

It seems Cajuns have very particular tastes: at their snack bar, inside the market, the Arceneaux's serve 1,800 of their famous shrimp- or crab-stuffed fritters and 6,000 Cajun-style hot dogs smothered in an explosive meat and tomato sauce every week!

---

rinds are cooked on. You can't eat there but with all the wonderful provisions you've acquired, you can easily improvise a picnic in one of Lafayette's pleasant parks. The owner is the brother and manager of Nathan Williams, the famous zydeco singer and musician.

Breaux's Mart *(every day, 7am to 9pm; 2600 Moss St., at Alexander, Lafayette, ☎ 234-4398)*. Grocery store-delicatessen. Particularly handy for campers at nearby Acadiana Park.

Gift Baskets

Fruit World *(6404 Johnston St., Lafayette)*. Everything you need for a picnic or for a gourmet Cajun gift basket, packed with okra, kazoos, preserves and hot pepper jelly.

Wine

Marcello's Wine Market *(2800 Johnston St., Lafayette, ☎ 318-264-9520)*. The largest selection of wines in the area. They specialize in California wines.

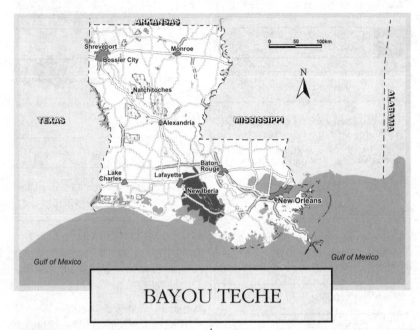

BAYOU TECHE

Bayou Teche runs through the heart of Cajun Country; the first colonists from France and Acadia settled on its banks. The region is located on the edge of the Atchafalaya River basin, into which flow the Red River, the floodwaters of the Mississippi and countless waterways that rise up in the north. The Atchafalaya basin, one of the most impressive swamps on earth, stretches hundreds of kilometres. This gigantic maze of turbid water is teeming with plant and animal life. Half-land, half-water, this is the realm of the cypress, which is draped with garlands of Spanish moss and water hyacinth, and is home to snakes, wild pigs and rabbits, opossums, armadillos, nutrias, raccoons, herons, snowy egrets, alligators, crayfish and numerous freshwater fish. The residents of the towns and countryside along the Teche are dynamic people who take pride in their cultural heritage, be it native, French, African, Creole, Spanish or Acadian.

Lafayette, Breaux Bridge, Henderson, Butte La Rose, St. Martinville, New Iberia, Avery Island, Jefferson Island… these are the kinds of names you'll encounter on this tour, which can be completed in two legs, both starting out from Lafayette. The first leads eastward to Breaux Bridge, Henderson and Butte La Rose; the other, southward through St. Martinville, New Iberia, Avery Island and Jefferson Island, all the way to the Gulf of Mexico.

FINDING YOUR WAY AROUND

Breaux Bridge

From Louisiana Avenue or East Pinhook in downtown Lafayette, take Carmel Drive/LA 94 15 kilometres east to Breaux Bridge. You can also take I-10 East.

Car Rentals

Martin Chevrolet-Geo Rentals, 1315 Rees Street, Breaux Bridge, ☎ (318) 332-2132

Henderson

From Breaux Bridge, take LA 347 East eight kilometres, then LA 352 seven kilometres to Henderson. A quicker route is to take I-10 and then LA 352 (Exit 115).

McGee's Landing - Butte La Rose

Take the 352 East (the main street) out of Henderson, turn right and follow Levee Road for four kilometres. McGee's Landing will be on the left, on the Atchafalaya basin. Farther south, you'll reach a small bridge leading to Butte La Rose. An alternative route to Butte La Rose is to take I-10, then LA 3177 South (Exit 122). It is also possible to get there from McGee's Landing; simply head south on picturesque Levee Road, then take LA 96 West for 15 kilometres.

Parks

From Breaux Bridge, take LA 31 South for 11 kilometres, or LA 347 South, which runs along the left bank of the Teche.

Broussard

From Lafayette, take the SE Evangeline Thruway/US 90 for 15 kilometres.

St. Martinville

From Broussard, take LA 96 East for 11 kilometres.

To get to St. Martinville from Breaux Bridge, take LA 31 South (along the right bank of the Teche) or LA 347 South (left bank) for 20 kilometres.

New Iberia

From St. Martinville, take LA 31 or LA 347 South, then pick up LA 86. From US 90, take LA 14 East, which runs through the town.

Car Rentals

Rent-A-Wreck, 1314 Hangar Drive, New Iberia, ☎ (318) 367-5568

Enterprise Rent-A-Car, 501 Admiral Doyle Drive, New Iberia, ☎ (318) 364-5851

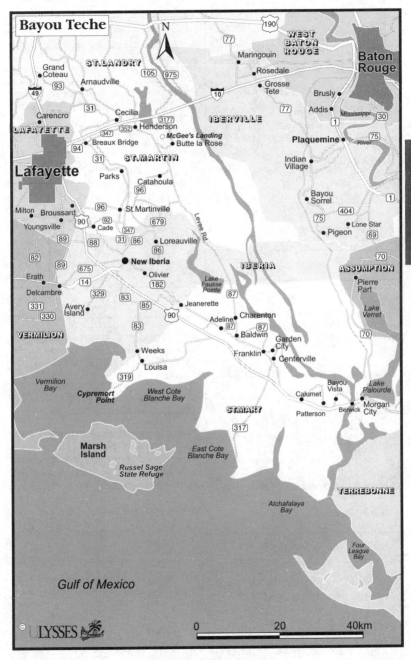

Buses

The only towns in the Bayou Teche region served by buses are those located along LA 182.

Bus information:

Greyhound/Trailways, 101 Terry Street, New Iberia, ☎ (318) 364-8571

Trains

Train information:

Amtrack, ☎ (800) 872-7245

Loreauville

Take LA 86 East out of New Iberia. This road runs along the Teche to Loreauville, 14 kilometres away.

Jefferson Island

From New Iberia (Center Street), take LA 14 West for 24 kilometres, then LA 675 North for a few kilometres.

Car Rentals

Musson-Patout Automotive Group, New Iberia, ☎ (318) 365-3411, 1-800-960-AUTO

Avery Island

Avery Island is located 10 kilometres southwest of New Iberia (LA 329).

Cypremort Point

Cypremort Point is located on the Gulf of Mexico. From New Iberia, take LA 83 South for 32 kilometres to Louisa, then LA 319 for about 12 kilometres. US 90 intersects with LA 83 40 kilometres south of Lafayette.

Jeanerette

Take LA 182 South (Main Street) out of New Iberia and continue for 16 kilometres. This road is known as the Old Spanish Trail. Jeanerette lies on the banks of the Teche. US 90 will also take you there.

Charenton

From Jeanerette, take LA 182 South eight kilometres to Adeline, then take LA 87 for six and a half kilometres.

Lake Fausse Pointe

From Charenton, take Levee Road north for eight kilometres. Lake Fausse Pointe is part of a state park that stretches over 15 kilometres along the east side of the highway. Farther north, you'll reach McGee's Landing, then Henderson.

Franklin

Franklin is located 20 kilometres from Jeanerette off LA 182 South.

Morgan City

From Franklin, take US 90 for 45 kilometres or LA 182, which follows the Teche, passing the villages of Centerville, Patterson and Bayou-Vista.

Lake Palourde - Lake Verret

From Morgan City, head northward on LA 70 to Lake Palourde, a few kilometres away. If you continue, you'll reach Lake Verret, located 25 kilometres from Morgan City.

PRACTICAL INFORMATION

Emergencies

For the police, the fire department or ambulance service, dial 911.

Tourist Information

Breaux Bridge Area Chamber of Commerce, 314 Bridge Street, Breaux Bridge, ☎ (318) 332-5406 or (318) 332-6655

City of Franklin Tourist Department, 200 Iberia Street, Franklin, ☎ (318) 828-6323, or 1-800-962-6889 within the U.S.

The Tourist Department distributes maps showing the major places of interest in Franklin (historic area and plantation houses) *(Mon to Fri 9am to 4:30pm)*.

St. Mary Parish Tourist Commission, 1600 Northwest Boulevard, Franklin, ☎ (504) 395-4905, or 1-800-256-2931 within the U.S. *(Mon to Fri 8:30am to 4:30pm)*

Morgan City Tourist Information Center, 725 Myrtle Street, Morgan City, ☎ (504) 384-3343 *(every day 9am to 4pm)*

St. Martinville Tourism Commission, P.O. Box 379, St. Martinville, ☎ (318) 394-2233 or 394-2232

Iberia Parish Tourist Commission, 2704 Abbeville Highway, New Iberia, LA 70560, ☎ (318) 365-1540

Mayor's Office, 101 Bernard Street, Breaux Bridge, LA 70517, ☎ (318) 332-2172

Mayor's Office, 120 New Market South, St. Martinville, LA 70582, ☎ (318) 394-2230

Mayor's Office, 457 E. Main St., New Iberia, LA 70560, ☎ (318) 369-2300

Guided Tours

Cajun "FUN" Tours of New Iberia *(701 Parkview Dr., New Iberia, LA 70560, ☎ (318) 369-6777)*. Guided group or private tours of Iberia, Lafayette and St. Martin Parishes. Multilingual guides.

Hunting and Fishing Guides

Aventures Provost *(P.O. Box 31892, Lafayette, LA 70593, ☎ 988-6531)* hires out guides for deer-, alligator-, partridge-, duck- and turkey-hunting, and for freshwater and ocean fishing.

Pick-up trucks may be rented for these outings.

The **Service de Pêche Richard Legnon** *(Cypremort Point, ☎ (318) 867-4443)* will do everything possible to make sure that your fishing expedition is a success.

 EXPLORING

Breaux Bridge ★★

Though Cajuns say "Pont-Breaux", the original name of the town, most road signs made by "Americans" read Breaux Bridge. At the town limits, however, the signs are bilingual ("Pont-Breaux/Breaux Bridge").

Named after Agricole Breaux, who had a bridge over Bayou Teche, Breaux Bridge is the crawfish capital of the world. There are many French-speaking blacks here, so you're likely to hear some Cajun and Creole. The local **Crawfish Festival** (see p 266), held each May, is very famous, as is the restaurant **Mulate's** (see p 129), *the* place to get together in Breaux Bridge.

In fall, the sugarcane is cut and brought to the mill to be processed. The procedure has evolved considerably since Étienne de Boré first started marketing granulated sugar two centuries ago, and several hundreds of thousands of tons of sugarcane are processed each year in Breaux Bridge.

The **Louisiana Sugar Co-op** is located on Mills Avenue. During the harvest season, you don't even have to know the address; just let your nose follow the sweet smell. During quieter periods,

the manager, Jack Thériot, gives tours of the mill.

Henderson

Henderson is the western gateway to the Atchafalaya basin. The only road that runs along the shores of the basin, Levee Road, leads to Morgan City. The abundance of seafood, one of the region's natural riches, accounts for the large number of quality restaurants in Henderson. Crawfish reigns on the menus. There are guided tours of the basin and boat-launching ramps for fishermen. The region was hit by major floods in 1927, prompting a significant portion of the population to leave.

The Atchafalaya Basin ★★★

You can embark on a tour of the swamps and bayous at **McGee's Landing** *(adults $12, seniors $10, children $6; departures at 10am, 1pm, 3pm and 5pm; boat rental, motor and gas included, $30/two hours, $40/six hours or $50 a day; with fishing guide for two people: $100 for half a day or $185 for a full day; 1337 Levee Rd., Henderson; ask for Marc or David Allemond, ☎ (318) 228-2384, (800) 445-6681 within the U.S.).* On this boat ride, you'll get to see a tiny part of the huge Atchafalaya basin; the I-10, which spans it on concrete piles; and the plant and animal life that thrives here (bring your camera): bald cypress trees, Spanish moss, water hyacinth, snakes, etc. At McGee's Landing, there is an outdoor café that serves a number of typical dishes, including alligator (see "Restaurants" section: McGee's Atchafalaya Café, p 259).

Angelle's Atchafalaya Basin Swamp Tours *(every day; departures at 10am, 1pm, 3pm and 5pm; adults $12, seniors $10, children under 12 $6; no tour if ticket sales total less than $25; Levee Rd., Henderson, Exit 115 off I-10,* ☎ *(318) 228-8567 or 667-6135)* offers 45-minute guided excursions on the Whisky River and through the otherworldly swamps of the Atchafalaya basin. On Sunday, from 4pm to 8pm, there is live Cajun music on board.

Errol Verret, a Henderson resident, also offers boat tours. Between shows with the group Beausoleil, this accordion-player will take you on a short outing in some of the better-known swamps. To set up a time, call him at (318) 394-7145. Competitive prices that vary according to the length of the tour (read: how much he likes your face!).

Wiltz's "Cajun" Boat Landing *(canoe $12 a day, boat $35 a day, motor and gas included; Levee Rd., Henderson,* ☎ *(318) 228-2430)* is located on the first landing stage on the other side of the levee. In addition to renting out canoes and motor boats, this place also issues fishing permits and sells bait.

Cypress Cove *($145 a night Mar to Oct, $100 a night Nov to Feb; just past McGee's Landing, Henderson,* ☎ *(800) 491-4662 within the U.S.)* offers adventurous types a chance to stay on a houseboat in the heart of the Atchafalaya basin. You are provided with a motorboat to get to your "aquahome", surrounded by flowers and swamp birds and equipped with all the necessaries, including kitchenware, bed linen, towels and an outdoor grill on which to cook the fish you'll catch through a hole in the hull. All four

houseboats are air-conditioned. This outfit, run by Doug Sabatier, also rents out a fully-equipped cottage with two bedrooms, two bathrooms, a kitchen and a living room *($150 a night Mar to Oct, $100 a night Nov to Feb; three-night minimum)*.

Butte La Rose ★

Butte La Rose is a vacation spot on the Atchafalaya basin where many Cajuns have their second homes; a few others live here year-round. Make sure to stop at Mr. and Mrs. Doucet's appealing **General Store**, which sells just about everything and is also the local fishermen's and hunters' favourite hangout.

Broussard

Pelican Aviation's Flight "Seaing" Tours ★ *($90/hour for two people aboard a Cessna 172; 13 km south of Lafayette on US 90; after the LA 182 viaduct, near Broussard, turn left onto LA 3013; ask the pilot, Jeff Ayo, for particulars,* ☎ *(318) 235-7303)* offers visitors a chance to take in a bird's-eye view of the Atchafalaya basin, the sugarcane plantations along the coast, Avery Island, Jefferson Island and Lake Peigneur during an hour-long plane tour.

Parks

A large number of Creoles live in this town between Breaux Bridge and St. Martinville. Parks was originally named "Pâques" (Easter) in reference to the day the railway reached the town.

BAYOU TECHE

St. Martinville ★★★

Many aristocrats took up residence here after the French Revolution of 1789. In an effort to re-create the atmosphere of evenings at Versailles in this still French land, they held balls and hosted operas, earning St. Martinville the nickname "Petit Paris d'Amérique". However, in the early 18th century, when a military fort was built here (1714), trappers from the northern part of New France settled in the area.

Then, after years of wandering, thousands of Acadians who had been deported in 1755 made this area their new home. St. Martin Parish now has a large Creole population as well.

The poet Henry Wadsworth Longfellow immortalized "Evangeline", whose real name was Emmeline Labiche. She is buried in the cemetery of the oldest Catholic church in Louisiana, **St. Martin de Tours** ★★ *(100 S. Main St., St. Martinville, ☎ (318) 394-6021)*. The building was erected in 1765, while the brick facing dates from 1832. Inside, the inscriptions of the Stations of the Cross are written in French. It was in this church that the cardinal of Paris, Monseigneur Lustiger, chose to celebrate Mass when he visited Louisiana. The **Evangeline Monument** beneath which lie Emmeline's remains, was a gift from the actors who played in a 1927 film about the tragic events of her life. Actress Dolores del Río was the sculptor's model.

To the left of the church, on the **Grand'Place** (St. Martin Square), facing Main Street (Rue Principale), a 19th-century house has been converted into the **Petit Paris Museum** ★★, which displays a collection of Mardi Gras costumes and typical objects from the French colonial era. The neoclassical **Presbytère** ★ adjacent to the church dates from 1857.

Farther along, in the park alongside Bayou Teche, stands the very same oak tree where, according to Longfellow, Evangeline waited desperately for her beloved Gabriel to return. The tree, now three centuries old, was very nearly destroyed when a spotlight fell and burned the base of the venerable oak until dawn. This is a favourite meeting place for old Cajuns, storytellers, singers and musicians. Famous brothers Lennis and Ophe Romero often stop here to play a little traditional music on the accordion and the "ti-fer", sing a song or tell a few colourful local tales in French. Ask them to sing *Les maringoins ont mangé ma belle* (The Mosquitoes Ate My Sweetheart) or ask groundskeeper Emmet Charles about the funny things he's seen happen in the park.

The **Maison Du Champ** ★ *(every day 10am to 4pm; at the corner of Main and Evangeline, St. Martinville, ☎ (318) 394-2229)* was built in 1876 by Eugène Du Champ de Chastaignier.

The **Old Courthouse** ★ *(400 S. Main St.)* of St. Martin Parish was built in 1859. This neoclassical building houses a large collection of documents dating from the French and Spanish regimes.

The **Longfellow - Evangeline State Commemorative Area** ★ *(cars $2; every day 9am to 5pm; tourist information office on site, 1200 N. Main St., ☎ (318) 394-3754)*, whose handsome oak trees covered with Spanish moss line the shores of Bayou Teche, is well worth a stop. It is home

Acadian Memorial - Acadian House Museum ★★★

In 1755, Acadians were driven from their land in New France, in the northeastern part of North America (now Nova Scotia, New Brunswick and Prince Edward Island). This *"Grand Dérangement"* was the start of a never-ending saga for the deportees, who were scattered all over the world, their families often fragmented. For many Acadians, far-off Louisiana seemed like a promised land, a "Nouvelle-Acadie" where they could start their lives over. In 1784, Louisiana came under Spanish rule, and a treaty between France and Spain made it possible for many of these exiles to realize their dream and settle. The following year, thousands of Acadians did just that, setting out from the port of Nantes to join their compatriots in St. Martinville.

The **Acadian House Museum**, established in honour of the Acadians who came to Louisiana after the Deportation, is still a moving place to visit and should not be missed. The two-story building is the former town hall, which was restored by architect Robert Barras and is on loan to the museum free of charge from the municipality of St. Martinville. Inside, there is a mural measuring ten metres by four metres, beside which burns an **eternal flame** lit during the inauguration ceremonies on December 10, 1995. Five bronze plaques, each two metres high and one metre wide, bear the names of about 3,000 people identified as Acadian refugees in the Louisiana records from that period. Above the plaques is the following inscription: *Arrête-toi, mon ami, lis mon nom et souviens-toi de moi - Pause friends, read my name and remember*. It is written in both French and English, for it is intended to be read not only by French-speakers, but also by the many Americans of all different origins who visit the museum.

Some of the more common names are LeBlanc, Landry, Comeau, Dugas, Guédry, Pitre, Trahan and Hébert. These are joined by names that are rare nowadays, such as Arosteguy, Semer and Longuepée.

The Acadian Monument Committee, based in St. Martinville since its creation in 1990, strives to highlight the originality of Cajun culture, which is vanishing into the great American melting-pot. Its choice has made St. Martinville a pilgrimage site for Acadians from all over, and one of the main attractions of the World Acadian Congress of August 1999.

The designer of the mural, Louisiana artist Robert Dafford, did much more than simply execute a commission. When he heard about the Acadian Monument Committee, he contacted them and suggested painting a fresco. After two years of discussion, the project took its present shape – a mural showing nearly 300 historic figures involved in the estalishment of the Acadian community in Louisiana. It was their descendants who posed for the artist in period dress. For example, Eddie Richard, the former mayor of the town of Scott and father of musician Zachary, was the model for their ancestor Pierre Richard. A.P. Broussard, who sold farm machinery before he retired, was the model for the leader of the Acadian resistance, Joseph Broussard "Beausoleil".

BAYOU TECHE

J.P. Thibodaux, a car salesman, posed for his ancestor Armand Thibodeau. Olivier Thériault, who went to France to convince Acadians in Nantes to come join their brothers and sisters in Louisiana (despite the fact that it was under Spanish rule in 1784, Louisiana remained very French), is represented by Ronnie Thériault. Ronnie is a policeman and came to the inaugural ceremony is his uniform, standing beside his portrait in ancestral dress. Modeste Barras Bourque and Dolorès Guidry Respess were models for their ancestors Jeanne Chaillon Bourg and Marguerite Martin, respectively.

Acadian Memorial - Acadian House Museum *(adults $3, seniors $2, children 6-12 $1, free admission for children under 5; ticket is a membership card that is valid for one year; every day 10am to 4pm; guided tours in English and French; for more information contact the curator Jolene Adam at 121 S. New Market, P.O. Box 379, St. Martinville, LA 70582, ☎ 318-394-2233)*

to the **Acadian craft store** and the **Acadian plantation house**. The latter was built by Charles Olivier du Clozel at the beginning of the last century, in a style highly representative of the raised Creole country houses of the French colonial era in Louisiana and the West Indies.

The **Oak and Pine Alley** ★ *(LA 96, 5 km north of St. Martinville)*. Charles Durande's plantation house once stood at the end of this lane lined with century-old trees. A planter known to this day for his whims, Durande built his home here in 1829 and had his slaves plant this five-kilometre row of trees between the house and the bayou. Immensely wealthy, he indulged in all sorts of other extravagances as well. It is said, for example, that servants would fill the air around him with perfume before waking him each morning.

When his two daughters were to be married, Durande really let his imagination run wild. Some time before the ceremony, he imported a particularly industrious species of spider from China and set them loose to spin their webs between the trees along the lane. On the morning of the big day, his servants blew gold and silver dust onto the nearly invisible webs, creating a glittering archway for the future brides and grooms and their guests to walk beneath.

The Civil War ruined Durand, who died shortly thereafter. In a niche attached to one of the trees lining the lane, there is a sculpture of Christ on the cross. Others can be seen all along LA 96.

New Iberia ★★

New Iberia was thus named by its first Spanish residents in memory of their homeland. Many of their descendants still live here — Romeros, Viators, Seguras, Hernandezes and others.

New Iberia is truly the queen city of the Teche. A simple stroll along Main Street, with its lovely colonial houses surrounded by tropical parks and gardens, summons up images of the great steamboat era. New Iberia is also home to the famous **Shadows-on-the-Teche plantation** ★★★ and the **Konriko rice mill** ★★, whose name is a hybrid of its owner's name (Conrad) and the words "rice" and "company". New Iberia also hosts a **Sugar Cane Festival** (see p 266).

The **Iberia Parish Tourist Commission** *(every day 8am to 5pm; 2704 Hwy 14, New Iberia,* ☎ *(318) 365-1540)*, which occupies a small Cajun house, distributes maps for a walking tour of the historic district.

The **Bayou Art Gallery** ★ *(free admission; Mon to Fri 10am to 4pm; 143 W. Main St., New Iberia,* ☎ *(318) 369-3014)*. Local art and handicrafts; books on the region.

Trappey's Fine Foods ★ *(adults $1.75, seniors $1, children and teenagers under 17 $0.75; guided tours Mon to Fri 9am, 9:45am, 10:30am, 1pm, 1:45pm and 2:30pm; 900 E. Main St., New Iberia,* ☎ *(318) 365-8281)*. This factory makes typical Louisiana-style hot sauces. The guided tour includes an audiovisual presentation.

The **Justine Antebellum Home** ★★ *($4; by appointment; 2250 Loreauville Rd.; 4 km east of New Iberia on LA 86)*, built in 1822 and converted into a museum, contains a collection of typical Louisiana furniture and objects.

Shadows-on-the-Teche ★★★ *(adults $5, seniors $4, children 6 to 11 $3; every day 9am to 4:30pm; 317 E. Main St., New Iberia,* ☎ *318-369-6446)*. This superb antebellum house was built in 1834. The original owner's great grandson, William Weeks Hall, has restored it but maintained its exotic charm. A number of famous people have been guests here, including Hollywood giants D.W. Griffith, Cecil B. DeMille, Walt Disney and Elia Kazan, and writer Anaïs Nin.

The **Konriko Company Store/Conrad Rice Mill** ★★ *(adults $2.75, seniors $2.25, children under 12 $1.25; Mon to Sat 9am to 5pm; guided tours of the mill 10am, 11am, 1pm, 2pm and 3pm; 307 Ann St., New Iberia,* ☎ *(318) 367-6163 or 1-800-551-3245 within the U.S.)*. The Conrad Rice Mill is the oldest rice-processing factory in North America. A tour of the premises includes complimentary rice samples and coffee. And A 40-minute slide show winds things up.

Lifetime Memories *(Mon and Tue and Thu to Sat, or by appointment; 611 Ashton St., New Iberia,* ☎ *(318) 369-7571)* offers guided carriage rides.

The **William G. "Bunk" Johnson Memorial Plaza** ★ *(free admission; Hopkins St., in the heart of the historic African-American neighbourhood, New Iberia,* ☎ *318-365-1540)* was laid out in memory of the man who taught his unique way of trumpet-playing to none other than jazz great Louis Armstrong. A labourer at both the rice mill and the Shadows-on-the-Teche plantation, Johnson often went to New Orleans, where he played in cafés in and around the French Quarter. It was there, in the 1940s, that he met the man who was to become his best friend, Louis "Satchmo" Armstrong, in a popular gambling joint.

For your own safety, it is strongly recommended that you do not walk around here at night.

Bunk Johnson is buried in the St. Edward Cemetery in New Iberia.

BAYOU TECHE

Lake Peigneur Has Sprung a Leak!

On the morning of November 20, 1980, workers on the drilling platform in Lake Peigneur bored into the gallery of a salt mine under the lake. The drill jammed and the platform shifted, prompting the immediate evacuation of all workers. As if someone had pulled the plug in a giant bathtub, the water in the lake drained out in a huge whirlpool, sweeping along everything in its way and swallowing up over 25 hectares of land, a house and its five adjacent greenhouses. The lake emptied out in the space of seven hours and in the course of the catastrophe, 11 barges were sucked down, along with a number of small fishing boats and a tugboat on the Delcambre Canal. Witnesses say that it was incredible to feel the waterway change direction. The canal flowed in the opposite direction for two days, enough time to fill the subterranean gallery and the entire lake. Fortunately, no one died as a result of this extraordinary incident. All that remains of the house is the chimney and the columns, which stick up out of the water. To see them, take the path in Live Oak Gardens to the observation deck on the shore of the lake.

Loreauville

Originally called Picotville, this town was renamed after a Frenchman who gave the parish a piece of land for the cemetery. This little community of 100 does not get a lot of people passing through, as it lies on the big curve in the Teche, which motorists usually bypass, opting instead for US 90 or LA 192, which links the Teche to Jeanerette. This is a shame, since visitors to Loreauville, located at the southern end of the Atchafalaya, can enjoy a spectacular hovercraft ride on the basin.

There's good food to be had in Loreauville as well, and you can treat your ears to some zydeco, a style of music created by black Creoles, at a club formerly run by the widow of the town's most illustrious composer, Clifton Chenier.

Clifton Chenier, the "King of Zydeco" and "King of the Bayous" is buried in the little **Loreauville cemetery ★**. Fans who would like to pay their respects at his grave will have no easy time of it, since his name is not written on the tombstone *(from Loreauville, take LA 3242 for about 2 km to Landry Rd., then turn left and continue for 3 km. Use the second entrance, and go to the middle of the cemetery. The Chenier crypt is located near the path on the right, parallel to those of the Broussard and Verret families)*.

Clifton Chenier's influence is still very apparent here, especially at **Clifton's Club** *(Parish Rd. 409, Croche Lane, 800 metres from the cemetery, ☎ (318) 229-6576)*, which his widow Margaret ran up until a few years ago, when Bessie Mitchell took over. Like her predecessor, Bessie Mitchell hosts dancing nights at the club, always with excellent bands. Live zydeco Friday, Saturday and Sunday. Call beforehand.

Airboat Tours ★★ *($10 per person; no tours if ticket sales total less than $50; Tue to Sun 8am to 5pm; mailing address: P.O. Box 716, Loreauville, LA 70552; ask for Lon Prioux, ☎ 318-229-4457)* offers open-deck tours on meandering Lake Fausse Pointe. There are three boats, each able to carry six passengers. The tours start at Marshfield Boat Landing and last an hour.

Jefferson Island ★★★

Jefferson Island sits on a block of salt on the shores of Lake Peigneur. The former estate of the Jeffersons, a family of planters, is now a magnificent garden.

Azaleas, hibiscus and camellias abound at **Live Oak Gardens ★★★** *(adults $8.50, children under 15 $5; every day 9am to 5pm, 9am to 4pm during winter, 5505 Rip Van Winkle Rd., ☎ 318-367-3485 or 365-3332)*, along with a wide variety of subtropical plants. The gardens' age-old oaks are among their loveliest ornaments. The admission charge includes a tour of the gardens, a tour of the Joseph Jefferson Home, which was built in 1870 and still has its original furniture and decorations, as well as a boat ride on the lake and the Delcambre Canal. The cafeteria serves light meals and delicious home-made ice cream.

Avery Island ★★★

The **Tabasco Visitor's Center ★★★** *(free admission; Mon to Fri 9am to 4pm, Sat 9am to noon; McIlhenny Company, Avery Island, LA 70513 ☎318-365-8173)* welcomes thousands of people each year, and is an absolute must. Fans of spicy food can visit the factory where the famous Tabasco sauce has been made since 1868. The adjoining shop sells all sorts of food products (free tastings) and Tabasco souvenirs: canned red beans, strings of peppers, signs, aprons, ties, cups and even Tabasco-flavoured candy. The factory has always belonged to the McIlhennys, a family of French-speaking Creoles with Irish roots.

Romantics will find two magnificent natural areas to explore here, both laid out on the former McIlhenny estate: the **Jungle Gardens ★★★** *(adults $4.50, children $3.50; every day 8am to 5pm; ☎ 318-369-6243)*, filled with tropical and subtropical flora, and the **Bird City sanctuary ★★★** (observation tower), home to no fewer than 20,000 snowy egrets, an endangered species. The area is strewn with lovely ponds teeming with alligators.

The **McIlhenny estate** stretches over 80 hectares. Motorcycles and bicycles are not allowed here, but cars are permitted.

Cypremort Point ★★

Cypremort Point is a fishing village and seaside resort on the Gulf of Mexico, between Weeks Bay and Blanche Bay.

Jeanerette

Jeanerette, known as the "Heart of the Lower Teche", is a region full of sugar-cane plantations. During harvest-time, the air around the mills is heavy with sweet smells.

BAYOU TECHE

Jeanerette was named after John Jeanerette, the town's first postmaster (1830). The population is part Cajun (Hébert, Landry, Le Blanc, Boudreaux, etc.) and Creole (Provost, Estève, Le Jeune, Lançon, etc.)

The expansion of the cypress lumber industry later attracted a good number of English-speaking families to the area, while area plantations account for the large number of African Americans found here today.

Le Beau Petit Musée ★★ *(adults $3, children $1.50, students $1; Mon to Fri 10am to 4pm; 500 E. Main St., Jeanerette, ☎ 318-276-4408)* provides an excellent overview of life on the Teche. It displays a large number of objects and documents related to the sugar-cane and cypress industries, the area's two major economic activities. Among the items are moulds made of cypress for the gears used to move the canes along during the various stages of processing in the mills, as well as those for the historic steamboats.

Jeanerette is the hub of the region's sugar industry, and the harvesting period, from October to November, is a busy time. The mill of the Jeanerette sugar company is located almost in the middle of the village; it is not open to the public, but the museum shows a video on the evolution of the sugar industry. At harvest-time, you can also see "cutters" at work and watch them loading the cane onto trucks. Watch out, especially at nightfall, for slow-moving trucks.

The **Bayside Plantation House** *(closed to the public; on the north bank of the Teche, Old Jeanerette Rd.)*, surrounded by magnificent live oaks, is a fine example of the neoclassical style.

Magnolias grow around the bay from which the house takes its name. A little farther east, right after the curve before the Bayside Bridge, you'll see the family cemetery of the planters, the Richardsons, on a hillock overlooking the bayou. Supposedly, the mound is an old native burial ground.

A few kilometres northwest of Jeanerette lies the Creole community of Grand-Marais*(Forty-Arpent Rd., on LA 674)*. Like Olivier, St. Martinville, Parks, Breaux Bridge, Opelousas and Palmetto, Grand-Marais is largely inhabited by descendants of slaves who were freed after the Civil War. Most are farmers who grow sugarcane. The big annual event here is the **Mardi Gras parade**.

Five kilometres west of Jeanerette *(via LA 182 and LA 318)*, you'll see the **St. Mary Sugar Co-op mill**.

The **Moresi Foundry ★** *(506 E. Main St., Jeanerette, ☎ 318-276-4533)* is the same old building where the gears for the sugar mills and steamboats used to be made. It is still in operation, and its owner, Pierre Larroque, will greet you in French, and will gladly tell you about the old cemeteries on the estates of sugarcane planters and other unusual aspects of local life.

The **Albania Plantation House ★** *(by appointment; call 24 or 48 hours in advance; LA 182, exit east of Jeanerette, ☎ 318-276-4816)* is a lovely, four-story building with about 10 rooms. It is hidden behind a curtain of Spanish moss, amidst live oaks and magnolias. Its present owner, Emily Cyr Bridges, has decorated it with antebellum furniture. Her collection of old dolls makes a visit here that much more interesting.

There are two possible routes to Charenton and Franklin – along the north bank of the Teche, which is lined with sugarcane fields, or along the south bank, on LA 182, which runs through Albany. There are two bridges linking Jeanerette to Charenton. On the north bank, you'll go through a region little known to tourists. This strip of land between the Atchfalaya basin and the bayou is inhabited chiefly by farmers and plantation workers. A little closer to Charenton, most residents are fishermen. Almost everyone here has a boat and a truck.

Charenton

Jean Lafitte National Historical Park and Preserve, Chitimacha Cultural Center ★★★ *(free admission; Tue to Fri 8am to 4:30pm, Sat 9am to 5pm; mailing address: P.O. Box 609, Charenton, LA 70523, ☎ (318) 923-4830 or 923-7215).* The "motherland" of the Chitimacha, this is the only reserve in Louisiana that is officially recognized by the government. At the Cultural Center, there are exhibitions on tribal art, history and traditions.

Behind the Catholic church, there are **old Chitimacha tombs** ★ and a **monument** to the 200 victims of the hurricane that hit Isles Dernière on August 10, 1856, an event portrayed in the novel *Chita*, by Louisiana native Lafcadio Hearn.

Atchafalaya Expeditions ★★★ *(two hours: adults $20, children $5; four hours: adults $35, children $10; mailing address: P.O. Box 181, Charenton, LA 70523; after crossing the Teche, turn left onto LA 87, then immediately right onto Charenton Beach Rd.; at the dyke, turn left and drive 5 km to the entrance, on the left after the Anse-de-la-Grande-Avole landing; ask for Marcus de la Houssaye, ☎ 318-923-7149)* offers unusual guided tours, led by friendly Marcus de la Houssaye. Among other things, your guide will show you 500-year-old cypress trees, native tombs, abandoned saw mills, the ruins of a sugar refinery and even a village accessible only by water. In addition, you should be able to spot some of the region's characteristic plant and animal life while crossing Lakes Fausse Pointe and Chitimacha. Itineraries specifically tailored to the interests of photographers, naturalists, ecotourists and bird-watchers are available. Nocturnal outings, fishing trips, photosafaris at dusk or at dawn, camping, accommodations, meals and even scouting for movie locations can all be arranged upon request.

Franklin ★★

Franklin's Main Street easily rivals New Iberia's, though it is not as well known. Lined with an almost uninterruped series of historic homes, it is remarkably beautiful.

Arlington Plantation ★★ *(by appointment only, adults $4, free admission for children under 12; 56 Main St.; on LA 182, 2 km east of Franklin, ☎ 318-828-2644 or 1-800-279-2119 within North America)* features a neoclassical house built on the banks of the Teche in 1830. Inside, visitors will find a magnificent collection of antique furniture.

Grevemberg House ★★ *(adults $3, seniors and students $2.50, children $1.50; every day 10am to 4pm; 407 Sterling Rd., ☎ 318-828-2092* is another splendid neoclassical home (1851) furnished with antiques.

Sterling Mill ★★★ *(tours Sat am; LA 322,* ☎ *318-828-0620* is one of the only operational sugar mills that is open to the public.

Oaklawn Manor ★★★ *(adults $6, ages 7 to 17 $4; every day 10am to 4pm;* ☎ *318-828-0434)* is a gorgeous neoclassical house dating from 1837 and owned by Louisiana governor Mike Foster. It contains one of the largest collections of works by the celebrated American naturalist painter John James Audubon, who was actually born on the island of Santo Domingo (Haiti). The house is surrounded by flowers and magnificent live oaks.

The **Épicerie Médric Martin ★★** *(LA 322, 4 km east of Oaklawn Manor)* is a grocery store made entirely of cypress wood. Plantation workers used to buy their provisions here. Today, the two Martin brothers offer little else than drinks (with or without alcohol), and of course the magical stories of their youth.

If you take LA 182 from Franklin to Morgan City, you'll pass through a series of lovely villages along the Teche: **Garden City, Centerville, Calumet, Patterson, Bayou Vista** and **Berwick.**

Patterson

The **Wedell-Williams Memorial Aviation Museum ★★** *(adults $2, children free Wed and Sat 9am to 5pm; every day 9am to 4pm; 394 Airport Circle, near US 90, Patterson,* ☎ *504-395-7067)* presents the fascinating history of air transportation in Louisiana with the help of dioramas, information panels, audiovisuals and reconstructed airplanes. The museum is located on the former landing strip of the Wedell-Williams company, a pioneer in the Louisiana air industry.

Cajun Jack's Swamp Tour *(adults $20, children $10; every day at 9am and 2:30pm, "sunset cruise" from Jun to Aug; 118 Main St., Patterson,* ☎ *504-395-7420)* offers a two-hour tour of the Atchafalaya swamps.

Morgan City ★★

It was here, in the Atchafalaya basin, at the end of the Teche, that the Americans first started drilling offshore. Oil and natural gas are the region's economic mainstays.

The **Gathright Interpretive Center ★** *(free admission; every day until 4pm; 725 Myrtle St.,* ☎ *504-384-3343)* shows the role of the Atchafalaya basin in the development of Morgan City through documents, photographs and films. A visit takes about an hour.

The **International Petroleum Museum & Exposition** *(adults $5, children free; Mon to Fri 10am to 2pm, Sat by appointment; on Riverfront,* ☎ *504-384-3744* is an interpretive center focusing on the extraction of oil on land and offshore.

Cajun Houseboat Rentals *($95 per night, plus $10 for each additional person; P.O. Box 93, Morgan City, LA 70381, or at Bayou Long, on LA 70, in Stephensville,* ☎ *504-385-2738)* is located an hour and a half from Lafayette and two hours from New Orleans. This little outfit rents out a two-room houseboat called the

Magnolia, which can accommodate up to eight people (kitchenette, bathroom, television and telephone). The boat does not leave the dock.

Built along Front Street to keep back the floodwater of the basin, the seven-metre-high **Great Wall** ★ *(free admission; every day; ☎ 504-395-4905)* offers a sweeping view of the region.

The **Morgan City Historic District** ★★ *(☎ 504-385-0730)*, a collection of about fifty 19th-century houses, is one of the downtown area's loveliest attractions.

The Swamp Gardens & Wildlife Zoo ★★ *(adults $3, children $1.50, children under four free; every day, guided tours: Mon 11am, 1pm, 3pm and 4pm; Tue to Sat 10am, 11am, 1pm, 2pm, 3pm and 4pm; Sun 1pm, 2pm, 3pm and 4pm; 725 Myrtle St., ☎ 504-384-3343* is a natural cypress grove inhabited by alligators and other swamp creatures.

Lataniers, elephant's-ears, irises, cypresses and other species native to the swamps can be admired in the four-acre **Brownell Memorial Park** *(free admission; every day 9am to 5pm; LA 70, on Lake Palourde, ☎ 318-384-2283)*, where a carillon in a 30-metre-high tower rings at regular intervals.

Scully's Swamp Tours *(adults $20, children $10; Mon to Sat 10am, 12:30pm and 3pm, Sun by appointment; 3141 LA 70, ☎ 504-385-2388)* offers two-hour outings aboard different kinds of boats. Pedalboat rentals, restaurant.

PARKS

Henderson

Outings on the **Henderson swamp**, which is part of the Atchafalaya basin *(Levee Rd.)*. Boat and canoe rentals; guided barge tours.

Cypremort Point

Cypremort Point State Park ★ *($2 per car; Apr 1 to Sep 30, 7am to 8pm; Oct to Mar, 8am to 7pm; LA 319, south of Jeanerette, ☎ 318-386-4510)* has a picnic area, a sailing harbour and a small beach in a somewhat bare spot where there is little shelter from the sun.

Lake Fausse Pointe

Lake Fausse Pointe State Park ★★★ *(picnic areas $2 per car; Apr to Sep 7am to 8pm, Oct to Mar 8am to 7pm; ☎ 318229-4764 or 504-342-8111)* covers an area of 2,400 hectares and has eight kilometres of trails leading through a cypress grove. Those wishing to stay here will find eight well-equipped cabins able to accommodate up to eight people each; 50 campsites; picnic areas with restrooms and a grocery store.

The park boasts several lovely stretches of water, and if you take a boat ride, you can admire some 800-year-old cypress trees. There are guided tours of the swamps, and boats and canoes may be rented at **Captain Cleve's Landing and Grocery** *(excursion $20/hour; canoe $5/hour, motorboat*

BAYOU TECHE

$6/hour; ☎ 318-229-6333). Owner Cleve Bergeron has been fishing and hunting in the Atchafalaya basin all his life.

Evening outings offer a chance to learn about the nocturnal habits of reptiles and other inhabitants of the Louisiana waters. Credit cards accepted for reservations.

Burns Point

The **Burns Point Recreation Area** ★ *(camping $3-$7, picnic areas $1; E. Blanche Bay; from Centerville, take LA 317 South, ☎ 318-836-9784)* has several campsites with showers, picnic areas, a beach and fishing areas. Located in a swampy area, the beach is better suited to fishing than swimming.

Morgan City

Lake End Park ★★ *($2 per car; LA 70, 1.6 km north of Morgan City, ☎ 504-380-4623)* has a beach, a campground with restrooms and showers, and picnic areas. It is located near Lake Palourde, in an area shaded by magnificent cypress trees.

 ACCOMMODATIONS

Breaux Bridge

In addition to selling its famous Cajun boudin (blood pudding) on Sunday from 7am to 6pm, **Bayou Boudin & Cracklin** *($50-60; 100 Mills Avenue, near Mulates, ☎ 318-332-6158)* rents out attractive cypress cabins facing onto the Teche.

As indicated by its name, **La Galerie - Bed and Breakfast** *($75 bkfst incl.; downtown, above the Broussard hardware store, E. Bridge St., ☎ 318-332-4092* has a wraparound porch *(galerie in French)*; in this case it looks out onto the commercial artery of the "World Crawfish Capital". The sumptuous Jean-Lafitte and Bayou-Tèche rooms are tastefully decorated with Queen-Anne furnishings, while the ground floor is occupied by attractive antique and craft shops. Smoking is permitted on the porch, and guests enjoy breakfast at the neighbouring Café des Amis (see "Restaurants", p 259).

The **Maison Bérard** *($75-$95 bkfst incl.; pb or sb; 209 W. Bridge St.; Breaux Bridge, LA 70517, ☎ 318-989-0228 or pages 265-9168)* is a Victorian-style cottage that has a few studios in addition to its rooms. The French-speaking hosts, Kenneth and Kathleen LeBlanc Dugas, are members of the Action 'Cadienne cultural association.

Butte La Rose

The **Uncle Dick Davis Park** *(tents $3; 4 km from Butte La Rose, near the Levee Rd.)* is a small campground with restrooms. RVs welcome.

The **Frenchman's Wilderness Campground** *(tents $10-$11; Exit 122/Butte La Rose off the I-10, ☎ 318-228-2616)* is just far enough from the highway that you don't hear the traffic. Equipped with restrooms and showers, this campground is used mainly by urbanites from the Lafayette and Baton Rouge areas seeking an escape from the tropical heat of the cities. The place hosts evenings of Cajun music, and on Saturday nights there is traditional dancing ("fais do-do"). RVs welcome.

The **1-10 Rest Area** *(Butte La Rose exit)* is a popular spot for a break or a snack while on the road. There is no campground, but there are picnic tables and a boat ramp. There is also free waste-disposal for Rvs.

St. Martinville

Beno's Motel and Steakhouse *($31-$36; pb, ctv; LA 31, south of St. Martinville, ☎ 318-394-5523)* is popular with the people who live along the Teche.

The **Old Castillo Bed & Breakfast** *($45-$75 bkfst incl.; pb; 200 Evangeline Blvd.; Peggy Hulin, ☎ 318-394-4010 or 1-800-621-3017 within North America)* is a historic inn shaded by the famous oak tree where Evangeline used to dream about her beloved Gabriel. The little place has five rooms and is located in the heart of the old town. Credit cards accepted.

The **Maison Bleue Bed & Breakfast** *($75 bkfst incl.; pb or sb; 417 N. Main St., St. Martinville, LA 70582, ☎ 318-394-1215)*, run by Debbie LeBlanc Kranske, is a Queen-Anne house with two rooms (double or queen-sized bed) for rent, one of which has its own bathroom and private entrance. Those who wake with a big appetite are sure to enjoy the breakfasts here, which feature crawfish omelettes, crawfish étouffée on corn biscuits, eggs with boudin and all sorts of other typical Cajun dishes. Credit cards accepted.

The **Maison Dautreuil Bed & Breakfast** *($75 bkfst incl.; pb, ℝ; 517 E. Bridge St., St. Martinville, LA 70582, ☎ 318-394-1872, Sandra Martin)*, a charming house listed as a historic monument, was built in 1850. Known also as the Maison Louis Dautreuil, it has a studio appointed with lovely French furniture. The hostess gives her guests the warmest welcome imaginable, and has a bottle of wine waiting for them in the refrigerator. Depending on the day, the copious breakfast might include eggs with ham, pecan French toast with cane syrup, syrup cake and home-made fig preserves. Mrs. Martin's son is mayor of St. Martinville.

The **Bienvenue House** *($80-$105 bkfst incl.; pb or sb; 421 N. Main St., St. Martinville, LA 70582, ☎ 318-394-9100*, owned by Leslie Leonpacher, was built in 1830 and is listed as a historic monument. It has four rooms, each decorated according to a different theme. The Scarlet room is Victorian in style; the Evangeline has rustic Provençal furnishings; the Josephine has an Empire-style decor and the Montgomery, with its balcony overlooking the street, is more eclectic. The rooms contain double and king-size beds. Upon their arrival, guests are served snacks and a glass of "soco", an apéritif wine made with cranberries. The breakfasts are varied and include cranberry crêpes and eggs *á la provençale*; the super-fresh eggs come from the neighbouring henhouse. Guests with dietary restrictions are given special attention. Credit cards accepted.

BAYOU TECHE

New Iberia

The **Belmont Campground** *($2 for two people; RVs $12 in winter, $13 in summer or $72 per week; at the intersection of LA 31 and LA 86, 13 km north of New Iberia,* ☎ *318-369-3252)* is a lovely 200-site campground with restrooms and showers. Located on an old Creole plantation, it is shaded by live oaks. The place is clean and as peaceful as can be; you can even fish and swim in the bayou! For those who'd like to take a walk, there are paths as well.

The **Sher-Mac Campground** *(open year-round; ≈; 3104 Curtis Lane, LA 14, 2 km east of US 90,* ☎ *318-364-4256)* has 170 sites equipped with water and electricity and 25 sites for RVs, as well as restrooms, showers and laundry facilities. Campers can go fishing here or take a walk on one of the lovely nearby trails.

The **Harry Smith Lodge RV Park** *($12.50; LA 96, 5 km east of St. Martinville,* ☎ *318-837-6286)* is a lovely park with room for over 300 RVs. It is located midway between St. Martinville and US 90.

The **Estorge-Norton House** *($35-$80 bkfst incl.; pb or sb; 446 E. Main St.,* ☎ *318-365-7603)* is a three-story house with five pretty rooms with period furnishings. There is even an elevator. No smoking. Credit cards accepted.

🦐 **La Maison** *($50-$60 bkfst incl.; pb; 8317 Weeks Island Rd., LA 83, 3 km south of US 90; Eleanor Naquin,* ☎ *318-364-2970)* is a Cajun cottage surrounded by live oaks and fruit trees and set near the cane fields. Guests staying in its two rooms have access to the living room, dining room and kitchen. The house also has a pretty wraparound veranda. Credit cards accepted. During your stay, you can take a boat ride on the neighbouring swamps *(*☎ *1-800-CAJUNS-1 within the U.S.)*.

The **Pourtos House** *($50-$85 bkfst incl.; pb, ≈; 5610 Old Jeanerette Rd.; Emma Bassin Fox,* ☎ *318-367-7045, 1-800-336-7317 within the U.S.)* is nestled away on the banks of the Teche, on a luxuriant piece of property inhabited by swans, peacocks and other exotic birds. The owner rents out four rooms decorated with loving care. No credit cards.

🦐 The **Maison Marceline** *($60-$80 bkfst incl.; pb; 442 E. Main St.; Ernest Nereaux,* ☎ *318-364-5922)*, a splendid Victorian house that has been completely restored and adorned with period furnishings, is located in the historic district. One suite and one guest room are available for rent. Breakfast is served in royal style, with porcelain and crystal, in the magnificent tropical garden. No credit cards.

🦐 **La Maison du Tèche** *($85/two people plus $15 for each additional person, bkfst incl.; sb; 417 E. Main St., New Iberia, LA 70560,* ☎ *318-367-9456 or 1-800-667-9456 within the U.S.)*, located in the historic district, is a lovely, century-old Victorian that looks out onto the Teche. The famous Shadows-on-the-Teche plantation and the Konriko mill (see "Exploring", p 247) are located near by. A studio and two guest rooms are available for rent. Mary Livaudais serves a copious Cajun breakfast featuring French toast with sautéed apples and praline sauce and a crawfish souffle. Guests may smoke on the stoop. Credit cards accepted.

The **Sandoz House** *($100-$125 bkfst incl.; pb or sb, ctv; 775 E. Main St.,* ☎ *318-369-7737)* is an elegant house dating from the early 20th century (1906) and located in the heart of a historic neighbourhood. Owners John and Carolyn Hébert-Hutchison rent out a luxurious room complete with a private bath and a solarium on the upper floor, as well as a more modest room with a common bath. Each room has its own porch. No smoking inside, but your hosts will be glad to serve you drinks. Major credit cards accepted.

The three following places offer decent, traditional accommodations with all standard services (credit cards accepted):

The **Inn of New Iberia** *($34-$60; pb, ctv, ℜ; 924 E. Admiral Doyle Dr.,* ☎ *318-367-3211).*

Best Western Motel *($38-$86; pb, tv, ≈; 2700 Center St.,* ☎ *318-364-3030 or 1-800-528-1234).*

The **Holiday Inn New Iberia/Avery Island** *($47-$59; pb, tv, ≈, ℜ; 2801 Center St.,* ☎ *318-367-1201 or 1-800-HOLIDAY within North America)* is typical of the chain to which it belongs and offers the same modern comfort as its fellow members.

Jeanerette

At Barbara Patout's **Bed & Breakfast on Bayou Teche** *($40-$55, bkfst incl.; 2148½ W. Main St.,* ☎ *318-276-5061)*, there is a minimum stay of two nights in the house or an adjacent cottage. No credit cards.

The **Alice Plantation Bed & Breakfast** *($100-$125, bkfst incl.; pb or sb, ≈; 9217 Old Jeanerette Rd., Jeanerette, LA 70544,* ☎ *318-276-3187)* is the elegant Creole house of the former Fuselier plantation. Built in 1796, it was carried up the Teche by barge from Baldwin. Mr. and Mrs. Rodgers offer guests their choice of a studio or one of two cottages. The breakfasts are delicious. Tennis buffs can practise their game here. Visa and MasterCard accepted.

Lake Fausse Pointe

The lovely woodland setting of the **Lake Fausse Pointe State Campground** *(6-8-person cabins $65, campsites $10-$12, picnic areas $2 per car; Apr to Sep 7am to 8pm, Oct to Mar 8am to 7pm; Levee Rd.,* ☎ *318-229-4764 or 504-342-8111)* promotes rest and relaxation. The 2,400-hectare park includes a cypress grove with eight kilometres of maintained trails. Those wishing to stay here will find eight well-equipped cabins able to accommodate up to eight people each; 50 campsites, picnic areas with restrooms and a grocery store.

BAYOU TECHE

Franklin

The **Forest Best Western** *($45-$50; pb, ctv, ≈, ℜ; take LA 182, ☎ 318-828-1810 or 1-800-528-1234 within North America)* has the advantage of housing what is generally agreed to be the best restaurant (see p 263) in town.

 The **Hanson House** *($95-125, bkfst incl.; pb or sb; 114 E. Main St., Franklin, LA 70538, ☎ 318-828-3217 or 828-7675)* is a lovely cottage dating from 1849, set in the heart of the historic part of town. It was built by an English captain named Albert Hanson, who used to sail on the Teche. The present owner and host offers his guests a traditional plantation-style breakfast each morning.

Morgan City

The following places offer decent, standard accommodations with all the standard services (credit cards accepted):

The **Kemper Williams Park Campground** *(entrance fees; Sun to Thu 8am to 8pm, Fri and Sat 9am to 6pm; Cotton Rd.; take US 90, Patterson, 7 km west of Morgan City, ☎ 504-395-2298)* covers an area of several hundred hectares and has 26 sites with access to water, electricity, showers, restrooms and laundry facilities. There are picnic areas, and campers can go fishing or enjoy a game of golf or tennis. Guided tours of the swamp are also offered.

Scores of cypress trees draped with Spanish moss make the **Lake End Campground** *(tents and RVs $10; Lake Palourde; off LA 70, ☎ (504) 380-4623)*, on the shores of Lake Palourde, one of the loveliest campgrounds in the region. It has 135 sites for tents or RVs.

Lonely Oaks Campground-Airplane Tours *(tents $7, RVs $10; 30-minute plane ride $80, 1 hour $150; Bayou Vista, off LA 182, 4 km west of Morgan City ☎ 504-395-6765)* is equipped with restrooms and showers and has a boat-rental service.

The **Plantation Inn** *($33-$38; pb, ctv, ≈, ℜ; 815 US 90 E., ☎ 504-395-4511)* offers modest rooms at extremely attractive rates.

The **Acadian Inn** *($33-$61; pb, ctv, ≈, ℜ; 1924 US 90 E., ☎ 504-384-5750)* is a 155-room hotel.

The **Holiday Inn** *($43-$75; pb, ctv, ≈, ℜ; 520 Roderick St., ☎ 504-385-2200 or 1-800-HOLIDAY within North America)*, like all members of its chain, offers all the modern comforts.

✕ RESTAURANTS

Breaux Bridge

Bayou Boudin & Cracklin *($; Tue to Sun 7am to 6pm; 100 Mills Ave., on the banks of the Teche, just past Mulate's, ☎ 318-332-6158)* serves up tasty Cajun specialties like boudin blanc, porc rinds, head cheese and po-boys. Grill dishes and pork fricassee are available on Sundays. The building itself is an old Cajun house dating from 1869.

A Pleasant Stop on the Atchafalaya

At **McGee's Atchafalaya Café** *($-$$; Mon to Thu 10am to 5pm, Fri to Sun 10am to 10:30pm; 1339 Levee Rd., Henderson,* ☎ *318-228-7555 or 228-2384)*, brothers Marc and David Allemond offer their guests a boat ride on the bayou, followed by a stop at their family restaurant-café, which looks out onto the Atchafalaya basin. The cuisine was once superb here, and it's too bad the crab gumbo, frog's legs étouffée and alligator with hot sauce that people used to gobble down here are no longer served. There is dancing on Friday and Saturday nights, as well as on Sunday afternoon, when live Cajun music adds to the atmosphere. The friendliest place in the area.

Poché's Butcher's Shop and Restaurant *($; every day; lunch 11am to 2pm, dinner 5:30pm to 8pm; Exit 109 off I-10; take LA 31 North for 4 km, then take a left on Poché Bridge Rd.,* ☎ *318-332-2108)*. The butcher's shop is particularly proud of its pork rinds, which, like its boudin and meats, can be purchased to go or enjoyed on the premises. The cafeteria-style restaurant serves traditional cuisine for lunch and dinner.

The **Café des Amis** *($-$$; Tue to Fri 8am to 10pm; Sat 7:30am to 10pm; Sun 7:30am to 3pm; 140 E. Bridge St.,* ☎ *318-332-5273)* serves up sophisticated Creole and Cajun cuisine that scores high points with gourmets: turtle soup, seafood and corn bisque, grilled shrimp, beignets, crab, etc.

The **Crawfish Kitchen** *($-$$; Sun to Thu 9am to 9pm; Fri and Sat 9am to 10pm; Exit 109 off I-10,* ☎ *318-332-2687)*, a Cajun restaurant, caters to local families. People come here mainly for the nightly seafood buffet.

Mulate's *($$-$$$; Mon to Sat 7am to 10:30pm, Sun 11am to 11pm; 325 Mills Ave.,* ☎ *(318) 332-4648 or 1-800-42-CAJUN within the U.S.)* is open from breakfast through dinner. There is live Cajun music here every night of the week and during lunch on Saturday and Sunday.

The **Old Sugarmill Seafood Patio** *($$-$$$; every day 10am to 10pm; 282 Rees Rd.,* ☎ *318-332-4120 or 1-800-487-5820 within the U.S.)* offers traditional Cajun cuisine and gets everybody dancing to the sounds of the best Cajun bands on Fridays and Saturdays. You can purchase seafood to go here, and you might even find some gifts for the folks back home.

Henderson

Crawfish Town, USA *($-$$; every day 11am to 10pm; Grand Point Rd., Exit 115 off the I-10, then north for 800 m,* ☎ *318-667-6148)* serves up crawfish straight from the Atchafalaya basin – not farmed crawfish, which are smaller. Another house specialty is the chef's grilled catfish. The atmosphere is extremely rustic.

Las's *($-$$; every day 10am to 10pm; LA 352, just before Henderson,* ☎ *318-228-2209)* serves all the classics of Cajun cuisine.

BAYOU TECHE

Chez Robin *($-$$; Mon to Thu 10am to 10pm; Fri to Sun 10am to 11pm; LA 352,* ☎ *318-228-7594)* serves up seafood, steak, grill and home-made desserts.

🦐 The terrace of **Pat's Fisherman's Wharf Restaurant** *($$-$$$; every day 10am to 11pm; 1008 Levee Rd., at the end of LA 352, after the bridge on the left,* ☎ *318-228-7110)* offers an unforgettable view of Bayou Amy, but you're likely to have to share it with the *maringouins*, which are voracious mosquitoes. Guests of Pat's savour good Cajun and Creole food like crawfish pie, gumbo, jambalaya and tasty crawfish in court-bouillon.

St. Martinville

Danna's Bakery *($; Thu to Sun 5:30am to 5:30pm; 207 E. Bridge St., just before the bridge,* ☎ *318-394-3889)* sells excellent local pastries.

Little **Café Thibodeaux** *($; Mon to Sat 6am to 4pm; 116 S. Main St.,* ☎ *318-394-9268)*, located on Main Street, is a favourite with the locals. Local cuisine served at lunchtime.

🦐 **La Place d'Évangéline** *($$; Sun 8am to 2pm, Mon and Tue 8am to 5pm, Wed to Sat 8am to 9pm; 220 Evangeline Blvd.,* ☎ *318-394-4010 or 1-800-621-3017 within North America)* is the restaurant of the historic Old Castillo B&B, near the Evangeline Oak. It serves the best dishes from the Cajun and Creole repertoire.

Contrary to what you might think, **Possum's** *($$; LA 31 South, 1.6 km from St. Martinville,* ☎ *318-394-3233)*

serves good seafood dishes, not marsupials.

New Iberia

The **Freezo** *($; every day 10am to 10pm; 1215 Center St., New Iberia,* ☎ *318-369-9391)* is a must after a visit to nearby Jefferson and Avery "Islands". Center Street, which becomes LA 14, leads there. Freezo is a good place to treat yourself to a good meal without spending a lot of money. The specialties of the house are baked chicken and chili con carne.

🦐 **Legnon's Meat Market** *($; Tue to Fri 8am to 4pm, Sat 8am to noon; 513 Bank Avenue,* ☎ *318-367-3831)* is known for its boudin, pork rinds, sausages, head cheese and other delicatessen products. A good place to stock up for a picnic in the shade of the oak trees in the public park on the other side of the bayou.

Sandwiches - N - More *($; Mon to Sat 9am to 5pm; 106 E. Main St.,* ☎ *318-364-4138)* offers a table d'hôte and succulent Southern-style sandwiches. No credit cards.

Theriot's *($; Mon to Fri 11am to 1:30pm; 330 Julia St.,* ☎ *318-369-3871)* grocery prides itself on serving the best breakfasts in town. The house specialties are boudin and pork rinds.

Viator's Drive Inn *($; Mon to Sat 9am to 9pm; 1403 Hopkins St.,* ☎ *318-364-4537)* was a pioneer in the fast-food industry. Long before the trend took off, Viator's was already serving hurried, hungry customers its "mangeaille exprès". The hamburgers and hot dogs are served on French bread baked fresh every day.

The shopkeepers of downtown New Iberia have been eating at the **Victor's Cafeteria** *($; Mon to Fri 6am to 2pm, Sat 6am to 10am, Sun 11am to 2pm; 109 W. Main St.,* ☎ *318-369-9924)* for years. Popular Cajun food served in a decor that is pure Louisiana (exhibitions of paintings by Rodrigue and other artists featured at the Lockwood Gallery). Seafood dishes and first-rate crawfish, meat and chicken pies. No credit cards.

The **Lagniappe Too** *($-$$; breakfast 10am to 2pm, dinner Fri and Sat 6pm to 9pm; 204 E. Main St.,* ☎ *318-365-9419)* serves home-made soups, gumbos, salads, sandwiches and regional cuisine in a unique setting.

Dolores' Restaurant *($-$$; Mon to Thu 5:30am to 10pm, Fri 5:30am to 11pm, Sat 10am to 11pm, Sun 6:30am to 3:30pm; 617 S. Hopkins St.,* ☎ *318-365-9419)* serves up breakfast early in the morning. The place has good Creole dishes and a small table d'hôte, as well as a daily buffet. No credit cards.

The chef at the **Guiding Star** *($-$$; every day 3pm to 10pm; 4404 US 90,* ☎ *318-365-9113)* uses herbs from Avery Island in his delectable *potée d'écrevisses* (crawfish hotpot), whose secret recipe he naturally refuses to divulge! These tasty shellfish are simply presented: a piece of newspaper serves as a tablecloth, and there is a washbasin at hand for guests to rinse their fingers (a ritual practised by all Cajun families).

Parker's *($-$$; Tue to Thu 10am to 9pm, Fri and Sat 10am to 10pm; 600 W. Admiral Doyle Dr.,* ☎ *318-367-3737)* is best known for its boiled and fried seafood dishes. Breakfast special *($4; 10am to 4pm)*.

The **Picadilly's** *($-$$; every day 11am to 8:30pm; 723 S. Lewis St.,* ☎ *318-357-3171)* serves a good selection of regional dishes in a completely relaxed atmosphere.

People flock to **Top's Landing** *($-$$; Mon to Sat 11am to 10pm, Sun 1pm to 6pm; at the corner of Jefferson and Fulton Streets,* ☎ *318-364-8677)* for tasty po-boys, soups, salads, gumbos and a whole range of refreshing drinks. For a snack, we recommend the terrific crawfish étouffée po-boy.

The **Little River Inn** *($$-$$$; Mon to Thu 11am to 10pm, Fri 11am to 11pm, Sat 5pm to 11pm; 1000 Parkview Dr.,* ☎ *318-367-7466)* serves home-style cuisine: crab dishes, turbot, crawfish, alligator, steak and other grilled dishes.

Armand's *($$-$$$; Tue to Fri 11am to 2pm, Tue to Sat 5pm to 10pm; 111 E. Main St.,* ☎ *318-369-8029)* is located in the downtown historic district. A handsome wooden bar and big mirrors adorn this place, which is very popular with local residents, who love the traditional Cajun and Creole food served here.

Customers of **Pat's Fisherman's Wharf Restaurant** *($-$$; Sun to Thu 10am to 10pm; Fri and Sat 10am to 11pm; US 90, at LA 675,* ☎ *318-369-6429)* savour superb fresh oysters displayed on crushed ice. The place also serves seafood from the Gulf of Mexico, crawfish (in season), steak and grill.

🦫 **Le Rosier** *($$-$$$; Tue to Sat 6pm to 10pm; 314 E. Main St., ☎318-367-5306)*, a cottage built in the 1850s next to the splendid Shadows-on-the-Teche plantation, has the charm of an old country inn. The menu features creative New Acadian cuisine made with fresh produce from the vegetable garden. No smoking.

Jefferson Island

Café Jefferson - Live Oak Gardens *($-$$; every day 11am to 4pm; 5505 Rip Van Winkle Rd., ☎ 318-365-3332)*. The café is located near the Jefferson Home and the gardens, and also offers a sweeping view of Lake Peigneur. On the menu: gumbo, sandwiches, catfish dishes and a few Cajun specialties.

Loreauville

Le Patio *($-$$; Tue to Sat 11am to 2pm and 5pm to 9pm; Sun 11am to 2pm; 105 Main St., ☎ 318-229-8281)* serves up typical Louisiana dishes in a very relaxed atmosphere.

The Boiling Place *($$; Tue to Sat 5pm to 10pm; 102 Main St., ☎ 318-229-4172)* offers seafood prepared in three ways: grilled, fried or in court-bouillon.

Jeanerette

🦫 **LeJeune's Bakery** *($; 1510 W. Main St., ☎ 318-276-5960)* makes the best French bread between Lafayette and New Orleans. The LeJeune family have been baking in this region for 110 years, to everyone's delight. If you pass by the bakery around 11:30am, you'll see a small blinking red light, the signal that the next batch is about to come out of the oven. Knock on the side door to be served, then head over to the public park to enjoy the fresh bread in the shade of the big oak trees.

Landry's Seafood and Steakhouse *($-$$; Tue to Thu 11am to 9:30pm, Fri and Sat 11am to 10pm, Sun 11am to 2:30pm, big lunch buffet every day; 2045 US 90, 4 km east of Jeanerette, ☎ 318-376-4857)* serves Cajun specialties: crawfish, seafood, steaks and other grilled dishes.

🦫 **The Yellow Bowl** *($-$$; Tue to Thu 11am to 1:30pm and 5pm to 9pm, Fri 11am to 2pm and 5pm to 10pm, Sat 11am to 2:30pm and 5pm to 11pm, Sun 11am to 2:30pm; LA 182, 5 km east of Jeanerette, ☎ 318-276-5512 or 828-4806)*. In Cajun Louisiana, when someone says "Jeanerette", people immediately think of the Boulangerie LeJeune and the Yellow Bowl restaurant. The same family has been running the restaurant since 1961, and one of them is always at the stove. The Yellow Bowl has become a local institution. The house specialties are crawfish, seafood and steak.

Cypremort Point

The **Bayview Inn Restaurant & Bar** *($-$$; Tue to Thu 11am to 8pm; Fri and Sat 11am to 9pm; 141 Mitchel Lane, ☎ 504-867-4478)* is the only place to eat in Cypremort Point. Seafood. A good place to have a drink when the shrimp boats are coming back into port with their catch of the day.

Franklin

Charlie's Meat and Deli *($; Mon to Sat 11am and 2pm; 1803 W. Main St., ☎ 318-828-4169)* serves up a daily special and excellent regional cuisine.

The **Forest Restaurant** *($$; Mon to Sat 5:30am to 9:30pm; 1909 W. Main St., ☎ 318-828-3300)* is the best restaurant in Franklin, if not the entire area. Tuck into some good Cajun cuisine - gumbo or crawfish followed by a slice of Mississippi Mud Pie, that famous Louisiana concoction of pecans and chocolate.

Morgan City

The **Harbor Seafood Restaurant** *($$; Tue to Thu 11am to 2pm and 5pm to 9pm; Fri 11am to 10pm; Sat 5pm to 10pm; Sun 11am to 2pm; 500 Universe St., Bayou-Vista, just west of Morgan City, ☎ 504-395-3474)* is a family-style restaurant that serves seafood and Cajun cuisine.

Manny's *($$; every day 5am to 9pm; 7021 US 90 E., ☎ 504-384-2359)*. Pleasant ambiance. Cajun cuisine and local specialties. More health-conscious dishes are available upon request.

 The **Richard Restaurant and Lounge** *($$; Tue to Sat 4pm to 9pm; LA 182 E., ☎ 504-395-7282)* specializes in crawfish, crab and shrimp. Live Cajun music Sundays from 3pm to 7pm; Cajun dance lessons Thursdays from 7pm to 9pm.

Scully's Cajun Seafood Restaurant *($$; Mon to Sat 10:30am to 9pm; LA 70, 8 km north of Morgan City,* ☎ *504-385-2388)* offers a pretty view of the bayou.

The **Café Louisiane** *($-$$; 24 hours a day, US 90 E., ☎ 504-384-3245)* cooks up gumbo, Creole shrimp, crawfish étouffée, seafood, steak. Breakfast is served round the clock.

Landry's Seafood Inn *($$-$$$; Mon to Fri 11am to 10pm; Sat 5pm to 10pm; Colonial Plaza shopping mall, ☎ 504-385-2285)* serves Cajun cuisine and all sorts of good, fresh seafood from the Gulf of Mexico.

ENTERTAINMENT

Breaux Bridge

Mulate's *(325 Mills Ave., ☎ 318-332-4648)* is not only the most popular restaurant in the area, but also attracts large numbers of tourists. Meals are served here from 7am to 10:30pm. Cajun singers and musicians get the crowd singing and dancing every night. Though Mulate's is in fierce competition with Randol's (see p 229), a Lafayette club, the atmosphere here is as friendly and authentic as ever.

On the first Sunday of each month, starting at 8pm, it's time for Cajun dancing at **Harry's Club** *(519 Parkway Dr., Exit 109 S. off I-10, on the left, ☎ 318-332-9515)*. It is here, furthermore, that the **Cajun French Music Association** *(CFMA, ☎ 318-231-6597)* holds its meetings and its Mardi Gras dance.

La Poussière *(cover charge; 1301 Grand Point Rd. ☎ 318-332-1721)* is a

BAYOU TECHE

veritable institution as far as Cajun dancing is concerned. In keeping with tradition, the dance floor is sprinkled with cornstarch to make it less slippery. It was from this "dust" (*poussière*) that the club took its name. Cajun dance fanatics like to get together here, along with a loyal clientele of golden-agers. Live Cajun music on Saturday night from 10:30 until the wee hours.

Zydeco Music

The **Caffery Alexander Ranch** (*Au Large, Zin Zin Rd., between Breaux Bridge and Henderson, ☎ 318-332-5715*). Oddly enough, this temple of zydeco music is out in the middle of a sea of cane fields. The decor of the dance floor area, where fans alternate with window screens, was designed by the owner, Caffery Alexander, who knows the Creole language inside and out. The place is known as the Caffery Ranch because the Creole horsemen from the plantations like to stop here after a day of work in the fields. Live music from 9pm on on weekends (*$3-$6*); call beforehand to double-check. Free lunch on Fridays to the sounds of recorded music. The **Zydeco and Blues Festival**, held between mid-June and mid-July depending on the year, offers a chance to hear some of the best bands in all Louisiana. *The easiest way to get to the Ranch is to take I-10 to Exit 109. Turn left on Bridge Rd. and continue for about 2.6 km, then turn right onto Doyle-Melançon Rd. Finally, take a left on Zin Zin Rd., just under 3 km farther.*

Joseph Dural, Caffery Alexander's grandson, organizes **weekend trail rides** in the purest Creole tradition (*for rates call ☎ 318-332-5363*).

Davis' Disco and Lounge (*every night from 7pm until the wee hours; mailing address: Route 4, P.O. Box 258, Breaux Bridge, LA 70517; no telephone*) books zydeco bands.

Edmond's Club (*11am to 2pm; 667 Anderson St.; no telephone*) Friday to Sunday disco music; live zydeco Saturday and Sunday.

The **Valley Club** (*weekends from 5pm on; LA 31, north of Breaux Bridge, between Cecilia and Arnaudville; no telephone*). Live zydeco, sandwiches.

Henderson

Angelle's Atchafalaya Basin Bar (*Levee Rd., ☎ 318-228-8567 or 667-6135*). Dancing on weekends. On the third pier on the other side of the levee.

McGee's Atchafalaya Café (*1339 Levee Rd., ☎ 318-228-7555 or 228-2384*). Cajun dancing on weekends. Dining (see p 259).

Butte La Rose

At the **Frenchman's Wilderness Campground** (*free admission; 8pm; I-10, Butte La Rose exit, ☎ 318-228-2616*), campers and others eager to kick up their heels get together to waltz and dance the two-step beneath the stars.

Parks

Dauphine's Tuxedo Club (*St. Louis Rd.; take LA 31 over the bayou to LA 347 then turn right on St. Louis Rd., ☎ 318-394-9616 or 845-4880*) is a favourite with Creoles from the plantations and packs a full house every Saturday night with its live zydeco. Often referred to as the Double D Cotton Club, Dauphine's also has its own riding club, the **Double D Trail Ride Club**, whose activities are open to all.

St. Martinville

Podnuh's *(LA 96, Cade, a few kilometres from St. Martinville,* ☎ *318-394-9082)*. If a Cajun really likes you, he'll call you his "podnuh", meaning his partner. At Podnuh's, your partner might be Cajun, Creole or simply an "American" country music fan. The theme varies weekly, but the place is always packed.

Zydeco

Dalton Reed and the Musical Journey are in the spotlight every other Sunday at the **Candle Lite Lounge** *(3721 S. Main St.,* ☎ *318-394-9188)*.

People go to **Tee's Connection** *(weekends, 6pm until the wee hours; 704 S. Main St.; no telephone)* to hear zydeco and blues.

New Iberia

Club La Lou *(LA 14 W.,* ☎ *318-369-7020)* – "La Lou" being a familiar shortform for *La Louisiane* – is the most popular dance hall in the area. Country music is what's "in" here right now, and the latest stars come to play.

Between New Iberia and Lafayette, **Rainbeaux Club** *(8am to midnight, 1373 LA 182 W.,* ☎ *318-367-6731)* is

the place to kick up your heels to Cajun accordion music on Saturday night. Though the dance floor is huge, the place is always packed with fans of *La Valse du Bayou Tèche* or *Jolie Blonde*.

Charenton

Like the Tunica-Biloxi Indians in Marksville, the Chitimacha run a casino here in Charenton. The **Cypress Bayou Casino** *(Mon to Thu 10am to 2am, Fri to Sun 10am to 4am; 832 Martin Luther King Rd.,* ☎ *1-800-284-4386 within the U.S.)* has 850 slot machines and 39 gaming tables (black jack,etc.). There are two restaurants on the premises. Free shuttle service from Lafayette.

BAYOU TECHE

Tabasco Sauce

This famous hot sauce is produced on Avery Island, in the Gulf of Mexico. Cajun cuisine, a blend of Native American, French, African and Spanish culinary traditions, remains unchallenged as the best regional cooking style in the United States – and one of the spiciest, too! A simple visit to the grocery store will give you an idea of the huge selection of foodstuffs available here.

Calendar of Events

February

La Grande Boucherie des 'Cadiens *(on the Sunday before Mardi Gras; St. Martinville,* ☎ *318-394-5912)*. In the purest tradition of the Cajun heartland, this festival features an abundance of food and tastings of grilled meats prepared in all different ways.

Mardi Gras Parades

Loreauville *(☎ 318-229-6825)*

Grand Marais ★★ *(near Jeanerette, ☎ 318-276-4713)*

Franklin *(Debbie Melançon, P.O. Box 567, Franklin, LA 70538)*

May

The **Crawfish Festival** ★★★ *(first weekend in May; Breaux Bridge, ☎ 318-332-6655)* attracts over 100,000 people each year. Cajun and zydeco music, crawfish races and crawfish-eating competitions.

Le Festival du Poisson-Armé *(first weekend in May; Baldwin, between Jeanerette and Franklin)* is another cultural event that is very popular with the Cajun community.

June

The best zydeco and blues musicians perform for tens of thousands of fans from all over North America during the **Zydeco and Blues Festival** ★★★ *(mid-Jun; near Henderson, on Caffery Alexander's "Ranch", ☎ 318-233-4262)*.

July

Pirogue Races ★ *(Jul 4; at Victoria Park in Patterson)*. St. Mary Parish hosts these races on Independence Day.

September

The **Louisiana Shrimp & Petroleum Festival** ★ *(first weekend in September; Morgan City, ☎ 504-385-0703)*. Shrimp and petroleum are two of the region's greatest natural resources – that's reason enough for a festival!

The **Louisiana Sugar Cane Festival** ★★ *(last weekend in September; New Iberia, ☎ 318-369-9328)*. This event, held at harvest-time, always attracts thousands of visitors, who are always ready to have a good time!

 # SHOPPING

New Iberia

The Combined Effort *(Mon to Sat 9am to 5pm; 121 Burke St., ☎ 318-369-7569)* is a co-op run by local craftspeople.

The **Olivier Plantation Store** *(6811 Weeks Island Rd., 8 km south of New Iberia, ☎ 318-369-76960)* was the general store of the Olivier sugar-cane plantation from the late 19th century to the 1950s. It still belongs to the Olivier family, who have decorated it with reproductions of items that used to be sold here, as well as some leftover inventory. An interesting stop for those going to Cypremort Point.

Chez Gullotta *(Mon to Sat 8am to 6pm; 916 S. Lewis St., ☎ 318-364-4149)* is a western-wear shop that sells everything a cowboy might need for his wardrobe, starting with boots.

Franklin

House of Needlework *(every day 10am to 5pm; 610 St. Mary Parish Rd.,* ☎ *318-836-5442).* In her home on the banks of Bayou Teche, Ruth Weels, whose family has been handing down the art of needlework for five generations, makes magnificent creations with her needle and crochet hook.

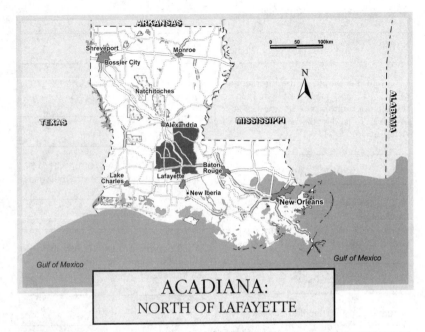

ACADIANA:
NORTH OF LAFAYETTE

 charming countryside of quaint little towns and magnificent spots, all accessible by train, surrounds Lafayette. This chapter covers the northern extremity of St. Martin Parish, where the Bayou Teche has its source (Cecilia, Arnaudville, Leonville), the parishes of Evangeline and St. Landry (Grand Coteau, Sunset, Cankton, Chretien Point, Opelousas, Port Barre, Krotz Springs, Plaisance, Washington, Palmetto, Grand Prairie, Ville Platte, Mamou, Eunice, Richard, Church Point, Branch) and the parish of Avoyelles (Bunkie, Cottonport, Mansura, Simmesport, Marksville). The area is largely populated by Cajuns and Creoles. The region is flat, ideal for the cultivation of rice and other crops such as yams and cotton.

 FINDING YOUR
WAY AROUND

Cecilia

Travel along Highway LA 31; Cecilia is 9 kilometres south of Arnaudville and 11 kilometres east of Lafayette. It is at the northern tip of St. Martin Parish, between LA 347 and LA 31, which follow the Bayou Teche.

Arnaudville

Arnaudville lies 11 kilometres east of Interstate 49 (I-49), on LA 31, which skirts the Bayou Teche, between Leonville to the north and Cecilia to the south. It is located at the southeastern tip of St. Landry Parish, nine kilometres east of Grand Coteau.

Leonville

Leonville is situated at the intersection of LA 103 and LA 31 (which follows the Bayou Teche), nine kilometres east of I-49. It is 11 kilometres north of Arnaudville.

Grand Coteau

Just outside Lafayette, the NW Evangeline Thruwy turns into I-49; head north to LA 93, then east to Grand Coteau. It lies on LA 182.

Sunset

Return to LA 93, heading west; Sunset is on the other side of the highway, a few kilometres west of Grand Coteau.

Cankton

Take LA 93, south of Sunset; Cankton is 14 kilometres from Lafayette.

Opelousas

Return to LA 182, heading north. Opelousas lies approximately 30 kilometres north of Lafayette, at the intersection of I-49 and US 190.

Port Barre

Port Barre is 11 kilometres east of Opelousas, off LA 103, just north of US 190.

Krotz Springs

Krotz Springs is located off US 190, 16 kilometres east of Port Barre.

Plaisance

Plaisance is off LA 10 or US 167, 11 kilometres northwest of Opelousas.

Washington

LA 182 turns into LA 10; Washington is located nine kilometres north of Opelousas.

Palmetto

Take US 71 to the Lebeau exit *(LA 10 East)*. It lies 16 kilometres east of I-49.

Grand Prairie

Grand Prairie is 9 kilometres west of Washington, off LA 103.

Ville Platte

From Washington, travel along LA 103, which runs through Grand Prairie, then along LA 10, heading west.

Mamou

From Ville Platte, take LA 10 for about 11 kilometres, and take a left on Highway 13 for 8 kilometres.

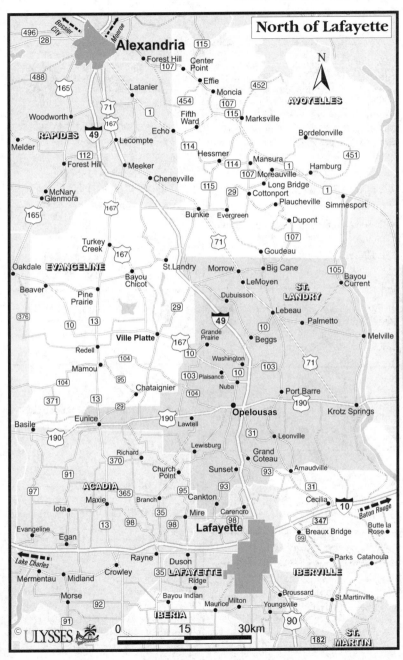

North of Lafayette

N

ACADIANA:
NORTH OF LAFAYETTE

© ULYSSES

0   15   30km

Eunice

Located 32 kilometres north of Interstate 10 (I-10) and 32 kilometres west of I-49, Eunice lies at the intersection of US 190. Eunice is approximately 30 kilometres west of Opelousas, in St. Landry Parish, between the parishes of Evangeline and Acadia.

Richard

Richard is situated off LA 370, south of Eunice, and 3 kilometres from LA 95.

Church Point

In Eunice, take US 190 heading east, then LA 95 south; follow the signposts to Church Point. LA 95 joins I-10 for a quick return (30 min) to Lafayette.

Branch

Branch is off LA 35, eight kilometres south of Church Point.

Bunkie

Take US 71, then the Bunkie Exit (LA 115 West).

Cottonport

Drive 13 kilometres northwest from Bunkie until you reach the junction of LA 29 and LA 107.

Mansura

From Bunkie, travel north along LA 115 for nine kilometres until you reach Hessmer, then follow LA 114 East for eight kilometres.

Simmesport

Drive for 25 kilometres along LA 1, east from Mansura.

Marksville

Take LA 1; Marksville lies eight kilometres north of Mansura.

PRACTICAL INFORMATION

Opelousas

Bus Station

Greyhound/Trailways, 255 East Landry Street, Opelousas, ☎ 318-942-2702

Travel Agencies

Gem Tours, *(415 North Market Street, Opelousas, LA 70570, ☎ 318-942-5767)* offers customized bus tours for southern Louisiana (including New Orleans and plantation country). Groups and individuals.

St. Landry Historical Tours, *(441 East Grolee Street, Opelousas, LA 70570, ☎ 318-948-6784)* offers individual or group tours of St. Landry Parish; meals are included and guides are bilingual.

Tourist Office

St. Landry Parish Tourist Commission, P.O. Box 1415, Opelousas, ☎ 1-800-424-5442 from the US.

Opelousas Tourist Information Center, East Vine Street, US 190 West, Opelousas, ☎ (318) 948-6263, ☎ 1-800-424-5442 from the US

Opelousas/St. Landry Chamber of Commerce, Opelousas, ☎ (318) 942-2683

Opelousas Town Hall, Opelousas, ☎ (318) 948-2531

Hospital

Opelousas General Hospital, 520 East Prudhomme Street, Opelousas, ☎ (318) 948-3676

Service Stations

Doucet's Towing, 1437 North Main Street, Opelousas, ☎ (318) 942-2662

Lafleur's Towing and Recovery, US 167, Opelousas, ☎ (318) 942-8363

Pat's Wrecker Service, 563 Laurent Street, Opelousas, ☎ (318) 948-6420

Palmetto

Service Station

Thomas Wrecker Service, Hwy LA 740, Leonville, ☎ (318) 879-2821

Ville Platte

Tourist Office

Ville Platte Chamber of Commerce, 306 West Main Street, Ville Platte, ☎ (318) 363-1878

Hospital

Ville Platte Medical Center, 800 East Main Street, Ville Platte, ☎ (318) 363-5684

Mamou

Hospital

Savoy Medical Center, 801 Poinciana Street, Mamou, ☎ (318) 457-3363 or 457-7943

Eunice

Tourist Office

Eunice Chamber of Commerce, P.O. Box 508, Eunice, LA 70535, ☎ (318) 457-2565 ☎ 1-800-C-ACADIA from the US

Cajun French Music Association - CFMA, Acadiana Charter Chapter, Eunice, ☎ (318) 457-4399

Hospital

Moosa Memorial Hospital, 400 Moosa Blvd., Eunice, ☎ (318) 457-5244

ACADIANA: NORTH OF LAFAYETTE

Service Station

Robbie's Speed Shop and Wrecker Service, Old Crowley Road, Eunice, ☎ (318) 457-4795

Bunkie

Hospital

Bunkie General Hospital, Evergreen Highway, Bunkie, ☎ (318) 346-6681

Service Station

Dan's Auto Service (general mechanics), US 71, Bunkie, ☎ (318) 346-6297

Marksville

Hospital

Avoyelles Hospital, Hwy 1192/Blue Town Road, Marksville, ☎ (318) 876-2555

Ambulance

Acadian Ambulance, Marksville, ☎ (318) 253-4000, ☎ 1-800-267-1111 from the US

Service Station

Earl's Body Shop, (24 hours/day towing service), Hwy LA 1 South, Marksville, ☎ (318) 563-4657

EXPLORING

Cecilia

Cecilia is part of a large agricultural region (beans, cabbage, yams, pecans).

Leonville

Leonville is the largest Creole community in St. Landry Parish and was established by free blacks. The land here is ideal for growing yams, sugar cane and cotton.

Grand Coteau

Grand Coteau is an idyllic village of 1,100 inhabitants with historic houses as well as old villas and small Creole farms. Worth visiting here, among others, is the Academy of the Sacred Heart, the oldest teaching establishment west of the Mississippi.

Founded in 1821, the **Academy of the Sacred Heart** ★ *($5, seniors $3; length of visit: 1 to 1.5 hr; Mon to Fri 10am to 3pm, Sat and Sun 1pm to 4pm; 1821 Academy Rd., ☎ 318-662-5275)*, a school for girls, has stayed true to its long tradition. It is the site of the only miracle in the U.S. to be officially recognized by the Vatican. The convent's park is, in fact, a magnificent garden flanked by a lane of majestic oaks and pine trees.

The **St. Charles Borromeo Roman Catholic Church** ★ *(admission fee; guided tours by appointment; Church St., ☎ 318-662-5279 or 662-3875)* is located next to the St. Charles college, run by the Jesuits. This magnificent wooden church, dating from 1880 and surrounded by hundred-year old oaks, caters to the Creole and Cajun communities.

The **St. Charles Borromeo Cemetery** behind the church is worth a visit. Burial vaults dating from the beginning of the last century can be admired here; some monuments have been damaged by bad weather and hurricanes, but most are in good shape.

Sunset

Sunset is part of a horse breeding area. The **Chretien Point Plantation Home** ★★ *($5.50; every day, 10am to 5pm; on the scenic "Real French Destination" Byway, or LA 93, 24 kilometres north of Lafayette, ☎ 318-662-5876)*, a house in the Greek Revival style, was built in 1831 by Hippolyte Chrétien and his wife Félicité. The residence, the main building of this 20,000 hectare plantation, was later abandoned and even served as a warehouse. Now restored to its original splendour, it remains a beautiful example of the elegant style old Louisiana architecture. The Chrétien family name comes up often in the history of the area. Legend has it that Lady Félicité shot a highwayman in the spiral staircase of this large residence, which became world-famous for having inspired the sets of the Tara property in the American film classic *Gone With the Wind*. The famous pirate Jean Lafitte is also said to have been a close friend of the Chrétiens and spent considerable time with the family. The property was furthermore the site of a great battle during the Civil War; indeed, the bulletholes are still visible.

The **Romain Castille Home** *(by appointment only; 254 Budd St., ☎ 318-662-5401)* is a Victorian house now occupied by the Francophone senator Armand Brinkhaus and his family.

Opelousas

The finest example of multicultural and multiethnic heritage in Louisiana (here described as a "cultural gumbo") can be observed in St. Landry Parish, and more particularly, in the Opelousas region. This Cajun and Francophone mosaic is made up of Native Americans, English, Germans and Irish. Opelousas is the third oldest city in Louisiana, following Natchitoches and New Orleans. The French settled here in 1720 and immediately named it "Poste des Opelousas", after the Opelousas Indians, who then occupied the territory. A trading post was immediately established. The region gradually specialized in agriculture, and still does. First the kingdom of cotton and livestock breeding, it is now that of rice and yams.

The meeting of different cultures, or "cultural gumbo", gave rise to several generations of Cajun and Creole musicians. The genesis of "zydeco" shot the music of black Creoles to the top of the charts. This musical form of expression, made famous by Clifton Chenier, has become as popular as Cajun music itself. Though the king of zydeco is no longer with us, his son keeps his memory alive by performing his music in Louisiana's many nightclubs and festivals.

Opelousas is also the birthplace of Cajun chef Paul Prudhomme, the

---

Food Processing Plants (visits by appointment)

The **Lou Ana Foods** plant *(call ahead; N. Railroad Ave., ☎ 318-948-6561)* specializes in the processing of vegetable oils.

The **Creole Foods** plant *(Lombard St., ☎ 318-948-4591, ☎ 1-800-551-9066 from the US)* makes "Tony Chachere" brand condiments and seasonings.

The **Savoie's Sausage and Food Products** plant *(free admission; Old Port Barre Rd., ☎ 318-942-7241)* prepares sausages, brown roux (used in many Cajun and Creole recipes), barbecue sauces and rice mixes.

---

darling of contemporary cuisine in the United States. We are indebted to him for the creation of "blackened fish" (Louisiana perch cooked in its skin on the grill; ask for the blackened redfish), as are American gourmets for his infusion of new flavours, inspired by Cajun culinary tradition and the rich mix of local ingredients available in Southern Louisiana.

In St. Landry Parish, yam farming dates back to the early days of the founding of Opelousas; the town actually calls itself the Yam Capital.

Cajuns are said to be great storytellers and to have such a particular fondness for jokes that their special wit is considered a real national treasure in these parts. And so was born the **International Cajun Joke Telling Contest** *(3rd weekend of April; Opelousas, ☎ 318-948-4731 or 942-3562)*.

The **Jim Bowie Museum** *(8am to 4pm; US 190 East, ☎ 318-948-6263, ☎ 1-800-424-5442 from the US)* exhibits artifacts linked to the career of this legendary hero, as well as documents, photographs and weapons all relating Acadian culture. The museum is also a tourist centre; pick up a map of the city's historic district

while you're there. Also worth seeing are the **Bowie Residence** *(S. Union St., Opelousas)* and the **Bowie Oak** *(Landry St., Opelousas)*.

The **Opelousas Museum and Interpretive Center ★** *(Tue to Sat 9am to 5pm; 329 N. Main St., ☎ 318-948-2589)* features exhibits on the life of native Americans living in the region, on agriculture, local culture and the American Civil War. An interesting collection of some 400 dolls is also on display here.

Le Vieux Village *(220 Academy St., ☎ 318-924-2683)* is a tourist information centre that presents a historical overview of St. Landry Parish.

The **Historic District Tour ★★** *(corner of St. Landry and Vine St.s, downtown)* features a visit to the Courthouse and to the fire station, where a donkey cart and a whole arsenal of old fire fighting tools are on display.

The **Michel Prudhomme House ★** *($3, by appointment; 1152 Prudhomme Dr., ☎ 318-942-2683 or 942-9602)*, the oldest building in Opelousas, was entirely restored by the celebrated chef Paul Prudhomme in order to preserve this magnificent plantation home's 18th century French Colonial architecture.

The **Mount Olive Baptist Church** *(corner of Market St. and Church St.)* was established in 1897, as the African-American Academy.

The **Holy Ghost Church** *(N. Union St.)* is the largest African-American Catholic church in the United States.

The **Little Zion Baptist Church** *(Academy St.)* was the first African-American church in Opelousas.

The **St. Landry Catholic Church** *(N.Main St.)* is named for the parish.

The **Estorge House** *(no visits; 427 N. Market St.)*, built in 1827, is a beautiful example of the Greek Revival style.

Built in 1853, the old **Ray Homestead** *(by appointment; 378 Bellevue St., ☎ 318-948-6784)* was once annexed to a small farm.

During the American Civil War, in 1862 Opelousas became the Confederate capital of Louisiana (the Northerners occupied Baton Rouge, the State Capital) and Governor Homer Mouton moved into the **Governor's Mansion** *(no visits; corner of Grolee St. and Liberty St.)*.

The **Yesterday House** ★ *(admission fee; by appointment; 441 E. Grolee St., ☎ 318-948-4731)*, a residence whose architecture dates back to the end of the last century, houses a beautiful collection of Louisiana antiques from the Empire period, as well as numerous historic and prehistoric artifacts.

Washington ★★★

Time seems to have come to a stop in 1880 in this city, where most buildings are registered landmarks. First named the "Church Landing" (Débarcadère-de-l'Église) because of its establishment on land donated by the French Government to the Catholic Church, the municipality welcomed its first steamboat in 1832 and quickly became the largest steamboat port between New Orleans and St. Louis, Missouri. Tons of cotton and sugar and thousands of animal hides were piled in its warehouses before being traded for other goods. The arrival of the railway in 1883 signalled the decline of this city, with its beautiful Victorian houses and plantations. The last steamboat chugged away in 1900.

The **Washington Museum and Tourist Center** *(Mon to Fri 10am to 3pm, Sat and Sun 9am to 4pm; between Main St. and Dejean St., ☎ 318-326-3622)* provides information about surrounding historic houses, as well as walking or driving tours. You can also flip through books and newspaper articles relating the flourishing era of steamboats; videos are also presented.

Built in 1700, the **Hinckley House** ★ *(by appointment; 405 E. Dejean St., ☎ 318-826-3906)* was owned by the same family for over two centuries. It is made of bald cypress wood and its walls are covered with the hides of horned animals. The property has its own family graveyard.

The **Nicholson House** *(by appointment; 303 Main St., at the corner of Vine St., ☎ 318-826-3670)*, built in 1835, served as a hospital during the Civil War.

The **De la Morandière House** *(by appointment; 515 St. John St., ☎ 318-826-3626)* dates from 1830.

The **Old Washington Cemetery** *(Vine St.)* has old tombstones dating from the beginning of the 19th century.

Visitors can also see antebellum houses (from before the Civil War) on the outskirts of the village.

The **Magnolia Ridge Plantation** ★ *(private residence, free admission to the park; LA 103, between Dejean St. and Prescott St.)* incorporates a beautiful Greek Revival building from 1830. During the war, this structure was used by turns as headquarters for Southern troops (Confederates) and Northern troops. A trail skirts the Bayou Courtableau.

Arlington House *(by appointment; LA 103, ☎ 318-826-3298)* was built in 1829.

The **Starvation Point House** *(at the confluence of Bayous Boeuf and Cocodrie)* dates from the late 18th century.

The **"Chêne Vent Lastrapes"** ★★ *(LA 10 South)* a unique tree made up of seven intertwined trunks, is considered a real jewel of its species by the Live Oak Society, an eminent association devoted to the preservation and protection of this tree in Louisiana.

In 1863, two years after the beginning of the Civil War, Lincoln's army, contemplating the invasion of Texas, occupied the entire south of Louisiana. Many confrontations between the Confederates and the federal militia took place in the Opelousas Prairie. The **Battle of Bayou Boubeux Reenactment Festival** ★ *($3/day; end of Sept; LA 103, ☎ 318-826-5256 or 826-7404)* runs for two days and recreates the battle with the help of actors in period costume. Shooting competitions and duels.

Palmetto

Palmetto was founded by freed slaves. Many of their descendants still live there, though a considerable number have gone west: to Houston, San Francisco, Los Angeles, etc.

Ville Platte

Evangeline Parish was founded in 1910. Its main city, Ville Platte, was founded by Lieutenant Marcellin Garand, a veteran of the French Empire Wars, who became an innkeeper; the tavern was later turned into a post office. The committee that drafted the city's charter wished to name it Garandville, but Garand refused and suggested the present name instead, on account of the town's "flat and muddy" topography.

Food Processing Plant

Cajun and Creole grilled meats just aren't the same without Jack Miller's famous sauce, a staple in any Louisiana kitchen. You can find out more about how this renowned sauce is prepared by visiting **Jack Miller's Barbecue Sauce Factory** *(Mon to Fri 7am to 4pm; 811 Humana Rd., next to the Humana Hospital, Ville Platte, ☎ 318-363-1541)*.

The many private residences in Ville Platte are fine examples of architecture and the Acadian style: **O. E. Guillory House**, built in 1835; **Maison De Ville** *(right near the junction of US 167 and I-10)*; **Jean Vidrine Residence** *(Hwy LA 29)*; **Aldes Vidrine House** *(Hwy LA 363 East)*; **Old Ardoin House**; **Octave Thompson House** and **Johnson Residence** *(US 167)*.

Mamou

Set in the heart of Cajun Country, the small village of Mamou is among the most popular cultural stops with visitors. Its name stems from the discovery of a mammoth's skeleton, unearthed in the vicinity. In the nineteenth century, Mamou integrated all non-Francophone immigrants to Cajun culture. This massive Acadianization means that many Cajuns bear names that are not necessarily of French origin. Such is the case with the greatly missed Revon Reed, author of *Lâche Pas la Patate!*, and the late Fred Tate, former owner of Fred's Lounge, as well as famed Cajun musicians Nathan Abshire and Dewey Balfa. Still an institution in the village, Fred's Lounge (see "Entertainment", p 293) remains Mamou's main attraction. The bar's motto is quintessentially Cajun: *Laisse le bon temps rouler!* "Let the good times roll!"

A small town of 3,200 inhabitants, Mamou is renowned for its **"Courir du Mardi Gras"** ★★★, one of the oldest Mardi Gras festivals in the area. It is also one of the most popular and impressive in Cajun Country. Festivities begin on the preceding day (Monday), with a *fais-do-do*, a dance through the streets of the village that gets your hips shaking and the party started. On the day itself, as early as 7am, villagers can watch costumed riders starting off, followed by another *fais-do-do* in a true Bastille Day atmosphere. The party continues all day long, with live Cajun music. Visitors can also follow the Mardi Gras revellers travelling through the countryside on horseback. Around 3pm, the merry-makers return to the village and the festivities resume.

Eunice

While devoid of the most popular tourist attractions, such as plantations to visit or water sports activities, this small town of 12,000 inhabitants, Louisiana's Prairie Cajun Capital, has still found the recipe for tourism success by promoting its greatest resource: its Cajun heritage.

The **Eunice Museum** ★ *(free admission; length of visit: 1 hour; Tue to Sat 8am to noon and 1pm to 5pm, Sun noon to 5pm; 220 S. C.C. Duson Dr., ☎ 318-457-6540)* is actually a converted train depot. It boasts a collection of artifacts and photographs from the early days on the Cajun Prairies.

By settling in the western part of the prairies of southwestern Louisiana, lands ideal for raising livestock and growing rice, the Acadians introduced a lifestyle to the region that persists to this day. At the **Jean Lafitte National Historical Park/Prairie Acadian Cultural Center** ★★★ *(Sun to Fri 8am to 5pm, Sat 8am to 6pm; 250 W. Park Ave., ☎ 318-457-8499)*, numerous exhibits highlight the history and culture of past and present Cajuns, as well as other aspects of their collective lives: pastimes, clothing, furniture, religion, cooking and farming. The region also boasts many other attractions: Cajun-music evenings featuring local musicians, film and video presentations, music and instrument-making workshops, as well as arts and crafts, and local cooking demonstrations *(Saturdays)*.

The **Eunice "Courir du Mardi Gras"** ★★★ *(Feb or Mar, day before Ash Wednesday;* ☎ *318-457-6502,* ☎ *1-800-222-2342 from the US)* attracts ever increasing numbers of people. In Eunice, the carnival lasts four days. Masked balls at St. Mathilda Church and Liberty Theater featuring Cajun and zydeco music are held on the weekend preceding Mardi Gras Day. Exhibitions with Mardi Gras themes at the Eunice Museum, the Prairie Acadian Cultural Center and the Liberty Theater run for eight days leading up to the festival. Not to be missed!

Just like in Mamou, Church Point and Iota, Eunice "runners" ride through the surrounding countryside on Mardi Gras Day *(departure at 8am, behind the National Guard Armory; return to the village around 3pm)*. More family-oriented than those of Mamou and Church Point but similar to the Iota version, Eunice's Mardi Gras is "good, clean fun", with costume competitions as well as cooking and handicraft stands. Cajun and zydeco music as well as the traditional parade are also *de rigueur* here on Mardi Gras.

The **CFMA Cajun Music Festival** ★★ *(2nd Sunday after Easter;* ☎ *318-457-3543)* is sponsored by the Cajun French Music Association (CFMA).

The **Louisiana Cajun Culture and Music Club Festival - "LCCMC"** *(beginning of spring;* ☎ *318-457-5106)* is a celebration of Cajun music and culture.

Faithful to the era of James Dean, Elvis Presley and Little Richard, the **Louisiana Raceway Park** car races *($5; Sun 8am, qualifying heat 1pm; 6 km east of Eunice on US 190,* ☎ *318-546-6031)* have changed little over the years. The best hot rods and drag races in the area. You can check out the pit for an extra $5. Hot dogs, hamburgers and soft drinks are served at the fast-food counter.

The **Fontenot Rice Mill** *(visits and demonstrations by appointment; corner of Vine St. and Hwy LA 13,* ☎ *318-457-7651)*.

Crawfish Processing Plants
(visits by appointment only)

Jeff Derouen Crawfish Supply *(west of Eunice, on LA 757,* ☎ *318-457-1138)*.

Riceland Crawfish Inc. *(101 South East St.,* ☎ *318-457-1811)*.

Richard

The small village of Richard lies about 16 kilometres southwest of Eunice. The **Gravesite of Charlene Richard** *(Friends of Charlene, P.O. Box 91623, Lafayette, LA 70509-1623)*, a 12-year-old Cajun girl who died of leukaemia in 1959, is here, in the St. Edward Parish Cemetery. Many Cajuns consider this child a saint and, since her death, between 8,000 and 10,000 pilgrims a year have come to pay their respects at her tomb and to ask her for a few favours.

Avoyelles Parish

This name comes from the Avoyel Indians, who preceded the Tunica-Biloxi nation. The region was colonized by the Spanish, who set up the "Avoyelles Post" here in 1783. In the 18th and 19th centuries, other colonists, the majority of them French immigrants including former soldiers who had served under Napoleon, settled here. The city of Mansura was named thus by the soldiers to whom this part of Louisiana recalled Mansera, where a famous battle took place during the Egyptian campaign. The cotton-growing in Avoyelles during the antebellum period was so widespread and lucrative that plantations sprung up everywhere. At the time, steamboats plying the waterways (the Red River and Bayou Boeuf) played an essential role. During the Civil War, the region was the scene of numerous military manoeuvres, particularly at the Fort de Russy and around Yellow Bayou.

The Avoyelles parish now has close to 40,000 inhabitants, many of whom still bear French names: Couvillon, Grémillion, Bordelon, Mayeux, Dauzat, Dupuy, LaBorde, etc. Former State Governor Edwin Edwards, who is also Cajun, was born in Marksville.

When the elderly from Avoyelles speak of a very distant place, they use the expression "Over there in Tchebec*". The current network of roads has largely reduced these distances, and today the feeling of belonging to the North American French-speaking community is stronger than ever in this northern region of Acadiana. Despite their proximity to Anglo-Saxon districts, towns like Marksville, Mansura and Bunkie are recognized as Francophone bastions where Cajun culture and traditions hold sway.

* From "Québec": under the French regime, Québec City was the capital of New France, some three thousand kilometres away to the northeast.

Church Point

This municipality once bore the lovely name of "Pointe-Plaquemine" because of its location on the Plaquemine Brulee waterway. In 1800, the Grand Coteau Jesuits built a church here, and the city was christened "Church Point" (Pointe-de-l'Église). Today, despite its English appellation, Church Point has become the bastion of Cajun culture and French language in Louisiana.

Resolutely Cajun and Francophone, this village is recognized as one of the hubs of regional Cajun music. The legendary Iry LeJeune, credited with giving the accordion its place in Cajun music was born here.

Two annual events held in Church Point are worth checking out:

The **"Courir du Mardi Gras"** ★★★ *(Sunday preceding Mardi Gras; LA 178, Saddle Tramp Riders Club, 1036 E. Abbey St.,* ☎ *318-684-2026 or*

The Antebellum Houses of Avoyelles ★★★

The Avoyelles parish boasts many houses in the antebellum style. In **Bunkie**, be sure to visit the **Epps House** *(Mon to Fri 8am to 5pm; US 71, ☎ 318-926-3944)*, where Solomon Northup suffered many long years of slavery at the hands of the vile tyrant Edwin Epps. Built entirely of bald cypress, this plantation residence is typical of those lining the Bayou Boeuf. It is now a tourist information centre.

Other antebellum houses in the area are still inhabited, but you can still admire them from the roadside. North of Bunkie, in the bend of US 71, the **Bubenzer House** is also quite a sight. In his book *Twelve Years a Slave* , Solomon Northup describes the lavish Christmas parties thrown by the masters of the plantation.

There is also the impressive **Ashland House**, built in 1857, nearby. Like the Bubenzer House, the Ashland House once belonged to the family of Jefferson Davis, president of the Confederate States of America during the Civil War.

South of Bunkie, between Eola and St. Landry, is the **White House**. It was built in 1835 and inspired by the colonial style. This house is surrounded by towering live oaks, a few of which have been listed by the Live Oak Society, which keeps track of all the live oaks in Louisiana.

East of Bunkie, the **Hillcrest House** (1840) and the **Frithland House** are representative of the Greek Revival (neoclassical) style; the latter was entirely rebuilt after the original house burnt to the ground. The ninth generation of the Frith family now resides there.

Still east of Bunkie, on LA 29, is the town of **Evergreen**, fortunately spared during the Civil War. Superb mansions such as the **Oakwold, Clarendon** *(1.5 km west of Oakwold on Hwy LA 29)*, **West, Cappel, Quirk, Karpe** (in the Victorian style), **Flournoy, Buck Muse, Foster Grimble** and **Robert Houses** still stand here. The building of the railway, which put an end to navigation, slowed down this small town's economy; the wonderful steamboat era is now nothing more than a memory.

Proceed to LA 29, then along LA 107 to **Mansura**, where you can visit the **Desfossé House** *(free admission)*, circa 1790.

684-3333) is a very popular event in Church Point. Mardi Gras riders set off from Saddle Tramp Riders, located right next to Richard's Feed Store. This livestock food store belongs to Joey Richard, who is also the captain of the Mardi Gras runners, a life-long position.

The masked and costumed horsemen arrive between 7am and 8am. The "capitaine" then reads out the rules to them and to anyone who wishes to join them. The whole scene is quite surreal; just about anything goes.

Visitors can follow the revellers by car or on horseback, stopping with them along the way at various homes, where they dismount and perform their peculiar antics in exchange for food. This ritual is repeated from house to house. The collected items are then thrown into a gargatuan gumbo.

The seventh stop brings them to the David house, where an outrageous "mad dash" takes place. Followers are advised to keep a safe distance. All of this exertion necessitates a short break with some music and even a short dance on horseback before setting off for the next escapade, the *"chasse aux 'tites poules grasses"* (hen-hunt).

Two stops later brings them to the Hanley House, where they stay for an hour. A great time is had by all here, boozing between the greased pig and the hen-hunting contests.

The riders then take to the road again (as the Mardi Gras theme song goes: *"Allons se mett' dessus le chemin..."*, or "Let's Take to the Road...") and, as tradition requires, make a stop at a retirement home before proceeding to the next village, where the eagerly awaited parade takes place.

The parade ends at the Saddle Tramp Club, where everyone is invited to share the famed gumbo and participate in the celebrations. Music, dancing and beer abound and, finally, trophies are awarded for the best and worst costumes.

Branch

The **Heritage Farm Village** ★ *(admission fee; Mon to Sat 11am to 5pm, Sun 9am to 6pm; LA 35, 8 km southwest of Church Point,* ☎ *318-334-2949)* is an Acadian house dating from 1852. It was restored and converted into an interpretive museum highlighting the day-to-day life of 19th-century Cajuns.

Anglers can enjoy their favourite sport at the **Acadiana Fish Farm** *(admission fee; close to Branch, on LA 365)*.

Bunkie

Bunkie is the gateway to Central Louisiana's Cajun country. Until the arrival of the railway, this region was covered with plantations. The name "bunkie" is said to have originated with the young son of a planter who was trying to say the word monkey.

The Bunkie region became famous prior to the Civil War due to the publication of Solomon Northup's book: *Twelve Years a Slave*. A freed slave, Northup made his way to New York State to a better life. Treacherously abducted, he was taken back to Washington in 1841 and sold as a slave once again. From there, he was packed off to New Orleans, where the Baptist minister of Cheneyville bought him. Two years later, he was sold once again, to a certain Edwin Epps, who tortured him brutally.

With the help of a Canadian cabinet-maker, he succeeded in dispatching a letter to white abolitionist friends in New York. One of these, a judge, travelled to Avoyelles to demand his immediate release. Northup was freed once and for all in January of 1853. A well-read individual, Northup proceeded to write his memoirs. The work became as successful as *Uncle Tom's Cabin*.

Visitors can now follow the illustrious writer's tracks along the **Solomon Northup Path** *($12.50; 105 Walnut St., speak to Debbie,* ☎ *318-346-7663)* thanks to the many commemorative plaques indicating the places he passed through along the way. Tour guides are available.

Marksville

Broken wagon wheels can be seen on the way into and out of Marksville. The story goes that one day, while travelling through this region neighbouring Avoyelles, the wagon of a merchant named Marc Eliché broke down. After receiving such a warm welcome from local inhabitants, he decided to open a business there. The townspeople chose to name the village that sprung after the generous investor to express their gratitude.

If the legend is to be believed, on October 23rd 1947, Marksville was the scene of a very strange occurrence. At the height of a storm, hundreds of fish from one of the neighbouring lakes were apparently sucked up by a whirlwind and then spit back out right in the middle of downtown. This, at least, is what Lady Eleanor Gremillon maintains, an employee at the Chamber of Commerce who claims to have witnessed the phenomenon and who gladly relates her version.

Built on the Tunica-Biloxi's native reservation, the **Tunica-Biloxi Indian Center & Museum** ★★★ *(700 Allen St.,* ☎ *318-253-8954)* features one of the most beautiful collections of native and European artifacts from the colonial period. Archaeological digs testify to the presence of Native Americans in the Marksville region at least 2,000 years ago. The funeral rites of these indigenous peoples, who buried their dead beneath small conical mounds of earth, have also been pieced back together.

The museum also enlightens visitors about other characteristics of Native American culture, such as the fact that they imported raw materials, the way in which they made decorative pottery and their complex trade system. About ten of the funeral mounds mentioned above can also be seen here. The museum is part of the Jean Lafitte National Historical Park and Preserve.

No visit to the Marksville region would be complete without seeing the Spring Bayou. **Fins & Feathers Bayou Tours** *(adults $30, children under 12 $10; Mon to Fri 6pm, Sat and Sun departures at 9am, noon and 3pm; 172 Fins and Feathers Rd., Spring Bayou, near Marksville,* ☎ *318-253-8709)* offers an interesting tour, lasting a few hours, through the Spring Bayou and surrounding cypress lakes. The highlight of this tour is certainly the wildlife of this forested and marshy environment, the realm of alligators, egrets, herons, deer and ducks.

The **Sarto Old Iron Bridge** ★ *(free for pedestrians; near LA 451, southeast of Marksville, Big Bend, near Bordelonville)*, a steel-reinforced bridge built in 1916, spans the Bayou Glaises. This was the first bridge to be listed as a historic monument in Louisiana.

Marksville's Architectural Heritage

In **Marksville**, the **Hypolite Bordelon House** *($2; Tue to Sat 11am to 3pm; LA 1, W. Tunica Dr.,* ☎ *318-253-7047 or 253-9222)*, built between 1790 and 1820 (at the end of the Spanish occupation), also serves as a tourist information centre. Built in 1843, the **Laborde House** *(817 Main St.)* was a hotel, a tavern and a school, before being converted into a private residence. The **Denux House** *(corner of Monroe and Tarleton Sts.)*, built in the early 1800s, boasts some 14 rooms; its ceilings are almost four-metres high. **The Corner School** *(215 W. Waddil St.)*, which served as a girl's school from the 1880s onward, is now a private residence. The **Dupuy's House** *(824 S. Main St.)* dates from 1868. North of Marksville, in the **Johnson** commune, is the **family residence of Wallace Edwards**, grandfather of Louisiana's former governor, Edwin Edwards. Many houses built after the Civil War and before the end of the last century can also be found in the Marksville region.

The **Black History Month Parade ★** *(in February, dates change from year to year;* ☎ *318-253-9208)* is an annual event.

Moncla

Mardi Gras in Moncla *(February; 8 km north of Marksville, on LA 107,* ☎ *318-253-9208)* is as lively and colourful as Mardi Gras in other villages in the region.

 PARKS

Port Barre

The **Bayou Teche**, the most famous in the State of Louisiana, has its source here. This romantic bayou draws its waters from the Bayou Courtableau. Lovely little park and a tiny Cajun museum *(*☎ *318-585-7646)*. Visitors can also camp here.

Washington

The **Thistlethwaite Wildlife Management Area ★** *(northeast of Washington, on LA 10,* ☎ *318-948-0255)* boasts 440 hectares of bottomland hardwoods (oaks, pecans, copals, maples, walnut trees, etc.), and no less than 17 kilometres of paths. Fauna also abounds here (deer, squirrels, swamp rabbits, ducks, woodcocks, raccoons, otters, boars, opossums, etc.). Hunting, wild game traps, day-hiking, birding. No camping.

Ville Platte

The **Louisiana State Arboretum**, the oldest in the country covering eight hectares and criss-crossed by paths, is situated approximately 12 kilometres north of Ville Platte, on Highway 3042 (next to Chicot State Park). This majestic property is planted with trees draped in Spanish moss. Magnolias, hickories and pecan trees, among others, grow here. The very uneven terrain is punctuated by many ravines.

The **Chicot State Park** ★ *(Apr 1 to Sep 30, 7am to 8pm; Oct 1 to Mar 31, 8am to 7pm; closed Dec 25 and Jan 1; 9 km north of Ville Platte on LA 42, ☎ 318-363-2403)* is the largest park in Louisiana *(200 camp sites; 27 cottages; fishing on a 4,000-hectare lake; picnic areas; beach; swimming pool; 12 km of paths)*. It was established in the thirties on the hills surrounding Lake Chicot and derives its name from the bald cypress tree stumps scattered throughout the swamps. Peculiar to Louisiana, the bald cypress, which grows in water, can live some 500 years before reaching maturity. The bald cypress forests were decimated by the forestry industry in the early 1900s. As a result of this excessive clear-cutting, numerous swamps in Louisiana are now desolate, a mere expanse of stark tree stumps. Visitors can stay in cottages or at the adjacent camping site. Boat rentals *($8/day)*. Credit cards accepted.

The **Crooked Creek Recreation Area** *(22 km northwest of Ville Platte, LA 13, then LA 3187; ☎ 318-599-2661)* has picnic areas, a camping site and a beach on the Crooked Creek Reservoir, where visitors can fish, rent a boat or go sailing.

The camp site around **Lake Cazan** *(east of the Chicot State Park, LA 29, ☎ 318-363-1558)* covers 40 hectares. Cottages and boat rentals; guests can also catch fish and shellfish here.

Lake Miller *(east of Ville Platte, Hwy LA 376)* is teeming with much-sought-after bass. Boat rentals.

Boar Busters Outfitters *(☎ 318-363-7019)* offers wild boar, deer and duck hunting, as well as fishing; they can also arrange accommodations.

Eunice

The **Eunice Country Club and Municipal Golf Course** *(US 190 West)* boasts a beautifully landscaped 18-hole golf course.

The **Eunice Municipal Park** *(US 190 West, 3 km west of LA 13)* is not much more than a small lake and picnic areas. Barbecues are available for cooking (crawfish perhaps) under the stars.

The **Cajun Prairie Restoration Project** ★★ *(corner Martin Luther King Dr. and Magnolia St., ☎ 318-457-2016 or 457-4497)* occupies a territory that has undergone ecological redevelopment. Endangered indigenous flora has been replanted in this protected zone. In his book *Twelve Years a Slave*, writer Solomon Northup describes seeing these Louisiana prairies in the mid-19th century while on his way to the sugar-cane fields. Bereft of trees even then, it was merely a broad savannah of tall grass. Intensive farming had ravaged the land; the gradual re-naturalization of the original habitat is now being attempted.

Branch

Anglers can enjoy their favourite sport at the **Acadiana Fish Farm** *(admission fee; right near Branch, on LA 365)*.

Simmesport

The **Yellow Bayou Civil War Memorial Park** *(25 km southeast of Marksville, LA 1, on the Atchafalaya River)* commemorates the last battle fought by the Northerners in the countryside surrounding the Red River. Camping and RV sites, picnic areas, paths, observation towers.

Marksville

Spring Bayou *(3 km southeast of Marksville, LA 1 or LA 107, ☎ 318-948-0255 or 253-7068)* is a wildlife zone, protected and managed by the State of Louisiana. A veritable fresh water fishing paradise, this territory is peppered with places of evocative-sounding names: Bayou Cocodrie, Point-Tournant, Perion-du-Chat, Lake Tête-de-Boeuf, Bayou-Creux, etc. Three different camp sites are accessible.

There are other wildlife zones protected and managed by the State in the Marksville region, though these are devoid of camp sites. Worthy of mention, among others, are those of **Pomme-de-Terre** (hunting and fishing; call Spring Bayou), **Lake Ophelia ★** (fresh-water-fowl habitat) and the **Grand Cote National Wildlife Refuge ★** (falcon and eagle ornithological reserve).

There is also the **Ben Routh Recreational Area** *(LA 1196, Vick)*, with picnic areas, a boat ramp and bathrooms.

The **Lock and Dam No. 1** *(19 km from Marksville, on LA 1196, Basse Brouillette)* has picnic and play areas, paths and washrooms; visitors can also fish here.

 ACCOMMODATIONS

Arnaudville

Vin-O-Lyn's - B & B *($85-$100, bkfst incl; pb, ≈; 1160 Joe Kidder Rd., Arnaudville, 70512, ☎ 318-754-8153)*. A dozen attractive rooms with resolutely Cajun decor, each with its own bath, have been fitted out on both floors of a charming house owned by Melvin and Carolyn Tate. When the weather is fine (par for the course in Louisiana), a traditional southern breakfast is served under the shade of stately live oaks. The place, which also offers a catering service and boasts its own chapel, is very popular with young, local newlyweds, who hold their wedding receptions here. There is also a small fish pond on the property. Bicycles are available. No smoking inside.

Sunset

Chretien Point Bed & Breakfast *($95 to $200, brkfst incl; pb, sb ,≈; Hwy 1, Box 162, Sunset, 70584; 24 km north of Lafayette off LA 93, ☎ 1-800-880-7050 from North America)*. In addition to its five luxurious rooms, this place offers cocktails and hors d'oeuvres, a tennis court, and a guided tour of the Chretien Point Plantation Home.

Opelousas

Acadiana Wilderness Campground *(tent $8, RV $12; 3 km south of Opelousas, I-49 South, Exit 15, ☎ 318-662-5154)* holds dances every second Saturday.

The **South City Park Campground** *($; 1489 S. Market St., ☎ 318-948-2560)* is a camping site in a quiet spot, close to downtown. Locations for RVs and tents, picnic areas and outdoor grills.

The **Quality Inn of Opelousas** *($50-$100; tv, ⊛, ℜ, ≈; I-49 South, 4501 Guilbeau Rd., ☎ 318-948-9500, ☎ 1-800-228-5151 from North America)* features a dining room, café, launderette, and health club.

🦐 The **Maison De Saizan** *($65-$75, bkfst incl; studios $75-$120, bkfst incl; pb or sb; 412 S. Court St., Opelousas, LA 70570, ☎ 318-942-1311)*. This large Victorian house built in 1889 is furnished with many antiques. There are three magnificent rooms, one of which has a private bathroom, and three studios. The former bourgeois residence boasts a lovely courtyard, a garden in full bloom, where smokers gather. No credit cards accepted.

Port Barre

The **Birthplace of the Teche Park Campgrounds** *($; 9 km east of Opelousas, LA 103, just north of US 190, City Hall: ☎ 318-585-7646)* offers all the usual amenities.

Krotz Springs

The **Country Store Bed and Breakfast Inn** *($$, bkfst incl; pb or sb; US 190, 24 km east of Opelousas; 200 N. Main St., ☎ 318-566-2331)* boasts four attractive rooms, three of which have private bathrooms.

Washington

Bell's Washington Campground *(RV $10; tent $6; Main St., near the bridge spanning the Bayou Courtableau, ☎ 318-826-9987)* features country music Friday and Saturday nights.

Washington has a few charming bed & breakfasts, from the humblest to the most luxurious:

🦐 **La Place De Ville - B & B** *($60, $5/add. pers., bkfst incl; sb; Box 6723, Washington, 70589, ☎ 318-826-3367)*. The De Villes offer a cozy, welcoming and tidy little two-room Cajun cottage, the whole furnished with magnificent antiques. Lovely pecan trees shade the garden. Because the hosts do not reside in the cottage, which is reserved exclusively for the use of guests, they take care to keep all necessary breakfast victuals in the fridge, including coffee. Credit cards accepted.

🦐 The **Country House** *($70, bkfst incl; pb; Box 11, Washington, 70589, ☎ 318-826-3052)* offers two rooms in the main house and a third in the annexed cottage, equipped with a kitchenette. Breakfasts are quite generous here: fresh fruit, eggs, sausage and cheese make up hearty, wonderfully presented dishes served with oven-baked French toast. Also a

ert Dafford's work, *L'Arrivée des Acadiens en Louisiane* ("the arival of the Acadians in Louisiana"), at the Acadian Memorial in St. Martinville - Steve Comeaux.

Dusk falls on a Louisiana swamp - R.N.

Snowy egrets in the ornithological reserve at Avery Island - R.N.

gallery, this pretty little house belongs to painter June Lowry, who exhibits her work here as well as that of other Louisiana artists.

The **Elter House Inn** *($70-$80, bkfst incl; pb; 603 S. Main St., Washington, 70589, ☎ 318-826-7362)* is a Victorian house with lovely period furniture, three bedrooms and four bathrooms. Fully stocked kitchen for self-catered breakfasts. Prepared breakfast can be arranged for $5/person.

The **Camellia Cove Bed and Breakfast** *($75, bkfst incl; pb; 205 W. Hill St., Washington, 70589, ☎ 318-826-7362)* has three rooms, each with its own private bathroom. The house was built in 1825 on land planted with camellias and myrtles. No credit cards accepted.

Ville Platte

At **Chicot State Park** *(9 km north of Ville Platte, LA 3042 North; mailing address: R.R. 3, Box 494, Ville Platte, 70586; ☎ 318-363-2403)*, cottages for four or six people *($45-$60; ≡)* or a camp site *($12, electricity, water; $10 no amenities)* are available.

The **Crooked Creek Recreation Area** *(RV $10, tent $7; 22 km northwest of Ville Platte, LA 13, then LA 3187, ☎ 318-599-2661)* boasts about one hundred sites with A/C for RVs, or simple campsites for tents.

Lake Cazan *($$; east of Chicot State Park, on LA 29, ☎ 318-363-1558)* features a camping site and fully-equipped cottages.

The **Platte Motel** *($22-$36; on W. Main St., ☎ 318-363-2148)* rents its rooms

at economical rates. Any lower, and you wouldn't want to stay here...

Mamou

The **Cazan Hotel** *($-$$; pb or sb; 6th St., opposite Fred's Lounge, ☎ 318-468-7187)* is housed in a former bank. The establishment is ideally situated, near local nightclubs. Charming establishment with decent facilities. Reservations are recommended, for the hotel has but 12 rooms.

Eunice

Cajun Campground *($; US 190 East, 5 km east of Eunice, ☎ 318-457-5753)* is a shaded spot offering a playground, lake, swimming pool, paths and fishing on the bayou.

Allen's Lakeview Park *($; US 190 West, ☎ 318-546-0502)* throws open its dance hall doors every Saturday night.

The **Fontenot House Bed and Breakfast** *($45, bkfst incl; pb or sb; 550 N. 4th St., close to downtown Eunice, 70535, ☎ 504-861-0082, for reservations ☎ 1-800-749-1928 from the US)* offers the choice of a cottage with private entrance, a room, or a studio with bathroom, living room and dining room.

The **Seale Guesthouse** *($65-$75, suite $85-$95, cottage $100; LA 13, 3 km south of Eunice, Box 568, Eunice, 70535, ☎ 318-457-3753)*. This inn from the late 1800s is furnished with magnificent antiques. Six rooms, two of which have private bathrooms, and a two-bedroom cottage. Continental breakfast. No credit cards accepted.

Howard's Inn Motel *($32-$36; tv; toward Opelousas, on US 190 East, US 1, Box 19-A, Eunice, 70535, ☎ 318-457-2066).* Coffee shop, launderette.

Potier's Prairie Cajun Inn *(110 Park Ave., ☎ 318-457-0440).* Small inn with old-time Cajun decor.

 RESTAURANTS

Note: Visitors should keep in mind that most fine restaurants (small, medium and large) in Louisiana are closed on Christmas Day.

Grand Coteau

Catahoula's *($$-$$$; Tue to Sat 11am to 2pm and 5pm to 10pm; Sun brunch 11am to 2pm; 235 King Dr., ☎ 318-662-2275)* is named after a dog originating in Louisiana, who is said to be cross-bred from an indigenous mutt and another brought over by the Spanish. The catahoula hound is, in fact, the State dog. The establishment is primarily renowned for its creative Cajun cuisine, a fusion, as it were, of new Californian flavours with the more classic southwestern Louisianian ones.

Sunset

Café Dugas *($; Mon to Fri 10:30am to 2pm; LA 182, downtown Sunset, next to the railway, ☎ 318-662-9208).* Family-style Cajun cuisine.

Opelousas

The Palace Café *($-$$; Mon to Sat 6am to 9pm, Sun from 5pm; 167 W. Landry St., opposite the Courthouse, ☎ 318-942-2142)* is a big favourite with locals. The owner, Pete Doucas, offers family cooking that is greatly appreciated by gourmets visiting the city's historic district, and home-made baklava that makes many a Greek restaurateur green with envy. Other specialties include chicken salad, French onion rings and a scrumptuous milkshake.

The Country Meat Block Diner *($; 1618 S. Union St.)* prepares it like at home: barbecued beef featured on Thursdays. Next door, butcher Kelly Cormier will be happy to share the secrets of all fine Cajun dishes.

Family cooking is also concocted at the **Jambalaya Creole Cajun Café** *(24 hrs/day, every day; US 190 East, ☎ 318-587-7697).* The lunch menu always features a regional dish.

Washington

The **Jack Womack's Steamboat Warehouse Restaurant** *($$-$$$; Main St.),* which offers Cajun and Creole cuisine, is a must. The chef's seafood dishes have made him a gold-medal winner. The restaurant is located in the only steamboat warehouse left in Louisiana. Among the goodies on the menu: stuffed fish or "Palmetto" catfish, with creamy crawfish and almond sauce. The establishment's most famous dish is the seafood gumbo, served with an oven-baked yam. This speciality, which is served in every home in the parish, is rarely seen in restaurants. This exception to the norm is a real treat for tourists.

Ville Platte

The **Pig Stand** *($; Tue to Thu 6am to 11pm, Fri and Sat 6am to 2am; 318 Main St.* ☎ *318-363-2883)* offers the entire repertoire of good authentic Cajun cooking, from tasso (dried meat) to spicy sausages, and from boudin to grilled and barbecued meats.

Elmand's Cajun Restaurant *($-$$; Thu to Sat, lunch to dinner; 5.8 km north of Ville Platte, on Tate Cove Rd./LA 1171,* ☎ *318-363-3768)* serves Cajun food. The establishment lays out a generous buffet at lunch as well as on Thursday evenings. Cajun music nights (see "Entertainment", p 293) is featured on all three nights.

The **Jungle Dinner Club** *($$; Sun to Thu 5:30pm to 11pm, Fri and Sat 5:30pm to midnight; US 167 West,* ☎ *318-636-6006)* is famous for its crawfish, served mild, hot, super hot or extra super hot! The Manuel family has been doing the cooking for over 40 years now. This establishment has been rated among the five best crawfish restaurants by *Jazz Festival* magazine.

Eunice

The **Pelican Restaurant** *($; Sun 6am to 2pm, Mon to Sat 6am to 10pm; W. Laurel St.,* ☎ *318-457-2323)*. On Sundays, the lunch menu features a choice of roast pork or beef, duck, chicken, barbecued cutlets and ribs, all served with corn bread, black-eyed peas and Cajun-style rice.

Ruby's Café *($; Mon to Sat 5am to 3pm; 221 W. Walnut St.* ☎ *318-457-2583)* prepares excellent family fare: roast pork with garlic, roasted or fried chicken.

At **Mama's Fried Chicken and Cajun Restaurant** *($; Sun to Wed 10am to 9pm, Thu to Sat 10am to 10pm; 1640 W. Laurel St.,* ☎ *318-457-9978)*, patrons can enjoy both family cooking and local dishes.

Allison's Hickory Pit *($; 501 W. Laurel St.,* ☎ *318-457-9218)* specializes in barbecued meats; the ribs are delicious.

Chatterbox Restaurant *($; 1141 E. Laurel St.,* ☎ *318-457-8255)* stands out for its Cajun family cooking.

Nick's on Second *($; 123 S. 2nd St.,* ☎ *318-457-4921)*. Restaurant and classic bar since 1930.

Crispy Cajun *($; Amy Shopping Centre, E. Laurel Ave.,* ☎ *318-546-0259)* prepares fried chicken, seafood and po'boys.

Chub's Bar-B-Que *($; 331 E. Laurel St.,* ☎ *318-457-0348)* features meats either grilled, barbecued, or cooked on a spit.

The **Crawfish Hut** *(in season; 1029 W. Laurel St.,* ☎ *318-457-9490)* prepares crawfish in every shape and form.

Debarge's Crawfish *(in season; 101 Veterans Dr., via LSUE Dr.,* ☎ *318-457-4252)* is yet another place where you can savour crawfish.

Golden Corral Family Restaurant *($$; Sun to Thu 11am to 10pm, Fri and*

Sat 11am to 11pm; 1601 W. Laurel Ave., ☎ *318-457-8988)* offers family fare as well as steak, chicken and seafood. An all-you-can-eat buffet is also laid out.

The **Restaurant l'Acadien** *($$; 1415 E. Laurel St.,* ☎ *318-457-4760)* specializes in seafood and steaks.

Marksville

Few places in town stand out for their cuisine, but visitors are sure to find one that will please among those listed below.

A and J's Café *($; LA 1 North,* ☎ *318-253-4991)* is a snack bar as well as a café.

Chico's Tacos *($; LA 1 South,* ☎ *318-253-9929)* serves Tex-Mex grub, which turns out to be more Texan (or American) than Mexican!

The **Mardi Gras Restaurant** *($; 7845 US 1 South,* ☎ *318-253-0417)* occasionally features some interesting dishes.

At **Nanny's Restaurant** *($; 207 W. Tunica St.,* ☎ *318-253-6058)*, the menu sometimes lists good family fare.

Roy's Cajun Cabin *($; Spring Bayou Rd.,* ☎ *318-253-7186)* will do in a pinch, but no more than that!

The **Lunch Box** *($; 208 Main St.,* ☎ *318-253-5290)* makes such a good sandwich, you will polish it off in minutes!

The **Tunica Café** *($; Tunica Dr.,* ☎ *318-253-7673)* has a bit of everything mentioned above.

The **Grand Tunica-Biloxi Native Reservation Casino** *($$-$$$; 24 hrs/day; 711 Tunica Dr.,* ☎ *318-253-2838)* has two restaurants. Those who hit the jackpot can eat at the posher of the two, while others can settle for the more reasonably priced alternative!

 ENTERTAINMENT

Cecilia - Arnaudville

The **Valley Club** *(weekends, from 5pm; LA 686, between Cecilia and Arnaudville, Dalton Singleton,* ☎ *318-228-2554)*. This nightclub in Creole country presents various zydeco bands. Snacks.

Opelousas

Slim's Y-Ki-Ki ★★★ *(US 167 North; N. Main St.,* ☎ *318-942-9980)*. Venerable zydeco dance hall with the best local bands. Dances held on weekends.

Richard's Club ★★★ *(weekends, from 7pm; 8 km west of Opelousas on US 190 West, Lawtell; Carman Richard,* ☎ *318-543-6596)*. You cannot visit Louisiana without checking out Richard's Club: it is the best place in town for zydeco music. This old dance hall offers a unique atmosphere, with Creole tunes and songs performed in Louisiana French.

The **Offshore Lounge** *(8 km west of Opelousas, US 190, Lawtell; Roy Carrier,* ☎ *318-543-9996)*. Zydeco nightclub *(Thu nights and weekends)*.

Bourque's Club *(12 km south of Opelousas: take LA 357, turn right on LA 759, and right again on Cedar St. in Lewisburg, ☎ 318-948-9904)*. Visitors are in for an unforgettable experience at this popular Cajun nightclub; it is *the* spot for Prairie Cajuns. Dance hall; bar and dancing on weekends.

Guidry's Friendly Lounge *(right before Bourque's Club, Lewisburg, ☎ 318-942-9988)*. If all other nightclubs are full (Prairie Cajuns go out in droves on weekends), you can always hit Guidry's! Cajun music, dancing on weekends *(Sun from 5pm)*.

Toby's Little Lodge Lounge *(LA 182, ☎ 318-948-7787)*. At Toby's, visitors can have dinner, then go dancing next door to Cajun music *(Thu nights)* or country and soul *(Wed, Fri, Sat nights)*.

Mamou

Fred's Lounge ★★★ *(Sat 9am to 1pm; 6th St., downtown Mamou, ☎ 318-468-5411)* celebrated its fiftieth anniversary in 1997 with great pomp and ceremony. Even Governor Mike Foster came for the occasion and spoke to the crowd of revellers. A veritable institution, this restaurant exudes genuine Cajun *joie de vivre*. You can meet everyone here from the village postilion to Australian television camera operators, for whom this place embodies the "mythical" Louisiana. Mornings at Fred's Lounge are broadcast live from 9am on KVPI 1250 AM. The legendary Wall of Fame, bearing the names of the most prestigious Cajun musicians who have played here, is quite impressive.

Ville Platte

At **Elmand's Cajun Restaurant** *(Thu to Sat nights; 5,8 km north of town, on Tate Cove Rd., LA 1171, ☎ 318-363-3768)*, a succession of Cajun bands play on weekend nights. Their Thursday night jam sessions, said to be "very distinct", attracts many fans. The establishment also serves meals and sets out a lavish buffet at lunch as well as on Thursday nights. (See "Restaurants", p 291).

Snook's Bar and Cajun Dance Hall *(US 190 West, ☎ 318-363-0451)*. Cajuns have been "hoofin' it" here on weekend nights for generations.

Eunice

When it comes to Cajun music and dancing, there is much to choose from in Eunice. You can spend a very pleasant evening dancing to live Cajun music at the **Lakeview Campground Lounge** *($1; Sat 8pm; LA 13 North, ☎ 318-457-9263)*. No cover charge for campers.

Cajuns also spend their evenings at the **VFW Restaurant and Dance Hall** *(US 190, E. Laurel St., ☎ 318-457-1055)* or at **Homer's** dance hall *(US 190, E. Laurel St., Eunice, ☎ 318-457-5922)*.

Fans of zydeco music throng the **Gilton's Lounge** *(8 km east of Eunice, intersection of US 190 East and LA 95, ☎ 318-457-1241)* for dancing and music.

Some prefer **Richard's and Slim's** *(St. Landry Parish)*, larger and more modern than most traditional zydeco nightclubs, where bands of the same calibre perform. Supper on Friday nights.

The **Savoy Musical Center** ★★★ *(Hwy 190, east of Eunice, ☎ 318-457-9563).* Musician and artisan Marc Savoy makes and repairs Cajun accordions, but is also a great supporter of Cajun culture and the French language. He organizes Cajun music concerts (accordion, violin and "ti-fer" (triangle)) in his accordion factory every Saturday morning around 10am. These events, which bring together musicians from all over Acadiana, spawn encounters, discussions, exchanges. Eunice Mayor Curtis Joubert is a regular.

The **Cajun French Music Association - CFMA** *(free admission; Tue to Sat 9am to 5pm; at the Cajun Music Hall of Fame and Museum; 210 S. C.C. Duson St., ☎ 318-457-6534)* offers fans of Cajun music the historical account of this cultural form of expression, putting an emphasis on French music from Louisiana.

Marksville

By virtue of their status, the majority of Louisianians are exempt from federal taxation laws. This enables them to operate gambling clubs such as the **Grand Casino Avoyelles** *(free admission, though it will cost you later!; 24 hrs/day; LA 1, ☎ 1-800-WIN-1-WIN).* Over 1,100 slot machines *(25¢; 50¢; $1 and $5),* 45 gaming tables, a poker room, three restaurants as well as shows *(Tue to Sun)* await in this large casino, the Las Vegas of Louisiana.

Calendar of Events

February

Mardi Gras is widely celebrated in the Opelousas countryside. Dates for the coming years are:

1998: February 24th
1999: February 16th
2000: March 7th
2001: February 26th
2002: February 12th
2003: March 4th

The **Ville Platte "Courir du Mardi Gras"** *(Mardi Gras Day; in downtown Ville Platte and surrounding countryside).*

Mamou is renowned for its **"Courir du Mardi Gras"** ★★★, one of the oldest. See "Exploring", p 279).

The **Eunice "Courir du Mardi Gras"** ★★★ *(Feb or Mar, day before Ash Wednesday; Eunice, ☎ 318-457-6502, ☎ 1-800-222-2342 from the US).* See "Exploring", p 280.

The **"Courir du Mardi Gras"** ★★★ *(Sunday before Mardi Gras; LA 178, Saddle Tramp Riders Club, 1036 E. Abbey St., Church Point, ☎ 318-684-2026 or 684-3333)* is a very popular event in **Church Point**. See "Exploring", p 281.

Mardi Gras in Moncla *(Feb; 8 km north of Marksville, on LA107, ☎ 318-253-9208).*

The **Black History Month Parade** ★ *(Feb; Marksville, ☎ 318-253-9208)* takes place every year, honouring African- American heritage.

March

The **Festival du Courtableau** ★★★ *(3rd weekend of Mar; Washington, ask for Mrs. James Fontenot,* ☎ *318-893-2936)*. Featuring traditional *fais do-do* and Cajun feasts, as well as special tours of Washington's lovely old homes.

The **World Championship Crawfish Étouffée Cook-Off** ★★ *(last Sunday of Mar or, if Easter falls on that day, the preceding Sunday; Northwest Community Center Pavilion, Samuel Dr., Eunice,* ☎ *318-457-6502,* ☎*1-800-222-2342 from the US)* brings together about a hundred very colourful teams of amateur and professional chefs, vying to create the best crawfish, Cajuns' favourite shellfish. Live Cajun and zydeco music is also featured.

April

At the **"Here's the Beef" Festival** ★ *(free admission; 3rd Sunday of Mar; Yambilee Ag-Arena, US 190, Opelousas,* ☎ *318-684-6751, ask for Daniel Lyons)*, the Breeders Association offers barbecue fans a smoky, Cajun-style village fair: music, dancing and sampling of grilled meats.

The **Eunice Festival of Arts and LSUE Community Day** ★ *(free admission; 1st weekend of April; Louisiana State University at Eunice - LSUE, Eunice,* ☎ *318-457-2156)* highlights native American handicrafts as well as regional music and cuisine.

The old custom of "pâcquer" for eggs persists among French-speaking Louisianians. The game is played by hitting one anothers' hard-boiled eggs, with the aim of cracking your opponent's egg shell. Certain crafty participants glaze their eggs to make them more resilient. In Marksville, this custom is the subject of the **Easter Egg Knocking Festival** *(Easter; Courthouse public garden, Marksville,* ☎ *318-253-9222)*, an annual event.

The **Goat Festival** *(3rd weekend of Apr; US 167, 16 km southwest of Ville Platte and 6 km east of I-49,* ☎ *318-942-2392 or 826-3431)*. This somewhat unusual festival, thought up by Creole stock breeder Wilbert Guillory, is as much an agricultural fair as it is an exclusive goat-festival. It takes place in the same location as the Southwest Louisiana Zydeco Festival (see below).

International Cajun Joke Telling Contest ★★ *(3rd weekend of Apr; Opelousas,* ☎ *318-948-6263)* attracts a large gathering of those who have a way with words and the gift of humour. An event that is certainly not for the dull and humourless.

May

The **Congé** *(dates change from year to year; Academy of the Sacred Heart, Grand Coteau)* is a festival of music, cooking, games, foot races, auctions, guided tours, and more.

Mansura is renowned for the quality of its livestock, and the **Cochon de Lait (Suckling Pig) Festival** ★★ *(May, Mother's Day weekend; Mansura,* ☎ *318-964-2152)* honours its quality goods.

ACADIANA: NORTH OF LAFAYETTE

June

The **Malaki Jubilee Festival** ★★ *(1st weekend of Jun; between Plaisance and Washington, ☎ 318-826-3934)* celebrates African-American culture and traditions through dance, music, song, arts and food. Gospel singers set things in motion at the crack of dawn, kicking off this increasingly popular festival.

The **Church Point Buggy Festival** ★★ *(1st weekend of Jun; in downtown Church Point, ☎ 318-684-4264 or 684-2739)*. Old-fashioned cars, buggies and others, which once roamed the streets and trails of the Prairies, hold a place of honour here. A fair, accordion and violin competitions and a parade, capping off the festival on Sunday, are organized.

The **Louisiana Corn Festival** *(2nd weekend of Jun; Bunkie, ☎ 318-346-2575)*. Corn-husking-n'-roasting-n'-crunching' party.

July

To get to the **Lebeau Zydeco Festival** ★ *(1st weekend of Jul; LA 10 East, at Immaculate Conception Church Park, Lebeau, ☎ 318-942-2392, ☎ 1-800-424-5442 from the US)*, one of the big music festivals in the region, take LA 10 East at the junction of US 71 and LA 10, and head to the church, just a little farther on the right.

The **Fourth of July Festival** ★ *(10am to 9pm; Tunica-Biloxi Native Reservation, ☎ 318-253-9222)*. These Native-American celebrations are among the best on Independance Day.

August

As its name suggests, the **Le Festival du Lapin de la Grand Prairie** *(end of Aug, early Sep; Fri 6pm to 11:30pm, Sat 10am to 11pm, Sun 9:30am to 3pm; St. Peter's Catholic Church, Grand Prairie, ☎ 318-826-3870)* pays homage to the rabbit. Requisite Cajun music and sampling of regional dishes.

September

The **Southwest Louisiana Zydeco Music Festival** ★★★ *(adults $10, children $2; last weekend of Aug or beginning of Sep; dates vary according to the year; on US 167, 16 km southwest of Ville Platte and 6 km east of I-49, ☎ 318-232-3803, ☎ 1-800-346-1958 from the US, ☎ 1-800-543-5340 from North America)*. This festival, the biggest of its kind in Louisiana and considered by many as a major event in the American South, celebrates Creole culture with 13 hours of music, good food and African-American arts and crafts.

Zydeco music: the term "zydeco" comes from the French word *"zarico"*, which stems from the expression *"les z'haricots sont pas salés!"* (literally, "the beans aren't salted!"), a common complaint among families too poor to afford traditional salted bacon. We are indebted to the sorely missed Clifton Chenier for having modernized the "lala" sound, drawn from blues and soul, with the requisite accompanying washboard and accordion. Storytellers, artisans and other artists of all kinds also take part in this grand festival. Accommodations available for visitors.

The **Harvest Festival** *(dates change from year to year; Tunica-Biloxi Native*

Reservation, ☎ *318-253-9767 or 253-8174).* This cultural event is another festival organized by native-Americans.

October

Eunice Cajun Capital Folklife Festival ★★ *(1st or 2nd weekend of Oct; at Liberty Theater, downtown Eunice,* ☎ *318-457-2265,* ☎ *1-800-222-2342 from the US).* Eunice is the proclaimed capital of Cajun popular culture. The focus of this festival is the venerable Liberty Theater and, despite the festival's name there is more going on than folklore. The Coushatta native community also takes part in this event, as cultural as it is folky, showing off their ancestral cuisine, handicrafts and dances. The Cajun contingent, for its part, sticks to their famous music and food, but also offers an exhibition of antique farm machinery. Finally, humourists and storytellers also participate in this very diverse festival.

Louisiana Cotton Festival ★ *(2nd weekend of Oct; Ville Platte,* ☎ *318-363-4521).* Various activities with a cotton theme celebrate one of the region's principal resources for over 200 years.

Louisiana Yambilee Festival ★ *(4th weekend of Oct, Sunday on Landry St., downtown, Opelousas,* ☎ *318-948-8848).* Opelousas is a great yam-producing region. Harvesting season is therefore a great excuse for organizing a party, complete with a "Yam Queen" and a colourful parade through city streets; it's a veritable carnival. There are also shows and all sorts of yam dishes to sample.

November

The **Louisiana Prairie Cajun Capital Folklife Festival** ★ *(free admission; mid-Nov; Eunice,* ☎ *318-457-7389).* This family-oriented festival runs for two consecutive days and reflects Louisiana's rich cultural traditions: music, arts and crafts, storytellers, food, etc.

December

During the **Grand Coteau Festival** *(in December, dates change from year to year; St. Charles Borromeo Church, Grand Coteau,* ☎ *318-662-5279)* all sorts of activities take place: cooking, music, tours, buggy drives.

 SHOPPING

Opelousas

Vidrine Records *(Hwy 4, Box 249, Opelousas, 70570,* ☎ *318-948-4249 or 684-5421)* specializes in Cajun music and zydeco albums and cassettes.

Washington

The **Antique School Mall** *(every day; old school in Washington;* ☎ *318-826-9909 or 826-7598)* is one of the biggest antique shops in the region.

ACADIANA:
NORTH OF LAFAYETTE

Boudin and Sausages

No self-respecting Cajun starts Saturday off without polishing off some boudin in anticipation of an evening of dancing. Several places in Eunice stock this spicy Prairie delight. And, since this region is also renowned for its sausages, why not stock up on these as well:

Épicerie Johnson *($; Mon to Fri 6am to 6pm, Sat 5am to 5pm; close to LA 13 South, 700 E. Maple St., ☎ 318-457-9314)*. The boudin here is worth lining up for!

At **LeJeune's Sausage** *(Old Crowley Rd., ☎ 318-457-8491)*, strings of tasty sausages tempt true gourmands. Irresistible!

Mowata Grocerie *(LA 13, south of Eunice, ☎ 318-457-1140)* is another place at which to purchase some piggy foodstuffs.

Eunice Superette Slaughter House *(1501 W. Maple Ave., ☎ 318-546-6041 or 457-9314)* gives its boudin and sausage rivals some stiff competition.

Ville Platte

Dupré's Grocery *($; 102 W. Hickory St., ☎ 318-363-4186)* is *the* place for Cajun boudin, pork rinds and smoked meats. You can sample these treats on the premises or get them to go.

Floyd's Record Store *(Mon to Sat 8am to 5pm; 434 E. Main St., ☎ 318-363-2138)* is a temple of Cajun and zydeco music, boasting the widest selection of such recordings. This shop has been around for close to forty years. The owner, Floyd Soileau, used to press the records of Louisiana's greatest recording artists under the *Swallow*, *House of Soul* and *Jin* labels. The old record factory was destroyed by fire in the summer of 1994, but the shop was spared. A few souvenirs, books and even musical instruments are also sold here. To obtain their catalogue, write to Floyd's Record Store, Mail Order and Tape Service, Box 10, Ville Platte, Louisiana - LA 70586, U.S.A.

Mamou

Ortego's Meat Market *($; Mon to Fri 7am to 5pm, Sat 7am to noon; South St., ☎ 318-468-3746)* offers house specialties, such as beef and pork tasso, Also available to go.

Eunice

Acadiana Records *(124 Bernard St., 70535, ☎ 318-546-6102)* has a good choice of Cajun music and zydeco records and tapes.

Music Machine and Video *(235 W. Walnut Ave., ☎ 318-457-4846)* stocks Cajun and zydeco music cassettes and CDs.

Watley's Store *(two streets north of US 190, on the right, before the railway, N. St. Mary St.,* ☎ *318-457-5140).* You can meet the very colourful owner, Preston Watley, provided he isn't off at one of the many Cajun music festivals somewhere in Louisiana. Mr. Watley is also a renowned artisan who makes traditional cowhide chairs. Mrs. Watley is a specialist when it comes to pies and blackberry jam, also sold here.

At **Potpourri** *(361 W. Maple Ave.,* ☎ *318-457-2683 or 457-9078),* Georgie and Allen Manuel make typical Mardi Gras masks.

Potier's Cajun Inn *(E. Park Ave.,* ☎ *318-457-0440)* is another place that stocks a multitude of souvenirs.

Designs *(N. 2nd St.,* ☎ *318-457-1433)* is a delightful shop with souvenirs of all kinds.

Potier's Pharmacy *(Amy Shopping Center, US 190 East,* ☎ *318-457-5698)* boasts a Cajun souvenir section.

Church Point

Lanor Records *(Box 233, Church Point, 70525,* ☎ *318-684-2176)* specializes in Cajun and zydeco music.

Bee Records *(Hwy 3, Church Point, 70525,* ☎ *318-684-5441 or 684-2331)* carries all Cajun music and zydeco records and tapes.

Bunkie

Downtown Bunkie is known for its many respectable antique shops.

Cottonport

The Bottle Shoppe *(N. Main St.,* ☎ *318-876-3885).* Seafood, and especially crawfish (live or boiled), can be procured at this grocer's.

Marksville

Panorama Foods Inc. *(815 W. Tunica Dr.,* ☎ *318-253-6403).* John Ed Laborde, the proprietor of this inviting grocery store, prepares beautiful "gift baskets", of crawfish-stuffed bread, sausage- stuffed bread, shrimp-stuffed bread and many other Cajun delights.

ACADIANA: NORTH OF LAFAYETTE

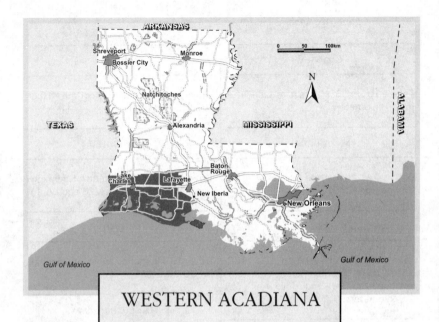

WESTERN ACADIANA

estern Acadiana is the region west of Lafayette. In Scott, just outside Lafayette, a sign informs motorists that the "Far West" starts here. The I-10 crosses the region in an almost straight line, from Crowley to Jennings and on to Lake Charles, located 55 kilometres from the Texas border. For a real taste of the landscape and local culture, you are better off taking US 90, the old road, also known as the Old Spanish Trail. To the north, at the top of the triangular Acadiana region, where the big pine forests start, visitors will find themselves surrounded by flat fields used for rice-growing and crawfish farming. To the south, along the Gulf of Mexico, lies a vast stretch of swampland strewn with lakes and wildlife refuges. Those who enjoy swimming and other water sports can stop at Lake Arthur. West Acadiana is also home to Highway 82 (Hug the Coast Highway), Holly Beach and Pecan Island, the coastline, saltwater swamps (*mèches*), oak groves and a number of fishing and hunting camps.

 FINDING YOUR WAY AROUND

US 90 runs parallel to I-10, straight through the Louisiana plains to the Texas border. From Lafayette (Cameron Street), the US 90 leads to Scott (8 km).

Rayne

Take I-10 or US 90 west of Lafayette for 25 kilometers.

Estherwood

South of I-10, on the US 90, Estherwood is halfway between Rayne and Jennings.

Crowley

Take I-10 or US 90 west of Lafayette for 44 kilometers.

Mermentau

Drive 14 kilometers southwest of Crowley on US 90.

Iota

Take Exit 76 off I-10 to LA 1120 North, drive nine kilometers then turn left on LA 98 and follow it for 2.5 kilometers.

Evangeline

Drive 16 kilometers north of I-10 on LA 97.

Jennings

Jennings is halfway between Lafayette and Lake Charles on I-10 or US 90.

Basile

Drive 27 kilometres north of Jennings on US 190.

Elton

From Jennings, drive 24 kilometres north on US 90.

Fenton

Drive 16 kilometres north of the I-10 on US 165 and LA 102.

Lake Arthur

Drive 17 kilometres south of Jennings at the intersection of LA 26 and LA 14.

Welsh

Drive 19 kilometres west of Jennings on US 90.

Lake Charles

Drive 112 kilometres west of Lafayette on I-10 or on US 90.

Quincy

Drive 32 kilometres northwest of Lake Charles on LA 27.

Sulfur

Take US 90 north of the I-10 and drive 11 kilometres west of Lake Charles.

Vinton

Near the Texas border on US 90, 29 kilometres west of Lake Charles.

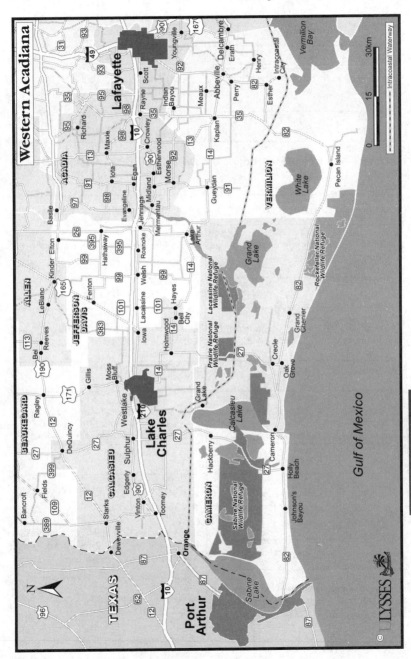

Holly Beach

Drive 57 kilometres south of Lake Charles on LA 82; on the Gulf of Mexico.

Johnsons Bayou

On LA 82, 19 kilometres west of Holly Beach.

Cameron

On LA 82, 53 kilometres south of Lake Charles.

Creole

Drive 21 kilometres east of Cameron to the junction on LA 27 and LA 82.

Grand Chenier

On LA 82, 14 kilometres east of Creole.

Pecan Island

On LA 82, 48 kilometres east of Grand Chenier then 64 kilometres southwest of Abbeville.

Kaplan

Drive 11 kilometres west of Abbeville then 27 kilometres south of Rayne to the intersection of LA 35 and LA 14.

Gueydan

Drive 22 kilometres west of Kaplan then 17 kilometres south of US 90 to the intersection of LA 14 and LA 91.

Abbeville

Drive 21 kilometres south of Lafayette on US 167.

Erath

Drive five kilometres east of Abbeville on LA 14.

Maurice

Drive six kilometres southwest of Lafayette on US 167.

 PRACTICAL INFORMATION

The area code for all cities covered in this chapter is 318.

Buses

Greyhound Bus, in Lafayette: ☎ 235-1541

Lafayette to Lake Charles: Six departures daily, at 5:45am, 10:25am, 1pm, 4:05pm, 7:15pm and 8:55pm; one way $11, return $22.

Lafayette to Jennings: Departures at 10:25am and 4:05pm.

Lafayette to Elton: Departure at 8:30am.

Emergencies

For the police, the fire department or ambulance service, dial 911.

Hospital

Jennings Hospital: Interstate 10, Jennings-Lake Arthur Exit, LA 26, ☎ 828-2490 *(24 hours a day)*

Roadside Assistance

Truman Abshire Towing, 1922 Cheryl Drive, Abbeville, ☎ 893-1608 or 893-2400 *(24 hours a day)*

Tourist Information

Crowley

The **Crowley Tourist Information Centre** *(Mon to Fri 9am to 4:30pm; 114 E. 1st St., ☎ 783-2108)* occupies a restored train station located at the beginning of Parkerson Avenue.

Iota

Tourist information is available at the local **Town Hall** *(☎ 779-2597 or 779-2456)*.

Jennings

Jeff Davis Tourist Commission *(P.O. Box 1209, Jennings, LA 70546, ☎ 264-5521)*.

Elton

The Koasatis (or Coushattas) Indian reservation *(5 km north of Elton)* lies in an isolated spot in the fragrant pine forest that dominates the landscape surrounding Acadiana. Due to the reservation's federal status, gas and cigarettes can be purchased at low prices at the local service station/grocery store *(Mon to Sat 6:30am to 8pm, Sun 8am to 8pm)*. A restaurant/souvenir shop *(Mon to Sun 9am to 4pm)* and a laundromat can also be found here.

The Roads

As a general rule, the farther you get from I-10, the harder it is to find complete auto-repair services. If you have mechanical problems after normal working hours or on the weekend, the gas stations near the highway are your best bet.

Though gas is sold in just about every town (service stations, grocery stores), it is advisable to fill up your tank before the end of the day, especially in remote rural areas.

On country roads, in the prairies, motorists should keep an eye out for stop signs, which often appear suddenly at intersections.

WESTERN ACADIANA

Lake Charles

To get your bearings and find out about the various activities and events taking place in the Lake Charles area, stop by the **Southwest Louisiana Visitors Center** *(Mon to Fri 8am to 5pm, Sat and Sun 10:30am to 3:30pm; 1211 N.*

Lakeshore Dr., ☎ *436-9588 or 1-800-456-SWLA within North America).* Take the Lakeshore Drive Exit off I-10.

The **Louisiana Visitors Center** *(☎ 589-7774),* for its part, is located in a cypress grove, where visitors can stroll through the swamps on an elevated walkway. Restrooms and picnic areas.

Cameron Parish Tourist Commission *(P.O. Box 388, Cameron, LA 70631,* ☎ *775-5145)*

 EXPLORING

Scott

A bedroom community outside Lafayette, Scott prides itself on being the gateway to the West. As in most towns located on a railway line, its old commercial centre is on the north side of the tracks (turn right on St. Mary Street). Scott lies on the **"Real French Destination" Scenic Byway ★★**, or LA 93, which starts at Arnaudville, in St. Landry Parish, and runs through the towns of Grand Coteau, Sunset, Cankton, Scott and Lafayette.

Scott is where "The West" starts, and the town's history (recounted fairly accurately in a renovated former saloon) contains all the traditional Far West ingredients. The "old saloon" looks like something out of an old spaghetti western. The bar has been converted into Cajun artist **Floyd Sonnier's studio and gallery ★★★** *(at St. Mary and Delhomme).* Poet, author, singer and composer Zachary Richard is

one of several Cajun artists who have taken up residence in Scott.

Finally, on St. Mary Street, there is a small green space commemorating Scott's relationship with its twin town, Saint-Aubin, France.

Rayne

This town of nearly 10,000 people is the self-proclaimed Frog Capital of the World. There are numerous murals showing the various kinds of frogs here (the locals call bullfrogs *ouaouarons*). **The Frog Festival ★** (see p 332), held during the third week of September, features all sorts of unusual activities, ranging from the preparation of frog-based dishes to a frog beauty competition.

Crowley

Louisiana is a major producer of rice, and Crowley, the state rice capital, lies in a sea of **paddies ★★**.

With the arrival of the railroad and the migration of farmers from the Midwest to the prairies west of Lafayette, communities like Crowley began adopting American customs and thus took on the appearance of mainstream America, though there are just as many Cajuns here as elsewhere in Acadiana. Today, with nearly 14,000 inhabitants (down from 16,036 in 1980), Crowley is the largest town between Lafayette and Lake Charles. The importance of the rice industry is obvious, what with the rice mills all over town. Recently, there have been exchanges between Crowley and a rice-producing town in Japan, an effort to establish a link between the communities of these two great rivals, located on opposite sides of the world. Part of this endeavor was the creation of a play, a collaborative piece written in Japanese, English and Cajun French, about the ups and downs in the lives of rice-growing families.

Near downtown Crowley, east of the Courthouse, is the **Historic District ★★★**, 33 blocks of houses, almost all Victorian in style. Many of these magnificent residences have drives lined with stately, age-old oak trees. A brief tour of the area, either on foot or by car, is well worth the time.

The **Rice Museum ★★** displays a fascinating collection of old and modern tools, as well as expounding on rice cultivation and local history. For more information, contact the Crowley Chamber of Commerce (☎ 788-0177).

Make sure to stop by the **Musée de la Rose Bleue - Maison Blanchet-Romero ★★** (*$4; by appointment; 8 km southwest of Crowley, ☎ 783-3096*), named after a kind of rice made popular by the Wright family. Erected around 1848, the Maison Blanchet-Romero is typical of Cajun architecture, built of hand-made bricks, cypress and cob (a mixture of mud and Spanish moss). Inside this 150-year-old house, visitors will find crystal and porcelain objects, Victorian furniture, a doll collection and a very impressive assortment of antique cars.

Given Crowley's nickname, the Rice Capital of Louisiana, it is hardly surprising that the town hosts an **International Rice Festival** (*1st or 2nd weekend in Oct; ☎ 788-0177*), the highlight of which is its *fais do-do*, which takes place through the streets of town.

Iota

Festival du Mardi Gras Tee-Mamou/Iota ★★

Located in the heart of Cajun country, way out in the countryside, the little town of Iota is known for its Mardi Gras festivities. The Cajuns from the prairies around Iota and Tee-Mamou (not to be confused with the town of Mamou, in Evangeline Parish) supposedly host the oldest Mardi Gras festival in the United States, dating back to 1750 – 90 years before New Orleans's. Carnival-lovers enjoy the local celebrations because they offer a different kind of atmosphere from the New Orleans festivities.

There are two Mardi Gras runs in Iota. The women's takes place on the Saturday before Mardi Gras, the men's on Fat Tuesday itself. The two events are very similar and follow more or less the same route. Each starts in the morning: at 7am, participants gather at the Frugés' barn (*LA 97, right near the restaurant D.I.'s*) to get ready. The beer starts flowing, the band starts playing, and everyone puts the final touches on their costumes.

All the costumes and masks – such as the *capuchon* (a tall, pointed hat reminiscent of medieval times and designed to poke fun at both the church and the nobility) – are made entirely by hand.

A captain then reads the rules; disobeying him is strictly forbidden. The distribution of beer is carefully controlled, and everyone is responsible for knowing his or her own limits. Each Mardi Gras participant is required to learn the rules and the traditional theme

WESTERN ACADIANA

song, and compulsory meetings are held to get it all straight.

All the "maskers" climb aboard a big wagon pulled by a truck. A long caravan of trucks then sets off on a journey of over 32 kilometres, with no fewer than 15 stops along the way. Elsewhere, in Mamou and in Church Point, for example, the traditional Mardi Gras parade is carried out mainly on horseback, but in Tee-Mamou/Iota, the custom changed in the forties, due to a shortage of horses and the proliferation of motor vehicles used for the rice industry. Like those of all towns in Acadiana, the Tee-Mamou/Iota Mardi Gras has its own symbolic colours: red, green and yellow. And what exactly do these colours represent? Well, they are none other than the colours of that famous manufacturer of tractors, the John Deere company.

Once the procession reaches a designated stop on its itinerary, the maskers climb down from the wagons, and their captain leads them in the singing of one of the traditional songs. Devotees of the Iota festivities claim that these songs are among the oldest in the Mardi Gras repertoire. In the midst of the commotion, you can hear the following song in Cajun French:

Les Mardi Gras quoi portes-tu,
Tour à l'entour du fond d'hiver?

On porte que la bouteille, O mon cher!
O mon cher!
On porte que la bouteille
Tout à l'entour du fond d'hiver.

Bonjour le maître et la maîtresse
On vous demande un peu de chose
On vous demande la fille aînée
On va la faire faire une bonne chose
On va la faire chauffer ses pieds.

Mardi Gras revellers, what are you wearing,
In the heart of winter?

We're only wearing the bottle, my dear!
My dear!
We're only wearing the bottle
In the heart of winter.

Hello, master and mistress
We'd like to ask a small favour
We'd like to ask for your eldest daughter
We're going to make her do something good
We're going to get her dancing.

After the song, the band joins in, along with just about everyone else. Tradition demands that every "mardi gras" then pretend to beg, extending one hand palm-up, and pointing into it with the index finger of the other hand. The scene is like something out of a Fellini film: the beggars shout "*Ti cinq sous!*" ("Five cents!") at the top of their lungs, then the frenzied music and dancing start up again. In the crazy scene that follows, everyone interprets the captain's rules in his or her own way, and "troublesome" revellers often get a taste of their captain's "whip". During the women's run, the ceremony is not unlike an ancient fertility ritual.

The residents thank the maskers by giving them rice, flour, onions or even money – the ingredients necessary to make a big pot of gumbo at the end of the day. The highlight of the stop, however, is definitely the "*chasse aux poules*" (the chicken run)...

The "*chasse aux poules*" is a crazy event. The host upon whom the horde of fun-seekers has descended has to throw the unfortunate chicken into the air. During this cathartic event, which involves no cruelty to the animal, the panic-stricken chicken starts running in all different directions, and the participants have to catch it. Catching the chicken is not just an extraordinary spectacle; each participant views this achievement as an act of both pride and bravura.

On an adrenalin high, the runners make their way to town to wind up the festival on Mardi Gras. They weave through the crowd, singing their song and waltzing and two-stepping.

At the end of the day, the community gathers in a dance hall, where the maskers sing and beg for the last time. Then, one by one, they are thrown out by the captains. They can come back once they have taken off their costumes, at which time everyone returns to his or her old self. During this ritual, the women give their captain a particularly hard time!

Finally, the maskers gather their families and friends around a nice bowl of gumbo and... everyone dances! Lent starts at midnight, however, and all the fun has to stop before the fateful hour. Many of the revellers go to church the very next morning for Ash Wednesday.

Estherwood

Built in 1900, the **pumping and irrigation station** (☎ 783-2108), on Bayou Plaquemine, was one of the first and the largest used for rice-growing in Acadia Parish.

Mermentau

Le Petit Château de Luxe ★★ *(adults $4.50, children $1; Tue to Sat by appointment; take US 90 to LA 92 and turn right; 4 km farther, there is a small gravel road on the right, which leads 3 km to the castle;* ☎ *783-3641)*, located on the banks of the Mermentau River, is reminiscent of the great French chateaux in the Loire Valley, complete with turrets, watchtowers and slate and copper roofs.

Lovic Desormeaux, who died a few years ago just shy of 100 years of age, had always wanted to build a big house on his property on the Mermentau. After taking all sorts of notes and conducting numerous studies on the subject, he finally drew up the plans for his future home.

Desormeaux began construction of his chateau in 1969. After 15 years of arduous work, however, he had to accept the fact that he would not be able to complete his project. His son Philippe took over, and after years of patience, the chateau finally became the family residence.

When Philippe took over from his father, he had a degree in horticulture. A man of many talents, he was also skilled in carpentry, mechanics, rice-growing, stockbreeding and residential construction.

Philippe Desormeaux was responsible for all the major work on the chateau, including the installation of the spiral staircase that dominates the lobby and the three marble mantelpieces, carved in France over 400 years ago and imported to Louisiana specifically for the chateau.

WESTERN ACADIANA

Philippe also laid the hundreds of wooden tiles that make up the magnificent parquet floor, which is almost identical to the one in the chateau at Fontainebleau, France. As well, we have him to thank for designing and planting the gardens, which are already 40 years old.

The ground floor is open to the public. There, visitors can admire period furniture and various Louis XV-style objects. The chateau is like a little piece of France in the middle of the Cajun prairie. Philippe Desormeaux and his family welcome visitors with the utmost kindness and an elegance of manner worthy of the highest ranks of the nobility.

Jennings

Here, there are plains as far as they eye can see. Though the area abounds in farmland and rice paddies, this is where the first oil well in Louisiana was drilled as well.

Visitors are greeted by the following statement, which could hardly be called a motto but is nonetheless funny and memorable: "Twelve thousand friendly people, and one or two grouches, welcome you". How could anyone resist?

The first inhabitants of this region were French, Acadian and Creole colonists, who settled on the banks of local bayous with decidedly French-sounding names like Nezpique, Grand Marais and Lacassine. The town of Jennings, founded in 1888, was named after Jennings McComb, a railroad builder.

The **Jean Lafitte Scenic Byway ★★** runs through Jefferson Davis Parish.

This route, which follows the Gulf of Mexico, is dotted with points of interest, historic sites and natural attractions.

The arrival of the railroad attracted large numbers of settlers and American farmers from the prairies of northern Iowa to these fertile plains. The population is still a mixture of English- and French-speakers.

Jennings is known as the birthplace of the oil industry in Louisiana. In 1901, the first oil well in the state was drilled here, on **Jules Clément's farm ★**, eight kilometres north of Jennings *(LA 97)*. This oil field, known as Evangeline, has yet to be exhausted nearly a century later. At the **Louisiana Oil and Gas Park** *(Exit 64 off I-10, 100 Acadian St.)*, visitors can see a replica of the first oil derrick.

The **Château des Cocodrils ★** *(free admission; every day 9am to 2pm; note: alligators are fed every Monday at 1:30pm from Jun to Aug)*. The word *cocodrie* (or *cocodril*) comes from the Spanish *cocodrilo*, and means "alligator" in the purest French of the Cajuns of West Acadiana. Visitors can photograph alligators here – up close and personal!

The **W.H. Tupper General Merchandise Museum ★** and the **Louisiana Telephone Pioneer Museum ★** *($3, guided tours; Tue to Sat 10am to 6pm; 311 N. Main St., ☎ 821-5532)* is a former rural general store that catered to Cajun, Creole, American and Native American locals during the first half of the 20th century. Visitors can admire some handsome merchandise displays and a magnificent collection of Native American hand-made baskets, which

Alligator

the store sells on consignment for the neighbouring community.

Creole Rose Manor ★ *($1; 214 W. Plaquemine St., ☎ 824-3145)* is a spacious, 14-room Victorian built in 1898 by one of the first French-speakers to settle in Jennings. Not only does the place have a superb antique and souvenir shop, but it also offers accommodations and serves breakfast.

The **Zigler Museum** ★★ *(adults $2, children free; Tue to Sat 9am to 5pm, Sun 1pm to 5pm; 411 Clara St., ☎ 824-0114)* displays lovely paintings and wooden sculptures and hosts travelling exhibitions of works by American and European artists. The **Museum of Natural History**, in the same building, contains reproductions of paintings and sketches from the celebrated naturalist John James Audubon's *Birds of America*.

The first Acadian settlers were known for having a way with horses. It is even said that the first real cowboys were Cajuns. The horsemen of the Louisiana prairies would drive their cattle to New Orleans by swimming across the Atchafalaya River.

West Louisiana is cowboy country just as much as Texas is. During summer, **rodeos** ★ are held in Jennings *(Jeff Davis Parish Fairground; ☎ 824-4452, ask for Billy Walker)*. It is also possible to sign up for a **trail ride** ★ *(rides include music, barbecue, etc.; ☎ 824-4452, after 5:30pm, ask for Dennis or Lena Landry)*.

County fairs are held all over the United States. The state of Louisiana, of course, is divided into parishes rather than counties, but the formula is the same. The **Jeff Davis Parish Fair** is held at the Jennings Fairgrounds on the first weekend of October (see p 333).

As farming is the main industry in the Jennings region, agricultural aviation services abound here. The twin-engine plane is still the aircraft of choice for spraying crops of rice and soybeans.

WESTERN ACADIANA

On the second weekend of October, there is an air show featuring old Stearman planes: the **Stearman Fly-In** *(at the Jennings airport, near I-10, across from the Oil and Gas Park)* (see p 333).

The **Musée Acadien** *(free admission; every day 10am to 5pm; LA 70546, ☎ 824-7380)*, run by the Association France-Louisiane, uses modern technology to show visitors various facets of the Cajun heritage.

Lake Arthur

A stroll along Pleasant Street on the shores of Lake Arthur is certainly pleasant: magnificent scenery with the lake on one side and some superb mansions on the other.

On July 4, **Independence Day** in the United States, the residents of Lake Arthur get together to celebrate in the shade of the town's stately, century-old oaks *(☎ 774-2211)*.

The **Lake Arthur Spring Regatta** *($5; 3rd weekend of May; ☎ 774-2211)* takes place at the Lake Arthur Park. Local bands take part in this popular event, which also includes crafts displays, on-water competitions, food, etc.

If you like bazaars, you'll have a great time at the **Our Lady of the Lake Catholic Church Bazaar** *(mid-Oct; at the Christian Unity Center, E. 8th St., ☎ 774-2614)*, which includes live music, an auction, a euchre competition and arm-wrestling matches.

Elton

Five kilometres north of town, is the autonomous **Koasatis reservation** ★★ *(☎ 584-2249)*. These Native Americans live in the pine forests, but earn their living as farm labourers. The Koasatis (or Coushattas) sell a variety of handicrafts, including pretty baskets woven out of long pine needles. They also offer tastings of sweets made with berries and other wild fruits, as well as Native American fried bread. Many of the Koasatis still speak their native language, and a few speak French.

The **Elton Rice Mill** ★ *(Tue to Thu 7am to 4pm; ☎ 584-2218)* is well-known in these parts. During the rice-harvesting season, from the end of summer to the end of autumn, guided tours of the facility are available. The owners, Tom LeJeune and David Bertrand, are proud of their mill and the various services it still provides for the community. At the mill, visitors can purchase, by the pound, enough aromatic rice and tac-tac rice (which smells like popcorn) to feed an army. The sacks *(poches)* are made on the premises; there is even a special one just for Mardi Gras.

Welsh

The **Welsh Threshing Days** ★ start sometime in October, depending on when the rice is ready to be harvested (see p 333). The rice is threshed the old way, using period equipment.

The Lake Charles Area

Lake Charles is the biggest town in this region and is located, as indicated by its name, on the shores of Lake Charles. It is known for its **carpenters' district**, 20 blocks of distinctive houses in the purest Victorian style.

The **De Quincy Railroad Museum** *(every day 9am to 5pm; north of Lake Charles, ☎ 786-7113)*, set up inside a former train station with Mission Revival architecture, displays a steam locomotive dating from 1913, as well as railway cars and equipment, telegraph equipment and period uniforms.

The **Brimstone Museum ★** *(free admission; Mon to Fri 9:30am to 5pm; 800 Picard Rd., Sulphur, ☎ 527-7142)* aims to familiarize visitors with the techniques used by the mining industry, with particular emphasis on the uses of the sulfur extracted in this area.

The **Fine Art Gallery of Southwest Louisiana ★** *(Mon to Fri 10am to 5:30pm, Sat 10am to 2pm, closed Sun; 1424 Ryan St., Lake Charles, ☎ 439-1430)* is a series of shops selling paintings, sculptures, pottery and porcelain by local artists and artisans.

The **Imperial Calcasieu Museum ★** *(adults $1, children $0.50; Tue to Fri 10am to 5pm, Sat and Sun 1pm to 5pm; 204 W. Sallier St., at Ether; ☎ 439-3797)* traces the history of Lake Charles. The museum is located on the estate where Charles Sallier (the founder of the original settlement) built his home. Visitors can see the 19th-century parlour, kitchen, bedroom (with a rosewood bed), dishes, utensils and patchwork quilt, as well as a pharmacy and barbershop. The museum also boasts a superb collection of prints by the great American naturalist John James Audubon.

Vermilion Parish

Vermilion Parish claims to be "the most Cajun place on the planet". For a unique, authentic experience in a truly Cajun environment, get in touch with the colourful Mrs. Pat Herpin of **Tour Masters** *(402 N. Irving Ave., Kaplan, LA 70548, ☎ 643-8481)*, who, as a "100% cotton" Cajun herself, knows the ins and outs of everyday Cajun life better than anyone. Though this outfit mainly handles group tours, it is nonetheless possible to enlist Mrs. Herpin's services for a personalized outing. Tour Masters also offers packages for various hunting and fishing trips (duck, goose, alligator, etc.); tours of different kinds of industrial facilities and farms (rice, soybean, sugar cane, crawfish, "cocodril" (alligator), burbot dairy, emu); cooking demonstrations; horse races; tours of historic Abbeville, and last but not least, a stop at Madame Cocodril and the Vagabond Cowboy's.

The **Jean Lafitte Scenic Byway ★★** crosses Vermilion, Acadia, Jeff Davis, Cameron and Calcasieu parishes.

Intracoastal City

In addition to its industrial facilities, the Intracoastal City oil and natural gas company is known for its locks on the Intracoastal Waterway. At the **Leland Bowman Locks ★** *(free admission; Mon to Fri, Sat by appointment only; 24 km south of Abbeville, on LA 333, ☎ 893-6790 or 893-4412, ask for Harold Trahan)*, visitors learn that they are "at the end of the world". Administered by the U.S. army corps of engineers this place teaches the public

WESTERN ACADIANA

about the waterway and how the locks work, as well as being an important station for the U.S. Coast Guard. There is an observation tower, where visitors can watch the numerous barges at work. You can also come here for a picnic and observe the *"cocodrils"* in their natural habitat while you eat.

Kaplan

Stockbreeding plays a major role in the economy of the prairies bordering the swamplands of southern Louisiana. A visit to Charles Broussard's **Flying J Ranch ★** *(admission fee; LA 82, south of Kaplan; ☎ 642-5287)* is a must and promises to be memorable. Broussard's family of stockbreeders earned their living driving herds of cattle to market along the Old Spanish Trail (now US 90) long before the first Texan cowboys appeared. Mr. Broussard, a proud descendant of the legendary head of the Acadian resistance, Joseph Broussard dit Beausoleil, can give you an interesting account of the introduction of Brahmin and Charolais cattle to Louisiana.

There are two other interesting places to visit in Kaplan: the **Liberty Rice Mill** *(tour by appointment; 200 W. Mill St., ☎ 643-6380)*, the area's biggest rice mill, and the **Beaux Gators Farm** *(107 Bea's Dr., Kaplan, LA 70548, ☎ 643-2745)*, which, as may be gathered by its name, is an alligator farm.

Abbeville ★

People first started settling in the Abbeville area around the 1730s. However, it wasn't until 1850 that the town was actually incorporated, thanks to Father Antoine Désiré Megret, who was dissatisfied with the administration in Vermilionville (Lafayette). Why he chose the name Abbeville remains a puzzle. There are two possible reasons: either he named the town after Abbéville, France, where he was born, or the name simply refers to the founder himself (*abbé* means "abbot" in French). Today, Abbeville is a charming town with public squares reminiscent both of the Far West and pretty provincial towns in France. You can take a walking tour of historic Abbeville with a guide from the Chamber of Commerce. If you'd rather go it alone, pick up a map of the downtown area at the local tourist information center *(Abbeville Tourist Information Center, 1905 Veterans Memorial Dr., ☎ 893-2596)*. Make sure to have a look at the eight blocks of historic houses. The Gothic Revival architecture of **St. Mary Magdalen Roman Catholic Church ★**, near Magdalen Square, is somewhat unusual in this part of southern Louisiana. Abbeville is twinned with Lasne, Belgium.

You can't miss the impressive **silos of the Riviana rice mill** *(visits by appointment; ☎ 893-2220)*, at the corner of Bas and 1st Streets. This is also a sugar-producing region. Grocery stores all over Louisiana sell Steen's cane syrup, in the yellow and black can and produced right here at **Steen's syrup mill** *(closed to the public; 119 N. Main St., just behind St. Mary Magdalen Church)*. The Steen family has been producing high-quality cane syrup, made with its famous "blue ribbon" sugar cane, since 1910. Not that long ago, everyone in the Louisiana countryside made their own cane syrup. Now, a handful of huge sugar refineries serve all of southern Louisiana. Steen's still uses the traditional method of making syrup, known as *roulaison*. Unfortunately, it is no longer possible to visit the mill. However, at *roulaison*-time *(Oct to Dec)*, you can still drink in the intoxicating odour of sugar and observe the bustling activity around the mill.

Not far from Abbeville is the **Bayou Légendaire ★★** *(1307 S. Henry St., ☎ 893-5760 or 893-1582)*, a cultural centre founded by Kathy and Johnny Richard in June 1997. It occupies an old barn formerly used for farm auctions. The vast space, where local Cajun cowboys used to come to examine and bid on livestock, has been converted into an amphitheatre. The place has excellent acoustics and is now a venue for concerts (bands and choirs), plays, dance performances and evenings of poetry. All shows are in French.

Horsy folk will appreciate the wide range of services offered by **Richard's Riding Center & Livery** *(11734 Hwy. 355 S., ☎ 898-1064 or 893-5701)*.

Erath

Stop by the **Musée Acadien ★★** *(Mon to Fri 1pm to 4pm; 203 S. Broadway, ☎ 233-5832 or 937-5486)*. The museum traces the history of Acadia, from the famous *Grand Dérangement* (Deportation) to the settling of Acadians in southern Louisiana. This foundation supported a human rights petition filed in 1990 demanding that all efforts be made to protect the people of the world from a persecution similar to that suffered by the Acadians.

Delcambre ★

The small port town of Delcambre straddles the boundary between Vermilion and Iberia Parishes. Watching the shrimp boats set out for the Gulf of Mexico from the docks of the Delcambre Canal is still an impressive spectacle. The fishermen come from all different ethnic backgrounds: Cajun, Asian, Native American (Houmas from the Bayou Lafourche area), Latin American, etc. If you talk to them, you can learn more about their way of life and the fishing techniques they use.

When you get back from the docks, you can stock up on good, fresh shrimp at **Vinet's Shrimp Inc.** *(604 Wilfrid Landry St., Delcambre, LA 70528, ☎ 685-2530)*.

 PARKS

Lake Arthur

Visitors can enjoy a variety of outdoor activities at **Lake Arthur**, located in the southeast part of Lake Arthur Parish. The small **park ★** on the shore of the lake, studded with live oaks and bald cypresses draped with Spanish moss, is a terrific place for a picnic. It has a small beach, but swimming is prohibited on some days during the rice-harvesting season, due to pollution. For more information, contact the **Municipality of Lake Arthur** *(710 1st St., Lake Arthur, LA 70549, ☎ 774-2211)*. During summer, the park is open from 7am to 9pm.

The Lake Charles Area

Though Allen Parish isn't located within the triangle formed by Acadiana, it is close enough to merit a detour, especially if you're an avid canoeist. **Whiskey Chitto Creek**, scattered with impressive sandbanks and recognized by the Louisiana Office of Tourism as the most scenic river in the state, is extremely popular with paddlers. **Arrowhead Canoe Rentals** *(every day; ☎ 639-2086 or 1-800-637-2086 within the U.S.)* is located 14 kilometres northwest of Oberlin, on LA 26.

The license plates in Louisiana read "Sportsman's Paradise", and with good reason: the state is truly a heaven on earth for hunters and fishermen. **Southern Traditions** *(13 km south of I-10, between Sulphur and Vinton, and 5 km south of LA 108, on Charley Ross Rd.; ☎ 436-0214 or 583-GRAY)* is an outfitter. You can try fishing for bass, a fish known for its aggressiveness, from March to September, or hunting for teal on the last weekend in September. The duck- and goose-hunting season lasts from November to January. Alligator-hunting is another possibility.

In some parts of Louisiana, it is also possible to fish at private ponds, even if you don't have a fishing permit. All the necessary equipment (fishing tackle, bait, etc.) is available at these fishing holes, and you're likely to reel in plenty of fine fish. At **Beausoleil Lake** *(5588 LA 14 E., 11 km southeast of Lake Charles, ☎ 433-1688 or 474-7777)*, there are at least eight different kinds to be caught.

Calcasieu and Cameron Parishes are linked by the **Creole Nature Trail** ★★, which starts at the Gulf of Mexico and runs through the Sabine National Wildlife Refuge. To reach the trail, you have to take Highway 27 for 160 kilometres, heading south to the Gulf of Mexico from Sulphur. On the way, you'll pass through **Hackberry**, the crab capital, as well as the famous Sabine National Wildlife Refuge.

All sorts of wild animals can be found in the vast **Sabine National Wildlife Refuge** *(free admission; Mon to Fri 7am to 4pm, Sat and Sun noon to 4pm; ☎ 762-3816)*, particularly migratory birds. The best bird-watching periods are from mid-April to mid-May for the spring and from early September to early October and from mid-November to late January for the fall and winter migrations. There is an **interpretive center** *(40 km south of I-10)* on the ecological importance of the swamplands, complete with three kilometres of trails *(allow between an hour and an hour and a half)*. A perfect place for amateur ornithologists.

There is another interesting viewing area on the **Sabine Trail** *(6 km south of the interpretation center)*. At the end of a two-and-a-half-kilometre footbridge, which leads over the swamp on a series of piles, you'll find an observation tower. Be careful! There are lots of reptiles around during summer. Furthermore, because there are so many mosquitoes, it is wise to bring along a good insect repellent. This advice applies to any outing in the swamps and forests of Louisiana.

This route leads to **Holly Beach** ★ *(☎ 436-9588)*, a seaside resort and fishing port whose waters are teeming with shrimp and oysters. You can stock up on these fresh treats by purchasing them straight from the fishermen on the docks. The locals call Holly Beach the Cajun Riviera. One look at the cabins and the way residents mark their property with garish signs complete with their phone numbers, you'll know you've found a cheerful vacation spot filled with fun-loving people. Holly Beach, the Cajun Riviera on the Gulf of Mexico, has over 40 kilometres of beaches, 10 of which are open to the public. The only real beach in Louisiana between the Texas border and Grand Isle, south of New Orleans, Holly Beach is fairly crowded during summer. Possible activities include swimming, fishing, crabbing, shellfish gathering (October through March) and bird-watching. Campgrounds, cabins; information available at the **Cameron Parish Tourist Office** *(P.O. Box 388, Cameron, LA 70631, ☎ 775-5493).*

Upon leaving this delightful, friendly haven, the road runs along the shore toward Lake Charles, through a magnificent, unspoiled landscape of swamplands sprinkled with aquatic plants and teeming with alligators, crabs and wild ducks and geese.

We should also mention the **beaches** at **Constance**, between Holly Beach and Johnsons Bayou; **Rutherford**, at Oak Grove; and **Hackberry** on Calcasieu Lake.

LA 82 and LA 27 intersect at Creole, 22 kilometres east of Cameron. If you head north on the 27, you'll follow the Creole Nature Trail, which ends at Lake Charles. If you head east on the 82, you'll continue along the coast of the Gulf of Mexico, ending up south of Lafayette, at Kaplan or Abbeville.

To complete the Creole Nature Trail, head north. Right after the bridge over the Intracoastal Waterway, you'll reach the **Cameron Prairie Wildlife Refuge** *(free admission; Mon to Fri 8am to 4:30pm; ☎ 598-2216),* which opened on January 1, 1994 and shows slides on the local wildlife and dams.

By taking LA 82 East to Oak Grove, south of Creole, you'll enter the coastal oak grove region, filled with forests of oaks that have been twisted and bent by the violent winds and frequent hurricanes that pass through here. Residents of this coastal part of the state were once extremely isolated, and outlaws used to hide out in the forests here. Later, the region was inhabited by farmers, who slowly cleared the land. Many local residents still earn their living farming and stockbreeding to this day.

Hunting and fishing still play an important role in the region's economy, as does the oil industry, with its numerous drilling sites and its offshore platforms. Fourteen kilometres west of Oak Grove is the community of Grand Chenier. The first French settlers used to call the coastal woodlands *"chêniers"* (oak groves); these islands are actually old mounds of sand piled on the beaches by the waves and the ocean currents, as well as by the flow of the Mississippi.

The **Rockefeller Wildlife Refuge and Game Preserve** ★★ *(every day, Mar 1 to Oct 30, from sunrise to sunset; admission $2 for those without a Wild Louisiana Stamp hunting and fishing permit, sold at the Preserve's office in Grand Chenier and at area stores; ☎ 528-2168)* covers over 33,600 hectares. It is a wonderful place for bird-watching, as the surrounding marshes are a stopping place for many migratory species that spend the winter in Central and South

WESTERN ACADIANA

America. Of course, there are permanent animal residents to observe as well: muskrats, nutrias, raccoons, otters and alligators. The best time for alligator-watching is from April to mid-July. At the end of summer in particular, it is important to be careful, as alligators don't like to be disturbed in the middle of their mating season! To take advantage of the activities offered at the refuge - fishing, crabbing or observing the wildlife from various viewing stations, take **Price Lake Road** *(closed Dec 1 to Mar 1)* from Highway 8.

At Pecan Island, LA 82 starts heading northward. Visitors can either follow it all the way to Abbeville or pick up LA 35 and go to Kaplan.

Abbeville

Hunting buffs are sure to appreciate the **Ace Hunting Club** *($250 per day: hunting, lodgings, meals, drinks and hunting dog included; Hwy 1, P.O. Box 1465, Abbeville, LA 70510, ☎ 643-2910)*. Owner Hammy Patin, a renowned storyteller with a knack for being the life of the party, presides over a veritable paradise of 2,600 hectares inhabited by thousands of ducks and wild geese. You'll never forget the wonderful evenings of bourrée (a card game) and poker, the gargantuan meals and the successful hunting expeditions that the master hunter enjoys as much as his dog. You can bring your own dog or choose one at the club.

 ACCOMMODATIONS

Rayne

The little **Acadian Oaks Campground** *($10 per night; Hwy 98 N. Exit off I-10, 1.5 km north of Rayne)*, located near the Interstate 10, has equipped sites and all essential facilities, as well as R.V. hook-ups.

La Maison de Mémoire - Bed and Breakfast *($60 for one person, $75 for two, bkfst incl..; pb; 403 E. Louisiana Ave., ☎ 334-2477)*, owned by Mr. and Mrs. Guidry, has been listed as a historic building. Only one room is available for rent, thus guaranteeing an intimate atmosphere. The couple loves to share their Cajun culture with their guests. Guests are requested to refrain from smoking.

La Maison Daboval *($65-$100 bkfst incl.; pb; 305 E. Louisiana Ave., ☎ 334-3489)* is an inviting old house built in 1892 and now listed as a historic building. Cajun owners Gene and Martha Royer offer five lovely rooms, each with its own bathtub and shower.

Crowley

The **Cajun Haven Campground** *($10 per night; on I-10, 13 km west of Crowley, Exit 72, Egan ☎ 783-2853)* offers all standard services and facilities for both tent and R.V. camping.

The **Trail's End Campground** *($16.50 per night; ≈; 2.5 km south of I-10, Exit 72, Egan, ☎ 783-8587)*, owned by

Dorothé Luquette Dailey, is definitely the best place to camp in Crowley.

Built in 1910, when the Crowley region was renowned as a major rice-growing centre, the **Rice Hotel** *($27 one queen bed, $38 two queen beds; 125 3rd St., one street west of Parkerson,* ☎ *783-6471)* is still a downtown institution. The place might be a bit outmoded but is positively spotless. Adam Primeaux, a French-speaking Cajun, has owned the hotel since the 1930s.

The **Crowley Inn** *($38 double occ.; LA 13,* ☎ *788-1970)* is an economical option perfect for travellers on a tight budget.

Jennings

Paradise Park *($$; Fri to Mon; 1108 S. Lake Arthur Ave., Exit 64 S off I-10, drive 4.8 km, the place will be on the left; for more information, contact Mr. and Mrs. Ellsworth or Deanna Duhon,* ☎ *774-3675)* is a full-service R.V. park.

The **Thrifty Inn** *($30 double bed, $31.95 queen bed, extra person $4; LA 26, Exit 64 off 1-10,* ☎ *824-8576)* is a dependable choice for standard accommodations.

The **Sundown Inn** *($30 double bed, $35 queen bed; special weekly rates for two people; LA 26,* ☎ *824-7041)* is another economical place that is very popular with families.

The **Holiday Inn** *($41, extra person $5; ≈, ℜ, ≡; LA 26, Exit 64 off I-10,* ☎ *824-5280 or 1-800-HOLIDAY within North America)* offers the same standard level of comfort that has made this international American chain so popular.

The **Days Inn** *($50 for two queen beds, $55 plus tax for two king-size beds; ≈, ℜ; 2502 Port Dr., Exit 65 off I-10;* ☎ *824-6550 or 1-800-329-7466 within North America)*, a modern establishment with 132 rooms, located on the highway, offers complimentary coffee.

The **Creole Rose Manor Bed and Breakfast** *($65 bkfst incl.; pb, four guest rooms; 214 W. Plaquemine St.,* ☎ *824-3145)* is a big, beautiful Victorian.

Lake Charles

The **Camping Jamie Mobile** *(tent $8, R.V. $12; 3256 Hwy. 27, at Opelousas St.,* ☎ *439-4422)* has 49 sites for tents or R.V.s. The owner, Earl Fontenot Ryder, is a proud descendant of one of the militiamen sent to Louisiana by Napoleon.

On the banks of the Calcasieu River, **Sam Houston Jones State Park ★** *($45 per night for a six-person cabin; K, ≡, ≴; 11 km north of Lake Charles: I-10, then LA 171 for 6 km; left on LA 378 for 5 km then right on the park road,* ☎ *855-2665)* has 73 magnificent, fully equipped campsites.

During the Civil War, a fort stood on the present site of **Niblett's Bluff Park and Campground** *(6am to 10pm; on the Texas border: I-10, Exit 4 for Toomey/Starks; take LA 109 North for 5 km, then turn left on LA 3063,* ☎ *589-7117)*. The Union troops, having occupied all of southern Louisiana, were trying to ward off an invasion from the west by Emperor Louis

WESTERN ACADIANA

Napoleon's soldiers, who had gathered in Mexico. The redoubt of the fort is still visible today. Visitors enjoy free access to paths and picnic areas. On the banks of the Sabine River, vacationers or visitors simply passing through can stay in a cabin *($20 for four adults;* ≡*)* or, for those who prefer something more rustic, in a tent *($5, $10 with amenities)*. R.V. sites. Niblett's Bluff is located near the Delta Downs racecourse.

The **Travel Inn** *($25-$30; 1212 N. Lakeshore Dr.,* ☎ *433-9461)* has the advantage of being located along the lake.

The **Days Inn - Lake Charles** *($34-$40; ℜ, ≈; 1010 US 171 N., Lake Charles, LA 70601,* ☎ *433-1711 or 1-800-325-2525 within North America)* is another inexpensive place to stay in Lake Charles.

The **Inn on the Bayou** *($42-$80; ≈; 1101 W. Prien Lake Rd.,* ☎ *474-5151 or 1-800-642-2768 within the U.S.)*, which offers all the comforts of a modern hotel, is an excellent choice for visitors exploring the Lake Charles region or the area around Prien Lake.

The **Holiday Inn** *($56-$76; ≈, ℜ; 505 N. Lakeshore Dr., Lake Charles, LA 70601,* ☎ *433-7121 or 1-800-367-1814 within North America)* is pleasantly located on the shores of Lake Charles.

The **Chateau Charles** *($70-$80; ≡, ctv, ℝ, microwave, video poker, free shuttle to the casino boat, shows every night; I-10, Exit 26, on Southern Columbia Road)* is a large hotel that was recently renovated for the inauguration of the casino boat that now cruises the waters of Lake Charles.

The **Best Western Richmond Suites** *($80-$125; at the intersection of I-10 and US 171,* ☎ *433-5213)* is conveniently located for getting back on the road early to beat the morning traffic.

Sulphur

The two hotels below offer the amenities and level of comfort people have come to expect from major mid-range hotel chains:

Holiday Inn *($40-$70; ≈, ℜ; 2033 Ruth St., Sulphur, LA 70663,* ☎ *528-2061 or 1-800-645-2525 within North America)*.

The **La Quinta Inn** *($48-$65; ≈; 2600 Ruth St., Sulphur, LA 70663-6465,* ☎ *527-8303 or 1-800-531-5900 within North America)*.

Vinton

Best Western Delta Downs Motor Inn *($37-$55; ≈, ℜ; LA 2, P.O. Box 125, Vinton, LA 70668, Toomey Exit off I-10,* ☎ *589-7492 or 1-800-282-8081 within North America)* offers standard accommodations.

Kaplan

The **Sunnyside Motel** *($30-$50; ≈, ⊛, ctv, K; 700 W. 1st St., Kaplan, LA 70548,* ☎ *643-7181)* has a room for guests travelling with their pets. The owner, Brenda Hoffpauir, is descended from the first German families who settled in Louisiana in the 18th century under the French regime and were assimilated into the Cajun community.

Abbeville

The **Coulee Kinney Camping** *($4 per night; LA 14 West Business, Charity St., then about 0.8 km past the bridge over the Bayou Vermilion and finally left on a small dirt road immediately after La Fourche Rd., a sign indicates 0.8 km to the campground)* has 52 sites with running water and electricity. No laundry facilities or grocery store.

The **Kisinoaks Bed and Breakfast** *($70-$80; Hwy. 2, P.O. Box 86, on N. Bayou Rd., 2 km north of the Abbeville McDonald's, ☎ 893-8888)* is a luxurious cottage set on a magnificent piece of property shaded by live oaks; the building was moved here from Jeanerette by a barge on the Teche.

The **Sunbelt Lodge Motel** *($37-$41; 1903 Veterans Memorial Dr., ☎ 898-1453)* offers standard accommodations.

Scott

According to camping enthusiasts who belong to the Kampgrounds of America association, the **KOA-Scott-LA** *(8 km west of Lafayette by I-10, Exit 97 for Scott; reservations ☎ 235-2739 or 1-800-244-7724 within the U.S.)* is the best in the country. It has about a dozen little log cabins *($27 for one room, $35 for two rooms; ≡; bedding not included; reservations required)*, tent sites *($15.50 for two people)* and 180 R.V. sites. Campers can also go fishing, as there's a fairly large lake here. From October to April, the campground hosts a Cajun dinner every Wednesday night. Furthermore, a 20-minute video on the local tourist attractions is shown until 6pm.

Lake Arthur

The charming little **Lorrain Bridge Campground** *($8 per night; six sites, running water and electricity; west of Lake Arthur, near Hayes; take LA 14 North, then LA 101 for 3 km; east of Lorrain Rd., continue for another 1.5 km then turn right at the fork)* is hidden away in the cypress and oak groves at the confluence of Bayou Lacassine and Bayou Chene. In 1860, François, Louis and Eugène Lorrain came here from France, the first members of the family after whom the town was named to settle in the area. At that time, the region was enjoying an economic boom, and scores of schooners loaded with wood travelled the region's bayous, swamplands and lakes en route to Galveston, Texas. In the heart of the town of Lorrain, there was a bridge specifically for horse-drawn carriages. The present bridge was built in 1920; it, too, is due to be replaced; despite its less than reassuring appearance, it is still in use. With the arrival of the railroad and the advent of trucking, Lorrain became a ghost town, and the only vestige of its glory days is its bridge. The Lorrain Bridge Campground is a perfect place for fishing, picnicking and canoeing (it has a boat landing).

The **Lake RV Park** *($12.50 per night; from the north, take LA 26 to the town of Lake Arthur, turn left on 3rd St. and continue half a block to Pelican St., then turn left; 222 LA 14, ☎ 774-3675)* has six fully equipped RV sites.

WESTERN ACADIANA

Meyer's Landing *(11 km west of Lake Arthur, on LA 14, then left on Lowry Rd.; LA 3056,* ☎ *774-2238 or 774-9992)*is in a clump of oak trees on the banks of the Mermenteau River. Grocery, tackle store, boat landing.

Welsh

John Blank Sportsman's Park *($8 per night; 10 R.V. sites, picnic areas, standard amenities; I-10, S. Welsh Exit, drive 2.5 km, then take Adams St., the main street; for more information, contact the town hall,* ☎ *734-2231, Mon to Fri 8am to 5pm, or, after working hours and on weekends, the police department,* ☎ *734-2626).*

Fenton

At the **Mobile City Campground** *($14 per night; I-10 Exit 44 N., then 19 km north of the highway to Fenton, and two blocks west of US 165,* ☎ *765-2230)* has between 30 and 35 equipped sites.

Holly Beach, Cameron

There are numerous motels and campgrounds on **Holly**, **Cameron** and **Rutherford Beaches**.

The rooms at the **Motel Rutherford** *($22-$35; K; Hwy 1, P.O. Box 2, Creole,* ☎ *542-4148)*, located an hour from Lake Charles, have kitchenettes with patios. Hunting and fishing guides may be hired here.

The **Motel Cameron** *($32-$50; P.O. Box 447, Cameron, LA 70631,* ☎ *775-5442)* lies just a kilometre and a half from the Gulf of Mexico and offers fully equipped rooms.

The **Broussard Apartments** *($40-$80 for an apartment for 4-10 people; R.V. $12; P.O. Box 117, Cameron, LA 70631,* ☎ *569-2375)* are located on the beach.

The **Motel Holly Beach** *($45 per night in summer during the week, $55 on the weekend; $35 in winter; K; P.O. Box 67, Cameron, LA 70631,* ☎ *569-2352)* is located near the Holly Beach grocery store. Each room has a fully equipped kitchenette.

At the **Cabines Tommy** *($45-$75; Holly Beach,* ☎ *569-2426)*, Anita Miguez rents out cabins by the night and offers attractive weekly rates.

The **Motel Joe Nick** *($50 during summer, $30 during winter; K; P.O. Box 49, Cameron, LA 70631,* ☎ *569-2421)* stands 65 metres from the beach, and all its rooms have kitchenettes.

Locations Irène *($50; K; LA 82, before Port Arthur, 64 km south of Lake Charles; P.O. Box 121 D, Cameron, LA 70631,* ☎ *569-2473)* rents out two four-person apartments, each with a fully equipped kitchenette.

The **Gulfview Apartments** *($50-$65 during summer, $30 to $45 during winter; R.V. $15; K; P.O. Box 66, Cameron, LA 70631,* ☎ *569-2388)* face onto the beach. Each has a kitchenette with all the standard amenities.

RESTAURANTS

Scott

The regional cuisine served at the **Cajun Cone** *($; Mon to Fri 6:30am to 3pm; 5802 Cameron St., ☎ 235-8772)* is very popular with Scott residents. Just stop by after the 6:30am Mass and you'll see how much the locals appreciate the breakfasts and the home-made biscuits, which disappear by the dozen. At lunchtime, the cook, Mrs. Fontenot, prepares full meals. The menu changes daily *(Mon to Thu, jambalaya, steak, grilled chicken, etc.; Fri, seafood)*.

Rayne

Michael's and Sun's *($-$$; Mon to Thu 7am to 3:30pm, Fri and Sat 7am to 10pm, Sun 11am to 2pm; ☎ 334-5539)* has an altogether unusual menu; the dishes, as pleasing to the eye as they are to the palate, are a blend of Cajun and Korean cuisines, with specialties that taste both Creole and Asian.

If there is one restaurant that is both folksy and unique, it's **Hawk's** *($$; mid-Nov to mid-Jun, Wed to Sat 5pm to 10pm)*, reputed to serve the best crawfish in all Louisiana. The crustaceans are soaked before being cooked. Hawk's is said to be a seafood-lovers paradise. Getting to the famous restaurant is like a treasure hunt, however: from I-10, take the exit for Rayne, turn left at the McDonald's on LA 98 and continue for 9 km, then take a right on parish road 2-7. The restaurant lies about a kilometre and a half farther on the left.

Crowley

After exploring Crowley's historic district, visitors can stop by the **Frosto Drive-in** *($; E. 3rd St. and N. G Ave., ☎ 783-0917)* to tuck into some fast food and choose from a whole slew of desserts and refreshing snacks.

The chef at **Chef Roy** *($-$$; Fri and Sat 5:30pm to 11pm, Tue to Thu 5:30pm to 10pm, Fri and Sat 5pm to 11pm; 2307 N. Parkerson St., ☎ 783-3256)* is a well-known figure in this area, whose residents appreciate the authenticity of his Cajun cuisine.

Free Meals

You don't have to worry about finding a good restaurant at dinnertime once you know which bars serve free meals, and when: it happens every night, all over Cajun Country! Nearly all Cajun and Creole bars serve simple dinners, some on Monday nights, others on Tuesday...

Jennings

The **Cajun Dragon** *($; every day, Sun to Thu 11am to 9:30pm, Fri 11am to 10pm, Sat 5pm to 10pm; 3014 Frontage Rd.; take I-10 north of the Oil and Gas Park, ☎ 824-4280)*, near Jennings, serves Chinese-American cuisine. Guests can order à la carte from a selection of Americanized Chinese dishes or opt for the buffet *($6.99)*. Some novel Cajun-Chinese offerings, such as imperial roll gumbo, are also available.

WESTERN ACADIANA

The **Corner Store Deli** *($; every day, 4:30am to 2:30pm; 314 N. Cutting Ave., ☎ 824-7702)* sells breakfast biscuits, po-boys, boudin and salads, to go or to be eaten on the premises.

At the **Rocket Drive Inn** *($; 1118 S. State St., ☎ 824-2120)*, you can step back in time to the 1950s; even the food has a retro look about it. Beware, however: because the place is so popular, the wait is longer here than elsewhere. The burgers, prepared in the good old-fashioned way, are fantastic and bear little resemblance to the mass-produced burgers we consume today. Make sure to try the sinfully delicious milk shakes as well.

The Courthouse crowd gets together at **Ruth's Coffee Shop** *($; 918 N. Main St., ☎ 824-9219)*. There is a nonstop flow of candid conversation in this cramped space packed with regulars – magistrates and workers alike. For some, this is the place to come and catch up on the latest news and gossip. Ruth's is known for its terrific cat eye cookies, made according to a secret recipe.

The **Winn Dixie** *($; Elton Rd., ☎ 824-3793)* supermarket sells deli products and all sorts of prepared dishes that can serve as full meals.

Le Roi du Boudin *($-$$; Mon to Sat 8am to 9pm; 906 W. Division St., ☎ 824-6593)* serves Cajun cuisine: boudin, chicken and sausage gumbo, crawfish, catfish, rice with red beans, head cheese, etc. Owner Ellis Cormier was named Louisiana chef of the year in 1985.

The Cajun owners of **Donn E.'s Cooking** *($-$$; Mon to Thu 6am to 8:30pm, Fri and Sat 6am to 10pm, Sun 7am to 7pm; 0.4 km north of I-10, on LA 26, ☎ 824-3402)* proudly display their slogan: *"Viens nous voir où le manger est tout le temps bon"* (Come eat where the food is always good!) Even if you love fried food, so many restaurants serve so little else that you can end up getting tired of it. If this is your case, you'll find the cure for your palate's ills at Donn E.'s, which serves a good choice of excellent grilled and baked seafood dishes. The Sunday buffet *(11am to 2pm)*, whose southwest Louisiana-style barbecue (*barbèque*) packs them in, is not to be missed.

Landry's Restaurant *($-$$; Tue and Wed 6am to 2pm, Thu and Fri 6am to 2pm and 5pm to 9pm, Sat 5pm to 9pm; US 90, ☎ 824-4744)* serves up Cajun specialties.

The **Golden Dragon** *($-$$; LA 26, ☎ 824-4280)* offers Cantonese and Chinese-American specialties.

Basile

Though restaurants are scarce in this rice-producing area, all is not lost, thanks to the Frugé family's renowned **D.I.'s Cajun Restaurant** *($$; Tue to Sat 5pm to 10pm; 19 km north of Jennings on LA 97, ☎ 432-5141)*. Owner and Chef D.I. Frugé is recognized as a true master in the art of preparing crawfish. The atmosphere is as homey as can be, and even better on Tuesday, Wednesday and Saturday nights, when you can dance the two-step between bites. Mr. Frugé welcomes runners during the Tee Mamou/Iota Mardi Gras festivities (in fact, the restaurant is their headquarters). One of his brothers, Gérald, is a Mardi Gras captain, and another, Rooney, is a representative for Acadia Parish, and escorts the merrymakers as they make their rounds.

Lake Arthur

🦐 Make sure to stop by the **Lake Sausage House** *($; Mon to Wed 9:30am to 2pm, Thu and Sat 9:30am to 9:30pm; 108 Arthur Ave., ☎ 774-3703)*, which serves sausages made on the premises, daily specials, seafood, steak and other grilled fare.

Fans of regional cuisine who don't have much time to eat or simply want to avoid the traditional restaurant routine will be glad to discover that most supermarkets in Lake Arthur have well-stocked deli counters. Breakfast is served from 11am to 2pm at the **Market Basket** *($; every day; LA 26, north of town, ☎ 774-3467)*.

🦐 Those nostalgic about the not-so-distant past will be thrilled by the 11 different flavours of milk shakes and the generously topped burgers at **Pappy's Drive Inn** *($; Mon to Sat 5:30am to 9pm, Sun 8:30am to 9pm; 323 Calcasieu St., ☎ 774-3334)*. The menu also includes a seafood platter, catfish etouffee, crab and all sorts of other Louisiana-style fast foods. You'll never wind up with a big bill here.

🦐 It would hard to miss **Nott's Corner** *($-$$; Sat to Thu 7am to 9pm, Fri to Sun 7am to 9:30pm; 639 Arthur Ave., ☎ 774-2500)*, since it has a giant crawfish as its sign. Among the house specialties the bisque, the crawfish court-bouillon, the fried shrimp, the oysters, the catfish, the frog's legs and the stuffed crab are particularly tasty.

Welsh

The **Cash & Carry** *($; US 90, ☎ 734-2126)* supermarket has a prepared-food and deli counter.

Cajun Tales *($$; Mon to Sun 7am to 10pm; 501 N. Adams, ☎ 734-4772)* serve house specialties, mainly seafood dishes and grilled fare, including good steaks. It is also known for its copious buffets.

Lacassine

If you take US 90 for 19 kilometres east of Lake Charles, you'll pass through this little village, which owes its popularity to its wildlife sanctuary (Lacassine National Wildlife Refuge). Here, you'll find **Restaurant Chez Pierre** *($$; ☎ 588-4507)*, another place that specializes in seafood.

Hayes

Harris Seafood *($$; Wed to Sat 11am to 11pm, Sun 5pm to 10pm; LA 14 West, ☎ 622-3582)* serves up fish and seafood prepared in a variety of ways: on the grill, fried, in sauce or fritters.

Lake Charles

🦐 **Smokey Joe's Bar-B-Que** *($; Mon to Sun 10am to 8pm; 406 W. McNeese St., ☎ 478-3352)* serves up barbecued fare in simple style outside on picnic tables. Take-out orders are accepted as well.

The **Acadian Delight/Barbeque Geyen** *($; 2007 Moeling St.)* is a popular restaurant that serves homestyle Creole cooking. House specialties: grill; bread and pastries from the bakery.

Hackett's Cajun Kitchen *($; Mon to Fri 7:30am to 6pm, Sat 7:30am to 3pm; 5614 Hwy. 14, ☎ 474-3731)* offers homestyle cooking, with boudin and seafood as the house specialties.

🦀 **Miller's Café** *($; Mon to Fri 7am to 8pm and Sat 7am to 7pm; 138 Louisiana Ave., one street north of I-10, ☎ 433-9184)* is very popular with local African-Americans. Homestyle Creole cuisine.

🦀 The **Crab Palace** *($-$$; Wed to Sat 10:30am to 9pm; 2218 Enterprise Blvd., ☎ 433-4660)*, as you might already have guessed, specializes in crab prepared in a variety of ways.

The **Picadilly Cafeterias** *($-$$; Mon to Fri 11am to 8:30pm, Prien Lake Mall, 316 W. Prien Lake Dr., ☎ 477-7010; Mon to Fri 11am to 8:30pm, Sat and Sun 7am to 10am, 3539 Ryan St., ☎ 477-8695)*, located near Highway 1-210, serve regional cuisine.

Pat's of Henderson *($$-$$$; Mon to Thu 11am to 10pm, Fri and Sat 11am to 10:30pm; 1500 Siebarth Dr., ☎ 439-6618)* is a family restaurant offering seafood specialties.

According to the magazine *Louisiana Life*, the **Café Margaux** *($$-$$$; Mon to Fri 11am to 2pm and 6pm to 10pm, Sat 6pm to 10pm; 765 E. Pines Bayou Rd., ☎ 433-2902)* is the best French and Continental restaurant in the state.

Abbeville

The shrimp and oysters from the Gulf of Mexico, fished off the shores of Louisiana, are renowned. In New Orleans, the uncontested po-boy capital, oyster po-boys are sold all over the place (the oysters are breaded, fried and seasoned with hot sauce, then served on French bread). Poor children used to feast on these inexpensive sandwiches, hence their name. Though New Orleans is the gastronomic mecca of the United States, the best po-boys are not found in the French Quarter. Supposedly, Chez Dupuy, on Quai des Français Street, in Abbeville, makes the best po-boys in Cajun country.

It is amazing that such a small town has so many good restaurants. Those listed below are not only popular with locals, but also with the many gourmets and gourmands who come here from all over Louisiana and even from the neighbouring states. In short, where food is concerned, Abbeville's reputation is on a par with New Orleans'.

Its breakfasts, traditional Cajun cuisine, delicious shrimp po-boys and old-fashioned hamburgers have made **Park Restaurant** *($; Mon to Sat 5am to 8:30; 204 Park Ave., ☎ 893-9957)* a favourite with Abbeville residents.

Bertrand's Charity Street *($; 24 hours a day; downtown, east of the Courthouse; 400 Charity St., ☎ 898-9008)*, owned by the affable Robert Bertrand, serves regional cuisine. The breakfast menu contains a hidden treasure: a crawfish étouffée omelette.

Mexican food is very popular in Louisiana, and **El Camino** *($-$$; 124 Concord St., ☎ 898-2710)* serves a variety strongly influenced by Cajun country cuisine.

🦪 Succulent oysters from the Gulf of Mexico can be savoured at two excellent Abbeville restaurants, which attract patrons from all over Louisiana and even beyond. The older of the two, **Dupuy** *($-$$; Mon to Sat 11am to 9pm; 108 S. Main St., on the right after the bridge over Bayou Vermilion, ☎ 893-2336)* opened in 1887. It is run by a descendant of founder Joseph Dupuy, who was the first person to rent sites on the Gulf for his own oyster supply; today, the family continues that tradition. The welcome is warm, the atmosphere, extremely congenial and the service, characterized by Cajun friendliness. As oyster is the house specialty, it is best to choose a dish featuring these tasty mollusks: fried oysters, oysters au gratin, gumbo, po-boys, etc. It is worth coming here just to see the oyster shuckers; many employees of Dupuy's have won competitions in that department. Honouring the custom that oysters must not be eaten during those months with no "R" in their name, the restaurant is closed from May to August. Its reopening always coincides with the new moon in August.

The other oyster-lover's paradise is **Black's Oyster Bar** *($-$$; Tue to Thu 10am to 9:30pm, Fri and Sat 10am to 10pm, closed May to Aug; 319 Père Megret St., ☎ 893-4266)*, which hasn't been around for as long as Dupuy's. It was originally modelled after the famous oyster bars in New Orleans. As at Dupuy's, you have to wait in line or sit patiently on the bench installed right on the sidewalk in order to enter this

august gastronomic shrine, especially on weekends. Riding the wave of its success, Black's has purchased the former hardware store next door in order to expand its dining room.

🦪 The newest establishment on Abbeville's fine-dining scene is **Shucks! The Louisiana Seafood House** *($-$$; Mon to Thu 11am to 9pm, Fri and Sat 11am to 10pm; 701 W. Port St., ☎ 898-3311)*, which is giving Dupuy's and Black's a serious run for their money in terms of both the quality of its food and its reasonable prices. For example, a half-dozen oysters and fried shrimp goes for $9.25; a dozen oysters on the half-shell for $4. The restaurant is becoming more and more popular with residents of Abbeville and the surrounding area.

Crawfish-lovers can pamper their palates at **Richard's Seafood Patio** *($$; Nov to Jun, Mon to Sun 5pm to 10:30pm; by LA 355 S., follow the Bayou Vermilion for 4 km; 1516 S. Henry St., ☎ 893-1693)*. The atmosphere is typical of a country restaurant, homey and as unpretentious as can be, the way locals like it.

Nunez

Hébert's Steak House *($$-$$$; Tue to Sat 5pm; LA 14, ☎ 643-2933)*. Between Abbeville and Kaplan, there is a little town called Nunez, which doesn't make it onto every map. However, the name "Goulou" (the former owner, Mr. Hébert's, nickname) is well-known to gourmets, and especially steak-lovers. This place is extremely popular with local carnivores; Texans even flock here for Janelle and Gérald Le Maire's comfort food. The

WESTERN ACADIANA

menu is pretty straighforward: seafood gumbo, crab salad, oyster po-boys, crab in its shell, mussels étouffée, rib steak, steak and shrimp, grilled partridge, etc. On weekends, there is dancing at the bar next door.

Kaplan

 Suire's Grocery and Restaurant *($; Mon to Thu 7am to 7pm, Fri and Sat 7am to 8:30pm; 4.8 km south of Kaplan by LA 35 South, ☎ 643-8911)* is a friendly little place on the road to the Rockefeller Wildlife Refuge. Suire's is so popular that soldiers on manoeuvres sometimes land their helicopters here to eat. The menu includes traditional gumbo, fried alligator, turtle in spicy sauce, crawfish *pistolettes*, catfish, po-boys, steak and fries and Cajun boudin.

The **Homestead** *($; Mon to Fri and Sun 6am to 9pm, Sat 6am to 10am and 4pm to 10pm; 303 Cushing Ave., at 5th St., ☎ 643-6660)* is a popular café and local hangout, where people get together over good, freshly ground coffee and mouthwatering biscuits made in the traditional Southern manner. The food, as copious as it is delicious, consists of local specialties.

Erath

Perate's Seafood Patio *($-$$; Wed to Sun from 5pm on; LA 14, ☎ 937-5037)* might not make it on a list of gourmet restaurants – its menu, made up of fresh seafood dishes (crab, shrimp, crawfish), is somewhat dull – but as far as Cajun dancing is concerned it is one of the best and most authentic places in the region.

Maurice

Soop's à Maurice *($-$$; Mon to Thu 9am to 8pm; US 167, ☎ 893-2462)* serves traditional cuisine.

ENTERTAINMENT

Basile

At first glance, the little town of Basile looks very desolate. This is misleading, however; as soon as you look beyond this apparent tranquillity, you'll discover that Basile has produced several prominent Cajun musicians. The best-known of these, Nathan Abshire and the Balfa brothers, used to thrill audiences right here in Basile. On US 190 (16 km west of Eunice), at the north intersection of LA 97, you'll enter the town. You then have to cross the railroad tracks north of US 190 (on Lewis Street), just before the Easy Mart. You'll end up at Stagg Street, the main drag. The façades of the old buildings will make you feel like you're in the Far West.

The best-known place in town is the **Main Street Lounge** *(every day 9am to midnight; 670 Stagg St., at the corner of Lewis, ☎ 432-6697)*, a veritable local institution owned by Juanita Fontenot. In this old dance hall, the heirs of the great masters of Cajun music continue to inspire new generations to kick up their heels. After the harvests and throughout winter, when the farm workers who are also musicians aren't labouring in the rice paddies or the bean fields, they come here to jam *(free admission; Mon to Thu 3pm to 1am, Fri and Sat 3pm to*

2am, Sun 3pm to 1am; dancing Saturday at 7pm, cover charge).

If you ask Jennings residents which is the best place to go to dance to live Cajun music, they are sure to tell you, "D.I.'s!". And the reason locals hang out at **D.I.'s** ★★ *(Wed, Fri and Sat eve, from 8pm on; 19 km north of Jennings on LA 97)* is that the best-known bands in the region, like Nonc Allie Young's group, play here. At the restaurant, the Frugé family not only serve excellent local cuisine but also host evenings of music that are always memorable and keep fans coming back for more.

Lake Arthur

The VFW (Veterans of Foreign Wars) asociation has a centre in almost every village in southern Louisiana. When the veterans aren't playing bingo, they can be found two-stepping or waltzing away to the sounds of a local Cajun band. At the Lake Arthur **VFW Center** *($2; take N. 3rd St. and drive 1.5 km toward the cypress grove; the Center will be on your right)*, as everywhere else, the dances start at 8pm on Saturday night and draw crowds of local Cajuns.

Lake Charles

There are two boats here that offer cruises for gambling buffs. The first, the *Players (Mon to Thu and Sun $2, Sat $5;* ☎ *437-1500 or 1-800-ASK-MERV within the U.S.)*, takes passengers out on Lake Charles six times a day. The second, the *Star Casino*, is also a hotel and restaurant and offers seven cruises a day *(24*

hours a day; I-10, Exit 29 or 30 A, ☎ 1-800-977-PLAY within the U.S.)

The petrochemical industry has attracted a lot of Cajuns to the Lake Charles area, along with their traditional music and dances, which come in all different forms nowadays. At Lake Charles, the **Cajun French Music Association (CFMA)** remains one of the most active groups on that score. The **Grand Ole Opry** *(Sat from 8pm on; 2130 Country Club Rd.,* ☎ *477-9176)* of Cajun music is broadcast by the VFW Center's radio station. The Center is located on the south side of town, where University Drive merges into Country Club Road.

Vinton

What distinguishes the **Delta Downs racecourse** *($1.50; free parking; Thu to Sat 6:30pm, Sun 5:15pm; I-10, Exit 4 North, 5 km on LA 109, then right on LA 3060 for 1.5 km;* ☎ *433-3206 or 1-800-589-7441 within the U.S.)* is that it is located in a positively bucolic setting. Bets may be placed at the racecourse or at an off-track betting station.

Horses aren't the only thing people bet on in southwest Louisiana; unfortunately, cock-fighting, cruel though it may be, is also popular. One of the biggest gladiator arenas is the **Circle Club Cockpit**, located on the Texas border. These degrading spectacles, which we can only denounce, take place from October to August. Unless you are unmoved by cruelty to animals, steer clear of these events!

WESTERN ACADIANA

Kaplan

The bars in Kaplan, like those of all towns in Vermilion Parish, are veritable socio-cultural centres. At Paul and Virley Duhon's **L'Il Tavern** ★★ *(Mon to Thu 10am to 2am, Fri to Sun 10am to 4am; 300 N. Cushing St., next to the post office,* ☎ *643-9810)*, visitors will find a friendly crowd proud of their Cajun roots. For a taste of Cajun culture, there is nothing like mingling with this big gang. There is a juke box with old Cajun tunes, and every two weeks, on Fridays, Cajun bands play here. Free supper on Wednesday nights; on the menu: hot sauce, chicken fricassee, gumbo, etc. Gourmets won't want to miss the traditional butcher on Sunday morning or the crawfish boil on Friday night.

Erath

At **Perate's Seafood Patio** *(LA 14)*, local Cajun bands get folks two-stepping and waltzing. Over the decades, the wooden floor of this old building has received thousands of cheerful kicks. The atmosphere at Perate's is very convivial, and it is easy to make friends with the locals.

Maurice

It's not complicated: there's only one traffic light in Maurice, and the **City Bar** *(every day 8am to 2am; 19 km south of Lafayette, on US 167,* ☎ *893-1968)* is right near it. Located on the east side of the highway, this bar has been around for 60 years and has been the favourite local watering hole throughout its existence. Its patrons are

from all walks of life: farmers, businessmen, politicians, students, workers, etc. On Saturday morning, people come here to play *bourrée*, a traditional card game. The owner, Mr. Trahan, enjoys chatting with visitors. Free supper on Thursday nights.

Calendar of Events

January

The **Louisiana Fur and Wildlife Festival** ★★ is held each January in Cameron. A tribute to the hunting industry featuring all sorts of competitions: best trap, best hunting dog, nutria- and muskrat-skinning, duck- and goose-calls, etc.

February

Iota Mardi Gras see description in "Exploring" section, p 307.

The little community of Grand Marais, located between Jennings and Lake Arthur, also has a **Mardi Gras festival** ★. To find out more about the *Coureurs du Mardi Gras* event, call the tourist office *(☎ 821-5521 or 1-800-264-5521 within the U.S.)*.

The **Elton Mardi Gras Run** ★ *(☎ 584-2218, ask for David Bertrand)* is held on the Koasatis reservation, five kilometres north of town. The revellers set up a base camp for the Mardi Gras festivities. On Fat Tuesday itself, the participants set out to the neighbouring areas on horseback, and at each stop they rouse everyone to sing, dance and make generous contributions to the traditional kitty.

Throughout the United States, people pay tribute to Reverend Martin Luther King, Jr. in February. The **Black Heritage Festival of Louisiana** ★★ *(Feb; Lake Charles,* ☎ *478-2127)* features African-American artists from church choirs, as well as gospel and jazz concerts.

Southwest Louisiana District Livestock Show and Rodeo ★ *(1st week of Feb; Lake Charles,* ☎ *477-2827).*

Local women organize the **Krewe des Femmes**, one of the most popular parts of the **Kaplan Mardi Gras Festival** *(Main St., Kaplan,* ☎ *643-2440).*

April

The **Cajun Food and Fun Festival** ★ is held in Welsh on the last weekend in April. As you might have concluded, there are lots of food and lots of laughs to be had at this event.

The **Louisiana Railroad Days Festival** *(De Quincy,* ☎ *786-8211),* an agricultural fair, is held on the second weekend of April.

The **Marsh Island, Forked Island and Pecan Island Festival** *(☎ 643-2298).* These sandbanks aren't really islands. They were created thousands of years ago by the toing and froing of the waves in the Gulf of Mexico. Still, due to the relatively flat topography of this region, these mounds of sand were erroneously labelled islands.

The **Festival des 'Cadiens** *(Recreation Centre, Kaplan,* ☎ *643-2190)* is aimed at anyone interested in partying to the music and songs of local Cajun bands.

May

Contraband Days ★ *(first two weeks of May; Lake Charles,* ☎ *436-9588 or 1-800-456-SWLA within the U.S.).* Lake Charles is the only town in Louisiana that celebrates (elaborately) the memory of the legendary pirate Jean Lafitte. All along the Louisiana coast people say that the buccaneer buried his treasures in various spots, especially in the swamps. The festivities include an assortment of events: concerts, parades, boat races, regattas, etc.

The **Louisiana Cajun Country Music Festival** ★ *(D. White House Festival Grounds, Kaplan,* ☎ *643-7456)* is another of the many music festivals held all over Louisiana.

July

On July 4, **Independence Day** in the United Sates, a big fête is held in the shade of Lake Arthur's century-old oak trees *(☎ 774-2211).*

Independence Day *(free admission; downtown parade at 9am,* ☎ *734-3330),* July 4, has been celebrated with great enthusiasm in Welsh for over 100 years. The festivities include horseshoe competitions, baseball, bingo, watermelon contests and pastries.

The **Cajun French Music and Food Festival** ★★★ *(3rd weekend of July, Sat 9am to midnight, Sun 10am to 5pm; Burton Coliseum, Lake Charles,* ☎ *478-2831, ask for Johnny Lacombe).* The experts are unanimous: this festival wins the prize for the best music and food in the region. Violin, accordion, waltz, two-step and jitterbug competitions. Sponsored by the Lake Charles chapter of the Cajun French Music Association (CFMA).

The **Southwest Louisiana Fishing Club Deep Sea Fishing Rodeo** *(July 2-4; Lake Charles)* involves deep-sea fishing competitions. Fish and seafood are displayed in a hall.

At the **Marshland Festival ★** *(last weekend in July; Burton Coliseum, Lake Charles, ☎ 762-3876)*, you can hear Cajun music, zydeco, country and swamp pop.

The **Cameron Fishing Rodeo ★** *(July 4; Grand Chenier)* is a deep-sea fishing tournament held in the bay and on the beach.

Like every other community in the country, rural and urban alike, Erath celebrates July 4, **Independence Day** *(☎ 937-6895 or 1-800-346-1958 within the U.S.)*, with a mass gathering; here, it is held downtown.

Bastille Day ★ *(Jul 14, at the Kaplan Recreation Center)*. Kaplan is the only town in Louisiana to celebrate the storming of the Bastille. The festivities take place on July 14, the French national holiday.

August

The **Blessing of the Fleet ★** takes place in Cameron in August. The event features a boat parade, music and food.

The **Festival de la Riviera 'Cadienne ★** *($1; Fri to Sun 10am to 11pm; Holly Beach, ☎ 569-2474)* is held on the second weekend in August. Rodeos, carousels, Cajun music and zydeco.

The **Festival de la Chevrette ★** *(2nd weekend in Aug, Festival Building, Delcambre, ☎ 685-2653)* is centred around the blessing of the fleet, a tradition that dates back nearly half a century here. The trawlers and shrimp boats are elaborately decorated and lit up for the event, making for an impressive spectacle (*Chevrette* is the Cajun word for shrimp.)

August 15 - Acadian National Holiday. Assumption Day is the Acadian national holiday all over the world and is marked by numerous events in most villages, towns and rural parts of Acadiana.

September

The **Frog Festival** *(3rd weekend in Aug, Rayne)* involves all sorts of unusual activities, ranging from frog-based cuisine to *ouaouaron* (frog) beauty contests.

The **Fenton Red Beans and Rice Festival** is held in September. Red beans and rice are a traditional accompaniment to many Cajun and Creole dishes and Fenton residents need no better excuse than that to throw a big shindig!

The **Calca Chew Food Festival**, another celebration of Cajun food and music, is held on the third weekend in September at the Burton Coliseum, on Gulf Road, near the airport. At the same time, there is an auction and a craft show featuring the work of local artisans.

The **Alligator Harvest Festival ★★** *(Sep; Grand Chenier)* features all sorts of alligator-centred activities: sales of alligator products, viewing of live alligators, tastings of alligator dishes, as well as boat races and music.

The **Duck Festival** *(Duck Festival Park, Gueydan,* ☎ *536-6780 or 1-800-346-1958 within the U.S.).*

The **Cajun Island Fête** *(Recreation Center, Kaplan,* ☎ *643-2400)* is another large-scale event showcasing the best Cajun bands and singers.

October

Given Crowley's nickname, the Louisiana Rice Capital, it is hardly surprising that the town hosts an **International Rice Festival** (1st or 2nd weekend in Oct; ☎ 788-0177). The festival's highlight is the fais do-do dance through the streets of town.

County fairs (parish fairs in Louisiana) are held throughout the United States. The **Jeff Davis Parish Fair** takes place on the first weekend of October at the Jennings Fairgrounds.

As farming is the main industry in the Jennings region, agricultural aviation services abound here. The twin-engined plane is still the aircraft of choice for spraying crops of rice and soybeans.

On the second weekend of October, there is an air show featuring about 50 fully restored twin-engined Stearman planes from World War II: the **Stearman Fly-In** *(at the Jennings airport, near the I-10, across from the Oil and Gas Park,* ☎ *824-5280).*

The **Lake Arthur Home Grown Music Fest & Craft Show** takes place on the second-to-last weekend in October. The Lake Arthur area is renowned for its Cajun musicians, such as the legendary Varice Conner and Hollywood and Nashville star Doug Kershaw.

The **Welsh Threshing Days** ★ start sometime in October, depending on when the rice is ready to the harvested. The rice is threshed the old way, using period equipment.

The **Louisiana Livestock Festival** ★★ *(downtown Abbeville)* includes live music, cooking events, livestock shows and a well-known rodeo.

During **Oktoberfest** *(Maltrait Memorial School, Kaplan,* ☎ *643-6472)*, beer flows freely and there is some serious partying in Kaplan.

November

At the **Omelette Festival** ★ *(Abbeville courthouse,* ☎ *893-2491)*, French chefs and Cajun cooks combine their talents to serve up big gastronomic meals. The highlight of the event is the preparation of a gigantic omelette containing several hundred eggs.

December

The **Lake Arthur Christmas Festival** *(2nd weekend of Dec;* ☎ *774-2211)* features a night-time shrimp boat "parade". The vessels are decorated for the occasion and twinkle with multicoloured lights.

The **Lumières du Village** *(Abbeville historic district,* ☎ *893-2491)* light up local houses throughout the holidays.

SHOPPING

Scott

The **Galerie d'Art Beau Cajun** *(Mon to Fri 10am to 5pm, Sat 10am to 4pm;*

1012 St. Mary St., ☎ 237-7104) is owned by artist Floyd Sonnier, known for his magnificent pen and ink drawings of rural Cajun scenes.

Fans of top-quality Cajun sausage and boudin swear by the **Boucherie Best Stop** *(Mon to Sat 6am to 8pm, Sun 6am to 6pm; I-10, Scott/Cankton Exit, then 1.5 km north on LA 93, ☎ 233-5805)*.

Rayne

The lovely **Rayne Antique Mall** *(9am to 5pm; 1st and 3rd weekends of the month; 411 E. Texas Ave., US 90 East, ☎ 334-2508 or 334-8416)* is owned by Peter Comeaux, one of the best antique dealers in the area. An excellent place to find souvenirs and unusual items from Louisiana.

In downtown Rayne, there is another antique shop, called **Antiques and Collectibles** *(113 Louisiana St., right near the railroad tracks, ☎ 334-2508 or 334-8416)*.

Crowley

The **Modern Music Center** *(Mon to Fri 8:30am to 5pm, Sat 8am to noon; downtown, 413 N. Parkerson Ave., ☎ 783-1601)* has the best selection of Cajun and zydeco recordings. Owned by Jay Miller, the place also has its own recording studio, used by many local singers and musicians.

The **Crowley Flea Market** *(9am to 5pm; 1st and 2nd weekends of the month; 210 E. 1st St., beside the railroad tracks, ☎ 783-3944)* sells everything, from unusual objects and collector's items to the bare necessities.

Iota

At **Bon Cajun Instruments** *(Hwy 1, P.O. Box 396, Iota, LA 70543, ☎ 779-2456)*, Larry Miller makes Cajun accordions (with diatonic scales), *"ti-fers"* (triangles) and spoons by hand. He can ship his instruments to you anywhere in the world.

Jennings

Reon's T.V. *(402 W. Plaquemine St., ☎ 824-3907)* has a good selection of Cajun and zydeco music.

Marcantel's *(203 W. Railroad Ave., ☎ 824-0445)*, which sells food for pets and farm animals, has a clothing section with Western hats, belts, boots, etc.

On Main Street, in Jennings, there are about a dozen shops selling various kinds of merchandise: crafts, cookbooks, pot-pourri, etc. **Jennings Antique Mall** is also located here *(1st and 3rd weekends of the month, Tue to Sat 10am to 5pm; 1019 N. Main St., ☎ 824-3360)*.

Lake Arthur

Lake Sausage *(Mon to Fri 7am to 6pm, Sat 7am to 4pm; LA 26, on the north side of town, behind the Exxon station, ☎ 774-3704)* sells home-made Cajun boudin, sausages and pork rinds.

Elton

The **Entreprises Bayou Indian** *(Mon to Sat 9am to 5pm; US 190, ☎ 584-2653)* sell highly prized Koasatis crafts. The craftsmanship of the pieces is meticulous, and many of the objects are unique (basketry, jewellery, dolls, leathergoods, etc.). The Koasatis' ancestral dances are shown on a giant screen.

Lake Charles

The **Galerie Melançon** *(Mon to Fri 9:30am to 5:30pm, Sat 10am to 3pm; 241 Place Sallier, ☎ 433-0766)* has a rich collection of paintings, sculptures, pottery, jewellery and countless other items.

The **Boutique Cottage** *(at the intersection of Hodges, Alamo and Common Streets)* sells magnificent antiques, patchwork quilts, stained glass, collectible dolls, handcrafted pottery and a lovely assortment of fine Cajun and Creole foodstuffs, as well as excellent blends of coffee.

Factory outlets can be found throughout the southern United States, mainly because there are so many textile factories here. The **VF Factory Outlet** *(Jan to May: Mon to Thu 9am to 7pm, Fri and Sat 9am to 9pm, Sun noon to 6pm; Jun to Dec: Mon to Sat 9am to 9pm, Sun noon to 6pm; I-10, Exit 43, 800 Factory Outlet Dr., suite 100, Iowa, ☎ 582-3568 or 1-800-772-8336 within the U.S.)*, located 13 kilometres east of Lake Charles, in Iowa, offers savings of up to 50% on jeans, shirts, shoes, sportswear and other kinds of clothing.

The owner of **Goldband Records** *(313 Church St., ☎ 439-8839)*, Eddie Shuler, is very well-known among collectors of Cajun and zydeco music. The store looks a bit rundown from the outside, but the disorder that prevails inside is sure to appeal to anyone who enjoys rummaging about. There are all sorts of finds to be made in this delightfully chaotic place, including a whole collection of old 45s.

Gueydan

As Louisiana is a hunter's paradise, craftsmen Mervis and Kendall Saltzman make duck and goose calls, which are sold at **Chien-Caille Duck & Goose Calls** *(LA 2, P.O. Box 187-A, Gueydan, LA 70542, ☎ 536-9852)*.

Handicrafts reflect the both the geographic environment and the customs of the people who make them. Cathy Broussard and her husband John Richard run a cultural centre on the banks of a bayou near Abbeville, where they make crafts for a living. A renowned jeweller, Cathy creates magnificent, delicate pieces of jewellery out of alligator teeth ("bayou ivory"), which she carves with beautiful results.

Johnny, for his part, is a master saddler – the best in all Louisiana. In his skilled hands, each piece of leather becomes a work of art. The Richards' original creations, each a little piece of Louisiana, make terrific gifts. Johnny also collects old saddles, some of the finest of which are more than a century old. Another curious sight – not for the faint of heart – is the alligator cemetery behind the Richards' home.

WESTERN ACADIANA

At **Vermilion Gator Farms** *(every day, from sunrise to sunset; 12906 Community Rd., Abbeville, LA 70510, ☎ 538-2168)*, the Sagrera brothers sell alligator meat and, for those who prefer the creatures' outsides to their insides, alligator clothing, accessories and crafts.

Louisiana Shell & Driftwood *(12702 Francis St., ☎ 893-4480 or 542-4702)* sells crafts made with shells and driftwood from the Louisiana coast.

Hébert's Meat Market *(Mon to Fri 7am to 6pm, Sat 7am to noon; Lafitte Rd., LA 338 N., ☎ 893-5688)*, opposite Cajun Downs, is one of the most popular butcher's shops in the Abbeville area. In addition to traditional boudin *blanc*, the store sells "red" boudin, made with pig's blood, a product hard to come by in Acadiana.

Maurice

Hébert's Specialty Meats *(Mon to Sat 7:30am to 6:30pm, Sun 6:30am to* noon; US 167, 19 km south of Lafayette, ☎ 893-5062)* is known for its wonderful way of preparing boneless fowl, and the dishes sold here are products of pure culinary artistry. There is no lack of inspiration here: boneless chicken stuffed with rice; pork, shrimp and crawfish dishes, and alligator cooked in all sorts of ways *(less than $10)*. Then, there is the famous "tur-duck-en", a boneless turkey stuffed with a layer of boneless duck, a layer of pork and a layer of boneless chicken. Then, to top it all off, a layer of cornbread stuffing is added. The tur-duck-en weighs eight kilograms when it is ready to go in the oven, where it is slowly roasted for a good five hours. Some 25 ravenous guests can feast on this hearty dish *($55)*. Everyone who tries this tasty concoction loves it. The butchers, Sammy and Widley Hébert, take pleasure in telling those who sample this positively unique gastronomic creation the various steps involved in making it.

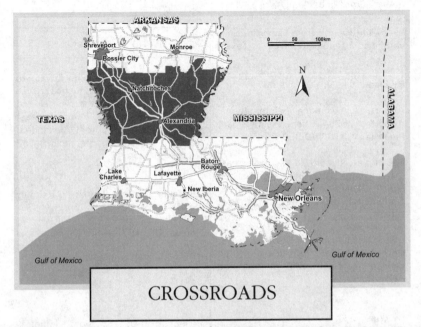

CROSSROADS

T he hills of the north slowly give way to plains as you head south and to bayous as you head east. Vast forests (**Kisatchie National Forest**) and lakes in the area make it a favourite of outdoor enthusiasts.

Alexandria is the main city in this central Louisiana area called Crossroads. In fact, whether it be from Baton Rouge, Lafayette, Lake Charles, Shreveport, Ruston or Monroe, from Texas or Mississippi, all roads lead to or pass through here.

 FINDING YOUR WAY AROUND

Alexandria - Pineville

Alexandria is located in the centre of Louisiana, almost an equal distance from many of the state's major cities. Taking I-49 from Alexandria, Lafayette is 140 kilometres to the south and Shreveport is 200 kilometres to the northwest. Other routes going through Alexandria include the US 165 which takes you to Lake Charles (150 km south) and Monroe (150 km north); US 167 takes you to Lafayette (140 km) and Ruston (155 km) and LA 1 goes to Baton Rouge (175 km) and Shreveport (200 km).

LA 28 crosses the state from east to west, from Natchez, Mississippi, through Alexandria (120 km) to

Leesville (80 km); from Leesville, LA 8 continues 30 kilometres west to Texas.

By Plane

Airport: Alexandria International Airport; 7625 Esler Field Road, Pineville, ☎ 318-449-3504

The airport, located 24 kilometres east of Alexandria, is serviced by American Eagle, Atlantic Southeast Airlines, Continental Express and Northwest Airlink.

Esler Limousine Service *($8; ☎ 318-487-2889)* provides a shuttle service between the airport and Alexandria.

By Bus

Greyhound/Trailways *(530 Jackson Street, Alexandria, ☎ 318-445-4524)* offers service linking Alexandria and towns on the national highways. The Alexandria-Shreveport trip costs $23, Alexandria-Lafayette $27.50, and the fare is about $40 to New Orleans.

By Car

Car Rental: Avis: ☎ 1-800-331-1212; Budget: ☎ 1-800-527-0700; National: ☎ 1-800-227-7368. All of these companies have rental offices at the airport.

By Public Transit

Atrans: ☎ 318-473-1273.

North of Alexandria

From Alexandria, to go northwest to Shreveport via Natchitoches, take either LA 1 or I-49 on the west side of the Red River, or US 71 on the east side. Heading north from Alexandria, US 165 leads to Monroe and US 167 leads to Ruston.

Kisatchie National Forest, Catahoula District

Routes US 167 and US 165 travel through the forest, which begins 15 kilometres north of Alexandria.

Pollock

Pollock is on US 165, eight kilometres into the forest.

Bentley - Williana - Winnfield

When leaving downtown Alexandria on Fulton Street, you will come to US 167 on the other side of the bridge; it is a divided highway until the intersection with US 71. Staying on US 167 North, you will come to Bentley (25 km), Williana (42 km) and Winnfield (75 km).

Colfax

To reach Colfax, 28 kilometres north of Alexandria, take either LA 1 or I-49, on the west side of the Red River, to Boyce, then LA 8 East; or take the US 71 North, on the east side of the river, to LA 123 and then go west for three kilometres.

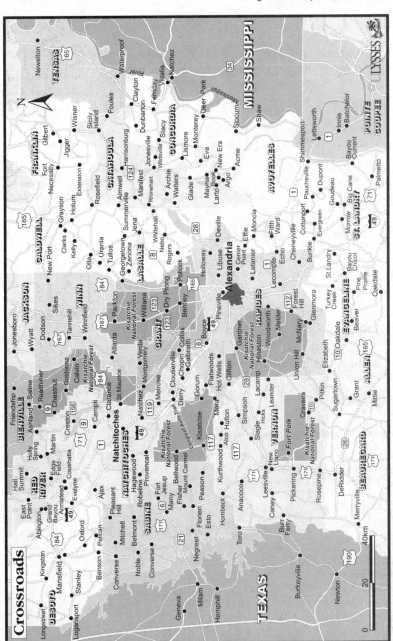

Derry

Both I-49 and LA 1 go to Derry, 48 kilometres from Alexandria.

Cloutierville

From Derry, take LA 1 South in the direction of Alexandria for 2 kilometres; then take LA 491 one and a half kilometres to Cloutierville.

Melrose - Natchez

Melrose is 10 kilometres north of Derry on LA 119. Continuing on LA 119 another 15 kilometres you will arrive at Natchez, which can also be reached by LA 1.

Natchitoches

Natchitoches, 95 kilometres north of Alexandria, can be reached by LA 1. You can also take I-49 to LA 6 and then go east.

Creston

Creston is 33 kilometres north of Natchitoches. From Natchitoches, take US 84 East to Clarence. From there take US 71 North for 13 kilometres and then LA 9 North for 11 kilometres.

Saline

Continuing on LA 9, Saline is 24 kilometres north of Creston.

Goldonna - Winnfield

From Creston, take LA 156 East for 15 kilometres. Goldonna is in Kisatchie National Forest, in Winn Parish. Winnfield is 28 kilometres further along the same road.

Hagewood - Robeline - Many

From the south exit of Natchitoches, take LA 6 West 12 kilometres to Hagewood, 22 kilometres to Robeline, 35 kilometres to Fort Jesup and 45 kilometres to Many.

Kisatchie National Forest, Kisatchie District

From Hagewood, LA 117 South goes through Kisatchie National Forest on the way to Leesville.

Longleaf Auto Trail (Forest Road 59)

This road crosses Kisatchie Forest from east to west. In the east it can be reached from Derry by taking LA 119 south to Bayou Pierre. In the west, the forest road intersects LA 117 16 kilometres south of Hagewood.

Kisatchie

From Hagewood, take the LA 117 South 37 kilometres. The same road continues to Leesville, 35 kilometres further south.

West of Alexandria

Hot Wells

Leave Alexandria on Rapides Avenue, which becomes LA 496, and travel 24 kilometres to Hot Wells. If you leave Alexandria on I-49, take the Boyce exit and then LA 1200 West for eight kilometres.

Kisatchie National Forest, Evangeline District - Gardner - Woodworth

To reach Gardner, leave Alexandria via Monroe Street, and then take LA 28 West, toward Leesville, 20 kilometres.

To reach Woodworth, leave Alexandria via Masonic Drive and take US 165 South 15 kilometres.

Leesville

From Alexandria, take Monroe Street or MacArthur Drive; then take LA 28 West 82 kilometres to Leesville, a good home base from which to tour the area.

Anacoco

Anacoco is 13 kilometres from Leesville on US 171 North.

Pickering

US 171 South takes you to Pickering, 12 kilometres from Leesville.

Kisatchie National Forest, Vernon District

To get here, either take LA 10 East from Pickering or LA 467 South from Leesville.

Fort Polk

From Pickering, travel east on LA 10 to LA 467; take LA 467 a few kilometres to Fort Polk.

Cravens

From Pickering, take LA 10 East 30 kilometres to Cravens.

De Ridder

De Ridder is 33 kilometres south of Leesville on US 171.

Merryville

Merryville is 27 kilometres west of De Ridder on US 190.

South of Alexandria

Lecompte

Leave Alexandria either on MacArthur Drive or Lee Street; then take US 71 South 20 kilometres to Lecompte, or take I-49 South to LA 112 and then take LA 112 East three kilometres to Lecompte.

CROSSROADS

Cheneyville

Cheneyville is 13 kilometres south of Lecompte, on US 71 or I-49.

Forest Hill

From Lecompte, take LA 112 west 15 kilometres to Forest Hill.

East of Alexandria

Whitehall - Jena

From Fulton Street in Alexandria, past the bridge, take US 167 to LA 28. Take LA 28 for 50 kilometres, then take US 84 west nine kilometres to Whitehall or 20 kilometres to Jena.

Jonesville

From Jena, take US 84 east 34 kilometres to Jonesville.

Harrisonburg

From Jonesville, take LA 124 North 16 kilometres to Harrisonburg.

Ferriday

From Jonesville, take US 84 East 28 kilometres to Ferriday.

Waterproof

Waterproof is 25 kilometres north of Ferriday on US 65.

Vidalia

Vidalia is 17 kilometres east of Ferriday on US 84, right on the Mississippi border.

PRACTICAL
INFORMATION

Safety and Emergencies

Police, fire department, ambulance:
☎ 911

Hospital:

St. Frances Cabrini Hospital, 3330 Masonic Drive, Alexandria, LA 71301, ☎ 318-487-1122.

Police:

Rapides Parish Sheriff's Department, P.O. Box 1510, Alexandria, LA 71309, ☎ 318-473-6700.

Tourist Information

Alexandria

Alexandria-Pineville Area Convention & Visitors Bureau: Mon to Fri 8am to 5pm, Sat 9am to 5pm; 201 Johnston St., suite 405, Alexandria, LA 71306, ☎ 318-443-7049 or 1-800-742-7049 from North America, ≈ 318-443-1617.

North of Alexandria

Natchitoches Parish Tourist Commission: Mon to Sat 9am to 5pm, Sun 10am to 3pm; 781 Front St.,

Natchitoches; mailing address: P.O. Box 411, Natchitoches, LA 71458; ☎ 318-352-8072 or 1-800-259-1714 from the U.S.

Winnfield Chamber of Commerce: 107 Court St., Winnfield, LA 71483, ☎ 318-628-4461.

East of Alexandria

Catahoula Tourist Commission: 106 Jasmine St., Jonesville, ☎ 318-339-8498.

Vidalia Tourist Commission: ☎ 318-336-5206.

West of Alexandria

Vernon Parish Tourist & Recreation Commission: Mon to Fri 8am to noon and 1pm to 4:30pm; US 171 North, Leesville; mailing address: P.O. Box 1228, US 171 N., Leesville, LA 71496-1228; ☎ 318-238-0349 or 238-0783.

Beauregard Parish Tourist Commission: Mon to Thu 9am to 4pm, Fri 10am to 5pm; 624 High School Dr., De Ridder; Mailing Address: P.O. Box 1174, De Ridder, LA 70634; ☎ 318-463-5534.

Guide Services

Alexandria

Verdis Dowdy Tour Services: for groups of 20 or more people; 810 Tanglewood, Alexandria, LA 71303, ☎ 318-442-7852.

Natchitoches

Ducournau Square Receptive Services: welcomes groups of visitors; 8 Ducournau Square, Natchitoches, LA 71457, Ms. Melissa Cloutier, ☎ 318-352-5242.

Tours by Jan: For groups or individuals; rates by the hour or day; by reservation; 434 2nd Street, Natchitoches, ☎ 318-352-2324.

Unique Tours of Historic Natchitoches: for groups; Route 2; P.O. Box 346-C, Natchitoches, LA 71457; ☎ 318-357-8698 or 352-4192.

Once Upon a Time Tours: Legendary tales are told and life during the Colonial period is described; Natchitoches; Ms. Vicki Martin, ☎ 318-352-9215.

 EXPLORING

Alexandria - Pineville ★

Alexandria was founded on the banks of the Red River by plantation owners in the 19th century and has grown into a city of 50,000 residents. In 1837 the first railway west of the Mississippi was built here, and, since then, the city has become a hub of train traffic. Alexandria is also the county seat of Rapides Parish. The Red River runs through a magnificent park, and a number of bayous snake through the area: Rapides, Robert, Hynson, Sandy, etc. Many plantations and antebellum houses, some of which have been converted into bed and breakfasts, are located on the banks of these waterways. Pineville is across the river

CROSSROADS

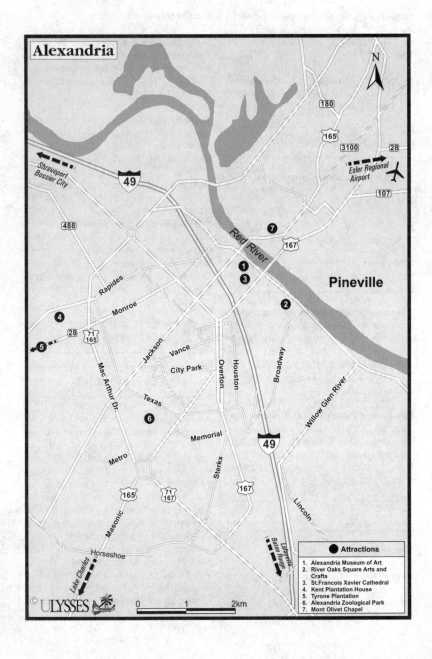

from Alexandria. These twin towns are home to many historical sites that recall the days of French explorers, the events of the Civil War, and the locations of old native villages. Attractions of interest include the cathedral, the Museum of Art, Hotel Bentley, local arts & crafts, Mont Olivet Chapel, and, of course, the natural beauty of the many surrounding lakes and rivers.

Alexandria Museum of Art ★★ (1) *(adults $1, seniors 75¢, children 50¢; Tue to Fri 9am to 5pm, Sat 10am to 4pm; 933 Main St., Alexandria, ☎ 318-443-3458)* regularly presents exhibitions of works by contemporary Louisiana artists and also has a permanent collection of works from the 19th and 20th centuries. The visit takes one hour.

River Oaks Square Arts & Crafts ★ (2) *(free admission; Tue to Sat 10am to 4pm; 1330 Main St., Alexandria, ☎ 318-473-2670)*. An attractive Queen-Anne house from 1899 has been transformed into a centre for artists and artisans.

St. Francois Xavier Cathedral ★ (3) *(Mon to Fri 9am to 4pm and Sat and Sun during church services; 626 4th St., Alexandria, ☎ 318-445-1451)* was built in 1895. This Gothic church has dazzling stained-glass windows.

Kent Plantation House ★★ (4) *(adults $4, seniors $3, children 6-12 $2; Mon to Sat 9am to 4pm, Sun 1pm to 4pm; cooking demonstrations Oct to Apr, Wed 9am to 2pm; 3601 Bayou-des-Rapides Road, Alexandria, ☎ 318-487-5998)* is the oldest building in central Louisiana (1796). It houses impressive Empire and Sheraton furniture, precious documents and decorative objects. The main building is surrounded by outbuildings (former slave quarters, kitchen and dairy) and attractive gardens on a property that extends over two hectares. The duration of the visit is one hour.

At the **Tyrone Plantation ★ (5)** *(adults $4, seniors $3, Tue to Sun 10am to 5pm; 6576 Bayou des Rapides Road, 8 km from Alexandria on LA 496 in the direction of Hot Wells, ☎ 318-442-8528)* the neoclassical-style cottage built in 1843 has been raised to protect it from high water levels.

Alexandria Zoological Park (6) *(adults $2, children 5-12 $1, children under 5 and seniors free; every day 9am to 5pm; Bringhurst Park, past Masonic Dr., Alexandria, ☎ 318-473-1385)* is home to mammals, birds, reptiles and some endangered species. Set aside about two hours for the visit.

Mont Olivet Chapel (7) *(Main St., Pineville)*, built in 1850, was used as a headquarters for Union soldiers during the Civil War.

Alexandria National Cemetery *(free admission; every day 8am to 5pm; 209 Shamrock St. East, Pineville, ☎ 318-473-7588)* was classified as a national military cemetery after the Spanish-American War and the American Civil War.

Rapides Cemetery *(free admission; every day; at the corner of Main and David Sts., Pineville, ☎ 318-443-7049)* is one of the oldest cemeteries in Louisiana. There are graves of French and Spanish pioneers from the 18th and 19th centuries here along with beautiful monuments.

CROSSROADS

North of Alexandria

Colfax ★

Colfax, a small harbour village on the Red River, is the county seat of Grant Parish which was created in 1869 during the Reconstruction period following the Civil War. The parish was named in honour of American President Ulysses S. Grant and includes a large part of Kisatchie National Forest.

Hotel Le Sage ★ was the favourite inn of captains during the steamship era. This neoclassical building continues to welcome travellers.

The **McNeely House**, built in 1883, is another lovely example of neoclassical architecture.

Cloutierville - Melrose - Natchez

One of the most interesting driving tours in the region is on the road along the Cane River. During French colonial times, the area was called "Cane Island Valley" ("Vallée de l'île-aux-Cannes"). This 55-kilometer-long "island", which is 10 kilometers across at its widest point, reaches from Cloutierville north to Natchitoches. During the era of New France, noble families lived here and left prestigious reminders of their presence: **Magnolia**, **Melrose**, **Oakland**, **Beau Fort**, **Cherokee** and **Oak Lawn** plantations, **Saint Augustine Cemetery** and **Kate Chopin Home**. All these places can be reached from LA 1.

Bayou Folk Museum/Kate Chopin Home ★★ *(adults $3, disabled $2.50, children 13-18 $2, 6-12 $1 ; every day noon to 4pm; Cloutierville, ☎ 318-379-2736 or 1-800-909-7907 from the U.S.)* is a site dedicated to the famous feminist writer from 19th-century Louisiana, Kate Chopin. At the museum, antique ploughing equipment and replicas of an old ironwork shop and of the old country medical office are reminders of the history of Cane River. The visit takes about one an a half hours.

Magnolia Plantation ★★ *(adults $5, students $4, children 8 to 11 $2; every day 1pm to 4pm; Natchez, ☎ 318-379-2221)* has a lovely main house that was first built in 1830 on land that had been granted to Jean Baptiste Le Comte 80 years earlier. The building was burned down during the Civil War and was reconstructed on the same foundation with the original walls in 1896. It was refurnished in Empire style and has been open to the public ever since. The current owners, descendants of Jean Baptiste Le Comte (the plantation has always stayed in the family), still cultivate cotton.

Melrose Plantation ★★ *(adults $4, students $2, children $1; every day noon to 4pm; LA 119, Melrose, ☎ 318-379-0055 or 352-4411)* is the setting of the storybook tale of the life of Marie-Thérèse "Coin-Coin". She was born a slave on this property owned by Louis Juchereau de Saint-Denis, founder of Natchitoches. Marie had 14 children whose descendants still live along the Cane River. The plantation has three sections: Yucca, the original house built in 1796; the African house built in 1800, which is reminiscent of Congolese huts; and the large residence with bachelor apartments from 1833. Clementine Hunter, a Louisiana artist whose primitive paintings have become famous, also lived here.

Historic **Saint Augustine Catholic Cemetery** ★ *(LA 494, Melrose)* has beautiful monuments engraved with French inscriptions and cast iron crosses. The tombs reflect the Creole character of "Bresville Island".

Oakland Plantation *(LA 119, 9 km north of Melrose)* reveals a very attractive example of Creole architecture (1821). This was the first cotton plantation in Louisiana. Not open to the public.

Beau Fort Plantation ★ *(adults $4, adolescents $3, children $2; every day 1pm to 4pm; LA 119, Natchez, ☎ 318-352-9580 or 352-5340)*, whose "Luclora" house was built in 1830, has a row of century-old oaks. The elegant residence also has a magnificent garden and an impressive collection of objects related to local history.

Cherokee Plantation ★ *(LA 494, Natchez)* which has a cottage built on pillars to protect it from floods, was built in 1839 and is a registered historic landmark. A famous duel between Bossier and Galenni took place here.

Oak Lawn Plantation ★★ *(LA 494, 1 km north of Cherokee, Natchez)* has a plantation house the walls of which are built with cob, a mixture of Spanish moss and mud. The oak lane that leads to it is 200 metres long and ranks as the third longest in Louisiana. Not open to the public.

Natchitoches ★★★

Natchitoches is a city of 17,000 on the Cane River, founded in 1714 by Louis Juchereau de Saint-Denis. It was the first community in Louisiana settled by French colonists. It is called "New Orleans of the North" because there are still many residences dating back to the 18th and 19th centuries; approximately fifty of these are grouped together in a neighbourhood that is classified in its entirety as a National Historic Landmark. **Fort St. Jean Baptiste**, which was completely rebuilt, is evocative of the French regime, whereas the buildings and houses, with their wrought-iron balconies, are reminiscent of the era of great cotton plantations during which Natchitoches was a major port. There are lovely houses along Front and Jefferson Streets as well as some superb landscaping throughout the city. Also of interest are **Ducournau Square, Cloutier House** and **Roque House**.

Museum of Historic Natchitoches ★ *(adults $2, children $1; every day 9am to 5pm; 840 Washington St., ☎ 318-357-0070)* illustrates the history of the area with objects of Native American and French origin and articles from the Civil War. The visit takes about 35 minutes.

Steel Magnolias Tour ★ *(Natchitoches Parish Tourism Office, ☎ 318-352-8072 or 1-800-259-1714 from the U.S.).* The city of Natchitoches was popularized by the comedy film *Steel Magnolias*. You can visit the locations used for the film on foot or by car.

Cloutier Townhouse and Ducournau Square ★★ *(Front St., ☎ 318-352-5242 or 1-800-351-7666 from the U.S.).* The town house, dating back to 1837, has been restored and furnished in the style of that period. They organize tours and dinners for groups.

Prudhomme-Roquier House ★ *($3; 446 Jefferson St., ☎ 318-352-6723 or 352-4411)*, built in 1800, is made

CROSSROADS

entirely of Spanish moss and mud. The furniture dates back to the French regime. Group tours by appointment.

Tante Huppé House ★ *(adults $4, children $2; Tue to Sat 10am to noon, ☎ 318-352-5342 or 1-800-482-4276 from the U.S.)* was built in 1827 for Suzette Prudhomme, a young Creole woman who was engaged and ended up marrying three times. Suzette welcomed many visiting family members and became known as "Aunt Huppé". The house, with its 11 exterior doors and nine fireplaces, is now a bed and breakfast.

The **Caspiana Plantation Store** ★ *(Mon to Fri 8am to 5pm, Sat 8am to 1pm; 1300 Texas St., ☎ 318-352-7688)* is highly representative of the architectural style of 19th-century plantation stores. They now sell livestock feed in this old building.

Kaffie-Frederick's General Hardware Store ★★★ *(Mon to Fri 7am to 5pm, Sat 7am to 4pm; 758 Front Street, ☎ 318-352-2803)*. The slogan of the Kaffie-Frederick hardware store is "Anything, a bit of everything, any time". This house, built in 1863 with one-metre-thick walls, is definitely worth a visit for its old-time charm. In the good old days, steamships loaded up on cotton here and unloaded various other products, including coffins, in exchange. You can pick up curios and souvenirs typical of Louisiana here.

Lemée House *(Mon to Fri 10am to noon; 310 Jefferson St., ☎ 318-352-8072)* can be visited by appointment only.

Fort Saint-Jean-Baptiste ★★ *(adults $2, free for seniors and children under 12; every day 9am to 5pm;* 130 Moreau St., ☎ 318-357-3101)*, on the edge of the Cane River, is a replica of the original fort with commander's quarters, chapel, teepees, etc.

The Natchitoches National Aquarium and Fish Farm ★ *(free admission; every day 8am to 3pm; 615 LA 1 South, ☎ 318-352-5324)* houses fish and reptiles from the waters of Louisiana. The visit takes 45 minutes.

Cruises on Cane River *(every day 10am to 10pm; 612 Williams Avenue, ☎ 318-352-7093 or 352-2577)* offers cruises on the river, visits by streetcar to the historic district and plantation tours.

Winnfield ★

The hills in this area provide a contrast to the Louisiana flat lands. With close to 7,000 inhabitants, Winnfield, located at the edge of the forest, is the county seat of Winn Parish. Before the 1920s, rich plantation owners reigned supreme in the area. They created laws that were detrimental to small farmers and country people, who were motivated, out of frustration, to join forces in creating farming cooperatives and associations.

The Long family of famous politicians (brothers Earl and Huey, and Huey's son Russell) originates in Winnfield.

The Museum of Politics and Famous People of Louisiana *($2; Mon to Sat 10am to 5pm, Sun 2pm to 5pm; 499 Main St. East, ☎ 318-628-5928)* is a reminder that Winnfield is the birthplace of former state governor Huey Long. Considered a demagogue at the time, Long left his mark on both local and national politics. He is responsible for the construction of the Louisiana capital, Baton Rouge (see p 166), where he was assassinated in 1935.

The **Ruins of Plantation Saint-Maurice** *(US 84)* are what is left of the original house, built in 1840, which was destroyed by a fire. There are still some interesting vestiges to admire. Many illustrious visitors passed through here such as Robert E. Lee, commander of the Confederate Army, and Ulysses S. Grant, of the opposing camp.

The **Southern Colonial** *($2; every day 9am to 6pm; 801 Main St. East,* ☎ *318-628-6087)*, an attractive colonial house built at the beginning of the century, is now a bed and breakfast.

Saline ★

Saline is located north of Winn Parish. The exceptionally picturesque road that leads there cuts through beautiful, vast and wonderfully aromatic pine forests. The Saline River threads through this undulating terrain, cuts through Kisatchie National Forest and then flows into Lake Iatt.

Briarwood ★ (The Caroline Dorman Local Plant Reserve) *($5; Mar to May and Aug to Nov, Sat 9am to 5pm, Sun noon to 5pm; 3 km south of Saline,* ☎ *318-576-3379)* is a hilly, wooded area. Both botanists and horticulturalists are attracted to its 50-hectare natural garden. You can easily spend two hours here.

West of Alexandria

Leesville - Anacoco

Since US 171 runs along the whole west side of the state, including the Leesville-De Ridder area, it's called the "western corridor". Leesville is the county seat of Vernon Parish. Like its neighbouring areas, it benefits from nature's generosity. Immense pine forests, the **Toledo Bend Reservoir ★★** and **Vernon, Anacoco and Fullerton Lakes ★** make it a hunting and fishing paradise, and if you enjoy outdoor activities there are beautiful sandy beaches and places to swim and boat. But there's more... swamps and forests are rich in indigenous aquatic and terrestrial plants, including some that are carnivorous. Wildlife is equally abundant. Amateur botanists will discover dazzling orchids and ornithologists can spot species such as the unfortunately endangered red woodpecker.

The **Museum of West Louisiana ★** *(free admission; Tue to Sun 1pm to 5pm; 803 Third St. South, Leesville,* ☎ *318-239-0927)* has memorabilia from the railway and paper-mill era, prehistoric objects and various collections that all recall the history of western Louisiana and Vernon Parish.

Holly Grove Methodist Church *(US 171, 6 km south of Anacoco)* was built in 1834 and is the oldest Methodist church west of the Mississippi. It is still an active place of worship.

Fort Polk

Close to Leesville, Fort Polk is one of the most important military training centres in the United States. During the Second World War, this was an area of intense paramilitary activity on the part of the American army.

Fort Polk Military Museum ★★ *(free admission; Wed to Fri 10am to 2pm, Sat and Sun 9am to 4pm; 917 S. Carolina Ave., ☎ 318-531-7905 or 531-4840)*, whose collection includes the current military installation, illustrates the history of the manoeuvres that took place at Fort Polk during the Second World War.

De Ridder - Merryville

With Bundick and Longville Lakes, this is another area well suited to camping, hunting and fishing. Beauregard Parish, next to the Texas border, was founded by Scottish and Irish settlers who had come from North and South Carolina. It is named for Pierre-Gustave Toutant Beauregard, a Louisianian Creole who made it into the history books for ordering the attack on Fort Sumter in South Carolina, the shot that started the U.S. Civil War.

This area is bounded by the Sabine River, which flows into the Gulf of Mexico and marks the border between Louisiana and Texas. Being so close Texas affects the mentality of local residents who are more like Texans than like outgoing Louisianians.

There are a few interesting buildings and a historic district in town.

Beauregard Museum ★ *(free admission; Tue to Fri 1pm to 4pm; 120 S. Washington Street De Ridder, ☎ 318-463-8148)* is located in an old brick Kansas Southern train station with a tile roof. It houses a collection

of porcelain as well as furniture and various other objects related to the history of southwest Louisiana, particularly that of De Ridder and Beauregard Parish.

Prison and **Courthouse ★** *(free admission; Mon to Fri 8:30am to 4:30pm; 210 W. 1st St., De Ridder, ☎ 318-463-5534)*. These imposing buildings were built in 1915 and are linked by a tunnel. The courthouse is still active but the jail isn't (visits to prison cells by appointment). A statue pays tribute to Pierre-Gustave Toutant Beauregard, the man who ordered the first shots of the American Civil War, on April 12, 1862 at Fort Sumter, South Carolina.

Burk's Log Cabin and Museum ★ *(free admission, donations accepted; Thu, Sat and Sun 2pm to 4pm; Merryville, ☎ 318-463-2979 or 825-8026)*, a rustic cottage built in 1883, has become an interesting museum containing objects of the Natchitoches Indians from the 19th and early-20th centuries.

South of Alexandria

Cheneyville

Here the plains stretch as far as the eye can see. As with all the regions surrounding Alexandria, this area, crossed by the Bayou Boeuf, has enchanting antebellum cotton plantations; many are still operational, others have been transformed into bed and breakfasts. This area saw many bloody clashes throughout the Civil War.

Loyd Hall Plantation ★ *($5 adults, every day, 9am to 4pm; exit 61 from*

I-49, Lecompte, ☎ 318-776-5641 or 1-800-240-8135 from the U.S.), on a pre-war plantation, is next to an aromatic herb garden. As legend has it, during the Civil War, the owner was a spy for the Confederates and was hung here by his enemies. The house rents a few rooms (watch out for ghosts!) and they serve good breakfasts.

Lecompte School was built in 1924 by the best craftspeople of the time.

Trinity Episcopal Church ★ *(free admission; by appointment; 1024 Bayou Rd.,* ☎ *318-279-2470)* was built in 1860. It has preserved its original decor including the "Slave Gallery".

Walnut Grove Plantation House ★★ *($4; Tue only 1pm to 4pm; on the Bayou Boeuf,* ☎ *318-279-2203 or 279-2291)* is a two-story structure built entirely of brick in 1840; original gardens, paths and furniture. The outbuildings are also interesting to see: a **Cajun house** and the old **slave huts**. The visit takes 45 minutes.

Producer's Mutual Cotton Gin Company *(free admission; Mon to Wed and Fri 9am to 3pm; US 71,* ☎ *318-279-2145).* This factory is particularly fascinating to visit during harvest time *(Sep to Nov)* but is open for visits out of season too. Some visits are allowed at ginning time. The visit takes from 30 to 45 minutes.

East of Alexandria

Whitehall - Jena

Between Whitehall and Jena, is **Lake Catahoula ★**, an ideal spot for fishing and duck hunting. Jena is the county seat of La Salle Parish, named in honour of the French-Canadian explorer Robert Cavelier de La Salle, who was born in Rouen in 1643 and died in Texas in 1687. La Salle explored the Mississippi River and the territory, naming it Louisiana in honour of King Louis XIV.

Jonesville

This area has both forests and fields. Jonesville, in Catahoula Parish, is where, in 1542, the Spanish explorer Hernandez de Soto last did battle (commemorative plaque at the US 84 and LA 124 intersection).

An extremely rare phenomenon exists at the **Jonesville Riverfront Park ★** *(by LA 124)*: the meeting of four rivers. They are the Black, Tensas, Ouachita and Little Rivers.

King Tortoise Farm *(just north of Jonesville)* raises up to 50,000 tortoises per year. Visits available except in May and June (during egg-laying season).

Harrisonburg

Harrisonburg was bustling with activity during the days of steamships and also during the Civil War. Not surprising that all points of interest relate to one of these two periods.

The **Catahoula Parish Museum of Natural History** *(Mon to Fri 8am to 4pm; Courthouse,* ☎ *318-339-7898)* is overflowing with prehistoric Native American objects and memorabilia from the Civil War.

Sargeant House *(by appointment; Catahoula St.)* is an old residence that

CROSSROADS

served as an inn during the steamship days.

The façade of **Harrisonburg Methodist Church** *(LA 8)* is marked with Civil War bullet holes.

Harrisonburg Ridge ★, in Catahoula Parish, is a native burial site. In the language of the Tensa Indians, *cataoola* means "large lake with clear water".

Lake Catahoulais now part of La Salle Parish.

Fort Beauregard ★ *(north of Harrisonburg, on LA 124 North, ☎ 318-435-9238)* was the site of many Civil War battles. On the first weekend of November, they recreate the battle that took place here in August of 1863.

Fort Hill Park *(May 21 to Oct 21; next to Fort Beauregard, ☎ 318-744-5397)* has an 1860s-inspired reconstructed fort. You can camp, go for a hike on the trails or go swimming, hunting or fishing.

Ferriday

This town is a commercial crossroads of sorts for cotton and soya growers. Ferriday, in Concordia Parish, is the birthplace of country singer Mickey Gillie, TV evangelist Jimmy Swaggart and his cousin, Jerry Lee Lewis, the king of rock and roll.

Lisburn Plantation *(LA 3196, exit midway between Ferriday and Vidalia)*, whose house was built in 1852 and is an attractive example of neoclassical architecture, is unfortunately not open to visitors.

Frogmore Plantation *(from the US 84 West)* was established in 1843. This cotton plantation is still active. There is also a native burial ground here.

Waterproof ★

St. John Lake and Concordia Lake draw quite a few tourists to Waterproof; camping and fishing are among the activities practised here.

Pecan Plantation and Gift Company *(free admission; Aug to Dec, Mon to Sat 8am to 5pm; postal address: HC 62, P.O. Box 139, Waterproof, LA 71375; ☎ 318-749-5421 or 1-800-47-PECAN from the U.S.)* allows visitors the opportunity to visit the kitchens where their famous pralines and other pecan delicacies are prepared. Length of the visit: kitchen 15 minutes, orchards and hickory trees, one hour.

Also see the **Alabama (1854)** and **Canebrake (1812) plantation houses**.

Vidalia ★

Concordia Parish borders the state of Mississippi. It's a forested area with abundant lakes and rivers; a real paradise for hunters and fishers.

Vidalia, a small town with 5,000 inhabitants, was the site of a duel whose survivor, James Bowie, had to escape to Texas. At the time of the duel, Bowie or his brother Rezin invented the "Bowie knife", made to effectively disembowel someone with its 24-centimetre blade, which is still manufactured today. Bowie is remembered by Americans for a better reason, however. He became a member of the movement to liberate Texas from Mexico and distinguished himself on a number of occasions by his courage and audacity right up to his death in 1836, on the battlefield at the famous Alamo. A number of popular songs tell the story of his exploits.

Every year, Vidalia organizes a **James Bowie Festival**. Contact the **Vidalia Tourism Office** (☎ 318-336-5206), for information about dates. You can also contact them regarding the **Black Heritage Festival**.

 PARKS

Kisatchie National Forest

The only national forest in Louisiana, Kisatchie has always been a favourite with nature enthusiasts. It is open to the public and almost all its sectors are accessible year round. Its well-maintained facilities are very popular, but there are also areas where you can take full advantage of the calm and beauty of nature. Kisatchie National Forest has nature centres, docks for fishing or water sports, beaches, picnic grounds, picturesque roads, horseback riding trails and marked hiking trails. There are also quite a few camp-sites. The funds raised from camp-site rental fees go to the conservation and maintenance of the park.

Kisatchie National Forest consists of different wooded zones in the north and centre of Louisiana, and includes five districts: Catahoula, Winn, Kisatchie, Evangeline and Vernon, each with its own administration headed by a forest ranger. Each local office supplies information about the unique character of their district as well as maps.

Certain parts of the forest are dedicated to the conservation of local flora and fauna. Campfires are authorized but individuals are responsible for any damage their fire might cause. For more information, contact the **Supervisor's Office, Kisatchie National Forest** (*2500 Shreveport Hwy, Pineville, LA 71360, ☎ 318-473-7160*).

North of Alexandria

Kisatchie National Forest, Catahoula District

Mailing address: Catahoula Ranger District, Box 307, Pollock, LA 71567; ☎ 318-765-3554.

Lake Stuart (*entrance fee; from Bentley, follow LA 8 East for 6 km, then turn right on Forest Rd. 144, drive for 1.5 km*) is in a lovely, absolutely calm, wooded environment. It has a campground, a picnic area and a beach. A delightful nature trail reveals the local plant and wildlife.

White Sulphur Springs (*17 km from Pollock, by LA 8*). Native Americans who discovered its benefits called it "the spring of healing waters". The gravel road at the exit from LA 8 leads to the beautiful Trout River.

Kisatchie National Forest, Winn District

Mailing Address: Winn Ranger District, Box 30, Winnfield, LA 71483; ☎ 318-628-4664.

CROSSROADS

The Dogwood Trail *(from Winnfield, take US 84 West for 25 km, follow the signs)* is a pleasant two-kilometre nature trail lined with dogwood trees.

Cloud Crossing *(from Goldonna, take LA 156 East for 4 km, then LA 1233 North to Forest Road 513, heading west)*, on Bayou Saline, is an ideal site and *the* place for canoe-camping and fishing. There are campsites and picnic grounds.

Saline Creek Canoe Trips *($20 with shuttle, $15 without shuttle; mailing address: Box 213, Goldonna, LA 71031; ☎ 318-727-4865)* organizes eight-hour canoe trips on Saline Creek.

Kisatchie National Forest, Kisatchie District

Mailing address: Kisatchie Ranger District, Box 2120, Natchitoches, LA 71457; ☎ 318-352-2568.

Bayou Kisatchie *(follow Forest Road 59 East for 11 km, at Longleaf Trail, go right on Forest Road 321 for 6 km, then go right on Forest Road 366 to the end)*, set in a forest of both coniferous and deciduous trees, offers a great panoramic view of the rapids and of the white sand beaches. There are picnic areas, a campsite and trails. Fishing and canoeing are possible. **Kisatchie Cajun Expeditions** *($20/canoe; Kisatchie, ☎ 318-239-0119)* organizes canoe excursions on the Bayou Kisatchie; they also rent out canoes.

Longleaf Vista *(on Forest Road 59, 5 km from LA 119)* is a 2.5-kilometre nature trail with excellent views of the **Kisatchie Hills Wilderness Area**, 3,500 hectares of exceptionally steep terrain for Louisiana, which even includes high volcanic plateaus (mesas). Picnic grounds, water and washrooms but no camping.

West of Alexandria

Kisatchie National Forest, Evangeline District

Mailing address: Evangeline Ranger District, 3727 Government St., Alexandria, LA 71301; ☎ 318-445-9396.

Wild Azalea National Recreation Trail. From mid-March to mid-April, this 50-kilometre trail cuts through a magnificent landscape of azaleas and dogwood trees among the long pines. It takes two or three days to cover it completely, but many people do shorter walks of a few hours from Woodworth or Valentine Lake, near Gardner.

Kincaid Lake *(entrance fee; from Gardner, take LA 121 South for 0.5 km to Forest Rd. 279, take that for 5.5 km to Forest Rd. 205; the park entrance is to the left)* covers an area of about 1000 hectares. There is a sandy beach, marked trails, picnic grounds and equipped campgrounds.

Valentine Lake *(admission fee; from Gardner, LA 121 South takes you to Forest Rd. 279, take that for 1 km, then turn right on Forest Rd. 282)*. This beautiful 20-hectare lake, located in a longleaf pine forest, has a sandy beach, with showers and washrooms, and marked trails. Camping, picnic areas.

Cotile Recreation Area *(Hot Wells, ☎ 318-793-8995)* has over 800 hectares of lakes and 100 camp sites. Fishing, water sports.

Leesville

Tack-A-Paw Expeditions *(canoe $25/day, kayak $15/day; mailing address: Box 1565, Leesville, LA 71446; ☎ 318-286-9337 or 238-0821 or 1-800-256-9337 from the U.S.)* organizes canoe-camping trips on Bayou Toro and the possibility of exploring 150 kilometres of rivers. They offer a choice of excursions lasting from two hours to several days.

Kisatchie National Forest, Vernon District

Mailing address: Vernon Ranger District, P.O. Box 678, Leesville, LA 71446; ☎ 318-239-6576.

Longleaf Scenic Area *(from Pickering, take LA 10 East for 11 km to Forest Road 421; turn left, east, and continue for 6.5 km to Longleaf Scenic Area which is on the right)*. This age-old, 100-hectare forest is the natural habitat of the red cockaded woodpecker, an endangered species. Trails; no water or washrooms.

Fullerton Lake *(from Cravens, take LA 10 for 1.5 km to LA 399 North, take that for 8 km to Forest Road 427, turn left, that takes you to Fullerton Lake)* is located in a remote forest. One of the largest sawmills in the South used to operate here but now only the ruins remain; they can be seen from the many trails around the lake. Camping, picnic areas, washrooms.

East of Alexandria

Catahoula Lake *(southwest of Whitehall)* is the largest natural lake in the southern United States. Ideal spot for fishing.

Ferriday

Concordia Lake *(east of Ferriday by LA 568)* is a lovely 400-hectare lake, great for fishing, camping and watersports.

 # ACCOMMODATIONS

Note: Scores of hotels and motels line the main roads in Louisiana, making it fairly easy to find accommodation. These establishments, which focus more on modern comforts than on charm, aren't ideal for long stays. They are all virtually identical and so there isn't much to say about each. The following list will prove helpful on that one unlucky night (during the tourist season), when you don't have any alternative. Most of these places do, however, offer breakfast (not always included in the price of the room). Except where mentioned, the following hotels don't necessarily stand out, but do provide standard, comfortable lodging. They all accept credit cards.

Alexandria

Alexandria West/Kincaid Lake campground *(from Alexandria LA 28 West for 15 km and turn Kisatchie Lane, ☎ 318-445-5* open year round. Fifty-seve trails, grocery store and facilities.

Country Living Camping *Pineville, ☎ 318-442-*

camp sites, water, electricity and a grocery store.

Days Inn Motel *($35-$45; ≡, pb, ctv, ≈, ℜ; 2300 N. MacArthur Dr., ☎ 318-443-7331 or 1-800-325-2525 from North America)* is actually located on US 71 and is close to the LA 1, in the north part of the city.

The **Rodeway Inn** *($33-$65; ≡, pb, ctv, ≈; 742 MacArthur Dr., ☎ 318-448-1611 or 1-800-228-2000 from North America)* is close to LA 28 and Monroe Street which leads downtown.

The **Alexandria Travelodge** *($35-$46; ≡, pb, ctv, ≈; 1146 MacArthur Dr., ☎ 318-443-1841 or 1-800-255-3050 from North America)* is a comfortable hotel. Downtown is accessible via Jackson Street. There are more hotels and motels further along MacArthur.

Bentley Hotel *($58-$195; ≡, pb, ctv, ⊛, ⊘, ≈, ℜ; 200 De Soto St., ☎ 318-448-9600 or 1-800-356-6835 from North America)* is a palace built in 1908 in the style of grand European hotels. It retains all its original charm: spacious rooms, upscale dining room, original stained-glass windows depicting historic scenes, etc. Its 178 rooms and suites and its evenings of dancing explain its longstanding good reputation as does its relaxing, get-you-back-on-your-feet ambiance. The hotel is downtown, near the Red River.

Tyrone Plantation House *($65-$75, kfst incl.; pb; 6576 Bayou-Des-pides Rd., speak to Marion, 318-442-8528)* is located on an old, e plantation on the bayou. The se, built in 1843, is extremely uil and has two spacious rooms.

They'll provide you with a synopsis of its history. Animals are not allowed. Credit cards are accepted.

North of Alexandria

Kisatchie National Forest, Catahoula District

Stuart Lake *(entrance fee; from Bentley, take LA 8 East for 6 km, then go right on Forest Road 144 for 1.5 km)*. This peaceful lake, located in a pleasant wooded area, has eight camp sites, picnic areas, a beach, water and washrooms. There's a delightful nature trail.

Bayou Saddle campground *(from Williana, take Forest Road 155 North for 4 km)* has the advantage of a great location in a deciduous forest, there's no water supply, however.

At **Pearson** campground *(on US 167, 8 km north of Williana; the campground is located east of the road)*, you can set up your tent in a forest of coniferous and deciduous trees but there is no water supply.

Bankston campground *(from Williana, take LA 472 for 6 km, then take Forest Road 145 for 3 km; the campground is on the right)* is very popular with visitors to the national forest. Unfortunately, it doesn't have any facilities.

The **Highway 472** campground *(from Williana, take LA 472 northeast for 10 km; the campground is on the right)* is another backwoods campground located in a pine forest.

Natchitoches

Nakatosh campground *(at the intersection of I-49 and LA 6 West, ☎ 318-352-0911)* offers 44 sites. Located next to the highway, it is more convenient than it is restful.

Sibley Lake campground *(on Sibley Lake, a few kilometres from Natchitoches by LA 6, ☎ 318-352-6708)* is equipped with washrooms, showers and a grocery store. Fishing.

At the **Lakeview Inn** *($32-$50; ≡, pb, ctv, ≈; 1316 Washington Ave., ☎ 318-352-9561 or 1-800-535-5672 from the U.S.)*, try to get a room with a balcony facing the river.

Jefferson House *($45-$55 bkfst incl.; 229 Jefferson St., ☎ 318-352-3957 or 352-5756)* is a large residence in old Natchitoches. Its lovely dining room with old-fashioned decor, looks onto the river. There are three rooms, two of which have bathrooms.

Chez Martin *($50 single, $60 double bkfst incl.; pb, ≈; 1735½ Washington St., ☎ 318-352-9215)*. In this charming setting with a terrace, a fountain and an aviary, you can enjoy a "gourmet" breakfast. Meals are also available here in the evening for under $15.

The **Fleur-de-Lis Inn** *($65-$70 bkfst incl; pb; 336 2nd St., ☎ 318-352-6621 or 1-800-489-6621 from North America)* is another beautiful Victorian house, with five rooms. They have a large communal table where breakfast is served, just like back on the plantation. The campus and downtown Natchitoches are very close.

Breazeale House *($65-$75 bkfst incl.; pb, sb, ≈; 926 Washington St.; Ms. Willa Freeman, ☎ 318-352-5630)*, in pure Victorian style, has four rooms for rent. Particularly impressive are the balconies, the stained-glass in the windows and doors, and the eleven original fireplaces.

River Oaks *($65-$75 bkfst incl.; pb, tv, ≈; 112 S. Williams St., ☎ 318-352-2776)*. This two-room bed and breakfast is on the Cane River, across from famous Fort St. Denis, built by the French. Restrictions on smoking. Children under 10 are not admitted; and animals are forbidden... in other words, just sit down and keep quiet!

Cloutier Townhouse *($65-$85 bkfst incl.; pb, ⊛, tv, ℜ; 8 Ducournau Sq.,☎ 318-352-5242)*, on Front St., doesn't go unnoticed with its large salon, high ceilings, French doors and balcony opening onto the river. On top of that, the interior is also enhanced by the charm of Empire furniture, period pieces and paintings. From the terrace there is a view of Ducournau Square.

Starlight Plantation *($75-$160 bkfst incl.; pb, sb, ctv; 4 km south of Natchitoches on the Cane River; mailing address: Route 1, Box 239, Natchitoches, LA 71457; ☎ 318-352-3775)* is an elegant country house, with two magnificent rooms. It has a number of attractive features: intimate environment, dock, small-boat rental, guided tours of the plantations. They serve dinner by reservation only.

Kisatchie National Forest, Kisatchie District

Dogwood *(close to the intersection of LA 117 and Forest Road 59)*. This campground, set up among dogwood trees, has useful facilities for recreational vehicles.

Bayou Kisatchie *(take Forest Road 59 East for 11 km; at Longleaf Trail, go right on Forest Road 321 for 6 km, then go right on Forest Road 366 until the end).* This coniferous and deciduous forest boast a wonderful panoramic view of the rapids and white-sand beaches. The campground has picnic areas, trails and 18 sites. Fishing and canoeing are possible.

Red Bluff *(take Forest Road 59 for 7 km, then go left on Forest Road 345 for 4 km, you will see the sign)* is a campground in the least sandy area of Bayou Kisatchie. Washrooms but no running water.

Lotus *(Forest Road 59, 6.5 km from LA 171)* has a limited set up but there are washrooms and running water. In this area *(Forest Road 59)* there are also five more campgrounds: **Coyote**, **Corral**, **Custis**, **Cane** and **Oak**. They have washrooms but no running water.

Winnfield

Governor's Country Inn *($40 bkfst incl.; pb, sb; N. 201 Abel St., ☎ 318-628-6780)*, built in 1903, has five rooms furnished with beautiful antiques. No children.

Best Western Motel *($40-$45; ≡, pb, tv, ≈, ℜ; 700 W. Court St., ☎ 318-628-3993 or 1-800-256-4494 from North America).*

The **Southern Colonial** *($45-$55, bkfst incl; pb, sb; E. Main St., ☎ 318-628-6087)* is a Colonial-style

house. Three of the four rooms have private bathrooms.

Kisatchie National Forest, Winn District

Cloud Crossing *(from Goldonna, take LA 156 East for 4 km, then go north on the LA 1233 to Forest Road 513 going west)* is a campground with 13 sites on the Bayou Saline; this is an ideal spot for canoe-camping. Water, washrooms, fishing, picnic areas.

Gum Springs *(from Winnfield, take US 84 for 13 km)* has 13 campsites in a coniferous and deciduous forest on picturesque hilly terrain. Running water, washrooms, picnic areas.

South of Alexandria

Lecompte

The charm of **Hardy House** *($65-$110 bkfst incl.; pb; in the historic town, ☎ 318-776-5896)* has not been diminished in the least by its many restorations. Built in 1888, it has three rooms and a suite; they supply bicycles for trips around the surrounding countryside.

Cheneyville

Loyd Hall Plantation *($85-$115 bkfst incl.; pb, K; on Bayou Boeuf, 24 km south of Alexandria, close to the intersection of US 71, US 167 and I-49, Exit 61, ☎ 318-776-5641 or 1-800-240-8135 from the U.S.)* offers fully equipped cottages: living room with a fireplace, two bedrooms and a kitchenette. Since this plantation is still operational, you can even go cotton-picking in season! No smoking.

Sunnyside *($125 bkfst incl.; pb, K; on Bayou Boeuf,* ☎ *318-279-2203 or 279-2291)* is located in the Walnut Grove plantation's park. This restored house has two rooms. Traditional big breakfast.

East of Alexandria

Vidalia

Oak Harbor *(open year round; from Ferriday, take LA 84 east for 3 km, turn left and follow the signs,* ☎ *318-757-2397).* This campground has a lovely location on the lake and many trails.

🏠 **Lisburn Plantation** *($100-$125 bkfst incl.; pb; from LA 3196, between Ferriday and Vidalia; mailing address: Box 1152, Vidalia, LA 71373,* ☎ *318-336-5457 or 1-800-972-0127 from the U.S.).* This rich mid-19th-century plantation is particularly well situated close to Concordia Lake and a few minutes away from Natchez city, Mississippi. Old furniture in their four rooms. Beaches, golf, water sports. No pets.

West of Alexandria

Kisatchie National Forest, Evangeline District

Evangeline campground *(from Alexandria, take LA 28 West for 13 km, then Forest Road 273 South for 6.5 km,* ☎ *318-443-0683),* which is an excellent home base for exploring the Wild Azalea National Recreation Trail, is reserved for tents only. Limited facilities but they do offer washrooms and running water.

Kincaid Lake *(entrance fee; from Gardner, take LA 121 South for 0.5 km to Forest Road 279, take that for 5.5 km to Forest Road 205; the park entrance is to the left).* This campsite has many marked trails, 41 sites for recreational vehicles, picnic areas with barbecues, sandy beaches, docks and paved roads. Washrooms and showers at the beach.

Valentine Lake *(entrance fee; from Gardner, take LA 121 south for 0.5 km to Forest Road 279, take that for 1 km, then go right on Forest Road 282).* This 20-hectare lake, located in a pine forest, has 34 campsites but no facilities for recreational vehicles. Picnic areas, beach with showers and washrooms.

Indian Creek Recreation Area *($10; Woodworth, on US 165, 15 km south of Alexandria,* ☎ *318-487-5058).* Set around a beautiful 38-hectare lake, this campground has 71 sites for recreational vehicles. Picnic areas, playgrounds and fishing areas.

Leesville - Anacoco

Diamond "S" Campground and Trailer Park *(6 km north of Leesville by the US 171,* ☎ *318-239-3256),* close to Vernon Lake, is open all year. There's a grocery store and a laundromat here.

Dive Toledo Scuba Center & Campground *(55 Perch Dr., Anacoco, LA 71403; 4.2 km north of Toledo Barge,* ☎ *318-286-9362),* which accommodates both campers and recreational vehicles, has a dock, a pool and a grocery store. The "party barge" keeps things hopping.

The **Country Inn** *($34-$41; ≡, pb, ctv, ≈; 3075 Lake Charles Highway, Leesville, ☎ 318-238-3506 or 1-800-256-2210 from the U.S.)* is a small, reasonably-priced hotel on a busy road.

Days Inn *($40-$50 bkfst incl.; pb, ctv, ≈; on LA 172 South, Leesville, ☎ 318-239-2612 or 1-800-329-7466 from North America)* is a modern hotel with 70 rooms and a restaurant.

Kisatchie National Forest, Vernon District

Vernon campground *(from Pickering, take LA 10 East for 8 km to Forest Road 405, go east until you reach the sign, where you turn right)*. There are 50 campsites and it's open all year. No running water and no washrooms. There are, however, walking trails and cycling paths.

Fullerton Lake *(from Cravens, take LA 10 for 1.5 km to LA 399, go north for 8 km to Forest Road 427, go left, this takes you to Fullerton Lake)* has only eight campsites but there are picnic areas and trails in a protected forest that used to run one of the largest sawmills in the South – now it gives great pleasure to campers.

 RESTAURANTS

Alexandria

There are many **Piccadilly Cafeterias** *($-$$; every day, 11am to 8:30pm; Alexandria Mall, 3437 Masonic Dr., ☎ 318-445-9574 and at 1400 MacArthur Dr.)* in Louisiana. In true-cafeteria style, diners choose from whole spread of choices and then take their loaded trays to a table to eat.

Tunk's Cypress Inn *($-$$; Mon to Fri 5pm to 10pm; 14 km from Alexandria on LA 28 West, ☎ 318-487-4014)* offers an attractive view of Kincaid Lake. Among the enticing specialties: alligator, gumbo and crawfish.

Catfish Shack Family Plantation Restaurant *($-$$; Sun to Thu 11am to 9:30pm, Fri and Sat 11am to 10pm; 3800 Coliseum Blvd., ☎ 318-473-8125)* is at the west exit from Alexandria on LA 28. Besides home-style cooking, this family restaurant offers catfish, seafood, crawfish and steaks.

North of Alexandria

Natchitoches

Grayson's Barbecue *($; 5849 US 71, ☎ 318-357-0166)*, established over 35 years ago, is an institution. Besides their famous Louisiana barbecue, Grayson's serves cutlets, smoked turkey and ham, sandwiches, homemade bread, cookies and pies.

Lasyone's *($; Tue to Sat 7am to 7pm; 622 2nd Street, ☎ 318-352-3353 or 352-2174)*. This restaurant is known throughout the United States for its famous Natchitoches meat pies. They serve family fare: meat fritters, beans and sausages, cream pies. Credit cards not accepted.

Just Friends Restaurant *($; Mon to Fri 8:30am to 5pm; 746 Front St., ☎ 318-352-3836)* is very popular with locals. Their famous "La Coste bread pudding" with rum sauce, is worth the visit.

Blake's Spicy Chicken *($; Mon to Fri 9am to 6:30pm; Sat 10am to 6:30pm; 442 Martin Luther King Drive, ☎ 318-352-9763)* prepares soul food, authentic southern cuisine: gumbo, chicken and seafood.

The **Tin House** *($; Mon to Fri 10:30am to 9pm; Sat 10:30am to 2pm and 6pm to 9pm; 400 Si. Denis St., at 4th St., ☎ 318-352-6164)* specializes in "smoked barbecue", as they say in Louisiana, and steak.

🦐 The **Merci Beaucoup Restaurant and Boutique** *($-$$; Sun to Wed 10am to 5pm, Thu to Sat 10am to 9:30pm; 127 Church St., ☎ 318-352-6634)*, as their sign says, offers both good Cajun cuisine at the restaurant and attractive souvenirs at the shop next door.

The Courtyard Café, Market and Pub *($-$$; Mon to Sat 7am to 7pm; Sun 1pm to 5pm; 1 Ducournau Sq., across from Front St., ☎ 318-352-3197)* serves Southern meals for lunch and dinner. Their "po-boys" are absolutely delicious.

Creston

Lakewood Inn *($$; Mon to Sat 4pm to 10pm, Sun 11am to 10pm; LA 9, ☎ 318-875-2263)* has succulent shrimp, stuffed crab, crawfish, frog's legs and oysters on the menu. Specials on Tuesdays, Wednesdays and Thursdays.

Winnfield

Lynda's Country Kitchen *($; Mon to Sat 6am to 10pm; LA 84 East, ☎ 318-628-3222)*. Home-style cooking and family atmosphere.

The Pink House *($; Tue to Sat 10am to 5pm; 105 S. Pineville St., ☎ 318-628-1515)* provides a Victorian atmosphere in which to enjoy your tea. Home-made desserts, salads and coffees. Souvenir shop.

Pea Patch Gallery *($-$$; Tue to Thu 4pm to 10pm; Fri and Sat 10am to 10pm, Sun 10am to 4pm; 109 S. Abel St., ☎ 318-628-3560)* offers home-style meals on its daily menu. Pea Patch was the name of the place that the famous governor Earl K. Long chose as his place of retirement. His brother, also a governor, Huey P. Long, was assassinated at the legislature building in Baton Rouge. Paul Newman played the colourful Earl K. Long in the movie *Blaze*, filmed in Winnfield.

West of Alexandria

Leesville

Catfish Junction *($$; Sun to Thu 5pm to 9pm; Fri and Sat 5pm to 10pm; 1004 N. Fifth St., Leesville, ☎ 318-239-0985)*, located in an old renovated train station, serves seafood and steaks.

De Ridder

Reichley's Bakery-Delicatessen *($; 219 N. Washington St., ☎ 318-463-6856)*. A good place to get German bread and brioches, sausages and smoked meats.

Thib's Pecan House *($; 29 km south of De Ridder, on US 171 South, south of Longville, ☎ 318-725-3958)* sells pecans, candy and souvenirs.

CROSSROADS

South of Alexandria

Forest Hill

Vivian's Vittles *($; Mon 6am to 2pm, Tue to Thu 6am to 8pm, Fri 6am to 9pm, Sat 10am to 8pm, Sun 10am to 2pm; LA 112, ☎ 318-748-6873)* offers country cooking including complete breakfasts, a lunch buffet, catfish, steaks, "po-boy" sandwiches and meat pies. Credit cards not accepted.

East of Alexandria

Vidalia

Sandbar Restaurant *($; every day 11am to 10pm; 106 Carter St., ☎ 318-336-5173)*. In a warm atmosphere with rustic decor, you can sample steak, seafood or catfish.

West Bank Eatery *($$; Mon to Sat 11am to 10pm; Levee Dr., ☎ 318-336-9669)*. From the dining room there's a superb view of the Mississippi. On the menu: seafood, Creole dishes, lunch specials.

 ENTERTAINMENT

Unlike other regions, particularly New Orleans and Lafayette, the Crossroads are somewhat isolated in terms of entertainment. Nonetheless, there is a handful of annual festivals, which add to the list of options.

Alexandria

Bentley Hotel *(Mon to Sat; 200 DeSoto St., ☎ 318-448-9600 or 1-800-356-6835)* presents shows and bands to liven up the dance floor.

Calendar of Events

March

Uncle Earl's Hot Dog Trials *(Fri to Sun of the third week in March; for more information, contact the Winnfield Chamber of Commerce, 107 Court St., Winnfield, LA 71483, ☎ 318-628-4461)*, a festival of wild-boar-hunting dogs, takes place in Winn Parish. The tradition of this hunt goes back four generations. The name comes from Governor Earl Long, who had a passion for hunting wild boars on his expansive property.

May

The **Shady Dell Bluegrass Festival** *(first weekend in May; Pollock, ☎ 318-765-9092)*, a gathering devoted to bluegrass music, takes place at the local campgrounds.

June

The **Melrose Arts and Crafts Festival** *($2 adults, $1 children; beginning of June 10am to 5pm)* brings together over 100 artists and craftspeople from Louisiana and neighbouring states. Exhibition, craft sale and cooking demonstrations.

July

Caddo-Adai Indian Pow Wow ★ *(free admission; July 5th, in the St. Anne Church hall, by LA 485, approximately 10 km north of Robeline, and close to 20 km west of Natchitoches).* Iberville and Joutel made mention of their encounters with Adai natives in the 17th century. Today, many speak French and some also speak Spanish. For the event, which only lasts one day, members of native bands set up teepees on the property, and there is a visit to the historic St. Anne Church, traditional dancing by the Caddo of Louisiana and Oklahoma, sampling of Native American cooking, craft demonstrations and sales.

Natchitoches Folklore Festival *(one day during the third week in July, on the campus of the University of Southwest Louisiana, Natchitoches, ☎318-357-4332)* has a different theme each year chosen from the many facets of Louisiana's cultural heritage. Exhibitions, cooking and craft demonstrations, music and dancing are all on the program on this busy day.

October

During the **Natchitoches Pilgrimage** ★ *(visits in the city and on plantations: $10 adults, $5 13-18 years old, $3 children; second weekend of October, 8:30am to 5pm; Lemee House, 310 Jefferson St., Natchitoches, ☎ 318-357-0447, 352-8604 or 352-8052)* all of the grand residences that are otherwise closed to the public or only accessible by appointment are open to visitors.

November

During the first weekend of November Colfax holds the **Pecan Festival**, in honour of the star ingredient of those wonderful pies. Craftspeople from the region come to sell their wares.

December

One of the most popular events in Louisiana is the **Christmas Festival of Lights** ★★★ *(first Saturday of December; Natchitoches, ☎ 318-352-4411, 352-8072 or 1-800-259-1714 from the U.S.).* A magnificent show including a procession of illuminated boats on the Cane River and the proud residences of the historic town.

 SHOPPING

North of Alexandria

Natchitoches

Gibb's Antiques and Treasures *(732 2nd St.).* This is a real treasure trove, where you are sure to find some frivolous item that you can't do without!

Gray's Antiques *(Oak Grove Dr., ☎ 318-352-4226)* promises some interesting finds, especially in 19th-century American furniture.

Carriage House Market *(720 Front St., ☎ 318-352-4578)* is a good spot for some antiquing nd picking!

Jefferson Street Mall *(Mon to Sat 9:30am to 4:30pm; 400 Jefferson St.,*

☎ *318-352-4011)* is overflowing with antiques of all sorts: attractive works by local artists and industrial quantities of junk.

At **Bayou Antique and Collectibles** *(Wed to Sat 9:30am to 5pm; at LA 6 and US 84, 15 min. from Natchitoches)*, you will find old furniture, glassware, linens, etc.

Granny's Antique Emporium *(every day, 10am to 5pm; 310 Texas St., ☎ 318-357-0807)* sells old books, antiques, retro furniture and glassware.

At **La Fournée Bakery** *(Mon to Fri 8am to 5pm, Sat 9am to 6pm; 119 St. Denis St., ☎ 318-352-9040)* you can stop for a quick snack during the course of a gruelling day of shopping!

At **Bayou Books and Coins** *(558 Front St.)* you'll find reading material, coins, all sorts of souvenirs, t-shirts, etc..

The **Craft Connection** *(Mon to Sat 10am to 5pm; 113 St. Denis St., ☎ 318-357-0064)* brings together 45 craft shops and has something for everyone.

Georgia's Gift Shop *(Mon to Sat 10am to 5pm, Sun 10am to 4pm; ☎ 318-352-5833)*. At Georgia's they sell recipe books, handmade dolls and a whole assortment of souvenirs and knick-knacks.

Cane River Crafts *(612 Front St., ☎ 318-352-1718)* exhibits and sells the work of about sixty artisans.

Choate's Interiors and Gifts *(Mon to Sat 10am to 5pm; 600 Front St., ☎ 318-352-2403)*, like all gift stores, has some pieces that are more appealing than others. In other words,

there's something to make everyone happy.

The **Kaffie-Frederick's General Hardware Store** *(758 Front St., ☎ 318-352-2525)* has a collection of unusual bric-a-brac. There are pruning shears, baby rattles, monkey wrenches, and a cane for grandpa; any practical thing you need, you'll find it here.

Merci Beaucoup *(127 Church St., ☎ 318-352-6634)*. "Thank you very much" for stopping by and picking up a little something to take home with you. The marvellous objects on display are a real sight; you're sure to find something irresistible!

Olivier's Woodworks *(177 2nd St., ☎ 318-352-1427)* sells beautiful Creole furniture made of cypress wood.

Robeline

Hesitation Station *(9068 Texas Dr., ☎318-472-9072)* is a good spot for all kinds of gifts: food baskets overflowing with fine regional products, crafts, etc..

West of Alexandria

De Ridder

The Three Sisters *(Tue to Sat 10am to 5:30pm; 113 S. Washington Ave., ☎ 318-463-7379)* sells a wide assortment of cowboy boots.

J.C.'s *(115 S. Washington Ave., ☎ 318-463-4549)*. This shop offers western-style clothing and Native American crafts.

Harper's Record Shop *(115 W. 1st St., ☎ 318-463-8278)*. Are you looking for some old 45's or LP's? You will probably find them here if you have the patience to flip through their stock!

Hook's Big "D" Corral *(119 N. Washington Ave.,* ☎ *318-463-4141)*. According to some specialists in the field, it's the preferred shop for real cowboys and cowgirls.

Uptown Antiques *(113 N. Washington Ave.,* ☎ *318-463-7200)* is a shop with superb antiques and rare collectibles.

The **Native American Center** *(Country Square Shopping Center,* ☎ *318-463-6437)*. Everything on display is made by native artists.

Treasure City Mall *(121 S. Washington Ave.,* ☎ *318-462-5777)* is worth investigating for flea-market lovers.

Merryville

Mrs. Gussie Townsley's *(mailing address: Route 1, Box 379, Merryville;* ☎ *318-825-8473)*. Ms. Gussie is both a poet and a folklorist and she sells precious works of poetry and texts on the traditions of Louisiana.

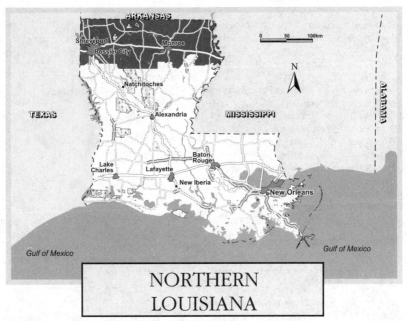

NORTHERN LOUISIANA

Northern Louisiana is bordered by Texas to the west, Arkansas to the north and skirted by the Mississippi River, which separates it from the state of the same name, to the east. Markedly different from the flat region to the south, its undulating terrain is interrupted by lakes, bayous and rivers, making it a veritable paradise for fishing and water sports enthusiasts. Its pine forests are suitable for hunting; its outdoor facilities appeal to campers, picnickers and cyclists as they do to golfers and simple walkers. The land is graced with majestic bald cypresses shrouded in Spanish moss, conferring a touch of melancholy to the landscape that will undoubtedly charm dreamers.

Part of the Ark-La-Tex axis - that is the point where the States of Arkansas, Louisiana and Texas meet - this region covers several hundred square kilometres of territory and is home to nearly 290,000 people.

The main urban area is made up of the twin cities of Shreveport and Bossier City, transected by the Red River, which meets up with the Atchafayala in Avoyelles Parish.

Founded in 1839 by Pierre Bossier, Shreveport is now the third largest city in Louisiana thanks to its annexation with the neighbouring suburb of Bossier City.

FINDING YOUR WAY AROUND

The region is traversed from east to west by Interstate 20 (I-20) and by Interstate 49 (I-49), from north to south. I-20, which runs from Dallas (Texas) to Atlanta (Georgia), runs through the cities of Shreveport/Bossier City and Monroe. I-49 extends from

Shreveport/Bossier City toward Alexandria and ultimately, to Lafayette.

On the outskirts of West Shreveport/Bossier City lies the city of Greenwood, in Caddo Parish; from here, Mooringsport, Oil City and Vivian lie to the north. South of Shreveport/Bossier City, along the Texas border, is Mansfield, in De Soto Parish, then Pleasant Hill, Marthaville, Zwolle, Many, Fisher and Florien, in Sabine Parish. Between East Shreveport/Bossier City and the Mississippi border lie the cities of Minden, Ruston, Monroe and Tallulah.

Shreveport/Bossier City

Shreveport and Bossier City, which have made up a single urban area for the last few years, are separated by the Red River. Exit 19A off I-20 leads to the downtown area (Market Street); LA 1 reaches downtown after running through the Highland Historic District.

Airport

Shreveport/Bossier Regional Airport, 5103 Hollywood Street, Shreveport/Bossier City, ☎ 318-673-5370

The regional airport is serviced by American, Continental Express, Delta, Gulf States Air, Northwest, Trans World Airlines and USAir.

Bus

The **Greyhound/Trailways** bus company has offices in the Mansfield, Many, Minden, Ruston, Monroe and Shreveport/Bossier City train stations

(one way Shreveport/Bossier City to Alexandria $23, Shreveport/Bossier City to Monroe $18). For further information, contact one of the company's offices:

408 Fannin Street, Shreveport, ☎ 318-221-4205

2229 Beckett Street, Bossier City, ☎ 318-746-7511

Car Rentals

All the following agencies have booking offices at the airport. Avis and Budget can be reached free of charge from North America; Hertz and National's 1-800 numbers are only valid from the United States.

Avis: ☎ 318-631-1839,
☎ 1-800-831-2847
Budget: ☎ 318-636-2846
☎ 1-800-527-0700
Hertz: ☎ 318-636-1212
☎ 1-800-654-3131 from the US
National: ☎ 318-636-1212
☎ 1-800-227-7368 from the US

Taxis

Casino Cabs, ☎ 318-425-3325

Yellow Checker Cab, ☎ 318-425-7000

Public Transport

Sportran City Transit System, Shreveport/Bossier City, ☎ 318-221-RIDE

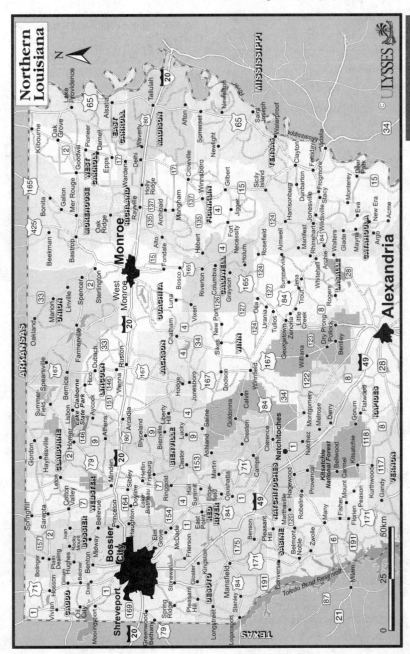

West of Shreveport/Bossier City

Greenwood

Greenwood is 20 kilometres from Shreveport/Bossier City. Take Exit 5 off I-20 or US Hwy 80.

Mooringsport

From Greenwood, take LA 169 heading north for 30 kilometres. From downtown Shreveport/Bossier City (Market Street), follow LA 1 North over 30 kilometres, then LA 169 for 2 kilometres.

Oil City

From Mooringsport, take LA 530 heading north for eight kilometres.

Vivian

From Oil City, follow LA 1 North for 12 kilometres.

South of Shreveport/Bossier City

Mansfield

From Shreveport/Bossier City, travel along I-49 South until you reach US 84; head west for 13 kilometres. Mansfield is the seat of the De Soto Parish.

Pleasant Hill

From Mansfield, take US 84 heading east for 1.5 kilometres; turn right onto LA 175. Pleasant Hill lies 35 kilometres away.

Marthaville

From Pleasant Hill, continue along LA 175 to Belmont, then take LA 120 heading east for 13 kilometres.

Zwolle

From Marthaville, get back on LA 120 West and travel 30 kilometres; here you will hit US 171, which is one kilometre north of Zwolle.

Many

From Zwolle, continue along US 171 South for 16 kilometres.

Fisher - Florien

From Many, drive eight kilometres along US 171 South to reach Fisher, or 15 kilometres for Florien.

East of Shreveport/Bossier City

Ringgold

Ringgold is situated 48 kilometres southeast of Shreveport/Bossier City. From Bossier City, take US 71 (Barksdale Blvd.) to Elm Grove (16 kilometres away), then LA 154 heading east for 31 kilometres.

Princeton

From Bossier City, travel 20 kilometres heading east on I-20, then take LA 157 North for 4 kilometres.

Doyline

From Princeton, follow LA 157 South for 6.5 kilometres, then take LA 164 heading east for 11 kilometres.

Minden

The Minden exit is 31 kilometres east of Shreveport/Bossier City on I-20.

Sibley

From Minden, take LA 7 South for eight kilometres.

Homer

At the north exit of Sibley, follow US 79 over 30 kilometres.

Haynesville

From Homer, continue along US 79 North for 21 kilometres.

Athens

In Homer, take US 79 South for five kilometres, then LA 9 for 13 kilometres.

Arcadia

From Athens, LA 9 South leads to Arcadia, 13 kilometres away. Arcadia is 56 kilometres from Shreveport/Bossier City via US 80.

Ruston

From Arcadia, I-20 and US 80 lead to Ruston, 30 kilometres away. Ruston lies 155 kilometres from Alexandria via US 167 South.

Jonesboro

In Ruston, take US 167 South for 24 kilometres.

Caney Lake - Chatham

From Jonesboro, travel along LA 4 East for 9.5 kilometres to reach Weston, 15 kilometres for Caney Lake and 25 kilometres for Chatham.

Farmerville

From Ruston, follow LA 33 North (Farmerville Highway) for 35 kilometres.

Monroe/West Monroe

Monroe/West Monroe is situated 154 kilometres from Shreveport/Bossier City via I-20 East or US 80, and 150 kilometres from Alexandria via US 165 South.

Airport

Monroe Regional Airport *(5400 Operations Road, Garrett Rd Exit off I-20 East, Monroe, ☎ 318-329-2461)* is serviced by American Eagle,

Continental, Delta, Northwest Airlink and USAir.

Car Rentals

All car rental agencies have booking offices at the Monroe Regional Airport.

Avis: ☎ 1-800-331-1212
Hertz: ☎ 1-800-654-3131
National: ☎ 1-800-227-7368

Columbia

From Monroe, take US 165 South, heading toward Alexandria, for 48 kilometres.

Rayville - Delhi

From Monroe, both US 80 and I-20 reach Rayville 35 kilometres to the east and Delhi, 60 kilometres farther east.

Winnsboro - Gilbert

In Rayville, take LA 137 South for 35 kilometres to reach Winnsboro, and 53 kilometres for Gilbert.

Newellton

From Winnsboro, take LA 4 East for 45 kilometres. From Tallulah, follow US 65 South for 42 kilometres.

Epps

From Delhi, take LA 17 heading north for 17 kilometres.

Tallulah

From Delhi, get back on US 80 East and travel 30 kilometres.

PRACTICAL INFORMATION

Area code: 318

Climate

The average temperature in the region is 30°C (84°F) in July and 11°C (48°F) in January.

Emergencies

Police, firefighters, ambulance ☎ 911

Hospitals

Schumpert Medical Center, 1 St. Mary Place, Shreveport, ☎ 681-4500

Willis-Knighton Medical Center, 2600 Greenwood Road, Shreveport, ☎ 632-4600

LSU Medical Center, 1541 King's Highway, Shreveport, ☎ 675-5000

Bossier Medical Center, 2105 Airline Drive, Bossier City, ☎ 741-6000

Doctor's Hospital, 1130 Louisiana Avenue, Shreveport, ☎ 227-1211

Lincoln General Hospital, 401 Vaughn Avenue, Ruston, ☎ 254-2100

Tourist Information

Shreveport/Bossier City

Shreveport/Bossier City Convention & Tourist Bureau, Mailing address: P.O. Box 1761, Shreveport, LA 71166, ☎ 222-9391
Internet address: tourism@shreveport-bossier.org

Riverfront Visitors Center, 405 Clyde Fant Parkway, Shreveport, ☎ 226-8884

Mall Information Center, 2950 East Texas Street, Bossier City, ☎ 747-5000, *(information: tax-free shopping)*

South Park Mall Customer Service Center, 8924 Jewella Street, Shreveport, ☎ 686-7627, *(information: tax-free shopping)*

Business Office, 626 Spring Street, Shreveport, ☎ 222-9391, ☎ 1-800-551-8682 from North America, *(for business people)*

Mansfield

De Soto Parish Tourist Bureau, Mailing address: P.O. Box 1327, Mansfield, LA 71052, ☎ 872-1177

Many

Sabine Parish Tourist & Recreation Commission, 920 Fisher Road, Many, LA 71449, ☎ 256-3419, ☎ 1-800-256-3523 from North America

Ruston

Ruston/Lincoln Convention & Visitors Bureau, Mailing address: P.O. Box 150, Ruston, LA 71273-0150, ☎ 255-2031

Monroe/West Monroe

Monroe/West Monroe Convention & Visitors Bureau, 1333 State Farm Drive, Monroe, LA 71202, ☎ 387-5691, ☎ 1-800-843-1872 from the US

 EXPLORING

Shreveport/Bossier City ★★

Founded in 1839, Shreveport has done much to preserve its old district, **Old Shreve Square ★★ (1)**, which stretches along Texas Street. Magnificent Victorian homes from the last century as well as many shops, hotels and saloons from the same era line this square. Over the years, up to 70 steamboats weighed anchor in this city's port, where the import-export industry flourished. Both retailers and wholesalers liquidated their wares here, on what is now known as Commerce Street, in a district then teeming with cotton mills.

Bossier City, so called to pay homage to Pierre Bossier, the founder of Shreveport, is the site of a major air force base (Eighth Air Force). It also ranks fifth among American cities for its thoroughbred horse races, which take place at the Louisiana Downs racetrack.

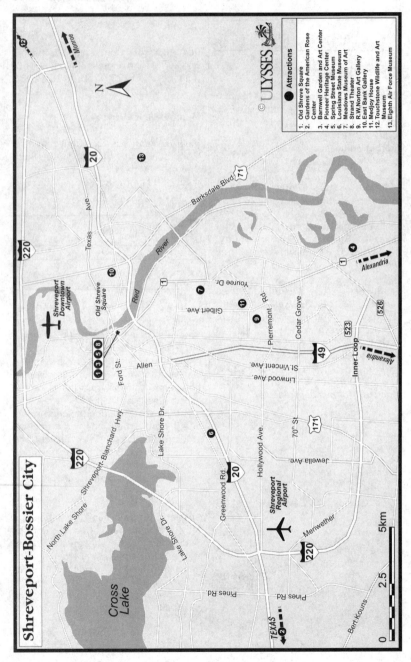

Shreveport-Bossier City

N

© ULYSSES

● Attractions

1. Old Shreve Square
2. Gardens of the American Rose Center
3. Barnwell Garden and Art Center
4. Pioneer Heritage Center
5. Spring Street Museum
6. Louisiana State Museum
7. Meadows Museum of Art
8. Strand Theater
9. R.W. Norton Art Gallery
10. East Bank Gallery
11. Medjoy House
12. Touchstone Wildlife and Art Museum
13. Eighth Air Force Museum

Cross Lake

Monroe

20

220

Shreveport Downtown Airport

Old Shreve Square

Red River

River

Barksdale Blvd.

71

Texas Ave.

220

13 5 8

Ford St.

Allen

Linwood Ave.

St. Vincent Ave.

49

523

526

Inner Loop

Alexandria

1

4

Alexandria

Youree Dr.

Gilbert Ave.

7

11

9

Pierremont Rd.

Cedar Grove

Lake Shore Dr.

6

Greenwood Rd.

20

Hollywood Ave.

70th St.

171

Jewella Ave.

Shreveport Regional Airport

Meriwether

220

Shreveport-Blanchard Hwy.

North Lake Shore

Lake Shore Dr.

Pines Rd.

Pines Rd.

Bert Kouns

TEXAS

2

0   2.5   5km

The **Shreveport/Bossier City Convention & Tourist Bureau** *(929 Spring St., Shreveport, LA 71101, ☎ 222-9391 or 1-800-551-8682 from North America)* will graciously provide you with a brochure that lays out an interesting tour of the city's historic district.

The **Texas Street Bridge** ★ *(☎ 222-9391)*, which spans the Red River between Shreveport and Bossier City, is entirely illuminated by lasers and neon lights at night.

The **Gardens of the American Rose Center** ★★★ **(2)** *(adults $5, package deal for groups and children; cars $5, RVs $10; Nov to Apr, Mon to Fri 9am to 6pm, Sat and Sun 10am to 6pm; Apr to Nov 8:30am to 4:30pm, holiday season 8:30am to 10pm; 16 km west of Shreveport/Bossier City, Exit 5 off I-20, ☎ 938-5402)* is the largest park dedicated to the rose in the United States. It extends over close to 48 hectares and boasts over 20,000 roses. The property includes 60 individual gardens with every variety of rose from around the world, these are generally in full bloom just in time for Christmas. There is also a Japanese garden ornamented with statues, waterfalls, fountains, gazebos, small pavilions and an inviting tea house. Touring the gardens can take from 30 minutes to 90 minutes, depending on the visitor.

The **R.S. Barnwell Memorial Garden & Art Center** ★ **(3)** *(free admission; Mon to Fri 9am to 4:30pm, Sat and Sun 1pm to 5pm; 601 Clyde Fant Parkway, Shreveport, ☎ 673-7703)* hosts most of the city's cultural activities. In addition to its magnificent floral arrangements, the **botanical garden** presents different exhibitions featuring local artists and artisans.

The **Pioneer Heritage Center** ★ **(4)** *($1, free admission for children; Wed and Thu 10am to 2pm, Sun 1pm to 4:30pm; 8515 Youree Dr., Shreveport, ☎ 797-5332)* is located on the Louisiana State University at Shreveport campus. Here, visitors can see how early settlers who came to these shores between 1830 and 1860 lived: reconstituted grocer's, doctor's office, ironworks etc. Count on spending about 45 minutes here.

The **Spring Street Museum** ★ **(5)** *(admission fee; Tue, Oct to June, 1:30pm to 4:30pm, reservations in summer; 525 Spring St., Shreveport, ☎ 869-0022 or 424-0964)* occupies one of the oldest buildings in the city. This former bank, whose interior is entirely fashioned of sculpted rosewood, has retained its original Victorian furnishings, its Chippendale chairs (a style in fashion in the 1760s) and a collection of French 19th-century paintings. A video on the history of Shreveport and Bossier City and various exhibitions are featured here.

The **Louisiana State Exhibit Museum** ★ **(6)** *(free admission; Mon to Sat 9am to 4:30pm, Sun 1pm to 5pm; 3015 Greenwood Rd., Shreveport, ☎ 632-2020)* depicts noteworthy events of Louisiana's history from the pre-Columbian era to the present. Count on spending 45 minutes to one hour here.

The **Meadows Museum of Art** ★ **(7)** *(free admission; Tue to Fri noon to 4pm, Sat and Sun 1pm to 4pm; 2911 Centenary Blvd, Shreveport, ☎ 869-5169)* is located on the Centenary College campus. Interesting collection of 360 works by American painter Jean Despujols depicting Indochina in the thirties. Documentary video on the artist. Length of visit: 30 minutes to one hour.

The dazzling neo-baroque **Strand Theater ★★ (8)** *(Mon to Fri 9am to 5pm; 619 Louisiana Ave., at Crocker St., Shreveport, ☎ 226-1481)* boasts 1,640 seats. The Strand's imposing cupola makes it easy to spot. It opened its doors in 1925 with the *Chocolate Soldier*, an opera that enjoyed considerable success. The old theatre was entirely restored in 1984. It is graced with, among other things, an 939-pipe organ, crystal chandeliers, gilt mirrors and boxes richly decorated in shades of gold and burgundy.

The **R. W. Norton Art Gallery ★ (9)** *(free admission; Tue to Fri 10am to 5pm, Sat and Sun 1pm to 5pm; 4747 Creswell Ave., Shreveport, ☎ 865-0435)* is a museum dedicated to American art, spotlighting art of the American West by Frederick Remington and Charles M. Russell. The gallery-museum also has a few paintings by European artists.

The **East Bank Gallery ★ (10)** *(free admission; Mon to Fri 8am to 5pm; 630 Barksdale Blvd, Bossier Arts Council, Bossier City, ☎ 741-8310)* features rotating exhibits by local artists.

The **Medjoy House ★ (11)** *($3,50; by appointment; 601 Ockley Dr., Shreveport, speak to Virginia Joyner, ☎ 865-5752 or 861-4424)* is a lovely, listed colonial-style residence in the South Highlands District. The guided tour lasts approximately 45 minutes.

The **Touchstone Wildlife and Art Museum ★ (12)** *(adults $1, free admission for children under 6; Tue to Sat 9am to 5pm, Sun 1pm to 5pm; 3386 US 80 East, Haughton,* *approximately 4 km east of Louisiana Downs in Bossier City, ☎ 949-2323)* offers dioramas and over 1,000 specimens of wildlife in natural habitats. Weapons and artifacts used by Native Americans or dating from the Civil War are also on display.

The **Eighth Air Force Museum (13)** *(free admission; Wed to Sun 10am to 4pm; Barksdale Air Force Base, Bossier City, ☎ 456-3067)* features period uniforms, dioramas and planes from World War II.

Boothill Speedway *(admission fee; Mar to Nov, Sat night; I-20, Exit 3, West Shreveport, ☎ 398-5373)*. Nothing in the world could keep local fans from attending this event.

West of Shreveport/Bossier City

Oil City

This region's economic activity revolves around the exploitation of oil and natural gas. The surrounding area is covered in pine forests and attracts those who enjoy the great outdoors, particularly in the vicinity of Caddo Lake and Black Bayou.

The **Caddo Pine Island Oil and Historical Society Museum ★** *(adults $1, children $0,50; Mon to Fri 9am to 5pm; 200 S. Land Ave., ☎ 995-6845)* is situated north of Shreveport/Bossier City, on LA 1. The history of the first oil wells is recounted here: replica of the first derrick, erected in 1906, near the museum. Oil City experienced the oil boom of the early 1900s. Every spring, the importance of the oil industry is highlighted through the **Gusher Days ★** festival, during which there is street dancing, a parade, an arts and crafts exhibit, a beard and moustache contest and more.

The museum also contains period railway artifacts, old photographs, Native American relics left by the Caddo Indians and other artifacts related to the history of the region.

Tours of Agricultural and Industrial Facilties

The **LSU Cooperative Extension Service** *(free admission; Apr to Nov; 501 Texas St., Shreveport, speak to Jon Lowe,* ☎ *226-6805)* offers groups (by appointment only) a display of cotton gins, a visit to a fully operational farm as well as crop dusting demonstrations.

The **Red River Research Station** *(Apr to Nov, 7:30am to 4:30pm; at the junction of US 71 and Curtis Rd.; mailing address: P.O. Box 8550, Bossier City, LA 71113; speak to Dr. Jere McBride,* ☎ *741-7430)* is an agricultural research centre that focuses on the growing of cotton, vegetables, soybeans and cereal, as well as livestock breeding.

South of Shreveport/Bossier City

Mansfield ★★

This region is greatly appreciated by hunting, fishing and water-sports enthusiasts. The De Soto Parish is bordered by the **Toledo Bend Reservoir** (73,000 hectares) to the west and by the Red River to the east. The central part of the region is covered with lush forests.

During the Civil War, Mansfield was the site of the Confederates' last great victory. This historic event is commemorated at the **Mansfield Commemorative Area** as well as at the **Confederates Cemetery**. Also worth seeing: the historic **Rock Chapel**, near Bayou Pierre in Carmel, built by the Carmelites in 1891; the Ferguson Cemetery, where you will find the **gravesite of Moses Rose**, the only survivor of the famous "Battle at the Alamo". For further information, contact the **De Soto Parish Tourist Bureau** *(mailing address: P.O. Box 1327, LA 71052,* ☎ *872-1177)*.

The **Mansfield State Commemorative Area** ★ *(adults $2, free for seniors and children under 12; every day 9am to 5pm; LA 175,* ☎ *872-1474)* is a commemorative park dedicated to the Confederates' last victory in Louisiana, during a battle led by Cajun General Alexandre Mouton, from Lafayette (Vermilionville). Dioramas and audiovisual presentation.

The **Old Log Courthouse** ★ *(free admission; open by appointment; corner of Polk and Madison Streets,* ☎ *872-1177)* was built in 1843 out of hand-carved logs. Its chimney is made of dried mud, and its original bell is still in place.

The **Rock Chapel** ★ *(free admission; key available at Lafitte's General Store, Carmel; to visit the chapel built by the Carmelites:* ☎ *872-3378; picnic area, LA 509 east of Carmel,* ☎ *872-1177)*, built from masonry by monks, dates from 1891. It is picturesquely situated on an escarpment overlooking Bayou

Sabine Parish

The region has a very colourful history. After the Spanish sold what they had left of Louisiana to the Americans in 1803, the delimitation of the new borders became a source of dispute between the two nations. The Americans claimed the eastern part of Texas. The Spanish responded by demanding they return the western part of Louisiana.

Neither nation, however, showed interest in the Sabine River region, which thus became "no man's land". It was referred to as "The Sabine Strip".

The Sabine Strip quickly turned into a refuge for bandits, murderers and outlaws of all kinds: Spaniards, French, Creoles and American slaves on the run who became smugglers. Fort Jesup, was therefore set up by the two nations in order to maintain some semblance of order. Nevertheless, anarchy prevailed until the famous treaty of 1819 between Spain and the United States. To this day, the faces of its inhabitants reflects its multicultural history.

Lou, behind the Carmel Roman Catholic Church.

Marthaville

This is Confederate country. Its proximity to Texas is palpable and confers a state of mind to its population altogether in keeping with Texan culture and traditions.

The **Rebel State Commemorative Area ★** *(adults $2, free for children under 12; every day 9am to 5pm; LA 1221,*

5 km north of Marthaville, ☎ 472-6255) recalls the fact that this region, situated near Texas, which was non-occupied at the time, experienced intense military activity. Many of its inhabitants still consider themselves proud descendants of rebel Confederates. The site pays homage to an unknown Confederate soldier. It includes an interpretive centre, an amphitheatre and a museum dedicated to Louisiana country music. Country music concerts are featured here throughout the summer, and an annual violin competition takes place in October.

Southeast of Marthaville, just east of the Robeline village, is the **Los Adaes State Commemorative Area** *(adults $2, free for children under 12; every day 9am to 5pm; LA 6, ☎ 256-4117)*. The Spanish fort of the same name was erected here in 1721.

Zwolle, Many, Fisher and Florien

The recreational activities offered in this region, whether in the heart of it's lush forests or on the Toledo Bend Reservoir, make it a popular destination.

The **Toledo Bend Reservoir ★★**, or lake, was created by the Sabine River dams. It enjoys an excellent reputation on a national scale, as much for the variety of fishing practised here as for the abundance of fish in its waters, including a delicious white-fleshed species known here as "wide-mouthed bass".

The **Fort Jesup State Commemorative Area** ★ *(adults $2, free for seniors and children under 12; every day 9am to 5pm; LA 6, about 10 km east of Many, ☎ 256-4117)* comprises a fort built in 1822 on the ruins of an 18th-century Spanish fortification. This was done on the initiative of Zachary Taylor, the only American president to originate from Louisiana. Fort Jesup was used to protect the United States' western border.

Tours of Agricultural and Industrial Facilities

The **Zwolle Tamale Factory** *(free admission; all year round; by appointment; mailing address: P.O. Box 157, Zwolle, LA 71486; speak to E. B. Malmay, ☎ 645-9086)*. Zwolle (pronounced "*zwalee*") produces tons upon tons of *tamales*, Mexican "pancakes" that prove very popular in Louisiana.

The **Village of Fisher** ★ *(free admission, donations accepted for guided tours; US 171, 8 km south of Many, ☎ 256-6745 or 256-5374)* is listed as a historic district and has preserved its original church, opera, post office, railway station, venerable houses and all the memorabilia of its bygone sawmills.

The **Hodges Gardens** ★★ *(adults $6.50, seniors $5.50, 6-17 years old $3; every day 8am to 5pm, US 171, 17 km south of Fisher, ☎ 586-3523 or 424-9513)* have been designed with

great care in the heart of a hilly 1,800-hectare pine forest. Greenhouses, wilderness park, picnic areas.

East of Shreveport/Bossier City

Minden

In the Webster Parish, the city of Minden takes pride in its numerous antebellum houses, its **Historic Residential District** as well as its **old business district**, whose streets are still paved as in days of old.

The **Germantown Colony Museum** ★ *(adults $3, couples $4, families $7, children $1; Tue to Sat 9am to 5pm, Sun 1pm to 6pm; north of Minden, approximately 13 km east of Shreveport/Bossier City, on LA 114, ☎ 377-6061)* is a replica of a communal village founded in 1835 by German immigrants under the leadership of Countess von Leon. The museum boasts the latter's archives as well as authentic letters, tools and furnishings from the time of these pioneers. Length of visit: 45 minutes.

Homer

A region of magnificent wooded hills, the Claiborne Parish includes the cities of Homer, Haynesville and Junction City, as well as the villages of Athens, Lisbon and Summerfield. Hunting and fishing enthusiasts are sure to appreciate **Lakes Corney and Claiborne**. For further information, contact the **Claiborne Parish Tourist Commission** *(mailing address: P.O. Box 83, Homer, LA 71040, ☎ 258-5863)*.

The **H. S. Ford Museum** *(adults $1, children $0,50; Mon to Fri 9am to noon and 1pm to 4pm, Sat 10am to 2pm, Sun 2pm to 4pm; 519 S. Main St., ☎ 927-3271)* is dedicated to local history, particularly that of the Claiborne Parish. The museum includes a Native American canoe, a wooden house, a still, a forge, a cotton scale, and more.

The **Claiborne Parish Courthouse** *(Mon to Fri 9am to 5pm; 187 Main St., ☎ 927-2223)* was built in 1861 in the Greek Revival style.

Athens

Fans of bluegrass music, one of the many current musical forms of expression in Louisiana, will certainly enjoy the **Homeplace Acres Bluegrass Festival** *(in the evening; first Fri, Sat and Sun of June and second Fri, Sat and Sun of Sept; ☎ 258-4943)*.

Rodeo fans are sure appreciate those organized by the **Mount Olive Christian School LRCA Rodeo** *(last weekend of July, 8pm; Gantt's Arena, near Athens, ☎ 927-2222)* during the summer.

Arcadia

County seat of the Bienville Parish, Arcadia boasts an interesting **Historic Monuments Museum**. The **Bienville Warehouse Museum** *(Hwy 2, P.O. Box 12, Exit 61 off I-20, or 6.4 km south of LA 154, Gigsland-Arcadia, LA 71028, ☎ 263-7420)*, for its part, is dedicated to the memory of famous gangsters Bonnie and Clyde. A commemorative plaque shows where the couple was gunned down by the law. The museum features permanent exhibits of memorabilia linked to the tumultuous life of the legendary duo, immortalized in the movie starring Warren Beatty and Faye Dunaway.

You can also visit the **Mount Lebanon Baptist Church** *(LA 154)* in Arcadia, and take advantage of the many lakes in this enchanting natural setting. For more information, contact the **Arcadia Chamber of Commerce** *(1001 N. Hazel St., Arcadia, LA 71001, ☎ 263-9897)*.

The **Bonnie & Clyde Trade Days** *($2/vehicle; weekend before the third Mon of the month, from dawn to dusk; LA 9, 6 km south of I-20 via Exit 69, ☎ 263-2437)* offers some 1,100 lots, kiosks or points of sale: it is Louisiana's largest flea market. Antiques, handicrafts, souvenirs, tools, ready-cooked dishes, trinkets and more: something for everyone!

Tours of Agricultural and Industrial Facilities

The **Back Forty Peaches** *(free admission; May 15 to July 31, Mon to Sat 8am to 5pm; 2 km north of I-20 on LA 151; mailing address: Hwy 2, P.O. Box 907, Arcadia, LA 71001, ☎ 263-2184)*. Northwestern Louisiana is renowned for the quality of its peaches, and numerous kiosks offering this delicious fruit (when in season) line the highways here and there. Mr. E. E. Letlow, market farmer, reveals to visitors his secrets for obtaining abundant crops of peaches and blackberries.

Ruston

The Lincoln Parish is home to two major universities: **Louisiana Tech**

University and **Grambling State University**. The latter is one of the biggest African-American universities in the United States.

Several artists and artisans exhibit and sell their work at the **Piney Hills Gallery ★★**. Also worth checking out: the **Lincoln Parish Museum**, the **Dixie Jamboree** and the **Lincoln Parish Park**, with 100 hectares of gardens and nature trails (picnic areas and swimming). For further information about sports activities, contact the **Ruston/Lincoln Convention & Visitors Bureau** *(900 N. Trenton St., Ruston, LA 71270, ☎ 255-2031)*.

The **North Louisiana Military Museum** *(adults $1, children $0.50; Thu, Fri and Sun 1pm to 5pm, Sat 10am to 5pm; corner of Georgia Street and Memorial Drive; contact the Ruston/Lincoln Visitors Bureau, ☎ 255-2031)* houses a prodigious collection of artillery and memorabilia from the American Civil War, the Spanish-American War, the First and Second World Wars, the Korean War, the Vietnam War as well as the Persian Gulf War, the latter (also called Operation Desert Storm) having occurred in the wake of a conflict between Iraq and Kuwait.

The **Lincoln Parish Museum ★** *(free admission; Tue to Fri 10am to 4pm; 609 N. Vienna St., ☎ 251-0018)* is a stately house, adorned with beautiful murals, in which visitors can see a multitude of objects linked to the history of the parish.

The *Louisiana Passion Play ★ (adults $8, seniors $6, children $5; Jun to Aug Fri and Sat 8:30pm, Sep, Fri and Sat 8pm)*. A particular dramatic interpretation of Christ's last days.

Built in 1924 in the Gothic style, the **Presbyterian Church of Ruston USA** *(212 N. Bonner St., ☎ 255-2542)* boasts attractive stained-glass windows.

The **Piney Hills Gallery** *(Tue to Sat 10am to 4pm; 206 W. Park Ave., ☎ 255-7234)* features beautiful works of art and handicrafts from North Louisiana: sculptures, musical instruments, furniture, pottery, patchwork quilted bedspreads, dolls, lamps and photographs.

Two pottery studios in Ruston are worth visiting: **Odell Pottery** *(Mon to Thu 9am to 6pm, Fri and Sat 9am to 7pm; 1705 W. Kentucky St., ☎ 251-3145)* and the **Follette Pottery Studio** *(Mon to Sat 8am to 5pm; 455 Parish Rd., north of Ruston upon exiting LA 33, ☎ 251-1310)*.

Tours of Agricultural and Industrial Facilities

Louisiana Tech Horticulture Center *(free admission; Mon to Fri 8am to 5pm; on the Louisiana Tech University campus, corner of US 80 and Tech Farm Rd.; mailing address: P.O. Box 10198, T. S., Ruston, LA 71772; ask for Dr. Peter Gallagher, ☎ 257-3275)*. Permanent exhibits of tropical plants. The facility is particularly renowned for its azaleas and poinsettias. Tours of research and growing greenhouses. Length of visit: 45 minutes.

Jonesboro

Jonesboro is in the Jackson Parish. Of interest here is the **Jimmy Davis Tabernacle**, deemed a mystical place.

Other attractions include the **Jackson Parish Heritage Museum**, the **Fine Arts Center** and **Caney Lake**. Information at **Jonesboro City Hall** *(128 Allen Ave., Jonesboro, LA 71251, ☎ 259-2385)*.

Monroe/West Monroe ★

The Ouachita Parish encompasses the twin cities of Monroe and West Monroe. It is a bustling tourist centre where everything from rodeos and concerts to ballet performances take place. The city was formerly known as Fort Miro, named after the first steamboat to go up the Ouachita River. Its **Historic District ★★ (1)** skirts the river. Further tourist information can be obtained at the **Monroe/West Monroe Convention and Visitors Bureau** *(1333 State Farm Dr., Monroe; mailing address: P.O. Box 6054, Monroe, LA 71211, ☎ 387-5691 or 1-800-843-1872 from the US, ☎ 324-1752)*.

It should be noted that the **Bienville Trace Scenic Byway - LA 2 ★★** runs through the parishes of Ouachita, Union, Claiborne and Webster.

The **Layton Castle ★★ (2)** *(adults $5, children $2; every day, by appointment only, 10am to 5pm; 1133 S. Grand St., ☎ 322-4869)* recalls the stately homes of long ago with its pillars, monumental tower, turret and carriage entrance. The splendid structure houses a collection of prints by John James Audubon, the great Franco-American naturalist painter who moved to Louisiana from the French colony of Santo Domingo (Haiti), where he was born. Length of visit: 1 hour 30 minutes.

Rebecca's Doll Museum ★ (3) *(adults $1, children $0.50; 4500 Bonaire Dr., ☎ 343-5627)* boasts over 2,000 dolls made of a great variety of materials, including wood, paper, fabric, papier mâché and metal. These dolls, dating from the 1850s, come from France, Germany, China and many other countries.

The **Masur Museum of Art ★ (4)** *(free admission; Fri to Sun 2pm to 5pm, Tue to Thu 9am to 5pm; 1400 S. Grand St., ☎ 329-2237)* is housed in an English Tudor-style building. The museum is dedicated to the visual arts: painting, sculpture and photography. Permanent collection and a dozen travelling exhibits per year.

The **Ouachita River Art Guild (5)** *(free admission; Tue to Sat 10am to 6pm; 102 Thomas Rd., Glenwood Mall, Suite 611, ☎ 322-2380)* is a fine arts guild as well as a gallery.

The **Emy-Lou Biedenharn Foundation ★ (6)** *(free admission; Tue to Fri 10am to 4:30pm, Sat and Sun 2pm to 5pm; 2006 Riverside Dr., ☎ 387-5281 or 1-800-362-0983 from the US)* occupies the house built by Joseph Biedenharn, who first bottled world-famous Coca-Cola in 1894. It houses a remarkable collection of bibles, old books, musical instruments and antiques. The house is surrounded by a garden in which numerous species of flowers grow.

The **Boscobel Cottage ★ (7)** *(groups of 10 to 30 people; by reservation only; 185 Cordell Lane, via LA 165, approx. 24 km south of Monroe, ask for Kay LaFrance, ☎ 325-1550)* is a plantation house listed as a historic monument. One room functions as a bed and breakfast. The largest pecan tree in the

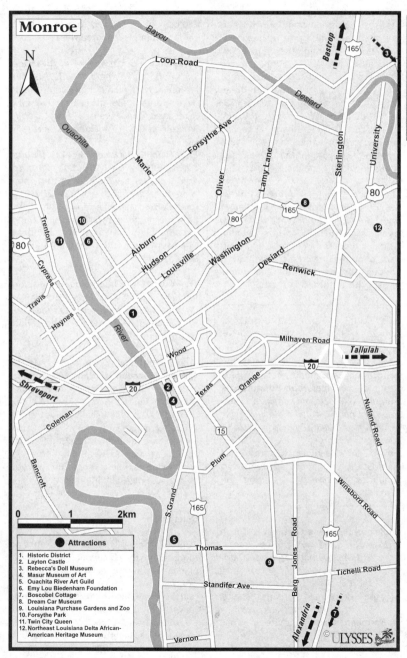

Monroe

N

Bayou

Loop Road

Desiard

Ouachita

Forsythe Ave.

Marie

Oliver

Lamy Lane

Sterlington

University

80

165

Bastrop

165

80

Trenton

80

Cypress

Auburn

Hudson

Louisville

Washington

Desiard

Renwick

12

Travis

Haynes

River

Wood

Milhaven Road

Tallulah

Shreveport

20

Texas

Orange

20

Coleman

15

Nutland Road

Bancroft

Plum

S. Grand

165

Winsbord Road

0   1   2km

Thomas

Berg

Jones Road

165

Tichelli Road

Standifer Ave.

Alexandria

● **Attractions**

1. Historic District
2. Layton Castle
3. Rebecca's Doll Museum
4. Masur Museum of Art
5. Ouachita River Art Guild
6. Emy Lou Biedenharn Foundation
7. Boscobel Cottage
8. Dream Car Museum
9. Louisiana Purchase Gardens and Zoo
10. Forsythe Park
11. Twin City Queen
12. Northeast Louisiana Delta African-
    American Heritage Museum

Vernon

© ULYSSES

State of Louisiana stands in its park. Count on spending one to one and a half hours touring the house and grounds.

The **Cotton Country Cooking School** *(2811 Cameron St., ☎ 322-3236, ☎ 1-800-256-4888 from the US)* specializes in southern Louisiana cuisine. Visitors can sample dishes prepared by students. Prices vary according to the menus.

The **Dream Cars Museum ★ (8)** *(adults $3, children $1; Mon to Sat 9am to 6pm, Sun 1pm to 6pm; 3000 Louisville Ave., ☎ 388-1989)*. This museum contains a collection of road and sports cars, about a hundred motorcycles from various eras, miniature cars and works of art with automotive themes.

Tours of Agricultural and Industrial Facilities

Forestry plays a vital role in the State of Louisiana's economy. A tour of the **Riverwood International paper mill** *(free admission; by appointment; 14 years old and over; mailing address: P.O. Box 35800, West Monroe, LA 71294, ☎ 362-2000)* initiates visitors to this industry. Count on spending 45 minutes to one hour touring the facilities.

Louisiana Purchase Gardens & Zoo (9) *(adults $3.25, seniors and children $2; Mon to Sun 10am to 5pm; on Ticheli Rd., two streets west of LA 165 South, ☎ 329-2400)*. The vast zoological part of the botanical gardens shelters several hundred animals: herds of zebra-tailed maki, primates, African eagles, leopards and others. Picnic areas and landscaped gardens.

Forsythe Park (10) *(corner of Riverside and Forsythe Streets, ☎ 329-2879)* features lovely picnic areas surrounded by evergreens alongside the Ouachita River and the Forsythe Boat Dock, where the *Twin City Queen* is berthed.

The ***Twin City Queen ★ (11)*** *(adults $2.50, children $1.25; Sun 2pm to 4pm; speak to Obie Webster; see "Forsythe Park" above, ☎ 329-2879)*, a three-decker ship able to accommodate 240 passengers, offers cruises along the Ouachita River every Sunday. Departure from the Forsythe Boat Dock.

The **Twin City Drag Race** *(admission fee; Mar to Oct, Sat 7pm; 3695 Prairie Rd., ☎ 387-8563)* presents car races at a sanctioned National Hot Rod Association track.

The **Northeast Louisiana Delta African-American Heritage Museum ★ (12)** *(Tue, Thu and Sat 10am to 5pm; 503 Oplum St., ☎ 323-1167 or 387-5567)* is exclusively devoted to African-American art. The museum also organizes a host of cultural and social activities, such as art exhibitions and workshops as well as community work projects to help out the needy.

Columbia

Columbia lies 48 kilometres south of Monroe, in the Caldwell Parish. Two places here worth visiting are...

Martin Homeplace *(admission fee; Tue to Sat 9am to 4:30pm; 1.6 km north of Columbia, via LA 165, ☎ 649-6722)*. Listed as a historic monument, this former cotton plantation home (1880) was restored to house the LA Art & Folk Museum, which features a traditional collection of old artifacts from the South. The building also boasts beautiful gardens.

The **Schepis Museum** *(admission fee; Tue to Fri 10am to 4:30pm, Sat 10am to 3pm; 107 Main St., at the Ouachita River levee, ☎ 649-2138)* presents interesting exhibits on the history and talents of Caldwell Parish and the State of Louisiana.

Newellton

Newellton is in the Tensas Parish, right near the State of Mississippi. The **Winter Quarters State Commemorative Area** *(free admission; every day; on LA 1; P.O. Box 91, Newellton, LA 608, ☎ 467-5439)* is 4,8 kilometres southeast of the city. Built in 1803, the former plantation house served as winter quarters for Confederate troops during the Civil War. It has since been converted into ain interpretive centre and comprises a collection of unique cotton plantation period furniture, as well as historic pieces and documents related to the wretched war between the American North and South.

Epps

The **Poverty Point State Commemorative Area (Native American Archaeological Site)** ★★ *(adults $2, free for seniors and children under 12; every day 9am to 5pm; on LA 577, north of Epps, ☎ 926-5492)* was the main trade and ceremonial centre of a prehistoric Native American culture, which flourished here more than 3,000 years ago. It is one of the country's major archaeological sites. It stretches over approximately 160 hectares, and includes an interpretive centre, a museum and paths. Guided tours upon request.

Tallulah ★

The vast Mississippi Delta spreads out as far as the eye can see here. The landscape is peppered with prosperous cotton and soybean plantations. Madison Parish was named after the fourth American president, James Madison. This territory was once occupied by the Ouachita and Tensa indigenous peoples. Traces of their presence here can still be discerned. Home to 5,000 inhabitants, Tallulah is the county seat of Madison Parish.

 PARKS

Shreveport/Bossier City

The **Cypress Black Bayou Recreation Area** *(on LA 162, between Bossier City and Benton, ☎ 965-0007)* is a Nature Study Center, but also a place where visitors can practise their favourite outdoor sports activities: exploring nature trails, fishing, camping and swimming.

West of Shreveport/Bossier City

Oil City

Caddo Lake *(LA 1, near Oil City)* is prized by hunting, fishing, camping and water skiing enthusiasts.

Blanchard

The **Walter B. Jacobs Memorial Nature Park** *(free admission; Wed to Sat 8am to 5pm, Sun 1pm to 5pm; via LA 173, about 6 km north of Blanchard,* ☎ *929-2806)* nature trails: a wonderful place where visitors can encounter local wildlife (birds, deer, tortoises, snakes, opossums, raccoons). The nature preserve also boasts a study centre.

South of Shreveport/Bossier City

Zwolle

The **North Toledo Bend State Park** *(16 km southwest of Zwolle, on LA 3229,* ☎ *645-4715)* is situated on a peninsula that juts out into the lake of the same name. Fishing, camping and picnicking.

The **Sabine Wildlife Management Area** *(8 km south of Zwolle, US 171,* ☎ *487-5885)* is a park that extends over close to 6,000 hectares; visitors can camp in the northwest part.

East of Shreveport/Bossier City

Princeton

Norris Outfitters *(US 80, 11 km east of Louisiana Downs; mailing address: P.O. Box 40, Princeton, LA 71607,* ☎ *949-9522)* rents camping equipment and supplies hunting and fishing guides. Transportation to the parks is also provided.

Minden

North of Minden, **Caney Lake** is ideal for swimming and camping as is **Lake Bistineau**, to the south, for fishing. For further information concerning tourism or various sports activities, contact the **Webster Parish Tourist Commission** *(mailing address: P.O. Box 819, Minden, LA 71058,* ☎ *377-4240)*.

Homer

The **Lake Claiborne State Park** *(LA 146, 11 km southeast of Homer,* ☎ *927-2976)* features 87 camping sites, several nature trails and a beach. Rental boats available for fishing on the 2,560-hectare lake.

Kisatchie National Forest *(mailing address: District Ranger, Caney Ranger District, P.O. Box 479, Homer, LA 71040,* ☎ *927-2061, or Supervisor's Office, Kisatchie National Forest, 2500 Shreveport Highway, Pineville, LA 71360,* ☎ *473-7160)*.

Caney Lakes Recreation Area *(admission fee; seasonal; from Minden, take LA 159 North to Webster Parish Road 111, turn left and travel 3 km,* ☎ *927-2061)*. There are two lakes in the heart of the Kisatchie National Forest: Upper Caney Lake (50 hectares) and Lower Caney Lake (100 hectares). The park boasts a beach where you can fish or take a stroll along one of its nature trails. The 12-kilometre-long Sugar Cane National Recreation Trail winds its way around Lower Caney Lake. Visible remains of a sugar cane mill are also here; they date back to the time when sugar-cane farming flourished in the region, as did cotton growing.

Corney Lake *(admission fee; all year round; LA 9, 28 km north of Homer,* ☎ *927-2061).* This 900-hectare lake is surrounded by a forest of cypresses, copal trees and pines. Eight camping sites available. Picnicking and fishing.

Arcadia

Trails End Golf Course *(every day; LA 9 South,* ☎ *263-7420).* This 18-hole golf course is located in the undulating region of Piney Hills.

Plum Ridge Licensed Shooting Preserve & Quail Farm *(Oct to Apr, by reservation only; via LA 507, 5 km north of Bienville or 24 km south of Simsboro; mailing address: P.O. Box 364, Arcadia, LA 71001;* ☎ *263-2850 (day) or 263-2747 (night)).* Partridge hunting with guides and dogs.

Ruston

The **Lincoln Parish Park** *(admission fee; LA 33, north of Ruston,* ☎ *251-5156)* has no campsite, but visitors can stroll along the paths, go for a swim or rent a boat.

Caney Lake

Not to be confused with Upper and Lower Caney Lakes in the Webster Parish, this lake *(24 km south of Ruston and 10 km east of Jonesboro; speak to Raymond Richardson, fishing guide,* ☎ *249-2535)* is very popular among fishing enthusiasts due to its reputation as a lake with "a miraculous draught of fishes". The best month for bass fishing is July.

Farmerville

The **Lake D'Arbonne State Park** *($10-$12; LA 2, west of Farmerville,* ☎*368-2086)* is a veritable paradise for fishing buffs. There are 43 camp sites here. Credit cards accepted.

Visitors can camp in the eastern part of the **Union Wildlife Management Area** *(35 km north of Farmerville, via LA 549 or 551,* ☎ *343-4044),* a state park extending over more than 5,200 hectares. Facilities are rudimentary, however.

Monroe/West Monroe

Kiroli Park *(free admission; on Kiroli Rd., West Monroe,* ☎ *396-4016)* boasts paved trails, tennis courts, a playground, picnic shelters as well as fishing ponds *($0.50).*

The **Chemin-A-Haut State Park** *(26 camping sites, $10-$12; 6 cabins $45-$50; ≈; via LA 139, about 18 km north of Bastrop,* ☎ *238-0812)* was once a stopping place for indigenous peoples during their seasonal migrations. It lies where Bayous Chemin-A-Haut and Bartholomew meet. Fishing, boat rentals, treks on nature trails and picnicking.

The **Ouachita Wildlife Management Area** *(LA 15, 10 km southeast of Monroe,* ☎ *343-4044)* offers fishing, hunting, rudimentary camping (with running water). Ornithology buffs will delight in observing the birds living on this 320-hectare expanse of bottomland hardwood forest.

The **Russell Sage Wildlife Management Area** *(11 km east of Monroe via US 80 or I-20,* ☎ *343-4044)* is a

6,900-hectare wildlife reserve. Hunting and rather rudimentary camping.

Tallulah

The **Tensas River National Wildlife Refuge** *(free admission; Mon to Fri 8am to 4pm; 14 km west of Tallulah via US 80, ☎ 574-2664)*, whose 22,800 hectares of protected forests provide shelter for abundant wildlife including black bears, alligators, deer, waterfowl and wild turkeys, is also a study centre. Observation tower and interpretive trails.

 # ACCOMMODATIONS

Shreveport/Bossier City

Finding accommodations in Louisiana is easy thanks to the great number of hotels and motels located near trunk roads. These places, which put more stock in modern comfort than in charming surroundings, are hardly ideal for prolonged stays, however. There is not much else to be said about these virtually identical hotels and motels. The following list merely aims to provide visitors with options when finding accommodation during the tourist season proves somewhat difficult. One advantage, however: several establishments offer breakfast (added to your bill). This applies to other regions as well. All mentioned establishments accept credit cards.

Located south of Shreveport is **KOA Shreveport/Bossier City** *(6510 W. 70th St., Shreveport, ☎ 687-1010)*.

Camper's RV Center *(7700 W. 70th St., Shreveport, ☎ 687-4567)* features several sites equipped for recreational vehicles.

C & J RV Park *($10; 14.4 km north of I-220, 6941 LA 1, Shreveport, ☎ 929-3193)* provides excellent accommodations for those travelling in RVs. Public showers.

The **Cypress Black Bayou Recreation and RV Park** *($-$$; get off I-20 at Airline Dr., head north for 13 km then turn right onto Linton Road and travel 6 km, ☎ 965-0007)*, on Cypress Bayou Lake, provides both full hook-up RV sites and campsites for tents. Supplies all services, a grocery as well as a playground, a beach and nature trails. Rental boats for fishing.

Hilltop Campgrounds *($-$$; 200 Hilltop Rd., Princeton, 8 km east of Bossier, ☎ 949-8486)*. Camping site with over 100 fully equipped locations. Guests can swim or fish in the lake.

Pine Hill Mobile Home and RV Park *($-$$; 900 US 80, Haughton, ☎ 949-3916)*. The park boasts 42 RV spaces. Bathrooms, public showers and launderette.

The **Mid-City Motor Hotel** *($30-$50; K; 725 Jordan St., Shreveport, ☎ 425-7481)* offers 60 rooms, each equipped with a kitchenette. This hotel ranks among the most economical establishments in the region.

The **Sundowner Inn-West** *($33-$60; ≡, pb, tv, ℜ, ≈; 2134 Greenwood Rd., Shreveport, ☎ 425-7467)* is west of downtown and close to I-20.

The **Plantation Inn** *($35 to $45; ≡, pb, tv, ℜ, ≈; 4901 Greenwood Rd.,*

Shreveport, ☎ *635-0500)* lies at the city's west entrance. It is easily reached via I-20, running parallel to Greenwood Road.

The **Howard Johnson Lodge and Restaurant** *($40-80;* ≡*, pb, tv,* ℜ*,* ≈*; 1906 N. Market St., Shreveport,* ☎ *424-6621)* is situated at the city's exit, where Market Street turns into US 71; this highway leads to Oil City and Vivian.

Days Inn - Shreveport *($43;* ≡*, pb, tv,* ℜ*,* ≈*; 4935 W. Monkhouse Dr., Shreveport,* ☎ *636-0080 or 1-800-325-2525).* Altogether standard and inexpensive establishment west of town, on the main highway leading to the regional airport.

Best Western Château Suite Hotel *($50-$100, bkfst incl;* ≡*, pb, K; 201 Lake St., Bossier City, Exit 13 off I-20,* ☎ *222-7620 or 1-800-845-9334 from North America)* has 103 rooms with all modern comforts.

Best Western Airline Motor Inn *($65-$75;* ≡*, pb, tv,* ≈*,* ℜ*; 1984 Airline Dr., Bossier City,* ☎ *742-6000 or 1-800-635-7639 from the US)* is by the main highway, upon entering Bossier City.

Located in the historic district, **The Columns on Jordan** *($85, bkfst incl;* ≡*, pb,* ⊛*, tv,* ℝ*,* ≈*,* ℜ*; 615 Jordan St., Shreveport,* ☎ *222-5912)* is a beautiful restored manor with five rooms boasting period furniture.

A lovely Victorian home dating from 1870, situated in the Highland Historic District, **Fairfield Place** *(single $95-$150, bkfst incl;* ≡*, pb, tv; 2221 Fairfield Ave., Shreveport,* ☎ *222-0048)* has nine rooms and studios with

European and American period furniture. No smoking.

🏠 The **2439 Farfield - A Bed & Breakfast** *($98-$149, bkfst incl;* ≡*, pb,* ⊛*,* ℝ*; 2439 Fairfield Ave., Shreveport,* ☎ *424-2424)* is another Victorian mansion built in the early 1900s. This establishment offers four rooms, each with its own private balcony overlooking English gardens.

West of Shreveport/Bossier City

Greenwood

The **Country Inn** *($30-$80;* ≡*, pb, tv,* ≈*; Exit 5 off I-20, 8489 Greenwood Rd.,* ☎ *938-7952)* is a 128-room hotel located near the highway, on the way out of Shreveport.

Vivian

The **Rose B & B** *(314 W. Tennessee St.,* ☎ *375-5607 or 375-3300).* Attractive house, dating from the end of the last century, with warm and friendly ambiance.

South of Shreveport/Bossier City

Mansfield

Burton's Gatehouse Inn *($30-$50; pb,* ≈*; 604 S. Washington St.,* ☎ *872-3601)* is another economical place in which to spend the night.

Zwolle

North Toledo Bend State Park *(camping $10-$12; cabin $65;* ≈*; picnic areas;*

16 km southwest of Zwolle, on LA 3229, ☎ *645-4715)* is fishing paradise. The park has 70 campsites and 10 cabins.

Many

Miss Elaine E.S. *($50-$60, bkfst incl; pb; 1315 Blake St.,* ☎ *256-6478)* offers two rooms furnished with antiques. The establishment also boasts a souvenir shop and an art gallery. For adults only. No smoking.

The Turtle Beach Lodge *($$; LA 191; mailing address: HC 63, P.O. Box 1025, LA 71449,* ☎ *256-5595)* is situated in the Toledo Bend Reservoir region. Air-conditioned cabins available. Camping, nearby grocery (where guests can purchase fishing bait and rent a boat) and gas station.

Florien

Red's Point *(RV $12, cabin $45; LA 191; mailing address: HC 65, P.O. Box 4420, LA 71429,* ☎ *565-4256)*. Camping site situated right near the large Toledo Bend Reservoir. Provides all RV services. Small cabins are also available. There is also a grocer here, where guests can buy fishing bait.

Toro Hills Lodge *(single $60, double $65; shared studio-condo $135;* ≡*, pb,* ⊛*, tv,* ℛ*,* ≈*, tennis; LA 171 South,* ☎ *586-4661,* ☎ *1-800-533-5031 from the US)*. All-inclusive rates for fishing on the Toledo Bend Reservoir.

East of Shreveport/Bossier City

Doyline

Lake Bistineau State Park *($10-$12, cabins $60-$65;* ≈*, beach, fishing,*

picnic areas; LA 163, 14 km south of Doyline,* ☎ *745-3503)* is by a 16-kilometre-long lake. The park has 67 campsites and 13 cabins.

Minden

🦐 **Calloway Corners B & B** *($60-$80, bkfst incl; LA 7, Sibley, 6 km south of Minden,* ☎ *377-2058 or 1-800-851-1088 from the US)* is a country-style house built in 1883. Three rooms are available to guests. The one-hectare property is planted with beautiful holm oaks, stunning magnolias and enormous pecan trees.

Homer

Lake Claiborne State Park *(camping $10-$12; LA 146, 11 km southeast of Homer,* ☎ *927-2976)* comprises 87 campsites, nature trails and a beach. Guests can rent a boat here and go fishing on the 2,560-hectare lake.

The **Caney Lakes Recreation Area** *($-$$; seasonal; from Minden, take LA 159 North to Webster Parish Road 111, then turn left on LA 111 and travel 3 km,* ☎ *927-2061)* offers nature lovers two lakes in the heart of the Kisatchie National Forest: Upper Caney Lake (50 hectares) and Lower Caney Lake (100 hectares). Forty-eight campsites, beach, fishing, nature trails. Visitors can walk around Upper Caney Lake on the 12-kilometres-long Sugar Cane National Recreation Trail. Remains of a sugar cane mill, from the time when sugar cane farming flourished in the region, can still be seen here.

Corney Lake *($-$$; all year round; LA 9, 28 km north of Homer,* ☎ *927-2061)* is a lovely 900-hectare lake set amidst a forest of cypresses, copal trees and pines. Eight camp sites, picnic areas and fishing.

Bucktail Campgrounds *($; LA 520, 11 km north of Homer,* ☎ *927-2061).* Wilderness camp with 25 sites in the heart of a pine forest. Running water only and no managed picnic areas.

Turkey Trot Campgrounds *($; north of Homer, follow LA 9 for 7 km, turn left on Forest Road 940 and travel 4 km, turn left on Forest Road 909 and drive for 1 km, following road signs,* ☎ *927-2061).* Rudimentary facilities, 25 sites, running water, no managed picnic areas.

Sugar Creek Campgrounds *($; from Homer, head north on LA 9 and travel 34 km, turn left on Forest Road 904 and drive for 2.5 km,* ☎ *927-2061).* Rudimentary facilities, 10 sites, no running water or managed picnic areas.

Linder Motor Lodge *($35-$45; ⊛, pb, tv, ℜ; LA 79 North,* ☎ *927-2574).* On the road leading to Haynesville.

Tall Timbers Cabins *($45, bkfst incl; pb; Harris Rd., 1.5 km from US 79 South,* ☎ *927-5260).* Situated in the hills; with private lake. Four units. All-inclusive price for deer hunting and fishing. Tennis and golf.

Haynesville

The **Burnham Plantation** *($40-$60, bkfst incl; pb; Parish Road 21,* ☎ *624-0695),* whose entrance is a carriage gateway, is a 6-hectare park with private lake. A paved path leads to the main house, a lovely Victorian residence offering four rooms with period furniture.

Athens

Home Place Acres Campgrounds *($$; 24 km northwest of Minden,* ☎ *358-4943)* offers many sites for RVs.

Arcadia

Nob Hill Inn *($31-$40, bkfst incl; pb, ℜ, ≈; Exit 69 off I-20,* ☎ *263-2013)* started out as an inn. The old building has been completely renovated and offers board and lodging once again.

Ruston

Comfort Inn *($40-$45; ⊛, pb, tv, ℝ, ≈; Exit 86 North off I-20,* ☎ *251-2360,* ☎ *1-800-228-5150 from North America).*

Best Western Kings Inn *($43-$66; ⊛, pb, tv, ≈; 1111 N. Trenton St.,* ☎ *251-0000,* ☎ *1-800-528-1234 from North America).* Trenton Street is Ruston's main thoroughfare.

Farmerville

D'Arbonne Lake State Park *($-$$; LA 2, west of Farmerville,* ☎ *368-2086)* features excellent fishing and water sports. Forty-three camp sites.

The **D'Arbonne Lake Motel** *($-$$; all-inclusive price for senior citizens; ⊛, tv, ℜ, ≈; Lake D'Arbonne,* ☎ *368-2236)* has 40 rooms as well as a marina with a gas station where guests can rent fishing gear.

Monroe/West Monroe

The **Cheniere Lake Park** *($; 112 Edwards Rd., West Monroe, ☎ 325-8327)*, situated close to the highway via LA 838, has several camping sites for tents.

The **Ouachita Wildlife Management Area** *($; LA 15, 10 km southeast of Monroe, ☎ 343-4044)* covers 320 hectares. Fishing, hunting, rudimentary camping with running water and observation tower for ornithology buffs.

The **Chemin-A-Haut State Park** *($10-$12; cabins $45-$50; ≈; 14656 State Park Rd., via LA 139, about 18 km north of Bastrop, ☎ 238-0812)* is another stopping place once used by Native Americans during their seasonal migrations. The park is at the intersection of Bayous Chemin-A-Haut and Bartholomew. Guests here can fish in a freshwater lake, rent a boat, stroll along one of the nature trails and go picnicking. Twenty-six camp sites and six cabins.

Budget Inn *($25-$35; ⊛, pb, tv, ≈; 2115 Louisville Ave., Monroe, ☎ 322-8161)*. The hotel is reached via Mill Sreet, downtown *(Exit 115 off I-20)*, which later turns into Bridge Street, then Louisville Avenue on the other side of the river. The establishment is one of the most reasonable in the region. You wouldn't want to stay anywhere cheaper.

The **Guest House Inn** *($38-$52; ⊛, pb, tv, ≈; 610 Civic Center Blvd, Monroe, ☎ 323-4452, ☎ 1-800-827-4451 from the US)* is located right near the highway, at Exit 117.

The **Travel Lodge** *($43-$47; ⊛, pb, tv, ℜ, ≈; 2102 Louisville Ave., Monroe, ☎ 325-5851, ☎ 1-800-325-2525 from North America)* is by the main thoroughfare leading to downtown and to the highway; in the opposite direction, it leads to US 165.

The **Holiday Inn Express** *($52-$62; ⊛, pb, tv, ℜ, ≈; at the junction of I-20 and Thomas Rd., West Monroe, ☎ 388-3810, ☎ 1-800-HOLIDAY from North America)* is situated west of the city; from the highway, take Exit 114.

The **Rosa Lee Inn** *($65-$95; reservations required; ⊛, pb; 318 Trenton St., West Monroe, ☎ 322-4090, after 6pm ☎ 322-5998)* was built in 1895. The hotel is located above Chandler's antique shop. The rooms are graced with antique furnishings. No children; no smoking. Trenton Street, in downtown Monroe, skirts the Ouachita River.

The **Boscobel Cottage B & B** *($75, bkfst incl; ⊛, pb, tv; 185 Cordell Lane; on US 165, 24 km south of Monroe, ☎ 749-1928)* is a lovely historic house from 1820 located by the Ouachita River. The residence boasts beautiful antique furniture, and the cottage is surrounded by stately pecan trees. Several cotton plantations are in this region.

Southwest of Tallulah

Lake Bruin State Park *($-$$; west of Winnsboro, close to St. Joseph and the State of Mississippi, LA 604, ☎ 1-888-677-1400 from the US)*. This region was explored by the Spaniard Hernando De Soto in the 16th century. The vast expanse of water covering 1,560 hectares, Bruin Lake, was once joined to the river bed. This lovely spot, where visitors can fish and swim (beach), boasts 25 campsites with picnic areas.

 RESTAURANTS

Shreveport

Café Bon Appetit *($; Mon to Sat 11am to 2:30pm; 4832 Line Ave., ☎ 868-1438)* offers honest cooking such as soups, salads, crepes and sandwiches. Chocolates and Louisiana gift baskets (assortment of spices, sweets, Creole and Cajun treats) can also be purchased here.

Julie Anne's Bakery and Café *($; Mon and Wed to Sat 6:30am to 7pm; 3110 Line Ave., ☎ 424-4995)* is a small place resembling a tea shop. Quiches and crepes are served here as is home-made bread with which succulent and hearty sandwiches are prepared. These can be enjoyed with the delicious soup of the day. This charming café also serves treats like milk shakes and ice cream.

Jacquelyn's Café *($; Mon to Sat 11am to 3pm; 1324 Louisiana Ave., ☎ 227-8598)* serves Cajun family-style daily specials as well as soups, sandwiches, salads and pies.

The **Noble Savage Tavern** *($; Mon to Fri 8:30am to 2am; 417 Texas Ave., ☎ 221-1781)* is a downtown restaurant where regional cuisine is prepared: gumbo, pasta and home-made pastries. Live music in the evenings.

A little out of the way, south of the downtown core, **Dudley and Gerald's**

($; every day 11:30am to 10pm; 2421 E. 70th St., ☎ 797-3010) offers Cajun and southern Louisiana cuisine: court-bouillon, stuffed crab, crawfish, shrimp or oyster po-boys, jambalaya, fried oysters.

Murrell's *($; every day 24 hours a day; 539 E. King St., ☎ 868-2620)* has been run by the same family for over 40 years. The establishment offers regional specialties.

Leon's Smoked Turkey *($-$$; Mon to Sat 10:30am to 8pm, Sun 11am to 8pm; 4723 Monkhouse Dr., ☎ 635-5700)* is a famous place. Excellent smoked turkey is prepared here, and it is said they make the best barbecue in town.

According to a local newspaper, the **Stumpwater Inn Restaurant** *($-$$; Sun and Tue to Thu 10am to 9pm, Fri and Sat 10am to 10pm; intersection of LA 169 and Blanchard-Furrh Rd., ☎ 929-3725)* makes the best traditional desserts around. Lobster Thermidor, catfish and grilled meats are also on the menu.

The **Piccadilly Cafeterias** *($-$$; every day 11am to 8:30pm; 57 S. Park Mall St., ☎ 686-6282; 1133 Mall St. Vincent St., ☎ 222-8057; 789 Shreveport-Barksdale Highway, ☎ 861-0967)* are all by the highway. Self-service restaurants, offering simple fare, especially regional dishes.

The **Cajun Seafood Gardens** restaurant *($-$$; every night 5pm to 10pm; 2441 E. 70th St., ☎ 797-6522)* prepares seafood, crawfish, steaks and catfish. Live music.

The **Pete Harris Café** *($-$$; Sun to Thu 8am to 1pm, Fri and Sat 11am to*

10pm; 1355 Milam St., ☎ 425-4277) attracts lovers of seafood (delicious stuffed shrimp), grilled meats and soul food. This place, which is said to be the oldest African-American restaurant in the United States, is very popular with locals.

La Paloma Mexican Restaurant *($-$$; Mon to Thu 11am to 9pm, Fri and Sat 11am to 10pm, Sun 11am to 2pm; 3110 Bert Kouns Industrial Loop, suite B, ☎ 687-6084)* makes Mexican food for American tastes; also features a daily menu.

The **Crescent Landing** *($$; Wed and Thu 11am to 2pm, Sun to Tue 11am to 2pm and 5pm to 8pm, Fri and Sat 11am to 2pm and 5pm to 9pm; 2530 Bert Kouns Industrial Loop, ☎ 686-4450)* has a wonderful rustic ambiance. All-you-can-eat catfish, said to be "the best in town". Steaks, chicken and shrimp are also on the menu.

At **Don's Seafood and Steakhouse** *($$; Sun to Thu 11am to 10pm, Fri and Sat 11am to 11pm; 3100 Highland Ave., ☎ 865-4291)*, seafood is prepared in southern Louisiana fashion.

At **Smith's Cross Lake Inn** *($$; Mon to Sat 5pm to 10pm; 5301 S. Lakeshore Dr., ☎ 631-0919)*, patrons opt for seafood or steak; a health menu is also provided. The view of the lake from the dining room is spectacular.

Monsieur Patou *($$$; Tue to Fri 11:30am to 2pm, every day 5pm to 11pm; 855 Pierremont Rd., ☎ 868-9822)*. Delicious authentic French cuisine in a Louis XV decor: chandeliers, crystal glasses, silverware.

Bossier City

Darrell's *($; every day 6am to midnight; 1964 Airline Dr., at I-20, ☎ 742-1999)* is a classic fifties diner, all painted in shades of blue and red and very popular with the locals. Their all-dressed hamburgers, home-made fries, milkshakes and strawberry pie are great favourites among regulars. Old photographs of Shreveport and Bossier City adorn the walls.

Cypress Inn *($-$$; Tue to Thu 5pm to 9pm, Fri and Sat 5pm to 10pm; S. Lakeshore Dr., Benton; 16 km north of Bossier City on LA 3, ☎ 965-2396)*. This restaurant offers a lovely view of Cypress Lake. Catfish, cooked in every conceivable way, is the house specialty. One such dish very prized by fish lovers is the catfish, served whole or in fillets, with marinated green tomatoes.

The **Louisiana Bar & Grill** *($-$$; Mon to Sat 11am to 10pm; 1701 Old Minden Rd., ☎ 741-1947)*, whose ambiance is that of a tavern from the twenties, serves beer, of course, and a choice of seafood or sandwiches; there is also an oyster bar.

Luby's Cafeteria *($-$$; Mon to Fri 10:45am to 2:30pm and 4:15pm to 8pm, Sat and Sun 10:45am to 8pm; 2958 E. Texas St., ☎ 741-3666)* is a regular haunt of residents, who wolf down salads, starters, vegetables, desserts and home-made bread here.

The **Pelican Room** at the Louisiana Downs racetrack *($$-$$$; Apr 24 to Nov 15, Wed to Sun 11am to 5pm; 8000 E. Texas St., ☎ 742-5555, ☎ 1-800-648-0712 from the US)*, whose dining room accommodates up to 700 guests, serves à-la-carte meals.

The **Sky Club** at the Louisiana Downs racetrack *($$$; Apr 24 to Nov 15; 8000 E. Texas St.,* ☎ *742-5555,* ☎ *1-800-648-0712 from the US)* lays out a lavish buffet. Sophisticated ambiance .

West of Shreveport/Bossier City

Greenwood

El Chico Restaurant *($$; Sun to Thu 11am to 10pm, Fri and Sat 11am to 11pm; 2127 Greenwood Rd.,* ☎ *425-7928)* is part of a large family-restaurant chain. Very Americanized Mexican (Tex-Mex) food and a few grilled meats are also on the menu.

Mooringsport

The **Summer Point Landing** Restaurant *($-$$; Tue to Thu 5pm to 9pm, Fri and Sat 5pm to 10pm; 7930 Boy Scout Camp Rd.,* ☎ *996-6045)* on Caddo Lake, close to the dam and 1 kilometre from LA 1 North, serves regional specialties, catfish, seafood and grilled meats.

Vivian

Big Boy's Diner *($; Mon to Sat 11am to 2pm and 5pm to 8pm; Stagecoach Junction Mall, downtown Vivian,* ☎ *375-3007)* prepares regional cuisine. Portions are substantial and desserts home-made.

The Hill Family Restaurant *($-$$; Mon to Sat 7am to 9pm, Sun 7am to 2pm; buffet 11am to 2pm; 1107 S. Pine St.,*

☎ *375-5700)* prepares hearty breakfasts, all kinds of sandwiches, steaks, seafood and Tex-Mex food.

South of Shreveport/Bossier City

Mansfield

At **Cole's** *($-$$; Tue to Sat 5pm to 10pm; LA 509, Lake Rd., close to Carmel,* ☎ *872-2404)*, the menu consists of grilled meats, seafood, crawfish and salads. Senior citizens' night on Tuesdays and all-you-can-eat catfish on Wednesdays.

Zwolle

Ethyl's Driftwood Restaurant *($; every day 5am to 10pm; Carter Ferry Rd.,* ☎ *645-6455)*. Family restaurant located by the Toledo Bend Reservoir. The menu features seafood, steaks and chicken.

Many

Sam's Restaurant *($-$$; Mon to Sat 7am to 9pm, Sun 7am to 2pm; US 171 South,* ☎ *256-9248)*. Varied menu, buffet on Sundays and catfish-based specialties on Fridays and Saturdays.

The Big Bass Marina *($$; Tue to Thu 6am to 9pm, Fri and Sat 5am to 10pm; on LA 476,* ☎ *586-4721,* ☎ *1-800-426-2809 from the US)* is also by the large Toledo Bend Reservoir. The restaurant has modelled itself after a seaside resort. Seafood, Asian dishes, hamburgers.

Country Boy *($$; every day 10am to 10pm; US 171 South,* ☎ *256-3953)*. A sign tells you all you need to know straight off: "The best food in Many is the spicy fried chicken, catfish fillets, shrimp and oysters!"

East of Shreveport/Bossier City

Doyline

At **Bobbie's Grocery** *($; every day 5am to 10pm; LA 163, State Park Rd., ☎ 745-3367)*, you can eat in the company of fishermen, as this place rents all necessary fishing gear.

Ringgold

Billy's Place *($; Mon to Thu 6am to 10pm, Fri 6am to midnight, Sat 7am to midnight; LA 7, ☎ 894-9234)* serves breakfast, grilled meats, minced meat pies and sandwiches as well as beer. Gas station.

Minden

Vivian Antique Mall and Tea Garden *($-$$; 142 W. Louisiana Ave., ☎ 375-3300)* is a charming tea shop surrounded by a Victorian-style garden. Crepes, quiches, milk pancakes, salads, sandwiches and desserts are among the delights served here. Afternoon English tea.

Bayou Inn Restaurant *($$; Sun to Thu 5pm to 9pm, Fri and Sat 11am to 10pm; ☎ 371-0287)*. This restaurant with rustic decor serves all-you-can-eat catfish in every shape or form, as well as steaks.

Arcadia

Luigi's Restaurant *($-$$; Tue to Sat 10am to 10pm; 811 Railroad Ave., downtown, ☎ 263-2248)* offers Italian food, steaks and sandwiches as well as a salad bar.

Ruston

The **Boiling Point** *($; Mon to Thu 11am to 9pm, Fri 11am to 10pm, Sat and Sun noon to 9pm; 381 W. California Ave., ☎ 255-8506)*, a very popular little restaurant where patrons eat at picnic tables, specializes in boiled crawfish enjoyed in the traditional way with corn on the cob, potato and an onion cooked in the shellfish court-bouillon. The whole is served with hot sauces. Many other freshwater- or ocean-fish-based dishes are also offered here, as is seafood from the Gulf of Mexico.

Bee's *($; Mon to Fri 5:30am to 7pm, Sat 5:30am to 5pm; 805 Larson St., ☎ 255-5610)* offers Creole food, cornbread, various grilled meats and breakfast.

Potluck *($; Mon to Sat 9:30am to 5:30pm, Fri and Sat 10am to midnight; 202 N. Vienna St., ☎ 254-1331)* specializes in breakfasts. Relaxed ambiance.

The **Sundown Tavern** *($; every day 11am to 9pm; 107 E. Park Ave., ☎ 255-8028)* serves a few good deli-style sandwiches.

Anthony's Pasta and Seafood *($-$$; Mon to Thu 11am to 9pm, Fri and Sat 11am to 11pm, Sun 8:30am to 10pm; 109 N. Trenton St., ☎ 255-9000)* prepares every conceivable

Italian-American pasta dish as well as seafood dishes to order.

Monroe/West Monroe

Catfish King Restaurant *($; Sun to Thu 11am to 9pm, Fri and Sat 11am to 10pm; 305 Sterlington Rd., Monroe,* ☎ *322-6115).* Family restaurant specializing in seafood and, as its name suggests, catfish reigns supreme here!

Ma and Pa's Kitchen *($; Mon to Fri 6am to 2pm; 310 Wood St., West Monroe,* ☎ *325-3442)* specializes in regional dishes and breakfasts; daily lunch specials are also offered.

West Monroe Coney Island *($; Mon to Sat 8:30am to 6pm; 410 Natchitoches St., West Monroe,* ☎ *323-7610)* makes the best hot dog in town!

Joe Bob's Seafood *($-$$; Tue to Sat 5pm to 10pm; 1100 Bayou D'Arbonne Dr., West Monroe,* ☎ *396-1818)* offers a lovely view of Lake D'Arbonne. Seafood and steaks.

The **Depot** *($-$$; Mon to Fri 11am to 2pm, Fri and Sat 5:30am to 10pm; 100 Trenton St., West Monroe,* ☎ *323-8996)* lays out an impressive and lavish self-serve, all-you-can-eat buffet!

Enoch's Café *($-$$; Mon to Sat 11am to 2am; 717 N. 6th St., Monroe,* ☎ *323-3455)* is a friendly place offering Louisiana and Texan cuisine. Wide range of live music: American, European and Cajun music.

Mohawk Seafood Tavern *($-$$; Tue to Thu 11am to 9pm, Fri and Sat 11am to 10pm; 704 Louisville Ave., Monroe,* ☎ *322-5481)* remains one of the best oyster bars north of New Orleans.

Morrison's Cafeteria *($-$$; Mon to Sat 11am to 8:30pm, Sun 11am to 6:30pm; 4700 Millhaven Rd., Monroe,* ☎ *322-5230).* Self-serve regional cooking.

Swartz Smokehouse & Grill *($-$$; 1882 LA 139, Swartz, 3 km north of Monroe,* ☎ *345-0486)* is a very popular place in which to savour a real Louisiana-style barbecue.

Cascio's Seafood Tavern *($$; Mon to Thu 11am to 10pm, Fri and Sat 11am to 11pm; 1210 N. 18th St., Monroe,* ☎ *387-3670).* The Cascios were one of the first families to launch out into the restaurant business in Monroe. Italian specialties, seafood and steaks.

Captain Avery Seafood Restaurant *($$-$$$; every day 5pm to 10pm; 1500 Hwy 165 North, Monroe,* ☎ *345-0100)* was granted several awards for its Louisiana-style seafood and steaks. The establishment has its own bar.

Winnsboro

Papa Wayne's *($; Sun to Thu 10am to 11pm, Fri and Sat 10am to midnight; 302 Front St.,* ☎ *435-3884).* Authentic American diner serving chicken and fried fish as well as regional cooking.

Gilbert

R.V.'s Food & Fun *($; Mon to Sat 5am to 10pm; LA 15 South,* ☎ *435-4650)* prepares steaks and grilled or fried fish. This rural restaurant also offers hearty breakfasts and a generous lunch buffet.

ENTERTAINMENT

Shreveport/Bossier City

The **Ark-La-Tex Round-up** *(adults $4, children 5-12 $2; Airline High School auditorium, 2801 Airline Dr., Bossier City,* ☎ *688-5463 or 869-3675 or 688-1130)* features country and gospel music with local professional musicians or amateurs on the first and third Saturdays of the each month. The programme is inspired by the Louisiana Hayride, an extraordinarily popular show in the fifties and sixties that saw the debuts of Hank Williams and Elvis Presley, among others.

At **James Burton's Rock n' Roll Café** *(cover charge; live music Wed to Sat 4pm to 4am; 616 Commerce St., Shreveport,* ☎ *424-5000)*, a fifties-, sixties- and seventies-retro café, favourite stars such as Elvis Presley and John Denver (who passed away in October, 1997) hold an exalted place.

The **Marjorie Lyons Playhouse** *(box office open Tue to Sat noon to 4pm; Centenary College campus, 2911 Centenary Blvd, Shreveport,* ☎ *869-5242)* presents six to eight big productions every year.

Shreveport Captains Baseball *(2 adults $10, children under 12 $2; Apr to Aug; Fair Grounds Field, Shreveport,* ☎ *636-5555,* ☎ *1-800-467-3230 from the US)*. The Captains are the AA-affiliate of the San Francisco Giants, a Major League Baseball team.

Shreveport Storm - Basketball Games *(admission fee; Nov to Mar; Centenary College campus, Shreveport; for schedule information:* ☎ *425-SLAM)*. The college's semi-professional basketball team competes against rival teams from other schools on a regular basis.

At the **Louisiana Downs** racetrack *($2-$8; Apr 24 to Nov 15; east of Bossier City, at the junction of I-20 and I-220,* ☎ *742-5555,* ☎ *1-800-551-RACE from the US)*, lucky backers can win up to $150,000 US! Children under 12 are not admitted to the racetrack, and impulsive gamblers must abstain from placing bets. Variety of restaurants on the premises.

Harrah's Shreveport Casino *(Shreveport Rose riverboat casino, Red River Dock, Clyde Fant Parkway, Shreveport,* ☎ *1-800-HARRAHS from the US)* is on a dockside riverboat casino, a faithful reproduction of a steamboat from the last century. It boasts 945 slot machines and 37 gaming tables.

Water Town U.S.A. *(May to Aug; Mon and Tue 10am to 6pm, Wed to Sat 10am to 8pm, Sun noon to 6pm; 7670 W. 70th St., Shreveport,* ☎ *938-5475)* has a swimming pool and a water park, allowing visitors to cool off and find temporary relief from the Louisiana heat and humidity. The park also features picnic areas and playgrounds.

At the colossal **Hamel's Amusement Park** *(spring, Sat 1pm to 10pm, Sun 1pm to 6pm; summer, Wed to Fri 6pm to 10pm, Sat 1pm to 10pm, Sun 1pm to 7pm; E. 70th St., Shreveport,* ☎ *869-3566)*, a host of rides and games await visitors. Fun entertainment in store for kids of all ages. Food is also available.

West of Shreveport/Bossier City

Greenwood

Boothill Speedway *(adults $8, free for children; Mar to Nov, Sat nights; Exit 3 off I-20, Cemetery Rd.,* ☎ *938-9373)*. Stock car races on the South's fastest quarter-mile oval dirt track.

East of Shreveport/Bossier City

Homer

The **North Louisiana Hayride** *(adults $5, 6-11 years old $2; Sat 8pm to 11:30pm; P & W Ranchouse, LA 9, north exit of Homer)* has been presenting shows and country dancing for about thirty years on what remains the largest dance floor in the Ark-La-Tex (Arkansas-Louisiana-Texas) region.

Ruston

The **Dixie Jamboree** *(adults $5, children and seniors $3; Sat from 7:30pm; 206 N. Vienna St.,* ☎ *255-0048)* stomps away at the Dixie Theater, an old cinema dating from 1920. Country music, gospel and blues can be enjoyed here. Comedians and shows are also presented.

Monroe/West Monroe

The **Honky Tonk** *(2003 Tower Dr.)* is the mecca of country music and one of the biggest dance halls in the region. Dance lessons on Wednesday nights.

There are two African-American nightclubs featuring good blues in Monroe/West Monroe:

Member's Club *(cover charge; nights; 1922 Tichelli Rd., for information regarding featured musical guests and show times:* ☎ *387-1050)*.

T's Lounge & Diner *(cover charge; nights; 2407 De Siard Avenue; for information regarding featured musical guests and show times:* ☎ *387-2279)*.

Calendar of Events

April

One of the biggest battles fought during the Civil War is commemorated in the northeast part of Sabine Parish, in Pleasant Hill *(weekend around Apr 9;* ☎ *256-5880)*.

June

The **Louisiana Peach Festival** *(*☎ *255-2031)* is held the second weekend of June, in the market-gardening town of Ruston. The festival's theme is "the spirit of the peach", a fruit that grows in profusion in the region. The **Mitcham Farms** orchard *(Hwy 2, Ruston,* ☎ *255-3409)* is open to the public.

In Louisiana, the blueberry flourishes in the Toledo Bend Reservoir region – just as it does in the Lac-Saint-Jean region of Québec. The **Louisiana Blueberry Festival** takes place on the third weekend of June in downtown Mansfield.

Fans of bluegrass music, one of the many current musical forms of expression in Louisiana, can attend the **Homeplace Acres Bluegrass Festival**, near Athens *(at night, first Fri, Sat and Sun of Jun,* ☎ *927-2222).*

July

Louisiana Watermelon Festival *(last weekend of Jul; Farmerville, 32 km north of West Monroe,* ☎ *368-3390).*

September

The **Southern Pickin' and Grinnin' Festival**, which celebrates the cotton industry, is held every year *(third Sat of Sep)* in Rayville, in the Richland Parish. For all pertinent information, contact the **Southern Pickin' and Grinnin' Festival Head Office** *(mailing address: P.O. Box 873, Rayville, LA 71268;* ☎ *728-3380 or 728-4127).*

Bluegrass music fans can get a second chance to attend the **Homeplace Acres Bluegrass Festival**, near Athens *(at night, second Fri, Sat and Sun of Sep;* ☎ *927-2222),* during its second run of the year.

The **Louisiana Folklife Festival** *(free admission; by the Ouachita River; 2nd weekend of Sep;* ☎ *1-800-843-1872 from the US)* celebrates a hodgepodge of cultures, Namely Cajun, native American and Creole. Music, arts and crafts, the gastronomy of Louisiana, not to mention cowboys, are all featured!

October

Zwolle Tamale Fiesta Festival *(Oct;* ☎ *256-5880).* Celebration of the Hispano-American heritage recalling the time when the region was united with Texas, on the other side of the Sabine River.

November

Florien Free State Festival *(Nov;* ☎ *256-5880).* After the Louisiana Purchase in 1803, the Florien region remained "no man's land" for about twenty years. The festival relates the different stages of Florien's rich history since that time.

 SHOPPING

Shreveport/Bossier City

The Line Avenue *(Common St., north of I-20, Shreveport,* ☎ *868-3651).* In the heart of Shreveport, this avenue encompasses about fifty businesses, boutiques, galleries and restaurants.

The Antique Mall *(Tue to Sat 10am to 5pm; 542 to 546 Olive St., Shreveport,* ☎ *425-8786)* is the biggest antique shop in North Louisiana.

Libbey Glass Factory Outlet *(Tue to Sat 10am to 5pm, Sun 1pm to 5pm; 4302 Jewella St., Shreveport,* ☎ *621-0228).* All items are available at wholesale prices in this shop owned by the famous Libbey Glass Factory.

The **Mall St. Vincent** *(Mon to Thu 9am to 7pm, Fri and Sat 9am to 9pm, Sun noon to 5pm; corner of St. Vincent and Southern Avenues, Shreveport,* ☎ *227-9880)* comprises shops that sell well-known brand-name linens and household items at half-price.

West of Shreveport/Bossier City

Greenwood

The **Greenwood Flea Market** *(Sat and Sun 10am to 6pm; Exit 5 off I-20, ☎ 938-7201)* boasts close to 150 kiosks and boutiques specializing in the sale of antiques.

Vivian

The **Re-Creations Musicke Shoppe** *(Tue to Sat 11am to 6pm; 136 W. Louisiana St., ☎ 375-5995)* sells antique musical instruments and makes instruments used by traditional folk musicians.

East of Shreveport/Bossier City

Monroe/West Monroe

Antique Alley *(Tue to Sat 10am to 5pm; from 100 through 200 Trenton St., West Monroe, ☎ 322-2691)* looks like a genuine antique village with its three-block array of shops in 1880s buildings. American and European furniture and vintage artifacts, carpets from the Middle East, Chinese vases, china, silverware, crystal, paintings and a multitude of decorative objects are all to be found here.

Rayville

There is a very interesting confectioner's shop west of Monroe/West Monroe:

Irene White's Café *(every day; 302 Rescue St., Rayville, ☎ 728-2499)*. In 1945, Irene White ran a café in this very place; the candy store that now occupies the premises has kept the original name. It is a favourite haunt of locals – young and old alike. A small museum relates the history of Irene's Café.

INDEX

1850 House (Greater New Orleans) 78
Abbeville (Western Acadiana) . . . 314
    Accommodations 321
    Finding Your Way Around . . . 304
    Restaurants 326
Abita Brewery (Abita Springs) . . 102
Abita Springs (Greater New
    Orleans) 99
    Finding Your Way Around . . . 61
Academy of the Sacred Heart
    (Grand Coteau) 274
Acadian craft store (St.
    Martinville) 246
Acadian Cultural Center
    (Lafayette) 218
Acadian House Museum (St.
    Martinville) 245
Acadian Memorial (St. Martinville) 246
Acadian plantation (St. Martinville) 246
Acadian Village (Lafayette) 220
Acadiana 25
Acadiana Fish Farm (Branch) . . . 283
Acadiana Park Nature Station
    (Acadiana: Lafayette) 221
Acadiana Zoo (Broussard) 221
Acadiana: Lafayette 211, 218
    Accommodations 223
    Calendar of Events 233
    Entertainment 231
    Finding Your Way Around . . . 212
    Guided Tours 217
    Parks 221
    Practical Information 214
    Restaurants 226
    Shopping 234
Acadiana: North of Lafayette . . . 269
    Accommodations 287
    Entertainment 292
    Finding Your Way Around . . . 269
    Parks 285
    Practical Information 272
    Restaurants 290
    Shopping 297
Acadians 20
Accommodations 48

Adams House (Greater New
    Orleans) 92
Afton Villa Gardens (St. Francisville
    Area) 170
Airports
    Alexandria International Airport 338
    Baton Rouge Metropolitan
        Airport 158
    Lafayette Regional Airport . . . 213
    Lakefront Airport 57
    Moisant Airport 42, 57
    Monroe Regional Airport 371
    New Orleans International
        Airport 42, 57
    Shreveport/Bossier Regional
        Airport 368
Alabama Plantation House
    (Ferriday) 352
Albania Plantation House
    (Jeanerette) 250
Albany (Greater New Orleans) . . 103
    Finding Your Way Around . . . 62
Aldes Vidrine House (Ville Platte) 279
Alexandre Mouton House
    (Lafayette) 220
Alexandria (Crossroads) 343
    Accommodations 355
    Entertainment 362
    Finding Your Way Around . . . 337
    Guide Services 343
    Practical Information 342
    Restaurants 360
Alexandria International Airport . 338
Alexandria Museum of Art
    (Alexandria - Pineville) 345
Alexandria National Cemetery
    (Alexandria - Pineville) 345
Alexandria Zoological Park
    (Alexandria - Pineville) 345
Algiers Point (Greater New Orleans) 85
Allendale Plantation (Port Allen) . 175
American Queen (Greater New
    Orleans) 100
Americans 21
Amistad Research Center (Greater
    New Orleans) 93

Amite (Greater New Orleans) . . . 103
    Accommodations 120
    Finding Your Way Around . . . 62
    Practical Information 67
    Restaurants 138
Anacoco (Crossroads) 349
    Accommodations 359
    Finding Your Way Around . . . 341
Andouille 30
Angola (Plantations, Baton Rouge) 171
    Finding Your Way Around . . . 159
Angola Crafts Fair (Angola) 171
Angola Rodeo (Angola) 171
Aquarium of the Americas (Greater
    New Orleans) 70
Arboretum (Houma) 196
Arcadia (Northern Louisiana) . . . 380
    Accommodations 391
    Finding Your Way Around . . . 371
    Parks 387
    Restaurants 396
Arlington House (Washington) . . 278
Arlington Plantation (Franklin) . . 251
Armstrong, Louis 29
Arnaudville (Acadiana: North of
    Lafayette)
    Accommodations 287
    Entertainment 292
    Finding Your Way Around . . . 269
Ascension Catholic Church
    (Donaldsonville) 173
Atchafalaya Basin (Henderson) . . 242
Athens (Northern Louisiana) 380
    Accommodations 391
    Finding Your Way Around . . . 371
Aubrey, Charles-Phillipe 19
Audubon Park (Greater New
    Orleans) 95
Audubon State Commemorative
    Area (St. Francisville) 169
Audubon Zoological Gardens
    (Greater New Orleans) 95
Audubon, John James 96
Avery Island (Bayou Teche) 249
    Finding Your Way Around . . . 240
Azalea Trail (Lafayette) 221
B. Lemann & Brothers Inc.
    (Donaldsonville) 174

Back Forty Peaches (Arcadia) . . . 380
Banks 47
Banque de la Louisiane (Greater
    New Orleans) 74
Barataria (Greater New Orleans)
    Finding Your Way Around . . . 63
Barrow House (St. Francisville) . . 169
Bars and Nightclubs 50
Basile (Western Acadiana)
    Entertainment 328
    Finding Your Way Around . . . 302
    Restaurants 324
Baton Rouge (Plantations, Baton
    Rouge) 164
    Accommodations 178
    Entertainment 186
    Finding Your Way Around . . . 158
    Restaurants 182
Baton Rouge Zoo (Plantations, Baton
    Rouge) 177
Battle of Baton Rouge (Baton
    Rouge) 166
Bayou Art Gallery (New Iberia) . . 247
Bayou Bourbeux Battle
    (Washington) 278
Bayou Folk Museum (Cloutierville) 346
Bayou Goula (Plantations, Baton
    Rouge) 174
    Finding Your Way Around . . . 160
Bayou Kisatchie (Crossroads) . . . 354
Bayou Lacombe Museum
    (Lacombe) 99
Bayou Lafourche and Terrebonne 191
    Accommodations 201
    Calendar of Events 206
    Entertainment 206
    Finding Your Way Around . . . 191
    Guided Tours 194
    Parks 201
    Practical Information 194
    Restaurants 204
    Shopping 209
    Tourist Information 194
Bayou Légendaire (Abbeville) . . . 315
Bayou St. John (Greater New
    Orleans) 85

INDEX

Bayou Teche 242
  Accommodations 254
  Calendar of Events 265
  Entertainment 263
  Finding Your Way Around . . . 238
  Guided Tours 241
  Parks 253
  Practical Information 241
  Restaurants 258
  Shopping 266
  Tourist Information 241
Bayside Plantation House
  (Jeanerette) 250
Beaches
  Holly Beach (Western Acadiana)316
Beau Fort Plantation (Natchez) . . 347
Beauregard House (Chalmette) . . 104
Beauregard Museum (De Ridder) . 350
Beauregard Parish (Crossroads)
  Practical Information 343
Beauregard Town (Baton Rouge) 166
Beauregard, Pierre Gustave Toutant 22
Beauregard-Keyes House (Greater
  New Orleans) 79
Beausoleil Lake (Western
  Acadiana) 316
Beaux Gators Farm (Kaplan) 314
Béchet, Sidney 26
Beignet 30
Ben Routh Recreational Area
  (Acadiana: North of
  Lafayette) 287
Bentley (Crossroads)
  Finding Your Way Around . . . 338
Bicycle 42
Bienville Warehouse Museum
  (Arcadia) 380
Bird City Sanctuary (Bayou Teche) 249
Black Heritage Festival (Vidalia) . 353
Black History Month Parade
  (Marksville) 285
Blanchard
  Parks 386
Blue Bayou Water Park (Plantations,
  Baton Rouge) 177
Bluffs on Thompson Creek (St.
  Francisville) 177
Blythewood Plantation (Amite) . . 103

Bogalusa (Greater New Orleans) . 102
  Finding Your Way Around . . . 61
  Practical Information 67
Bogue Lusa Pioneer Museum
  (Bogalusa) 102
Bogue-Chitto National Wildlife
  Reserve (Greater New Orleans) 98
Bohemia (Greater New Orleans)
  Finding Your Way Around . . . 62
Bonnie & Clyde Trade Days
  (Arcadia) 380
Bonnie Glen (New Roads Area) . . 176
Boothill Speedway (Shreveport) . 376
Boscobel Cottage (Monroe) 382
Bossier City (Northern Louisiana) 373
  Accommodations 388
  Entertainment 398
  Finding Your Way Around . . . 368
  Parks 385
  Practical Information 373
  Restaurants 394
  Shopping 400
Boudin 31
Boudreaux Canal General Store
  (Chauvin) 198
Bowie Oak (Opelousas) 276
Bowie Residence (Opelousas) . . . 276
Bragg, Braxton 22
Branch (Acadiana: North of
  Lafayette) 283
  Finding Your Way Around . . . 272
Breaux Bridge (Bayou Teche) . . . 242
  Accommodations 254
  Entertainment 263
  Finding Your Way Around . . . 238
  Restaurants 258
Brennan House (Greater New
  Orleans) 91
Briarwood (Saline) 349
Briggs-Staub House (Greater New
  Orleans) 89
Brimstone Museum (Sulfur) 313
Broussard (Acadiana: Lafayette) . 221
  Accommodations 226
  Finding Your Way Around . . . 214
  Restaurants 231
Broussard (Bayou Teche) 243
  Finding Your Way Around . . . 238

Broussard, Joseph 20
Brownell Memorial Park (Morgan
    City) 253
Brusly (Plantations, Baton Rouge) 175
    Finding Your Way Around . . . 160
    Restaurants 185
Bunkie (Acadiana: North of
    Lafayette) 283
    Finding Your Way Around . . . 272
    Practical Information 274
    Shopping 299
Buras (Greater New Orleans) . . . 105
    Finding Your Way Around . . . 62
Burk's Log Cabin and Museum
    (Merryville) 350
Burns Point Recreation Area (Bayou
    Teche) 254
Burnside (Plantations, Baton
    Rouge) 163
    Accommodations 177
    Finding Your Way Around . . . 156
    Restaurants 182
Bus 41
Bush (Greater New Orleans)
    Restaurants 137
Business Hours 49
Butler Greenwood (St. Francisville
    Area) 170
Butte La Rose (Bayou Teche) . . . 243
    Accommodations 254
    Entertainment 264
    Finding Your Way Around . . . 238
Cabildo (Greater New Orleans) . . 78
Caddo Lake (Northern Louisiana) 385
Caddo Pine Island Oil and Historical
    Society Museum (Oil City) . . 376
Café au lait 31
Cajun Prairie Restoration Project
    (Acadiana: North of
    Lafayette) 286
Cajun Queen (Greater New
    Orleans) 100
Calas 31
Cameron (Western Acadiana)
    Accommodations 322
    Finding Your Way Around . . . 304
Cameron Prairie Wildlife Refuge
    (Western Acadiana) 317

Camp Moore State Commemorative
    Area (Greater New Orleans) . 103
Cancellation Insurance 43
Canebrake Plantation House
    (Ferriday) 352
Caney Lake (Northern Louisiana) . 386
    Finding Your Way Around . . . 371
    Parks 387
Caney Lakes Recreation Area
    (Northern Louisiana) 386
Cankton (Acadiana: North of
    Lafayette)
    Finding Your Way Around . . . 270
Canoeing
    Greater New Orleans 105
Capote, Truman 27
Car 39
Car Rental 40
Carencro (Acadiana: Lafayette)
    Accommodations 226
    Entertainment 232
    Finding Your Way Around . . . 214
    Restaurants 230
Carroll-Crawford House (Greater
    New Orleans) 92
Carville (Plantations, Baton Rouge)163
    Finding Your Way Around . . . 156
Casa de Comercio (Greater New
    Orleans) 76
Casa Faurie (Greater New Orleans) 75
Caspiana Plantation Store
    (Natchitoches) 348
Catahoula (Crossroads)
    Practical Information 343
Catahoula Dogs (Denham) 168
Catahoula Lake (Crossroads) . . . 355
Catahoula Parish Museum of Natural
    History (Harrisonburg) 351
Catalpa Plantation (St. Francisville
    Area) 170
Cathedral Garden (Greater New
    Orleans) 77
Cecilia (Acadiana: North of
    Lafayette) 274
    Entertainment 292
    Finding Your Way Around . . . 269

INDEX

Central Business District (Greater
    New Orleans) 83
    Accommodations 115
    Restaurants 128
CFMA Cajun Music Festival
    (Eunice) 280
Chackbay (Bayou Lafourche and
    Terrebonne)
    Finding Your Way Around . . . 193
    Restaurants 206
Chalmette (Greater New Orleans) 104
    Finding Your Way Around . . . 62
    Practical Information 68
    Restaurants 139
Charenton (Bayou Teche) 251
    Entertainment 265
    Finding Your Way Around . . . 240
Charity Hospital (French Quarter)   74
Château des Cocodrils (Jennings) 310
Chatham (Northern Louisiana)
    Finding Your Way Around . . . 371
Chauvin (Bayou Lafourche and
    Terrebonne) 197
    Accommodations 202
    Finding Your Way Around . . . 192
    Restaurants 205
Chemin-A-Haut State Park (Northern
    Louisiana) 387
Chêne Vent Lastrapes
    (Washington) 278
Cheneyville (Crossroads) 350
    Accommodations 358
    Finding Your Way Around . . . 342
Chérie Districts (New Roads Area) 177
Cherokee Plantation (Natchez) . . 347
Chicot State Park (Acadiana: North
    of Lafayette) 286
Chipola (Greater New Orleans)
    Finding Your Way Around . . . 62
Chretien Point Plantation Home
    (Sunset) 275
Christ Church (Covington) 99
Church Point (Acadiana: North of
    Lafayette) 281
    Finding Your Way Around . . . 272
    Shopping 299
Church Point Mardi Gras (Acadiana:
    North of Lafayette) 281

Cinclare Plantation (Brusly) 175
City Park (Greater New Orleans) . 87
Civil War 22
Claiborne Parish Courthouse
    (Homer) 380
Clay House (Greater New Orleans) 81
Clifton's Club (New Iberia) 248
Climate 46
Clinton (Plantations, Baton Rouge) 171
    Finding Your Way Around . . . 159
Cloud Crossing (Crossroads) . . . 354
Cloutier Townhouse and Ducournau
    Square (Natchitoches) 347
Cloutierville (Crossroads) 346
    Finding Your Way Around . . . 340
Cocodrie (Bayou Lafourche and
    Terrebonne) 197
    Finding Your Way Around . . . 192
    Restaurants 205
Code Noir 21
Codrescu, Andrei 27
Colfax (Crossroads) 346
    Finding Your Way Around . . . 338
Colonel Short's Villa (Greater New
    Orleans) 89
Columbia (Northern Louisiana) . . 384
    Finding Your Way Around . . . 372
Concordia Lake (Crossroads) . . . 355
Confederate Museum (Greater New
    Orleans) 84
Conrad Rice Mill (New Iberia) . . . 247
Consulates 38
    Foreign Consulates and Delegations
        in New Orleans 38
    United States Consulates Abroad 38
Contemporary Arts Center (Greater
    New Orleans) 83
Convent (Plantations, Baton
    Rouge) 162
    Finding Your Way Around . . . 156
Corner School (Marksville) 285
Corney Lake (Northern Louisiana) 387
Cornstalk Fence (Greater New
    Orleans) 83
Cotile Recreation Area
    (Crossroads) 354
Cottage (St. Francisville Area) . . . 170

Cotton Blossom (Greater New
   Orleans) 100
Cotton Country Cooking School
   (Monroe/West Monroe) 384
Cottonport (Acadiana: North of
   Lafayette)
   Finding Your Way Around . . . 272
   Shopping 299
Coudrenière, Peyroux de La 21
Court of Two Lions (Greater New
   Orleans) 76
Court-bouillon 31
Covington (Greater New Orleans) 99
   Accommodations 120
   Finding Your Way Around . . . 61
   Practical Information 67
   Restaurants 137
Cravens (Crossroads)
   Finding Your Way Around . . . 341
Crawfish Processing Plants
   (Eunice) 280
Credit Cards 47
Creole 17, 31
Creole (Western Acadiana)
   Finding Your Way Around . . . 304
Creole Foods (Opelousas) 276
Creole House Museum (French
   Settlement) 164
Creole Queen (Greater New
   Orleans) 100
Creole Rose Manor (Jennings) . . 311
Crepe Myrtle Trail (Lafayette) . . . 221
Creston (Crossroads)
   Finding Your Way Around . . . 340
   Restaurants 361
Crooked Creek Recreation Area
   (Acadiana: North of
   Lafayette) 286
Crossroads 337
   Accommodations 355
   Entertainment 362
   Finding Your Way Around . . . 337
   Guide Services 343
   Parks 353
   Practical Information 342
   Restaurants 360
   Shopping 363

Crowley (Western Acadiana) . . . 306
   Accommodations 318
   Finding Your Way Around . . . 302
   Practical Information 305
   Restaurants 323
   Shopping 334
Crown Point (Greater New Orleans)
   Finding Your Way Around . . . 62
   Restaurants 139
Cuisine 30
Culture 26
Customs 37
Cut Off (Bayou Lafourche and
   Terrebonne)
   Accommodations 203
   Finding Your Way Around . . . 193
   Shopping 209
Cycling
   Greater New Orleans 105
Cypremort Point (Bayou Teche) . 249
   Finding Your Way Around . . . 240
   Restaurants 262
Cypremort Point State Park (Bayou
   Teche) 253
Cypress Black Bayou Recreation
   Area (Northern Louisiana) . . 385
Cypress Cove (Henderson) 243
Dansereau House (Thibodaux) . . 199
Darrow (Plantations, Baton Rouge)163
   Finding Your Way Around . . . 156
Davis, Jefferson 22
Davis-De Bachelle Seebold House
   (Greater New Orleans) 91
De la Morandière House
   (Washington) 278
De Quincy Railroad Museum (Lake
   Charles) 313
De Ridder (Crossroads) 350
   Finding Your Way Around . . . 341
   Restaurants 361
   Shopping 364
De Ulloa, Antonio 19
Degas, Edgar 90
Delacroix (Greater New Orleans)
   Accommodations 121
Delcambre (Western Acadiana) . . 315
Delhi (Northern Louisiana)
   Finding Your Way Around . . . 372

INDEX

Delta Queen (Greater New
  Orleans) 100
Denham Springs (Plantations, Baton
  Rouge) 168
  Accommodations 179
  Finding Your Way Around ... 159
  Restaurants 184
Denux House (Marksville) 285
Derry (Crossroads)
  Finding Your Way Around ... 340
Des Allemands (Bayou Lafourche
  and Terrebonne) 200
  Finding Your Way Around ... 193
  Restaurants 206
Destrehan (Plantations, Baton
  Rouge) 161
  Finding Your Way Around ... 156
Destrehan Plantation (Destrehan) 161
Disabled Travellers 45
Donaldsonville (Plantations, Baton
  Rouge) 173
  Finding Your Way Around ... 160
  Restaurants 185
Doyline (Northern Louisiana)
  Accommodations 390
  Finding Your Way Around ... 371
  Restaurants 396
Dream Cars Museum (Monroe/West
  Monroe) 384
Driver's License 39
Driving Code 39
Drugs 50
Ducayet House (Greater New
  Orleans) 87
Dulac (Bayou Lafourche and
  Terrebonne) 197
  Finding Your Way Around ... 192
  Restaurants 205
Dupré Library of USL (Lafayette) 220
Dupuy's House (Marksville) 285
East Bank Gallery (Bossier City) . 376
Economy 24
Eighth Air Force Museum (Bossier
  City) 376
Electricity 50

Elton (Western Acadiana) 312
  Finding Your Way Around ... 302
  Practical Information 305
  Shopping 335
Elton Rice Mill (Elton) 312
Embassies 38
  United States Embassies Abroad 38
Emergencies 45
Emigrating to the United States . 50
Empire (Greater New Orleans) .. 104
Emy-Lou Biedenharn Foundation
  (Monroe/West Monroe) 382
Entrance Formalities 37
Épicerie Médric Martin (Franklin) . 252
Epps (Northern Louisiana) 385
  Finding Your Way Around ... 372
Erath (Western Acadiana) 315
  Entertainment 330
  Finding Your Way Around ... 304
  Restaurants 328
Esplanade Avenue (Greater New
  Orleans) 85
Estherwood (Western Acadiana) . 309
  Finding Your Way Around ... 301
Estorge House (Opelousas) 277
Étouffée 31
Eunice (Acadiana: North of
  Lafayette) 279
  Accommodations 289
  Entertainment 293
  Finding Your Way Around ... 272
  Practical Information 273
  Restaurants 291
  Shopping 298
Eunice Mardi Gras (Acadiana: North
  of Lafayette) 280
Eunice Municipal Park (Acadiana:
  North of Lafayette) 286
Eunice Museum (Eunice) 279
Evangeline 27
Evangeline (Western Acadiana)
  Finding Your Way Around ... 302
Evangeline Monument (St.
  Martinville) 244
Exchange Rates 48
Exchanging Money 47

Farmerville (Northern Louisiana)
   Accommodations 391
   Finding Your Way Around . . . 371
   Parks 387
Faubourg Marigny (Greater New
   Orleans)
   Accommodations 107
   Bars and Nightclubs 139
   Restaurants 122
Fauna 15
Fenton (Western Acadiana)
   Accommodations 322
   Finding Your Way Around . . . 302
Ferriday (Crossroads) 352
   Finding Your Way Around . . . 342
Festivals 50
Festivals (Greater New Orleans) . 143
Filé 31
Fine Art Gallery of Southwest
   Louisiana (Lake Charles) . . . 313
Fine Arts Center (Jonesboro) . . . 382
First Skyscraper (Greater New
   Orleans) 76
First Ursulines Convent - Charity
   Hospital (Greater New Orleans) 74
Fisher (Northern Louisiana) 379
   Finding Your Way Around . . . 370
Fishing
   Greater New Orleans 105
Fitzgerald, F. Scott 26
Flechier House (Greater New
   Orleans) 76
Flora 14
Florien (Northern Louisiana) 378
   Accommodations 390
   Finding Your Way Around . . . 370
Floyd Sonnier's Studio and Gallery
   (Scott) 306
Flying J Ranch (Kaplan) 314
Follette Pottery Studio (Ruston) . 381
Folsom (Greater New Orleans) . . 102
   Accommodations 120
   Finding Your Way Around . . . 61
Fontainebleau State Park (Greater
   New Orleans) 99
Fontenot Rice Mill (Eunice) 280

Forest Hill (Crossroads)
   Finding Your Way Around . . . 342
   Restaurants 362
Forsythe Park (Monroe/West
   Monroe) 384
Fort Beauregard (Harrisonburg) . . 352
Fort Hill Park (Harrisonburg) 352
Fort Jackson (Buras) 105
Fort Jesup State Commemorative
   Area (Many) 379
Fort Livingston (Grande Terre
   Island) 201
Fort Polk (Crossroads) 349
   Finding Your Way Around . . . 341
Fort Polk Military Museum (Fort
   Polk) 350
Fort Saint-Jean-Baptiste
   (Natchitoches) 348
Fort San Carlos (Baton Rouge) . . 166
Fort Sumter 22
FrancoFête 1999 (Acadiana:
   Lafayette) 216
Franklin (Bayou Teche) 251
   Accommodations 258
   Finding Your Way Around . . . 240
   Restaurants 263
   Shopping 267
Franklinton (Greater New Orleans) 102
   Finding Your Way Around . . . 61
French 17, 25
French Market (French Quarter) . 70
French Market (Greater New
   Orleans) 70
French Quarter (Greater New
   Orleans) 68
   Accommodations 107
   Bars and Nightclubs 139
   Restaurants 122
French Quarter Folklore Center
   (Greater New Orleans) 73
French Settlement (Plantations,
   Baton Rouge) 164
   Finding Your Way Around . . . 158
   Restaurants 182
Frogmore Plantation (Ferriday) . . 352
Fullerton Lake (Crossroads) 355
Gaines, Ernest 26

Gallery for Fine Photography (Greater New Orleans) 72
Galliano (Bayou Lafourche and Terrebonne)
Accommodations 203
Finding Your Way Around . . . 193
Guided Tours 194
Gallier House (Greater New Orleans) 82
Garden District (Greater New Orleans) 87
Accommodations 113
Gardens of the American Rose Center (Shreveport/Bossier City) . . . 375
Gardner (Crossroads)
Finding Your Way Around . . . 341
Gas Stations 40
Gathright Interpretive Center (Morgan City) 252
Gay Bars and Nightclubs (Greater New Orleans) 142
Geography 13
Fauna 15
Flora 14
Geology 14
Geology 14
Geology Building (Baton Rouge) . 167
Germans 19
Germantown Colony Museum (Minden) 379
Gheens (Bayou Lafourche and Terrebonne)
Finding Your Way Around . . . 194
Gibson (Bayou Lafourche and Terrebonne) 198
Accommodations 203
Finding Your Way Around . . . 192
Guided Tours 197
Gilbert (Northern Louisiana)
Finding Your Way Around . . . 372
Restaurants 397
Gillis W. Long Hansen's Disease Center (Carville) 163
Girard Park (Acadiana: Lafayette) 222
Glencoe Plantation (Wilson) 172
Global Wildlife Center (Greater New Orleans) 102

Golden Meadow (Bayou Lafourche and Terrebonne) 201
Finding Your Way Around . . . 193
Guided Tours 195
Restaurants 206
Shopping 209
Goldonna (Crossroads)
Finding Your Way Around . . . 340
Golf
Acadiana: Lafayette 222
Greater New Orleans 106
Gonzales (Plantations, Baton Rouge) 164
Finding Your Way Around . . . 158
Governor's Mansion (Opelousas) . 277
Governor's Mansion (Baton Rouge)166
Grace Episcopal Church (St. Francisville) 169
Grand Chenier (Western Acadiana)
Finding Your Way Around . . . 304
Grand Cote National Wildlife Refuge (Acadiana: North of Lafayette) 287
Grand Coteau (Acadiana: North of Lafayette) 274
Finding Your Way Around . . . 270
Restaurants 290
Grand Isle (Bayou Lafourche and Terrebonne) 201
Accommodations 204
Finding Your Way Around . . . 193
Parks 201
Restaurants 206
Grand Isle State Park (Bayou Lafourche and Terrebonne) . 201
Grand Point (Plantations, Baton Rouge) 162
Grande Terre Island (Bayou Lafourche and Terrebonne) . 201
Grant, Ulysses 22
Great Wall (Morgan City) 253
Greater New Orleans 53
Accommodations 107
Calendar of Events 146
Entertainment 139
Finding Your Way Around . . . 56
Outdoors 105
Practical Information 63

Greater New Orleans, cont'd.
  Restaurants 122
  Shopping 149
  Tourist Information 63
Greenwood (Northern Louisiana)
  Entertainment 399
  Finding Your Way Around . . . 370
  Restaurants 395
  Shopping 401
Greenwood Plantation (St.
    Francisville Area) 170
Gretna (Greater New Orleans)
  Restaurants 138
Grinnan-Riley House (Greater New
    Orleans) 92
Grosse Tete (Plantations, Baton
    Rouge)
  Finding Your Way Around . . . 160
  Shopping 188
Gueydan (Western Acadiana)
  Finding Your Way Around . . . 304
  Shopping 335
Guillory House (Ville Platte) 279
Gumbo 31
Gumbo z'herbes 31
H. J. Smith's Son Museum
    (Covington) 99
H. S. Ford Museum (Homer) 380
H.C. Bergeron Pecan Shelling Plant
    (New Roads) 176
Hagewood (Crossroads)
  Finding Your Way Around . . . 340
Hahnville (Plantations, Baton
    Rouge) 172
  Finding Your Way Around . . . 159
Hammond (Greater New Orleans) 102
  Accommodations 120
  Finding Your Way Around . . . 61
  Restaurants 137
Harrisonburg (Crossroads) 351
  Finding Your Way Around . . . 342
Harrisonburg Methodist Church
    (Harrisonburg) 352
Harrisonburg Ridge (Harrisonburg) 352
Haunted House (Greater New
    Orleans) 81
Hayes (Western Acadiana)
  Restaurants 325

Haynesville (Northern Louisiana)
  Accommodations 391
  Finding Your Way Around . . . 371
Health 44
Health Insurance 44
Henderson (Bayou Teche) 242
  Entertainment 264
  Finding Your Way Around . . . 238
  Restaurants 259
Henderson Swamp (Bayou Teche) 253
Henry Sullivan Buckner House
    (Greater New Orleans) 92
Heritage Farm Village (Branch) . . 283
Hermann-Grima House (Greater New
    Orleans) 75
Highland Plantation House (St.
    Francisville Area) 171
Hinckley House (Washington) . . . 277
Historic Monuments Museum
    (Arcadia) 380
Historic New Orleans Collection
    (Greater New Orleans) 72
History 16
Hitchhiking 42
Hodges Gardens (Fisher) 379
Holidays 50
Holly Beach (Western Acadiana) . 316
  Accommodations 322
  Finding Your Way Around . . . 304
Holly Grove Methodist Church
    (Anacoco) 349
Holy Ghost Church (Opelousas) . 277
Homeplace Acres Bluegrass Festival
    (Athens) 380
Homer (Northern Louisiana) 379
  Accommodations 390
  Entertainment 399
  Finding Your Way Around . . . 371
  Parks 386
Horseback Riding
  Acadiana: Lafayette 222
Hospitals 65
Hot Wells (Crossroads)
  Finding Your Way Around . . . 341
Hotel Le Sage (Colfax) 346

INDEX

Houma (Bayou Lafourche and
    Terrebonne) 195
    Accommodations 201
    Finding Your Way Around . . . 191
    Guided Tours 195, 196
    Parks 201
    Restaurants 204
    Shopping 209
    Tourist Information 194
Houma Aquatic Park (Houma) . . 201
Houma Historic District 195
Houmas House Plantation and
    Gardens (Darrow) 163
Houmas Indian Center (Dulac) . . 197
Hungarian Harvest Festival
    (Albany) 103
Hunting and Fishing
    Acadiana: Lafayette 222
Hypolite Bordelon House
    (Marksville) 285
Imperial Calcasieu Museum (Lake
    Charles Area) 313
Independence (Greater New
    Orleans) 103
    Finding Your Way Around . . . 62
Indian Camp (Carville) 164
Indian Ridge shrimp processing
    company (Bayou
    Lafourche) 199
Insect Bites 44
Insurance 43
International Petroleum Museum &
    Exposition (Morgan City) . . . 252
Intracoastal City (Western
    Acadiana) 313
Iota (Western Acadiana) 307
    Finding Your Way Around . . . 302
    Practical Information 305
    Shopping 334
Ira Nelson Horticultural Center
    (Lafayette) 221
Isle de Jean-Charles (Bayou Lafourche
    and Terrebonne)
    Finding Your Way Around . . . 192
Italian Museum (Independence) . 103
Jack Miller's Barbecue Sauce Factory
    (Ville Platte) 279

Jackson (Plantations, Baton
    Rouge) 171
    Accommodations 180
    Finding Your Way Around . . . 159
    Restaurants 185
    Shopping 189
Jackson Brewery (Greater New
    Orleans) 70
Jackson Parish Heritage Museum
    (Jonesboro) 382
Jackson Square (Greater New
    Orleans) 78
Jambalaya 31
James Bowie Festival (Vidalia) . . 353
Jane Schlesinger House (Greater
    New Orleans) 91
Jazz 28
Jazz and Heritage Festival 147
Jean Lafitte (Greater New Orleans)
    Finding Your Way Around . . . 62
Jean Lafitte National Historic Park
    and Preserve (Greater New
    Orleans) 104
Jean Lafitte National Historical Park
    (Eunice) 279
Jean Lafitte National Historical Park
    and Preserve (Bayou
    Lafourche and Terrebone) . . 199
Jean Lafitte National Historical Park
    and Preserve (Bayou Teche) . 251
Jean Lafitte National Historical Park
    and Preserve (Greater New
    Orleans) 73
Jean Lafitte National Historical Park
    and Preserve, Chalmette Unit
    (Greater New Orleans) 104
Jean Lafitte National Historical Park
    and Preserve, Isleños Unit
    (Greater New Orleans) 104
Jean Lafitte Prairie Acadian Cultural
    Center (Eunice) 279
Jean Lafitte Scenic Byway (Western
    Acadiana) 310, 313
Jean Pascal House (French Quarter)83
Jean Vidrine Residence (Ville
    Platte) 279

Jeanerette (Bayou Teche) 249
  Accommodations 257
  Finding Your Way Around . . . 240
  Restaurants 262
Jeff Derouen Crawfish Supply
  (Eunice) 280
Jefferson Downs Racetrack
  (Kenner) 98
Jefferson Island (Bayou Teche) . . 249
  Finding Your Way Around . . . 240
  Restaurants 262
Jefferson Parish (Greater New
  Orleans)
  Practical Information 67
Jena (Crossroads) 351
  Finding Your Way Around . . . 342
Jennings (Western Acadiana) . . . 310
  Accommodations 319
  Finding Your Way Around . . . 302
  Practical Information 305
  Restaurants 323
  Shopping 334
Jim Bowie Museum (Opelousas) . 276
Jimmy Davis Tabernacle
  (Jonesboro) 381
Johnson Residence (Ville Platte) . 279
Johnsons Bayou (Western Acadiana)
  Finding Your Way Around . . . 304
Jonesboro (Northern Louisiana) . 381
  Finding Your Way Around . . . 371
Jonesville (Crossroads) 351
  Finding Your Way Around . . . 342
Jonesville Riverfront Park
  (Jonesville) 351
Joyce Wildlife Refuge (Greater New
  Orleans) 103
Judge Perez Lake (Greater New
  Orleans) 104
Judge Poche Plantation House
  (Convent) 163
Jules Clément's Farm (Jennings) 310
Jungle Gardens (Jefferson Island) 249
Justine Antebellum Home (New
  Iberia) 247
Kaffie-Frederick's General Hardware
  Store (Natchitoches) 348

Kaplan (Western Acadiana) 314
  Accommodations 320
  Entertainment 330
  Finding Your Way Around . . . 304
  Restaurants 328
Kate Chopin Home (Cloutierville) 346
Keller Home Place Plantation House
  (Hahnville) 172
Kenner (Greater New Orleans) . . 98
  Accommodations 119
  Finding Your Way Around . . . 60
  Practical Information 67
  Restaurants 135
Kent Plantation House (Alexandria -
  Pineville) 345
Kentwood (Greater New Orleans)
  Accommodations 121
  Finding Your Way Around . . . 62
Kincaid Lake (Crossroads) 354
King Tortoise Farm (Jonesville) . . 351
Kiroli Park (Northern Louisiana) . . 387
Kisatchie (Crossroads)
  Finding Your Way Around . . . 340
Kisatchie Hills Wilderness Area
  (Crossroads) 354
Kisatchie National Forest
  (Crossroads) 353
  Accommodations 357
  Finding Your Way Around . . . 338
Kisatchie National Forest (Northern
  Louisiana) 386
Kliebert's Turtle & Alligator Farm
  (Hammond) 102
Koasatis Reservation (Elton) 312
Kolly Townhouse (Greater New
  Orleans) 74
Konriko Company Store (New
  Iberia) 247
Konriko rice mill (New Iberia) . . . 246
Kraemer (Bayou Lafourche and
  Terrebonne) 199
  Finding Your Way Around . . . 193
  Guided Tours 200
  Restaurants 206
Krotz Springs (Acadiana: North of
  Lafayette)
  Accommodations 288
  Finding Your Way Around . . . 270

La Laurie House (Greater New
    Orleans) 81
Labadieville (Bayou Lafourche and
    Terrebonne)
  Finding Your Way Around . . . 192
  Restaurants 205
Laborde House (Marksville) 285
Labranche Building (Greater New
    Orleans) 68
Lacassine (Western Acadiana)
  Restaurants 325
Lacombe (Greater New Orleans) . 98
  Finding Your Way Around . . . 60
  Restaurants 136
Lafayette (Acadiana: Lafayette) . 218
  Accommodations 223
  Entertainment 231
  Finding Your Way Around . . . 212
  Restaurants 226
  Shopping 234
Lafayette Cemetery No. 1 (Greater
    New Orleans) 89
Lafayette International Center
    (Lafayette) 220
Lafayette Moments in Time
    (Lafayette) 220
Lafitte (Greater New Orleans)
  Finding Your Way Around . . . 62
Lafitte's Blacksmith Shop (Greater
    New Orleans) 82
Lafourche Courthouse (Thibodaux)199
Lafreniere Park (Metairie) 96
Lake Arthur (Western Acadiana) . 312
  Accommodations 321
  Entertainment 329
  Finding Your Way Around . . . 302
  Restaurants 325
  Shopping 334
Lake Bistineau (Northern
    Louisiana) 386
Lake Cazan (Acadiana: North of
    Lafayette) 286
Lake Charles (Western Acadiana) 312
  Accommodations 319
  Entertainment 329
  Finding Your Way Around . . . 302
  Practical Information 305

Lake Charles (Western Acadiana),
    cont'd.
  Restaurants 325
  Shopping 335
Lake Claiborne State Park (Northern
    Louisiana) 386
Lake D'Arbonne State Park (Northern
    Louisiana) 387
Lake End Park (Bayou Teche) . . . 254
Lake Fausse Pointe (Bayou Teche)
  Accommodations 257
  Finding Your Way Around . . . 240
Lake Fausse Pointe State Park
    (Bayou Teche) 253
Lake Hermitage (Greater New
    Orleans) 104
Lake Miller (Acadiana: North of
    Lafayette) 286
Lake Ophelia (Acadiana: North of
    Lafayette) 287
Lake Palourde (Bayou Teche)
  Finding Your Way Around . . . 241
Lake Pontchartrain Causeway
    (Greater New Orleans) 87
Lake Stuart (Crossroads) 353
Lake Verret (Bayou Teche)
  Finding Your Way Around . . . 241
Lakefront (Greater New Orleans) . 85
Lakefront Airport 57
Lakeshore Drive (Greater New
    Orleans) 87
LaPlace (Plantations, Baton Rouge)
  Finding Your Way Around . . . 156
Larose (Bayou Lafourche and
    Terrebonne)
  Accommodations 203
  Finding Your Way Around . . . 193
LASC Riverside Museum (Baton
    Rouge) 166
Lastrapas Live Oak (Washington) 278
Laura Plantation (Vacherie) 172
Laurel Valley Plantation Village
    (Thibodaux) 199
Laurens H. Cohn Memorial
    Arboretum (Baton Rouge) . . 168
Lavinia C. Dabney House (Greater
    New Orleans) 92

Layton Castle (Monroe/West
    Monroe) 382
Le Beau Petit Musée (Jeanerette) 250
Le Monnier House (Greater New
    Orleans) 76
Le Petit Château de Luxe
    (Mermentau) 309
LeBeau House (Jarreau) 176
Lecompte (Crossroads)
    Accommodations 358
    Finding Your Way Around . . . 341
Lecompte School (Cheneyville) . . 351
Lee, Robert E. 22
Leesville (Crossroads) 349
    Accommodations 359
    Finding Your Way Around . . . 341
    Restaurants 361
Leeville (Bayou Lafourche and
    Terrebonne)
    Finding Your Way Around . . . 193
    Guided Tours 195
Leland Bowman Locks (Intracoastal
    City) 313
Lemée House (Natchitoches) . . . 348
Leonville (Acadiana: North of
    Lafayette) 274
    Finding Your Way Around . . . 270
Liberty Rice Mill (Kaplan) 314
Life Insurance 43
Lincoln Parish Museum (Ruston) . 381
Lincoln Parish Park (Northern
    Louisiana) 387
Lincoln, Abraham 22
Lisburn Plantation (Ferriday) 352
Literature 26
Little Zion Baptist Church
    (Opelousas) 277
Live Oak Gardens (Jefferson
    Island) 249
Live Oaks Plantation (Rosedale) . 175
Livonia (Plantations, Baton Rouge)
    Finding Your Way Around . . . 160
    Restaurants 186
Lock and Dam No. 1 (Acadiana:
    North of Lafayette) 287

Lockport (Bayou Lafourche and
    Terrebonne) 201
    Guided Tours 201
    Restaurants 206
Locust Grove State Commemorative
    Area (St. Francisville Area) . 171
Longfellow - Evangeline State
    Commemorative Area (St.
    Martinville) 244
Longfellow, Henry Wadsworth
    Longfellow 27
Longleaf Scenic Area (Crossroads) 355
Longleaf Vista (Crossroads) 354
Longue Vue House and Gardens
    (Greater New Orleans) 87
Loranger (Greater New Orleans)
    Finding Your Way Around . . . 62
Loreauville (Bayou Teche) 248
    Finding Your Way Around . . . 240
    Restaurants 262
Los Adaes State Commemorative
    Area (Marthaville) 378
Lou Ana Foods (Opelousas) 276
Louis Armstrong Park (Greater New
    Orleans) 73
Louise McGehee School (Greater
    New Orleans) 92
Louisiana Cajun Culture and Music
    Club Festival (Eunice) 280
Louisiana Center for Political and
    Government History (Baton
    Rouge) 167
Louisiana Children's Museum (Greater
    New Orleans) 85
Louisiana Museum of Ancient Indian
    Culture (Bogalusa) 102
Louisiana Oil and Gas Park
    (Jennings) 310
Louisiana Passion Play (Ruston) . 381
Louisiana Purchase Gardens & Zoo
    (Monroe/West Monroe) 384
Louisiana Raceway Park (Eunice) 280
Louisiana Seafood Exchange
    (Kenner) 98
Louisiana State Arboretum (Acadiana:
    North of Lafayette) 285
Louisiana State Archives (Baton
    Rouge) 167

INDEX

Louisiana State Arsenal (Greater New
    Orleans) 76
Louisiana State Bank (Greater New
    Orleans) 74
Louisiana State Capitol (Baton
    Rouge) 166
Louisiana State Exhibit Museum
    (Shreveport) 375
Louisiana State Museum (Greater
    New Orleans) 72
Louisiana State University (Baton
    Rouge) 167
Louisiana Superdome (Greater New
    Orleans) 85
Louisiana Tax Free Shopping . . . 149
Louisiana Tech Horticulture Center
    (Ruston) 381
Louisiana Telephone Pioneer Museum
    (Jennings) 310
Louisiana Toy Train Museum
    (Kenner) 98
Louisiana Universities Marine
    Consortium (Chauvin) 198
Louisiana Wildlife and Fisheries
    Museum (Kenner) 98
Lower Garden District (Greater New
    Orleans) 96
Loyd Hall Plantation (Cheneyville) 350
Loyola University (Greater New
    Orleans) 93
LSU Cooperative Extension Service
    (Shreveport) 377
LSU Hilltop Arboretum (Baton
    Rouge) 168
LSU Museum of Art (Baton Rouge)167
LSU Stadium (Baton Rouge) 167
Lutcher (Plantations, Baton Rouge)162
    Finding Your Way Around . . . 156
Lyle S. Saint-Amant Marine
    Laboratory (Grande Terre
    Island) 201
Madame John's Legacy (Greater
    New Orleans) 83
Madewood Plantation
    (Napoleonville) 199

Madisonville (Greater New Orleans) 99
    Accommodations 119
    Finding Your Way Around . . . 61
    Restaurants 136
Madisonville Museum (Madisonville)99
Madonna Chapel (Bayou Goula) . 174
Magnolia Cemetery (Houma) . . . 195
Magnolia Mound (Baton Rouge) . 167
Magnolia Plantation (Natchez) . . 346
Magnolia Ridge Plantation
    (Washington) 278
Maison Blanchet-Romero
    (Crowley) 307
Maison De Ville (Ville Platte) . . . 279
Maison Du Champ (St. Martinville)244
Maison du CODOFIL (Lafayette) . 220
Mamou (Acadiana: North of
    Lafayette) 279
    Accommodations 289
    Entertainment 293
    Finding Your Way Around . . . 270
    Practical Information 273
    Shopping 298
Manchac (Greater New Orleans) . 103
    Restaurants 138
Mandeville (Greater New Orleans) 99
    Accommodations 119
    Finding Your Way Around . . . 61
    Restaurants 136
Manresa House of Retreats
    (Convent) 163
Mansfield (Northern Louisiana) . . 377
    Accommodations 389
    Finding Your Way Around . . . 370
    Practical Information 373
    Restaurants 395
Mansfield State Commemorative
    Area (Mansfield) 377
Mansura (Acadiana: North of
    Lafayette)
    Finding Your Way Around . . . 272
Many (Crossroads)
    Finding Your Way Around . . . 340
Many (Northern Louisiana) 378
    Accommodations 390
    Finding Your Way Around . . . 370
    Practical Information 373
    Restaurants 395

Maque-choux 31
Marché Français (Greater New
    Orleans) 70
Mardi Gras (Bayou Teche) 266
Mardi Gras (Greater New Orleans) 145
Mardi Gras Museum (Kenner) . . . 98
Marksville (Acadiana: North of
    Lafayette) 284
    Entertainment 294
    Finding Your Way Around . . . 272
    Practical Information 274
    Restaurants 292
    Shopping 299
Marston House (Clinton) 171
Marthaville (Northern Louisiana) . 378
    Finding Your Way Around . . . 370
Martin Homeplace (Columbia) . . . 384
Masur Museum of Art (Monroe/West
    Monroe) 382
Mathews (Bayou Lafourche and
    Terrebonne)
    Finding Your Way Around . . . 193
    Shopping 209
Maurice (Western Acadiana)
    Entertainment 330
    Finding Your Way Around . . . 304
    Restaurants 328
    Shopping 336
Mayor Sullivan's Home (Bogalusa) 102
McGee's Landing (Bayou Teche)
    Finding Your Way Around . . . 238
McHugh House Museum (Zachary) 169
McIlhenny Estate (Jefferson
    Island) 249
McNeely House (Colfax) 346
Meadows Museum of Art
    (Shreveport) 375
Measures 51
Medjoy House (Shreveport) 376
Melrose (Crossroads) 346
    Finding Your Way Around . . . 340
Melrose Plantation (Melrose) . . . 346
Memorial Tower (Baton Rouge) . 167
Merieult House (Greater New
    Orleans) 75
Mermentau (Western Acadiana) . 309
    Finding Your Way Around . . . 302

Merryville (Crossroads) 350
    Finding Your Way Around . . . 341
    Shopping 365
Metairie (Greater New Orleans) . . 96
    Accommodations 119
    Finding Your Way Around . . . 60
    Restaurants 134
    Tourist Information 63
Methodist Church (St. Francisville) 169
Michel Prudhomme House
    (Opelousas) 276
Mid-City (Greater New Orleans) . 85
    Accommodations 115
    Restaurants 133
Middle American Research Institute
    & Art Gallery (Greater New
    Orleans) 93
Milbank Historic House (Jackson) 172
Mile Branch Settlement
    (Franklington) 102
Miltenberger Houses (Greater New
    Orleans) 83
Milton (Acadiana: Lafayette)
    Accommodations 226
    Finding Your Way Around . . . 214
Milton H. Latter Memorial Library
    (Greater New Orleans) 93
Minden (Northern Louisiana) . . . 379
    Accommodations 390
    Finding Your Way Around . . . 371
    Parks 386
    Restaurants 396
Mirliton 31
Mississippi Queen (Greater New
    Orleans) 100
Moisant Airport 42, 57
Moncla (Acadiana: North of
    Lafayette) 285
Money 47
Monroe (Northern Louisiana) . . . 382
    Accommodations 392
    Entertainment 399
    Finding Your Way Around . . . 371
    Parks 387
    Practical Information 373
    Restaurants 397
    Shopping 401

INDEX

Mont Olivet Chapel (Alexandria -
   Pineville) 345
Montegut (Bayou Lafourche and
   Terrebonne)
   Finding Your Way Around . . . 192
Montgomery-Hero House (Greater
   New Orleans) 91
Mooringsport (Northern Louisiana)
   Accommodations 389
   Finding Your Way Around . . . 370
   Restaurants 395
Moresi Foundry (Jeanerette) . . . 250
Morgan City (Bayou Lafourche and
   Terrebonne)
   Finding Your Way Around . . . 192
Morgan City (Bayou Teche) 252
   Accommodations 258
   Finding Your Way Around . . . 241
   Restaurants 263
Morgan City Historic District (Morgan
   City) 253
Morphy House (Greater New
   Orleans) 75
Morton, Jelly Roll 26
Motivatit Seafood (Houma) 196
Mount Lebanon Baptist Church
   (Arcadia) 380
Mount Olive Baptist Church
   (Opelousas) 277
Mount Olive Christian School LRCA
   Rodeo (Athens) 380
Muffaletta 31
Musée Acadien (Erath) 315
Musée Acadien (Jennings) 312
Musée Conti Wax Museum (Greater
   New Orleans) 72
Musée de la Rose Bleue (Crowley) 307
Museum of Geoscience (Baton
   Rouge) 167
Museum of Historic Natchitoches
   (Natchitoches) 347
Museum of Natural History
   (Jennings) 311
Museum of Natural History
   (Lafayette) 220
Museum of Natural Science (Baton
   Rouge) 167
Museum of Rural Life (Thibodaux) 199

Museum of the Mississippi Valley
   (Lafayette) 220
Museum of Politics and Famous
   People of Louisiana
   (Winnfield) 348
Museum of West Louisiana
   (Leesville) 349
Musson-Bell House (Greater New
   Orleans) 91
Myrtles (St. Francisville) 170
Napoleonic Code 24
Napoleonville (Bayou Lafourche and
   Terrebonne) 199
   Accommodations 203
   Finding Your Way Around . . . 192
Natchez (Crossroads) 346
   Finding Your Way Around . . . 340
Natchez (Greater New Orleans) . 100
Natchitoches (Crossroads) 347
   Finding Your Way Around . . . 340
   Guide Services 343
   Practical Information 342
   Restaurants 360
   Shopping 363
Natchitoches National Aquarium
   and Fish Farm (Natchitoches) 348
New Iberia (Bayou Teche) 246
   Accommodations 256
   Entertainment 265
   Finding Your Way Around . . . 238
   Guided Tours 241
   Restaurants 260
   Shopping 266
New Orleans 53
New Orleans Botanical Garden
   (Greater New Orleans) 87
New Orleans Court Building (Greater
   New Orleans) 75
New Orleans Fairgrounds and
   Racetrack (Greater New
   Orleans) 87
New Orleans Historic Voodoo
   Museum (Greater New Orleans)72
New Orleans International
   Airport 42, 57
New Orleans Museum of Art (Greater
   New Orleans) 85

New Orleans Pharmacy Museum
(Greater New Orleans) 72
New Roads (Plantations, Baton
Rouge) 175
Accommodations 181
Finding Your Way Around . . . 160
Restaurants 186
Newellton (Northern Louisiana) . . 385
Finding Your Way Around . . . 372
Nicholson House (Washington) . . 277
Nightclubs, see Bars
North Louisiana Military Museum
(Ruston) 381
North Toledo Bend State Park
(Northern Louisiana) 386
Northeast Louisiana Delta African-
American Heritage Museum
(Monroe) 384
Northern Louisiana 367
Accommodations 388
Calendar of Events 399
Entertainment 398
Finding Your Way Around . . . 367
Parks 385
Practical Information 372
Restaurants 393
Shopping 400
Northup, Solomon 26
Nottoway Plantation (White
Castle) 174
Nunez (Western Acadiana)
Restaurants 327
Oak Alley Plantation (Vacherie) . 173
Oak and Pine Alley (St. Martinville)246
Oak Lawn Plantation (Natchez) . . 347
Oakland Plantation (Melrose) . . . 347
Oakland Plantation (Wilson) 172
Oaklawn Manor (Franklin) 252
Oakley Plantation House (St.
Francisville) 169
Octave Thompson House (Ville
Platte) 279
Odell Pottery (Ruston) 381
Oil City (Northern Louisiana) . . . 376
Finding Your Way Around . . . 370
Parks 385
Old Ardoin House (Ville Platte) . . 279

Old Arsenal Museum (Baton
Rouge) 166
Old Bank of the United States
(Greater New Orleans) 74
Old Governor's Mansion (Baton
Rouge) 166
Old Log Courthouse (Mansfield) . 377
Old Shreve Square (Shreveport) . 373
Old State Capitol (Baton Rouge) . 167
Old Turnerville (Plaquemine) 174
Old United States Mint (Greater New
Orleans) 79
Old Ursuline Convent (Greater New
Orleans) 79
Old Washington Cemetery
(Washington) 278
Opelousas (Acadiana: North of
Lafayette) 275
Accommodations 288
Entertainment 292
Finding Your Way Around . . . 270
Practical Information 272
Restaurants 290
Shopping 297
Opelousas Museum and Interpretive
Center (Opelousas) 276
Ormond Plantation (Destrehan) . . 162
Otis House Museum (Madisonville) 99
Ouachita River Art Guild
(Monroe/West Monroe) 382
Ouachita Wildlife Management Area
(Northern Louisiana) 387
Our Lady of Mount Carmel Church
(St. Francisville) 169
Our Mother of Perpetual Help Chapel
(Greater New Orleans) 91
O'Reilly, Alejandro 19
Pain perdu 31
Paincourtville (Bayou Lafourche and
Terrebonne)
Finding Your Way Around . . . 192
Palmetto (Acadiana: North of
Lafayette) 278
Finding Your Way Around . . . 270
Practical Information 273
Papillote 31
Parish Prison (Donaldsonville) . . . 174

INDEX

Parks
Acadiana Park Nature Station
(Acadiana: Lafayette) 221
Baton Rouge Zoo (Plantations,
Baton Rouge) 177
Bayou Kisatchie (Crossroads) . 354
Bayou Teche (Acadiana: North of
Lafayette) 285
Ben Routh Recreational Area
(Acadiana: North of
Lafayette) 287
Blue Bayou Water Park
(Plantations, Baton Rouge) . 177
Bluffs on Thompson Creek (St.
Francisville) 177
Bogue-Chitto National Wildlife
Reserve (Greater New Orleans) 98
Burns Point Recreation Area
(Bayou Teche) 254
Caddo Lake (Northern
Louisiana) 385
Cajun Prairie Restoration Project
(Acadiana: North of
Lafayette) 286
Cameron Prairie Wildlife Refuge
(Western Acadiana) 317
Camp Moore State Commemorative
Area (Greater New Orleans) . 103
Caney Lake (Northern
Louisiana) 386
Caney Lakes Recreation Area
(Northern Louisiana) 386
Catahoula Lake (Crossroads) . 355
Chemin-A-Haut State Park
(Northern Louisiana) 387
Chicot State Park (Acadiana:
North of Lafayette) 286
Cloud Crossing (Crossroads) . . 354
Concordia Lake (Crossroads) . 355
Corney Lake (Northern
Louisiana) 387
Cotile Recreation Area
(Crossroads) 354
Crooked Creek Recreation Area
(Acadiana: North of
Lafayette) 286
Cypremort Point State Park (Bayou
Teche) 253

Parks, cont'd.
Cypress Black Bayou Recreation
Area (Northern Louisiana) . . 385
Eunice Municipal Park (Acadiana:
North of Lafayette) 286
Fontainebleau State Park (Greater
New Orleans) 99
Fullerton Lake (Crossroads) . . 355
Girard Park (Acadiana:
Lafayette) 222
Global Wildlife Center (Greater
New Orleans) 102
Grand Cote National Wildlife
Refuge (Acadiana: North of
Lafayette) 287
Grand Isle State Park (Bayou
Lafourche and Terrebonne) . 201
Henderson swamp (Bayou
Teche) 253
Houma Aquatic Park (Houma) . 201
Jean Lafitte National Historic Park
and Preserve (Greater New
Orleans) 104
Jean Lafitte National Historical
Park and Preserve, Chalmette
Unit (Greater New Orleans) . 104
Jean Lafitte National Historical
Park and Preserve, Isleños
Unit (Greater New Orleans) . 104
Joyce Wildlife Refuge (Greater
New Orleans) 103
Kincaid Lake (Crossroads) . . . 354
Kiroli Park (Northern Louisiana) 387
Kisatchie Hills Wilderness Area
(Crossroads) 354
Kisatchie National Forest (Northern
Louisiana) 386
Lake Cazan (Acadiana: North of
Lafayette) 286
Lake Claiborne State Park
(Northern Louisiana) 386
Lake D'Arbonne State Park
(Northern Louisiana) 387
Lake End Park (Bayou Teche) . 254
Lake Fausse Pointe State Park
(Bayou Teche) 253
Lake Miller (Acadiana: North of
Lafayette) 286

Parks, cont'd.

Lake Ophelia (Acadiana: North of
Lafayette) 287
Lake Stuart (Crossroads) 353
Lincoln Parish Park (Northern
Louisiana) 387
Lock and Dam No. 1 (Acadiana:
North of Lafayette) 287
Longleaf Scenic Area
(Crossroads) 355
Longleaf Vista (Crossroads) . . 354
Louisiana State Arboretum
(Acadiana: North of
Lafayette) 285
North Toledo Bend State Park
(Northern Louisiana) 386
Ouachita Wildlife Management
Area (Northern Louisiana) . . 387
Pomme-de-Terre (Acadiana: North
of Lafayette) 287
Rockefeller Wildlife Refuge and
Game Preserve (Western
Acadiana) 317
Russell Sage Wildlife Management
Area (Northern Louisiana) . . 387
Sabine National Wildlife Refuge
(Western Acadiana) 316
Sabine Wildlife Management Area
(Northern Louisiana) 386
Spring Bayou (Acadiana: North of
Lafayette) 287
Tensas River National Wildlife
Refuge (Northern Louisiana) . 388
Thistlethwaite Wildlife Management
Area (Acadiana: North of
Lafayette) 285
Union Wildlife Management Area
(Northern Louisiana) 387
Valentine Lake (Crossroads) . . 354
Walter B. Jacobs Memorial Nature
Park (Northern Louisiana) . . 386
Whiskey Chitto Creek (Western
Acadiana) 316
White Sulphur Springs
(Crossroads) 353
Wild Azalea National Recreation
Trail (Crossroads) 354

Parks, cont'd.

Yellow Bayou Civil War Memorial
Park (Acadiana: North of
Lafayette) 287
Parks (Bayou Teche) 243
Entertainment 264
Finding Your Way Around . . . 238
Parlange Plantation (New Roads
Area) 176
Patterson (Bayou Teche) 252
Pecan Island (Western Acadiana)
Finding Your Way Around . . . 304
Pecan Plantation and Gift Company
(Waterproof) 352
Pentagon Barracks (Baton Rouge) 166
Père Antoine Alley (Greater New
Orleans) 77
Perique Tobacco Farm (Grand
Point) 163
Petit Paris Museum (St.
Martinville) 244
Petit-Caporal (Golden Meadow) . 201
Pickering (Crossroads)
Finding Your Way Around . . . 341
Pierre-Part (Bayou Lafourche and
Terrebonne) 198
Finding Your Way Around . . . 192
Pineville (Crossroads) 343
Finding Your Way Around . . . 337
Practical Information 342
Piney Hills Gallery (Ruston) 381
Pioneer Heritage Center
(Shreveport) 375
Pirate Alley (Greater New Orleans) 77
Plaisance (Acadiana: North of
Lafayette)
Finding Your Way Around . . . 270
Plane 41
Planetarium (Lafayette) 220
Plantations, Baton Rouge 155
Accommodations 177
Calendar of Events 187
Entertainment 186
Finding Your Way Around . . . 155
Parks 177
Practical Information 160
Restaurants 181
Shopping 188

INDEX

Plaquemine (Plantations, Baton
    Rouge) 174
    Accommodations 181
    Finding Your Way Around . . . 160
Plaquemine Locks (Plaquemine) . 174
Plaquemines Parish (Greater New
    Orleans) 104
    Practical Information 67
Pleasant Hill (Northern Louisiana)
    Finding Your Way Around . . . 370
Pointe a la Hache (Greater New
    Orleans)
    Finding Your Way Around . . . 62
Pointe Coupée Antique Show & Sale
    (New Roads) 176
Pointe Coupée Parish Museum (New
    Roads Area)
    Finding Your Way Around . . . 176
Pointe-aux-Chênes (Bayou Lafourche
    and Terrebonne) 197
    Finding Your Way Around . . . 192
Politics 24
Pollock (Crossroads)
    Finding Your Way Around . . . 338
Pomme-de-Terre (Acadiana: North of
    Lafayette) 287
Ponchatoula (Greater New Orleans)
    Finding Your Way Around . . . 62
    Restaurants 138
Pontalba Buildings (Greater New
    Orleans) 78
Poplar Grove Plantation (Port
    Allen) 175
Population 24
Port Allen (Plantations, Baton
    Rouge) 175
    Accommodations 181
    Finding Your Way Around . . . 160
    Restaurants 185
Port Allen Locks (Port Allen) . . . 175
Port Barre (Acadiana: North of
    Lafayette)
    Accommodations 288
    Finding Your Way Around . . . 270
Port Hudson National Cemetery
    (Zachary) 169
Port Hudson State Commemorative
    Area (Zachary) 169

Port Sulphur (Greater New Orleans)
    Finding Your Way Around . . . 62
    Practical Information 67
Port Vincent (Plantations, Baton
    Rouge)
    Finding Your Way Around . . . 158
Port-Fouchon (Bayou Lafourche and
    Terrebonne) 201
    Finding Your Way Around . . . 194
Portrait of Louisiana 13
Poverty Point State Commemorative
    Area (Epps) 385
Po'boy 31
Prairieville (Plantations, Baton Rouge)
    Accommodations 178
    Finding Your Way Around . . . 158
Pralines 31
Presbytère (Greater New Orleans) 77
Presbytère (St. Martinville) 244
Presbyterian Church of Ruston USA
    (Ruston) 381
Princeton (Northern Louisiana)
    Finding Your Way Around . . . 370
    Parks 386
Producer's Mutual Cotton Gin
    Company (Cheneyville) 351
Propinquity (St. Francisville) 169
Prudhomme-Roquier House
    (Natchitoches) 347
Public Holidays 50
Pumping and Irrigation Station
    (Estherwood) 309
Quadroon Ballroom (Greater New
    Orleans) 77
Quincy (Western Acadiana)
    Finding Your Way Around . . . 302
R. W. Norton Art Gallery
    (Shreveport) 376
R.S. Barnwell Memorial Garden & Art
    Center (Shreveport) 375
Raceland (Bayou Lafourche and
    Terrebonne)
    Finding Your Way Around 193, 194
Rapides Cemetery (Alexandria -
    Pineville) 345
Ray Homestead (Opelousas) 277

Rayne (Western Acadiana) 306
   Accommodations 318
   Finding Your Way Around . . . 301
   Restaurants 323
   Shopping 334
Rayville (Northern Louisiana)
   Finding Your Way Around . . . 372
   Shopping 401
Real French Destination Scenic
   Byway (Scott) 306
Rebecca's Doll Museum
   (Monroe/West Monroe) 382
Rebel State Commemorative Area
   (Marthaville) 378
Red River Research Station (Bossier
   City) 377
Republic of West Florida Museum
   (Jackson) 172
Reserve (Plantations, Baton Rouge)161
   Finding Your Way Around . . . 156
Rice Museum (Crowley) 307
Rice, Anne 27
Riceland Crawfish Inc. (Eunice) . 280
Richard (Acadiana: North of
   Lafayette) 280
   Finding Your Way Around . . . 272
Richard's Riding Center & Livery
   (Abbeville) 315
Ringgold (Northern Louisiana)
   Finding Your Way Around . . . 370
   Restaurants 396
River Boat Tours (Greater New
   Orleans) 100
River Oaks Square Arts & Crafts
   (Alexandria - Pineville) 345
River Road African-American Museum
   & Gallery (Burnside) 163
Riverwood International Paper Mill
   (West Monroe) 384
Riviana Rice Mill (Abbeville) 314
Robeline (Crossroads)
   Finding Your Way Around . . . 340
   Shopping 364
Robert (Greater New Orleans)
   Accommodations 120
   Finding Your Way Around . . . 61
Rock Chapel (Carmel) 377

Rockefeller Wildlife Refuge and Game
   Preserve (Western Acadiana) 317
Romain Castille Home (Sunset) . . 275
Rosedale (Plantations, Baton
   Rouge) 175
   Finding Your Way Around . . . 160
Rosedown Plantation and Gardens
   (St. Francisville) 170
Roux 31
Ruins of Plantation Saint-Maurice
   (Winnfield) 349
Rural Life Museum (Baton Rouge) 168
Russell Sage Wildlife Management
   Area (Northern Louisiana) . . 387
Ruston (Northern Louisiana) 380
   Accommodations 391
   Entertainment 399
   Finding Your Way Around . . . 371
   Parks 387
   Practical Information 373
   Restaurants 396
Sabine National Wildlife Refuge
   (Western Acadiana) 316
Sabine Wildlife Management Area
   (Northern Louisiana) 386
Sacred Heart Academy (Greater New
   Orleans) 96
Safety 45
Saint Augustine Catholic Cemetery
   (Melrose) 347
Saline (Crossroads) 349
   Finding Your Way Around . . . 340
San Francisco Plantation House
   (Destrehan) 162
Sargeant House (Harrisonburg) . . 351
Sarto Old Iron Bridge (Marksville) 284
Sauce Piquante 31
Savoie's Sausage and Food Products
   (Opelousas) 276
Schepis Museum (Columbia) . . . 385
Scott (Western Acadiana) 306
   Accommodations 321
   Restaurants 323
   Shopping 333
Seignouret House (Greater New
   Orleans) 75
Shadows-on-the-Teche (New
   Iberia) 247

Shopping 49
Shreveport (Northern Louisiana) . 373
    Accommodations 388
    Entertainment 398
    Finding Your Way Around . . . 368
    Parks 385
    Practical Information 373
    Restaurants 393
    Shopping 400
Shriever (Bayou Lafourche and
    Terrebonne) 196
    Shopping 209
Sibley (Northern Louisiana)
    Finding Your Way Around . . . 371
Simmesport (Acadiana: North of
    Lafayette)
    Finding Your Way Around . . . 272
Slaves 21
Slidell (Greater New Orleans) . . . 98
    Accommodations 119
    Finding Your Way Around . . . 60
    Restaurants 135
Snake Bites 44
Soft-Shell Crab 32
Solomon Northup Path (Bunkie) . 284
Soniat House (Greater New
    Orleans) 79
Sorrento (Plantations, Baton
    Rouge) 164
    Finding Your Way Around . . . 158
Southdown Plantation House
    (Houma) 195
Southern Colonial (Winnfield) . . . 349
Southern University (Baton Rouge)168
Spanish 19
Spanish Town (Baton Rouge) . . . 166
Sportman's Paradise (Chauvin) . 198
Spring Bayou (Acadiana: North of
    Lafayette) 287
Spring Street Museum
    (Shreveport) 375
Springfield (Greater New Orleans) 103
    Finding Your Way Around . . . 62
St. Andrews Episcopal Church
    (Clinton) 172
St. Bernard Parish (Greater New
    Orleans) 104
    Practical Information 68

St. Charles Borromée Cemetery
    (Grand Coteau) 275
St. Charles Borromée Roman Catholic
    Church (Grand Coteau) 274
St. Charles Borromeo Catholic Church
    (Destrehan) 162
St. Francis Chapel (New Roads
    Area) 177
St. Francis de Sales Cathedral
    (Houma) 195
St. Francisville (Plantations, Baton
    Rouge) 169
    Accommodations 179
    Finding Your Way Around . . . 159
    Parks 177
    Restaurants 184
St. Francois Xavier Cathedral
    (Alexandria - Pineville) 345
St. Gabriel (Plantations, Baton
    Rouge) 164
    Finding Your Way Around . . . 156
St. Gabriel Church (St. Gabriel) . 164
St. James (Plantations, Baton
    Rouge) 172
    Finding Your Way Around . . . 159
St. James Catholic Church (St.
    James) 173
St. James Cemetery (St. James) 173
St. James Episcopal Church (Baton
    Rouge) 168
St. James Historical Society Culture
    & Heritage Center Museum
    (Lutcher) 162
St. John Cathedral (Lafayette) . . 220
St. Joseph Abbey (Covington) . . 99
St. John's Espiscopal Church
    (Thibodaux) 199
St. John the Baptist Church
    Cemetery (Brusly) 175
St. Joseph's Cathedral
    (Thibodeaux) 199
St. Joseph's Catholic Cemetery
    (Thibodaux) 199
St. Landry Catholic Church
    (Opelousas) 277
St. Louis Cathedral (Greater New
    Orleans) 78
St. Louis Plantation (Plaquemine) 174

St. Martin de Tours (St.
   Martinville) 244
St. Martinville (Bayou Teche) . . . 244
   Accommodations 255
   Entertainment 265
   Finding Your Way Around . . . 238
   Restaurants 260
St. Mary Magdalen Roman Catholic
   Church (Abbeville) 314
St. Mary Sugar Co-op Mill
   (Jeanerette) 250
St. Mary's Catholic Church (New
   Roads) 176
St. Matthew's Episcopal Church
   (Houma) 195
St. Michael's Catholic Church
   (Convent) 163
St. Peter's Methodist Church
   (Donaldsonville) 174
St. Stephen's Episcopal Church
   (New Roads Area) 177
St. Tammany Parish (Greater New
   Orleans)
   Practical Information 67
Starvation Point House
   (Washington) 278
Statuary of New Orleans 80
Steel Magnolias Tour
   (Natchitoches) 347
Steen's Syrup Mill (Abbeville) . . . 314
Stennis Space Center (Slidell) . . . 98
Sterling Mill (Franklin) 252
Strand Theater (Shreveport) 376
Sulfur (Western Acadiana)
   Accommodations 320
   Finding Your Way Around . . . 302
Sun Oak (Greater New Orleans) . 85
Sunset (Acadiana: North of
   Lafayette) 275
   Accommodations 287
   Finding Your Way Around . . . 270
   Restaurants 290
Supreme (Bayou Lafourche and
   Terrebonne) 199
   Finding Your Way Around . . . 192
Swamp Gardens & Wildlife Zoo
   (Morgan City) 253

Swimming
   Greater New Orleans 105
Tabasco Visitor's Center (Jefferson
   Island) 249
Table of Distances 40
Tallulah (Northern Louisiana) . . . 385
   Accommodations 392
   Finding Your Way Around . . . 372
   Parks 388
Tangipahoa (Greater New Orleans) 103
   Finding Your Way Around . . . 62
   Practical Information 67
Tante Huppé House
   (Natchitoches) 348
Tasso 32
Taxes 49
Tee Joe Gonzales Museum
   (Gonzales) 164
Telecommunications 42
Temperature 46
Tennis
   Greater New Orleans 106
Tensas River National Wildlife Refuge
   (Northern Louisiana) 388
Terrebonne Museum (Houma) . . 195
Texas Street Bridge
   (Shreveport/Bossier City) . . . 375
Tezcuco Plantation (Burnside) . . 163
Theft Insurance 43
Thériault, Olivier 20
Thibodaux (Bayou Lafourche and
   Terrebonne) 199
   Accommodations 202
   Finding Your Way Around . . . 192
   Restaurants 206
   Shopping 209
Thibodaux Chamber of Commerce
   (Thibodaux) 199
Thierry House (Greater New
   Orleans) 82
Thistlethwaite Wildlife Management
   Area (Acadiana: North of
   Lafayette) 285
Time Difference 50
Tipping 49
Toby-Westfeldt House (Greater New
   Orleans) 92

INDEX

Toby's Corner (Greater New
    Orleans) 92
Touchstone Wildlife and Art Museum
    (Bossier City) 376
Tourist Information 39
Train 41
Trappey's Fine Foods (New Iberia) 247
Trinity Episcopal Church
    (Cheneyville) 351
Trinity Episcopal Church (Greater New
    Orleans) 93
Tulane University (Greater New
    Orleans) 93
Tunica (Plantations, Baton Rouge) 171
    Finding Your Way Around . . . 159
Tunica-Biloxi Indian Center & Museum
    (Marksville) 284
Twin City Drag Race (Monroe/West
    Monroe) 384
Twin City Queen (Monroe/West
    Monroe) 384
Tyrone Plantation (Alexandria -
    Pineville) 345
U.S.S. Kidd (Baton Rouge) 167
Union Gallery (Baton Rouge) . . . 168
Union Wildlife Management Area
    (Northern Louisiana) 387
University of Southwest Louisiana
    (Lafayette) 220
Uptown (Greater New Orleans) . . 93
    Accommodations 113
    Bars and Nightclubs 142
    Restaurants 130
Vacherie (Plantations, Baton
    Rouge) 172
    Accommodations 180
    Finding Your Way Around . . . 159
    Restaurants 185
Valentine Lake (Crossroads) 354
Variety Plantation Cottage
    (Plaquemine) 174
Venice (Greater New Orleans)
    Accommodations 121
    Finding Your Way Around . . . 62
Ventress (Plantations, Baton Rouge)
    Finding Your Way Around . . . 160
    Restaurants 186
Vermilionville (Lafayette) 221

Vernon Parish (Crossroads)
    Practical Information 343
Vidalia (Crossroads) 352
    Accommodations 359
    Finding Your Way Around . . . 342
    Practical Information 343
    Restaurants 362
Villa de Mon Cœur (Oscar) 176
Village 'Cadien (Sorrento) 164
Ville Platte (Acadiana: North of
    Lafayette) 278
    Accommodations 289
    Entertainment 293
    Finding Your Way Around . . . 270
    Practical Information 273
    Restaurants 291
    Shopping 298
Villeré-Carr House (Greater New
    Orleans) 89
Vinet's Shrimp Inc. (Delcambre) . 315
Vinton (Western Acadiana)
    Accommodations 320
    Entertainment 329
    Finding Your Way Around . . . 302
Violet (Greater New Orleans)
    Finding Your Way Around . . . 62
Virlane Foundation Collection (Greater
    New Orleans) 83
Visitors' Center (Baton Rouge) . . 166
Vivian (Northern Louisiana)
    Accommodations 389
    Finding Your Way Around . . . 370
    Restaurants 395
    Shopping 401
W.H. Tupper General Merchandise
    Museum (Jennings) 310
Walker (Plantations, Baton Rouge)
    Entertainment 187
    Finding Your Way Around . . . 159
Walking
    Greater New Orleans 106
Wallace Edwards Family Residence
    (Marksville) 285
Walnut Grove Plantation House
    (Cheneyville) 351
Walter B. Jacobs Memorial Nature
    Park (Northern Louisiana) . . 386

Warehouse District (Greater New
    Orleans) 83
    Bars and Nightclubs 142
    Restaurants 128
Washington (Acadiana: North of
    Lafayette) 277
    Accommodations 288
    Finding Your Way Around . . . 270
    Restaurants 290
    Shopping 297
Washington Museum and Tourist
    Center (Washington) 277
Waterproof (Crossroads) 352
    Finding Your Way Around . . . 342
Wedell-Williams Memorial Aviation
    Museum (Patterson) 252
Weights and Measures 51
Welsh (Western Acadiana) 312
    Accommodations 322
    Finding Your Way Around . . . 302
    Restaurants 325
West Baton Rouge Museum (Port
    Allen) 175
West Feliciana Historical Society
    Museum (St. Francisville) . . 169
West Monroe (Northern Louisiana) 382
    Accommodations 392
    Entertainment 399
    Finding Your Way Around . . . 371
    Parks 387
    Practical Information 373
    Restaurants 397
    Shopping 401
West Pointe a la Hache (Greater New
    Orleans) 104
Western Acadiana 301
    Accommodations 318
    Beaches 316, 317
    Calendar of Events 330
    Entertainment 328
    Finding Your Way Around . . . 301
    Parks 315
    Practical Information 304
    Restaurants 323
    Shopping 333
Westwego (Greater New Orleans)
    Accommodations 121
    Restaurants 139

Wetlands Acadian Cultural Center
    (Thibodaux) 199
Whiskey Chitto Creek (Western
    Acadiana) 316
White Castle (Plantations, Baton
    Rouge) 174
    Accommodations 180
    Finding Your Way Around . . . 160
White Sulphur Springs
    (Crossroads) 353
Whitehall (Crossroads) 351
    Finding Your Way Around . . . 342
Wickliffe Plantation (New Roads
    Area) 176
Wild Azalea National Recreation Trail
    (Crossroads) 354
Wildlife Gardens (Gibson) 198
William G. "Bunk" Johnson Memorial
    Plaza (New Iberia) 247
Williams Residence (Greater New
    Orleans) 76
Williams, Tennessee 27
Williana (Crossroads)
    Finding Your Way Around . . . 338
Wilson (Plantations, Baton Rouge) 171
    Finding Your Way Around . . . 159
Winnfield (Crossroads) 348
    Accommodations 358
    Finding Your Way Around 338, 340
    Practical Information 343
    Restaurants 361
Winnsboro (Northern Louisiana)
    Finding Your Way Around . . . 372
    Restaurants 397
Winter Quarters State
    Commemorative Area
    (Newellton) 385
Women's Guild of the New Orleans
    Opera Association (Greater
    New Orleans) 91
Woodside Cottage (Clinton) 172
Woodside House (Clinton) 172
Woodworth (Crossroads)
    Finding Your Way Around . . . 341
World Acadian Congress of
    Louisiana in 1999 (Acadiana:
    Lafayette) 216

Yellow Bayou Civil War Memorial
  Park (Acadiana: North of
  Lafayette) 287
Yesterday House (Opelousas) . . . 277
Zachary (Plantations, Baton
  Rouge) 169
  Finding Your Way Around . . . 159
Zemurray Gardens (Folsom) 102
Zigler Museum (Jennings) 311

Zion Lutheran Church (Greater New
  Orleans) 96
Zwolle (Northern Louisiana) 378
  Accommodations 389
  Finding Your Way Around . . . 370
  Parks 386
  Restaurants 395
Zwolle Tamale Factory (Zwolle) . 379